DISCOVERING COMPUTERS 2002

Concepts for a Digital World
Web Enhanced

Brief

DISCOVERING COMPUTERS 2002

Concepts for a Digital World
Web Enhanced

Brief

Gary B. Shelly
Thomas J. Cashman
Misty E. Vermaat

Contributing Authors
Susan L. Sebok
Dolores J. Wells

COURSE
TECHNOLOGY
THOMSON LEARNING

COURSE TECHNOLOGY
25 THOMSON PLACE
BOSTON MA 02210

SHELLY
CASHMAN
SERIES®

Australia • Canada • Denmark • Japan • Mexico • New Zealand • Philippines • Puerto Rico • Singapore
South Africa • Spain • United Kingdom • United States

COURSE TECHNOLOGY

THOMSON LEARNING

Asia (excluding Japan)
Thomson Learning
60 Albert Street, #15-01
Albert Complex
Singapore 189969

Latin America
Thomson Learning
Seneca, 53
Colonia Polanco
11560 Mexico D.F. Mexico

Canada
Nelson/Thomson Learning
1120 Birchmount Road
Scarborough, Ontario
Canada M1K 5G4

Japan
Thomson Learning
Palaceside Building 5F
1-1-1 Hitotsubashi, Chiyoda-ku
Tokyo 100 0003 Japan

South Africa
Thomson Learning
Zonnebloem Building,
Constantia Square
526 Sixteenth Road
P.O. Box 2459
Halfway House, 1685
South Africa

UK/Europe/Middle East
Thomson Learning
Berkshire House
168-173 High Holborn
London, WC1V 7AA United Kingdom

Australia/New Zealand
Nelson/Thomson Learning
102 Dodds Street
South Melbourne, Victoria 3205
Australia

Spain
Thomson Learning
Calle Magallanes, 25
28015-MADRID
ESPANA

ISBN 0-7895-6187-5

1 2 3 4 5 6 7 8 9 10   BC   05 04 03 02 01

DISCOVERING COMPUTERS *2002*
Concepts for a Digital World
Web Enhanced

CONTENTS

Preface   ix

CHAPTER 1
Introduction to Computers

OBJECTIVES	**1.2**
THE DIGITAL REVOLUTION	**1.2**
WHAT IS A COMPUTER?	**1.4**
Data and Information	1.4
Information Processing Cycle	1.5
THE COMPONENTS OF A COMPUTER	**1.5**
Input Devices	1.5
Output Devices	1.6
System Unit	1.6
Storage Devices	1.6
Communications Devices	1.8
WHY IS A COMPUTER SO POWERFUL?	**1.8**
Speed	1.8
Reliability	1.9
Accuracy	1.9
Storage	1.9
Communications	1.9
COMPUTER SOFTWARE	**1.10**
System Software	1.12
Application Software	1.13
Software Development	1.14
NETWORKS AND THE INTERNET	**1.16**
CATEGORIES OF COMPUTERS	**1.19**
PERSONAL COMPUTERS	**1.19**
Desktop Computers	1.20
Notebook Computers	1.22
HANDHELD COMPUTERS	**1.23**
INTERNET APPLIANCES	**1.24**
MID-RANGE SERVERS	**1.25**
MAINFRAMES	**1.26**
SUPERCOMPUTERS	**1.26**
ELEMENTS OF AN INFORMATION SYSTEM	**1.27**
EXAMPLES OF COMPUTER USAGE	**1.28**
Home User	1.29
Small Office/Home Office User	1.31
Mobile User	1.32
Large Business User	1.33
Power User	1.35
COMPUTER USER AS A WEB PUBLISHER	**1.36**
CHAPTER SUMMARY	**1.37**
Help Desk Specialist	1.37
E-FUN E-ENTERTAINMENT	**1.38**
THAT'S ENTERTAINMENT	**1.38**

Surf's Up for Fun Web Sites	1.38
In Summary	1.40
Key Terms	1.42
Learn It Online	1.43
Checkpoint	1.44
In The Lab	1.46
Web Work	1.47

SPECIAL FEATURE   **1.48**

TimeLine 2002 — Milestones in Computer History

CHAPTER 2
The Internet and World Wide Web

OBJECTIVES	**2.2**
THE INTERNET	**2.2**
HISTORY OF THE INTERNET	**2.3**
HOW THE INTERNET WORKS	**2.4**
Service Providers	2.5
Connecting to the Internet	2.6
How Data Travels the Internet	2.6
Internet Addresses	2.8
THE WORLD WIDE WEB	**2.9**
Browsing the Web	2.9
Navigating Web Pages	2.11
Using a URL	2.12
Searching for Information on the Web	2.14
Types of Web Pages	2.16
Multimedia on the Web	2.18
Webcasting	2.23
ELECTRONIC COMMERCE	**2.24**
WEB PUBLISHING	**2.26**
Planning the Web Site	2.26
Analyzing and Designing the Web Site	2.26
Creating a Web Site	2.28
Deploying a Web Site	2.29
Maintaining the Web Site	2.29
OTHER INTERNET SERVICES	**2.29**
E-Mail	2.30
FTP	2.32
Newsgroups and Message Boards	2.33
Mailing Lists	2.34
Chat Rooms	2.35
Instant Messaging	2.36

NETIQUETTE   **2.37**
CHAPTER SUMMARY   **2.37**
  Webmaster   2.37
E-TRAVEL   **2.38**
GET PACKING!   **2.38**
  Explore the World without Leaving Home   2.38
  In Summary   2.40
  Key Terms   2.42
  Learn It Online   2.43
  Checkpoint   2.44
  In The Lab   2.46
  Web Work   2.47

SPECIAL FEATURE   **2.48**

GUIDE TO WORLD WIDE WEB SITES AND SEARCHING TECHNIQUES

CHAPTER   3

Application Software

OBJECTIVES   **3.2**
APPLICATION SOFTWARE   **3.2**
  The Role of the System Software   3.3
  The Role of the User Interface   3.4
  Starting a Software Application   3.4
PRODUCTIVITY SOFTWARE   **3.7**
  Word Processing Software   3.8
DEVELOPING A DOCUMENT   **3.10**
  Spreadsheet Software   3.12
  Database Software   3.15
  Presentation Graphics Software   3.18
  Personal Information Managers   3.20
  Software Suite   3.20
  Project Management Software   3.21
  Accounting Software   3.21
GRAPHICS AND MULTIMEDIA SOFTWARE   **3.22**
  Computer-Aided Design   3.22
  Desktop Publishing Software (Professional)   3.23
  Paint/Image Editing Software (Professional)   3.24
  Video and Audio Editing Software   3.25
  Multimedia Authoring Software   3.25
  Web Page Authoring Software   3.25
SOFTWARE FOR HOME, PERSONAL,
  AND EDUCATIONAL USE   **3.26**
  Integrated Software   3.27
  Personal Finance Software   3.27
  Legal Software   3.28
  Tax Preparation Software   3.28
  Desktop Publishing (Personal)   3.28
  Paint/Image Editing Software (Personal)   3.29
  Clip Art/Image Gallery   3.30
  Home Design/Landscaping Software   3.30
  Educational/Reference/Entertainment Software 3.30
SOFTWARE FOR COMMUNICATIONS   **3.32**
  E-Mail   3.32
  Web Browsers   3.32
  Chat Rooms   3.32
  Newsgroups   3.32

  Instant Messaging   3.32
  Groupware   3.33
  Videoconferencing   3.33
APPLICATIONS ON THE WEB   **3.33**
  Web-Based Training   3.34
  Application Service Providers   3.35
LEARNING AIDS AND SUPPORT TOOLS
  WITHIN AN APPLICATION   **3.36**
CHAPTER SUMMARY   **3.37**
  Word Processing Technician   3.37
E-FINANCE   **3.38**
KA-CHING, KA-CHING   **3.38**
  Cashing In on Financial Advice   3.38
  In Summary   3.40
  Key Terms   3.42
  Learn It Online   3.43
  Checkpoint   3.44
  In The Lab   3.46
  Web Work   3.47

CHAPTER   4

The Components of the System Unit

OBJECTIVES   **4.2**
THE SYSTEM UNIT   **4.2**
  The Motherboard   4.4
CENTRAL PROCESSING UNIT   **4.5**
  The Control Unit   4.5
  The Arithmetic/Logic Unit   4.6
  Pipelining   4.7
  Registers   4.7
  The System Clock   4.8
  Comparison of Personal Computer Processors   4.9
  Processor Installation and Upgrades   4.11
  Heat Sinks and Heat Pipes   4.12
  Coprocessors   4.13
  Parallel Processing   4.13
DATA REPRESENTATION   **4.13**
MEMORY   **4.15**
  RAM   4.16
  Cache   4.19
  ROM   4.20
  Flash Memory   4.21
  CMOS   4.21
  Memory Access Times   4.22
EXPANSION SLOTS AND EXPANSION CARDS   **4.23**
  PC Cards and Flash Memory Cards   4.24
PORTS   **4.25**
  Serial Ports   4.27
  Parallel Ports   4.27
  Universal Serial Bus Port   4.28
  Special-Purpose Ports   4.28
BUSES
  4.29
  Expansion Bus   4.31
BAYS   **4.32**
POWER SUPPLY   **4.32**
MOBILE COMPUTERS   **4.33**
PUTTING IT ALL TOGETHER   **4.35**
CHAPTER SUMMARY   **4.35**

Software Engineer   4.35
E-RESOURCES   **4.36**
LOOK IT UP   **4.36**
Web Resources Ease System Concerns   4.36
In Summary   4.38
Key Terms   4.40
Learn It Online   4.41
Checkpoint   4.42
In The Lab   4.44
Web Work   4.45

CHAPTER 5

Input

OBJECTIVES   **5.2**
WHAT IS INPUT?   **5.2**
WHAT ARE INPUT DEVICES?   **5.4**
THE KEYBOARD   **5.4**
Keyboard Types   5.5
POINTING DEVICES   **5.7**
MOUSE   **5.7**
Mouse Types   5.7
Using a Mouse   5.8
OTHER POINTING DEVICES   **5.10**
Trackball   5.10
Touchpad   5.10
Pointing Stick   5.11
Joysticks and Wheels   5.11
Light Pen   5.12
Touch Screen   5.12
Stylus   5.13
VOICE INPUT   **5.14**
Audio Input   5.16
INPUT DEVICES FOR HANDHELD COMPUTERS   **5.16**
DIGITAL CAMERAS   **5.18**
VIDEO INPUT   **5.21**
PC Video Cameras   5.22
Web Cams   5.23
Videoconferencing   5.24
SCANNERS AND READING DEVICES   **5.24**
Optical Scanner   5.25
Optical Readers   5.27
Magnetic Ink Character Recognition Reader   5.30
Wireless Input   5.31
INPUT DEVICES FOR PHYSICALLY CHALLENGED USERS   **5.31**
PUTTING IT ALL TOGETHER   **5.32**
Webcasting   5.33
E-COMMUNITIES   **5.34**
PICTURE THIS   **5.34**
Share Your Community Pride   5.34
In Summary   5.36
Key Terms   5.38
Learn It Online   5.39
Checkpoint   5.40
In The Lab   5.42
Web Work   5.43

CHAPTER 6

Output

OBJECTIVES   **6.2**
WHAT IS OUTPUT?   **6.2**
WHAT ARE OUTPUT DEVICES?   **6.4**
DISPLAY DEVICES   **6.4**
CRT Monitors   6.5
LCD Monitors and Displays   6.5
Gas Plasma Monitors   6.8
Quality of Display Devices   6.8
Video Cart and Monitors   6.10
Monitor Ergonomics   6.11
Televisions   6.12
PRINTERS   **6.12**
Impact Printers   6.14
Nonimpact Printers   6.15
Ink-Jet Printers   6.15
Laser Printers   6.16
Thermal Printers   6.19
Photo Printers   6.20
Label and Postage Printers   6.21
Portable Printers   6.22
Plotters and Large-Format Printers   6.22
SPEAKERS AND HEADSETS   **6.23**
OTHER OUTPUT DEVICES   **6.24**
Data Projectors   6.25
Facsimile (Fax) Machine   6.25
Multifunction Devices   6.26
TERMINALS   **6.27**
OUTPUT DEVICES FOR PHYSICALLY CHALLENGED USERS **6.29**
PUTTING IT ALL TOGETHER   **6.31**
CHAPTER SUMMARY   **6.31**
Graphics Designer/Illustrator   6.31
E-GOVERNMENT   **6.32**
STAMP OF APPROVAL   **6.32**
Making a Federal Case for Useful Information   6.32
In Summary   6.34
Key Terms   6.36
Learn It Online   6.37
Checkpoint   6.38
In The Lab   6.40
Web Work   6.41

SPECIAL FEATURE   **6.42**
MULTIMEDIA a VIRTUAL experience

CHAPTER 7

Storage

OBJECTIVES	**7.2**
MEMORY VERSUS STORAGE	**7.2**
Memory	7.3
Storage	7.4
FLOPPY DISKS	**7.6**
Floppy Disk Drives	7.6
How a Floppy Disk Stores Data	7.8
Care of Floppy Disks	7.9
HIGH CAPACITY DISKS	**7.9**
HARD DISKS	**7.10**
How a Hard Disk Works	7.11
Hard Disk Controllers	7.13
Removable Hard Disks	7.13
RAID	7.14
Maintaining Data Stored on a Disk	7.15
Internet Hard Drives	7.16
COMPACT DISCS	**7.17**
CD-ROMs	**7.20**
CD-ROM Drive Speed	7.20
PhotoCDs and Picture CDs	7.21
CD-R AND CD-RW	**7.22**
DVD-ROMS	**7.24**
DVD Variations	7.25
TAPES	
7.26	
ENTERPRISE STORAGE SYSTEMS	**7.27**
PC CARDS	**7.28**
MINIATURE MOBILE STORAGE MEDIA	**7.28**
Smart Cards	7.29
MICROFILM AND MICROFICHE	**7.30**
PUTTING IT ALL TOGETHER	**7.31**
CHAPTER SUMMARY	**7.31**
Computer Technician	7.31
E-SHOPPING	**7.32**
CYBERMALL MANIA	**7.32**
Let Your Mouse Do Your Shopping	7.32
In Summary	7.34
Key Terms	7.36
Learn It Online	7.37
Checkpoint	7.38
In The Lab	7.40
Web Work	7.41

CHAPTER 8

Operating Systems and Utility Programs

OBJECTIVES	**8.2**
SYSTEM SOFTWARE	**8.2**
OPERATING SYSTEMS	**8.3**
OPERATING SYSTEM FUNCTIONS	**8.4**
Starting a Computer	8.4
The User Interface	8.7
Managing Programs	8.8
Managing Memory	8.10
Scheduling Jobs	8.10
Configuring Devices	8.11
Accessing the Web	8.13
Monitoring Performance	814
Providing Housekeeping Services	8.14
Controlling a Network	8.15
Administering Security	8.16
TYPES OF OPERATING SYSTEMS	**8.17**
STAND-ALONE OPERATING SYSTEMS	**8.17**
DOS	8.17
Windows 3.x	8.18
Windows 95	8.18
Windows NT Workstation	8.18
Windows 98	8.18
Windows 2000 Professional	8.18
Windows Millennium Edition	8.20
Mac OS	8.21
OS/2 Warp	8.22
NETWORK OPERATING SYSTEMS	**8.22**
NetWare	8.22
Windows NT Server	8.22
Windows 2000	8.22
OS/2 Warp Server for E-business	8.23
UNIX	8.23
Linux	8.24
Solaris	8.25
EMBEDDED OPERATING SYSTEMS	**8.25**
Windows CE	8.25
Pocket PC OS	8.26
Palm OS	8.26
UTILITY PROGRAMS	**8.27**
File Viewer	8.27
File Compression	8.28
Diagnostic Utility	8.28
Uninstaller	8.29
Disk Scanner	8.29
Disk Defragmenter	8.30
Backup Utility	8.30
Screen Saver	8.31
CHAPTER SUMMARY	**8.31**
Network Administrator	8.31
E-WEATHER E-SPORTS E-NEWS	**8.32**
WHAT'S NEWS?	**8.32**
Weather, Shorts, and News Web Sites Score Big Hits	8.32
In Summary	8.34
Key Terms	8.36
Learn It Online	8.37
Checkpoint	8.38
In The Lab	8.40
Web Work	8.41

SPECIAL FEATURE   **8.42**

Buyer's Guide 2002
How to Purchase, Install, and Maintain a Personal Computer

PREFACE

The Shelly Cashman Series® offers the finest textbooks in computer education. We are proud of the fact that the previous six editions of this textbook have been runaway best-sellers. Each of the these editions included new learning innovations, such as integration of the World Wide Web, WebCT, Interactive Labs, online learning games, MyCourse.com, and Teaching Tools that set it apart from its competitors. *Discovering Computers 2002: Concepts for a Digital World, Web Enhanced* continues with the innovation, quality, timeliness, and reliability that you have come to expect from the Shelly Cashman Series. This latest edition of *Discovering Computers* includes these enhancements:

- Eight-chapter Brief edition, twelve-chapter Introductory edition, and sixteen-chapter Complete edition lets you choose the version of the textbook that fits your teaching needs
- Three new chapters round out the concepts students need to know: (1) E-Commerce; (2) Computers and Society; and (3) Careers and Certification
- Students can relate to the Picture Yourself chapter openers that set the stage by providing conversational chapter-related situations
- E-Revolution two-page spreads at the end of each chapter provide a fascinating perspective of Web applications, such as e-finance, e-travel, e-arts, e-learning, e-entertainment, and e-government
- Learn It Online exercise section at the end of each chapter includes practice tests and learning games that offer a unique way for students to solidify, reinforce, and extend the concepts presented in the chapter
- Two cutting-edge companies and two technology trailblazers are spotlighted in each chapter to help students recognize the leaders and major companies in the field of computers
- Career Corner at the end of each chapter pinpoints career opportunities for all levels of students
- Apply It boxes throughout chapters help students apply the concepts presented to everyday life

OBJECTIVES OF THIS TEXTBOOK

The Brief edition of *Discovering Computers 2002: Concepts for a Digital World, Web Enhanced* is intended for use as a stand-alone textbook or in combination with an applications, Internet, or programming textbook in a one-quarter or one-semester introductory computer course. No experience with computers is assumed. The material presented provides an in-depth treatment of introductory computer subjects. Students will finish the course with a solid understanding of computers, how to use computers, and how to access information on the World Wide Web. The objectives of this book are as follows:

- Teach the fundamentals of computers and computer nomenclature, particularly with respect to personal computer hardware and software, and the World Wide Web
- Give students an in-depth understanding of why computers are essential components in business and society in general
- Present the material in a visually appealing and exciting manner that invites students to learn
- Provide exercises and lab assignments that allow students to interact with a computer and actually learn by using the computer and the World Wide Web
- Offer alternative learning techniques with streaming audio and video on the Web, learning games, WebCT, Blackboard, and MyCourse.com
- Present strategies for purchasing, installing, and maintaining a desktop computer, a notebook computer, and a handheld computer
- Assist students in planning a career in the computer field

DISTINGUISHING FEATURES

The Complete edition of *Discovering Computers 2002: Concepts for a Digital World, Web Enhanced* includes the following distinguishing features.

A Proven Book

More than five million students have learned about computers using Shelly and Cashman computer fundamentals textbooks. With the additional World Wide Web integration and interactivity, streaming up-to-date audio and video, extraordinary step-by-step visual drawings and photographs, unprecedented currency, and the Shelly and Cashman touch, this book will make your computer concepts course exciting and dynamic.

World Wide Web Enhanced

This book uses the World Wide Web as a major supplement. The purpose of integrating the World Wide Web into the book is to (1) offer students additional information and currency on topics of importance; (2) make available alternative learning techniques with Web-based learning games, practice tests, and interactive labs; (3) underscore the relevance of the World Wide Web as a basic information tool that can be used in all facets of society; and (4) offer instructors the opportunity to organize and administer their traditional campus-based or distance-education-based courses on the Web using WebCT, Blackboard, or MyCourse.com.

This textbook, however, does not depend on Web access in order to be used successfully. The Web access adds to the already complete treatment of topics within the book. The World Wide Web is integrated into the book in seven ways:

■ Streaming audio speaks the end-of-chapter In Summary sections to students

■ End-of-chapter pages and the special features in the book are stored as Web pages on the World Wide Web; see page xv for more information

■ Streaming up-to-date, computer-related CNN videos on the Web are in the end-of-chapter Web Work sections

■ Throughout the text, marginal annotations titled Web Links provide suggestions on how to obtain additional information via the Web on an important topic covered on the page

■ Eighteen Interactive Labs on the Web in the end-of-chapter Web Work sections

■ WebCT and Blackboard Web-based course management systems for use in a traditional classroom setting or in a distance education environment

■ MyCourse.com offers instructors and students an opportunity to supplement classroom learning with additional content on the Web.

A Visually Appealing Book that Maintains Student Interest

The latest technology, pictures, drawings, and text are artfully combined to produce a visually appealing and easy-to-understand book. Many of the figures show a step-by-step pedagogy, which simplifies the more complex computer concepts. Pictures and drawings reflect the latest trends in computer technology. Finally, the text is set in three columns, which research indicates is the easiest design for students to read. This combination of pictures, step-by-step drawings, and text sets a new standard for computer textbook design.

Technology Trailblazer and Company on the Cutting Edge Boxes

All students graduating from an institution of higher education should be aware of the leaders and major companies in the field of computers. Thus, interspersed throughout each chapter are boxed write-ups on two leaders in technology and two computer companies. The titles of these boxes are Technology Trailblazer and Company on the Cutting Edge. The Technology Trailblazer feature presents people who have made a difference in the computer revolution, such as Bill Gates, Lavonne Luquis, Andy Grove, Carly Fiorina, Marc Andreessen, and Tim Berners-Lee. The Company on the Cutting Edge feature presents the major computer companies, such as Microsoft, Intel, Yahoo!, Sun Microsystems, Gateway, and IBM.

COMPANY ON THE CUTTING EDGE

YAHOO!

Indexing the World Wide Web

The Yahoos were a primitive society in Jonathan Swift's *Gulliver's Travels*. Like those Yahoos, the contemporary Yahoo!'s co-founders, Jerry Yang and David Filo, were involved in the early phases of a

TECHNOLOGY TRAILBLAZER

DONNA DUBINSKY

As if being the president and CEO of 3Com's Palm Computing Division were not enough of a challenge, Donna Dubinsky founded Handspring with Jeff Hawkins in 1998 with the goal of becoming the leading handheld computing device maker for the consumer market. Before coming to Palm Computing, Dubinsky had served as director of distribution at Apple Computer and as an international vice president at Claris. At Palm, she and Hawkins introduced the PalmPilot personal organizer in 1996; sales of more than two million units make it the most rapidly adopted new computing product ever manufactured. In an effort to learn how consumers actually use the PalmPilot boxes they bought, she watched customers open the PalmPilot boxes and read the manuals. She even took some technical support calls herself to see what questions they were asking. Craving her independence and autonomy at Handspring, Dubinsky is using the Palm operating system on its Visor handheld computer. She stresses that size, connectivity to a personal computer, usability, and an economical price are the factors that make handheld computers successful. For more information on Donna Dubinsky, visit the Discovering Computers 2002 People Web page (scsite.com/dc2002/people.htm) and click Donna Dubinsky.

operation to large comp Communications Corporation.

Today, the lists still are maintained by Yahoo!'s employees. More than 166 million visitors access 180 million pages daily, including the network's e-mail, chat rooms, shopping site, and personal Web pages. These services, which are supported by 3,000 advertisers, are free to users.

For more information on Yahoo!, visit the Discovering Computers 2002 Companies Web page (scsite.com/dc2002/companies.htm) and click Yahoo!.

Latest Computer Trends

The terms and technologies your students see in this book are those they will encounter when they start using computers. Only the latest application software packages are shown throughout the book. New topics and terms include: digital divide; wireless service provider; microbrowser; spider; wireless portal; MP3 player; m-commerce (mobile commerce); latest version of Microsoft Office; online print service; .NET; input devices for handheld computers; digital video camera; video telephone call; digital watermarks; Web bar codes; gesture recognition; Pentium 4; high-performance addressing (HPA); Internet appliance; electronic book (e-book); Digital Display Working Group (DDWG); Digital Visual Interface (DVI); Video Electronics Standards Association (VESA); interactive TV; Internet printing; Internet stamps; optically-assisted hard drive; Internet hard drive; multiread CD-ROM drive; miniature mobile storage media; Picture CD; Active Directory; Microsoft Windows 2000; Solaris; embedded operating system; Pocket PC; Pocket PC OS; utility suite; Web-based utility service.

End-of-Chapter Exercises

We dedicate as many resources to create the end-of-chapter material as we do to the chapter content. We believe strongly in offering exciting, rich, and thorough end-of-chapter material to reinforce the chapter objectives and assist you in making your course the finest ever offered. As indicated earlier, each of the end-of-chapter pages is stored as a Web page on the World Wide Web to provide your students in-depth information and alternative methods of preparing for examinations. Each chapter ends with the following:

- **E-Revolution** A two-page E-Revolution spread introduces students to Web applications such as e-finance, e-travel, e-arts, e-learning, e-auctions, e-entertainment, and much more. At the end of each E-Revolution are exercises that allow students to apply the topics described.

- **In Summary** This section summarizes the chapter material in the form of questions and answers. Each question addresses a chapter objective, making this section invaluable in reviewing and preparing for examinations. Links on the Web page provide additional current information. With a single-click on the Web page, the In Summary section is spoken to students using streaming audio.

- **Key Terms** This list of the key terms found in the chapter together with the page numbers on which the terms are defined will aid students in mastering the chapter material. A complete summary of all key terms in the book, together with their definitions, appears in the Index at the end of the book. On the corresponding Web page, students can click terms to view a definition and a picture and then click a link to visit a Web page that offers additional information.

- **Learn It Online** These all-new Web-based exercises include exciting activities that maintain student interest. Exercises include a scavenger hunt, search sleuth, practice tests, and learning games.

- **CheckPoint** These pencil-and-paper exercises have been expanded to two pages. Exercises include label the figure, matching, multiple choice, short answer, and working together. Students accessing the Web page can answer the questions in an interactive forum.

- **In The Lab** A series of Windows lab exercises begins with the simplest exercises within Windows. Students then are led through additional activities that, by the end of the book, enable them to be proficient using Windows.

- **Web Work** In this section, students gain an appreciation for the online technology available with the Web. The At The Movies exercise includes streaming video. The Shelly Cashman Series Interactive Labs exercises uses the latest Web technologies. Other exercises in this section, such as working with newsgroups and reviewing the latest news in technology, also use the World Wide Web.

Timeline 2002: Milestones in Computer History

A colorful, highly informative 13-page timeline following Chapter 1 steps students through the major computer technology developments during the past 60 years, including the most recent advances in 2001.

Guide to World Wide Web Sites and Searching Techniques

More than 150 popular up-to-date Web sites are listed and described in this guide to Web sites that follows Chapter 2. This guide also introduces the students to basic searching techniques.

Multimedia: A Virtual Experience

Multimedia is changing the way people work, learn, and play. This special feature following Chapter 6 introduces the students to multimedia applications, such as business presentations, computer-based training, Web-based training, electronic books, entertainment, and edutainment.

Buyer's Guide 2002

A 10-page guide following Chapter 8 introduces students to purchasing, installing, and maintaining a desktop computer, notebook computer, and handheld computer.

A World Without Wires

This special feature presents a pictorial introduction of the wireless revolution. It describes the growth of wireless technology and the latest in hardware and applications. This special feature is available in the Introductory and Complete editions.

Trends 2002: A Look to the Future

Following Chapter 16, an 11-page feature examines several trends that will influence the direction of the computer field. This special feature is available only in the Complete edition.

Shelly Cashman Series Interactive Labs

The Shelly Cashman Interactive Labs have been redone completely for this edition using the latest technologies. See page xvi for more information.

SHELLY CASHMAN SERIES TEACHING TOOLS

Three basic ancillaries accompany this textbook: Teaching Tools (ISBN 0-7895-6261-8), Course Presenter (ISBN 0-7895-6191-3), and MyCourse.com. These ancillaries are free to adopters through your Course Technology representative or by calling one of the following telephone numbers: Colleges and Universities, 1-800-648-7450; High Schools, 1-800-824-5179; Private Career Colleges, 1-800-477-3692; Canada, 1-800-268-2222; and Corporations and Government Agencies, 1-800-340-7450.

Teaching Tools

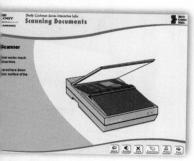

The Teaching Tools for this textbook include both teaching and testing aids. The contents of the Teaching Tools CD-ROM are listed below.

■ **Instructor's Manual** The Instructor's Manual consists of Microsoft Word files that include the following for each chapter: chapter objectives; chapter overview; detailed lesson plans with page number references; teacher notes and activities; answers to the exercises; test bank (100 true/false, 50 multiple-choice, and 70 fill-in-the-blank questions per chapter); and figure references. The figures are available in the Figures in the Book. The test bank questions are numbered the same as in the Course Test Manager. You can print a copy of the chapter test bank and use the printout to select your questions in Course Test Manager. Using your word processing software, you can generate quizzes and exams.

■ **Figures in the Book** Illustrations for every picture, table, and screen in the textbook are available in electronic form. Use this ancillary to present a slide show in lecture or to print transparencies for use in lecture with an overhead projector. If you have a personal computer and LCD device, this ancillary can be an effective tool for presenting lectures.

- **Course Test Manager** Course Test Manager is a powerful testing and assessment package that enables instructors to create and print tests quickly from the 3,500 question test bank. Instructors with access to a networked computer lab (LAN) can administer, grade, and track tests online. Students also can take online practice tests, which generate customized study guides that indicate where in the textbook students can find more information for each question.
- **ExamView** ExamView is a state-of-the-art test builder. ExamView enables you to create printed tests, Internet tests, and computer (LAN-based) tests quickly. You can enter your own test questions or use the 3,500 question test bank that accompanies ExamView.
- **Course Syllabus** Any instructor who has been assigned a course at the last minute knows how difficult it is to develop a course syllabus. For this reason, a sample syllabus is included that can be customized easily to a course.
- **Student Files** A few of the exercises in the end-of-chapter In The Lab section ask students to use these files. You can distribute the files on the Teaching Tools CD-ROM to your students over a network, or you can have them follow the instructions in this preface to obtain a copy of the Discovering Computers 2002 Data Disk.
- **Interactive Labs** These are the non-audio versions of the 18 hands-on Interactive Labs exercises. Students can step through each Lab in about 15 minutes to solidify and reinforce computer concepts. Assessment requires students to answer questions about the contents of the Interactive Labs.
- **Interactive Lab Solutions** This ancillary includes the solutions to the Interactive Labs assessment quizzes.

Course Presenter with Figures, Animations, and CNN Video Clips

Course Presenter is a multimedia lecture presentation system that provides PowerPoint slides for every subject in each chapter. Use this presentation system to give well-organized lectures that are both interesting and knowledge-based. A presentation is provided for each chapter. Each file contains PowerPoint slides for every subject in each chapter together with optional choices to show any figure in the chapter as you introduce the material in class. More than 50 current, two- to three-minute up-to-date, computer-related video clips, many from CNN, and more than 35 animations that reinforce chapter material also are available for optional presentation. Course Presenter provides consistent coverage for multiple lecturers.

MyCourse.com

MyCourse.com offers instructors and students an opportunity to supplement classroom learning with additional course content. You can use MyCourse.com to expand traditional learning by accessing and completing readings, tests, and other assignments through the customized, comprehensive Web site. For additional information, visit mycourse.com and click the Help button.

SUPPLEMENTS

Five supplements can be used in combination with *Discovering Computers 2002: Concepts for a Digital World, Web Enhanced.*

Audio Chapter Review on CD-ROM

The Audio Chapter Review on CD-ROM (ISBN 0-7895-6192-1) speaks the end-of-chapter In Summary pages. Students can use this supplement with a CD player or personal computer to solidify their understanding of the concepts presented. It is a great tool for preparing for examinations. This same Audio Chapter Review also is available at no cost on the Web by clicking the Audio button on the In Summary page at the end of any chapter.

Shelly Cashman Series Interactive Labs with Audio on CD-ROM

The Shelly Cashman Series Interactive Labs with Audio on CD-ROM (ISBN 0-7895-6111-5) may be used in combination with this textbook to augment your students' learning process. See page xvi for a description of each Lab. These Interactive Labs also are available at no cost on the Web by clicking the appropriate button on the Web Work exercise pages (see page 1.47) and as a non-audio version on the Teaching Tools CD-ROM. A companion student guide for the Interactive Labs, titled *A Record of Discovery for Exploring Computers, Fourth Edition* (ISBN 0-7895-6372-X), enhances the Interactive Labs presentation, reinforces concepts, shows relationships, and provides additional facts.

Study Guide

This highly popular *Study Guide* (ISBN 0-7895-6189-1) includes a variety of activities that help students recall, review, and master introductory computer concepts. The *Study Guide* complements the end-of-chapter material with a guided chapter outline; a self-test consisting of true/false, multiple-choice, short answer, fill-in, and matching questions; an entertaining puzzle; and other challenging exercises.

WebCT Users Guide and Blackboard Users Guide

The *WebCT Users Guide* (ISBN 0-7895-6163-8) and the *Blackboard Users Guide* (ISBN 0-7895-6165-4) show students how to navigate through these course management tools.

ACKNOWLEDGMENTS

The Shelly Cashman Series would not be the leading computer education series without the contributions of outstanding publishing professionals. First, and foremost, among them is Becky Herrington, director of production and designer. She is the heart and soul of the Shelly Cashman Series, and it is only through her leadership, dedication, and tireless efforts that superior products are made possible. Becky created and produced the award-winning Windows series of books.

Under Becky's direction, the following individuals made significant contributions to these books: Doug Cowley, production manager; Ginny Harvey, series specialist; Ken Russo, senior Web and graphic designer; Mike Bodnar, associate production manager; Mark Norton, Web designer; Meena Moest, production editor; Michele French, Christy Otten, Stephanie Nance, Chris Schneider, Hector Arvizu and Kenny Tran, graphic artists; Jeanne Black and Betty Hopkins, Quark experts; Laurie Sullivan and Lyn Markowicz, copyeditors; Nancy Lamm and Rich Hansberger, proofreaders; Jeff Quasney, Teaching Tools developer; Tim Walker, Instructor's Manual and MyCourse.com author; Floyd Winters, Web content analyst; Robert Safdie, Course Presenter author; Cristina Haley, indexer; Sarah Evertson of Image Quest, photo researcher; Richard Keaveny, associate publisher; Jim Quasney, series consulting editor; Lora Wade, product manager; Erin Roberts, associate product manager; Francis Schurgot, Web product manager; Marc Ouellette, associate Web product manager; Rachel VanKirk, marketing manager; and Erin Runyon, associate product manager.

Our sincere thanks go to Dennis Tani, who together with Becky Herrington, designed this book. In addition, Dennis designed the cover, performed all the initial layout and typography and executed the magnificent drawings contained in this book.

Finally, thanks to Judy Brown, Paul Bartolomeo, Jeff Corcoran, Dr. Wil Dershimer, Susan Fry, Dr. Homa Ghajar, John G. Hoey, Joyce King, Sherry Lenhart, Dana Madison and Ed Mott, for reviewing the manuscript and to William Vermaat for researching, reviewing the manuscript, and taking photographs. Special thanks to Erin Runyon for recruiting and managing the reviewer process. We hope you find using this book an exciting and rewarding experience.

Gary B. Shelly
Thomas J. Cashman

Misty E. Vermaat
Dolores J. Wells
Susan L. Sebok

NOTES TO THE STUDENT

If you have access to the World Wide Web, you can obtain current and additional information on topics covered in this book in the five ways listed below.

1. Throughout the book, marginal annotations called Web Link (Figure 1) specify subjects about which you can obtain additional current information. Enter the designated URL and then click the appropriate term on the Web page.

2. Each chapter ends with six sections titled In Summary, Key Terms, Learn It Online, Checkpoint, In The Lab, and Web Work. These sections in your textbook are stored as pages on the Web. You can visit them by starting your browser and entering the URL listed in the Web Instructions at the top of the end-of-chapter pages. When the Web page displays, you can click links or buttons on the page to broaden your understanding of the topics and obtain current information about the topics.

3. Each chapter ends with a two-page E-Revolution spread that describes a Web application. Included in this section are URLs that let you apply what you have learned.

4. Throughout the chapters, you will find Apply It, Technology Trailblazer, Company on the Cutting Edge, and Issue boxes. Most of these boxes include URLs that point you to additional information on the topic presented.

5. More than 150 popular up-to-date Web sites are listed and described in the Guide to World Wide Web sites that follows Chapter 2. This guide also describes basic searching techniques.

> Web Link provides additional current information on a topic
>
> ## Web Link
> For more information on submission services, visit the Discovering Computers 2002 Chapter 2 WEB LINK page **(scsite.com/dc2002/ ch2/weblink.htm)** and click Submission Services.
>
> **Figure 1**

Each time you reference a Web page from the textbook's Web site, a navigation system displays at the top of the page (Figure 2). To display one of the Student Exercises, click the chapter number and then click the Student Exercises title at the top. To display one of the Special Features, click the desired Special Feature title at the top.

Figure 2

TO DOWNLOAD PLAYERS

For best viewing results of the Web pages referenced in this book, download Shockwave and Flash Player. To play the audio in the In Summary section and view the movie in the Web Work section at the end of each chapter, you must download RealPlayer. Follow the steps below:

Shockwave and Flash Player— (1) Start your browser; (2) enter the URL macromedia.com; (3) click DOWNLOADS at the top of the Macromedia home page; (4) click Macromedia Shockwave Player; (5) click the button in the Step box; (6) respond to the dialog boxes.

RealPlayer — (1) Start your browser; (2) enter the URL real.com; (3) scroll down and click RealPlayer 8 Basic (this is the free version of RealPlayer); (4) step through and respond to the forms, requests, and dialog boxes; (5) when the File Download dialog box displays, click the Save this program to disk option button; (6) save the file to a folder and remember the folder name; (7) if necessary, start Windows Explorer and double-click the file downloaded in Step 6.

SHELLY CASHMAN SERIES INTERACTIVE LABS WITH AUDIO

Each of the 8 chapters in this textbook includes the Web Work exercises, which utilize the World Wide Web. The 13 Shelly Cashman Series Interactive Labs described below are included as exercises in the Web Work section. These Interactive Labs are available on the Web (see page 1.47) or on CD-ROM. The audio version on CD-ROM (ISBN 0-7895-6111-5) is available at an additional cost. A non-audio version also is available on the Shelly Cashman Series Teaching Tools CD-ROM that is available free to adopters.

A student guide for the Interactive Labs is available at an additional cost. The student guide is titled *A Record of Discovery for Exploring Computers, Fourth Edition* (ISBN 0-7895-6372-X), which reviews the Interactive Labs content, shows relationships, and provides additional facts.

Each Lab takes students approximately 15 minutes to complete using a personal computer and helps them gain a better understanding of a specific subject covered in the chapter.

Shelly Cashman Series Interactive Labs with Audio		
Lab	*Function*	*Page*
Using the Mouse	Master how to use a mouse. The Lab includes exercises on pointing, clicking, double-clicking, and dragging.	1.47
Using the Keyboard	Learn how to use the keyboard. The Lab discusses different categories of keys, including the edit keys, function keys, ESC, CTRL, and ALT keys and how to press keys simultaneously.	1.47
Connecting to the Internet	Learn how a computer is connected to the Internet. The Lab presents using the Internet to access information.	2.47
The World Wide Web	Understand the significance of the World Wide Web and how to use Web browser software and search tools.	2.47
Word Processing	Gain a basic understanding of word processing concepts, from creating a document to printing and saving the final result.	3.47
Working with Spreadsheets	Learn how to create and utilize spreadsheets, including entering formulas, creating graphs, and performing what-if analysis.	3.47
Understanding the Motherboard	Step through the components of a motherboard. The Lab shows how different motherboard configurations affect the overall speed of a computer.	4.45
Scanning Documents	Understand how document scanners work.	5.43
Setting Up to Print	See how information flows from the system unit to the printer and how drivers, fonts, and physical connections play a role in generating a printout.	6.41
Configuring Your Display	Recognize the different monitor configurations available, including screen size, display cards, and number of colors.	6.41
Maintaining Your Hard Drive	Understand how files are stored on disk, what causes fragmentation, and how to maintain an efficient hard drive.	7.41
Evaluating Operating Systems	Evaluate the advantages and disadvantages of different categories of operating systems.	8.41
Working at Your	Learn the basic ergonomic principles that prevent back and neck pain, eye strain, and other	8.41

DISCOVERING COMPUTERS 2002

Concepts for a Digital World
Web Enhanced

CHAPTER 1

Introduction to Computers

Your last final exam is complete; the semester is over! Tonight, you finally will get a good night's sleep. This semester was the most intense yet. You are a bit anxious about your grades in sociology and psychology; but ... no more waiting for mail delivery! For the first time, the school's registration department will post grades on the Internet. They should be available by the weekend.

On Friday morning, you access the Internet from your home computer to find the grades have not been posted. When you meet your sister for lunch, you discuss the anticipation of receiving your grades via the Internet. She reaches for a computer in her briefcase and accesses the Internet. Still no grades. Then while visiting a friend, you ask if he has Internet access. He pulls a handheld computer out of his coat pocket and uses it to connect to the Internet. No grades yet.

Saturday finds you relaxing with friends at the beach. With a cellular telephone in hand, one friend shouts, "Our grade reports made it to the Internet!" You cross your fingers while entering your student identification number on the telephone keypad. Yes! Three As and two Bs. Now you can enjoy the summer.

OBJECTIVES

After completing this chapter, you will be able to:

- Explain the importance of computer literacy

- Define the term computer

- Identify the components of a computer

- Explain why a computer is a powerful tool

- Differentiate among the various categories of software

- Explain the purpose of a network

- Discuss the uses of the Internet and the World Wide Web

- Describe the categories of computers and their uses

- Identify the various types of computer users

- Understand how a user can be a Web publisher

THE DIGITAL REVOLUTION

Computers are everywhere ... at home, at work, and at school. Most of our daily activities either involve the use of or depend on information from a computer. Activities such as learning to read, contacting a senator, looking up a stock quote, visiting a museum, or planning a trip, could involve the use of computers (Figure 1-1).

With a home computer, you can balance your checkbook, pay bills, track personal income and expenses, transfer funds, buy or sell stocks, and evaluate financial plans. People deposit or withdraw funds through an ATM (automated teller machine). At the grocery store, a computer tracks your purchases and calculates the amount of money you owe. It also usually generates coupons customized

to your buying patterns. Many cars today include an onboard navigation system that provides directions, signals for emergency services, and tracks the vehicle if it is stolen.

In the workplace, people use computers to create correspondence such as memos and letters, calculate payroll, track inventory, and generate invoices. Both schools and homes have computers for educational purposes. Teachers use them to assist with the instruction. Students complete assignments and do research on computers in lab rooms and at home.

Many people find hours of entertainment on the computer. They play games, listen to music, watch a video or a movie, read a book or magazine, make a family tree, compose a video, re-touch a photograph, or plan a vacation.

Through computers, society has access to information from all around the globe. Instantaneously, you can find local and national news, weather reports, sports scores, stock prices, your medical records, your credit report, and countless forms of educational material. At your fingertips, you can send messages to others, meet new friends, shop, fill prescriptions, file taxes, or take a course.

Figure 1-1 Computers are present in every aspect of daily living.

Computers have become a primary tool people use to communicate with others. The brilliance of these communications is they are not limited to text. With today's technology, you also can transmit voice, sounds, video, and graphics. Use the computer to see others while you talk to them. Send family, friends, or clients videos or photographs.

The digital revolution is upon us. Technology continues to advance and computers extend into more facets of daily living. To be successful in this digital world, it is essential you are computer literate. Being **computer literate** means you have knowledge and understanding of computers and their uses.

The purpose of this book is to present the knowledge you need to understand how computers work and how computers are used. While you read, remember this chapter is an overview and many of the terms and concepts introduced will be discussed further in later chapters.

WHAT IS A COMPUTER?

A **computer** is an electronic machine, operating under the control of instructions stored in its own memory, that can accept data, manipulate the data according to specified rules, produce results, and store the results for future use.

Data and Information

Data is a collection of raw unprocessed facts, figures, and symbols. Computers process data to create information. **Information** is data that is organized, meaningful, and useful. As shown in Figure 1-2, a computer processes several data items to produce a paycheck. Another example of information is a grade report, which is generated from data items such as a student name, course names, and course grades.

A **user** is someone that communicates with a computer or uses the information it generates.

Hardware is the electric, electronic, and mechanical equipment that makes up a computer. **Software** is the series of instructions that tells the hardware how to perform tasks. Without software, most hardware is useless. The hardware needs instructions from software to process data into information.

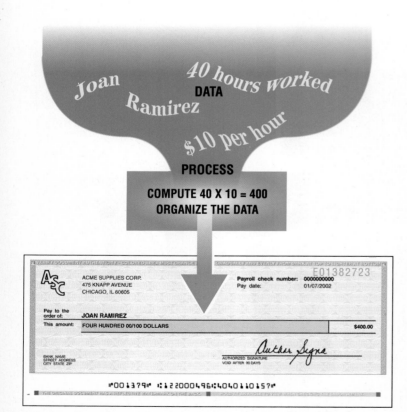

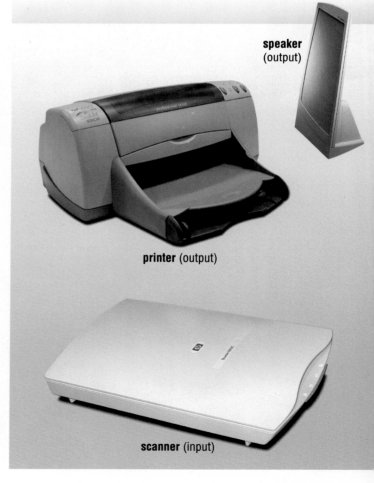

speaker (output)

printer (output)

scanner (input)

Figure 1-2 A computer processes data into information. In this example, the employee name, number of hours worked, and hourly pay rate each represent data. The computer processes these items to produce the paycheck.

Information Processing Cycle

Input is any data or instructions you enter into a computer. **Output** is data that has been processed into information. Computers process input (data) into output (information). **Storage** is an area in a computer that can hold data and information for future use. This series of input, process, output, and storage activities sometimes is called the **information processing cycle**.

Most computers today have the capability of communicating with other computers. Thus, communications also has become an important element of the information processing cycle.

THE COMPONENTS OF A COMPUTER

A computer consists of a variety of hardware components that work together with software to perform calculations, organize data, and communicate with other computers.

These hardware components include input devices, output devices, a system unit, storage devices, and communications devices. Figure 1-3 shows some common computer hardware components.

Input Devices

An **input device** is any hardware component that allows a user to enter data and instructions into a computer. Six commonly used input devices are the keyboard, mouse, microphone, scanner, digital camera, and PC camera (see Figure 1-3).

A computer keyboard contains keys that allow you to type letters of the alphabet, numbers, spaces, punctuation marks, and other symbols. A computer keyboard also contains other keys that allow you to enter data and instructions into the computer.

A mouse is a small handheld device that contains at least one button. The mouse controls the movement of a symbol on the screen called a pointer. For example, as you move the mouse across a flat surface, the pointer on the screen also moves. With the mouse, you can make choices, initiate a process, and select objects.

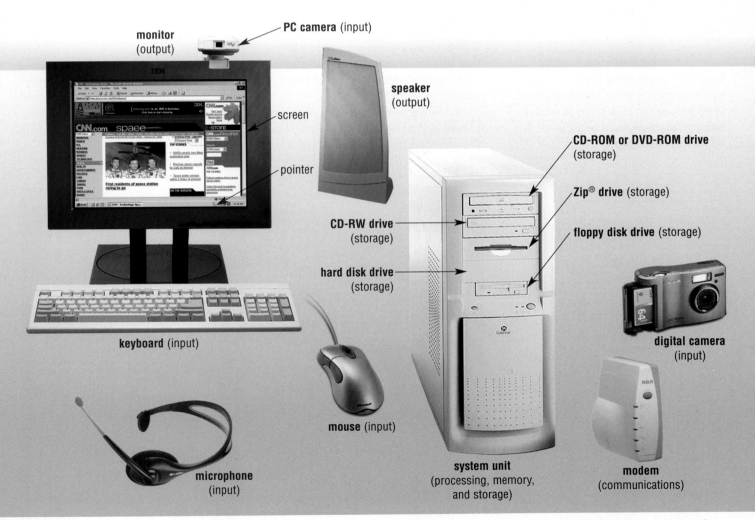

Figure 1-3 Common computer hardware components include a keyboard, mouse, microphone, PC camera, scanner, digital camera, system unit, disk drives, printer, monitor, speakers, and modem.

A microphone allows a user to speak to the computer to enter data and instructions into the computer. A scanner reads printed text and pictures and then translates the results into a form the computer can use. For example, you can scan a picture, and then include the picture when creating a brochure.

With a digital camera, you can take pictures and transfer the photographed image to the computer, instead of storing the images on traditional film. A PC camera is a digital video camera attached to a computer. This technology allows home users to edit videos, create a movie, and take digital still photographs on their computer. With a PC camera, you also can have video telephone calls — where someone can see you while communicating with you.

Output Devices

An **output device** is any hardware component that can convey information to a user. Three commonly used output devices are a printer, a monitor, and speakers (see Figure 1-3 on the previous page).

A printer produces text and graphics on a physical medium such as paper or transparency film. A monitor, which looks like a television screen, displays text, graphics, and video information. Speakers allow you to hear music, voice, and other sounds generated by the computer.

System Unit

The **system unit**, sometimes called a **chassis**, is a box-like case made from metal or plastic that protects the internal electronic components of the computer from damage (see Figure 1-3). The circuitry in the system unit usually is part of or is connected to a circuit board called the motherboard.

Two main components on the motherboard are the central processing unit and memory. The **central processing unit** (**CPU**), also called a **processor**, is the electronic device that interprets and carries out the basic instructions that operate the computer.

During processing, the processor places instructions to be executed and data needed by those instructions into memory. **Memory** is a temporary holding place for data and instructions.

Both the processor and memory consist of chips. A chip is an electronic device that contains many microscopic pathways that carry electrical current. Chips, which usually are no bigger than one-half inch square, are packaged so they can be attached to a motherboard or other circuit board (Figure 1-4).

Some computer components, such as the processor and memory, are internal and reside inside the system unit. Other components, such as the keyboard, mouse, microphone, monitor, printer, scanner, digital camera, and PC camera, often are located outside the system unit. These devices are considered external. A **peripheral** is any external device that attaches to the system unit.

Storage Devices

Storage holds data, instructions, and information for future use. Storage differs from memory, in that it can hold these items permanently. Memory, by contrast, holds items only temporarily while the processor interprets and executes them.

Figure 1-4 Chips are packaged so they may be attached to a circuit board.

A storage medium (media is the plural) is the physical material on which a computer keeps the data, instructions, and information. A **storage device** records and retrieves items to and from a storage medium. Storage devices often function as a source of input because they transfer items from storage into memory.

Six common storage devices are a floppy disk drive, a Zip® drive, a hard disk drive, a CD-ROM drive, a CD-RW drive, and a DVD-ROM drive (see Figure 1-3 on page 1.5). A drive is a device that reads from and may write onto a storage medium. This media includes floppy disks, Zip® disks, hard disks, and compact discs.

A floppy disk consists of a thin, circular, flexible disk enclosed in a plastic shell. A floppy disk stores data, instructions, and information using magnetic patterns. You insert and remove a floppy disk into and from a floppy disk drive (Figure 1-5). A Zip® disk is a higher capacity disk that can store the equivalent of up to 170 standard floppy disks.

A hard disk provides much greater storage capacity than a floppy disk. A hard disk usually consists of several circular platters that store items electronically. These disks are enclosed in an airtight, sealed case, which often is housed inside the system unit (Figure 1-6). Some hard disks are removable, which enables you to insert and remove the hard disk from a hard disk drive, much like a floppy disk (Figure 1-7). Removable disks are enclosed in plastic or metal cartridges so you can remove them from the drive. The advantage of removable media such as a floppy disk and removable hard disk is you can take the media out of the computer and transport or secure it.

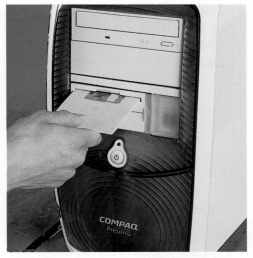

Figure 1-5 A floppy disk is inserted and removed from a floppy disk drive.

Web Link

For more information on processors, visit the Discovering Computers 2002 Chapter 1 WEB LINK page (**scsite.com/dc2002/ch1/ weblink.htm**) and click Processors.

Web Link

For more information on storage devices, visit the Discovering Computers 2002 Chapter 1 WEB LINK page (**scsite.com/dc2002/ch1/ weblink.htm**) and click Storage Devices.

self-contained hard disk

Figure 1-6 Most hard disks are self-contained devices housed inside the system unit.

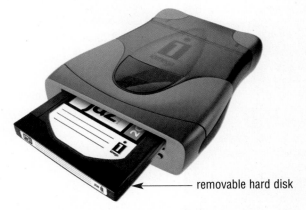

removable hard disk

Figure 1-7 Removable hard disks are inserted and removed from a drive.

A compact disc is a flat, round, portable medium that stores data using microscopic pits, which are created by a laser light. One type of compact disc is a CD-ROM, which you access using a CD-ROM drive. A Picture CD is a special type of CD-ROM that stores digital versions of photographs for consumers.

A variation of the standard CD-ROM is the rewriteable CD, or CD-RW. In addition to accessing data, you also can erase and store data on a CD-RW. To use a CD-RW, you need a CD-RW drive. Another type of compact disc is a DVD-ROM, which has tremendous storage capacities —

enough for a full-length movie. To use a DVD-ROM, you need a DVD-ROM drive (Figure 1-8).

Some devices, such as digital cameras, use miniature storage media (Figure 1-9). One popular type of miniature storage media is a card. You then can transfer the items, such as the digital photographs, from the media to your computer using a device called a card reader.

Communications Devices

Communications devices enable computer users to communicate and to exchange items such as data, instructions, and information with another computer.

A modem is a communications device that enables computers to communicate via telephone lines or cable. Modems are available as both external and internal devices.

Communications devices, such as modems, allow you to establish a connection between two computers and transmit items over transmission media, such as cables, telephone lines, or satellites.

WHY IS A COMPUTER SO POWERFUL?

A computer derives its power from its capability of performing the information processing cycle operations (input, process, output, and storage) with amazing speed, reliability, and accuracy; storing huge amounts of data and information; and communicating with other computers.

Speed

Inside the system unit, operations occur through electronic circuits. When data, instructions, and information flow along these circuits, they travel at close to the speed of light. This allows billions of operations to be carried out in a single second.

Figure 1-8 To use a DVD-ROM, you need a DVD-ROM drive.

miniature storage media

Figure 1-9 Many smaller devices, such as digital cameras, use miniature storage media.

Reliability

The electronic components in modern computers are dependable because they have a low failure rate. The high reliability of the components enables the computer to produce consistent results.

Accuracy

Computers can process large amounts of data and generate error-free results, provided the data is entered correctly and the program works properly. If data is inaccurate, the resulting output will be incorrect. A computing phrase — known as **garbage in, garbage out (GIGO)** — points out that the accuracy of a computer's output depends on the accuracy of the input.

Storage

Many computers can store enormous amounts of data and make this data available for processing any time it is needed. Using current storage devices, the computer can transfer data quickly from storage to memory, process it, and then store it again for future use.

Communications

Most computers today have the capability of communicating with other computers. Computers with this capability can share any of the four information processing cycle operations — input, process, output, and storage — with another computer. For example, two computers connected by a communications device such as a modem can share stored data, instructions, and information.

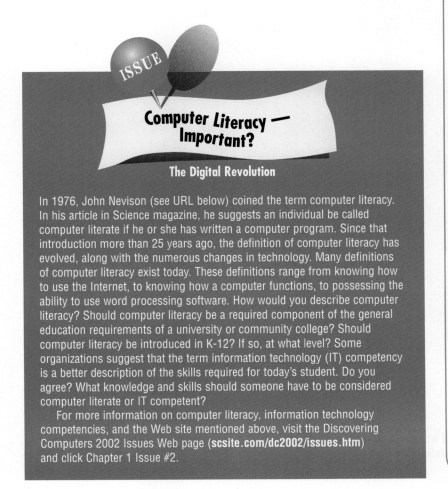

ISSUE
Computer Literacy — Important?

The Digital Revolution

In 1976, John Nevison (see URL below) coined the term computer literacy. In his article in Science magazine, he suggests an individual be called computer literate if he or she has written a computer program. Since that introduction more than 25 years ago, the definition of computer literacy has evolved, along with the numerous changes in technology. Many definitions of computer literacy exist today. These definitions range from knowing how to use the Internet, to knowing how a computer functions, to possessing the ability to use word processing software. How would you describe computer literacy? Should computer literacy be a required component of the general education requirements of a university or community college? Should computer literacy be introduced in K-12? If so, at what level? Some organizations suggest that the term information technology (IT) competency is a better description of the skills required for today's student. Do you agree? What knowledge and skills should someone have to be considered computer literate or IT competent?

For more information on computer literacy, information technology competencies, and the Web site mentioned above, visit the Discovering Computers 2002 Issues Web page (**scsite.com/dc2002/issues.htm**) and click Chapter 1 Issue #2.

Web Link

For more information on communications devices, visit the Discovering Computers 2002 Chapter 1 WEB LINK page (**scsite.com/dc2002/ch1/weblink.htm**) and click Communications Devices.

TECHNOLOGY TRAILBLAZER

BILL GATES

What advice does one of the richest men in the world have for students? *Get the best education you can. Take advantage of high school and college. Learn how to learn.* As Microsoft's chairman and chief software architect, Bill Gates receives hundreds of e-mail messages from students asking for insight on education. He emphasizes that college graduates know about a multitude of subjects and group dynamics. Gates dropped out of Harvard during his junior year, but he stresses that students should not quit going to school unless they are facing extraordinary prospects.

Gates began programming computers when he was 13. Early in his career he developed the BASIC programming language for the MITS Altair, one of the first microcomputers. He founded Microsoft in 1975 with Paul Allen, and five years later they developed the first operating system for the IBM PC, called MS-DOS. Under Gates' leadership, Microsoft continued to update MS-DOS and then develop Windows, Internet Explorer, and the MSNBC cable television news network and corresponding Web site. Today he is regarded as the most powerful person in the computer industry.

Gates has written two books: *Business @ the Speed of Thought* and *The Road Ahead*. All proceeds have been donated to non-profit organizations. He and his wife have endowed more than $21 billion to the Bill and Melinda Gates Foundation, which supports global health and learning.

For more information on Bill Gates, visit the Discovering Computers 2002 People Web page (**scsite.com/dc2002/people.htm**) and click Bill Gates.

When two or more computers are connected together via communications media and devices, they form a network. The most widely known network is the Internet (Figure 1-10).

COMPUTER SOFTWARE

Software, also called a **computer program** or simply a **program**, is a series of instructions that tells the hardware of a computer what to do. Some instructions allow you to input data from the keyboard and direct the computer to store the data in memory. Other instructions cause data in memory to be used in calculations such as adding a series of numbers to obtain a total. Some instructions compare two values in memory and direct the computer to perform alternative operations based on the results of the comparison. Other instructions direct the computer to print a report, display information on the monitor, draw a color picture on the monitor, or store information on a disk.

A computer carries out, or **executes**, the instructions in a program by first placing, or loading, the instructions in the memory of the computer. Usually, the computer loads the instructions from storage into memory. For example, a program might load into memory from the hard disk each time you execute the program.

When you purchase a program, such as one shown in Figure 1-11, you typically receive media such as a CD-ROM(s) or a DVD-ROM that contains the software. Some programs

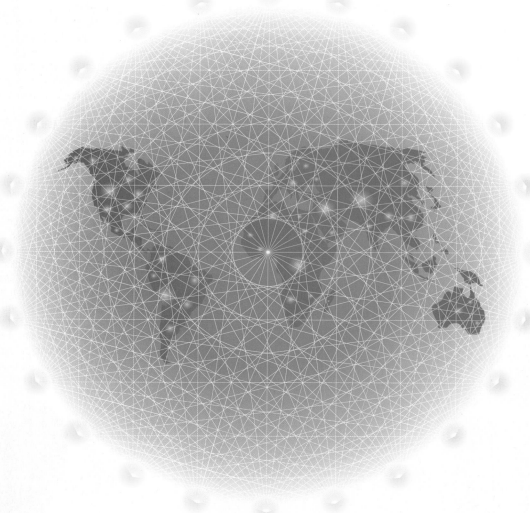

Figure 1-10 The Internet is a worldwide collection of networks that links together millions of businesses, government agencies, educational institutions, and individuals.

Figure 1-11 When you buy software, you receive media such as CD-ROMs or a DVD-ROM that contains the software program.

can load in memory directly from the media. With other programs, you must **install** a part or all of the software on the computer's hard disk before you can use the program. Some programs also require you insert the media, such as a CD-ROM, into the drive while you use, or run, the program. Others do not. Figure 1-12 shows the steps a user follows to run a computer program that allows you to create a greeting card. This program requires a CD-ROM in the CD-ROM drive.

When you buy a computer, it usually has some software pre-installed on its hard disk. This enables you to use the computer as soon as you set it up.

Software is the key to productive use of computers. With the proper software, a computer can become a valuable tool. Two types of software exist: system software and application software. The following pages describe these categories of software.

Web Link

For more information on computer programs, visit the Discovering Computers 2002 Chapter 1 WEB LINK page (**scsite.com/dc2002/ch1/weblink.htm**) and click Computer Programs.

Figure 1-12 RUNNING A COMPUTER PROGRAM FROM A CD-ROM

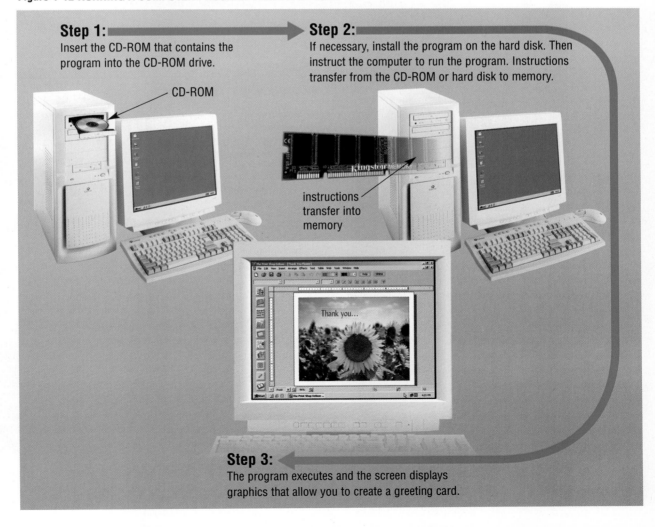

Step 1:
Insert the CD-ROM that contains the program into the CD-ROM drive.

CD-ROM

Step 2:
If necessary, install the program on the hard disk. Then instruct the computer to run the program. Instructions transfer from the CD-ROM or hard disk to memory.

instructions transfer into memory

Thank you...

Step 3:
The program executes and the screen displays graphics that allow you to create a greeting card.

1.12

System Software

System software consists of the programs that control the operations of the computer and its devices. System software serves as the interface between the user, the application software, and the computer's hardware. Two types of system software are the operating system and utility programs.

OPERATING SYSTEM An **operating system (OS)** is a set of programs containing instructions that coordinate all the activities among computer hardware devices. The operating system also contains instructions that allow you to run application software. Many of today's computers use the Microsoft Windows operating system.

When you start a computer, the operating system loads into memory from the computer's hard disk. It remains in memory while the computer is running and allows you to communicate with the computer and other software.

UTILITY PROGRAMS A **utility program** is a type of system software that performs a specific task, usually related to managing a computer, its devices, or its programs. An example of a utility program is an uninstaller, which removes a program that has been installed on a computer. Most operating systems include several utility programs for managing disk drives, printers, and other devices. You also can buy stand-alone utility programs to perform additional computer management functions.

USER INTERFACE You interact with software through its user interface. The user interface controls how you enter data and instructions and how information displays on the screen. Many of today's software programs have a graphical user interface. With a **graphical user interface (GUI** pronounced gooey), you interact with the software using visual images such as icons. An **icon** is a small image that represents a program, an instruction, or some other object. You can select icons with the mouse to perform operations such as starting a program. Figure 1-13 shows the graphical user interface of the Microsoft Windows operating system.

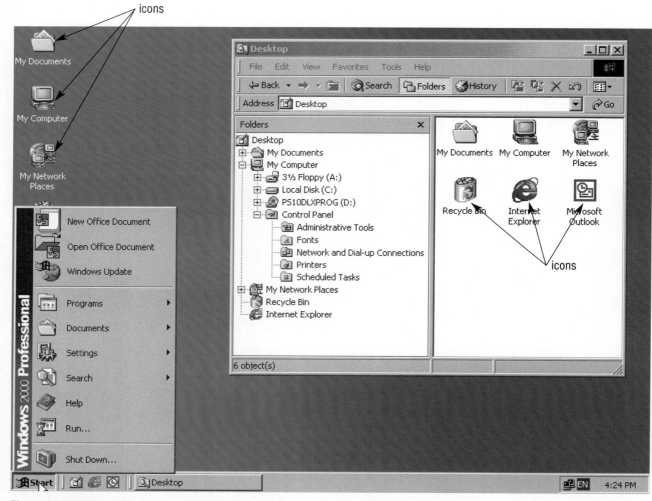

Figure 1-13 Microsoft Windows is an operating system that has a graphical user interface.

Application Software

Application software consists of programs that perform specific tasks for users. Popular application software includes word processing software, spreadsheet software, database software, and presentation graphics software. Word processing software allows you to create documents such as letters, memorandums, and brochures. Spreadsheet software allows you to calculate numbers arranged in rows and columns. Users perform financial tasks such as budgeting and forecasting with spreadsheet software. Database software allows you to store data in an organized fashion, as well as retrieve, manipulate, and display that data in a variety of formats. With presentation graphics software, you create documents called slides that add visual appeal to presentations. Software vendors often bundle and sell these four applications together as a single unit. This bundle, called a suite, costs

much less than if you purchased the applications individually.

Many other types of application software exist that enable users to perform a variety of tasks. Some widely used applications include the following: reference, education, and entertainment; desktop publishing; photo and video editing; multimedia authoring; network, communications, electronic mail (e-mail), and Web browsers; accounting; project management; and personal information management. Chapter 2 discusses Web browsers and e-mail, and Chapter 3 discusses the other applications.

Application software is available in a variety of forms: packaged, custom, freeware, public domain, shareware, and from application service providers.

PACKAGED SOFTWARE Packaged software is copyrighted retail software that meets the needs of a wide variety of users, not just a single user or company. You can purchase packaged software from stores that sell computer products (Figure 1-14a). You also can purchase packaged software from companies on the Internet (Figure 1-14b).

Figure 1-14a (computer store)

Figure 1-14b (online computer store)

Figure 1-14 Packaged software programs can be purchased from computer stores, office equipment suppliers, retailers, and software vendors. Many stores, such as OfficeMax shown in this figure, allow you to purchase software programs on the Internet.

Web Link

For more information on application software, visit the Discovering Computers 2002 Chapter 1 WEB LINK page (**scsite.com/dc2002/ch1/ weblink.htm**) and click Application Software.

CUSTOM SOFTWARE Sometimes a user or company with unique software requirements cannot find packaged software that meets all its needs. In this case, the person or company can opt for custom software. **Custom software**, written by a programmer, is a tailor-made program developed at a user's request to perform specific functions.

FREEWARE, PUBLIC-DOMAIN SOFTWARE, AND SHAREWARE
Freeware is software provided at no cost to a user by an individual or company. Freeware is copyrighted. You cannot resell it as your own. **Public-domain software** also is free software, but it has been donated for public use and has no copyright restrictions.

Shareware is copyrighted software that is distributed free for a trial period. If you want to use a shareware program beyond that period of time, you send a payment to the person or company that developed the program. Companies that develop shareware rely on the honor system. The company trusts you to send payment if you continue to use the software beyond the stated trial period. Upon sending this small fee, the developer registers you to receive service assistance and updates.

Examples of shareware, freeware, and public-domain software include utility programs, graphics programs, and games. Thousands of these programs are available on the Internet to download, or copy to your computer. You also can obtain copies of these programs from the developer, a coworker, or a friend.

APPLICATION SERVICE PROVIDER
Storing and maintaining programs can be a costly investment for individuals and businesses. Some opt to use an application service provider for their software needs. An **application service provider** (**ASP**) is a third-party company that manages and distributes software and services on the Internet. That is, instead of installing the software on your computer, you run the programs from the Internet. Some vendors provide access to the software at no cost. Others charge for use of the program.

Software Development

A **computer programmer**, also called a **programmer**, is someone who writes software programs. Programmers write the instructions that direct the computer to process data into information. A programmer must place instructions in the correct sequence so the computer generates the desired results. Complex programs can require hundreds of thousands of program instructions.

When writing complex programs for large businesses, programmers often follow a plan developed by a systems analyst. A **systems analyst** designs a program, working with both the user and the programmer to determine the desired output of the program.

Programmers use a programming language to write computer programs. Some programming languages, such as JavaScript, allow programmers to develop applications that run on the Internet. Figure 1-15 shows an Internet application and the instructions the programmer writes to create the application.

Figure 1-15a (JavaScript program)

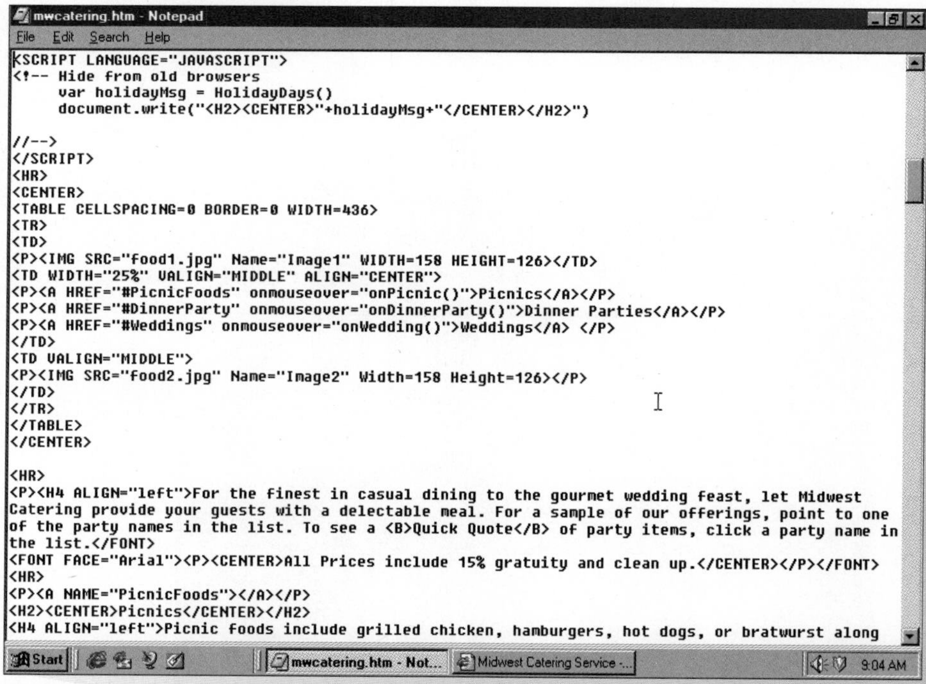

```
<SCRIPT LANGUAGE="JAVASCRIPT">
<!-- Hide from old browsers
     var holidayMsg = HolidayDays()
     document.write("<H2><CENTER>"+holidayMsg+"</CENTER></H2>")

//-->
</SCRIPT>
<HR>
<CENTER>
<TABLE CELLSPACING=0 BORDER=0 WIDTH=436>
<TR>
<TD>
<P><IMG SRC="food1.jpg" Name="Image1" WIDTH=158 HEIGHT=126></TD>
<TD WIDTH="25%" VALIGN="MIDDLE" ALIGN="CENTER">
<P><A HREF="#PicnicFoods" onmouseover="onPicnic()">Picnics</A></P>
<P><A HREF="#DinnerParty" onmouseover="onDinnerParty()">Dinner Parties</A></P>
<P><A HREF="#Weddings" onmouseover="onWedding()">Weddings</A> </P>
</TD>
<TD VALIGN="MIDDLE">
<P><IMG SRC="food2.jpg" Name="Image2" Width=158 Height=126></P>
</TD>
</TR>
</TABLE>
</CENTER>

<HR>
<P><H4 ALIGN="left">For the finest in casual dining to the gourmet wedding feast, let Midwest
Catering provide your guests with a delectable meal. For a sample of our offerings, point to one
of the party names in the list. To see a <B>Quick Quote</B> of party items, click a party name in
the list.</FONT>
<FONT FACE="Arial"><P><CENTER>All Prices include 15% gratuity and clean up.</CENTER></P></FONT>
<HR>
<P><A NAME="PicnicFoods"></A></P>
<H2><CENTER>Picnics</CENTER></H2>
<H4 ALIGN="left">Picnic foods include grilled chicken, hamburgers, hot dogs, or bratwurst along
```


Figure 1-15 This figure illustrates an Internet application and the instructions a programmer writes in JavaScript to create the application.

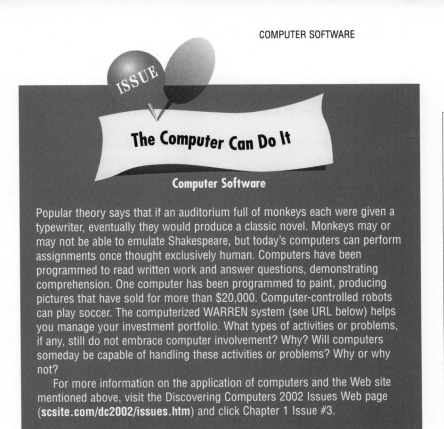

ISSUE

The Computer Can Do It

Computer Software

Popular theory says that if an auditorium full of monkeys each were given a typewriter, eventually they would produce a classic novel. Monkeys may or may not be able to emulate Shakespeare, but today's computers can perform assignments once thought exclusively human. Computers have been programmed to read written work and answer questions, demonstrating comprehension. One computer has been programmed to paint, producing pictures that have sold for more than $20,000. Computer-controlled robots can play soccer. The computerized WARREN system (see URL below) helps you manage your investment portfolio. What types of activities or problems, if any, still do not embrace computer involvement? Why? Will computers someday be capable of handling these activities or problems? Why or why not?

For more information on the application of computers and the Web site mentioned above, visit the Discovering Computers 2002 Issues Web page (**scsite.com/dc2002/issues.htm**) and click Chapter 1 Issue #3.

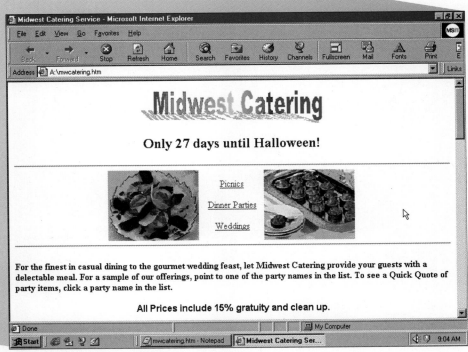

Figure 1-15b (Internet application)

APPLY IT!

Software – Purchase it Packaged, Subscribe, or Download?

Buying software used to be simple — you either purchased it from a local store or ordered it for delivery. You still have these options, but others have emerged. Providing the consumer the option to purchase and download software via the Internet, for example, is becoming standard practice for many online companies. Alternatively, Microsoft.NET is Microsoft's recent business strategy aimed at making Microsoft's existing software available on the Internet. With the Microsoft option, the user subscribes to and uses only the programs and data needed. If you are in the market to purchase or upgrade software and are unsure which option is best for you, consider the following:

- Purchasing packaged software
  - Pros: physical media in hand, easy to reinstall, does not require online access
  - Cons: limited to one computer, requires registration for upgrades, media may become damaged or lost
- Downloading from the Internet
  - Pros: easy to do, accessible 24 hours — the store is always open, easy to upgrade
  - Cons: service interruption while downloading, requires credit card information be posted online, hardware problems — reinstallation, need to download user manual
- Subscribing to and using Internet-based software
  - Pros: latest versions, accessible from any location with Internet access, access to online help, subscription not limited to one computer, use only the program and features you need
  - Cons: online access required, requires credit card information be posted online, data security, need to download user manual

For more information on software downloading or purchasing, visit the Discovering Computers 2002 Apply It Web page (**scsite.com/dc2002/apply.htm**) and click Chapter 1 Apply It #1.

NETWORKS AND THE INTERNET

A **network** is a collection of computers and devices connected together via communications devices and media. A modem is an example of a communications device. Examples of communications media are cables, telephone lines, cellular radio, and satellites. Some of these media, such as satellites and cellular radio, are wireless, which means they have no physical lines or wires. When your computer connects to a network, you are considered **online**.

Networks allow users to share **resources**, such as hardware devices, software programs, data, and information. Sharing resources saves time and money. For example, instead of purchasing one printer for every computer in a company or in a home, you can connect a single printer and

all computers via a network (Figure 1-16). This type of network enables all of the computers to access the same printer.

Most businesses network their computers together. These networks can be relatively small or quite extensive. A local area network (LAN) is a

network that connects computers in a limited geographic area, such as a school computer laboratory, office, or group of buildings. A wide area network (WAN) is a network that covers a large geographical area, such as one that connects the district offices across the country (Figure 1-17).

Figure 1-16 This local area network (LAN) enables two separate computers to share the same printer.

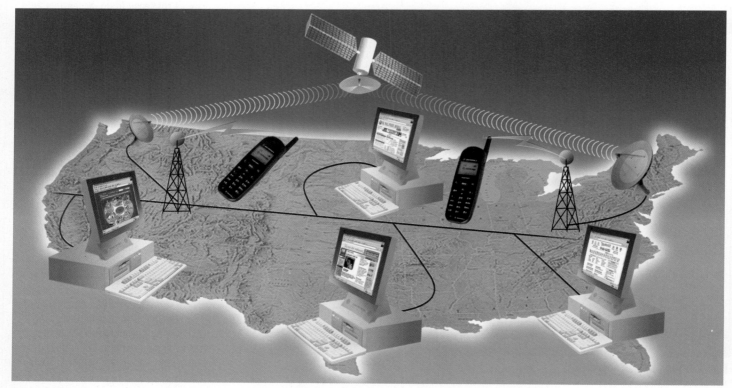

Figure 1-17 A network can be quite large and complex, connecting users in district offices around the country.

The world's largest network is the Internet. The **Internet** is a worldwide collection of networks that links together millions of businesses, government agencies, educational institutions, and individuals. With an abundance of resources and data accessible via the Internet, more than 360 million users around the world are making use of the Internet for a variety of reasons, some of which include the following (Figure 1-18):

- Sending messages to other connected users
- Accessing a wealth of information, such as news, maps, airline schedules, and stock market data
- Shopping for goods and services
- Meeting or conversing with people around the world
- Accessing sources of entertainment and leisure, such as online games, music, books, magazines, and vacation planning guides

Figure 1-18a (send a message)

Figure 1-18e (entertainment)

Figure 1-18b (access information)

Figure 1-18d (meet people)

Figure 1-18 Users access the Internet for a variety of reasons: to send messages to other connected users, to access a wealth of information, to shop for goods and services, to meet and converse with people around the world, and for entertainment.

Figure 1-18c (shop)

Most users connect to the Internet in one of two ways: through an Internet service provider or through an online service provider. An Internet service provider (ISP) is a company that supplies connections to the Internet, usually for a monthly fee. An online service provider (OSP) also provides access to the Internet, as well as a variety of other specialized content and services such as financial data, hardware and software guides, news, weather, legal information, and other similar commodities. For this reason, the fees for using an OSP sometimes are slightly higher than fees for using an ISP. Two popular OSPs are America Online and The Microsoft Network.

One of the more popular segments of the Internet is the World Wide Web, also called the Web. The Web contains billions of documents called Web pages. A Web page contains text, graphics, sound, or video, and has built-in connections, or links, to other Web documents. Computers throughout the world store Web pages. The screens shown in Figure 1-18 on the previous page are examples of Web pages.

A Web site is a collection of related Web pages. You access and view Web pages using a software program called a Web browser. The two most popular Web browsers are Microsoft Internet Explorer and Netscape Navigator. Figure 1-19 illustrates one method of connecting to the Web and displaying a Web page.

Web Link

For more information on the Internet, visit the Discovering Computers 2002 Chapter 1 WEB LINK page (**scsite.com/dc2002/ch1/ weblink.htm**) and click Internet.

Figure 1-19 CONNECTING TO THE INTERNET AND DISPLAYING A WEB PAGE

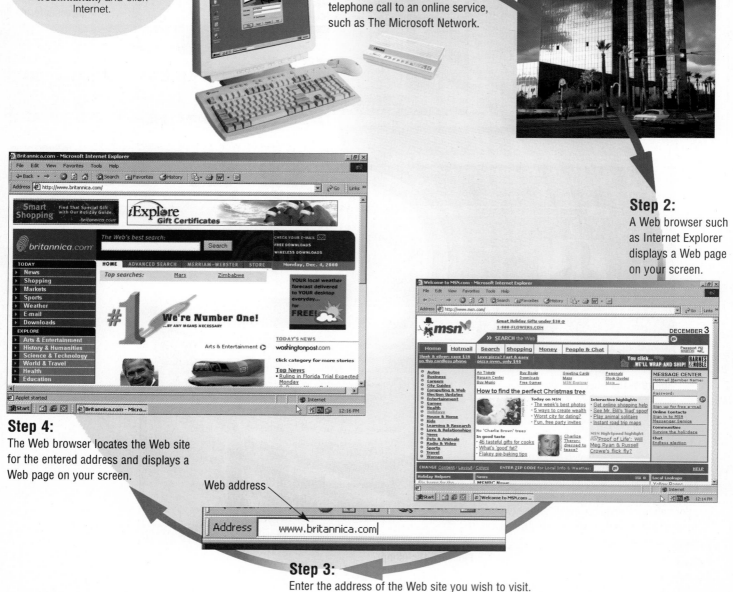

Step 1:
Use your computer and modem to make a local telephone call to an online service, such as The Microsoft Network.

Step 2:
A Web browser such as Internet Explorer displays a Web page on your screen.

Step 4:
The Web browser locates the Web site for the entered address and displays a Web page on your screen.

Web address

Address   www.britannica.com

Step 3:
Enter the address of the Web site you wish to visit.

CATEGORIES OF COMPUTERS

The six major categories of computers are personal computers, handheld computers, Internet appliances, mid-range servers, mainframes, and supercomputers. These categories are based on the differences in the size, speed, processing capabilities, and price of computers. Due to rapidly changing technology, the categories cannot be defined precisely. For example, the speed that defines a mainframe today may define a mid-range server next year. Some characteristics may overlap categories. Still, many people refer to these categories when discussing computers.

Figure 1-20 summarizes the six categories of computers, and the following pages discuss them.

PERSONAL COMPUTERS

A **personal computer** is a computer that can perform all of its input, processing, output, and storage activities by itself. A personal computer contains at least one input device, one output device, one storage device, memory, and a processor. On a personal computer, all of the processor's functions typically reside on a single chip, often called a microprocessor. The processor is the basic building block of a personal computer.

Two popular series of personal computers are the PC (Figure 1-21) and the Apple Macintosh (Figure 1-22). These two types

Category	Physical size	Number of simultaneously connected users	General price range
Personal computer (desktop or notebook)	Fits on a desk or on your lap	Usually one, or many networked	Several thousand dollars or less
Handheld computer	Fits in your hand	Usually one	Several hundred dollars or less
Internet appliance	Fits on a countertop	Usually one	Several hundred dollars or less
Mid-range server	Small cabinet	Two to thousands	$5,000 to $150,000
Mainframe	Partial room to a full room of equipment	Hundreds to thousands	$300,000 to several million dollars
Supercomputer	Full room of equipment	Hundreds to thousands	Several million dollars and up

Figure 1-20 This table summarizes some of the differences among the categories of computers. These should be considered general guidelines only because of rapid changes in technology.

Figure 1-21 The PC and compatibles use the Windows operating system.

Power Mac G4 Cube

Figure 1-22 The Apple Macintosh uses the Macintosh operating system.

of computers have different processors and use different operating systems. The PC and compatibles use the Windows operating system. The Apple Macintosh uses the Macintosh operating system (Mac OS). Today, the terms PC and compatible refer to any personal computer that is based on specifications of the original IBM personal computer. Companies such as Gateway, Compaq, Dell, and Toshiba all sell PC-compatible computers.

Two major categories of personal computers are desktop computers and notebook computers. The next two sections discuss these types of personal computers.

Desktop Computers

A **desktop computer** is designed so the system unit, input devices, output devices, and any other devices fit entirely on or under a desk or table (Figure 1-23). In some models,

the monitor sits on top of the system unit, which is placed on top of the desk. A **tower model**, by contrast, has a tall and narrow system unit that can sit on the floor vertically — if space is limited on your desktop. Tower model desktop computers are available in a variety of heights: a full tower is at least 24 inches tall, a mid-tower is about 16 inches tall, and a mini-tower is usually 13 inches tall. The model of desktop computer you use often depends on the design of your workspace.

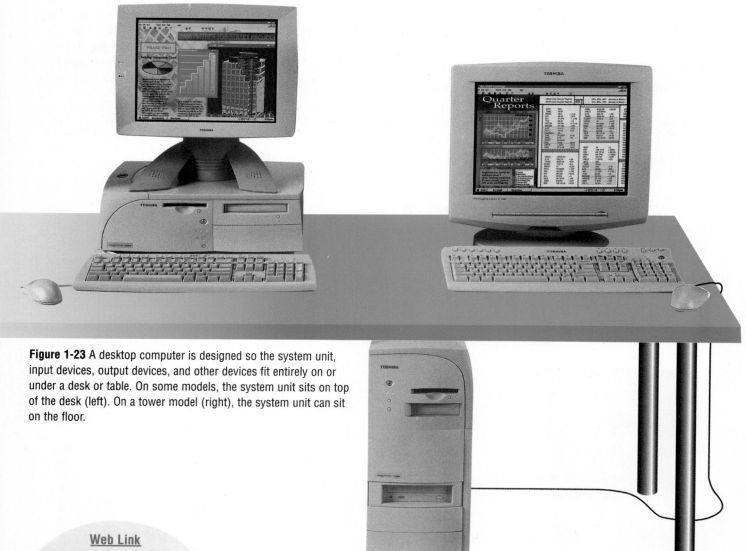

Figure 1-23 A desktop computer is designed so the system unit, input devices, output devices, and other devices fit entirely on or under a desk or table. On some models, the system unit sits on top of the desk (left). On a tower model (right), the system unit can sit on the floor.

An **all-in-one computer** is a less expensive desktop computer that combines the monitor and system unit into a single device (Figure 1-24). These compact computers are ideal for the casual home user.

A **workstation** is a more expensive and powerful desktop computer designed for work that requires intense calculations and graphics capabilities. Users in fields such as engineering, desktop publishing, and graphic art use workstations. An architect uses a workstation to view and create maps. A graphic artist uses a workstation to create computer-animated special effects for Hollywood movies.

A **stand-alone computer** is a computer that can perform the information processing cycle operations (input, process, output, and storage) without being connected to a network. Most stand-alone desktop computers today also have networking capabilities.

Some desktop computers also are powerful enough to function as a server on a network. A **server** is a computer that manages the resources on a network. Servers control access to the software, printers, and other devices on the network. Servers also provide a centralized storage area for software programs and data. The other computers on the network, called

Figure 1-24 An all-in-one computer is a less expensive desktop computer that combines the monitor and system unit into a single device.

clients, can access the contents of the storage area on the servers (Figure 1-25). Instead of clients, some people refer to these attached computers as workstations — giving the term workstation two entirely separate meanings.

In a network, one or more computers usually are designated as the server(s). The major difference between the server and client computers is the server ordinarily has more power and more storage space.

Notebook Computers

A **notebook computer**, also called a **laptop computer**, is a portable, personal computer small enough to fit on your lap. Today's notebook computers are thin, lightweight, and can be as powerful as the average desktop computer. Notebook computers generally are more expensive than desktop computers with equal capabilities.

On a typical notebook computer, the keyboard is located on top of the system unit, the monitor attaches to the system unit with a hinge, and the drives are built into the system unit (Figure 1-26). Weighing on average between 4 and 10 pounds, you easily can transport these computers from place to place. Most notebook computers can run either on batteries or a standard power supply. Users with mobile computing needs, such as business travelers, often have a notebook computer.

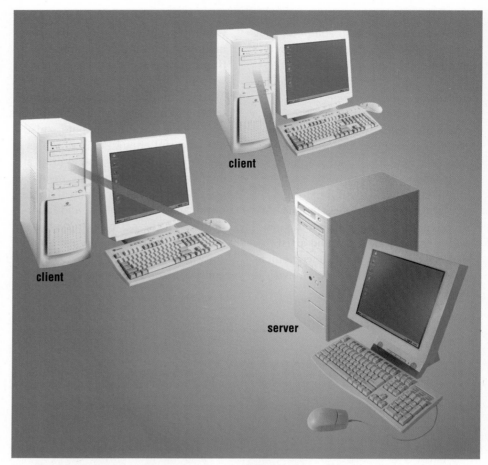

Figure 1-25 A server is a computer that manages resources on a network. Other computers on the network are called clients.

DVD-ROM and CD-RW drives

Figure 1-26 On a typical notebook computer, the keyboard is on top of the system unit, the monitor attaches to the system unit with a hinge, and the drives are built-in to the system unit.

HANDHELD COMPUTERS

A **handheld computer**, sometimes called a **palmtop computer**, is a small computer that fits in your hand (Figure 1-27). Because of their reduced size, the screens on handheld computers are quite small. Some have small keyboards. Others have no keyboard at all. Computers in the handheld category usually do not have disk drives. Instead, programs and data are stored on chips inside the system unit or on miniature storage media.

You typically can connect a handheld computer to a larger computer to exchange information between the two computers. A business traveler or other mobile user might use a handheld computer if a notebook computer is too large. Employees whose jobs require them to move from place to place such as parcel delivery people and meter readers also use specific industry-related handheld computers.

Handheld computers often include a stylus for input. A stylus looks like a ballpoint pen, but uses pressure, instead of ink, to write text and draw lines. With the stylus, also called a pen, you write on the screen instead of typing on a keyboard. These computers contain special software that permits the computer to recognize handwritten characters and other symbols. As an alternative to typing or writing, some handheld computers support voice input so you can enter text and instructions by speaking into the computer.

Figure 1-28 shows one of the most popular handheld computers in use today. Sometimes called a **PDA (personal digital assistant)**, these

Figure 1-27 A handheld computer is a small personal computer designed to fit in your hand.

Figure 1-28 With some handheld computers, you write directly on the screen with the stylus.

APPLY IT!
Lease or Purchase?

Your computer is old, and you are ready to upgrade. You discover many companies now offer a lease option — somewhat similar to what many automobile companies offer. The question is: When considering the obsolescence factor of a personal computer, does it make sense to lease rather than buy? Consider the following advantages and disadvantages when making your decision.

- Purchase Advantages
  - You own it
  - Tax deductions if used for business-related activities
  - Upgrade options
- Purchase Disadvantages
  - Obsolescence
  - Drains cash
  - Responsible for repairs
  - Interest payments
- Lease Advantages
  - Obsolescence not a factor
  - Conserves cash
  - Increases technological flexibility
- Lease Disadvantages
  - Generally more expensive
  - Will be charged for damage
  - Lease agreement might be confining or have penalty clause

Before making a decision, consider a Lease/Buy Analyzer program. Several of these are free online (see URL below).

For more information on leasing versus purchasing and the Web site mentioned above, visit the Discovering Computers 2002 Apply It Web page (scsite.com/dc2002/apply.htm) and click Chapter 1 Apply It #2.

lightweight handheld computers provide personal organizer functions such as a calendar, appointment book, address book, calculator, and notepad. Most of these handheld computers also offer basic software applications such as word processing and spreadsheet. Because of all these added features, many people have replaced their pocket-sized appointment book with these small handheld computers.

Some handheld computers are Web-enabled, allowing you also to access the Internet wirelessly. Other Web-enabled devices include cellular telephones and pagers (Figure 1-29). A **Web-enabled cellular telephone**, sometimes called a **smart phone**, allows you to send and receive messages on the Internet and browse Web sites specifically configured for display on the telephone. A **Web-enabled pager**, also called a **smart pager**, is a two-way radio that allows you to send and receive messages on the Internet.

INTERNET APPLIANCES

A **Internet appliance**, also called an **information appliance**, is a computer with limited fuctionality whose main purpose is to connect to the Internet from home. Internet appliances are available in a variety of styles, sizes, colors, and sleek designs.

Some Internet appliances look much like a desktop computer (Figure 1-30). Manufacturers typically preinstall all software on these Internet appliances, making it very easy for the novice user to work on the

Figure 1-29 These handheld computers and devices are small enough to fit in the palm of your hand.

Figure 1-30 This Internet appliance is equipped with all the software you need to access the Internet easily from any room in the house.

Web Link
For more information on handheld computers, visit the Discovering Computers 2002 Chapter 1 WEB LINK page (**scsite.com/dc2002/ch1/ weblink.htm**) and click Handheld Computers.

Internet. Another popular Internet appliance is a set-top box. A set-top box, such as WebTV™, sits on top of or next to a television set and allows you to access the Internet and navigate Web pages using a device that resembles a remote control (Figure 1-31).

MID-RANGE SERVERS

A **mid-range server** is more powerful and larger than a workstation computer (Figure 1-32). Mid-range servers often can support up to 4,000 connected users at the same time. In the past, these types of computers were known as **minicomputers**.

Users typically access a mid-range server via a personal computer or a terminal. A **terminal** is a device with a monitor and keyboard. Terminals, sometimes called **dumb terminals** because they have no processing power, cannot act as stand-alone computers and must be connected to a server to operate.

Figure 1-31 With a device such as WebTV™, you can access the Internet from the comfort of your family room or any room that has television access.

Figure 1-32 A mid-range server is more powerful than a workstation, but less powerful than a mainframe.

ISSUE

A Double-Edged Sword?

Handheld Devices

Many technological innovations are double-edged swords, with both positive and negative effects on society. Some sources say that extended use of Web-enabled cellular telephones, for instance, could lead to health problems. Storing obsolete equipment in basements and landfills is not healthy for you or the environment. Research from some health institutions indicates that people who have cardiac pacemakers could be affected by radio signals. Drivers using handheld devices are more likely to be involved in a crash. Media reports that mobile telephones have caused explosions at gasoline stations. Is the overall impact of computers and technology positive or negative for society? Do you agree adverse health effects could be related to the signals produced by the mobile devices? Should there be a law against driving and using a handheld device? What are some other negative issues related to technology?

For more information on computer effects on society, visit the Discovering Computers 2002 Issues Web page (**scsite.com/dc2002/issues.htm**) and click Chapter 1 Issue #4.

MAINFRAMES

A **mainframe** is a large, expensive, very powerful computer that can handle hundreds or thousands of connected users simultaneously (Figure 1-33). Mainframes also can act as a server in a network environment.

Mainframes can store tremendous amounts of data, instructions, and information. Users often access the mainframe with terminals or personal computers.

SUPERCOMPUTERS

A **supercomputer** is the fastest, most powerful computer — and the most expensive (Figure 1-34). Supercomputers are capable of processing more than 12 trillion instructions in a single second. Applications requiring complex, sophisticated mathematical calculations use supercomputers. For example, weather forecasting, nuclear energy research, and petroleum exploration applications use a supercomputer.

COMPANY ON THE CUTTING EDGE

IBM

Big Blue PC

Checkmate. That is the word World Chess Champion Garry Kasparov heard when IBM's Deep Blue supercomputer defeated him in 1997. This six-game match marked the first time a computer had beaten a reigning world-renown chess player. But rather than emphasize the victory, IBM executives used the opportunity to focus on technology's potential.

Indeed, IBM has altered our lives since its incorporation in 1911. IBM's long record of computer successes include financial support for the Mark I in 1944, which took about 12 seconds to perform a division operation; the System/360 in 1964, which was the first family of computers with interchangeable software and peripherals; the IBM PC in 1981, with a base price of $1,565 and 16 KB of memory, a floppy disk drive, and an optional color monitor; and the ThinkPad notebook computer in 1992. For the past 40 years, IBM has been noted for its mainframe computers.

Today, IBM is the world's largest information technology company and has received numerous honors for its corporate policies, including being named by *WE Magazine* as the Top Employer of the Year for People with Disabilities and by the *Financial Times* as one of the World's Most Respected Companies.

For more information on IBM, visit the Discovering Computers 2002 Companies Web page (**scsite.com/dc2002/ companies.htm**) and click IBM.

Figure 1-33 Mainframe computers are large, expensive, powerful machines that can handle thousands of connected users simultaneously and process up to millions of instructions per second.

Figure 1-34 This IBM supercomputer, which covers an area the size of two basketball courts, can process up to 12 trillion calculations per second.

ELEMENTS OF AN INFORMATION SYSTEM

Obtaining useful and timely information from a computer requires more than just the hardware and software discussed thus far. Other elements include the input of accurate data, trained information technology (IT) personnel, knowledgeable users, and documented procedures. Together, these elements (hardware, software, data, people, and procedures) comprise an **information system** (Figure 1-35).

For an information system to provide accurate, timely, and useful information, each element in the system must be present and all of the elements must work together. The hardware must be reliable and capable of handling the expected workload. The software must be developed carefully and tested thoroughly. The data entered must be accurate. If the data is incorrect, the information it generates also will be incorrect.

Properly trained IT personnel are required to run most mid-size and large computers. Even small networks of personal computers usually have a

system administrator to manage the network. Users are taking increasing responsibility for the successful operation of information systems. This includes responsibility for the accuracy of both the input and output. In addition, users are taking a more active role in the development of computer applications. They work closely with IT personnel in the development of computer applications that relate to their areas of work. Finally, all the IT applications should have documented procedures covering not only the computer operations but any other related procedures as well.

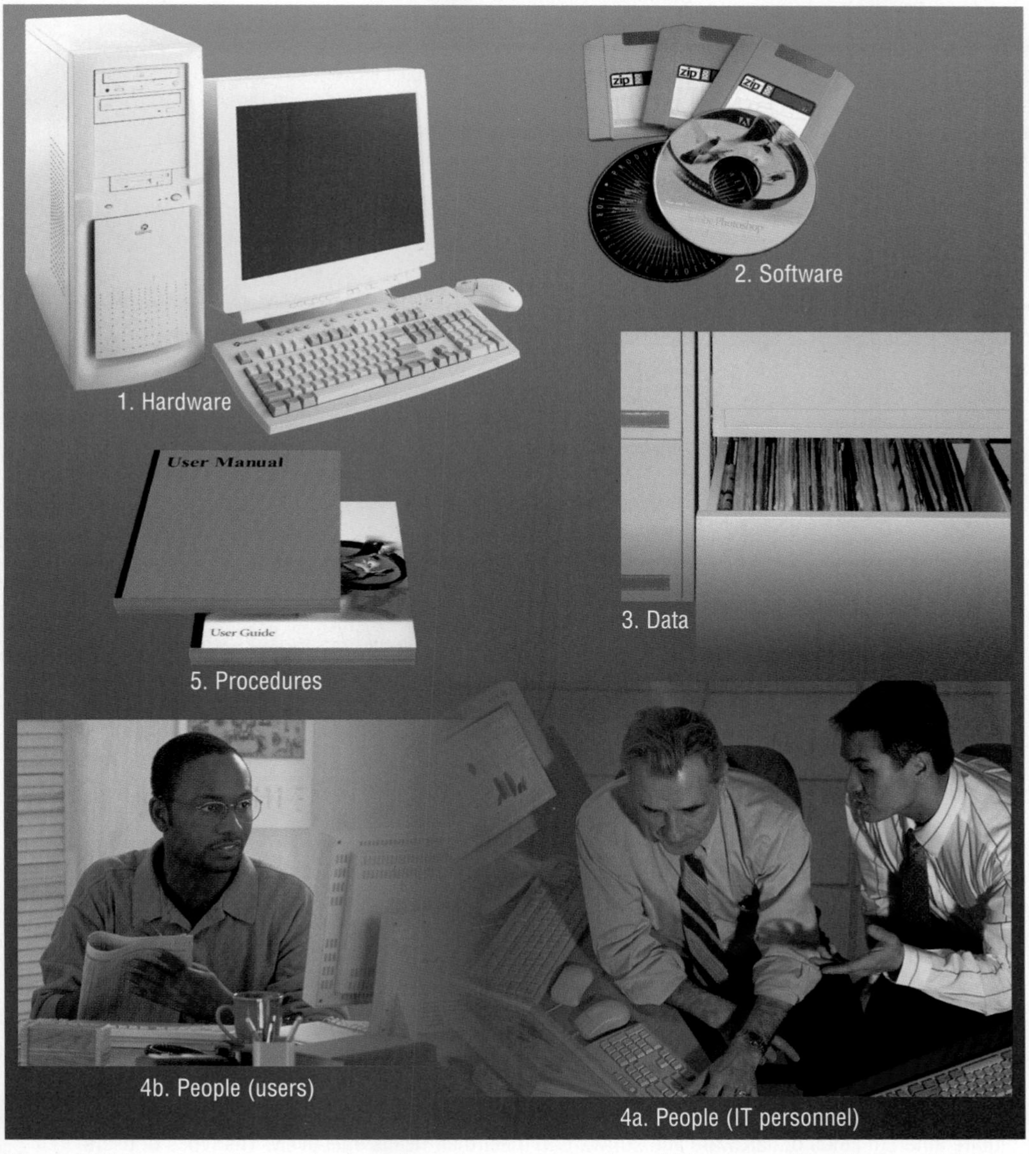

Web Link

For more information on women in technology, visit the Discovering Computers 2002 Chapter 1 WEB LINK page (**scsite.com/dc2002/ch1/ weblink.htm**) and click Women in Technology.

Web Link

For more information on minorities in technology, visit the Discovering Computers 2002 Chapter 1 WEB LINK page (**scsite.com/dc2002/ch1/ weblink.htm**) and click Minorities in Technology.

1. Hardware
2. Software
3. Data
5. Procedures
4b. People (users)
4a. People (IT personnel)

Figure 1-35 Five elements combine to make an information system: (1) hardware, (2) software, (3) data, (4) people, and (5) procedures.

EXAMPLES OF COMPUTER USAGE

Every day, numerous users rely on different types of computers for a variety of applications. Whether running complex application software, connecting to a network, or performing countless other functions, computers are powerful tools at home, at work, and at school.

To illustrate the variety of uses for computers, this section takes you on a visual and narrative tour of five categories of users: a home user, a small office/home office (SOHO) user, a mobile user, a large business user, and a power user (Figure 1-36). The following pages present examples of hardware and software listed in the table.

USER	HARDWARE/NETWORK	SOFTWARE
Home 	• Desktop computer • Handheld computer • Web-enabled devices • Internet	• Reference (e.g., encyclopedias, medical dictionaries, road atlas) • Entertainment (e.g. games, music composition, greeting cards) • Educational (e.g. foreign language tutorials, children's math and reading software) • Computer-based training • Productivity (word processing, spreadsheet) • Personal finance, online banking • Communications and Web browser • E-mail and instant messaging
Small Office/Home Office 	• Desktop computer • Handheld computer • Shared network printer • Local area network • Internet	• Productivity software (word processing, spreadsheet, database) • Company specific (e.g. accounting, legal reference) • Communications and Web browser • May use network versions of some software packages • E-mail
Mobile 	• Notebook computer equipped with a modem • Video projector • Web-enabled handheld computer • Internet • Local area network	• Productivity (word processing, spreadsheet, presentation graphics) • Personal information management • Communications and Web browser • E-mail
Large Business 	• Mid-range server or mainframe • Desktop or notebook computer • Handheld computer • Kiosk • Local area network or wide area network, depending on the size of the company • Internet	• Productivity (e.g., word processing, spreadsheet, database, presentation graphics) • Personal information management • Desktop publishing • Accounting • Network management software • Communications and Web browser • May use network versions of some software packages • E-mail
Power 	• Workstation or other powerful computer with multimedia capabilitities • Local area network • Internet	• Desktop publishing • Multimedia authoring • Photo, sound, and video editing • Communications and Web browser • Computer-aided design • E-mail

Figure 1-36 Today, computers are used in millions of businesses and homes to support work tasks and leisure activities. Depending on their intended usage, different computer users require different kinds of hardware and software to meet their needs effectively. The types of users are listed here together with the hardware, software, and network types mostly commonly used by each.

Home User

In a growing number of homes, the computer no longer is a convenience. Instead, it has become a basic necessity. Each family member uses the computer for different purposes. A **home user** spends time on the computer for research and education, budgeting and personal financial management, home business management, entertainment, personal and business communications, and Web access (Figure 1-37).

Once online, users can retrieve a tremendous amount of information, take college classes, pay bills, buy and sell stocks, shop, download music or movies, read a book, file taxes, book a flight, and communicate with others around the world. Some home users access the Web through the desktop computer, while others use Internet appliances and Web-enabled handheld computers and devices.

Home users also have a variety of other software. Most computers today are sold with word processing software already installed. Personal finance software helps to prepare taxes, balance a checkbook, and manage investments and family budgets. This software also allows you to connect to your bank via the Internet to pay bills online. Other software assists in organizing names and addresses, setting up home and automobile maintenance schedules, and preparing legal documents.

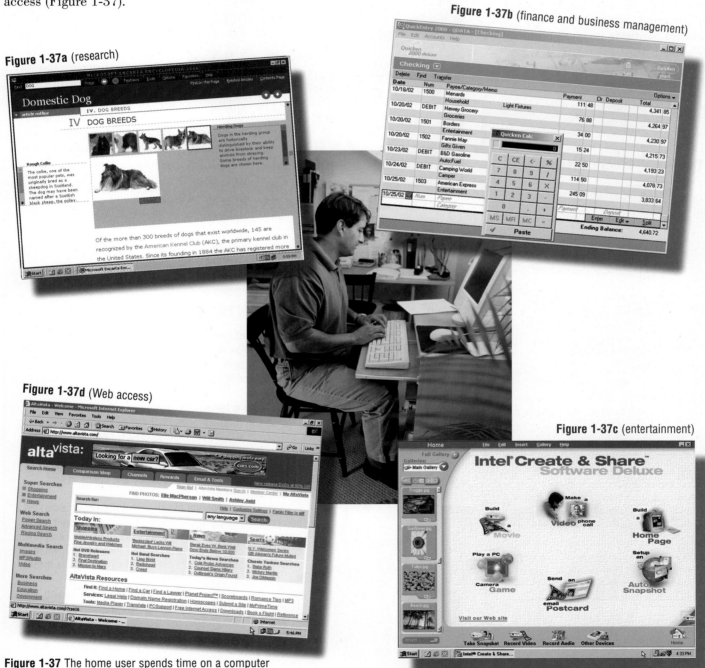

Figure 1-37a (research)

Figure 1-37b (finance and business management)

Figure 1-37d (Web access)

Figure 1-37c (entertainment)

Figure 1-37 The home user spends time on a computer for a variety of reasons.

Reference software, such as encyclopedias, medical dictionaries, or a road atlas, provides valuable and thorough information for everyone in the family. Software also provides hours of entertainment. For example, you can play games such as solitaire, chess, and Monopoly™; compose music; make a family tree; or create a greeting card. Educational software helps adults learn to speak a foreign language and youngsters to read, write, count, and spell. To make computers easier for younger people to use, many companies design special hardware just for children (Figure 1-38).

Many home users also have handheld computers to maintain daily schedules and address lists. Other special-purpose handheld computers manage and monitor the health condition of a family member.

A major concern of the United States government and many citizens around the world is the digital divide.

Figure 1-38 Many manufacturers design hardware especially for younger children.

The **digital divide** is the idea that you can separate people of the world into two distinct groups: (1) those who have access to technology with the ability to use it and (2) those who do not have access to technology or are without the ability to use it. The concern is that some of the less fortunate people in the world are not able to take advantage of the very technology that makes much of our society prosper and grow.

To narrow the gap in the digital divide, the United States government and many organizations have efforts in progress to improve the way society interacts with computers. These efforts include establishing community training centers and supplying teachers and students with necessary technology.

ISSUE

Does Technology Discriminate?

Computer Usage

In California, the Technology Training Foundation of America (TTFA) (see URL below) is trying to help bridge the digital divide by providing all California public and private schools and non-profit organizations access to donated computer equipment. A study completed by the Gartner Group suggests, however, the introduction of computer technology and the Internet into the schools has served to widen the gap in educational opportunity. Michael Fleisher, Gartner chief executive, says the study indicates an experience gap exists, and an entire socioeconomic group is now one generation behind in terms of that experience. The findings of the report further imply that even if this socioeconomic group has access to computers and to the Internet at school and public libraries, they cannot catch up to their experienced counterparts. Do you agree with these findings? Does a digital divide exists? Will the gap continue to widen? What measures can be taken to eliminate the digital divide?

For more information on technology discrimination, the digital divide, and the Web site mentioned above, visit the Discovering Computers 2002 Issues Web page (**scsite.com/dc2002/issues.htm**) and click Chapter 1 Issue #5.

TECHNOLOGY TRAILBLAZER

SHAWN **FANNING**

Frustrated about not being able to download good songs, Shawn Fanning decided to take matters in his own hands. Why not allow music lovers to swap individual songs from each other? Starting in January 1999, he spent sleepless nights feverishly writing the source code on his Dell notebook computer, fearful that someone would steal his idea before he could complete the program.

One semester earlier, Fanning had been a 19-year-old freshman computer science major at Boston's Northeastern University. But he dropped out to devote his full energy toward developing the Napster software and company, named after his nappy hair. The program he wrote was an instant success, even before it was complete. More than 32 million people, including an estimated 73 percent of all U.S. students, had downloaded the software and songs in less than one year.

Fanning's pioneering file-sharing concept has extended beyond the music industry. Media moguls in the print media, photography, and movie industries are battling to keep their copyrighted digital information under their control, while information-age zealots claim that information is meant to be exchanged freely.

For more information on Shawn Fanning, visit the Discovering Computers 2002 People Web page (**scsite.com/dc2002/people.htm**) and click Shawn Fanning.

Small Office/Home Office User

Computers also play an important role in helping small business users manage their resources effectively. A **small office/home office** (**SOHO**) includes any company with fewer than 50 employees, as well as the self-employed people that work out of their home. Small offices include local law practices, accounting firms, travel agencies, and florists. SOHO users typically have a desktop personal computer to perform some or all of their duties (Figure 1-39). Many also have handheld computers to manage appointments and contact information.

SOHO users access the Web to look up information on addresses, postal codes, flights, package shipping, and rates. Nearly all SOHO users communicate with others through e-mail. Many are entering the **e-commerce** arena by conducting their financial business on the Web.

These SOHO users have their own Web sites to advertise their products and services and take orders and requests from customers. Some of these Web sites use a **Web cam**, which is a video camera with output that can be displayed on a Web page. A Web cam allows the SOHO user to show the world a live view of some aspect of their business.

Small offices often have a local area network to connect the computers in the company. Networking the computers saves money on both hardware and software. For example, the small office avoids the expense of buying multiple printers by connecting a single shared printer to the network. The company also can purchase a network version of a software package.

A network version usually costs less than purchasing a separate software package for each individual desktop computer. Employees then access the software on a server as needed.

For business document preparation, finances, and tracking, SOHO users often purchase basic productivity software such as word processing and spreadsheet software. They also may use other types of software, specific to their industry or company. An accounting firm, for example, will have accounting software to prepare journals, ledgers, income statements, balance sheets, and other accounting documents.

(Web access)

(spreadsheet)

Figure 1-39 People with a home office and employees in small offices typically use a desktop personal computer for some or all of their duties.

Mobile User

As businesses expand to serve customers across the country and around the world, more and more employees have become **mobile users**, traveling to and from a main office to conduct business (Figure 1-40). Mobile users include a range of people such as sales representatives, marketing managers, real estate agents, insurance agents, meter readers, package delivery people, journalists, consultants, and students.

Mobile users often have a notebook computer equipped with a modem, which enables them to transfer information between their computer and another computer such as one at the main office. Sometimes they connect wirelessly to the Internet using a Web-enabled handheld computer or device such as a cellular telephone.

Other software utilized by mobile users includes basic productivity software such as word processing and spreadsheet software. They also use presentation graphics software to create and deliver presentations. To deliver the presentation to a large audience, the mobile user connects a notebook computer to a video projector that displays the presentation on a full screen.

Figure 1-40 Mobile users have notebook computers, handheld computers, and Web-enabled cellular telephones, so they can work while on the road.

Large Business User

A large business can have hundreds or thousands of employees in offices across a region, the country, or the world. The company usually has an equally large number of users (the **large business user**) and computers connected in a network (Figure 1-41).

This network — a local area network or a wide area network depending on the size of the company — enables communications among employees at all locations.

Almost all large businesses today have their own Web sites to showcase products, services, and selected company information (Figure 1-42). Customers, vendors, and any other interested parties can access the information on the Web without having to speak to a company employee. Many large businesses also participate in e-commerce, allowing customers to conduct financial business through the Web site.

Throughout a large business, computers help employees perform a variety of job-related tasks. For example, users in a typical large company use an automated telephone system to route calls to the appropriate department or person. The inside sales representatives enter orders into desktop personal computers while on the telephone with a customer.

Figure 1-41 A large business can have hundreds or thousands of users in offices across a region, the country, or the world. Throughout the business, computers help employees perform a variety of job-related tasks.

Figure 1-42 Large businesses usually have their own Web site to showcase products, services, and company information. Many allow customers to transact business on the Web, as well.

Outside sales representatives — the mobile users in the firm — use notebook computers to conduct business while on the road. The marketing department uses desktop publishing software to prepare marketing literature such as newsletters, product brochures, and advertising material. The accounting department uses software to pay invoices, bill customers, and process payroll. The employees in the information systems department have a huge responsibility: to keep the computers and the network running and determine when and if it requires new hardware or software.

In addition to word processing, spreadsheet, database, and presentation graphics software, employees in a large firm also may use calendar programs to post their schedules on the network and handheld computers to maintain personal or company information. Electronic mail and Web browsers enable communications among employees and others around the world.

Some large businesses also use a kiosk to provide information to the public. A **kiosk** is a freestanding computer, usually with a touch screen that serves as an input device (Figure 1-43). More advanced kiosks allow customers to place orders, make payments, and access the Web.

Many employees of a large business often telecommute (Figure 1-44). **Telecommuting** is a work arrangement in which employees work away from a company's standard workplace, and often communicate with the office using some communications technology.

Figure 1-43 A kiosk is a freestanding computer, usually with multimedia capabilities and a touch screen.

Figure 1-44 Many employees of large businesses often telecommute, and communicate with the office using some form of communications technology.

Power User

Another category of user, called a **power user**, requires the capabilities of a workstation or other powerful computer. Examples of power users include engineers, architects, desktop publishers, and graphic artists (Figure 1-45). Power users typically work with **multimedia**, in which they combine text, graphics, sound, video, and other media elements into one application. All of these users need computers with extremely fast processors that have multimedia capabilities because of the nature of their work.

In addition to powerful hardware, a workstation contains software specific to the needs of the power user. For example, engineers and architects use software to draft and design items such as floor plans, mechanical assemblies, and computer chips. The desktop publisher uses specialized software to prepare marketing literature such as newsletters, brochures, and annual reports. This software usually is quite expensive because of its specialized design.

Power users are found in all types of businesses, both large and small. Some also work at home. Depending on where they work, power users might fit into one of the previously discussed categories, as well. Thus, in addition to their specific needs, these users often have additional hardware and software requirements such as network capabilities and Internet access.

Figure 1-45 Examples of power users are engineers, architects, desktop publishers, graphic artists, and multimedia authors.

COMPUTER USER AS A WEB PUBLISHER

Individuals in each of the five categories of users (home, SOHO, mobile, large business, and power) access the Internet for a wealth of information and to shop for goods

APPLY IT!

Share Your Photos Online

Digital cameras have opened a new world of photo sharing online. Photo communities are all the rage. At these photo sharing Web sites, you store and share pictures. You can elect to share your Web site with the world, protect it with a password, or keep the site private. Many of the Web sites offer a variety of other services, including advice on how to take better pictures, tools, products, and more. Some let you share other items too, including calendars and stories.

WebShots (see URL below) is one of the many popular photo communities. To join WebShot and other free photo communities, you first must complete a registration process. Most of these sites require you provide your name and e-mail address, and that you select a user name and password. Some communities, such as WebShot, require you to download a software program, which includes an automatic Web connection that downloads new photos each day from a category of your choice. PhotoPoint (see URL below) is another popular community. This site provides helpful links and how-to guides and does not require a software download. Some sites limit the amount of space, while others offer unlimited space. Before joining one of these communities (see URLs below), evaluate several of them and determine the one or ones that best meets your needs.

For more information on photo communities, photo albums online, and the Web sites mentioned above, visit the Discovering Computers 2002 Apply It Web page (**scsite.com/dc2002/apply.htm**) and click Chapter 1 Apply It #3.

and services. In addition to being a recipient of information, however, users have the ability to *provide* information to other connected users around the world. Embracing this growing service of the Internet, users now can be active participants that provide personal and business information, photographs, items for sale, and even live conversation.

To accomplish this, many users create Web pages with word processing software or with Web page authoring software. Once you have created a Web page, you publish it. **Publishing** a Web page is the process of making it available on the Internet. Many Internet service providers (ISPs) and online service providers (OSPs) will store personal Web pages for their subscribers and members at no cost. Through your application software, you can copy Web pages from your computer to the ISPs or OSPs to make your Web pages available to the world.

Users publish Web pages for a variety of reasons:

- Home users publish Web pages that provide information about their family
- Small business users publish Web pages that provide information about their business
- Job seekers often publish Web pages that resemble a resume (Figure 1-46)
- Educators publish online courses, called distance-learning courses

Home and small business users also display photographs, videos, artwork, and other images on personal Web pages or as advertisements on other's Web pages. To display photographs, you use a scanner, a digital camera, or a PC camera. To create and modify graphical images, many easy-to-use paint/image editing programs exist. Some of these programs even include photo-editing capabilities so you can touch-up digital photographs such as removing red-eye. Some Web sites are called **photo communities** because they allow you to create an online photo album, and they store your digital photographs free of charge.

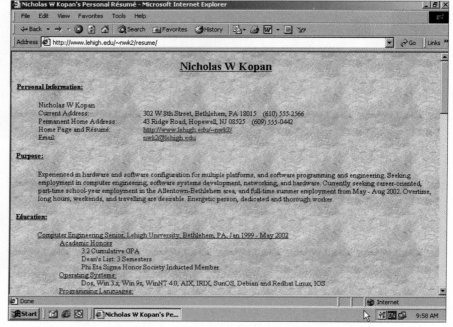

Figure 1-46 Job seekers often publish Web pages, so potential employers easily can locate their resume on the Web.

If you are a small business and you would like to advertise and take orders on the Web, you can sell your products at an electronic storefront. Some Web sites provide a means for you to create a storefront directly at their site, from which users around the world can view and make purchases (Figure 1-47). If you have only a single item for sale, you instead might consider putting it for sale on an online auction.

If you simply want to communicate with others on the Web, you can use e-mail, chat rooms, or instant messaging. Many Web sites offer online calendars and address books so that you can share your appointments and contacts with others. The next chapter presents a more detailed discussion of these Internet services.

CHAPTER SUMMARY

Chapter 1 introduced you to basic computer concepts such as what a computer is, how it works, and what makes it a powerful tool. You learned about the components of a computer. Next, the chapter discussed computer software, networks, and the Internet. The many different categories of computers and computer users also were presented. This chapter was an overview. Many of the terms and concepts introduced will be discussed further in later chapters.

Career Corner

Help Desk Specialist

A Help Desk Specialist is an entryway into the information technology (IT) field. Almost all organizations provide their employees with some type of help desk assistance. Within most companies, this job is one of the least technical. Some of the job requirements may include the following:

- Solve procedural and software questions both in person and over the telephone
- Develop and maintain Help Desk Operations Manuals
- Assist in training new Help Desk personnel

The type of questions one may encounter as a Help Desk Specialist depends on the setting. Someone who works in the computing center of a school would be required to have a broad knowledge of each computing platform used. In most instances, regardless of the setting, this job requires the specialist to be knowledgeable about major software packages in use.

Educational requirements are not as stringent as they are for other jobs in the computer field. In some cases, a high school diploma is sufficient. Advancement within the field requires a minimum of a two-year degree, while management generally requires a bachelor's degree in Information Systems or a related field. Entry-level salaries average $20,000 per year. Managers average between $42,000 and $50,000.

To learn more about the field of Help Desk Specialist as a career, visit the Discovering Computers 2002 Careers Web page (**scsite.com/dc2002/careers.htm**) and click Help Desk Specialist.

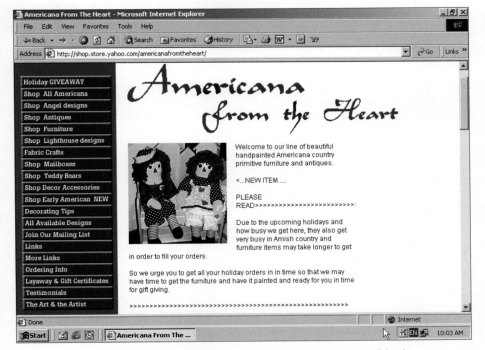

Figure 1-47 Users can create an electronic storefront for their home or small business.

E·FUN E·ENTERTAINMENT

THAT'S ENTERTAINMENT

Surf's Up for Fun Web Sites

Girls just want to have fun, according to singer Cindy Lauper. The Internet abounds with fun sites for both gals and guys, with everything from the Rock and Roll Hall of Fame and Museum to the Rock of Gibraltar.

Do you want to see the attractions at Walt Disney World? Or, how about wild animals at a game preserve in Africa, pandas at the San Diego Zoo, and surfers in Hawaii (Figure 1-48)? Travel to the South Pole and hear the frigid wind blow, to Yellowstone Park to see the Old Faithful geyser, and to Loch Ness for a possible glimpse of the famous monster. Web cams take armchair travelers across the world for views of natural attractions, historical monuments, colleges, and cities. Some of the world's Web cams are listed in Figure 1-49.

Figure 1-48 Web cams provide a glimpse of locations throughout the world, including famous surfing beaches in Hawaii.

FUN AND ENTERTAINMENT WEB SITES	URL
Web Cams	
AfriCam - The World's First Virtual Game Reserve	africam.com/
Discovery.com Cams	discovery.com/cams/cams.html
Iowa State Insect Zoo Live Camera	zoocam.ent.iastate.edu
Nesse on the Net! (Loch Ness Monster)	www.lochness.co.uk/livecam
OnlineWeather.com Webcams Index	onlineweather.com/webcams
Panda Cam San Diego Zoo	sandiegozoo.org/special/pandas/pandacam/index.html
The Automated Astrophysical Site-Testing Observatory (AASTO) (South Pole)	bat.phys.unsw.edu.au/~aasto
The Old Faithful Geyser WebCam	www.nps.gov/yell/oldfaithfulcam.htm
Walt Disney World - Theme Park Live Camera	home.disney.com/DisneyWorld/cgi-bin/oneShot.cgi?type=st&park=ds
Wild Birds Unlimited Bird FeederCam	wbu.com/feedercam_home.htm
World Map of Live Webcams	dove.mtx.net.au/~punky/World.html
World Wide Surf Cameras	goan.com/surfcam.shtml
Entertainment	
AMG All Music Guide	allmusic.com
Entertainment Tonight Online	etonline.com
Entertainment Weekly Online	ew.com/ew
Mr. Showbiz: Celebrities	mrshowbiz.go.com/celebrities/index.html
RadioDigest.com	radiodigest.com
Rock and Roll Hall of Fame and Museum	rockhall.com
Spinner.com	spinner.com
The Internet Movie Database (IMDb)	imdb.com
Welcome to E! Online	eonline.com
World Radio Network WRN	wrn.org

For an updated list of fun and entertainment Web sites, visit scsite.com/dc2002/e-rev.htm.

Figure 1-49 When you visit Web sites offering fun and entertainment resources, you can be both amused and informed.

If you need an update on what happened to Victor and Nikki on *The Young and the Restless* or a preview of the upcoming Julia Roberts movie, the Web can satisfy your entertainment thirst. E! Online, Entertainment Tonight Online (Figure 1-50), and Mr. Showbiz provide the latest features on television and movie stars. The Internet Movie Database contains credits and reviews of more than 120,000 movies.

If your passion is music and radio, the AMG All Music Guide provides backgrounds on new releases and top artists. See and hear the musicians inducted into the Rock and Roll Hall of Fame and Museum (Figure 1-51). The World Radio Network features international public radio programs, such as *The Voice of Russia* and *UN Radio*.

For more information on fun and entertainment Web sites, visit the Discovering Computers 2002 E-Revolution Web page (scsite.com/dc2002/e-rev.htm) and click Fun/Entertainment.

Figure 1-50 The entertainment Web sites feature celebrity news and profiles.

Figure 1-51 Visitors exploring the Rock and Roll Hall of Fame and Museum Web site will find history, exhibitions, programs, and the names and particulars of the latest inductees.

E-FUN E-ENTERTAINMENT *applied:*

1. Visit the World Map of Live Webcams and the Culture Connect Web sites listed in Figure 1-49. View two of the Web cams closest to your hometown, and describe the scenes. Then, visit the Discovery.com Cams Web site and view two of the animal cams in the Cam Universe. What do you observe? Visit another Web site listed in Figure 1-49 and describe the view. What are the benefits of having Web cams at these locations throughout the world?

2. What are your favorite movies? Use The Internet Movie Database Web site listed in Figure 1-49 to search for information about two of these films, and write a brief description of the biographies of the major stars and director for each movie. Then, visit one of the entertainment Web sites and describe three of the featured stories. At the Rock and Roll Hall of Fame and Museum Web site, view the information on Elvis and one of your favorite musicians. Write a paragraph describing the information available on these rock stars.

1.40

DISCOVERING
COMPUTERS *2002*

Chapter 1 2 3 4 5 6 7 8 9 10 11 12 13 14 15 16 Index **HOME**

In Summary

SHELLY
CASHMAN
SERIES.

Student Exercises   Web Links   In Summary   Key Terms   Learn It Online   Checkpoint   In The Lab   Web Work

Special Features   ■ TIMELINE 2002 ■ WWW & E-SKILLS ■ MULTIMEDIA ■ BUYER'S GUIDE 2002 ■ WIRELESS TECHNOLOGY ■ TRENDS 2002 ■ INTERACTIVE LABS ■ TECH NEWS

Web Instructions: To display this page from the Web, start your browser and enter the URL scsite.com/dc2002/ch1/summary.htm. Click the links for current and additional information. To listen to an audio version of this In Summary, click the Audio button. To play the audio, RealPlayer must be installed on your computer (download by clicking here).

1 Why Is Computer Literacy Important?

To be successful in today's world, it is crucial to have knowledge and understanding of computers and their uses. Being computer literate is essential as technology advances and computers extend into every facet of daily living.

2 What Is a Computer?

A computer is an electronic machine that operates under the control of instructions stored in its own memory, that can accept data (input), manipulate the data according to specified rules (process), produce results (output), and store the results for future use (**storage**). **Data** is a collection of unorganized facts, figures, and symbols. Computers process data to create information. **Information** is data that is organized, meaningful, and useful. Examples are a paycheck or a student grade report. Data entered into a computer is called **input**. The processed results are called **output**. The cycle of input, process, output, and storage is called the **information processing cycle**.

3 What Are the Components of a Computer?

Hardware is the electric, electronic, and mechanical equipment that makes up a computer. An **input device** allows a user to enter data and commands into the memory of a computer. Six commonly used input devices are a keyboard, mouse, microphone, scanner, PC camera, and digital camera. An **output device** conveys information generated by a computer to the user. Three commonly used output devices are a printer, a monitor, and speakers. The **system unit**, sometimes called a **chassis**, is a box-like case made from metal or plastic that houses the computer circuitry. The two main components of the motherboard are the **central processing unit (CPU)**, which interprets

and carries out the instructions that operate a computer, including computations; and **memory**, which is a series of electronic elements that temporarily holds the data and instructions while the processor is processing them. A **storage device** records and retrieves data, information, and instructions to and from a storage medium. Six common storage devices are a floppy disk drive, hard disk drive, CD-ROM drive, Zip® drive, CD-RW drive, and DVD-ROM drive. **Communications devices** allow computer users to exchange items such as data, instructions, and information with another computer.

4 Why Is a Computer a Powerful Tool?

A computer's power is derived from its capability of performing the information processing cycle operations with speed, reliability, and accuracy; its capacity to store huge amounts of data, instructions, and information; and its ability to communicate with other computers.

5 What Are the Categories of Computer Software?

Software, also called a computer program, is the series of instructions that tells the hardware of a computer what to do. Software can be categorized into two types: system software and application software. **System software** controls the operation of the computer and its devices and serves as the interface between a user and the computer's hardware. Two types of system software are the **operating system (OS)**, which contains instructions that coordinate the activities of hardware devices; and **utility programs**, which perform specific tasks usually related to managing a computer. **Application software** performs specific tasks for users, such as creating word processing documents, spreadsheets, databases, or presentation graphics. A **computer programmer** writes software programs, often following a plan developed by a **systems analyst**.

DISCOVERING COMPUTERS 2002

Chapter 1 2 3 4 5 6 7 8 9 10 11 12 13 14 15 16 Index HOME 1.41

In Summary

SHELLY CASHMAN SERIES.

Student Exercises   Web Links   In Summary   Key Terms   Learn It Online   Checkpoint   In The Lab   Web Work

Special Features   ■ TIMELINE 2002 ■ WWW & E-SKILLS ■ MULTIMEDIA ■ BUYER'S GUIDE 2002 ■ WIRELESS TECHNOLOGY ■ TRENDS 2002 ■ INTERACTIVE LABS ■ TECH NEWS

6   What Is the Purpose of a Network?

A <u>network</u> is a collection of computers and devices connected together via communications media. Computers are networked so users can share **resources** such as hardware devices, software programs, data, and information. When your computer connects to a network, you are **online**.

7   How Are the Internet and the World Wide Web Used?

The world's largest network is the **Internet**, which is a worldwide collection of networks that links together millions of computers. The <u>Internet</u> is used to send messages to other users, obtain information, shop for goods and services, meet or converse with people around the world, and access sources of entertainment and leisure. The World Wide Web, which contains billions of Web pages with text, graphics, sound, video, and links to other Web pages, is one of the more popular segments of the Internet.

8   What Are the Categories of Computers and Their Uses?

The six major categories of computers are <u>personal computers</u>, <u>handheld computers</u>, Internet appliances, mid-range servers, mainframes, and supercomputers. These categories are based on differences in size, speed, processing capabilities, and price. A **personal computer** can perform all of its input, processing, output, and storage activities by itself. Two categories of personal computers are **desktop computers**, which are designed to fit entirely on or under a desk or table, and **notebook computers**, which are small enough to fit on your lap. A **handheld computer**, also called a **palmtop computer**, is a small computer that fits in your hand. One of the most popular handheld computers is the **PDA (personal digital assistant)**. An **Internet appliance** is a device designed specifically to connect to the Internet. A **mid-range server**,

formerly called a **minicomputer**, is larger and more powerful than a workstation computer and often can support up to 4,000 connected users. A **mainframe** is a large, expensive, very powerful computer that can handle hundreds or thousands of connected users simultaneously. A **supercomputer** — the fastest, most powerful, and most expensive computer — is capable of processing more than 12 trillion instructions in a single second.

9   Who Are Computer Users?

Every day, people depend on different types of computers for a variety of applications. A **home user** relies on the computer for entertainment; communications, Web access, and e-mail; reference, research, and education; personal finance; and productivity software. A **small office/home office (SOHO)** includes small companies (under 50 employees) and self-employed individuals working from home. These users access the Web; utilize productivity and specialized software; and use e-mail and communications software. **Mobile users** have notebook computers often equipped with a modem so they can work on the road. They often use presentation software and other productivity software. **Large business users** utilize computers to run their businesses by using productivity software, communications software, automated systems for most departments in the company, and large networks. **Power users** require the capabilities of workstations or other powerful computers to design plans, produce publications, create graphic art, and work with **multimedia** that includes text, graphics, sound, video, and other media elements.

10   How Can a User Be a Web Publisher?

Through the Internet, each category of user can access a wealth of information and has the ability to provide information to other connected users around the world. Many users create Web pages. <u>Publishing a Web page</u> is the process of making it available on the Internet.

Key Terms

SHELLY
CASHMAN
SERIES.

Student Exercises   Web Links   In Summary   Key Terms   Learn It Online   Checkpoint   In The Lab   Web Work

Special Features   ■ TIMELINE 2002   ■ WWW & E-SKILLS   ■ MULTIMEDIA   ■ BUYER'S GUIDE 2002   ■ WIRELESS TECHNOLOGY   ■ TRENDS 2002   ■ INTERACTIVE LABS   ■ TECH NEWS

Web Instructions: To display this page from the Web, start your browser and enter the URL scsite.com/dc2002/ch1/terms.htm. Scroll through the list of terms. Click a term to display its definition and a picture. Click the To WEB button for current and additional information about the term from the Web. To see animations, Shockwave and Flash Player must be installed on your computer (download by clicking here).

all-in-one computer (1.21)
application service provider (ASP) (1.14)
application software (1.13)
central processing unit (CPU) (1.6)
chassis (1.6)
communications devices (1.8)
computer (1.4)
computer literate (1.4)
computer program (1.10)
computer programmer (1.14)
custom software (1.14)
data (1.4)
desktop computer (1.20)
digital divide (1.30)
dumb terminals (1.25)
e-commerce (1.31)
executes (1.10)
freeware (1.14)
garbage in, garbage out (GIGO) (1.9)

home user (1.29)
icon (1.12)
information (1.4)
information appliance (1.24)
information processing cycle (1.5)
information system (1.27)
input (1.5)
input device (1.5)
install (1.11)
Internet (1.17)
Internet appliance (1.24)
kiosk (1.34)
laptop computer (1.22)
large business user (1.32)
mainframe (1.26)
memory (1.6)
mid-range server (1.25)
minicomputers (1.25)
mobile users (1.32)
multimedia (1.35)
network (1.16)
notebook computer (1.22)
online (1.16)
operating system (OS) (1.12)
output (1.5)
output device (1.6)
packaged software (1.13)
palmtop computer (1.23)
PDA (Personal Digital Assistant) (1.23)
peripheral (1.6)
personal computer (1.19)
photo communities (1.37)
power user (1.35)
processor (1.6)
program (1.10)
programmer (1.14)
public-domain software (1.14)
publishing (1.36)
resources (1.16)

INFORMATION
Information is data that is organized, meaningful, and useful. A computer processes data into information. (1.4)

To WEB

server (1.21)
shareware (1.14)
small office/home office (SOHO) (1.29)
smart pager (1.24)
smart phone (1.24)
software (1.4)
stand-alone computer (1.21)
storage (1.5)
storage device (1.7)
supercomputer (1.26)
system software (1.12)
system unit (1.6)
systems analyst (1.14)
telecommuting (1.34)
terminal (1.25)
tower model (1.20)
user (1.4)
utility program (1.12)
Web cam (1.29)
Web-enabled cellular telephone (1.24)
Web-enabled pager (1.24)
workstation (1.21)

WORKSTATION
Desktop computer designed for work that requires intense calculations and graphics capabilities; sometimes used to refer to any computer connected to a network. (1.21)

To WEB

graphical user interface (GUI) (1.12)
handheld computer (1.23)
hardware (1.4)

DISCOVERING
COMPUTERS *2002*

Learn It Online

SHELLY
CASHMAN
SERIES.

Student Exercises Web Links   In Summary   Key Terms   Learn It Online   Checkpoint   In The Lab   Web Work

Special Features ■ TIMELINE 2002 ■ WWW & E-SKILLS ■ MULTIMEDIA ■ BUYER'S GUIDE 2002 ■ WIRELESS TECHNOLOGY ■ TRENDS 2002 ■ INTERACTIVE LABS ■ TECH NEWS

Web Instructions: To display this page from the Web, start your browser and then enter the URL scsite.com/dc2002/ch1/learn.htm.

1. Web Guide

Click Web Guide to display the Guide to World Wide Web Sites and Searching Techniques Web page. Click Reference and then click AskEric Virtual Library. Click AskEric InfoGuides and search for Computer Literacy. Click a search results link of your choice. Use your word processing program to prepare a brief report on what you learned and submit your assignment to your instructor.

2. Scavenger Hunt

Click Scavenger Hunt. Print a copy of the Scavenger Hunt page; use this page to write down your answers as you search the Web. Submit your completed page to your instructor.

3. Who Wants to Be a Computer Genius?

Click Computer Genius to find out if you are a computer genius. Directions on how to play the game will display. When you are ready to play, click the PLAY button. Submit your score to your instructor.

4. Wheel of Terms

Click Wheel of Terms to reinforce important terms you learned in this chapter by playing the Shelly Cashman Series version of this popular game. Directions on how to play the game will display. When you are ready to play, click the PLAY button. Submit your score to your instructor.

5. Career Corner

Click Career Corner to display the Hire-Ed page. Search for jobs in your state. Write a brief report on the jobs you found. Submit the report to your instructor.

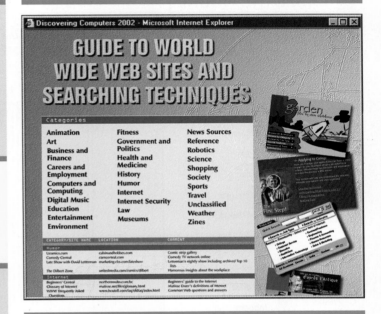

6. Search Sleuth

Click Search Sleuth to learn search techniques that will help make you a research expert. Submit the completed assignment to your instructor.

7. Crossword Puzzle Challenge

Click Crossword Puzzle Challenge. Complete the puzzle to reinforce skills you learned in this chapter. Directions on how to play the game will display. When you are ready to play, click the PLAY button. Submit the completed puzzle to your instructor.

8. Practice Test

Click Practice Test. Answer each question. When completed, enter your name and click the Grade Test button to submit the quiz for grading. Make a note of any missed questions. If required, print a copy to submit to your instructor.

DISCOVERING
COMPUTERS *2002*

Checkpoint

SHELLY
CASHMAN
SERIES.

Student Exercises   Web Links   In Summary   Key Terms   Learn It Online   Checkpoint   In The Lab   Web Work

Special Features   ■ TIMELINE 2002 ■ WWW & E-SKILLS ■ MULTIMEDIA ■ BUYER'S GUIDE 2002 ■ WIRELESS TECHNOLOGY ■ TRENDS 2002 ■ INTERACTIVE LABS ■ TECH NEWS

Web Instructions: To display this page from the Web, start your browser and enter the URL scsite.com/dc2002/ch1/check.htm. Click the links for current and additional information. To experience the animation and interactivity, Shockwave and Flash Player must be installed on your computer (download by clicking here.)

LABEL THE FIGURE | Instructions: Categorize these common computer hardware components.

Write the letter next to each component on the right in an appropriate blue box. Then write the words from the list on the left in the appropriate yellow boxes to identify the hardware components.

monitor

speakers

keyboard

mouse

printer

system unit

hard disk drive

CD-ROM or
DVD-ROM drive

floppy disk drive

Zip drive

modem

digital camera

microphone

PC video camera

scanner

INPUT   OUTPUT   STORAGE   COMMUNICATIONS

PROCESSING

a.
b.   i.
c.   j.
d.   k.
e.   l.
f.   m.
g.   n.
h.   o.
p.

MATCHING | Instructions: Match each term from the column on the left with the best description from the column on the right.

_____ 1. data
_____ 2. information
_____ 3. output
_____ 4. storage
_____ 5. input

a. An area in a computer that can hold data and information for future use.
b. Someone who communicates with a computer or uses the information it generates.
c. A collection of raw unprocessed facts, figures, and symbols.
d. Data or instructions a user enters into a computer.
e. Data that is organized, meaningful, and useful.
f. Data that has been processed into information.
g. The series of instructions that tells the hardware how to perform tasks.

DISCOVERING COMPUTERS 2002

Checkpoint

SHELLY CASHMAN SERIES.

Student Exercises   Web Links   In Summary   Key Terms   Learn It Online   Checkpoint   In The Lab   Web Work

Special Features   ■ TIMELINE 2002   ■ WWW & E-SKILLS   ■ MULTIMEDIA   ■ BUYER'S GUIDE 2002   ■ WIRELESS TECHNOLOGY   ■ TRENDS 2002   ■ INTERACTIVE LABS   ■ TECH NEWS

MULTIPLE CHOICE

Instructions: Select the letter of the correct answer for each of the following questions.

1. _____ is the electric, electronic, and mechanical equipment that makes up a computer.
   a. Hardware
   b. Software
   c. The operating system
   d. The GUI

2. A(n) _____ is software that consists of programs that perform specific tasks for users.
   a. operating system
   b. virus
   c. application
   d. GUI

3. Software donated for public use that has no software restrictions is _____ .
   a. shareware
   b. public domain software
   c. freeware
   d. copyrighted

4. Someone who writes software programs is called a _____ .
   a. systems analyst
   b. hardware specialist
   c. network manager
   d. programmer

5. A Web _____ is a collection of related **Web pages**.
   a. site
   b. browser
   c. interface
   d. set

SHORT ANSWER

Instructions: Write a brief answer to each of the following questions.

1. What are some ways people use computers in the home, at work, and at school? _____ What does it mean to be computer literate? _____
2. How is hardware different from software? _____ Why is hardware useless without software? _____
3. What is a peripheral device? _____ What hardware components are considered peripheral devices? _____
4. What are six common storage devices? _____ How are they different? _____
5. Why do people use the Internet? _____ How do most users connect to the Internet? _____

WORKING TOGETHER

Instructions: Working with a group of your classmates, complete the following team exercise.

Six commonly used input devices are listed in this chapter. These devices include a keyboard, mouse, microphone, scanner, PC camera, and digital camera. Using the Internet or other resources, prepare a report on each of the devices. Discuss how and when you would use one device instead of another. What are some of the different features available in each device? How would you determine which keyboard, mouse, and so on is the best for your particular needs? Share your reports with the class.

1.46

DISCOVERING
COMPUTERS *2002*

Chapter 1 2 3 4 5 6 7 8 9 10 11 12 13 14 15 16 Index **HOME**

In The Lab

SHELLY
CASHMAN
SERIES.

Student Exercises   Web Links   In Summary   Key Terms   Learn It Online   Checkpoint   In The Lab   Web Work

Special Features   ■ TIMELINE 2002   ■ WWW & E-SKILLS   ■ MULTIMEDIA   ■ BUYER'S GUIDE 2002   ■ WIRELESS TECHNOLOGY   ■ TRENDS 2002   ■ INTERACTIVE LABS   ■ TECH NEWS

Web Instructions: To display this page from the Web, start your browser and enter the URL scsite.com/dc2002/ch1/lab.htm. Click the links for current and additional information.

Using Windows Help

This exercise uses Windows 98 or Windows 2000 procedures. In the past, when you purchased computer software, you also received large printed manuals that attempted to answer any questions you might have. Today, Help usually is offered directly on the computer. To make it easy to find exactly the Help you need, Windows Help is arranged on three sheets: Contents, Index, and Search. Windows 2000 includes a fourth sheet, Favorites. Click the Start button on the taskbar and then click Help on the Start menu. Click the Contents tab in the Help window. What do you see? When would you use the Contents sheet to find Help? Click the Index tab. What do you see? When would you use the Index sheet to find Help? Click the Search tab. What do you see? When would you use the Search sheet to find Help? If you are using Windows 2000, click the Favorites tab. What do you see? When would you use the Favorites sheet to find Help? Close the Help window.

What's New in Microsoft Windows?

This exercise uses Windows 98 or Windows 2000 procedures. Click the Start button on the taskbar and then click Help on the Start menu. Click the Contents tab in the Windows Help window. Click the Introducing Windows 98 or Windows 2000 book, and then click the What's New in Windows 98 or Windows 2000 book.

Click a topic in which you are interested. Click each topic in the right pane. How is this version of Windows better than previous versions of Windows? Will the improvement make your work more efficient? Why or why not? What improvement, if any, would you still like to see? Close the Windows Help window.

Improving Mouse Skills

This exercise uses Windows 98 or Windows 2000 procedures. Click the Start button on the taskbar. Point to Programs on the Start menu, point to Accessories on the Programs submenu, point to Games on the Accessories submenu, and then click Solitaire on the Games submenu. When the Solitaire window displays, click the Maximize button. Click Help on the Solitaire menu bar, and then click Help Topics. Click the Contents tab. Click the The object of Solitaire topic and read the information. Click the Playing Solitaire topic. Read and print the information by clicking the Solitaire Help window's Options button, clicking Print, and then clicking the OK button. Click the Close button in the Solitaire Help window. Play the game of Solitaire. Close the Solitaire window.

Learning About Your System

You can learn some important information about your computer system by studying the system properties. Click the Start button. Point to Settings on the Start menu, and then click Control Panel on the Settings submenu. Double-click the System icon in the Control Panel window. Click the General tab in the System Properties dialog box. Use the General sheet to find out the answers to these questions:

- What operating system does your computer use?
- To whom is your system registered?
- What type of processor does your computer have?
- How much memory (RAM) does your computer have?

Close the System Properties dialog box. Close the Control Panel window.

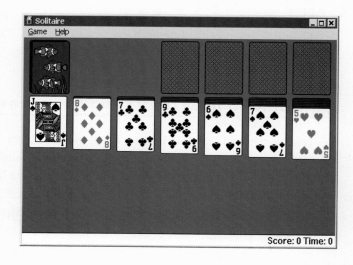

DISCOVERING COMPUTERS *2002*

Web Work

SHELLY CASHMAN SERIES.

Student Exercises   Web Links   In Summary   Key Terms   Learn It Online   Checkpoint   In The Lab   Web Work

Special Features   ■ TIMELINE 2002   ■ WWW & E-SKILLS   ■ MULTIMEDIA   ■ BUYER'S GUIDE 2002   ■ WIRELESS TECHNOLOGY   ■ TRENDS 2002   ■ INTERACTIVE LABS   ■ TECH NEWS

Web Instructions: To display this page from the Web, start your browser and enter the URL scsite.com/dc2002/ch1/web.htm. To view At The Movies in exercise 1, RealPlayer must be installed on your computer (download by clicking here). To use the Shelly Cashman Series Using the Mouse Lab and Using the Keyboard Lab from the Web, Shockwave and Flash Player must be installed on your computer (download by clicking here).

Technosaurs

To view the Technosaurs movie, click the button to the left or click the Play button to the right. Watch the movie, and then complete the exercise by answering the questions below. Just as rapid, massive climate changes are said to have rendered dinosaurs extinct, dizzying changes in computer technology challenge today's companies to evolve, adapt, or… die off. Traditional brokerages are losing billions of dollars to online trading. Travel Web sites on the Internet are siphoning billions of dollars from bricks-and-mortar travel agencies. Changes in communications hardware and software for sales and service functions threaten companies as well. What are some of the new technologies that radically can improve the competitiveness of a company's sales force? What are some of the new software programs to manage customer relationships better?

Shelly Cashman Series Using the Mouse Lab

1. To start the Shelly Cashman Series Using the Mouse Lab, complete the step that applies to you.
   a. Running from the World Wide Web: Enter the URL, www.scsite.com/sclabs/menu.htm; or display the Web Work page (see instructions at the top of this page) and then click the button to the left.
   b. Running from a CD-ROM: Insert the Shelly Cashman Series Labs with Audio CD-ROM in your CD-ROM drive.
   c. Running the No-Audio Version from a Hard Disk or Network: Click the Start button on the taskbar, point to Shelly Cashman Series Labs on the Programs submenu, and then click Interactive Labs.

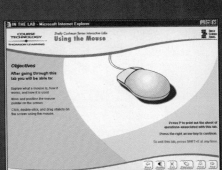

2. When the Shelly Cashman Series IN THE LAB screen shown in the figure to the right displays, follow the instructions on the screen to start the Using the Mouse Lab.
3. When the Using the Mouse screen displays, read the objectives.
4. If assigned, follow the instructions on the screen to print the questions associated with the Lab.
5. Follow the instructions on the screen to continue in the Lab.
6. When completed, follow the instructions on the screen to quit the lab.
7. If assigned, submit your answers for the printed questions to your instructor.

Shelly Cashman Series Using the Keyboard Lab

Follow the appropriate instructions in Web Work Exercise 2 above to start and use the Shelly Cashman Series Using the Keyboard Lab. If you are running from the Web, enter the URL, www.scsite.com/sclabs/menu.htm; or display the Web Work page (see instructions at the top of this page) and then click the button to the left.

Learn the Net

No matter how much computer experience you have, navigating the Net for the first time can be intimidating. How do you get started? Click the button to the left and complete this exercise to discover how you can find out everything you want to know about the Internet.

TiMe Line 2002

Milestones in Computer History

1946

1937 Dr. John V. Atanasoff and Clifford Berry design and build the first electronic digital computer. Their machine, the Atanasoff-Berry-Computer, or ABC, provides the foundation for advances in electronic digital computers.

Dr. John W. Mauchly and J. Presper Eckert, Jr. complete work on the first large-scale electronic, general-purpose digital computer. The ENIAC (Electronic Numerical Integrator And Computer) weighs thirty tons, contains 18,000 vacuum tubes, occupies a thirty-by-fifty-foot space, and consumes 160 kilowatts of power. The first time it is turned on, lights dim in an entire section of Philadelphia.

1945 Dr. John von Neumann writes a brilliant paper describing the stored program concept. His breakthrough idea, where memory holds both data and stored programs, lays the foundation for all digital computers that have since been built.

1943 During World War II, British scientist Alan Turing designs the Colossus, an electronic computer created for the military to break German codes. The computer's existence is kept secret until the 1970s.

Web Instructions: *To gain World Wide Web access to additional and up-to-date information regarding this special feature, start your browser and enter the URLs at the top of each page.*

William Shockley, John Bardeen, and Walter Brattain invent the transfer resistance device, eventually called the transistor. The transistor would revolutionize computers, proving much more reliable than vacuum tubes.

FORTRAN (FORmula TRANslation), an efficient, easy-to-use programming language, is introduced by John Backus.

1952

Dr. Grace Hopper considers the concept of reusable software in her paper, "The Education of a Computer." The paper describes how to program a computer with symbolic notation instead of the detailed machine language that had been used.

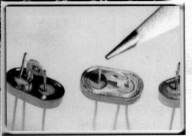

1947

1957

1953

The IBM model 650 is one of the first widely used computer systems. Originally planning to produce only 50 machines, the system is so successful that eventually IBM manufactures more than 1,000. With the IBM 700 series of machines, the company will dominate the mainframe market for the next decade.

1951

The first commercially available electronic digital computer, the UNIVAC I (UNIVersal Automatic Computer), is introduced by Remington Rand. Public awareness of computers increases when the UNIVAC I, after analyzing only 5 percent of the popular vote, correctly predicts that Dwight D. Eisenhower will win the presidential election.

Core memory, developed in the early 1950s, provides much larger storage capacity than vacuum tube memory.

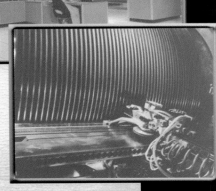

The IBM 305 RAMAC system is the first to use magnetic disk for external storage. The system provides storage capacity similar to magnetic tape that previously was used, but offers the advantage of semi-random access capability.

Dr. John Kemeny of Dartmouth leads the development of the BASIC programming language. BASIC will be widely used on personal computers.

BASIC

IBM introduces two smaller, desk-sized computers: the IBM 1401 for business and the IBM 1602 for scientists. The IBM 1602 initially is called the CADET, but IBM drops the name when campus wags claim it is an acronym for, Can't Add, Doesn't Even Try.

1960

COBOL, a high-level business application language, is developed by a committee headed by Dr. Grace Hopper. COBOL uses English-like phrases and runs on most business computers, making it one of the more widely used programming languages.

1965

Digital Equipment Corporation (DEC) introduces the first minicomputer, the PDP-8. The machine is used extensively as an interface for time-sharing systems.

More than 200 programming languages have been created.

1959

1958

Computers built with transistors mark the beginning of the second generation of computer hardware.

1964

The number of computers has grown to 18,000.

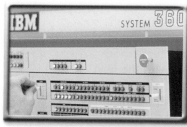

Third-generation computers, with their controlling circuitry stored on chips, are introduced. The IBM System/360 computer is the first family of compatible machines, merging science and business lines.

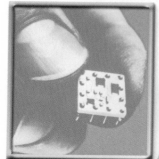

1968

Computer Science Corporation becomes the first software company listed on the New York Stock Exchange.

In a letter to the editor titled, "GO TO Statements Considered Harmful," Dr. Edsger Dijsktra introduces the concept of structured programming, developing standards for constructing computer programs.

Alan Shugart at IBM demonstrates the first regular use of an 8-inch floppy (magnetic storage) disk.

Ethernet, the first local area network (LAN), is developed at Xerox PARC (Palo Alto Research Center) by Robert Metcalf. The LAN allows computers to communicate and share software, data, and peripherals. Initially designed to link minicomputers, Ethernet will be extended to personal computers.

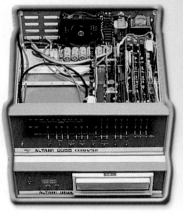

Fourth-generation computers, built with chips that use LSI (large-scale integration) arrive. While the chips used in 1965 contained as many as 1,000 circuits, the LSI chip contains as many as 15,000.

MITS, Inc. advertises one of the first microcomputers, the Altair. Named for the destination in an episode of Star Trek, the Altair is sold in kits for less than $400. Although initially it has no keyboard, no monitor, no permanent memory, and no software, 4,000 orders are taken within the first three months.

1970

1975

1976

1969

The ARPANET network, a predecessor of the Internet, is established.

Under pressure from the industry, IBM announces that some of its software will be priced separately from the computer hardware. This unbundling allows software firms to emerge in the industry.

1971

Dr. Ted Hoff of Intel Corporation develops a microprocessor, or micro-programmable computer chip, the Intel 4004.

Steve Wozniak and Steve Jobs build the first Apple computer. A subsequent version, the Apple II, is an immediate success. Adopted by elementary schools, high schools, and colleges, for many students the Apple II is their first contact with the world of computers.

1.52

Alan Shugart presents the Winchester hard drive, revolutionizing storage for personal computers.

Hayes introduces the 300 bps smart modem. The modem is an immediate success.

IBM offers Microsoft Corporation co-founder, Bill Gates, the opportunity to develop the operating system for the soon-to-be announced IBM personal computer. With the development of MS-DOS, Microsoft achieves tremendous growth and success.

COMPAQ

Compaq, Inc. is founded to develop and market IBM-compatible PCs.

3,275,000 personal computers are sold, almost 3,000,000 more than in 1981.

Instead of choosing a person for its annual award, TIME magazine names the computer Machine of the Year for 1982, acknowledging the impact of computers on society.

1980

1982

1983

1979

1981

The first public online information services, CompuServe and the Source, are founded.

VisiCalc, a spreadsheet program written by Bob Frankston and Dan Bricklin, is introduced. Originally written to run on Apple II computers, VisiCalc will be seen as the most important reason for the acceptance of personal computers in the business world.

The IBM PC is introduced, signaling IBM's entrance into the personal computer marketplace. The IBM PC quickly garners the largest share of the personal computer market and becomes the personal computer of choice in business.

Lotus Development Corporation is founded. Its spreadsheet software, Lotus 1-2-3, which combines spreadsheet, graphics, and database programs in one package, becomes the best-selling program for IBM personal computers.

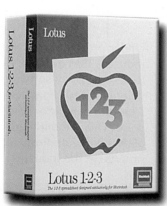

IBM introduces a personal computer, called the PC AT, that uses the Intel 80286 microprocessor.

Microsoft surpasses Lotus Development Corporation to become the world's top software vendor.

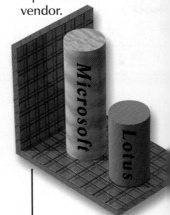

1987

Several personal computers utilizing the powerful Intel 80386 microprocessor are introduced. These machines perform processing that once only large systems could handle.

1988

1984

Apple introduces the Macintosh computer, which incorporates a unique, easy-to-learn, graphical user interface.

1989

The Intel 486 becomes the world's first 1,000,000 transistor micro-processor. It crams 1.2 million transistors on a .4" x .6" sliver of silicon and executes 15,000,000 instructions per second — four times as fast as its predecessor, the 80386 chip.

Hewlett-Packard announces the first LaserJet printer for personal computers.

While working at CERN, Switzerland, Tim Berners-Lee invents an Internet-based hypermedia enterprise for infor-mation sharing. Berners-Lee will call this innovation the World Wide Web.

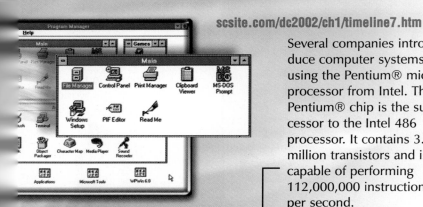

Several companies introduce computer systems using the Pentium® microprocessor from Intel. The Pentium® chip is the successor to the Intel 486 processor. It contains 3.1 million transistors and is capable of performing 112,000,000 instructions per second.

Jim Clark and Marc Andreessen found Netscape and launch Netscape Navigator 1.0, a browser for the World Wide Web.

Microsoft releases Windows 3.1, the latest version of its Windows operating system. Windows 3.1 offers improvements such as TrueType fonts, multimedia capability, and object linking and embedding (OLE). In two months, 3,000,000 copies of Windows 3.1 are sold.

1992

1993

1994

1991

World Wide Web Consortium releases standards that describe a framework for linking documents on different computers.

Linus Torvalds creates the Linux kernel, a UNIX-like operating system that he releases free across the Internet for further enhancement by other programmers.

Marc Andreessen creates a graphical Web browser called Mosaic. This success leads to the organization of Netscape Communications Corporation.

The White House launches its Web page. The site includes an interactive citizens' handbook and White House history and tours.

Sun Microsystems launches Java, an object-oriented programming language that allows users to write one application for a variety of computer platforms. Java becomes one of the hottest Internet technologies.

U.S. Robotics introduces PalmPilot, a handheld personal organizer. The PalmPilot's user friendliness and low price make it a standout next to more expensive personal digital assistants (PDAs).

Microsoft releases Windows NT 4.0, an operating system for client-server networks. Windows NT's management tools and Wizards make it easier for developers to build and deploy business applications.

The Summer Olympics in Atlanta makes extensive use of computer technology, using an IBM network of 7,000 personal computers, 2,000 pagers and wireless devices, and 90 industrial-strength computers to share information with more than 150,000 athletes, coaches, journalists, and Olympics staff members, and millions of Web users.

1995 **1996**

Microsoft releases Windows 95, a major upgrade to its Windows operating system. Windows 95 consists of more than 10,000,000 lines of computer instructions developed by 300 person-years of effort. More than 50,000 individuals and companies test the software before it is released.

Two out of three employees in the United States have access to a personal computer, and one out of every three homes has a personal computer. Fifty million personal computers are sold worldwide and more than 250,000,000 are in use.

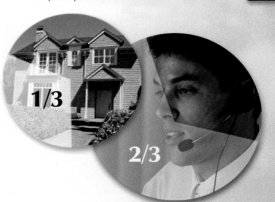

1/3

2/3

An innovative technology called webtv combines television and the Internet by providing viewers with tools to navigate the Web.

Intel introduces the Pentium® II processor with 7.5 million transistors. The new processor, which incorporates MMX™ technology, processes video, audio, and graphics data more efficiently and supports applications such as movie-editing, gaming, and more.

Deep Blue, an IBM super-computer, defeats world chess champion Gary Kasparov in a six-game chess competition. Millions of people follow the 9-day long rematch on IBM's Web site.

Fifty million users are connected to the Internet and World Wide Web.

More than 10,000,000 people take up telecommuting the capability of working at home and communicating with an office via computer. More and more firms embrace telecommuting to help increase productivity, reduce absenteeism, and provide greater job satisfaction.

1997

1998

Apple and Microsoft sign a joint technology development agreement. Microsoft buys $150,000,000 of Apple stock.

Microsoft releases Internet Explorer 4.0 and seizes a key place in the Internet arena. This new Web browser is greeted with tremendous customer demand.

E-commerce, or electronic commerce – the marketing of goods and services over the Internet – booms. Companies such as Dell, E*TRADE, and Amazon.com spur online shopping, allowing buyers to obtain everything from hardware and software to financial and travel services, insurance, automobiles, books, and more.

DVD (Digital Video Disc), the next generation of optical disc storage technology, is introduced. DVD can store computer, audio, and video data in a single format, with the capability of producing near-studio quality. By year's end, 500,000 DVD players are shipped worldwide.

Microsoft ships Windows 98, an upgrade to Windows 95. Windows 98 offers improved Internet access, better system performance, and support for a new generation of hardware and software. In six months, more than 10,000,000 copies of Windows 98 are sold worldwide.

The Department of Justice's broad antitrust lawsuit asks that Microsoft offer Windows 98 without the Internet Explorer browser or that it bundle the competing Netscape Navigator browser with the operating system.

Intel releases its Pentium® III processor, which provides enhanced multimedia capabilities.

Governments and businesses frantically work to make their computer systems Y2K (Year 2000) compliant, spending more than $500 billion worldwide. Y2K non-compliant computers cannot distinguish if 01/01/00 refers to 1900 or 2000, and thus may operate using a wrong date. This Y2K bug can affect any application that relies on computer chips, such as ATMs, airplanes, energy companies, and the telephone system.

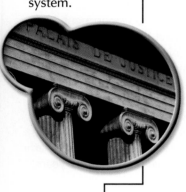

U.S. District Judge Thomas Penfield Jackson rules in the antitrust lawsuit brought by the Department of Justice and 19 states that Microsoft used its monopoly power to stifle competition.

1998

1999

Compaq Computer, the United States' leading personal computer manufacturer, buys Digital Equipment Corporation in the biggest take-over in the history of the computer industry. Compaq becomes the world's second largest computer firm, behind IBM.

Microsoft introduces Office 2000, its premier productivity suite, offering new tools for users to create content and save it directly to a Web site without any file conversion or special steps.

Apple Computer introduces the iMac, the latest version of its popular Macintosh computer. The iMac abandons such conventional features as a floppy disk drive but wins customers with its futuristic design, see-through case, and easy setup. Consumer demand outstrips Apple's production capabilities, and some vendors are forced to begin waiting lists.

Open Source Code software, such as the Linux operating system and the Apache Web server created by unpaid volunteers, begin to gain wide acceptance among computer users.

1.58

Shawn Fanning, 19, and his company, Napster, turn the music industry upside down by developing software that allows computer users to swap music files with one another without going through a centralized file server. The Recording Industry of America, on behalf of five media companies, sues Napster for copyright infringement.

Microsoft ships Windows 2000 and Windows Me. Windows 2000 offers improved behind-the-scene security and reliability. Windows Me is designed for home users and lets them edit home movies, share digital photos, index music, and create a home network.

According to the U.S. Commerce Department, Internet traffic is doubling every 100 days, resulting in an annual growth rate of more than 700 percent. It has taken radio and television 30 years and 15 years to reach 60 million people, respectively. The Internet has achieved the same audience base in three years.

2000

Intel unveils its Pentium 4 chip with clock speeds starting at 1.4 GHz. The Pentium 4 includes 42 million transistors, nearly twice as many contained on its predecessor, the Pentium III.

E-commerce achieves mainstream acceptance. Annual e-commerce sales exceed $100 billion, and Internet advertising expenditures reach more than $5 billion.

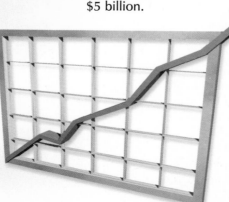

Dot.com companies (Internet based) go out of business at a record pace — nearly one per day — as financial investors withhold funding due to the companies' unprofitability.

Telemedicine uses satellite technology and videoconferencing to broadcast consultations and to perform distant surgeries. Robots are used for complex and precise tasks. Computer-aided surgery uses virtual reality to assist with training and planning procedures.

Microsoft introduces a new version of Office, which includes voice recognition and speech capabilities. Its Subscription mode lets users register the software over the Internet and renew or extend the amount of time it will run.

More than 25 million computer users subscribe to America Online and take advantage of its AOL Anywhere features, including Instant Messenger, e-mail, and customized news and information pages. AOL's merger with Time Warner combines the strengths of the Internet, entertainment, and communications industries.

Microsoft .net Microsoft launches its .NET strategy, which is a new environment for developing and running software applications featuring ease of development of Web-based services. As a user of applications, you will see the benefit of .NET as instant access to data and services in the context of your current task.

AOL Anywhere

TIME WARNER

2001

Application service providers offer a return to a centralized computing environment, in which large megaservers warehouse your data, information, and software, so it is accessible using a variety of devices from any location.

Avid readers enjoy e-books, which are digital texts read on compact computer screens. E-books can hold the equivalent of 10 traditional books containing text and graphics. Readers can search, highlight text, and add notes.

Wireless technology, especially handheld computers, achieves significant market penetration. Prices drop, usage increases, and wireless carriers scramble for new services, particularly for a mobile workforce that can access the Internet anywhere at any time.

CHAPTER 2

The Internet and World Wide Web

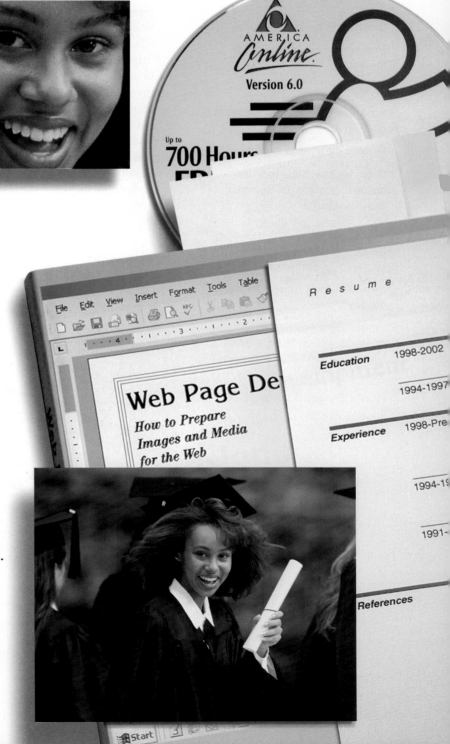

Ecstatic. Relieved. Exhausted. With graduation day approaching, these are only a few of your emotions. The day after commencement exercises, you and six friends from school are driving to Hidden Lake National Park to enjoy fresh air in the great outdoors on a two-week camping trip.

Before the semester ends, though, you plan to line up a job. This way, you can embark on your new career just as soon as you return from the outing. Today, you meet with an adviser in the Office of Career Development. Among other resources, the office maintains a Resume Forwarding system. The adviser shows you how to enter your resume into the system, and then automatically, it sends yours and all current resumes on file to potential employers. He also recommends that you attend the Campus Career Fair next week, and suggests you publish your resume on the Web.

Computer Technology was not your major. You tell the adviser that publishing on the Web sounds a little too high-tech for you. He says publishing a personal Web page is fairly simple … as long as you have the right tools. His office is conducting a three-hour seminar next Wednesday called How to Publish a Resume. You immediately sign up.

THE INTERNET

One of the major reasons business, home, and other users purchase computers is for Internet access. Through the Internet, society has access to information from all around the globe. Instantaneously, you can find local and national news, weather reports, sports scores, stock prices, your medical records, your credit report, and countless forms of educational material. The Internet also offers many conveniences. At your fingertips, you can send messages to others, meet new friends, bank, invest, shop, fill prescriptions, file taxes, take a course, play a game, listen to music, or watch a movie. The magnificence of the Internet is you can access it from a computer anywhere: at home, at work, at school, at the beach, in a restaurant, and even on an airplane.

Success today in the business world requires an understanding of the Internet. Without it, you are missing a tremendous resource for goods, services, information, and communications.

As discussed in Chapter 1, the Internet is the world's largest network. A **network** is a collection of computers and devices connected together via communications devices and media such as modems, cables, telephone lines, and satellites. The **Internet**, also called the **Net**, is a worldwide collection of networks that links millions of businesses, government agencies, educational institutions, and individuals. Each of the networks on the Internet provides resources that add to the abundance of goods, services, and information accessible via the Internet.

OBJECTIVES

After completing this chapter, you will be able to:

- Discuss how the Internet works
- Understand ways to access the Internet
- Identify a URL
- Know how to search for information on the Web
- Describe the types of Web pages
- Recognize how Web pages use graphics, animation, audio, video, and virtual reality
- Define Webcasting
- Describe the uses of electronic commerce (e-commerce)
- Identify the tools required for Web publishing
- Explain how e-mail, FTP, newsgroups and message boards, mailing lists, chat rooms, and instant messaging work
- Identify the rules of netiquette

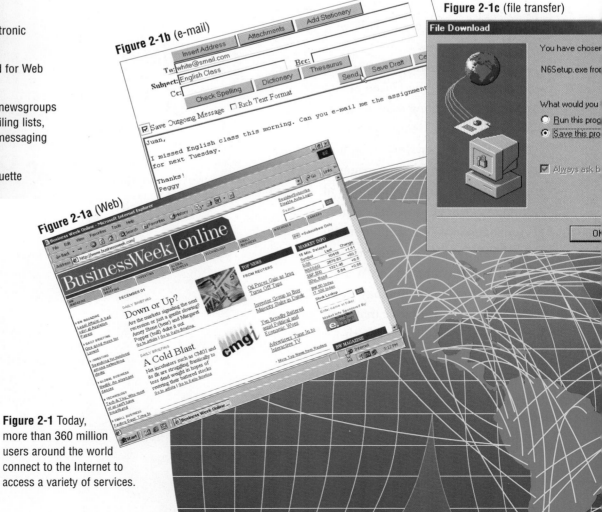

Figure 2-1b (e-mail)

Figure 2-1c (file transfer)

Figure 2-1a (Web)

Figure 2-1 Today, more than 360 million users around the world connect to the Internet to access a variety of services.

The Internet consists of many local, regional, national, and international networks. Although each of these networks on the Internet is owned by a public or private organization, no single organization owns or controls the Internet. Each organization on the Internet is responsible only for maintaining its own network.

Today, more than 360 million users around the world connect to the Internet for a variety of reasons. Some of the uses of the Internet are as follows:

- Access a wealth of information, news, and research material
- Communicate with others around the world
- Bank and invest

- Shop for goods and services
- Download and listen to music or download and watch movies
- Take a course or access other educational material
- Access sources of entertainment and leisure such as online games, magazines, and vacation planning guides
- Access other computers and exchange files
- Share and edit documents with others in real time
- Provide information, photographs, audio clips, or video clips

To support these and other activities, the Internet provides a variety of services (Figure 2-1). One of the most widely accessed of the

Internet services is the World Wide Web. Other services include electronic mail (e-mail), file transfer, newsgroups and message boards, mailing lists, chat rooms, and instant messaging. The following pages explain these services, along with a discussion of the history of the Internet and how the Internet works.

HISTORY OF THE INTERNET

The Internet has it roots in a networking project started by the Pentagon's **Advanced Research Projects Agency** (**ARPA**), an agency of the U.S. Department of Defense. ARPA's goal was to build a network that (1) would allow scientists at different

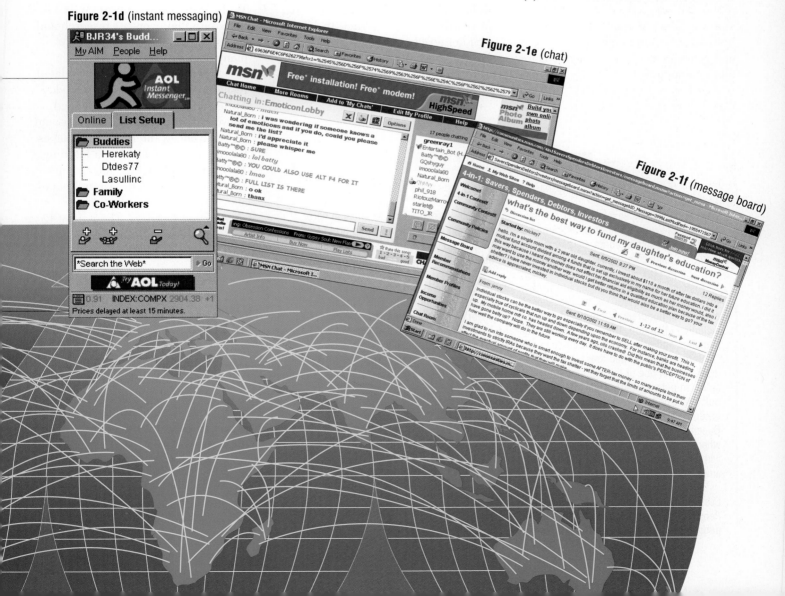

Figure 2-1d (instant messaging)

Figure 2-1e (chat)

Figure 2-1f (message board)

locations to share information and work together on military and scientific projects and (2) could function even if part of the network were disabled or destroyed by a disaster such as a nuclear attack. That network, called **ARPANET**, became functional in September 1969, linking scientific and academic researchers in the United States.

The original ARPANET was a wide area network (WAN) consisting of four main computers, one each located at the University of California at Los Angeles, the Stanford Research Institute, the University of California at Santa Barbara, and the University of Utah. Each of these four computers served as the network's host nodes. In a network, a host **node**, or **host**, is any computer that directly connects to the network. A host often stores and transfers data and messages on high-speed communications lines and provides network connections for other computers.

As researchers and others realized the great benefit of using ARPANET's electronic mail to share information, ARPANET underwent phenomenal growth. By 1984, ARPANET had more than 1,000 individual computers linked as hosts. (Today, more than 100 million hosts connect to the Internet.)

Some organizations connected entire networks to ARPANET to take advantage of the high-speed communications it offered. In 1986, for example, the National Science Foundation (NSF) connected its huge network of five supercomputer centers, called **NSFnet**, to ARPANET. This configuration of complex networks and hosts became known as the Internet.

Until 1995, NSFnet handled the bulk of the communications activity, or **traffic**, on the Internet. In 1995, NSFnet terminated its network on the Internet and returned its status to a research network.

Today, a variety of corporations, commercial firms, and other companies provide networks to handle the traffic on the Internet. These networks, along with telephone companies, cable and satellite companies, and the government all contribute toward the internal structure of the Internet. Many donate resources, such as servers, communications lines, and technical specialists — making the Internet truly collaborative.

Even as the Internet grows, it remains a public, cooperative, and independent network. Although no single person, company, institution, or government agency controls or owns the Internet, several organizations contribute toward its success by advising, defining standards, and addressing other issues. The **World Wide Web Consortium (W3C)** is the group that oversees research and sets standards and guidelines for many areas of the Internet.

Internet2 is an Internet-related research and development project. Through an extremely high-speed network, **Internet2 (I2)** develops and tests advanced Internet technologies for research, teaching, and learning. Members of I2 include more than 180 universities in the United States, along with several industry and government partners. The goal of I2 is to enhance tomorrow's Internet with its advanced technologies.

HOW THE INTERNET WORKS

Data sent over the Internet travels via networks and communications channels owned and operated by many companies. The following sections preset various ways to connect to these networks.

Service Providers

An **Internet service provider** (**ISP**) is a business that has a permanent Internet connection and provides temporary connections to individuals and companies for free or for a fee. The most common ISP fee arrangement is a fixed amount, usually about $10 to $20 per month for an individual account. For this amount, many ISPs offer unlimited Internet access. Others specify a set number of access hours per month. With these arrangements, you pay an additional amount for each hour you connect in excess of an allotted number of access hours.

If you use a telephone line to access the Internet, the telephone number you dial connects you to an access point on the Internet, called a **point of presence** (**POP**). When selecting a service provider, ensure it provides at least one local POP telephone number. Otherwise, you will pay long-distance telephone bills for the time you connect to the Internet.

Two types of ISPs are regional and national (Figure 2-2). A **regional ISP** usually provides access to the Internet through one or more telephone numbers local to a specific geographic area. A **national ISP** is a larger business that provides local telephone numbers in most major

cities and towns nationwide. Some national ISPs also provide a toll-free telephone number. Due to their larger size, national ISPs usually offer more services and generally have a larger technical support staff than regional ISPs. Examples of national ISPs are AT&T, Earthlink, and WorldCom.

Like an ISP, an **online service provider** (**OSP**) supplies Internet access, but an OSP also has many members-only features that offer a variety of special content and services such as news; weather; legal information; financial data; hardware and software guides; games; and travel guides. For this reason, the fees for using an OSP sometimes are slightly

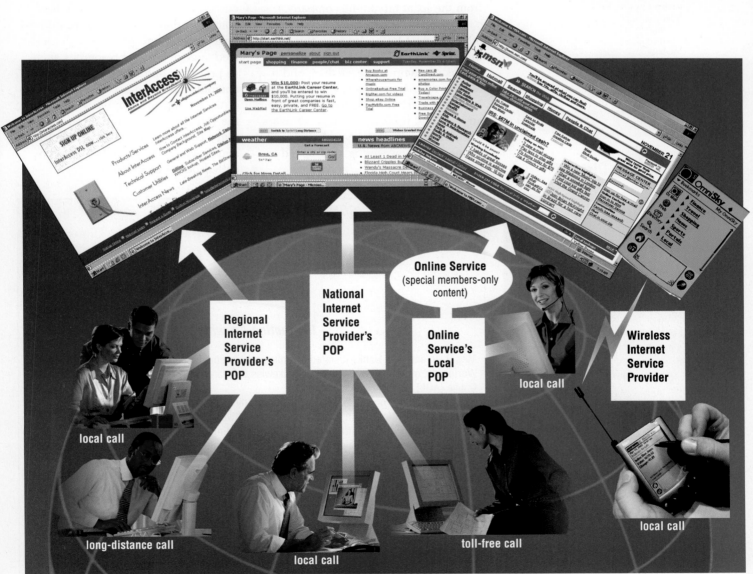

Figure 2-2 Common ways to access the Internet are through a regional or national Internet service provider, an online service provider, or a wireless service provider.

higher than fees for an ISP. The two most popular OSPs are America Online (AOL) and the Microsoft Network (MSN).

A **wireless service provider** (**WSP**) is a company that provides wireless Internet access to users with wireless modems or Web-enabled handheld computers or devices. Notebook computers can use wireless modems. Web-enabled devices include cellular telephones, two-way pagers, and hands-free (voice activated)

Web Link

For more information on service providers, visit the Discovering Computers 2002 Chapter 2 WEB LINK page (**scsite.com/dc2002/ch2/weblink.htm**) and click Service Providers.

ISSUE

Local or Long Distance?

Fees and Taxes for Internet Access

In early 1999, the Federal Communications Commission (FCC) (see URL below) ruled that dial-up Internet calls are interstate in nature and not local. The FCC concluded that calls to Internet service providers (ISPs) should be regarded as interstate transactions, because Internet traffic is not, strictly speaking, local. Many people feel this 4-0 vote by the FCC could open the way for new fees for ISPs, which eventually would be passed on to users. If this ruling is implemented, Internet users will pay a fee and tax similar to the charges for long-distance telephone calls. Should Internet users be required to pay a long-distance fee? Should they be taxed while online? Will Internet usage diminish if users are required to pay additional per minute charges?

For more information on Internet charges, online access, and the Web site mentioned above, visit the Discovering Computers 2002 Issues Web page (**scsite.com/dc2002/issues.htm**) and click Chapter 2 Issue #1.

Internet devices in automobiles. An antenna on the wireless modem or Web-enabled device typically sends signals through the airwaves to communicate with a WSP. Examples of WSPs include GoAmerica Communications, OmniSky, and SprintPCS.

Connecting to the Internet

Employees and students often connect to the Internet through a business or school network. In this case, the computers usually are part of a local area network (LAN) that connects to a service provider through a high-speed connection line leased from the local telephone company.

Home or small business users often connect to the Internet through dial-up access. With **dial-up access**, you use a computer, a modem, and a regular telephone line to dial into an ISP or OSP. Dial-up access provides an easy and inexpensive way for users to connect to the Internet. A dial-up connection, however, is slow-speed technology.

Some home and small business users opt for newer high-speed technologies such as digital subscriber lines or cable television Internet services. **DSL** (**digital subscriber line**) provides high-speed connections over a regular copper telephone line. A **cable modem** provides high-speed Internet connections through the cable television network. These services cost about twice as much as dial-up access.

How Data Travels the Internet

Computers connected to the Internet work together to transfer data and information around the world using servers and clients. As discussed in Chapter 1, a **server** is a computer that manages the resources on a network and provides a centralized storage area for resources such as programs and data. A **client** is a computer that can access the contents of the storage area on the server. On the Internet, for example, your computer is a client that can access files and services on a variety of servers, called **host computers**.

COMPANY ON THE CUTTING EDGE

Interacting Anywhere

Meg Ryan and Tom Hanks fostered an online relationship in their hit movie, *You've Got Mail.* Worldwide, more than 25 million users likewise cultivate associations by using America Online (AOL) for their interactive needs.

With a strategy of *AOL Anywhere*, the company is the world's leading online service provider, with features such as electronic mail, software, computer support services, and Internet access. Each day members send 110 million e-mail messages, seek 200 million stock quotes, and browse 5.2 billion Web pages. At any given time, nearly 1.2 million users can be online simultaneously.

Stephen M. Case founded the company in 1985 as Quantum Computer Services Corporation with a vision of simplifying the Internet for people other than computer scholars and specialists. He partnered with a series of companies, including Commodore International, Ltd., Tandy Corporation, and Apple Computer. Case changed the company name to America Online in 1991.

AOL experienced tremendous growth throughout the 1990s partly due to its aggressive marketing campaign using direct mail, membership kits, and magazine inserts. It acquired Netscape Communications in 1998 and proposed the largest corporate merger with Time Warner, one of the world's leading media conglomerates, in 2000.

For more information on America Online, visit the Discovering Computers 2002 Companies Web page (**scsite.com/dc2002/companies.htm**) and click AOL.

The inner structure of the Internet works much like a transportation system. Just as highways connect major cities and carry the bulk of the automotive traffic across the country, several main communications lines carry the heaviest amount of traffic on the Internet. These communications lines are referred to collectively as the Internet **backbone**.

In the United States, the communications lines that make up the Internet backbone exchange data at several different major cities across the country. The high-speed equipment in these major cities functions similar to a highway interchange, transferring data from one network to another until it reaches its final destination (Figure 2-3).

Web Link
For more information on the Internet backbone, visit the Discovering Computers 2002 Chapter 2 WEB LINK page (**scsite.com/dc2002/ch2/weblink.htm**) and click Internet Backbone.

Figure 2-3 HOW DATA MIGHT TRAVEL THE INTERNET USING A TELEPHONE LINE CONNECTION

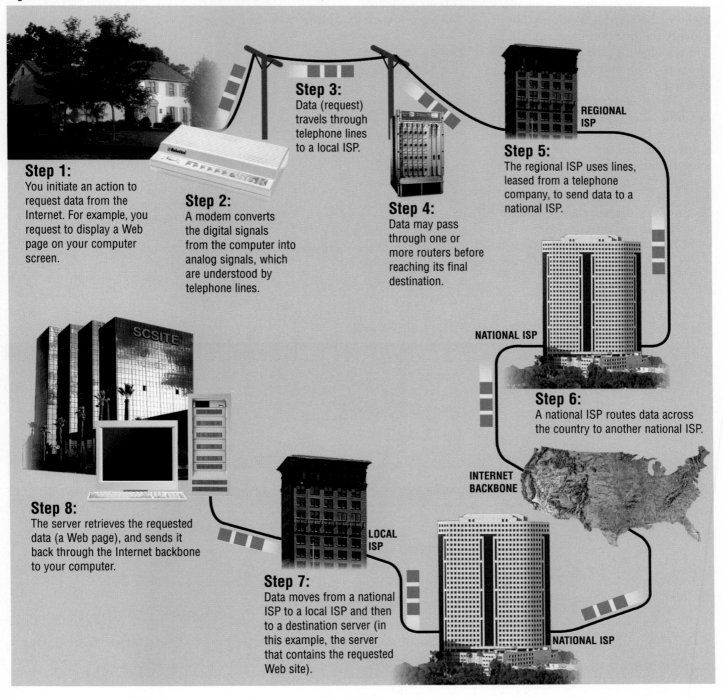

Step 1:
You initiate an action to request data from the Internet. For example, you request to display a Web page on your computer screen.

Step 2:
A modem converts the digital signals from the computer into analog signals, which are understood by telephone lines.

Step 3:
Data (request) travels through telephone lines to a local ISP.

Step 4:
Data may pass through one or more routers before reaching its final destination.

REGIONAL ISP

Step 5:
The regional ISP uses lines, leased from a telephone company, to send data to a national ISP.

NATIONAL ISP

Step 6:
A national ISP routes data across the country to another national ISP.

INTERNET BACKBONE

Step 8:
The server retrieves the requested data (a Web page), and sends it back through the Internet backbone to your computer.

LOCAL ISP

Step 7:
Data moves from a national ISP to a local ISP and then to a destination server (in this example, the server that contains the requested Web site).

NATIONAL ISP

Internet Addresses

The Internet relies on an addressing system much like the postal service to send data to a computer at a specific destination. An **IP address**, short for Internet protocol address, is a number that uniquely identifies each computer or device connected to the Internet. The IP address consists of four groups of numbers, each separated by a period. The number in each group is between 0 and 255. For example, the numbers 199.95.72.10 are an IP address. In general, the first portion of each IP address identifies the network and the last portion identifies the specific computer.

These all-numeric IP addresses are difficult to remember and use. Thus, the Internet supports the use of a text name that represents one or more IP addresses. A **domain name** is the text version of an IP address. Figure 2-4 shows an IP address and its associated domain name. Similarly to an IP address, the components of a domain name are separated by periods.

Every domain name contains a **top-level domain (TLD)** abbreviation that identifies the type of organization that is associated with the domain. In Figure 2-4, the abbreviation, com, is a top-level domain. **Dot com** is the name sometimes used to describe an organization that has a TLD of com.

The group that assigns and controls TLDs is the **Internet Corporation for Assigned Names and Numbers (ICANN** pronounced EYE-can). Figure 2-5 lists current TLD abbreviations. For international Web sites outside the United States,

the domain name also includes a country code. In these cases, the domain name ends with the country code, such as au for Australia or fr for France.

The **domain name system (DNS)** is the system on the Internet that stores the domain names and their corresponding IP addresses. Every time you specify a domain name, an Internet server called the **DNS server** translates the domain name into its associated IP address, so data can route to the correct computer.

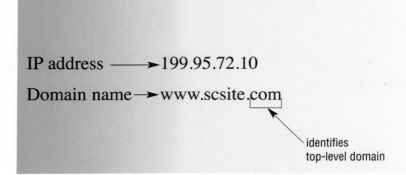

IP address ⟶ 199.95.72.10

Domain name ⟶ www.scsite.com

identifies top-level domain

Figure 2-4 The IP address and domain name for the Shelly Cashman Series® Instructional Web site.

TOP-LEVEL DOMAIN (TLD) ABBREVIATIONS

Original TLD Abbreviations	Type of Domain
com	Commercial organizations, businesses, and companies
edu	Educational institutions
gov	Government agencies
mil	Military organizations
net	Network provider
org	Non-profit organizations

Newer TLD Abbreviations	Type of Domain
museum	Accredited museum
biz	Business
info	Information service
name	Individuals or families
pro	Credentialed professional such as doctor or lawyer
aero	Air transport company
coop	Business cooperative such as credit unions and rural electric coops

Figure 2-5 With the explosion of Internet growth during the last few years, the Internet Corporation for Assigned Names and Numbers (ICANN) recently adopted seven new TLDs.

THE WORLD WIDE WEB

Many people use the terms World Wide Web and Internet interchangeably. The World Wide Web, however, is just one of the many services available on the Internet. The World Wide Web actually is a relatively new aspect of the Internet. While the Internet was developed in the late 1960s, the World Wide Web emerged less than a decade ago — in the early 1990s. Since then, however, it has grown phenomenally to become the most widely used service on the Internet.

The **World Wide Web** (**WWW**), or **Web**, consists of a worldwide collection of electronic documents. Each of these electronic documents on the Web is called a

Web page. A Web page can contain text, graphics, sound, and video, as well as built-in connections to other documents. A **Web site** is a collection of related Web pages.

Do not assume that information presented on a Web page is correct or accurate. You always should evaluate the value of a Web page before relying on its content.

Browsing the Web

A **Web browser**, or **browser**, is a software program that allows you to access and view Web pages. The more widely used Web browsers for personal computers are Microsoft Internet Explorer and Netscape. Figure 2-6 shows Netscape and

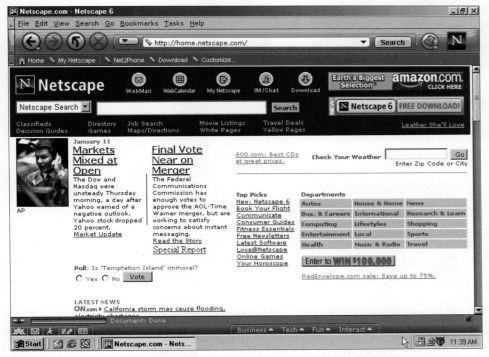

Figure 2-6 Netscape is a widely used Web browser. Shown here is the Netscape Web site, which displays when you start the Netscape browser.

the final screen in Figure 2-7 shows Internet Explorer, which in this case displays the AOL Web site.

To browse the Web, you need a Web browser and a computer that is connected to the Internet. To establish the connection and start the Web browser, you typically use the mouse to select an icon on your desktop (Figure 2-7). If you use a standard telephone line for an Internet connection, a modem dials the telephone number to the ISP or OSP. Once the telephone connection is established, the browser retrieves and displays a home page.

A **home page**, which is the starting page for a browser, is similar to a book cover or a table of contents for a Web site. It provides information about the site's purpose and content. The initial home page that displays is one selected by your Web browser.

Figure 2-7 ONE METHOD OF CONNECTING TO THE INTERNET

Step 1:

Double-click an icon on the desktop, such as Internet Explorer, to start your browser.

Step 2:

If you are not connected to the Internet already, your computer attempts to establish a connection with a service provider. If necessary, click the Connect button.

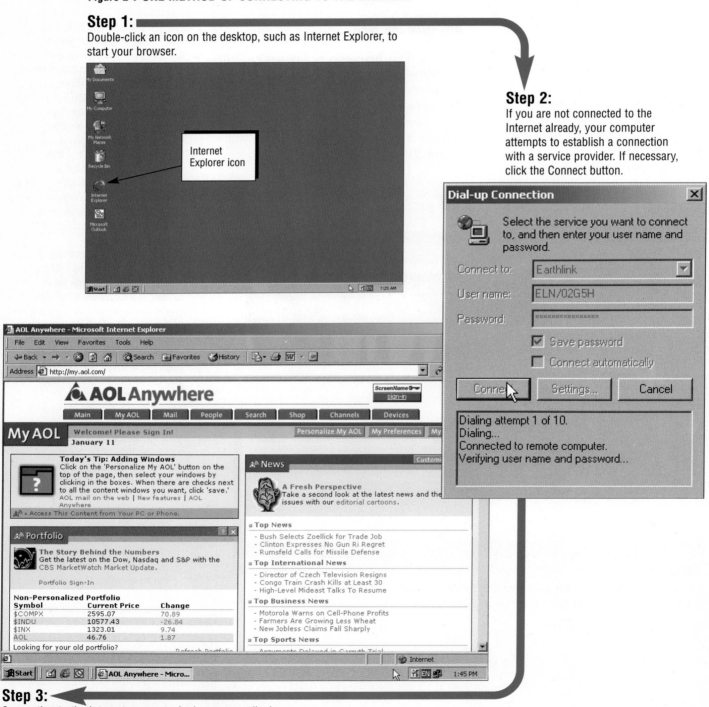

Step 3:

Connection to the Internet occurs and a home page displays.
Shown here is an AOL home page. Your home page may vary.

You can change the home page at any time. Many sites also allow you to personalize the home page so it displays areas of interest to you. Some Web sites also refer to their starting page as a home page.

Downloading is the process of receiving information, such as a Web page, onto your computer from a server on the Internet. While your browser downloads a page, such as the home page, it typically displays an animated logo or icon in the top-right corner of the browser window. When the download finishes, the animation stops.

Downloading a Web page can take from a few seconds to several minutes, depending on the speed of your Internet connection and the amount of graphics on the Web page. To speed up the display of pages, you can turn off the graphics and display only text in most Web browsers.

Web-enabled handheld computers and devices such as cellular telephones use a special type of browser designed for their small screens. A **microbrowser**, also called a **minibrowser**, is a software program that accesses and displays Web pages that contain mostly text (Figure 2-8). Many Web sites design Web pages specifically for display on a Web-enabled handheld computer or device.

Navigating Web Pages

Most Web pages contain hyperlinks. A **hyperlink**, also called a **link**, is a built-in connection to another related Web page or part of a Web page. Links allow you to obtain information in a nonlinear way. That is, you make associations between topics instead of moving sequentially through the topics. Reading a book from cover to cover is a linear way of learning. Branching off and investigating related topics as you encounter them is a nonlinear way of learning. Looking up definitions in a dictionary is a nonlinear way of learning.

While reading an article online about nutrition, you might want to learn more about counting calories. Having linked to and read information on counting calories, you might want to find several low-fat, low-calorie recipes. Reading these might inspire you to learn about a chef that specializes in healthy but tasty food preparation. The capability of branching from one related topic to another in a nonlinear fashion is what makes links so powerful, and the Web such an interesting place to explore.

Figure 2-8a (microbrowser for a Web-enabled handheld computer)

Figure 2-8 Sample microbrowser screens.

Figure 2-8b (microbrowser for a Web-enabled cellular telephone)

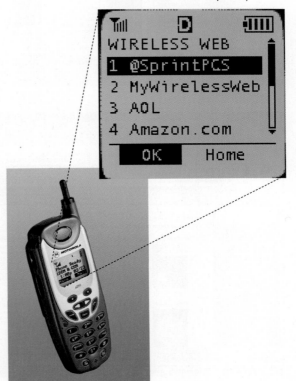

On the Web, a link can be a word, phrase, or image. You often can identify a link by its appearance. Text links usually are underlined or in a color different from the rest of the document. When you point to a graphical link, it may change its look in some way. As shown in Figure 2-9, the shape of the pointer on the screen changes to a small hand with a pointing index finger when you position it on a link, or point to the link.

To activate a link, you point to it and then press the mouse button, or click the link. This causes the item associated with the link to display on the screen. The link can point to an item on the same Web page, a different Web page at the same Web site, or a separate Web page at a different Web site in another city or country. In most cases, when you navigate using links, you are jumping from Web page to Web page. Some people refer to

this activity of jumping from one Web page to another as **surfing the Web**. To remind you visually that you have visited a location or document, some browsers change the color of a text link after you click it.

Using a URL

A Web page has a unique address, called a **Uniform Resource Locator (URL)**. A browser retrieves

Figure 2-9 NAVIGATING USING A VARIETY OF LINKS

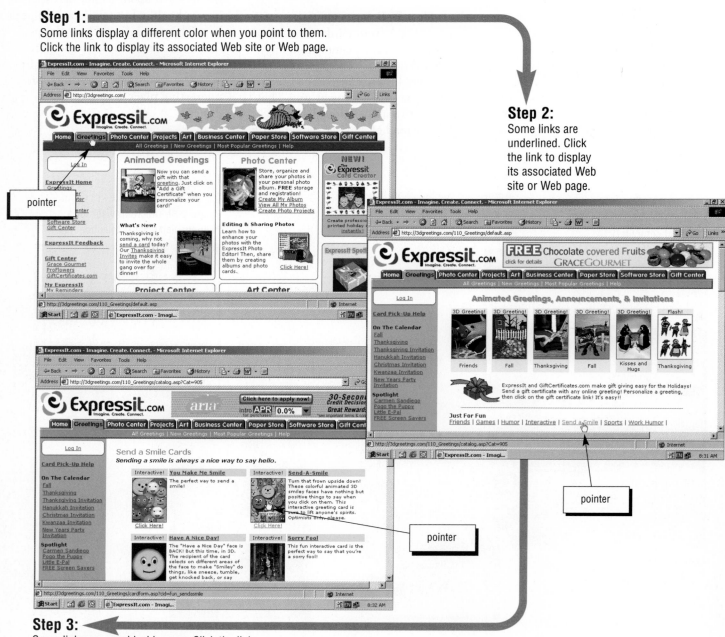

Step 1:
Some links display a different color when you point to them.
Click the link to display its associated Web site or Web page.

Step 2:
Some links are underlined. Click the link to display its associated Web site or Web page.

Step 3:
Some links are graphical images. Click the link to display its associated Web site or Web page.

a Web page by using its URL, also called a **Web address**. The URL tells the browser where to locate the document. URLs make it possible for you to navigate using links because a link is associated with a URL. When you click a link, you are issuing a request to display the Web site or the document associated with the URL.

Many companies and organizations assume the public is familiar with URLs. Web addresses appear on television, in radio broadcasts, in printed newspapers, magazines, and other forms of advertising.

If you know the URL of a Web page, you can type it into a text box at the top of the browser window. For example, if you type the URL of http://www.nationalgeographic.com/travel/index.html in the Address text box and then press the ENTER key, the browser downloads and displays the Travel page of the National Geographic Web site (Figure 2-10).

As shown in Figure 2-10, a URL consists of a protocol, domain name, and sometimes the path to a specific Web page or location on a Web page. Most Web page URLs begin with http://. The **http** stands for **hypertext transfer protocol**, which is the communications standard that enables pages to transfer on the Web.

If you do not enter a URL exactly, your browser will not locate the site or Web page you want to visit (view). To help minimize errors, most current browsers and Web sites allow you to omit the http:// and www portions of the URL. For example, you can type nationalgeographic.com/travel/index.html instead of http://www.nationalgeographic.com/travel/index.html. If you enter an incorrect URL, some browsers search for similar addresses and provide a list from which you can select.

A **Web server** is a computer that delivers (serves) Web pages you request. For example, when you enter the URL, nationalgeographic.com/travel/index.html in the browser, it sends a request to the server that stores the Web site of www.nationalgeographic.com. The server then retrieves the Web page named index.html in the travel path and sends it to your browser.

The same Web server can store multiple Web sites. For example, many Internet service providers grant their subscribers free storage space on a Web server for personal or company Web sites.

Web Link

For more information on URLs, visit the Discovering Computers 2002 Chapter 2 WEB LINK page (**scsite.com/dc2002/ch2/weblink.htm**) and click URLs.

ISSUE

Beware of Stealth URLs

Navigating the Web

A father sat down at a computer with his young child, typed what he thought was the URL for a site of national interest, and was surprised to encounter pornographic material. "I should have paid closer attention to the (URL) suffix," he admitted. Stealth URLs — addresses similar to those of other Web pages — attract visitors and potential subscribers. Some Web pages adopt the URLs of popular Web sites, with minor changes in spelling or domain name. Critics claim this misleads consumers and weakens the value of the original name. Defendants counter that restrictions on URLs would violate rights to free speech. Similar to stealth URLs, some *adult* Web sites include words such as Nintendo 64, Sega, Barbie, and others within the Web site descriptions, often called meta tags. Many search engines examine the meta tags content and return these Web sites as a suggested link. Do you think URLs should be regulated? Why or why not? How else can people deal with the problem of stealth URLs? Should Web site developers be permitted to include phrases within the meta tags that do not relate to the Web site? How could this be regulated?

For more information on stealth URLs and meta tags, visit the Discovering Computers 2002 Issues Web page (**scsite.com/dc2002/issues.htm**) and click Chapter 2 Issue #2.

protocol   domain name   path

http://www.nationalgeographic.com/travel/index.html

Figure 2-10 The URL for the Travel page of the National Geographic Web site is www.nationalgeographic.com/travel/index.html. When you enter this URL in the Address text box, the Web page shown displays.

Searching for Information on the Web

No single organization controls additions, deletions, and changes to Web sites. This means no central menu or catalog of Web site content and addresses exists. Several companies, however, maintain organized directories of Web sites to help you find information on specific topics.

A **search engine** is a software program you can use to find Web sites, Web pages, and Internet files. Search engines are particularly helpful in locating Web pages on certain topics or in locating specific pages for which you do not know the exact URL. To find a page or pages, you enter a word or phrase, called **search text** or **keywords**, in the search engine's text box. Many search engines use a program called a spider to display a list of all Web pages that contain the word or phrase you entered. A **spider**, also called a **crawler** or **bot**, is a program that reads pages on Web sites in order to create a catalog, or index, of hits.

A **hit** is any Web page name that lists as the result of a search. For example, if you want a listing of ski resorts in Colorado, you could enter Colorado ski resort as your search text. The search engine would return a list of hits, or Web page names, that contain the phrase Colorado ski resort (Figure 2-11). You then click an appropriate link in the list to display the associated Web site or Web page.

When you enter search text that contains multiple keywords, the search engine usually locates sites that

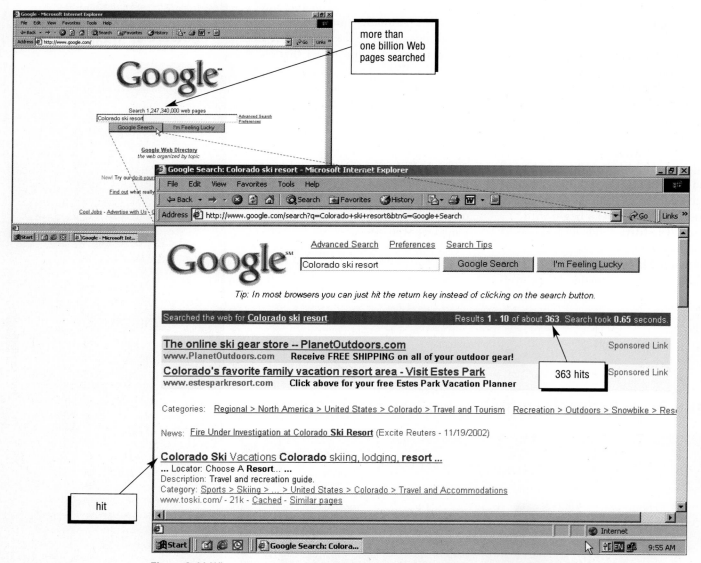

Figure 2-11 When you enter search text into a search engine, such as Google, a list of hits will display.

contain all of the words. For example, a search with the keywords, ski resort, results in 368,000 hits, or Web pages, that contain the word ski and the word resort. To reduce the number of hits, you should be more specific in the search. For example, the search text, Colorado ski resort, reduces the number of hits to 363.

The table in Figure 2-12 lists the Web site addresses of several Internet search engines. Most of these sites also provide directories of Web sites. On the Web, a **directory** is an organized set of topics, such as arts, reference, sports, and subtopics. Figure 2-13 shows Yahoo!'s directory Web page. If you wanted information on major league baseball parks, you could use a directory to display the topic sports, then the subtopic base-ball, and then the subtopic major league.

Widely Used Search Engines	
AltaVista	altavista.com
Excite	excite.com
Google	google.com
GoTo.com	goto.com
HotBot	hotbot.com
Lycos	lycos.com
WebCrawler	webcrawler.com
Yahoo!	yahoo.com

Figure 2-12 Widely used search engines.

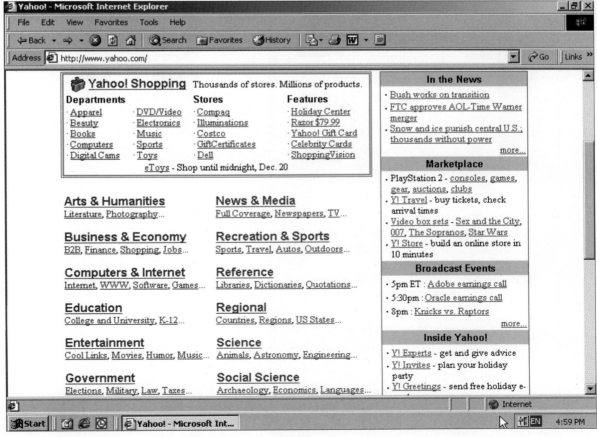

Figure 2-13 An example of a directory Web page.

Types of Web Pages

Six basic types of Web pages exist: advocacy, business/marketing, informational, news, portal, and personal (Figure 2-14). Many Web pages fall into more than one of these categories. The following paragraphs discuss each of these types of Web pages.

ADVOCACY WEB PAGE An **advocacy Web page** contains content that describes a cause, opinion, or idea. The purpose of an advocacy Web page is to convince the reader of the validity

Figure 2-14a (advocacy Web page)

Figure 2-14b (business/marketing Web page)

Figure 2-14c (informational Web page)

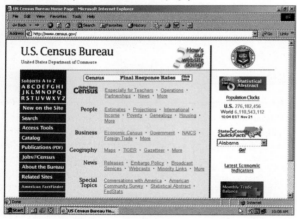

Figure 2-14d (news Web page)

Figure 2-14e (portal Web page)

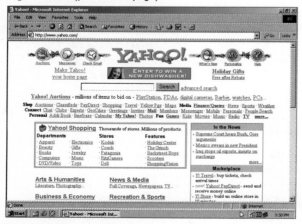

Figure 2-14f (personal Web page)

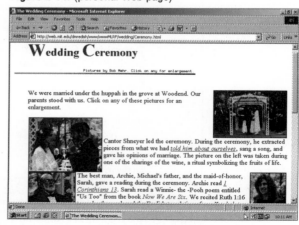

Figure 2-14 Types of Web pages.

of the cause, opinion, or idea. These Web pages usually present views of a particular group or association. Sponsors of advocacy Web pages include the Democratic Party, the Republican Party, the Society for the Prevention of Cruelty to Animals, and the Society to Protect Human Rights.

BUSINESS/MARKETING WEB PAGE

A **business/marketing Web page** contains content that promotes or sells products or services. Nearly every business today has a business/marketing Web page. AT&T, Dell Computer Corporation, General Motors Corporation, Kraft Foods Inc., and Walt Disney Company all have business/marketing Web pages. Many of these companies also allow you to purchase their products or services online.

INFORMATIONAL WEB PAGE An

informational Web page contains factual information. Many United States government agencies have informational Web pages providing information such as census data, tax codes, and the congressional budget. Other organizations provide information such as public transportation schedules and published research findings.

NEWS WEB PAGE A news Web

page contains newsworthy material including stories and articles relating to current events, life, money, sports, and the weather. Many magazines and newspapers sponsor Web sites that provide summaries of printed articles, as well as articles not included in the printed versions. Newspapers and television and radio stations are some of the media that maintain news Web pages.

PORTAL WEB PAGE A portal Web

page, often called a **portal**, offers a variety of Internet services from a single, convenient location. Most portals offer the following free services: search engine; local, national, and worldwide news; sports and weather; free personal Web pages; reference tools such as yellow pages, stock quotes, and maps; shopping malls and auctions; e-mail; instant messaging, newsgroups or message boards, calendars, and chat rooms.

Some portals also have Web communities. A **Web community** is a Web site that joins a specific group of people with similar interests or relationships. These communities usually offer a newsgroup or message board, chat room, e-mail, and online photo albums to facilitate communications among members.

Popular portals include AltaVista, America Online, Dogpile, Euroseek, Excite, GO.com, Google, HotBot, looksmart, Lycos, Microsoft Network, Netscape Netcenter, and Yahoo!. You may notice that many portals also are Internet service providers or online service providers, and offer search engines and directories. The goal of these portals is to be designated as your browser's home page, the first page that displays when you connect to the Internet.

A **wireless portal** is a portal specifically designed for Web-enabled handheld computers and devices. Wireless portals attempt to provide all information a wireless user might require. These portals offer services such as search engines, news, stock quotes, weather, maps, e-mail, calendar, instant messaging, and shopping.

PERSONAL WEB PAGE A private

individual who normally is not associated with any organization often maintains a **personal Web page**. People publish personal Web pages for a variety of reasons. Some are job hunting. Others simply want to share life experiences with the world.

Multimedia on the Web

Most Web pages include more than formatted text and links. In fact, some of the more exciting Web pages use multimedia. **Multimedia** refers to any application that integrates text with one or more of the following elements: graphics, sound, video, virtual reality, or other media elements. A Web page that uses multimedia has much more appeal than one with text on a gray background. It brings a Web page to life, increases the types of information available on the Web, expands the Web's potential uses, and makes the Internet a more entertaining place to explore. Multimedia Web pages often require more time to download because they contain large graphics and video or audio clips. These multimedia pages, however, usually are worth the wait.

The following sections discuss how the Web uses graphics, audio, animation, video, and virtual reality multimedia.

GRAPHICS A **graphic**, or **graphical image**, is a digital representation of information such as a drawing, chart, or photograph. Graphics were the first media used to enhance the text-based Internet. The introduction of graphical Web browsers allowed Web page developers to incorporate illustrations, logos, and other images into Web pages. Today, many Web pages use colorful graphical designs and images to convey messages (Figure 2-15).

The Web contains thousands of image files on countless subjects.

You can download many of these images at no cost and use them for noncommercial purposes. Recall that downloading is the process of transferring an object from the Web to your computer. For example, you can incorporate them into your own Web pages.

To use graphics files on the Web, they must be saved in a certain format (Figure 2-16). A saved image, known as a file, is stored on a medium such as a floppy disk or hard disk. The next chapter discusses files and saving in more depth.

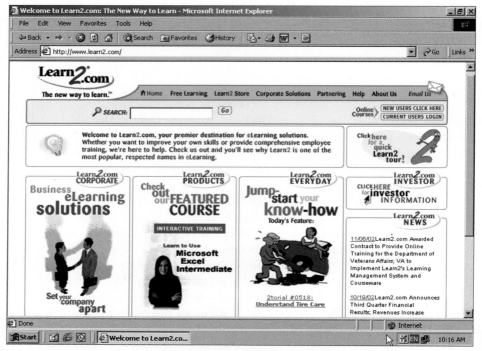

Figure 2-15 Many Web pages use colorful graphical designs and images to convey their messages.

GRAPHICS FORMATS USED ON THE INTERNET

Acronym	Name	File Extension
BMP	Bit Map	.bmp
GIF (pronounced JIFF)	Graphics Interchange Format	.gif
JPEG (pronounced JAY-peg)	Joint Photographic Experts Group	.jpg
PCX	PC Paintbrush	.pcx
PNG (pronounced ping)	Portable Network Graphics	.png
TIFF	Tagged Image File Format	.tif

Figure 2-16 Graphics formats used on the Internet. Some users look on their computer at a file's extension to determine the type of file.

Two of the more common file formats in Figure 2-16 for graphical images on the Web are JPEG and GIF. A **JPEG** (pronounced JAY-peg) file, which stands for **Joint Photographic Experts Group**, is a graphical image that uses compression techniques to reduce the file size. These smaller sizes result in faster downloading of Web pages. The more compressed the file, the smaller the file, but the lower the quality. The goal with JPEG files is to reach a balance between image quality and file size.

A graphical image saved as a **GIF** (pronounced jiff or giff) file, which stands for **Graphics Interchange Format**, also uses compression techniques to reduce file sizes.

The GIF format works best for images with only a few distinct colors, such as line drawings, single-color borders, and simple cartoons.

The BMP, PCX, and TIFF formats listed in Figure 2-16 have larger file sizes and thus are not used on the Web as frequently as JPEG and GIF.

Some Web sites use thumbnails on their pages because graphics files can be time consuming to display. A **thumbnail** is a small version of a larger graphical image you usually can click to display the full-sized image (Figure 2-17).

ANIMATION Many Web pages use animated graphics, or animation. **Animation** is the appearance of motion created by displaying a series of still images in rapid sequence. Animated graphics can make Web pages more visually interesting or draw attention to important information or links. For example, text that animates by scrolling across the screen, called a **marquee** (pronounced mar-KEE), can serve as a ticker to display stock updates, news, sports scores, weather, or other information. Web-based games often use animation. Some animations even contain links to a different page.

One popular type of animation, called an **animated GIF**, uses computer animation and graphics software to combine several images into a single GIF file.

Figure 2-17 If you click the thumbnail of the envelope with the stamp in the screen above, a full-sized image of the envelope displays in a separate window.

AUDIO On the Web, you can listen to audio clips and live audio. **Audio** is music, speech, or any other sound.

Simple audio applications on the Web consist of individual sound files that you download to your computer. Once downloaded, you can play (listen) to the contents of these files. As with graphics files, audio files must be saved in a certain format. A common format for audio files on the Web is MP3.

MP3 is a popular technology that compresses audio. MP3 reduces an audio file to about one-tenth of its original size — while preserving the original quality of the sound. You easily can copy these smaller files from the Web to your computer — even with a slow Internet connection.

This capability of transferring music across the Internet has stirred much controversy with respect to copyright infringement of music because it provides users with an easy method of copying MP3 music files from one computer to another.

Most current operating systems contain a program, called a **player**, that can play the audio in MP3 files on your computer. You also can buy portable audio devices, called **MP3 players**, that can play MP3 files stored on CD or miniature storage media (Figure 2-18).

More advanced audio applications on the Web use streaming audio. **Streaming** is the process of transferring data in a continuous and even flow. Streaming allows users to access and use a file while it is transmitting. Streaming is important because most users do not have fast enough Internet connections to download a large multimedia file quickly.

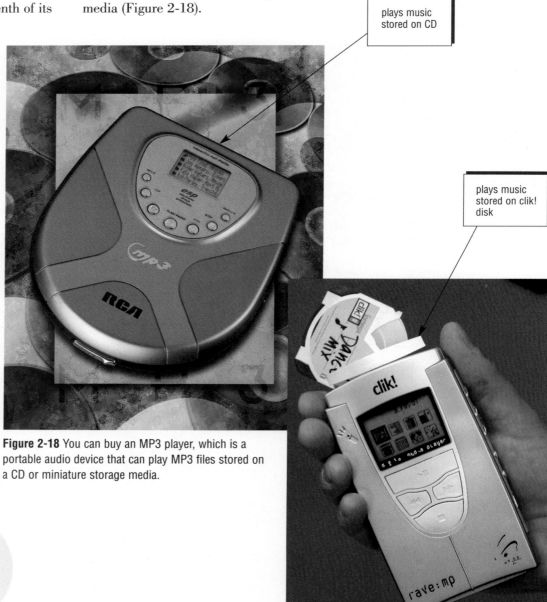

plays music stored on CD

plays music stored on clik! disk

Figure 2-18 You can buy an MP3 player, which is a portable audio device that can play MP3 files stored on a CD or miniature storage media.

Streaming audio, also called **streaming sound**, enables you to listen to the sound (the data) as it downloads to your computer. Many radio and television stations use streaming audio to broadcast music, interviews, talk shows, sporting events, music videos, news, live concerts, and other segments (Figure 2-19). Two accepted standards supported by most Web browsers for transmitting streaming audio data on the Internet are Windows Media Player and RealAudio. RealAudio is a component of RealPlayer, which is a streaming media program. You also can use MP3 for streaming audio.

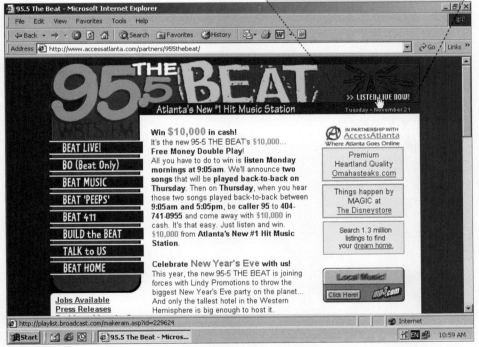

Figure 2-19 Many radio and television stations use streaming audio. Radio station 95.5 The Beat broadcasts using RealAudio, which is a component of RealPlayer.

APPLY IT!
Now Playing – Online Radio

Regardless of your taste in music — jazz, country, rock, classical, hip hop — you can find it on the Internet. Thousands of radio stations now are broadcasting in real-time on the World Wide Web. You can listen to almost any station in the world for free as long as you have the right software and an Internet connection. The three most popular software programs are RealNetwork's RealPlayer software (see URL below), Apple Computer's QuickTime (see URL below), and Microsoft's Windows Media Player (see URL below).

You can download each of these programs at no cost from the Internet. After downloading and installing the software, you are ready to tune in and listen to a radio station of choice. You can find online radio stations on the Web in a variety of places. Some sites, such as Yahoo! Broadcast.com (see URL below) and Starting Page (see URL below) function as clearinghouses, archiving many radio programs in one area for you to sample. Or, in a search engine, type `radio stations` and then click the Find or Search button to display hundreds of links. Select your favorite station, click the link to activate your software, and then listen to the music.

For more information on online radio and the Web sites mentioned above, visit the Discovering Computers 2002 Apply It Web page (**scsite.com/dc2002/apply.htm**) and click Chapter 2 Apply It #2.

VIDEO **Video** consists of full-motion images that are played back at various speeds. Most video also has accompanying audio. As with audio, many Web sites include video to enhance your understanding or for entertainment purposes. Watch a news report as it is being reported (Figure 2-20) or enjoy a live performance of your favorite vocalist.

Like audio, simple video applications on the Web consist of individual video files, such as movie or television clips, that you must download completely before you can play them on the computer. Video files often are compressed because they are quite large in size. These clips also are quite short in length because they can take a long time to download. The **Moving Pictures Experts Group** (**MPEG**) defines a popular video compression standard.

As with streaming audio, **streaming video** allows you to view longer or live video images as they download to your computer. Two widely used standards supported by most Web browsers for transmitting streaming video data on the Internet are RealVideo and Windows Media Player. Like RealAudio, RealVideo is a component of RealPlayer.

Another use of video on the Web is for a Web cam. A **Web cam**, also called a **cam**, is a video camera whose output displays on a Web page. A Web cam attracts Web site visitors by showing images that change regularly. Chapter 6 discusses Web cams in more depth.

VIRTUAL REALITY **Virtual reality** (**VR**) is the use of computers to simulate a real or imagined environment that appears as a three-dimensional (3-D) space. On the Web, VR involves the display of 3-D images that you can explore and manipulate interactively.

Using special VR software, a Web developer creates an entire 3-D site that contains infinite space and depth, called a **VR world**. A VR world, for example, might show a room with furniture. You can walk through such a VR room by moving an input device forward, backward, or to the side.

VR often is used for games, but it has many practical applications as well. Science educators can create VR models of molecules, organisms, and other structures for students to examine (Figure 2-21). Companies can use VR to showcase products or create advertisements. Architects can create VR models of buildings and rooms so clients can see how a completed construction project will look before it is built.

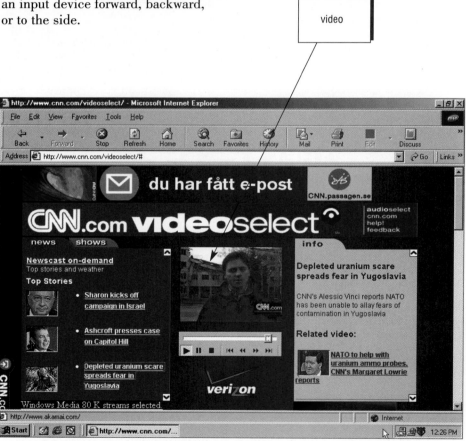

Figure 2-20 A live video broadcast.

Web Link

For more information on streaming media, visit the Discovering Computers 2002 Chapter 2 WEB LINK page (**scsite.com/dc2002/ ch2/weblink.htm**) and click Streaming Media.

Webcasting

When you want information from a Web site, you often request it from the site. This method of obtaining information, known as **pull technology**, relies on a client such as your computer to request a Web page from a server. For example, you enter a URL in your browser or click a link to display a particular Web page.

Today's browsers also support push technology. Using **push technology**, also called **Webcasting**, a server automatically downloads content to your computer at regular intervals or whenever updates are made to the site. A Web server can push an entire Web site or just a portion of one, such as the latest news, to your computer. For example, a Webcast can display stock prices and financial headlines on your desktop in the form of a continuously running ticker tape (Figure 2-22). Webcasting saves time by delivering information at regular intervals, without you having to request it.

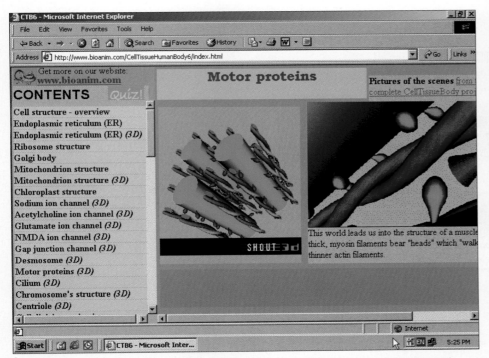

Figure 2-21 This instructional site uses VR to teach biology students about cells and body tissue.

Figure 2-22 On this screen, stock prices and financial headlines are pushed onto the desktop.

ticker tape pushed to desktop from Microsoft Investor Web site

Another advantage of Webcasting is that once the Web server pushes Web content to your computer, you can view it whether you are online or offline. (**Offline** means you are not connected to the Internet.) With Webcasting, the Web server downloads the contents of one or more Web sites to your hard disk while you are online. This downloaded information also is available for browsing while you are offline. Offline browsing is ideal for mobile users because they do not always have access to the Internet.

ELECTRONIC COMMERCE

Electronic commerce, also known as **e-commerce**, is a financial business transaction that occurs over an electronic network such as the Internet. Anyone with access to a computer, an Internet connection, and a means to pay for purchased goods or services can participate in e-commerce (Figure 2-23).

In the past, e-commerce transactions were conducted primarily through desktop computers. Today, many laptop computers, handheld computers, pagers, and cellular telephones also can access the Web wirelessly. Some people use the term **m-commerce** (**mobile commerce**) to identify e-commerce that takes place using mobile devices.

E-commerce has changed the way people conduct business. It virtually eliminates the barriers of time and distance that slow traditional transactions. Now, with e-commerce, transactions can occur instantaneously and globally. This saves time for participants on both ends.

Two of the most popular uses of e-commerce by consumers are investing and shopping. Through online investing, you buy and sell stocks or

Figure 2-23 E-commerce activities include shopping for goods from a retailer.

bonds without using a broker. Thus, the transaction fees for online trading usually are reduced greatly.

You can purchase just about any good or service on the Web. Examples include flowers, books, groceries, computers, prescription drugs, music, movies, cars, airline tickets, and concert tickets.

Today, three types of e-commerce exist: business to consumer, consumer to consumer, and business to business. **Business to consumer (B-to-C or B2C)** e-commerce consists of the sale of goods to the general public. For example, instead of visiting a computer retailer to purchase a computer, you can order one that meets your specifications directly from the manufacturer's Web site.

A customer (consumer) visits an online business through an electronic storefront. An **electronic storefront** contains descriptions, graphics, and a shopping cart. The **shopping cart** allows the customer to collect purchases. When ready to complete the sale, the customer enters personal and financial data through a secure Web connection.

Instead of purchasing from a business, consumers can purchase from each other. For example, with an **online auction**, you bid on an item being sold by someone else. The highest bidder at the end of the bidding period purchases the item. **Consumer to consumer (C-to-C or C2C)** e-commerce occurs when one consumer sells directly to another, such as in an online auction.

Most e-commerce, though, actually takes place between businesses, which is called **business to business (B-to-B or B2B) e-commerce**. Businesses often provide goods and services to other businesses, such as online advertising, recruiting, credit, sales, market research, technical support, and training.

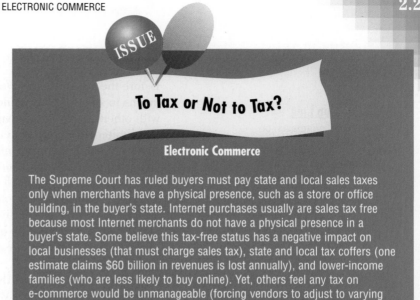

ISSUE

To Tax or Not to Tax?

Electronic Commerce

The Supreme Court has ruled buyers must pay state and local sales taxes only when merchants have a physical presence, such as a store or office building, in the buyer's state. Internet purchases usually are sales tax free because most Internet merchants do not have a physical presence in a buyer's state. Some believe this tax-free status has a negative impact on local businesses (that must charge sales tax), state and local tax coffers (one estimate claims $60 billion in revenues is lost annually), and lower-income families (who are less likely to buy online). Yet, others feel any tax on e-commerce would be unmanageable (forcing vendors to adjust to varying sales tax rates) and unjustified. Should a sales tax be applied to Internet purchases? Why or why not? How can the problems of taxing, or not taxing, Internet purchases be addressed?

For more information on e-commerce and taxing issues, visit the Discovering Computers 2002 Issues Web page (**scsite.com/dc2002/ issues.htm**) and click Chapter 2 Issue #4.

TECHNOLOGY TRAILBLAZER

MASAYOSHI **SON**

Often called "the Bill Gates of Japan," Masayoshi Son has helped bring that country to the forefront of the digital age.

When he was 16 years old, the second-generation Korean-Japanese moved from Japan to California to learn English. He then majored in economics at the University of California, Berkeley. While in school, he earned his first $1 million by importing arcade games from Japan for the campus, developing computer games, and selling a patent for a multilingual pocket translator to Sharp Corporation.

At age 23, he founded Softbank Corporation, a software distribution operation, in 1981. By 1995, the company controlled one-half of the personal computer software in Japan. Profits from this company have served as the primary basis for other profitable investments, including Yahoo!, Kingston Technologies, Ziff-Davis, and E*Trade. Besides these software investments, Son now has holdings in more than 50 international technology companies, including publishing, electronic banking, and broadcasting.

Son is a leading member of Japan's Prime Minister's IT Strategy Council. Though criticized for heavy investment in U.S. Internet companies, Son sees such alliances as helpful to both countries' economies.

For more information on Masayoshi Son, visit the Discovering Computers 2002 People Web page (**scsite.com/dc2002/ people.htm**) and click Masayoshi Son.

Web Link

For more information on
Web publishing, visit the
Discovering Computers 2002
Chapter 2 WEB LINK page
(**scsite.com/dc2002/
ch2/weblink.htm**) and
click Web Publishing.

Ink or Link?

Web Publishing

With the exception of the printed book,
the Twentieth Century was predominantly
visual — photography, film, television,
video. As we begin the Twenty-First
Century, are we entering a brave new
world of all digital media? Digital communications technologies no doubt are
spurring fundamental changes within all
publishing businesses. Many magazines
provide both a printed subscription
service and an online presence. A printed
version provides the flexibility of any
time, anywhere reading. Many people
who read for enjoyment assert they
prefer reading that includes the ability to
carry, hold, and manipulate the material.
On the other hand, the online version
offers benefits not found in the printed
version. For instance, one can search
and display an index of past articles or
link to other relevant and updated topics.
Do most people prefer reading online or
reading printed materials? What impact
will the Internet have on printed media
within the next five years? with books?
with magazines? with newspapers?
Which will be better for the environment
— online reading or printed media? Why?
    For more information on electronic
media and Web publishing, visit the
Discovering Computers 2002 Issues Web
page (**scsite.com/dc2002/issues.htm**)
and click Chapter 2 Issue #5.

WEB PUBLISHING

Before the advent of the Web, the
means to share opinions and ideas
with others easily and inexpensively
was limited to the media, classroom,
work, or social environments.
Generating an advertisement or
publication that could reach a massive
audience required much expense.
Today, businesses and individuals
can convey information to millions
of people by creating their own
Web pages.

      Web publishing is the develop-
ment and maintenance of Web pages.
To develop a Web page, you do not
have to be a computer programmer.
For the small business or home user,
Web publishing is fairly easy as long
as you have the proper tools.

      The five major steps to Web
publishing are as follows:
(1) planning the Web site
(2) analyzing and designing the
     Web site
(3) creating the Web site
(4) deploying the Web site
(5) maintaining the Web site
      Figure 2-24 illustrates these
steps with respect to a personal Web
site. The following paragraphs
describe these steps in more depth.

Planning the Web Site

      Planning a personal Web site
involves thinking about issues that
could affect the design of the Web
site. You should identify the purpose
of the Web site and the characteristics
of the people that you want to visit

the Web site. Determine ways to
differentiate your Web site from
similar ones. Decide how to keep the
content of the Web site current and
exciting. With these types of issues
resolved, you can move to the next
step of Analyzing and Designing the
Web Site.

Analyzing and Designing the Web Site

      A Web site can be simple or
complex. In this step, you determine
specific ways to meet the goals identified in the previous step. You design
the layout of elements of the Web
page such as text, graphics, audio,
video, and virtual reality. Decide if
you have the means to include all
the elements of the design into the
Web site.

      Hardware you may need
includes a digital camera, scanner,
sound card, microphone, and PC
camera. To incorporate pictures in
your Web pages, you can take digital
photographs with a digital camera or
scan existing photographs and other
graphics into a digital format with a
scanner. You also can download
images from the Web or purchase a
CD-ROM or DVD-ROM that contains
a collection of images. With a sound
card, you can add sounds to your
Web pages. A microphone allows
you to include your voice in a Web
page. To incorporate videos, you
could use a PC camera or purchase
special hardware that captures still
photographs from videos.

Figure 2-24 HOW TO PUBLISH YOUR RESUME ON THE WEB

Step 1:
Think about issues that could affect the design of the Web site.

Step 2:
Sketch a design of the Web page on paper.

Step 4:
Copy (upload) the Web site from your hard disk to a Web server.

Step 3:
Create the Web site in a software package such as word processing.

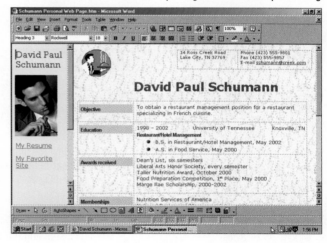

Step 5:
Visit and revise your Web site regularly to be sure it is working and current.

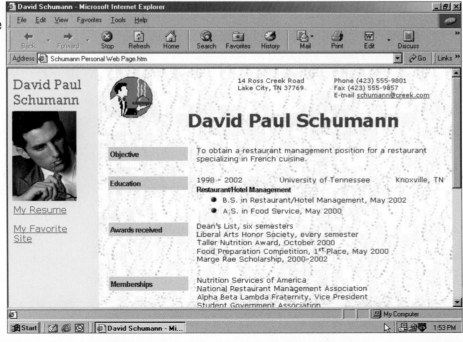

Most browsers have the capability of displaying basic multimedia elements on a Web page. Sometimes, a browser might need an additional program, called a plug-in. A **plug-in** is a program that extends the capability of a browser. You can download many plug-ins at no cost from various sites on the Web (Figure 2-25). If your Web page uses multimedia elements that require a plug-in, you may want to include a link to the Web site that contains the plug-in so that visitors can download it.

Creating a Web Site

Creating a Web site, sometimes called **Web page authoring**, involves working on the computer to compose the Web site. Many current word processing packages include Web page authoring features that help you to create basic Web pages that contain text and graphics. Millions of people use word processing software every day to develop documents, including Web pages.

To create more sophisticated Web pages that include video, sound, animation, and other special effects, you can use Web page authoring software. **Web page authoring software** is software specifically designed to help you create Web pages. Both new and experienced users can create fascinating Web sites with this software. Popular Web page authoring software packages include Microsoft FrontPage, Adobe GoLive, Lotus FastSite, Macromedia Dreamweaver, and Macromedia Flash.

When you save a Web page using word processing or Web page authoring software, the software saves the Web page in an HTML format.

Web Link

For more information on plug-ins, visit the Discovering Computers 2002 Chapter 2 WEB LINK page (**scsite.com/dc2002/ch2/weblink.htm**) and click Plug-ins.

POPULAR PLUG-IN APPLICATION

Plug-In Application		Description	Web Site
Get Acrobat Reader	Acrobat Reader	View, navigate, and print Portable Document Format (PDF) files — documents formatted to look just as they look in print	adobe.com
macromedia FLASH PLAYER	Flash Player	View dazzling graphics and animation, hear outstanding sound and music, display Web pages across entire screen	macromedia.com
supports mp3s liquid player five	Liquid Player	Listen and purchase CD-quality music tracks and audio CDs over the Internet; access MP3 files	liquidaudio.com
QuickTime icon	QuickTime	View animation, music, audio, video, and VR panoramas and objects directly in a Web page	apple.com
real jukebox FREE	RealJukebox	Play MP3 files; create music CDs	real.com
real player plus	RealPlayer	Listen to live and on-demand near-CD-quality audio and newscast-quality video; stream audio and video content for faster viewing	real.com
macromedia SHOCKWAVE	Shockwave	Experience dynamic interactive multimedia, graphics, and streaming audio	macromedia.com

Figure 2-25 Most plug-ins can be downloaded free from the Web.

HTML (hypertext markup language) is a set of special codes that format a file for use as a Web page. These codes, called tags, specify how the text and other elements display in a browser and where the links lead. For an example of HTML, see Figure 1-15a on page 1.14. Your Web browser translates the document with HTML tags into a functional Web page. Some experienced programmers modify the HTML generated by Web page authoring software or even write the entire HTML codes from scratch.

Deploying a Web Site

After your Web pages are created, you store them on a Web server. Many ISPs and OSPs provide their customers with a Web address and storage space on a Web server for the Web site at no additional cost. If your service provider does not include this service, companies called Web hosting services provide storage for your Web pages for a reasonable monthly fee. The fee charged by a Web hosting service varies based on factors such as the amount of storage your Web pages require, whether your pages use streaming or other multimedia, and whether the pages are personal or for business use.

If your service provider does not supply you with a Web address or if you want to obtain a different domain name, you apply to an official registrar for a specific domain name such as countryflorist.com. You then pay a small annual fee to continue using the domain name.

Once you have created a Web site and located a Web server to store it, you need to upload the Web site, or copy it from your computer to the Web server. One procedure used to upload files is FTP, discussed later in this chapter. Another procedure is to save the Web site to a Web folder, which is a location on a Web server. You must contact the network administrator or technical support staff at your ISP or OSP to determine if the Web server supports FTP or Web folders and then obtain necessary permissions to access the Web server.

To help others locate your Web site, you should register it with various search engines. Doing so ensures your site will appear in the hit lists for searches on related keywords. Many search engines allow you to register your URL and keywords at no cost.

Registering your site with the various search engines, however, can be an extremely time-consuming task. Instead, you can use a submission service. A submission service is a Web-based business that offers a registration package in which you pay to register with hundreds of search engines.

In addition to supplying a title for your site, the URL, and a site description, the submission service might require you to identify several features of your site, such as whether it is commercial or personal; a category and subcategory; and search keywords. For example, if your Web site business sells greeting cards, you could register under the Products and Services subcategory in the Business and Economy category, and specify keywords such as greeting cards, birthday cards, and anniversary cards.

Maintaining the Web Site

A Webmaster is the individual responsible for maintaining a Web site and developing Web pages. Webmasters and other Web page developers maintain Web sites using software products. Most Web page authoring software packages provide basic Web site management tools, allowing you to add and modify Web pages within the Web site. For more advanced features such as managing users, passwords, chat rooms, and e-mail, you need to purchase specialized Web site management software.

OTHER INTERNET SERVICES

Although the World Wide Web is the most talked about service on the Internet, many other Internet services are used widely. These include e-mail, FTP, newsgroups and message boards, mailing lists, chat rooms, and instant messaging. The following pages discuss each of these services.

E-Mail

E-mail (**electronic mail**) is the transmission of messages and files via a computer network. E-mail was one of the original services on the Internet, enabling scientists and researchers working on government-sponsored projects to communicate with colleagues at other locations. Today, e-mail quickly is becoming a primary communications method for both personal and business use.

You can create, send, receive, forward, store, print, and delete messages using an **e-mail program**. The steps in Figure 2-26 illustrate how to

Figure 2-26 HOW TO SEND AN E-MAIL MESSAGE

Step 1:
Start an e-mail program and point to the New Mail Message button.

Step 2:
Click the New Mail Message button to display the Message window.

Step 4:
Click the Insert File button to attach a JPG file containing a picture to the message. Locate the file on your hard disk and click its name. An icon for the file displays below the message. Click the Send button to send the message.

Step 3:
Enter the recipient's e-mail address, the subject, and the message in the Message window.

Step 5:
When Sally receives the e-mail message, she opens the JPG file to view the picture.

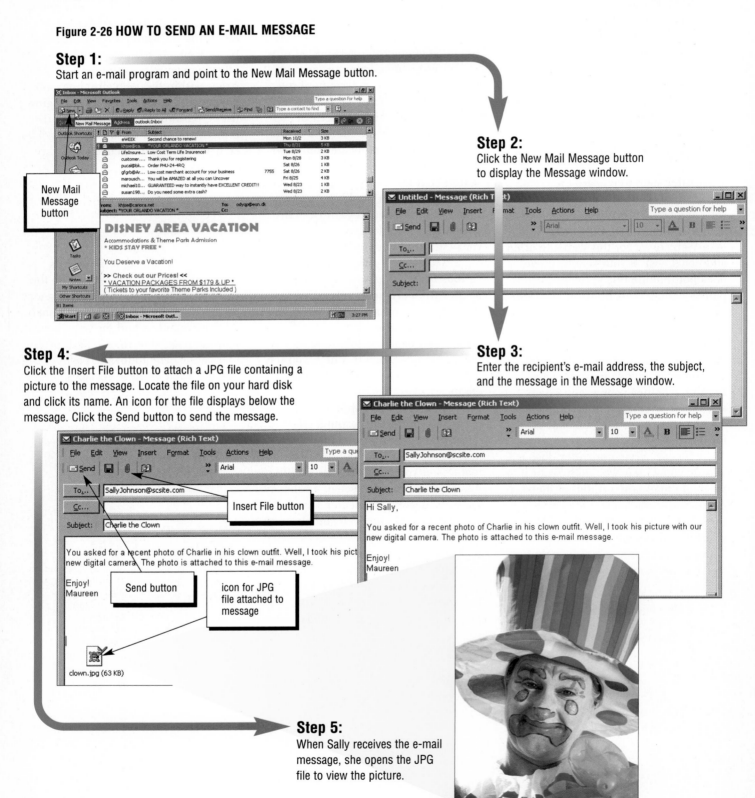

send an e-mail message. The message can be simple text or can include an attachment such as a word processing document, a graphical image, or an audio or video clip.

Just as you address a letter when using the postal system, you must address an e-mail message with the e-mail address of your intended recipient. To receive messages, you need an e-mail address. Likewise, when someone sends you a message, they must have your e-mail address. An **e-mail address** is a combination of a user name and a domain name that identifies a user, so he or she can receive Internet e-mail (Figure 2-27).

A **user name**, or **user-ID**, is a unique combination of characters, such as letters of the alphabet or numbers, that identifies you. Your user name must be different from the other user names in the same domain. For example, a user named Sally Johnson whose server has a domain name of scsite.com might select S_Johnson as her user name. If scsite.com already has a user S_Johnson (for Sam Johnson), Sally would have to select a different user name, such as SallyJohnson or Sally_Johnson. You select your user name. Although you can select a nickname or any other combination of characters for your user name, many users select a combination of their first and last names so others can remember it easily.

In an Internet e-mail address, an @ symbol (pronounced at) separates the user name from the domain name. Your service provider supplies you with the domain name. Using the example in Figure 2-27, a possible e-mail address would be SallyJohnson@scsite.com, which would be read as follows: Sally Johnson at s c site dot com. Most e-mail programs allow you to create an **address book**, which contains a list of names and e-mail addresses.

Although no complete listing of Internet e-mail addresses exists, several Internet sites list addresses collected from public sources. These sites also allow you to list your e-mail address voluntarily so others can find it. The site also might ask for other information, such as your high school or college, so others can determine if you are the person they want to reach.

Most e-mail programs have a mail notification alert that informs you via a message or sound when you receive new mail, even if you are working in another application. As you receive e-mail messages, they are placed in your mailbox. A **mailbox** is a storage location usually residing on the computer that connects you to the Internet, such as the server operated by your ISP or OSP. The server that contains the mailboxes often is called a **mail server**. Most ISPs and OSPs provide an Internet e-mail program and a mailbox on a mail server as a standard part of their Internet access services.

V APPLY IT!

Hello from Your Personal Computer

The convenience of voice communications now is available online. In traditional voice mail, the caller leaves a message in your voice mailbox; similarly, with voice e-mail, you speak instead of typing an e-mail message. Most computers can handle voice messages once you install the proper software or services. In addition to a computer, you will need software that can record sound, a sound card, and a microphone. Most likely, you will want a set of external speakers, though you can use the computer's internal speakers. Cool Edit Pro (see URL below) is a good software choice for the Windows user, and Sound Edit (see URL below) works well for the Macintosh user. You also can find many other software packages by searching on the term, voice messaging, at CNET's download site (see URL below). Most voice messaging software packages require you to pay a fee. Some software manufacturers, however, provide free versions, but they do not have as many capabilities as the full versions.

Once you are set up and ready to go, prepare your room for recording by making sure it is quiet. Speak directly into the microphone as though you are talking to someone else in the room. When you finish with a recording, reduce the file size by saving your message as a mono sound file. Generally, it is best to keep the message length no longer than 30 seconds.

To send a sound file, open your e-mail program and attach the sound file, using the same process you use to attach any other file. Click the Send button and the voice message is on its way.

For more information on computer voice messages and the Web sites mentioned above, visit the Discovering Computers 2002 Apply It Web page (**scsite.com/dc2002/apply.htm**) and click Chapter 2 Apply It #3.

SallyJohnson@scsite.com

Figure 2-27 An e-mail address is a combination of a user name and a domain name.

Web Link

For more information on e-mail, visit the Discovering Computers 2002 Chapter 2 WEB LINK page (**scsite.com/dc2002/ch2/weblink.htm**) and click E-Mail.

Some Web sites provide e-mail services free of charge. To use these Web-based e-mail programs, you connect to the Web site and set up an e-mail account, which typically includes an e-mail address and a password. Instead of sending e-mail messages, several Web sites provide services that allow you to send other items such as online invitations and greetings. These Web sites have a server that stores your messages, invitations, and greetings.

When you send an e-mail message, a program on the mail server determines how to route the message through the Internet and then sends the message. When the message arrives at the recipient's mail server, the message transfers to a POP or POP3 server. **POP (Post Office Protocol)** is a communications technology for retrieving e-mail from a mail server. The POP server holds the message until the recipient retrieves it with his or her e-mail software

(Figure 2-28). The newest version of POP is **POP3**, or **Post Office Protocol 3**.

FTP

FTP (File Transfer Protocol) is an Internet standard that allows you to upload and download files with other computers on the Internet. For example, if you click a link on a Web page that begins to download a file to

Figure 2-28 HOW AN E-MAIL MESSAGE TRAVELS FROM THE SENDER TO THE RECEIVER

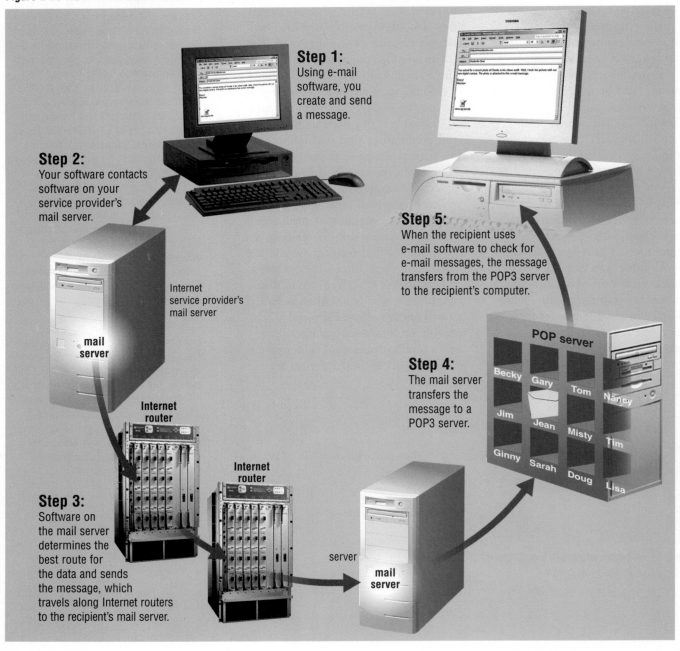

Step 1:
Using e-mail software, you create and send a message.

Step 2:
Your software contacts software on your service provider's mail server.

Internet service provider's mail server

mail server

Step 5:
When the recipient uses e-mail software to check for e-mail messages, the message transfers from the POP3 server to the recipient's computer.

Internet router

Internet router

Step 3:
Software on the mail server determines the best route for the data and sends the message, which travels along Internet routers to the recipient's mail server.

Step 4:
The mail server transfers the message to a POP3 server.

POP server

Becky | Gary | Tom | Nancy
Jim | Jean | Misty | Tim
Ginny | Sarah | Doug | Lisa

server

mail server

your hard disk, you probably are using FTP (Figure 2-29).

An **FTP server** is a computer that allows users to upload and download files using FTP. An **FTP site** is a collection of files including text, graphics, audio, video, and program files that reside on an FTP server. Some FTP sites limit file transfers to individuals who have authorized accounts (user names and passwords) on the FTP server. Many FTP sites allow **anonymous FTP**, whereby anyone can transfer some, if not all, available files. Many program files on anonymous FTP sites are freeware or public domain software. Others are shareware.

Large files on FTP sites often are compressed to reduce storage space and download time. Before you use a compressed file, you must expand it with a decompression program, such as WinZip. Such programs usually also are available for download from an FTP site (see Figure 2-29). Chapter 8 discusses compression and decompression programs.

In some cases, you may want to upload a file to an FTP site. For example, if you create a personal Web site, you will want to publish it on a Web server. Many Web servers require you to upload the files using FTP. To upload files from your computer to an FTP site, you use an FTP program. Some ISPs and OSPs include an FTP program as part of their Internet access service. You also can download FTP programs from the Web.

Newsgroups and Message Boards

A **newsgroup** is an online area in which users conduct written discussions about a particular subject. To participate in a discussion, a user sends a message to the newsgroup, and other users in the newsgroup read and reply to the message. The entire collection of Internet newsgroups is called **Usenet**, which contains thousands of newsgroups on a multitude of topics. Some major topic areas include news, recreation, business, science, and computers.

A computer that stores and distributes newsgroup messages is called a **news server**. Many universities, corporations, ISPs, OSPs, and other large organizations have a news server. Some newsgroups require you to enter your user name and password to participate in the discussion. Only authorized members can use this type of newsgroup. For example, a newsgroup for students taking a college course may require a user name and password to access the newsgroup. This ensures that only students in the course participate in the discussion.

To participate in a newsgroup, you use a program called a **newsreader**, which is included with most browsers. The newsreader enables you to access a newsgroup to read a previously entered message, called an **article**. You also can **post**, or add, an article of your own. The newsreader also keeps track of which articles you have and have not read.

Newsgroup members frequently post articles as a reply to another article — either to answer a question or to comment on material in the original article. These replies may cause the author of the original article, or others, to post additional articles related to the original article. A **thread** or **threaded discussion** consists of the original article and all subsequent related replies. A thread can be short-lived or continue for some time, depending on the nature of the topic and the interest of the participants.

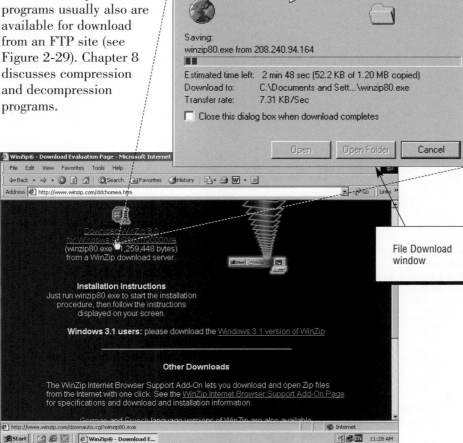

Figure 2-29 The File Download window indicates the estimated time for the download, as well as where the file is being saved on your hard disk.

Using a newsreader, you can search for newsgroups discussing a particular subject such as a type of musical instrument, brand of sports equipment, or employment opportunities. If you like the discussion in a particular newsgroup, you can **subscribe** to it, which means its location is saved in your newsreader for easy future access.

In some newsgroups, when you post an article, it is sent to a moderator instead of immediately displaying on the newsgroup. The **moderator** reviews the contents of the article and then posts it, if appropriate. Called a **moderated newsgroup**, the moderator decides if the article is relevant to the discussion. The

moderator may choose to edit or discard inappropriate articles. For this reason, the content of a moderated newsgroup is considered more valuable.

A popular Web-based type of discussion group that does not require a newsreader is a message board (Figure 2-30). Many Web sites provide a **message board**, also called a **discussion board**. Message boards typically are easier to use than newsgroups.

Mailing Lists

A **mailing list** is a group of e-mail names and addresses given a single name. When a message is sent to a mailing list, every person on the list receives a copy of the message in his or her mailbox. To add your e-mail name and address to a mailing list, you **subscribe** to it (Figure 2-31). To remove your name, you **unsubscribe** from the mailing list. Some mailing lists are called **LISTSERVs**, named

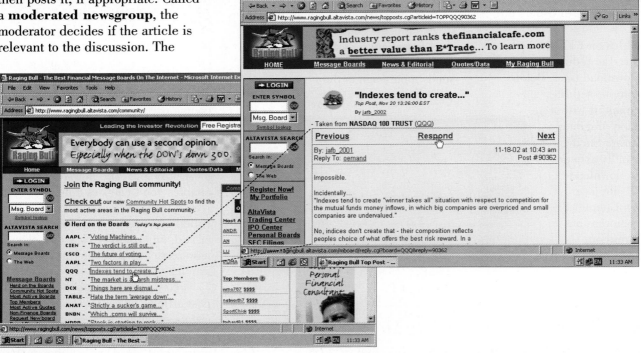

Figure 2-30 This message board allows users to discuss financial issues.

Figure 2-31 When you join a mailing list, you and all others on the mailing list receive an e-mail message from the Web site.

after a popular mailing list software product.

Thousands of mailing lists exist on a variety of topics in areas of entertainment, business, computers, society, culture, health, recreation, and education. To locate a mailing list dealing with a particular topic, you can search for the keywords, mailing lists or LISTSERVs, using your Web browser.

Chat Rooms

A **chat** is a real-time typed conversation that takes place on a computer. **Real-time** means that you and the people with whom you are

conversing are online at the same time. As you type on your keyboard, a line of characters and symbols display on the computer screen. Others connected to the same chat room server also can see what you have typed (Figure 2-32). In some chat rooms, you can click a button to see a profile of someone in the chat room.

A **chat room** is a location on an Internet server that permits users to chat with each other. Anyone in the chat room can participate in the conversation, which usually is specific to a particular topic. Some chat rooms support **voice chats** and **video chats**, where you hear or see others and they can hear or see you as you chat.

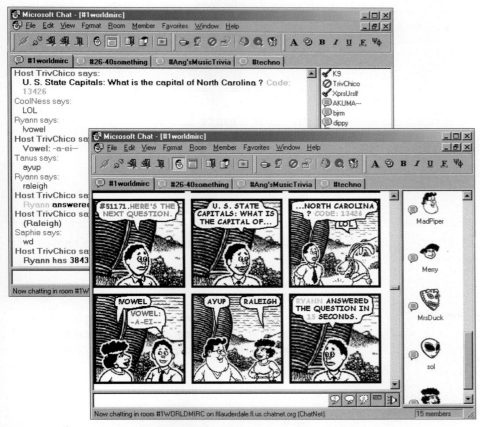

Figure 2-32 Most browsers include chat software. Some allow you to use a fictitious character.

Web Link

For more information on chat rooms, visit the Discovering Computers 2002 Chapter 2 WEB LINK page (**scsite.com/dc2002/ ch2/weblink.htm**) and click Chat Rooms.

To start a chat session, you connect to a chat server through a chat client. A **chat client** is a program on your computer. Today's browsers usually include a chat client. If yours does not, you can download a chat client from the Web. Some chat clients are text-based. Others support graphical chats also, where you can assume the appearance of a fictitious character.

Once you have installed a chat client, you can create or join a conversation on the chat server to which you are connected. The chat room should indicate the topic of discussion. The person who creates a chat room acts as the operator and has responsibility for monitoring the conversation and disconnecting anyone whom becomes disruptive. Operator status can be shared or transferred to someone else.

Instant Messaging

Instant messaging (IM) is a real-time Internet communications service that notifies you when one or more people are online and then allows you to exchange messages or files or join a private chat room with them (Figure 2-33). Many IM services also can alert you to information such as calendar appointments, stock quotes, weather, or sports scores. People use IM on all types of computers, including desktop computers, notebook computers, handheld computers, and Web-enabled devices.

To use IM, you install software from an instant messaging service, sometimes called an **instant messenger**, onto the computer or device with which you wish to use IM. No standards currently exist for IM. Thus, you and all those individuals on your notification list need to use the same or a compatible instant messenger to guarantee successful communications.

Web Link

For more information on instant messaging, visit the Discovering Computers 2002 Chapter 2 WEB LINK page (**scsite.com/dc2002/ch2/weblink.htm**) and click Instant Messaging.

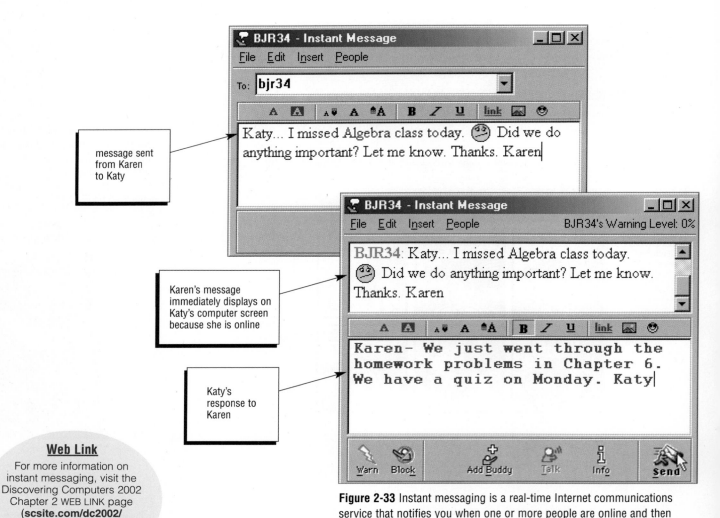

message sent from Karen to Katy

Karen's message immediately displays on Katy's computer screen because she is online

Katy's response to Karen

Figure 2-33 Instant messaging is a real-time Internet communications service that notifies you when one or more people are online and then allows you to exchange messages or files or join a private chat room with them.

NETIQUETTE

Netiquette, which is short for Internet etiquette, is the code of acceptable behaviors users should follow while on the Internet; that is, the conduct expected of individuals while online. Netiquette includes rules for all aspects of the Internet, including the World Wide Web, e-mail, FTP, newsgroups and message boards, chat rooms, and instant messaging. Figure 2-34 outlines the rules of netiquette.

CHAPTER SUMMARY

This chapter discussed the history and structure of the Internet. It discussed at length the World Wide Web, including topics such as browsing, navigating, e-commerce, and Web publishing. It also presented other various services available on the Internet, such as e-mail, FTP, newsgroups and message boards, chat rooms, and instant messaging. Finally, the chapter listed rules of netiquette.

Career Corner

Webmaster

What is a Webmaster? Although, typically, a Webmaster's responsibility is related to maintaining a company's Web site, no single definitive answer exists to this question. If your goal is to become a Webmaster, you will want to master most of these skills:

- Identify goals, objectives, and budget requirements
- Develop Web sites using HTML, Java, JavaScript, and other programming tools
- Determine the best software and hardware for presentation of information
- Work with others to coordinate the workflow of the Web site
- Develop a uniform standard for the company Web site
- Maintain the home page and certain other primary site documents as well as a Frequently Asked Questions (FAQ) document where necessary
- Actively participate in departmental advisory committees to provide input to help establish objectives and to establish standards and guidelines for content
- Promote the site

Many educational institutions offer Internet-related courses, certifications, and degrees. Salaries vary, depending on education and location. ZDNet (see URL below) reports that Webmasters earn an average annual salary of $40,000 to $53,000. Real Salary Survey (see URL below) shows a range of $40,000 to $93,000, with a median of $54,000.

To learn more about the field of Webmaster as a career and the Web sites mentioned above, visit the Discovering Computers 2002 Careers Web page (**scsite.com/dc2002/careers.htm**) and click Webmaster.

Netiquette

Golden Rule: *Treat others as you would like them to treat you.*

1. In e-mail, newsgroups, and chat rooms:
   - Keep messages brief using proper grammar and spelling.
   - Be careful when using sarcasm and humor, as it might be misinterpreted.
   - Be polite. Avoid offensive language.
   - Avoid sending or posting **flames**, which are abusive or insulting messages. Do not participate in **flame wars**, which are exchanges of flames.
   - Avoid sending spam, which is the Internet's version of junk mail. **Spam** is an unsolicited e-mail message or newsgroup posting sent to many recipients or newsgroups at once.
   - Do not use all capital letters, which is the equivalent of SHOUTING!
   - Use **emoticons** to express emotion. Popular emoticons include
:)	Smile
:(	Frown
:|	Indifference
:\	Undecided
:o	Surprised
   - Use abbreviations and acronyms for phrases such as
BTW	by the way
FYI	for your information
FWIW	for what it's worth
IMHO	in my humble opinion
TTFN	ta ta for now
TYVM	thank you very much
   - Clearly identify a **spoiler**, which is a message that reveals a solution to a game or ending to a movie or program.

2. Read the **FAQ** (frequently asked questions) document, if one exists. Many newsgroups and Web pages have a FAQ.

3. Use your user name for your personal use only.

4. Do not assume material is accurate or up to date. Be forgiving of other's mistakes.

5. Never read someone's private e-mail.

Figure 2-34 Some of the rules of netiquette.

e REVOLUTION

E·TRAVEL

GET PACKING!

Explore the World without Leaving Home

Balmy beaches. Majestic mountains. Exotic destinations. Just dreaming of experiencing these locales can lift your spirits. Researchers conclude that vacations are healthy for your mind and body because they help eliminate stress, offer opportunities to spend quality time with family and friends, and provide exercise. Whether you are ready to arrange your next travel adventure or just want to explore destination possibilities, the Internet provides ample resources to set your plans in motion.

Some good starting places are all-encompassing Web sites such as Travelocity, which is owned by Sabre, the electronic booking service travel agents use, Expedia (Figure 2-35), and TRIP.com (Figure 2-36). These general travel Web sites have tools to help you find the lowest prices and details on flights, cruises, car rentals, and hotels, and they include such features as airplane seating maps, local weather, popular restaurants, and photos. Each of the major airlines and cruise lines also has a Web site where you can check prices, purchase tickets and tour packages, and sign up for weekly e-mail alerts on specials and new services.

To discover exactly where your destination is on this planet, cartography Web sites, including MapQuest (Figure 2-37), maps.com, mapsindex.com, and

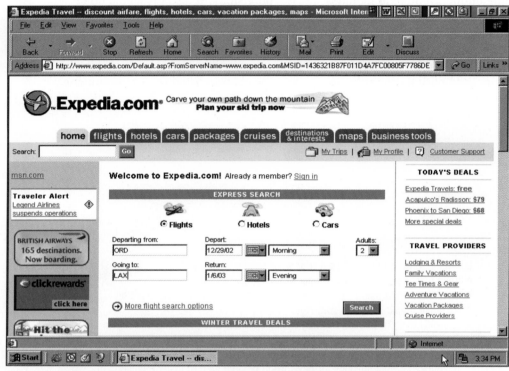

Figure 2-35 Book flights, cruises, and ski trips with all-encompassing travel resources.

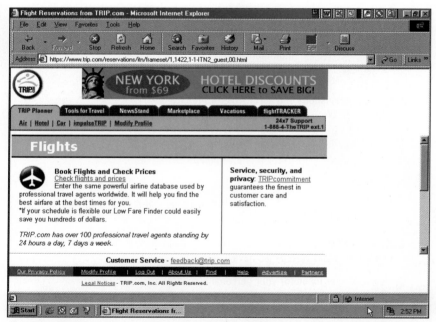

Figure 2-36 General travel Web sites allow users to check fares to your favorite destinations.

Rand McNally, let you pinpoint your destination. These Web pages generally are divided into geographical areas, such as North America and Europe. When you choose an area, you see a subject-based index that lists helpful tools such as route planners, subway maps, entertainment, and ski trails.

For more information on travel sites, visit the Discovering Computers 2002 E-Revolution Web page (scsite.com/dc2002/e-rev.htm) and click Travel.

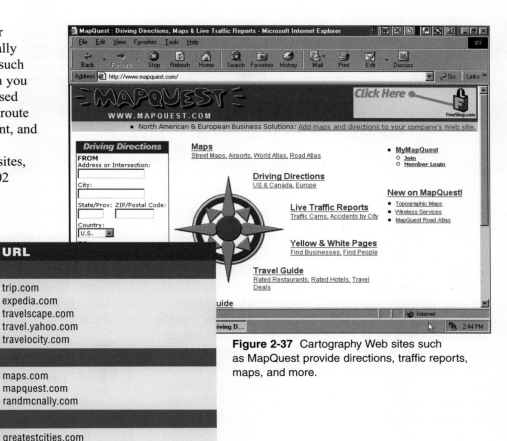

Figure 2-37 Cartography Web sites such as MapQuest provide directions, traffic reports, maps, and more.

TRAVEL WEB SITES	URL
General Travel	
TRIP.com	trip.com
Expedia Travel	expedia.com
Travelscape.com	travelscape.com
Yahoo! Travel	travel.yahoo.com
Travelocity.com	travelocity.com
Cartography	
Maps.com	maps.com
MapQuest	mapquest.com
Rand McNally	randmcnally.com
Travel and City Guides	
All the Greatest Cities of the World	greatestcities.com
U.S. National Parks Info	us-parks.com
10Best: City Guides	10best.com

For an updated list of travel Web sites, visit scsite.com/dc2002/e-rev.htm.

Figure 2-38 These travel resources Web sites offer travel information to exciting destinations throughout the world.

e REVOLUTION E-TRAVEL *applied:*

1. Visit one of the cartography Web sites listed in Figure 2-38 and print directions from your campus to one of these destinations: the White House in Washington, DC; Elvis's home in Memphis, Tennessee; Disney World in Orlando, Florida; or the Grand Old Opry in Nashville, Tennessee. How many miles is it to your destination? What is the estimated driving time? Then, visit one of the general travel Web sites listed in the table and plan a flight from the nearest major airport to one of the four destinations for the week after finals and a return trip one week later. What is the lowest coach fare for this round-trip flight? What airline, flight numbers, and departure and arrival times did you select? Finally, explore car rental rates for a subcompact car for this one-week vacation. What rental agency and rate did you choose?

2. Visit one of the travel and city guide Web sites listed in Figure 2-38, and choose a destination for a getaway this coming weekend. Write a one-page paper giving details about this location, such as popular hotels and lodging, expected weather, population, local colleges and universities, parks and recreation, ancient and modern history, and tours. Print a map of this place. Why did you select this destination? How would you travel there and back? What is the breakdown of expected costs for this weekend, including travel expenditures, meals, lodging, and tickets to events and activities? What URLs did you use to complete this exercise?

2.40

DISCOVERING
COMPUTERS 2002

Chapter 1 2 3 4 5 6 7 8 9 10 11 12 13 14 15 16 Index **HOME**

In Summary

SHELLY
CASHMAN
SERIES.

Student Exercises   Web Links   In Summary   Key Terms   Learn It Online   Checkpoint   In The Lab   Web Work

Special Features   ■ TIMELINE 2002 ■ WWW & E-SKILLS ■ MULTIMEDIA ■ BUYER'S GUIDE 2002 ■ WIRELESS TECHNOLOGY ■ TRENDS 2002 ■ INTERACTIVE LABS ■ TECH NEWS

Web Instructions: To display this page from the Web, start your browser and enter the URL scsite.com/dc2002/ch2/summary.htm. Click the links for current and additional information. To listen to an audio version of this In Summary, click the Audio button. To play the audio, RealPlayer must be installed on your computer (download by clicking here).

1 How Does the Internet Work?

The Internet, also called the **Net**, is a worldwide collection of networks that links millions of businesses, government agencies, educational institutions, and individuals. The Internet consists of many local, regional, national, and international networks. Although each of these networks on the Internet is owned by a public or private organization, no single organization owns or controls the Internet. Each organization on the Internet is responsible only for maintaining its own network. The Internet provides a variety of services, including access to the World Wide Web, electronic mail (e-mail), FTP, newsgroups and message boards, mailing lists, chat rooms, and instant messaging.

2 What Are the Ways to Access the Internet?

An **Internet service provider (ISP)** provides temporary Internet connections to individuals and companies. An **online service provider (OSP)** also supplies Internet access, in addition to a variety of special services. Those users with wireless modems or Web-enabled devices communicate through an antenna with a **wireless service provider (WSP)**. At a business or school, users connect to the Internet through a local area network (LAN) that is connected to an ISP. At home, individuals often use their computers and a modem to dial into an ISP or OSP over a regular telephone line. Some home and small businesses also use high-speed technologies such as a **DSL (digital subscriber line)** and cable modem.

Data is transferred over the Internet using a **server**, which is a computer that manages network resources and provides centralized storage areas, and a **client**, which is a computer that can access the contents of the storage areas. Each computer destination has a unique numeric address called an **IP address**, the text version of which is called a **domain name**.

3 How Do You Identify a URL?

The **Uniform Resource Local (URL)** is the Web page address. A URL consists of a protocol, a domain name, and sometimes the path to a specific Web page. Most Web pages begin with http://. The **http** stands for **hypertext transfer protocol**. The **domain name** is the text version of an IP address.

4 How Do You Search for Information on the Web?

To find Web sites, you use a **search engine** software program. To locate a Web page, you enter a keyword or **search text** in the search engine's text box. Another search option is a **directory**, which on the Web, is an organized set of topics and subtopics.

5 What Are the Types of Web Pages?

Six basic types of Web pages exist. An **advocacy Web page** contains content that describes a cause, opinion, or idea and attempts to convince the reader of the validity of the idea or opinion. A **business/marketing Web page** contains content that promotes or sells products or services. An **informational Web page** contains factual information. A **news Web page** contains stories and articles relating to current events, life, money, sports, and the weather. A portal Web page provides a variety of Internet services, many of which are free. These services may include search engines; local, national, and worldwide news; sports and weather; free personal Web pages; reference tools; shopping malls and auctions; e-mail; instant messaging, newsgroups, calendars, and chat rooms. A **wireless portal** is specifically designed for Web-enabled devices. Private individuals may maintain a **personal Web page** for a variety of general uses such as job hunting.

DISCOVERING
COMPUTERS 2002

Chapter 1 **2** 3 4 5 6 7 8 9 10 11 12 13 14 15 16 Index **HOME**   **2.41**

In Summary

SHELLY
CASHMAN
SERIES.

Student Exercises   Web Links   In Summary   Key Terms   Learn It Online   Checkpoint   In The Lab   Web Work

Special Features   ■ TIMELINE 2002   ■ WWW & E-SKILLS   ■ MULTIMEDIA   ■ BUYER'S GUIDE 2002   ■ WIRELESS TECHNOLOGY   ■ TRENDS 2002   ■ INTERACTIVE LABS   ■ TECH NEWS

6 How Are Graphics, Animation, Audio, Video, and Virtual Reality Used on the World Wide Web?

Most Web pages have built-in **links** to related Web pages. A Web page can contain **multimedia** features that include graphics, animation, audio, video, and virtual reality. A **graphic**, which is a digital representation of information, was the first medium used to enhance the text-based Internet. **Animation** is the appearance of motion that is created by displaying a series of still images in rapid sequence. Simple Web **audio** and Web **video** applications consist of individual sound and video files that must be downloaded completely before they can be played on your computer. <u>Streaming audio</u> and **streaming video** allow you to listen and/or view the sound and/or images as they download to your computer. **Virtual reality (VR)** is the simulation of a real or imagined environment that appears as a three-dimensional (3-D) space.

7 What is Webcasting?

Webcasting also is known as <u>push technology</u>. A server automatically downloads content to your computer at regular intervals or whenever updates are made to the Web site. Once the content is pushed to your computer, you can view it online or **offline**.

8 How Is Electronic Commerce Used?

Electronic commerce (e-commerce) is the performance of business activities online. Three types of e-commerce exist. **Business to consumer (B-to-C** or **B2C)** e-commerce consists of the sale of goods to the general public. <u>Consumer to consumer (C-to-C or C2C)</u> e-commerce occurs when one consumer sells directly to another, such as in an online auction. **Business to business (B-to-B** or **B2B)** e-commerce, which is the most prevalent type of e-commerce, takes place between businesses, with businesses typically providing services to other businesses.

9 What Tools Are Required for Web Publishing?

Web publishing is the development and maintenance of Web pages. Web pages are created and formatted using a set of codes called **HTML (hypertext markup language)**. These codes, called <u>tags</u>, stipulate how elements display and where links lead. Developers use tags to create <u>HTML documents</u> with a text editor or word processing software. Many word processing packages generate HTML tags and include authoring features that help users create basic Web pages. **Web page authoring software** can be used to create more sophisticated Web pages. Other Web publishing tools include digital cameras, scanners, and/or CD-ROM or DVD-ROM image collections to incorporate pictures; sound cards and microphones to incorporate sound; and PC cameras and video cameras to incorporate videos.

10 How Do E-Mail, FTP, Newsgroups and Message Boards, Mailing Lists, Chat Rooms, and Instant Messaging Work?

A variety of services are used widely on the Internet. **E-mail (electronic mail)**, which is the transmission of messages and files via a computer network, is a primary method of communication. <u>FTP (file transfer protocol)</u> is an Internet standard that allows you to upload and download files with other computers. A **newsgroup** is an online area in which users conduct written discussions about a particular subject. A **message board**, also called a **discussion board**, is a Web-based discussion group that is easier to use than newsgroups. A **mailing list** is a group of e-mail names and addresses given a single name. A **chat** is **real-time** typed conversation that takes place on a computer through a **chat room**, or communications medium. **Instant messaging (IM)** is a service that notifies you when one or more people are online and then allows you to exchange messages or join a private chat room.

11 What Are the Rules of Netiquette?

Netiquette, which is short for Internet etiquette, is the code of acceptable behaviors when using the Internet. Rules for e-mail, newsgroups, and chat rooms include keeping messages short and polite; avoiding sarcasm, **flames** (abusive messages), and <u>spam</u> (unsolicited junk mail); and reading the **FAQs** (frequently asked questions). When using the Internet, do not assume all material is accurate or up to date, and never read private e-mail.

2.42

DISCOVERING
COMPUTERS 2002

Chapter 1 2 3 4 5 6 7 8 9 10 11 12 13 14 15 16 Index HOME

Key Terms

SHELLY
CASHMAN
SERIES.

Student Exercises   Web Links   In Summary   Key Terms   Learn It Online   Checkpoint   In The Lab   Web Work

Special Features   ■ TIMELINE 2002 ■ WWW & E-SKILLS ■ MULTIMEDIA ■ BUYER'S GUIDE 2002 ■ WIRELESS TECHNOLOGY ■ TRENDS 2002 ■ INTERACTIVE LABS ■ TECH NEWS

Web Instructions: To display this page from the Web, start your browser and enter the URL scsite.com/dc2002/ch2/terms.htm. Scroll through the list of terms. Click a term to display its definition and a picture. Click the To WEB button for current and additional information about the term from the Web. To see animations, Shockwave and Flash Player must be installed on your computer (download by clicking here).

address book (2.31)
Advanced Research Projects Agency (ARPA) (2.3)
advocacy Web page (2.16)
animated GIF (2.19)
animation (2.19)
anonymous FTP (2.33)
ARPANET (2.4)
article (2.33)
audio (2.20)
backbone (2.7)
bot (2.14)
browser (2.9)
business/marketing Web page (2.17)
business to business (B-to-B or B2B) (2.25)
business to consumer (B-to-C or B2C) (2.25)
cable modem (2.6)
cam (2.22)
chat (2.35)
chat client (2.36)
chat room (2.35)
client (2.6)
consumer to consumer (C-to-C or C2C) (2.25)
crawler (2.14)
dial-up access (2.6)
directory (2.14)
discussion board (2.34)
DNS server (2.8)
domain name (2.8)
domain name system (DNS) (2.8)
dot com (2.8)
downloading (2.11)
DSL (digital subscriber line) (2.6)
e-commerce (2.24)
electronic commerce (2.24)
electronic storefront (2.25)
e-mail address (2.31)
e-mail (electronic mail) (2.30)
e-mail program (2.30)
emotions (2.37)
FAQ (2.37)
flames (2.37)
flame wars (2.37)
FTP (file transfer protocol) (2.32)
FTP server (2.33)
FTP site (2.33)
GIF (2.19)
graphic (2.18)
graphical image (2.18)
Graphics Interchange Format (2.19)
hit (2.14)
home page (2.10)
host (2.4)
host computers (2.6)
HTML (hypertext markup language) (2.29)
http (2.13)
hyperlink (2.11)
hypertext transfer protocol (2.13)
informational Web page (2.17)
instant messaging (IM) (2.36)
instant messenger (2.36)
Internet (2.2)

Internet Corporation for Assigned Names and Numbers (ICANN) (2.8)
Internet service provider (ISP) (2.5)
Internet2 (I2) (2.4)
IP address (2.8)
Joint Photographic Experts Group (2.19)
JPEG (2.19)
keywords (2.14)
link (2.11)
LISTSERVs (2.34)
mail server (2.31)
mailbox (2.31)
mailing list (2.34)
marquee (2.19)

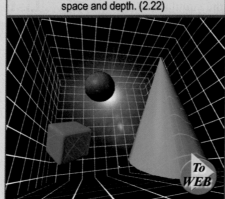
VR WORLD
3-D site that contains infinite space and depth. (2.22)
To WEB

m-commerce (mobile commerce) (2.24)
message board (2.34)
microbrowser (2.11)
minibrowser (2.11)
moderated newsgroup (2.34)
moderator (2.34)
Moving Pictures Experts Group (MPEG) (2.22)
MP3 (2.20)
MP3 players (2.20)
multimedia (2.18)
national ISP (2.5)
Net (2.2)
netiquette (2.37)
network (2.2)
news server (2.33)
news Web page (2.17)
newsgroup (2.33)
newsreader (2.33)
node (2.4)
NSFnet (2.4)
offline (2.24)
online auction (2.25)
online service provider (OSP) (2.5)
personal Web page (2.17)
player (2.20)

plug-in (2.28)
point of presence (POP) (2.5)
POP (Post Office Protocol) (2.32)
POP3 (2.32)
portal (2.17)
portal Web page (2.17)
post (2.33)
Post Office Protocol 3 (2.32)
pull technology (2.23)
push technology (2.23)
real-time (2.35)
regional ISP (2.5)
search engine (2.14)
search text (2.14)
server (2.6)
shopping cart (2.25)
spam (2.37)
spider (2.14)
spoiler (2.37)
streaming (2.20)
streaming audio (2.21)
streaming sound (2.21)
streaming video (2.22)
submission service (2.29)
subscribe (2.34)
surfing the Web (2.12)
tags (2.29)
thread (2.33)
threaded discussion (2.33)
thumbnail (2.19)
top-level domain (TLD) (2.8)
traffic (2.4)
Uniform Resource Locator (URL) (2.12)
unsubscribe (2.34)
upload (2.29)
Usenet (2.33)
user name (2.31)
user-ID (2.31)
video (2.22)
video chats (2.35)
virtual reality (VR) (2.22)
voice chats (2.35)
VR world (2.22)
Web (2.9)
Web address (2.13)
Web browser (2.9)
Web cam (2.22)
Web community (2.17)
Web hosting services (2.29)
Web page (2.9)
Web page authoring (2.28)
Web page authoring software (2.28)
Web publishing (2.26)
Web server (2.13)
Web site (2.9)
Webcasting (2.23)
Webmaster (2.29)
wireless portal (2.17)
wireless service provider (WSP) (2.6)
World Wide Web (WWW) (2.9)
World Wide Web Consortium (W3C) (2.4)

DISCOVERING
COMPUTERS *2002*

Learn It Online

SHELLY
CASHMAN
SERIES.

Student Exercises   Web Links   In Summary   Key Terms   Learn It Online   Checkpoint   In The Lab   Web Work

Special Features   ■ TIMELINE 2002   ■ WWW & E-SKILLS   ■ MULTIMEDIA   ■ BUYER'S GUIDE 2002   ■ WIRELESS TECHNOLOGY   ■ TRENDS 2002   ■ INTERACTIVE LABS   ■ TECH NEWS

Web Instructions: To display this page from the Web, start your browser, and then enter the URL scsite.com/dc2002/ch2/learn.htm.

1. Web Guide

Click Web Guide to display the Guide to World Wide Web Sites and Searching Techniques Web page. Click Reference and then click AskJeeves. Ask Jeeves about the history of the Internet. Click an answer of your choice. Use your word processing program to prepare a brief report on what you discovered and submit your assignment to your instructor.

2. Scavenger Hunt

Click Scavenger Hunt. Print a copy of the Scavenger Hunt page; use this page to write down your answers as you search the Web. Submit your completed page to your instructor.

3. Who Wants to Be a Computer Genius?

Click Computer Genius to find out if you are a computer genius. Directions on how to play the game will display. When you are ready to play, click the PLAY button. Submit your score to your instructor.

4. Wheel of Terms

Click Wheel of Terms to reinforce important terms you learned in this chapter by playing the Shelly Cashman Series version of this popular game. Directions on how to play the game will display. When you are ready to play, click the PLAY button. Submit your score to your instructor.

5. Career Corner

Click Career Corner to display the USA TODAY page. Scroll down, click Career Center, and click a link of interest. Write a brief report on what you discovered. Submit the report to your instructor.

6. Search Sleuth

Click Search Sleuth to learn search techniques that will help make you a research expert. Submit the completed assignment to your instructor.

7. Crossword Puzzle Challenge

Click Crossword Puzzle Challenge. Complete the puzzle to reinforce skills you learned in this chapter. Directions on how to play the game will display. When you are ready to play, click the PLAY button. Submit the completed puzzle to your instructor.

8. Practice Test

Click Practice Test. Answer each question. When completed, enter your name and click the Grade Test button to submit the quiz for grading. Make a note of any missed questions. If required, print a copy to submit to your instructor.

DISCOVERING
COMPUTERS *2002*

Checkpoint

SHELLY
CASHMAN
SERIES.

Student Exercises   Web Links   In Summary   Key Terms   Learn It Online   **Checkpoint**   In The Lab   Web Work

Special Features   ■ TIMELINE 2002 ■ WWW & E-SKILLS ■ MULTIMEDIA ■ BUYER'S GUIDE 2002 ■ WIRELESS TECHNOLOGY ■ TRENDS 2002 ■ INTERACTIVE LABS ■ TECH NEWS

Web Instructions: To display this page from the Web, start your browser and enter the URL <u>scsite.com/dc2002/ch2/check.htm</u>. Click the links for current and additional information. To experience the animation and interactivity, Shockwave and Flash Player must be installed on your computer (download by clicking <u>here</u>.).

LABEL THE FIGURE | **Instructions:** Identify each part of the URL and e-mail address.

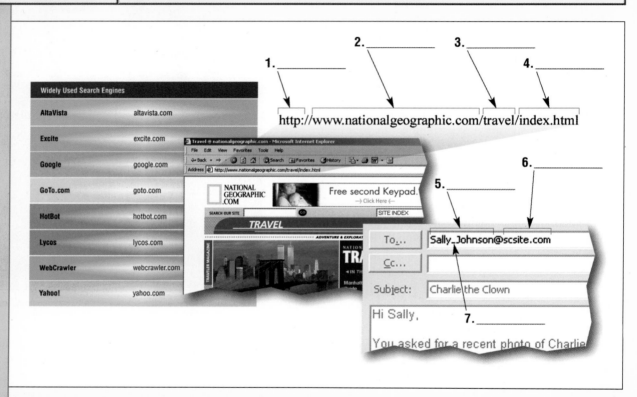

MATCHING | **Instructions:** Match each term from the column on the left with the best description from the column on the right.

_____ 1. FTP
_____ 2. chat
_____ 3. mailing list
_____ 4. newsgroup
_____ 5. e-mail

a. A <u>real-time typed conversation</u> that takes place on a computer.
b. A list of <u>names and addresses</u>.
c. An <u>Internet standard</u> that allows you to upload and download files with other computers.
d. The transmission of messages and files via a <u>computer network</u>.
e. A group of <u>e-mail names</u> and addresses given a single name.
f. A <u>real-time</u> Internet communications service that notifies you when one or more people are online.
g. An <u>online area</u> in which users conduct written discussions about a particular subject.

DISCOVERING
COMPUTERS *2002*

Checkpoint

SHELLY
CASHMAN
SERIES.

Student Exercises   Web Links   In Summary   Key Terms   Learn It Online   Checkpoint   In The Lab   Web Work

Special Features ■ TIMELINE 2002 ■ WWW & E-SKILLS ■ MULTIMEDIA ■ BUYER'S GUIDE 2002 ■ WIRELESS TECHNOLOGY ■ TRENDS 2002 ■ INTERACTIVE LABS ■ TECH NEWS

MULTIPLE CHOICE | Instructions: Select the letter of the correct answer for each of the following questions.

1. On a Web page, a(n) _____ is a built-in connection to another related Web page or part of a <u>Web page</u>.
   a. graphic
   b. animation
   c. link
   d. keyword
2. A(n) _____ is a <u>computer</u> that delivers Web pages you request.
   a. Web server
   b. client
   c. FTP server
   d. mail server
3. To participate in a <u>newsgroup</u>, you use a program called a _____ .
   a. discussion
   b. thread
   c. newsreader
   d. message board

4. A Web page that offers a variety of <u>Internet services</u> from a single, convenient location is called a(n) _____ .
   a. Web community
   b. informational Web page
   c. news Web page
   d. portal
5. _____ occurs when a <u>server</u> automatically downloads content to your computer at regular intervals.
   a. Pull technology
   b. Push technology
   c. Online technology
   d. M-commerce

SHORT ANSWER | Instructions: Write a brief answer to each of the following questions.

1. What is a network? _____ What is a <u>node</u>? _____ What is an ISP? _____
2. How are a Web page, Web site, and home page different? _____ What is a <u>URL</u>? _____
3. What is a search engine? _____ What is a <u>plug-in</u>? _____ Why would you need a plug-in? _____
4. What does it mean to subscribe to a <u>newsgroup</u>? _____ What is the difference between a newsgroup and Usenet? _____ What is a threaded discussion? _____
5. What is <u>FTP</u>? _____ What is an FTP site? _____ Why would someone use an FTP server? _____

WORKING TOGETHER | Instructions: Working with a group of your classmates, complete the following team exercise.

Your textbook lists six different types of Web pages. Use the Internet to find at least two examples of each type of Web page. Create a report listing the type of Web page, the URL or Web site address, and an explanation of why the Web page fits the particular category. Then, describe what <u>multimedia</u> elements your team found on each Web page. Share your report and/or a PowerPoint presentation with the class.

Student Exercises   Web Links   In Summary   Key Terms   Learn It Online   Checkpoint   **In The Lab**   Web Work

Special Features   ■ TIMELINE 2002 ■ WWW & E-SKILLS ■ MULTIMEDIA ■ BUYER'S GUIDE 2002 ■ WIRELESS TECHNOLOGY ■ TRENDS 2002 ■ INTERACTIVE LABS ■ TECH NEWS

Web Instructions: To display this page from the Web, start your browser and enter the URL scsite.com/dc2002/ch2/lab.htm. Click the links or current and additional information.

Online Services

This exercise uses Windows 98 procedures. What online services are available on your computer? Right-click the Online Services icon on the desktop and then click Open on the shortcut menu. What online services have shortcut icons in the Online Services window? Right-click each icon and then click Properties on each shortcut menu. Click the General tab. When was each icon created? Close the dialog box and then click the Close button to close the Online Services window.

Understanding Internet Properties

Right-click an icon for a Web browser that displays on your desktop. Click Properties on the shortcut menu. When the Internet Properties dialog box or Netscape Properties dialog box displays, click the General tab. Click the Question Mark button on the title bar and then click one of the buttons. Read the information in the pop-up window and then click the pop-up window to close it. Repeat the process

for other areas of the dialog box. Click the Cancel button in the Internet Properties dialog box.

Determining Dial-Up Networking Connections

This exercise uses Windows 98 procedures. Click the Start button on the taskbar. Point to Programs on the Start menu, point to Accessories on the Program submenu, point to Communications on the Accessories submenu, and then click Dial-Up Networking on the Accessories submenu. When the Dial-Up Networking window opens, right-click an icon displayed in the window and then click Connect on the shortcut menu. Write down the User name and the Phone number. Close the Connect To dialog box and the Dial-Up Networking window.

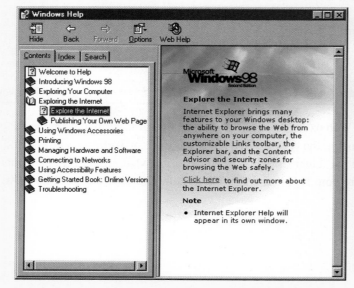

Using Help to Understand the Internet

This exercise uses Windows 98 procedures. Click the Start button on the taskbar and then click Help on the Start menu. Click the Contents tab. Click the Exploring the Internet book and then click the Explore the Internet topic. Click the Click here link to find out more about Internet Explorer. Answer the following questions:

• How can you update your favorite Web sites and view them at your leisure?

• How can you move around the Web faster and easier with the Explorer bar?

• How can you browse the Web safely?

• How can you view Web pages in other languages?

Close the Microsoft Internet Explorer Help window and the Windows Help window.

Streaming Audio and Streaming Video

Review the chapter section on streaming audio and streaming video. Use PowerPoint to create a presentation describing the basics of streaming media. Search the Web for additional information and include what you discover as part of your presentation. Share your presentation with your class.

DISCOVERING
COMPUTERS *2002*

Web Work

SHELLY
CASHMAN
SERIES.

:udent Exercises   Web Links   In Summary   Key Terms   Learn It Online   Checkpoint   In The Lab   **Web Work**

ecial Features   ■ TIMELINE 2002 ■ WWW & E-SKILLS ■ MULTIMEDIA ■ BUYER'S GUIDE 2002 ■ WIRELESS TECHNOLOGY ■ TRENDS 2002 ■ INTERACTIVE LABS ■ TECH NEWS

Web Instructions: To display this page from the Web, start your browser and enter the URL scsite.com/dc2002/ch2/web.htm. To view At The Movies in exercise 1, RealPlayer must be installed on your computer (download by clicking here). To use the Shelly Cashman Series Connecting to the Internet Lab and The World Wide Web Lab from the Web, Shockwave and Flash Player must be installed on your computer (download by clicking here).

Chat Room Lawsuit

To view the Chat room Lawsuit movie, click the button to the left or click the Play button to the right. Watch the movie, and then complete the exercise by answering the questions below. Many companies are fed up with being trashed online and are fighting back with lawsuits. Most chat room posters offer legitimate criticisms and warnings, but instances of outright lies and intentional sabotage are a reality. In some cases, unsubstantiated comments have caused a company's stock to nose-dive and even caused bankruptcy. Tracking down the anonymous posters (by filing subpoenas against Internet providers, such as Yahoo! or America Online) raises free speech issues and threatens the free flow of information on the Web. Who deserves greater protection: the companies and their products, or individuals and the free flow of information on the Web? What agency should be the judge?

Shelly Cashman Series Connecting to the Internet Lab

Follow the instructions in Web Work 2 on page 1.47 to start and use the Shelly Cashman Series Connecting to the Internet Lab. If you are running from the Web, enter the URL www.scsite.com/sclabs/menu.htm or display the Web Work page (see instructions at the top of this page) and then click the button to the left.

Shelly Cashman Series The World Wide Web Lab

Follow the instructions in Web Work 2 on page 1.47 to start and use the Shelly Cashman Series the World Wide Web lab. If you are running from the Web, enter the URL, www.scsite.com/sclabs/menu.htm or display the Web Work page (see instructions at the top of this page) and then click the button to the left.

Internet Newsgroups

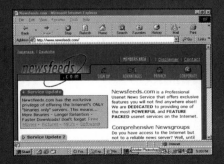

One of the more popular topics for Internet newsgroups is the Internet. Click the button to the left for a list of newsgroups. Find one or more newsgroups that discuss something about the Internet. Read the newsgroup postings and briefly summarize the topic under discussion. If you like, post a reply to a message.

In the News

In her book, *Caught in the Net*, Kimberly S. Young argues that the Internet can be addictive. Young's methodology and conclusions have been questioned by several critics, but Young remains resolute. She points out that at one time, no one admitted the existence of alcoholism. Click the button to the left and read a news article about the impact of Internet use on human behavior. What affect did the Internet have? Why? In your

2.48

"When I was a child in Philadelphia, my father told me that I didn't need to memorize the contents of the Encyclopedia Britannica; I just needed to know how to find what is in it."

— Richard Saul Wurman, "Information Anxiety," 1989

GUIDE TO WORLD WIDE WEB SITES AND SEARCHING TECHNIQUES

The World Wide Web is an exciting and highly dynamic medium that has revolutionized the way people access information. You can display information on virtually any topic you can imagine, if you know the URL. If you do not know the URL, you must use a search tool because the Web has no bibliographic control. Statistics from the NEC Research Institute indicate that every second, 25 new Web pages are added to the more than 5.5 billion Web pages already on the Internet. Given this, finding the information you want can be a massive chore if you don't know the URL or how to use Web search tools.

To help you locate information, this special feature provides three resources: a topical list of some of the more popular Web sites, an introduction to searching techniques, and a list of portals with search capabilities.

WEB INSTRUCTIONS: *To gain World Wide Web access to additional and up-to-date information regarding this special feature, start your browser and enter the URL shown at the top of this page.*

Categories

Animation
Art
Business and Finance
Careers and Employment
Computers and Computing
Digital Music
Education
Entertainment
Environment

Fitness
Government and Politics
Health and Medicine
History
Humor
Internet
Internet Security
Law
Museums

News Sources
Reference
Robotics
Science
Shopping
Society
Sports
Travel
Unclassified
Weather
Zines

CATEGORY/SITE NAME	LOCATION	COMMENT
Animation		
Animation Express	animationexpress.com	Cool animations
RGB gallery	hotwired.lycos.com/rgb	Art animations
Shockwave	shockwave.com	Cool Shockwave animations
Art		
Fine Art Forum	msstate.edu/fineart_online/home.html	Art and technology net news
Leonardo da Vinci	metalab.unc.edu/wm/paint/auth/vinci	Works of the famous Italian artist and thinker
The Andy Warhol Museum	warhol.org	Famous American pop artist
WebMuseum	www.louvre.fr/louvrea.htm	Web version of Louvre Museum, Paris
World Wide Arts Resources	wwar.com	Links to many art sites
Business and Finance		
All Business Network	all-biz.com	Links to Web business information
FinanCenter.com	financenter.com	Personal finance information
MSN MoneyCentral	moneycentral.msn.com	Microsoft's Financial portal
Morningstar, Inc.	morningstar.com	Mutual fund site
PC Quote	www.pcquote.com	Free delayed stock quotes
Quicken	quicken.com	Personal financial advice
Raging Bull	ragingbull.com	Real-time stock quotes
SiliconInvestor	siliconinvestor.com	Stock chat for technology investors
SmartMoney	smartmoney.com	Live snapshot of the stock market
Stockgroup Research	smallcapcenter.com	Investment information
The Wall Street Journal	interactive.wsj.com	Financial news page
Yahoo! Finance	quote.yahoo.com	Free delayed stock quotes
Careers and Employment		
CareerMagazine	careermag.com	Career articles and information
CareerBuilder	careerpath.com	Job listings from U.S. newspapers
Headhunter	headhunter.net	Jobs from around the world
Job Options	joboptions.com	Searchable job database
Monster.com	monster.com	Job finder

For an updated list: scsite.com/dc2002/ch2/websites.htm

CATEGORY/SITE NAME	LOCATION	COMMENT
Computers and Computing		
Computer companies	Insert name or initials of most computer companies before .com to find their Web sites. Examples: ibm.com, microsoft.com, dell.com	
Expertcity	expertcity.com	Live experts offer technical support
Internet.com	internet.com	E-Business and Technology Network
MIT Media Lab	www.media.mit.edu	Information on computer trends
The Computer Museum	computerhistory.org	Exhibits and history of computing
The PC Guide	pcguide.com	PC Reference Information
Virtual Computer Library	www.utexas.edu/computer/vcl	Information on computers and computing
Virtual Museum of Computing	www.museums.reading.ac.uk/vmoc	History of computing and online computer-base exhibits
ZDNet	zdnet.com	Downloads and product reviews
Digital Music		
Live Concerts	liveconcerts.com	RealMedia streamed concerts
MP3.com	mp3.com	Music files
Sonique	sonique.com	MP3 player made by aliens!!
This American Life	thislife.org	Public Radio program
Education		
CollegeNET	collegenet.com	Searchable database of more than 2,000 colleges and universities
EdLinks	webpages.marshall.edu/~jmullens/edlinks.html	Links to many educational sites
The Open University	www.open.ac.uk	Independent study courses from the U.K.
UMUC Distance Education	umuc.edu/distance	University of Maryland distance education
WiredScholar	www.wiredscholar.com	Information on financing an education
Entertainment		
Classics World	bmgclassics.com	Classical music information
Internet Movie Database	imdb.com	Movies
Internet Underground Music Archive	www.iuma.com	Underground music database
Mr. Showbiz	mrshowbiz.com	Information on latest films
Music Boulevard	musicblvd.com	Search for and buy all types of music
Playbill Online	playbill.com	Theater news
Rock & Roll Hall of Fame	rockhall.com	Cleveland museum site

For an updated list: scsite.com/dc2002/ch2/websites.htm

CATEGORY/SITE NAME	LOCATION	COMMENT
Environment		
EnviroLink Network	envirolink.org	Environmental information
Greenpeace	greenpeace.org	Environmental activism
U.S. Environmental Protection Agency (EPA)	epa.gov	U.S. government environmental news
Fitness		
24 Hour Fitness	24hourfitness.com	A health and fitness community
GlobalFitness.com	globalfitness.com	Health and fitness
Government and Politics		
CIA	www.odci.gov	Political and economic information on countries
Democratic National Committee	democrats.org	Democratic party news
FedWorld	fedworld.gov	Links to U.S. government sites
PoliSci.com	polisci.com	Politics on the Web
Republican National Committee	rnc.org	GOP party news
The Library of Congress	www.loc.gov	Variety of U.S. government information
The White House	www.whitehouse.gov	Take a tour and learn about the occupants
U.S. Census Bureau	www.census.gov	Population and other statistics
United Nations	www.un.org	Latest UN projects and information
Health and Medicine		
Centers for Disease Control and Prevention (CDC)	www.cdc.gov	How to prevent and control disease
Cornucopia of Disability Information (CODI)	codi.buffalo.edu	Resource for disability products and services
The Interactive Patient	medicus.marshall.edu/medicus.htm	Simulates visit to doctor
Women's Medical Health Page	cbull.com/health.htm	Articles and links to other sites
History		
American Memory	rs6.loc.gov/amhome.html	American history
Don Mabry's Historical Text Archive	geocities.com/Athens/Forum/9061/USA/usa.html	U.S. documents, photos, and databases
Virtual Library History	www.ukans.edu/history/VL	Organized links to history sites
World History Archives	www.hartford-hwp.com/archives	Links to history sites

For an updated list: scsite.com/dc2002/ch2/websites.htm

CATEGORY/SITE NAME	LOCATION	COMMENT
Humor		
Ucomics.com	calvinandhobbes.com	Comic strip gallery
Comedy Central	comcentral.com	Comedy TV network online
Late Show with David Letterman	marketing.cbs.com/lateshow	Letterman's nightly show including archived Top 10 lists
The Dilbert Zone	unitedmedia.com/comics/dilbert	Humorous insights about the workplace
Internet		
Beginners' Central	northernwebs.com/bc	Beginners' guide to the Internet
Glossary of Internet	matisse.net/files/glossary.html	Matisse Enzer's definitions of Internet
WWW Frequently Asked Questions	www.boutell.com/faq/oldfaq/index.html	Common Web questions and answers
Internet Security		
F-secure Hoax warnings	datafellows.com/news/hoax.htm	Industry standard information source for new virus hoaxes and false alerts
Secure Solutions Experts (SSE)	www.sse.ie/securitynews.html	Over 100 of the best information security news sites, many of which are updated daily
Law		
APB News.com	apbnews.com	Crime, justice, and safety news
Copyright Website	benedict.com	Provides copyright information
FindLaw	findlaw.com	Law resource portal
KuesterLaw	kuesterlaw.com	Technology law resource
Privacy Rights Clearinghouse	privacyrights.org	Information on privacy issues
Museums		
Smithsonian Institution	www.si.edu	Information and links to Smithsonian museums
The National Gallery of Art, Washington	aga.gov	Plan a visit or take an online tour
U.S. Holocaust Memorial Museum	ushmm.org	Dedicated to World War II victims
University of California Museum of Paleontology	www.ucmp.berkeley.edu	Information on dinosaurs and other exhibits

For an updated list: scsite.com/dc2002/ch2/websites.htm

CATEGORY/SITE NAME	LOCATION	COMMENT
News Sources		
CNET	cnet.com	Technology news
Cable News Network	cnn.com	CNN all-news network
Enews.com, Inc.	enews.com	An electronic newsstand
Time	time.com	Excerpts from Time-Warner magazines
USA TODAY	usatoday.com	Latest U.S. and international news
Wired News	wired.com	Wired magazine online and HotWired network
Reference		
About.com, Inc.	about.com	Search engine and portal
AskEric Virtual Library	askeric.org/Virtual	Educational resources
AskJeeves	askjeeves.com	Search engine
Bartlett's Quotations	www.columbia.edu/acis/bartleby/bartlett	Organized, searchable database of famous quotes
Internet Public Library	ipl.org	Literature and reference works
The New York Public Library	www.nypl.org	Extensive reference and research material
Webopedia	webopedia.com	Online dictionary and search engine
Robotics		
Remotebot.net	remotebot.net	Control a robot with your Netscape Web browser; interactive Robotic Museum
Robotics and Intelligent Machines Laboratory	robotics.eecs.berkeley.edu	Robotics and mechanical and electrical engineering
University of Massachusetts Robotics Information	www-robotics.cs.umass.edu/robotics.html	Robotics resource index page
Science		
American Institute of Physics	www.aip.org	Physics research information
Exploratorium	exploratorium.edu	Interactive science exhibits
Internet Chemistry Index	chemie.de	List of chemistry information sites
National Institute for Discovery Science (NIDS)	www.accessnv.com/nids	Research of anomalous phenomena
Solar System Simulator	space.jpl.nasa.gov	JPL's spyglass on the cosmos
The NASA Homepage	www.nasa.gov	Information on U.S. space program
The Nine Planets	www.nineplanets.org	Tour the solar system's nine planets

For an updated list: scsite.com/dc2002/ch2/websites.htm

CATEGORY/SITE NAME	LOCATION	COMMENT
Shopping		
Amazon.com	amazon.com	Books and gifts
Bartleby	bartleby.com	Great Books online
BizRate	bizrate.com	Rates e-commerce sites
BizWeb	bizweb.com	Search for products from more than 45,753 companies
CNET Shopper	shopper.com	Computer and electronic products
CommerceNet	www.commerce.net	Non-profit with focus on B2B e-commerce
Consumer World	consumerworld.org	Consumer information
Ebay	ebay.com	Online auctions
Greenlight	greenlight.com	Automobile buying site
Internet Bookshop	www.bookshop.co.uk	780,000 titles on more than 2,000 subjects
PriceLine.com	priceline.com	Merchandise from groceries to airfare; name your price
ShopNow	Shopnow.com	Specialty stores, hot deals, computer products
Society		
Association for Computing Machinery (ACM)	acm.org	World's first educational and scientific computing society
Center for Applied Ethics	www.ethics.ubc.ca/resources/computer	Computer and information ethic resources
Center for Computing and Society Responsibility	www.ccsr.cse.dmu.ac.uk/index.html	Social and ethical impacts of information and communication technologies
Civil Society Democracy Project	cpsr.org	A public-interest alliance of computer scientists and others concerned about the impact of computer technology on society
Computers and Society	acm.org/sigcas	Special interest group within Association for Computing Machinery (ACM)
Electronic Frontier Foundation	eff.org	Protecting rights and promoting freedom
Electronic Privacy Information Center	epic.org	Links to latest new regarding privacy issues
International Center for Information Ethics (ICIE)	infoethics.net	An academic Web site on information ethics
International Federation for Information Processing (IFIP)	www.info.fundp.ac.be/~jbl/IFIP/cadresIFIP.html	Computers and social accountability
ISWorld Net Professional Ethics	www.cityu.edu.hk/is/ethics/ethics.htm	Practice of ethics in the information systems profession
The Privacy Page	privacy.org	Current privacy issues

For an updated list: scsite.com/dc2002/ch2/websites.htm

CATEGORY/SITE NAME	LOCATION	COMMENT
Sports		
ESPN SportsZone	espn.com	Latest sports news
NBA Basketball	nba.com	Information and links to team sites
NFL Football	nfl.com	Information and links to team sites
Sports Illustrated	cnnsi.com	Leading sports magazine
Travel		
CitySearch	citysearch.com	United States and international city guides
Excite City.Net	excite.com/travel	Guide to world cities
InfoHub Specialty Travel Guide	infohub.com	Worldwide travel information
Lonely Planet Online	www.lonelyplanet.com	Budget travel guides and stories
Expedia.com	expedia.msn.com	Complete travel resource
Travelocity.com	travelocity.com	Online travel agency
TravelWebSM	travelweb.com	Places to stay
Unclassified		
Cool site of the Day	cool.infi.net	Different site each day
Cupid's Network™	cupidnet.com	Links to dating resources
Taxi Cam	ny-taxi.com	NYC from a taxi Web cam
Where's George?	wheresgeorge.com	Dollar bill locator
Zing	zing.com	Online photo community
Weather		
Intellicast	intellicast.com	International weather and skiing information
The Weather Channel	weather.com	National and local forecasts
Weather Underground	wunderground.com	Weather maps
Zines		
AFU & Urban Legends Archive	urbanlegends.com	Urban legends
Breakup Girl	breakupgirl.com	Saving love lives all over the world
Rock School	rockschool.com	Everything you need to know about being in a rock band
The Smoking Gun	thesmokinggun.com	Confidential documents

For an updated list: scsite.com/dc2002/ch2/websites.htm

WORLD WIDE WEB SEARCH TOOLS

Successful searching of the Web involves two key steps:

1. Briefly describe the information you are seeking. Start by identifying the main idea or concept in your topic and determine any synonyms, alternate spellings, or variant word forms for the concept.

2. Use the brief description with a search tool to display links to pages containing the desired information.

The two most common search tools are subject directories and search engines. You use a **subject directory** by clicking through its collection of categories and sub-categories until you reach the information you want. You use a **search engine** to search for a keyword. The following sections describe how to use a subject directory and a search engine.

Using a Subject Directory

A subject directory provides categorized lists of links. These categorized lists are arranged by subject and then displayed in a series of menus. Using this type of search tool, you can locate a particular topic by starting from the top and clicking links through the different levels, going from the general to the specific. Each time you click a category link, the search tool displays a page of sub-category links from which you again choose. You continue in this fashion until the search tool displays a list of Web pages on the desired topic. Browsing a subject directory requires that you make assumptions about the topic's hierarchical placement within the categorized list.

For the following example, assume you have been assigned the task of writing a research paper on Mark Twain's childhood. The assignment requires that you include at least one Web page citation. This example uses the Yahoo! (yahoo.com) search directory to locate information on Mark Twain's childhood.

1 Launch your browser and enter the URL yahoo.com in the Address box. When the Yahoo! home page displays, point to the Literature link below Arts & Humanities as shown in Figure 1. You point to Literature because that is the category in which Mark Twain made his contributions.

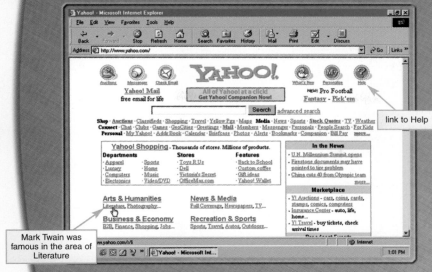

Figure 1 Yahoo! home page.

2 Click Literature. When the Literature page displays, scroll down and point to the Authors link as shown in Figure 2. You point to Authors because Mark Twain was an author. Each time you click a category link, you move closer to the topic.

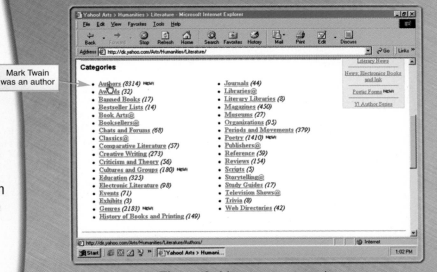

Figure 2 Literature categories.

3 Click Authors. When the Authors page displays, point to the Literary Fiction link as shown in Figure 3. You point to Literary Fiction because that is the area of literature in which Mark Twain specialized.

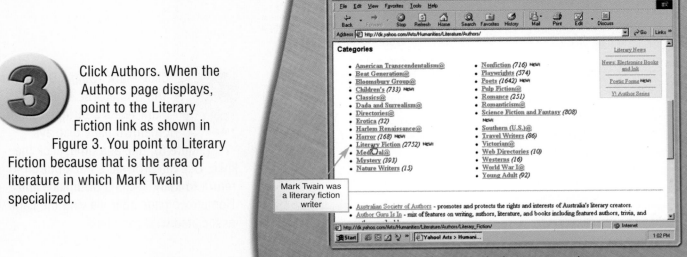

Figure 3 Authors categories.

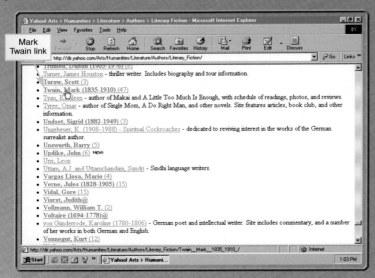

Figure 4 Literary Fiction categories.

4 Click Literary Fiction. When the Literary Fiction page displays, scroll down and point to the Twain, Mark (1835 - 1910) link as shown in Figure 4.

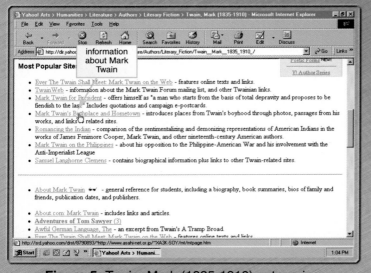

Figure 5 Twain, Mark (1835-1910) categories.

5 Click Twain, Mark (1835 - 1910). When the Twain, Mark (1835 - 1910) page displays, scroll down and point to the Mark Twain's Birthplace and Hometown link as shown in Figure 5.

Figure 6 Mark Twain's Birthplace and Hometown Web page.

6 Click Mark Twain's Birthplace and Hometown. When the Mark Twain's Birthplace and Hometown page displays (Figure 6), one at a time, click the links. Use the browser's Back button to return to Mark Twain's Birthplace and Hometown page after viewing the page associated with each link.

With just a few clicks, the Yahoo! search directory displays information about Mark Twain's childhood. The Mark Twain sub-category page in Figure 6 shows several links to his writings, as well as to pages describing his life and times.

The major problem with a search directory is deciding which categories to choose as you work through the menus of links presented. For additional information on how to use the Yahoo! search directory, click the Help link in the upper-right corner of its home page (Figure 1).

Using a Search Engine

Search engines require that you enter search text or keywords (single word, words, or phrase) that defines what you are looking for, rather than clicking through menus of links. Search engines often respond with results that include thousands of links to Web pages, many of which have little or no bearing on the information you are seeking. You can eliminate the superfluous pages by carefully crafting a keyword that limits the search. The following example uses the Google search engine to search for the phrase, mark twain childhood.

1 Launch your browser and enter the URL google.com in the Address box. When the Google home page displays, type mark twain childhood in the Search box and then point to the Google Search button as shown in Figure 7.

Figure 7 Google home page

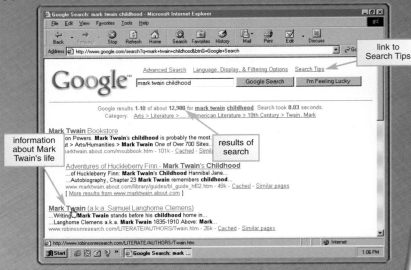

Figure 8 Google search results.

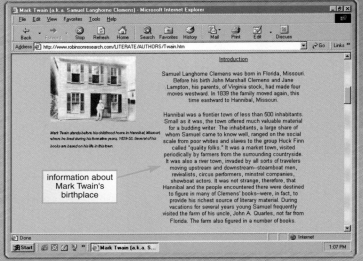

Figure 9 Web page describing Mark Twain's early years.

2 Click the Google Search button. When the results of the search display, scroll through the links and read the descriptions. Point to the Mark Twain (a.k.a. Samuel Langhorne Clemens) link as shown in Figure 8.

3 Click the Mark Twain (a.k.a. Samuel Langhorne Clemens) link. A Web page displays describing Mark Twain's birthplace (Hannibal, Missouri) and early life (Figure 9).

The results in Figure 8 include nearly 13,000 links to Web pages concerning Mark Twain's childhood. Most search engines sequence the results based on how close the words in the keyword are to one another in the Web page titles and their descriptions. Thus, the first few links probably contain more relevant information. For additional information on how to use the Goggle search engine, click the Search Tips link in the upper-right corner of its home page (Figure 8).

Limiting the Search

If you enter a phrase with spaces between the keywords, most search engines return links to pages that include all of the words. Figure 10 lists some common operators, commands, and special characters you can use to refine your search.

Guidelines to Successful Searching

You can improve your Web searches by following these guidelines.

1. Use nouns as keywords, and put the most important terms first in your keyword.

2. Use the asterisk (*) to find plurals of words. For example: retriev* returns retrieves, retrieval, retriever, and any other variation.

3. Type keywords in lowercase to find both lowercase and uppercase variations.

4. Use quotation marks to create phrases so the search engine finds the exact sequence of words.

5. Use a hyphen alternative. For example, use email e-mail.

6. Limit the search by language.

7. Use uppercase characters for Boolean operators in your search statements to differentiate between the words and operators.

8. Before you use a search engine, read its Help.

9. The Internet contains many search engines. If your search is unsuccessful with one search engine, try another.

Popular Portals

Most portals include both a search engine and subject directory. Figure 11 contains a list of portals and their URLs where you can access search engines and subject directories to search the Web.

CATEGORY OF OPERATOR	OPERATOR	KEYWORD EXAMPLES	DESCRIPTION
Boolean	AND (+)	art AND music smoking health hazards fish +pollutants +runoff	Requires both words to be in the page. No operator between words or the plus sign (+) are shortcuts for the Boolean operator AND.
	OR	mental illness OR insane canine OR dog OR puppy flight attendant OR stewardess OR steward	Requires only one of the words to be in the page.
	AND NOT (-)	auto AND NOT SUV AND NOT convertible computers -programming shakespeare -hamlet - (romeo+juliet)	Excludes page with the word following AND NOT. The minus sign (-) is a shortcut for the Boolean operator AND NOT.
Parentheses	( )	physics AND (relativity OR einstein)	Parentheses group portions of Boolean operators together.
Phrase Searching	" "	"harry potter" "19th century literature"	Requires the exact phrase within quotation marks to be in the page.
Wildcard	*	writ* clou*	The asterisk (*) at the end of words substitutes for any combination of characters.

Figure 10 Search engine keyword operators, commands, and special characters.

PORTALS	URL
Altavista	altavista.com
DirectHit	directhit.com
Excite	excite.com
Go	go.com
Google	google.com
Hotbot	hotbot.com
LookSmart	looksmart.com
Netscape Search	search.netscape.com
MSN	msn.search.com
Yahoo	yahoo.com

Figure 11 List of portals with search engines and directories.

CHAPTER 3
Application Software

The doorbell rings on Saturday afternoon. Surprised to see the mail carrier after opening the door, she hands you a huge stack of mail. She jokes about the quantity and that you are so popular the mail no longer fits in the mailbox. Sifting through the pile, you notice your bank statement and think back when it took hours to balance a statement.

Today, so much has changed. Checkbook registers are a thing of the past. Every other day you connect to the bank and copy your personal account transactions from the bank's computer to your computer. Your computerized checkbook balance always is up to date. It shows cleared checks, ATM withdrawals, debit card transactions, and automatic payments. Statement reconciliations literally take minutes.

The online payment feature also saves you time. Your bank automatically transfers the specified funds on certain dates from your checking account to the payees' accounts, assuring accurate and timely bill paying.

In the mail, you see an advertisement from your checkbook software vendor. Their new software version includes tax preparation capabilities. Now you can get help organizing and filing taxes electronically. This could mean no more endless days completing tax forms. You wonder what innovation might be next to help save you time.

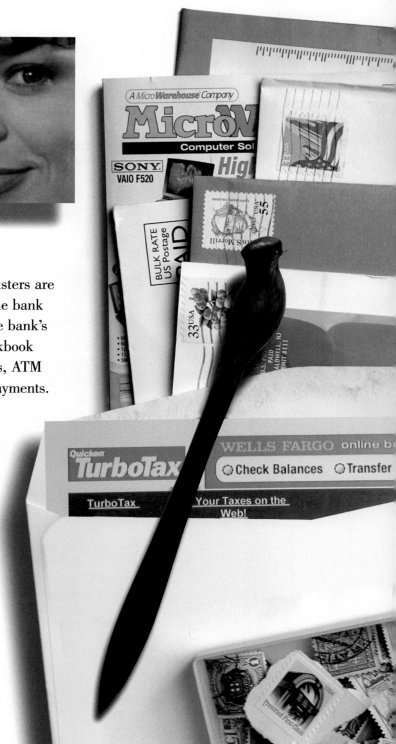

APPLICATION SOFTWARE

Application software, also called a **software application** or an **application**, consists of programs that perform specific tasks for users. Application software is used for a variety of reasons:

1. As a productivity/business tool
2. To assist with graphics and multimedia projects
3. To support household activities, for personal business, or for education
4. To facilitate communications

The table in Figure 3-1 categorizes popular types of application software by their general use. You likely will find yourself using software from more than one of these categories.

These four categories are not mutually exclusive. For example, an e-mail program is a communications tool and a productivity tool. A software suite is a productivity tool that also can include Web page authoring software. Both home users and business users have legal software.

A variety of application software is available as packaged software that you can purchase from software vendors in retail stores or on the Web. **A software package** is a specific software product, such as Microsoft Word. As discussed in Chapter 1, many software packages also are available as shareware, freeware, and public-domain software. These packages, however, usually have fewer capabilities than retail software packages.

OBJECTIVES

After completing this chapter, you will be able to:

- Define application software
- Understand how system software interacts with application software
- Identify the role of the user interface
- Explain how to start a software application
- Identify the widely used products and explain key features of productivity/business software applications, graphic design/multimedia software applications, home/personal/educational software applications, and communications software applications
- Identify various products available as Web applications
- Describe the learning aids available with many software applications

CATEGORIES OF APPLICATION SOFTWARE

Productivity/ Business	Graphic Design/ Multimedia	Home/Personal/ Educational	Communications
• Word Processing	• Computer-Aided Design	• Integrated Software	• E-Mail
• Spreadsheet	• Desktop Publishing (Professional)	• Personal Finance	• Web Browser
• Presentation Graphics	• Paint/Image Editing (Professional)	• Legal	• Chat Rooms
• Database	• Video and Audio Editing	• Tax Preparation	• Newsgroups
• Personal Information Management	• Multimedia Authoring	• Desktop Publishing (Personal)	• Instant Messaging
• Software Suite	• Web Page Authoring	• Paint/Image Editing (Personal)	• Groupware
• Project Management		• Home Design/ Landscaping	• Videoconferencing
• Accounting		• Educational	
		• Reference	
		• Entertainment	

Figure 3-1 This table outlines the four major categories of popular application software. You probably will use software from more than one of these categories.

The Role of the System Software

Like most computer users, you probably are somewhat familiar with application software. To run any application software, however, your computer must be running another type of software — system software.

As described in Chapter 1, **system software** consists of programs that control the operations of the computer and its devices. As shown in Figure 3-2, system software serves as the interface between the user, the application software, and the computer's hardware. One type of system software, the **operating system**, contains instructions that coordinate all the activities among computer hardware devices. The operating system also contains instructions that allow you to run application software.

Before a computer can run any application software, the operating system must load from the hard disk (storage) into the computer's memory. Each time you start the computer, the operating system loads, or copies, into memory from the computer's hard disk. Once the operating system loads, it tells the computer how to perform functions. These functions include controlling computer resources and transferring data among input and output devices and memory.

While the computer is running, the operating system remains in memory. The operating system continues to run until power is removed from the computer.

Another type of system software is a utility program. A **utility program**, also called a **utility**, is a type of system software that performs a specific task, usually related to managing a computer, its devices, or its programs. One utility that every computer should have is an antivirus program. An **antivirus program** is a utility that prevents, detects, and removes viruses from a computer's memory or storage devices. A **virus** is a program that copies itself into other programs and spreads through multiple computers. Some malicious programmers intentionally write virus programs that destroy or corrupt data

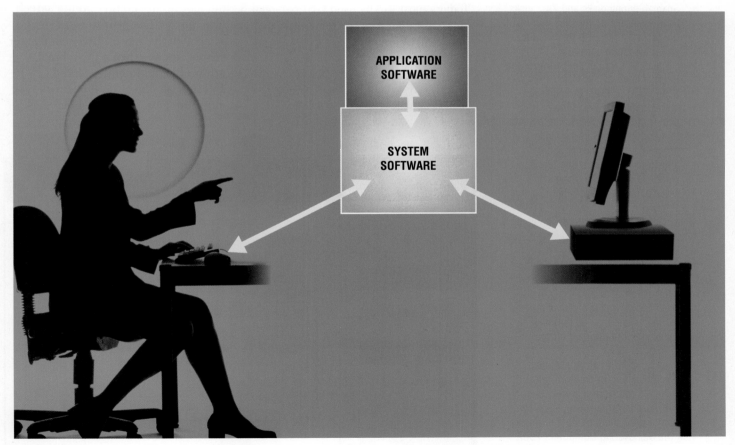

Figure 3-2 The user interacts with the system software or with the application software to control the hardware.

APPLY IT!
Virus Alert!

The number of computer viruses developed each day is astounding. Viruses can range from simply annoying ones to downright disastrous ones. If you read e-mail attachments, access shared files, insert disks into your computer, or download software from the Internet, you eventually will encounter a virus. Consider the following tips for preventing virus infections:

- Use a high-quality anti-virus program, and be sure to update it regularly. Use it to scan any files, programs, software, or floppy disks before you use them on your computer.
- Do not start your computer with a floppy disk in drive A, unless it is an uninfected rescue disk (see Chapter 8).
- Scan all floppy disks and Zip® disks. Scan every file on the disk, not just the program files. Do this even for shrink-wrapped software.
- Scan all files you download from the Internet.
- Scan Word or Excel e-mail attachments before you read them. It is best first to copy these attachments to a floppy disk. Some e-mail programs automatically open attachments. Disable this function within your e-mail program.
- Make backups of everything.

If you think your computer is infected, take special note of the following points:
- Do not panic.
- Do not erase or format everything in sight. You may lose valuable information. It is very likely that the virus is only in a few places on your computer and may be removed easily with the right anti-virus program.
- Keep a record of all your steps. It will help you to be thorough and will save you from duplicating work.

For more information on learning about and preventing computer viruses, visit the Discovering Computers 2002 Apply It Web page (**scsite.com/dc2002/ apply.htm**) and click Chapter 3 Apply It #1.

on a computer. When you purchase a new computer, it often includes an antivirus software program (Figure 3-3). Chapter 8 discusses other commonly used utility programs.

The Role of the User Interface

You interact with software through its user interface. The **user interface** controls how you enter data or instructions and how information displays on the screen. Many of today's software programs have a graphical user interface. A **graphical user interface** (**GUI**) combines text, graphics, and other visual images to make software easier to use.

In 1984, Apple Computer introduced the Macintosh operating system, which used a GUI. Many software companies recognized the value of this easy-to-use interface and developed their own GUI software. Today's most widely used GUI personal computer operating system is Microsoft Windows.

Starting a Software Application

Both the Apple Macintosh and Microsoft Windows operating systems use the concept of a desktop to make the computer easier to use. The **desktop** is an on-screen work area that can display graphical elements such as icons, buttons, windows, menus, links, and dialog boxes. The Windows desktop shown in Figure 3-4 contains many icons and buttons.

An **icon** is a small image that displays on the screen to represent a program, a document, or some other object. A **button** is a graphical element that you activate to cause a specific action to take place. For example, one button may start the Web browser and another may start an e-mail program. Buttons usually are rectangular or circular in shape.

One way to activate a button is to click it with a mouse. As you move the mouse, the pointer on the screen also moves. The **pointer** is a small symbol on the screen. Common pointer shapes are an I-beam (I), block arrow ( ), and pointing hand ( ). To **click** an object on the screen, you move the pointer to the object and

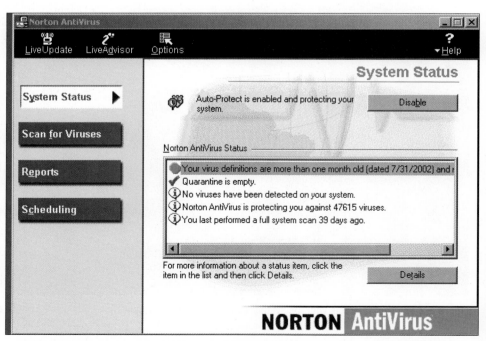

Figure 3-3 An antivirus program prevents, detects, and removes viruses from a computer's memory or storage devices.

then press and release a button on the mouse.

The Windows desktop contains a Start button in its lower-left corner. You can use the Start button to start an application. When you click the Start button, the Start menu displays on the desktop. A **menu** contains commands you can select. A **command** is an instruction that causes a computer program to perform a specific action.

Some menus have a submenu. A **submenu** is a menu that displays when you point to a command on a previous menu. As shown in Figure 3-5, when you click the Start button and point to the Programs command on the Start menu, the Programs submenu displays. Pointing to the Accessories command on the Programs submenu displays the Accessories submenu. Notice that the Accessories submenu contains several applications such as Calculator, Paint, and WordPad.

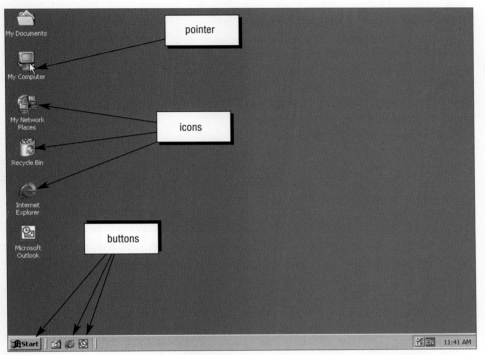

Figure 3-4 This Windows desktop shows a variety of icons and buttons.

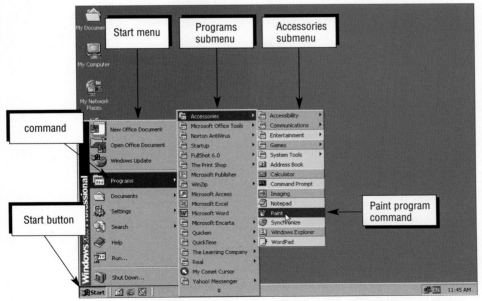

Figure 3-5 This figure shows the Start menu and the Programs and Accessories submenus. Some commands in menus are followed by a right arrowhead (▶), which indicates a submenu of additional commands exists.

PAUL **ALLEN**

Owning the Portland Trail Blazers and the Seattle Seahawks may seem unlikely investments for an individual who helped create one of the world's largest computer companies. But for Microsoft co-founder Paul Allen, these NBA and NFL franchises are opportunities to showcase his savvy business skills. So are Allen's 140 other diverse technology, entertainment, and new media enterprises. He is chairman of Vulcan Northwest, owns a 24 percent equity stake in Dreamworks SKG, and is responsible for Experience Music Project, a shrine for electric guitarist Jimi Hendrix. He also shares his expertise with the community through his six charitable foundations.

Allen met Bill Gates when they attended high school together in Seattle in the late 1960s. Allen was working in Boston in 1975 as a programmer at Honeywell when he saw an advertisement for the first microcomputer. He went to Gates' dorm room at Harvard and convinced Gates to help him develop software for this machine. Their creation laid Microsoft's foundation.

Allen became the company's head of research and new product development and helped bring many of the company's highest-profile products to market. Today he serves as a senior strategy adviser to top Microsoft executives.

For more information on Paul Allen, visit the Discovering Computers 2002 People Web page (**scsite.com/dc2002/people.htm**) and click Paul Allen.

You can start an application by clicking its program name on a menu or submenu. Doing so instructs the operating system to start the application by transferring the program's instructions from a storage medium into memory. For example, if you click Paint on the Accessories submenu, Windows transfers the Paint program instructions from the computer's hard disk into memory.

Once started, an application displays in a window on the desktop. A **window** is a rectangular area of the screen that displays a program, data, and/or information. The top of a window has a **title bar**, which is a horizontal space that contains the window's name. Figure 3-6 shows the Paint window. This window contains an image that has been photographed with a digital camera.

In some cases, when you instruct a program to perform an activity such as printing, a dialog box displays. A **dialog box** is a special window a program displays to provide information, present available options, or request a response (Figure 3-7). For example, a Print dialog box gives you many printing options such as specifying a different printer, printing all or part of a document, or printing multiple copies.

Many applications use shortcut menus. A **shortcut menu**, also called a **context-sensitive menu,** is a menu that displays a list of commonly used commands for completing a task related to the current activity or selected item.

Figure 3-6 The Paint program displays in a window on the desktop. Paint is an application included with Windows that allows you to work with, manipulate, and print graphical images. Many applications contain a toolbar, which is a row or column of buttons for commonly used tasks.

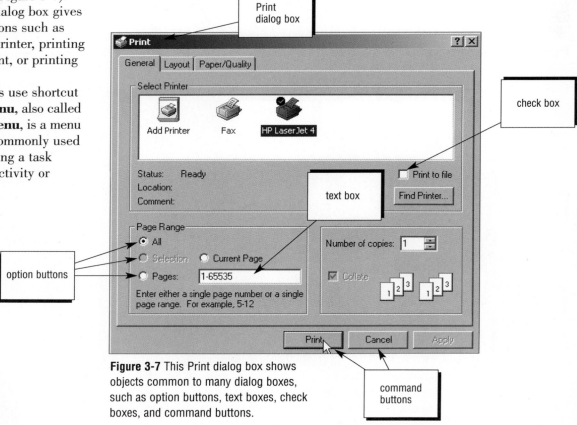

Figure 3-7 This Print dialog box shows objects common to many dialog boxes, such as option buttons, text boxes, check boxes, and command buttons.

Many elements shown on the previous pages, such as icons, buttons, and menus are part of the graphical user interface (GUI). One of the major advantages of a GUI is that these elements usually are similar across most applications. Once you learn the purpose and functionality of these elements, you can apply that knowledge to other software applications.

PRODUCTIVITY SOFTWARE

Productivity software is software that assists people in becoming more effective and efficient while performing daily activities. Productivity software includes applications such as word processing, spreadsheet, database, presentation graphics, personal information manager, software suite, accounting, and project management. Figure 3-8 lists popular software packages for each of these applications and the following sections discuss the features and functions of these applications.

POPULAR PRODUCTIVITY SOFTWARE PACKAGES

Software Application	Popular Packages
Word Processing	• Microsoft Word • Corel WordPerfect • Lotus Word Pro • Microsoft Pocket Word
Spreadsheet	• Microsoft Excel • Corel Quattro Pro • Lotus 1-2-3 • Microsoft Pocket Excel
Database	• Microsoft Access • Corel Paradox • Lotus Approach • Microsoft Visual FoxPro • Oracle
Presentation Graphics	• Microsoft PowerPoint • Corel Presentations • Lotus Freelance Graphics
Personal Information Manager	• Microsoft Outlook • CorelCENTRAL • Lotus Organizer • Palm Desktop
Software Suite	• Microsoft Office • Corel WordPerfect Suite • Lotus SmartSuite
Project Management	• Corel CATALYST • Microsoft Project • Primavera SureTrak Project Manager
Accounting	• Intuit QuickBooks • Peachtree Complete Accounting

Figure 3-8 Popular productivity software products.

COMPANY ON THE CUTTING EDGE

Microsoft®

Productivity Software Gives Directions

If someone asks "Where do you want to go today?" you might answer, "Microsoft." Indeed, Microsoft attributes its worldwide success to helping customers achieve their goals. Whether these people need help creating a letter, organizing their data, or playing a game, Microsoft supplies top-rated software to help them "any time, any place, and on any device."

Bill Gates, Microsoft's current chairman and chief software architect, founded the company in 1975 with Paul Allen, his former schoolmate. Today, the Redmond, Washington-based corporation employs nearly 40,000 people and has subsidiary offices in more than 55 countries.

Ninety-five percent of personal computers run at least one Microsoft application, making the company the world's leading productivity software developer. Equally popular is its family of operating system software, including Windows 2000 Professional for business customers and Windows Millennium Edition for consumers. Several million users across the globe use MSN, which includes Internet access, Hotmail e-mail, and instant messaging. Microsoft's games, especially Flight Simulator and Age of Empires, are best-sellers. The corporation also is making technological advances in the television, wireless, and small business fields.

For more information on Microsoft, visit the Discovering Computers 2002 Companies Web page (**scsite.com/dc2002/companies.htm**) and click Microsoft.

Word Processing Software

Word processing software is one of the most widely used types of application software. **Word processing software**, sometimes called a **word processor**, allows users to create and manipulate documents that contain text and graphics (Figure 3-9). Millions of people use word processing software every day to develop documents such as letters, memos, reports, fax cover sheets, mailing labels, newsletters, and Web pages.

Word processing software has many features to make documents look professional and visually appealing. You can change the shape and size of characters in headlines and headings, change the color of characters, and organize text into newspaper-style columns. When you use colors for characters, they will print as black or gray unless you have a color printer.

Most word processing software allows you to incorporate audio clips, video clips, and many types of graphical images into documents. One popular type of graphical image is clip art. **Clip art** is a collection of drawings, diagrams, and photographs that you can insert into documents. Figure 3-9 includes eight clip art images related to camping. Some clip art is stored on your hard disk, a CD-ROM, or a DVD-ROM. In other cases, you access the clip art on the Web.

All word processing software provides at least some basic capabilities to help you create and modify documents. For example, you can define the size of the paper on which to print. You also can specify the **margins** – that is, the portion of the page outside the main body of text, including the top, the bottom, and both sides of the paper. The word processing software automatically re-adjusts text so it fits within the adjusted paper size and margins.

Word wrap allows you to type words in a paragraph continually without pressing the ENTER key at

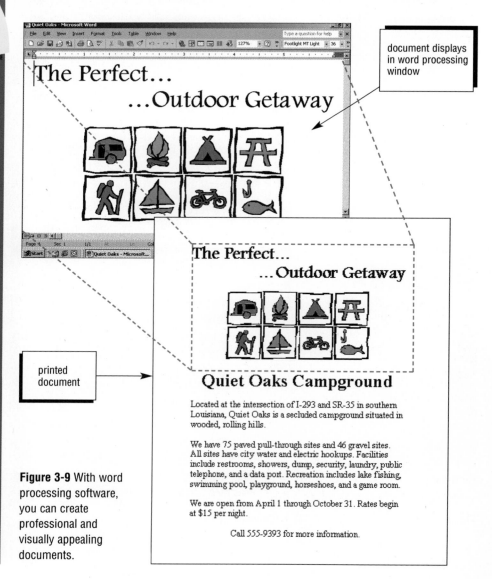

document displays in word processing window

printed document

Figure 3-9 With word processing software, you can create professional and visually appealing documents.

the end of each line. With **word wrap**, if you type text that extends beyond the right page margin, the word processing software automatically positions text at the beginning of the next line.

As you type more lines of text than can display on the screen, the top portion of the document moves upward, or scrolls, off the screen. **Scrolling** is the process of moving different portions of the document on the screen into view.

A major advantage of using word processing software is you easily can change what you have written. You can insert, delete, or rearrange words, sentences, paragraphs, or entire sections. The **find** or **search** feature allows you to locate all occurrences of a certain character, word, or phrase. This feature in combination with the **replace** feature allows you to substitute existing characters or words with new ones. The word processing software, for example, can locate the word, secluded, and replace it with the word, remote.

Current word processing packages even have a feature that automatically corrects errors and makes word substitutions as you type text. For instance, when you type the abbreviation asap, the word processing software replaces the abbreviation with the phrase, as soon as possible.

Word processing packages include a **spelling checker**, which reviews the spelling of individual words, sections of a document, or the entire document. The spelling checker compares the words in the document to an electronic dictionary that is part of the word processing software. You can customize the electronic dictionary by adding words such as companies, streets, cities, and personal names, so the software can check the spelling of those words too. Many word processing software packages allow you to check the spelling of a whole document at one time, or to check the spelling of individual words as you type them.

You also can insert headers and footers into a word processing document. A **header** is text that appears at the top of each page. A **footer** is text that appears at the bottom of each page. Page numbers, company names, report titles, and dates are examples of items often included in headers and footers.

In addition to these basic features, most current word processing packages provide numerous additional features. The table in Figure 3-10 lists these additional features.

POPULAR WORD PROCESSING FEATURES

AutoCorrect	As you type words, the AutoCorrect feature corrects common spelling errors. AutoCorrect also corrects capitalization mistakes.
AutoFormat	As you type, the AutoFormat feature automatically applies formatting to your text. For example, it automatically can number a list or convert a Web address to a hyperlink.
Collaboration	Collaboration includes discussions and online meetings. Discussions allow multiple users to enter comments in a document and read and reply to each other's comments. Through an online meeting, you share documents with others in real time and view changes as they are being made.
Columns	Most word processing software can arrange text in two or more columns to look similar to a newspaper or magazine. The text from the bottom of one column automatically flows to the top of the next column.
Grammar Checker	You can use the grammar checker to proofread documents for grammar, writing style, and sentence structure errors in a document.
Macros	A macro is a sequence of keystrokes and instructions that you record and save. When you wish to execute the same series of instructions, execute the macro instead.
Mail Merge	Create form letters, mailing labels, and envelopes.
Tables	Tables are a way of organizing information into rows and columns. Instead of evenly spaced rows and columns, some word processing packages allow you to draw the tables, any size or shape, directly into the document.
Templates	A template is a document that contains the formatting necessary for a specific document type. Templates usually exist for memos, fax cover sheets, and letters.
Thesaurus	With a thesaurus, you can look up a synonym (word with the same meaning) for a word in a document.
Tracking Changes	If multiple users work with a document, the word processing software can highlight or color-code changes made by various users. You also can add comments to a document, without changing the text itself. Comments allow you to communicate with the other users working on the document.
Voice Recognition	With some word processing packages, you can speak into the computer's microphone and watch the spoken words display on your screen as you talk. With these packages, you also can speak commands such as editing and formatting the document.
Web Page Development	Most word processing software supports Internet connectivity, allowing you to create, edit, and format documents for the World Wide Web. You automatically can convert an existing word processing document into the standard document format for the World Wide Web.

Figure 3-10 Some of the additional features included with word processing software.

DEVELOPING A DOCUMENT

Many software applications, such as word processing, allow you to create, edit, format, print, and save documents. During the process of developing a document, you likely will switch back and forth among all of these activities.

Creating involves developing the document by entering text or numbers, inserting graphical images, and performing other tasks using an input device such as a keyboard, mouse, or microphone. If you are designing an announcement in Microsoft Word, for example, you are creating a document.

Editing is the process of making changes to a document's existing content. Common editing features include inserting, deleting, cutting, copying, and pasting items into a document. In Microsoft Word, you can insert (add) text to a document, such as listing additional facilities at a campground. Deleting is the process of removing text or other content.

To cut involves removing a portion of the document and storing it in a temporary storage location called the **Clipboard**. Copying occurs when you duplicate a portion of the document and store it on the Clipboard. To paste items involves placing items stored on the Clipboard into the document.

When you **format** a document, you change its appearance. Formatting is important because the overall look of a document significantly can affect its ability to communicate effectively.

Examples of formatting tasks are changing the font, font size, or font style of text (Figure 3-11). A **font** is a name assigned to a specific design of characters. Times New Roman and Arial are examples of fonts. **Font size** specifies the size of the characters in a particular font. Font size is gauged by a measurement system called points. A single **point** is about 1/72 of an inch in height. The text you are reading in this book is 11 point. Thus, each character is about 11/72 of an inch in height. A **font style** adds

emphasis to a font. Examples of font styles are **bold**, *italic*, and <u>underline</u>.

While you create, edit, and format a document, the computer temporarily holds it in memory. Once you complete these steps, you may want to save your document for future use. **Saving** is the process of copying a document from memory to a storage medium such as a floppy disk or hard disk. While working on a document, you should save it frequently. Doing so ensures you will not lose much work in case of a power failure or other system failure. Many applications have an optional AutoSave feature that automatically saves open documents at specified time intervals.

Once you save a document, it exists as a file on a storage medium such as a floppy disk or hard disk. A **file** is a named collection of data, instructions, or information. To distinguish among various files, each file has a file name. A **file name** is a unique combination of letters of the alphabet, numbers, and other characters that identifies the file.

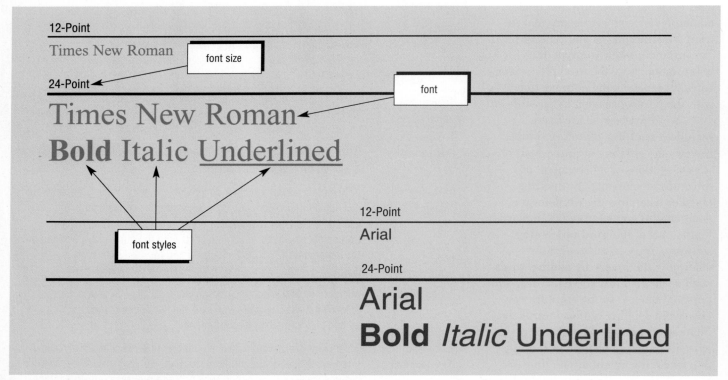

Figure 3-11 The Times New Roman and Arial fonts are shown in two font sizes and a variety of font styles.

The file name for the announcement in Figure 3-9 on page 3.8 is Quiet Oaks. The title bar of the document window usually displays a document's file name.

Once you have created a document, you can print it many times, with each copy looking just like the first. **Printing** is the process of sending a file to a printer to generate output on a medium such as paper. Instead of printing a document and mailing it, some users e-mail the document to others. That is, they send the document electronically to others on a network such as the Internet.

Many software applications support voice recognition. **Voice recognition**, also called **speech recognition**, is the computer's capability of distinguishing spoken words. You speak into the computer's microphone and watch the spoken words display on your screen as you talk. You also can edit and format a document by speaking or spelling instructions. Figure 3-12 shows how to dictate words and issue voice commands in Microsoft Word.

Figure 3-12 HOW TO DICTATE WORDS AND COMMANDS

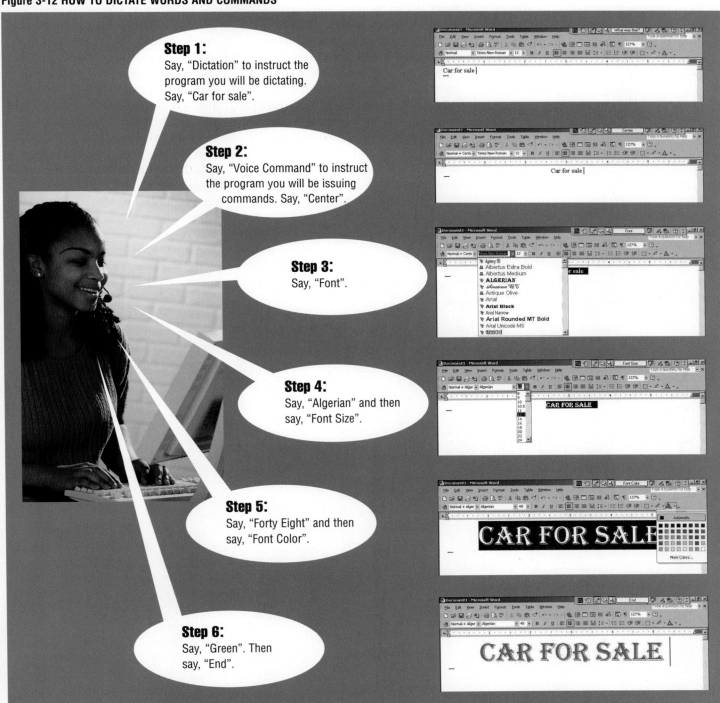

Spreadsheet Software

Spreadsheet software is another widely used application. With **spreadsheet software**, you can organize data in rows and columns and perform calculations on this data. These rows and columns collectively are called a **worksheet**. For years, people used manual methods, such as those performed with pencil and paper, to organize data in rows and columns. In an electronic worksheet, you organize data in the same manner as in a manual worksheet (Figure 3-13).

Web Link

For more information on spreadsheet software, visit the Discovering Computers 2002 Chapter 3 WEB LINK page (scsite.com/dc2002/ch3/weblink.htm) and click Spreadsheet Software.

As with word processing software, most spreadsheet software has basic features to help you create, edit, and format worksheets. The following sections describe the features that are included in several popular spreadsheet software packages.

SPREADSHEET ORGANIZATION A spreadsheet file is similar to a notebook with up to 255 related individual worksheets. Data is organized vertically in columns and horizontally in rows on each worksheet. Each worksheet typically has 256 columns and 65,536 rows. One or more letters identify each column, and a number identifies each row. The column letters begin with A and end with IV. The row numbers begin with 1 and end with 65,536. Only a small fraction of these columns and rows displays on the screen at one time. You scroll through the worksheet to display different parts of it on your screen.

A **cell** is the intersection of a column and row. Each worksheet has more than 16 million (256 x 65,536) cells in which you can enter data. The spreadsheet software identifies cells by the column and row in which they are located. For example, the intersection of column C and row 5 is referred to as cell C5. In Figure 3-13, cell C5 contains the number, 5,092.50, which represents the Sophomore Tuition & Books expenses.

Cells may contain three types of data: labels (text), values (numbers), and formulas. The text, or **label**, entered in a cell identifies the data and helps organize the worksheet. Using descriptive labels, such as Room & Board, Tuition & Books, and Clothes, helps make a worksheet more meaningful.

CALCULATIONS Many of the worksheet cells shown in Figure 3-13 contain a number, also called a **value**. Other cells, however, contain formulas that generate values. A **formula** performs calculations on the data in the worksheet and displays the resulting value in a cell, usually the cell containing the formula. When creating a worksheet, you can enter your own formulas. In Figure 3-13, for example, cell C9 could contain the formula =C4+C5+C6+C7+C8 to

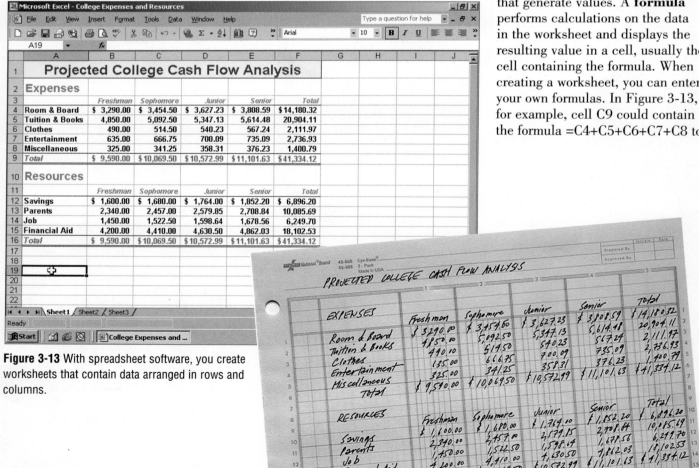

Figure 3-13 With spreadsheet software, you create worksheets that contain data arranged in rows and columns.

calculate the projected total expense for the student's sophomore year. A much more efficient way to sum the contents of cells is to use a function included with the spreadsheet software.

A **function** is a predefined formula that performs common calculations such as adding the values in a group of cells or generating a value such as the time or date. For example, instead of using the formula =C4+C5+C6+C7+C8 to calculate the projected total expense for the student's sophomore year, you should use the function =SUM(C4:C8), which adds, or sums, the contents of cells C4, C5, C6, C7, and C8. Figure 3-14 is a list of functions commonly included in spreadsheet software packages.

MACROS Spreadsheet software and other programs often include a timesaving feature called a macro. A **macro** is a sequence of keystrokes and instructions you record and save. When you run the macro, it performs the sequence of saved keystrokes and instructions. Creating a macro can help save you time by allowing you to enter a single character or word to perform frequently used tasks. For example, you can create a macro to format cells or print a portion of a worksheet.

RECALCULATION One of the more powerful features of spreadsheet software is its capability of recalculating the rest of the worksheet when data in a worksheet changes. To appreciate this capability, consider what happens each time you change a value in a manual worksheet. You must erase the old value, write in a new value, erase any totals that contain calculations referring to the changed value, and then recalculate these totals and enter the new results. When working with a manual worksheet, accurately making changes and updating the affected values can be time consuming and may result in new errors.

Making changes in an electronic worksheet is much easier and faster. When you enter a new value to change data in a cell, any value that is affected by the change is updated

SPREADSHEET FUNCTIONS

FINANCIAL	
FV (rate, number of periods, payment)	Calculates the future value of an investment
NPV (rate, range)	Calculates the net present value of an investment
PMT (rate, number of periods, present value)	Calculates the periodic payment for an annuity
PV (rate, number of periods, payment)	Calculates the present value of an investment
RATE (number of periods, payment, present value)	Calculates the periodic interest rate of an annuity
DAY & TIME	
DATE	Returns the current date
NOW	Returns the current date and time
TIME	Returns the current time
MATHEMATICAL	
ABS (number)	Returns the absolute value of a number
INT (number)	Rounds a number down to the nearest integer
LN (number)	Calculates the natural logarithm of a number
LOG (number, base)	Calculates the logarithm of a number to a specified base
ROUND (number, number of digits)	Rounds a number to a specified number of digits
SQRT (number)	Calculates the square root of a number
SUM (range)	Calculates the total of a range of numbers
STATISTICAL	
AVERAGE (range)	Calculates the average value of a range of numbers
COUNT (range)	Counts how many cells in the range have entries
MAX (range)	Returns the maximum value in a range
MIN (range)	Returns the minimum value in a range
STDEV (range)	Calculates the standard deviation of a range of numbers
LOGICAL	
IF (logical test, value if true, value if false)	Performs a test and returns one value if the result of the test is true and another value if the result is false

Figure 3-14 Functions typically found in spreadsheet software.

DAN **BRICKLIN**

The next time you use your calculator to balance your checkbook, think about Dan Bricklin. He used his Texas Instruments calculator constantly in the late 1970s while developing VisiCalc (Visible Calculator), the first electronic spreadsheet, in graduate school. He still owns that calculator, along with the original VisiCalc code.

Bricklin and his friend, Bob Frankston, formed a company called Software Arts and programmed the VisiCalc prototype using Apple Basic on an Apple II computer. The final version sold for $100 in 1979, and this small program included many of the features found in today's spreadsheet software. VisiCalc still runs on personal computers, and Bricklin includes the program on his personal Web site (see URL below).

Lotus Software purchased Software Arts in 1985. After serving as a consultant to Lotus, Bricklin turned his attention to starting a new company, Software Garden, Inc., and developing new software that focuses on pen-based computing and interactive videoconferencing. His current venture, Trellix, helps consumers and small businesses create and edit documents for the Internet.

For more information on Dan Bricklin and the Web site mentioned above, visit the Discovering Computers 2002 People Web page (**scsite.com/dc2002/people.htm**) and click Dan Bricklin.

automatically and instantaneously. In Figure 3-13 on page 3.12 for example, if you change the Room & Board Expenses for Sophomore from 3,454.50 to 3,554.50, the total in cell C9 automatically changes to $10,169.50.

Spreadsheet software's capability of recalculating data also makes it a valuable tool for decision-making by using what-if analysis. **What-if analysis** is a process in which you change certain values in a spreadsheet in order to reveal the effects of those changes.

CHARTING Charting, another standard feature of spreadsheet software, allows you to display data in a chart that shows the relationship of data in graphical form. A visual representation of data through charts often makes it easier for users to analyze and interpret information.

Three popular chart types are line charts, column charts, and pie charts. Figure 3-15 shows examples of these charts that were plotted from the data in Figure 3-13. **Line charts** show a trend during a period of time, as indicated by a rising or falling line. A line chart indicating college resources could show the total for each year the student attends college. **Column charts**, also called **bar charts**, display bars of various lengths to show the relationship of data. The bars can be horizontal, vertical, or stacked on top of one another. A column chart might show the college expense breakdown by category, with each bar representing a different category. **Pie charts**, which have the shape of round pies cut into pieces or slices, show the relationship of parts to a whole. You might use a pie chart to show what percentage (part) each

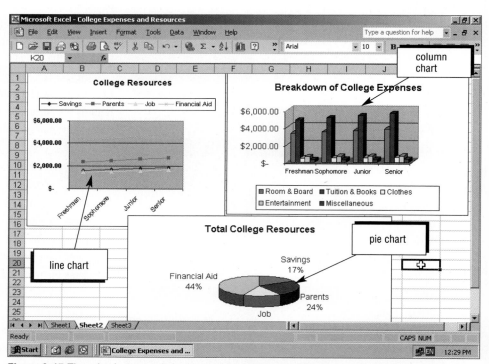

Figure 3-15 Three basic types of charts provided with spreadsheet software are line charts, column charts, and pie charts. The line chart, column chart, and pie chart were created from the data in the worksheet in Figure 3-13 on page 3.12.

resource category contributed to the total resources (whole) for a time period.

Spreadsheet software also incorporates many of the features found in word processing software such as checking spelling, changing fonts and font sizes, adding colors, tracking changes, recognizing voice input, including audio and video clips, and converting an existing spreadsheet document into a format for the World Wide Web.

Database Software

A **database** is a collection of data organized in a manner that allows access, retrieval, and use of that data. In a manual database, you might record data on paper and store it in a filing cabinet. With a computerized database, such as the one shown in Figure 3-16, the computer stores the data in an electronic format on a storage medium such as a floppy disk or a hard disk.

APPLY IT!

A Tip a Day

Today's software applications include many, many features that can improve your productivity. So how do you learn about all of these features? One option is to join a mailing list and receive daily or weekly tips for an application or applications of your choice. It is easy to subscribe to these newsletters. Just select the topics you want, fill in your e-mail address, and click the Subscribe button. Some of the more popular Web sites providing this free service are as follows:

- TipWorld (see URL below) offers daily tips. Tips on this site are not limited to software. Other categories include music, literature, cooking, business, science, personal finance, and entertainment.
- DummiesDaily (see URL below) offers daily eTips. Similarly to TipWorld, a variety of categories, in addition to computers, are available. Some other categories include Sports and Recreation, Pets, and Investing.
- CyberTips (see URL below) provides an option for how often you receive tips — daily, three times a week, or once a week. In addition to the Computers category, you also will find Health and Fitness, Home and Family, Golf, and other categories.
- PCShowAndTell (see URL below) is somewhat different from the other above listed services. This site offers multimedia tutorials for more than 100 different software applications, with a library of more than 35,000 tutorials. Signing up for their free newsletter brings random weekly tips to your mailbox. Ten tutorials per product are available free of charge. The company charges a $15 yearly fee, which provides access to their full library.

With the exception of PCShowAndTell, expect to see sponsor advertising within the newsletters you receive.

For more information on subscribing to an online tips service and the Web sites mentioned above, visit the Discovering Computers 2002 Apply It Web page (**scsite.com/dc2002/apply.htm**) and click Chapter 3 Apply It #2.

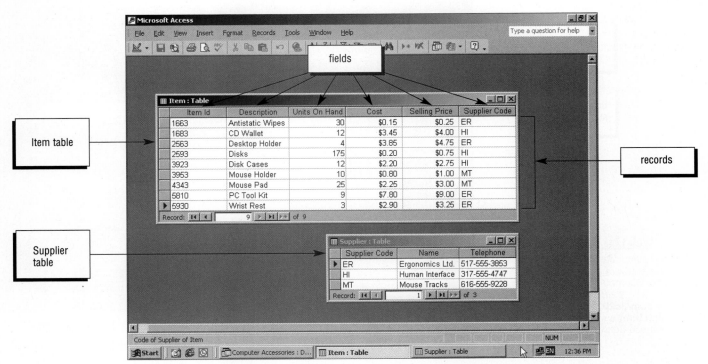

Figure 3-16 This database contains two tables: one for items and one for suppliers. The Item table has 9 records and 6 fields; the Supplier table has 3 records and 3 fields.

Database software, also called a **database management system** (**DBMS**), is software that allows you to create, access, and manage a database. Using database software, you can add, change, and delete data in the database; sort and retrieve data from the database; and create forms and reports using the data in the database.

With most popular personal computer database software packages, a database consists of a collection of **tables**, organized in rows and columns. A **record** is a row in a table that contains information about a given person, product, or event. A **field** is a column in a table that contains a specific piece of information within a record.

The Computer Warehouse database shown in Figure 3-16 on the previous page consists of two tables: an Item table and a Supplier table. The Item table contains nine records (rows), each storing data about one item. The item data exists in six fields

(columns): item identification number, description, units on hand, cost, selling price, and supplier code. The description field, for instance, contains a name of a particular item.

DATABASE ORGANIZATION Before creating a database, you should perform some preliminary tasks. Make a list of the data items you want to organize. Each of these data items will become a field in the database. To identify the different fields, assign each field a unique name that is short, yet descriptive. For example, the field name for an item identification number could be Item Id.

Once you determine the fields and field names, you also must decide the field size and data type for each field. The **field size** is the maximum number of characters that a particular field can contain. The Description field, for instance, may be defined as 25 characters in length. The **data type** specifies the kind of data a field

can contain and how the field is used. Common data types include the following:

- **Text**: letters, numbers, or special characters
- **Numeric**: numbers only
- **Currency**: dollar and cent amounts
- **Date**: month, day, and year information
- **Memo**: lengthy text entries
- **Hyperlink**: Web address that links to a document or a Web page
- **Object**: picture, audio, video, or a document created in other applications such as word processing or spreadsheet

Completing these steps provides a general description of the records and fields in a table, including the number of fields, field names, field sizes, and data types. These items collectively are known as the table **structure** (Figure 3-17).

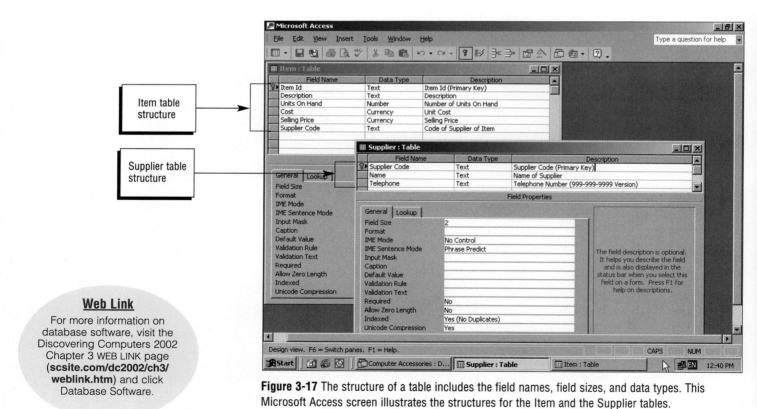

Figure 3-17 The structure of a table includes the field names, field sizes, and data types. This Microsoft Access screen illustrates the structures for the Item and the Supplier tables.

Web Link

For more information on database software, visit the Discovering Computers 2002 Chapter 3 WEB LINK page (**scsite.com/dc2002/ch3/weblink.htm**) and click Database Software.

ENTERING DATA After you create a table structure, the next step is to enter individual records into a table, called **populating** the table. The database software usually allows you to create a data entry form, through which you can enter or modify records using the keyboard (Figure 3-18). As you are entering the data, the database software checks, or validates, the data. **Validation** is the process of comparing the data to a set of rules or values to determine if the data is correct. For example, a field with a numeric data type restricts a user to entering only numbers into the field. Validation is important because it helps to ensure that data entered into the database is error free.

Another way to enter data into a database is to import data from an existing file. For example, you can import data from a spreadsheet file into a database.

MANIPULATING DATA Once the records are in the database, you can use the database software to manipulate the data to generate information. You can **sort**, or organize a set of records in a particular order, such as alphabetical or by date.

You also can retrieve information from the database by running a query. A **query** is a request for specific data from the database. You can specify which data the query retrieves by identifying **criteria**, which are

restrictions the data must meet. For example, suppose you wanted to generate a list of all items that have a selling price less than $15.00. You could set up a query to list the Supplier Code, Name, Item Id, Description, Units On Hand, Cost, and Selling Price for all records that meet the criteria. Then, you can sort the list by supplier name (Figure 3-19), and instruct the database software to print or store the results of the query.

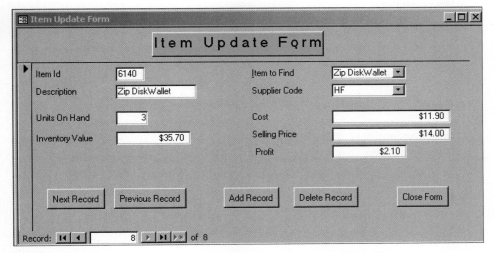

Figure 3-18 Once the table structure is defined, you can enter or modify data in a database using a data entry form. Most database software allows you to create a data entry form, based on the way you define fields. This data entry form allows you to enter or modify data in the Item table.

Supplier Code	Name	Item Id	Description	Units On Hand	Cost	Selling Price
ER	Ergonomics Inc.	2563	Desktop Holder	4	$3.85	$4.75
HF	Human Interface	1683	CD Wallet	8	$3.45	$4.00
HF	Human Interface	2593	Disks	145	$0.20	$0.75
HF	Human Interface	3923	Disk Cases	12	$2.20	$2.75
HF	Human Interface	6140	Zip DiskWallet	3	$11.90	$14.00
MT	Mouse Trails	3953	Mouse Holder	10	$0.80	$1.00
MT	Mouse Trails	4343	Mouse Pad-Plain	16	$2.25	$3.00
MT	Mouse Trails	5810	Mouse Pad-Logo	25	$3.45	$5.00

Figure 3-19 Database software can produce reports based on criteria a user specifies. This screen shows the result of a query to list the Supplier Code, Name, Item Id, Description, Units On Hand, Cost, and Selling Price fields for all records that have a Selling Price less than $15.00. The results of the query can be displayed or printed.

Presentation Graphics Software

Presentation graphics software allows you to create documents called presentations, which are used to communicate ideas, messages, and other information to a group. The presentations can be viewed as slides, sometimes called a **slide show**, that display on a large monitor or on a projection screen (Figure 3-20).

Presentation graphics software typically provides a variety of predefined presentation formats that define complementary colors for backgrounds, text, and other items on the slides. This software also provides a variety of layouts for each individual slide such as a title slide, a two-column slide, and a slide with clip art, a chart, or a table. You can enhance any text, charts, and graphical images on a slide with 3-D and other special effects such as shading, shadows, and textures.

Presentation graphics software typically includes a clip gallery, allowing you to create multimedia presentations. A **clip gallery** includes clip art images, pictures, video clips, and audio clips. A clip gallery can be stored on your hard disk, a CD-ROM, or a DVD-ROM. In some cases, you access the clip gallery on the Web. As with clip art collections, a clip gallery typically

is organized by categories that can include academic, business, entertainment, transportation, and so on. For example, the Healthcare & Medicine category may contain a clip art image of a treadmill, a photograph of a person jogging, a video clip of a person exercising, and an audio clip of a heartbeat.

If you have an artistic ability, you can create clip art and other graphics using Paint or a similar application. Then, you **import** (bring in) the clip art into the slide. Once you insert or import a clip art image or other graphical image into a document, you can move it, resize it, rotate it, crop it, and adjust its color.

When building a presentation, you also can set the slide timing so the presentation automatically displays the next slide after a preset delay. Presentation graphics software allows you to apply special effects to the transition between each slide. One slide, for example, might fade away slowly as the next slide displays.

To help organize the presentation, you can view small versions of all the slides in slide sorter view (Figure 3-21). Slide sorter view presents a screen view similar to how 35mm slides would look on a photographer's light table. The slide sorter allows you to arrange the slides in any order.

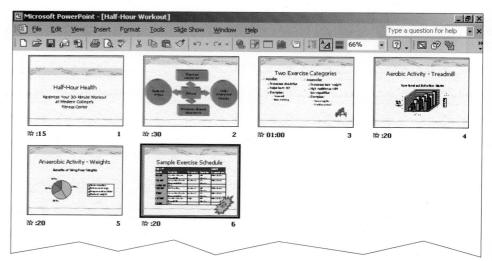

Figure 3-21 Slide sorter view shows a small version of each slide. Using a device, such as the mouse or the keyboard, you can rearrange the slides to change the sequence of the presentation.

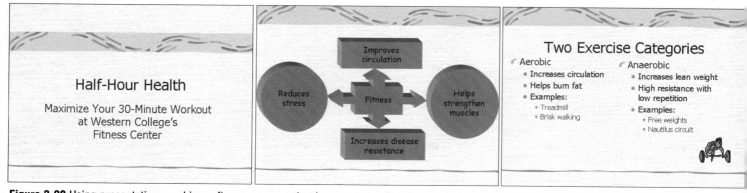

Figure 3-20 Using presentation graphics software, you can develop a presentation that can be projected onto a screen or displayed on a large monitor. This presentation consists of six slides.

Once a presentation is created, you can view or print the presentation as slides or in several other formats. An outline includes only the text from each slide such as the slide title and the key points (Figure 3-22a). Audience handouts include images of two or more slides on a page that you can distribute to audience members (Figure 3-22b). Speakers sometimes print a notes page to help them deliver the presentation. A notes page shows a picture of the slide along with any additional notes a presenter wants to see while discussing a topic or slide (Figure 3-22c).

Presentation graphics software incorporates some of the features found in word processing software such as checking spelling, formatting, recognizing voice input, and converting an existing slide show into a format for the World Wide Web.

Figure 3-22a (outline of presentation)

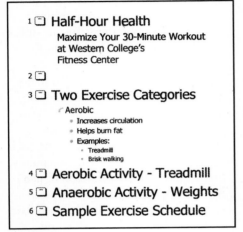

Figure 3-22c (notes page for speaker)

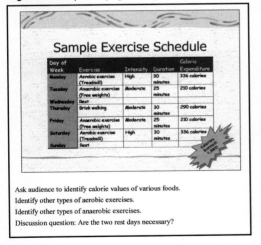

Figure 3-22b (audience handouts)

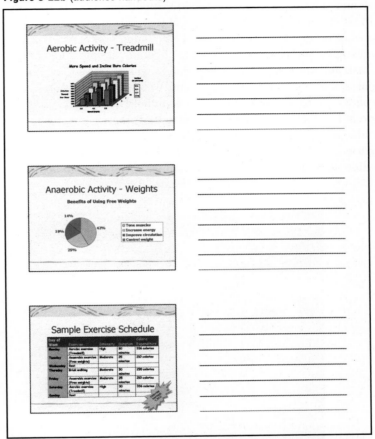

Figure 3-22 In addition to viewing the presentation as slides, presentation graphics packages allow you to view or print the presentation as an outline, as audience handouts, or as notes pages for the speaker.

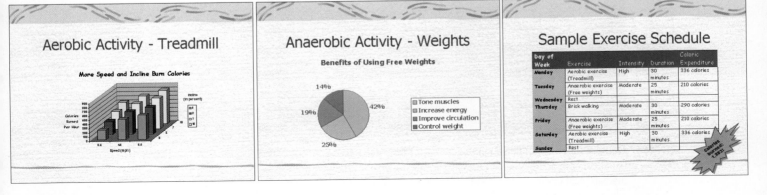

Personal Information Managers

A **personal information manager** (**PIM**) is a software application that includes an appointment calendar, address book, notepad, and other features to help you organize personal information. A PIM allows you to take information previously tracked in a weekly or daily calendar, and organize and store it on your computer. PIMs can manage many different types of information such as telephone messages, project notes, reminders, task and address lists, important dates, and appointments.

PIMs offer a range of capabilities. Most include at least an appointment calendar, address book, and notepad. An **appointment calendar** allows you to schedule activities for a

particular day and time. With an **address book**, you can enter and maintain names, addresses, and telephone numbers of customers, co-workers, family members, and friends. Instead of writing notes on a piece of paper, you can use a **notepad** to record ideas, reminders, and other important information.

Most handheld computers have PIM functions, as well as many other features. These features often include a calculator, simple word processing application, simple spreadsheet application, games, e-mail capabilities, and Web browsing capabilities. Using a handheld computer, you can **synchronize**, or transfer information between the handheld computer and a desktop computer so the same information is available on both computers (Figure 3-23).

Software Suite

A software **suite** is a collection of individual applications sold as a single package. When you install the suite, you install the entire collection of applications at once instead of installing each application individually. At a minimum, productivity suites typically include the following software applications: word processing, spreadsheet, database, and presentation graphics. Two popular software suites are Microsoft Office and Lotus SmartSuite.

Software suites offer two major advantages: lower cost and ease of use. Buying a collection of software packages in a suite usually costs significantly less than purchasing each of the application packages separately. Software suites provide ease of use because the applications within a suite normally use a similar interface and have some common features. Once you learn how to use one application in the suite, you are familiar with the interface in the other applications in the suite. For example, once you learn how to print using the suite's word processing package, you can apply the same skill to the spreadsheet, database, and presentation graphics software in the suite.

handheld computer

Figure 3-23 Most handheld computers have PIM functions. With most handheld computers, you can synchronize or transfer information from the handheld computer to your desktop computer, so your appointments, address lists, and other important information always are available.

Project Management Software

Project management software allows you to plan, schedule, track, and analyze the events, resources, and costs of a project (Figure 3-24). A general contractor, for example, might use project management software to manage a home-remodeling schedule. A publisher might use it to coordinate the process of producing a textbook.

Project management software helps users track, control, and manage project variables, allowing them to complete a project on time and within budget.

Accounting Software

Accounting software helps companies record and report their financial transactions (Figure 3-25). With accounting software, small and large business users perform accounting activities related to the general ledger, accounts receivable, accounts payable, purchasing, invoicing, job costing, and payroll functions. Accounting software also enables users to write and print checks, track checking account activity, and update and reconcile balances on demand.

Newer accounting software packages support online direct deposit and payroll services. These services make it possible for a company to deposit paychecks directly into employee's checking accounts and pay employee taxes electronically.

Some accounting software offers more complex features such as multiple company reporting, foreign currency reporting, and forecasting the amount of raw materials needed for products. The cost of accounting software for small businesses ranges from less than one hundred to several thousand dollars. Accounting software for large businesses can cost several hundred thousand dollars.

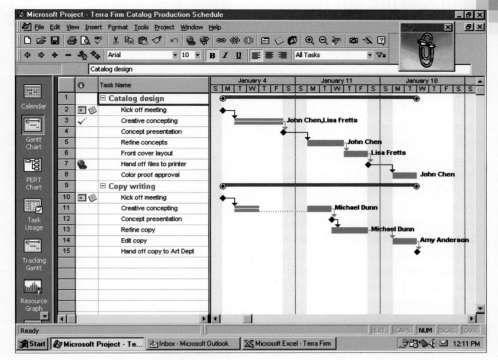

Figure 3-24 Project management software allows you to plan, schedule, track, and analyze the events, resources, and costs of a project.

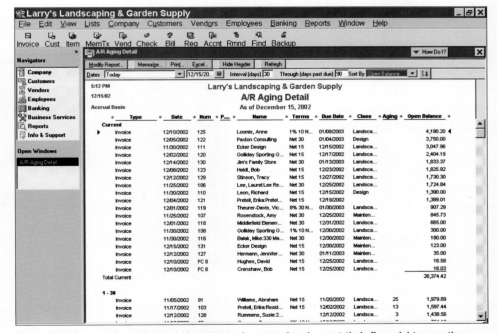

Figure 3-25 Accounting software helps companies record and report their financial transactions.

GRAPHICS AND MULTIMEDIA SOFTWARE

In addition to productivity software, many people work with software designed specifically for their field of work. Power users such as engineers, architects, desktop publishers, and graphic artists often use sophisticated software that allows them to work with graphics and multimedia. This software includes computer-aided design, desktop publishing, paint/image editing, video and audio editing, multimedia authoring, and Web page authoring. Figure 3-26 lists the more popular products for each of these applications. Some of these products incorporate user-friendly interfaces, so the home and small business user also can create documents in these applications.

The following sections discuss the features and functions of these applications.

Computer-Aided Design

Computer-aided design (CAD) software is a sophisticated type of application software that assists a professional user in creating engineering, architectural, and scientific designs. For example, engineers can create design plans for airplanes and security systems. Architects can design building structures and floor plans. Scientists can design drawings of molecular structures.

CAD software eliminates the laborious manual drafting that design processes can require. With CAD, designers can make changes to a drawing or design and immediately view the results. Three-dimensional CAD programs allow designers to rotate designs of 3-D objects to view them from any angle (Figure 3-27). Some CAD software even can generate material lists for building designs.

Some manufacturers of CAD software sell a scaled-down product that is designed for the home user or small business user.

POPULAR GRAPHICS AND MULTIMEDIA SOFTWARE PACKAGES

Software Application	Popular Packages
Computer-Aided Design (CAD)	• Autodesk AutoCAD • Microsoft Visio Technical
Desktop Publishing (Professional)	• Adobe InDesign • Adobe PageMaker • Corel VENTURA • QuarkXPress
Paint/Image Editing (Professional)	• Adobe Illustrator • Adobe Photoshop • CorelDRAW • Macromedia FreeHand
Video and Audio Editing	• Adobe Premiere • Ulead Systems MediaStudio Pro
Multimedia Authoring	• click2learn.com ToolBook • Macromedia Authorware • Macromedia Director
Web Page Authoring	• Adobe GoLive • Lotus FastSite • Macromedia Dreamweaver • Macromedia Flash • Microsoft FrontPage

Figure 3-26 Popular graphics and multimedia software products.

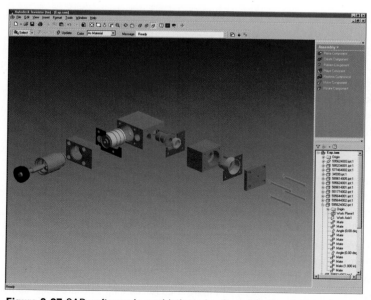

Figure 3-27 CAD software is sophisticated software that assists engineers, architects, and scientists in creating designs.

Desktop Publishing Software (Professional)

Desktop publishing (DTP) software enables professional designers to design and produce sophisticated documents that contain text, graphics, and brilliant colors (Figure 3-28). Professional DTP software is ideal for the production of high-quality color documents such as textbooks, corporate newsletters, marketing literature, product catalogs, and annual reports. In the past, documents of this type were created by slower, more expensive traditional publishing methods such as typesetting. Today's DTP software allows you to convert a color document into a format for use on the World Wide Web.

Although many word processing packages have some of the capabilities of DTP software, professional designers and graphic artists use DTP software because it supports page layout. **Page layout** is the process of arranging text and graphics in a document on a page-by-page basis.

With DTP software, users can add text and graphical images directly into the document or import existing text and graphics from other files. For example, text from a word processing file can be imported into a DTP document. Graphics files such as illustrations and photographs also can be imported into a DTP document. Another alternative is to use a scanner to convert printed graphics such as photographs and drawings into files that DTP software can use.

Once an artist or designer has created or inserted a graphical image into a document, the DTP software can crop, sharpen, and change the colors in the image by adding tints or percentages of colors. DTP software packages include color libraries to assist in color selections for graphical images and text. A **color library** is a standard set of colors used by designers and printers to ensure that colors will print exactly as specified.

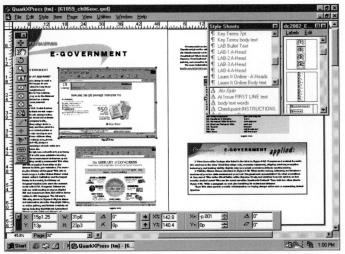

Figure 3-28 Professional designers and graphic artists use DTP software to produce sophisticated publications such as textbooks, marketing literature, product catalogs, and annual reports.

Paint/Image Editing Software (Professional)

Graphic artists, multimedia professionals, technical illustrators, and desktop publishers use paint software and image editing software to create and modify graphical images such as those used in DTP documents and Web pages. **Paint software**, sometimes called **illustration software**, allows these users to draw pictures, shapes, and other graphical images with various on-screen tools such as a pen, brush, eyedropper, and paint bucket. **Image editing software** provides the capabilities of paint software as well as the capability to modify existing images (Figure 3-29). For example, you can retouch photographs, adjust or enhance image colors, and add special effects such as shadows and glows.

Web Link

For more information on paint/image editing software, visit the Discovering Computers 2002 Chapter 3 WEB LINK page (**scsite.com/dc2002/ch3/weblink.htm**) and click Paint/Image Editing Software.

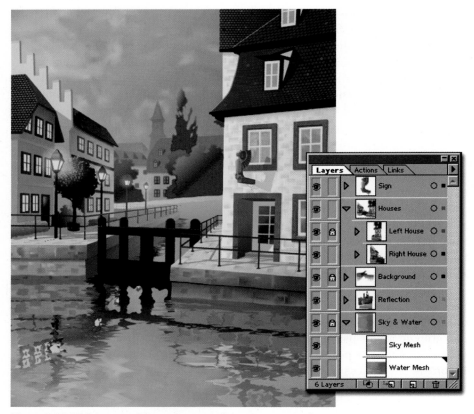

Figure 3-29 With image editing software, artists can create and modify a variety of graphic images.

Image Altering

Paint and Image Editing Software

Today, many photojournalists, commercial artists, creators of cartoons, book covers, and billboards designers use paint and image editing software. With this software, an artist can convert photographs to a digital form that can be colorized, stretched, squeezed, texturized, or otherwise altered. They can import graphics files and manipulate the images in ways that previously were unachievable. For example, you can add clouds to a blue sky, or manipulate a picture of a person so it appears the person is standing in front of the Great Pyramids of Egypt. The National Press Photographers Association endorses the following: "As [photo] journalists we believe the guiding principle of our profession is accuracy; therefore, we believe it is wrong to alter the content of a photograph in any way, electronically or in the darkroom, that deceives the public." Do you agree with this guideline? Should professional graphic artists be able to alter photographs or other existing illustrations with paint and image editing software? Is it ethical? Is altering someone else's photograph a copyright issue?

For more information on paint and image editing software and photograph altering, visit the Discovering Computers 2002 Issues Web page (**scsite.com/dc2002/issues.htm**) and click Chapter 3 Issue #2.

Video and Audio Editing Software

Video consists of full-motion images played back at various speeds. With **video editing software** (Figure 3-30), you can modify a segment of a video, called a clip. For example, you can reduce the length of a video clip, reorder a series of clips, or add special effects such as words that move horizontally across the screen. Video editing software typically includes audio editing capabilities.

Audio is any music, speech, or other sound stored and produced by the computer. With **audio editing software**, you can modify audio clips and produce studio quality soundtracks. Audio editing software usually includes filters, which are designed to enhance audio quality. A filter might remove a distracting background noise from the audio clip.

Some operating systems include audio editing and video editing capabilities. These operating systems give the home user the ability to edit home movies and share clips on the Web.

Multimedia Authoring Software

Multimedia authoring software, sometimes called **authorware**, allows you to combine text, graphics, audio, video, and animation into an interactive presentation (Figure 3-31). With this software, you can control the placement of text and images and the duration of sounds, video, and animation. Once created, multimedia presentations often take the form of interactive computer-based presentations or Web-based presentations designed to facilitate learning and elicit direct student participation. Multimedia presentations usually are stored and delivered via a CD-ROM or DVD-ROM, over a local area network, or via the Internet. The Multimedia special feature following Chapter 6 discusses multimedia authoring software in more depth.

Web Page Authoring Software

As discussed in Chapter 2, Web page authoring software helps users of all skill levels create fascinating Web pages that include graphical images, video, audio, animation, and other special effects. In addition, many Web page authoring packages allow users to organize, manage, and maintain Web sites.

Many application software packages include Web page authoring features. This allows home users to create basic Web pages using packages such as Microsoft Word or Microsoft Excel. For more sophisticated Web pages, users work with Web page authoring software. Many Web page developers also use multimedia authoring software along with, or instead of, Web page authoring software for Web page development.

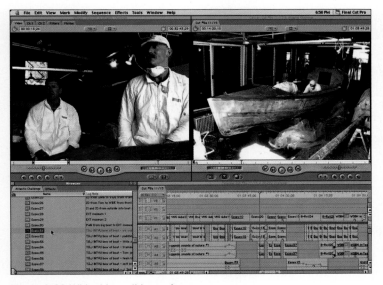

Figure 3-30 With video editing software, users can modify video images.

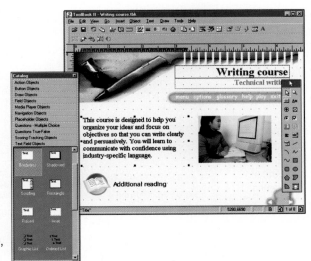

Figure 3-31 Multimedia authoring software allows you to create dynamic presentations that include text, graphics, audio, video, and animation.

SOFTWARE FOR HOME, PERSONAL, AND EDUCATIONAL USE

Many software applications are designed specifically for use at home or for personal or educational use. Integrated software is an example of a package for the home user that includes word processing, spreadsheet, database, and other software in a single package. Other packages for home, personal, and educational use include applications for finance, legal, tax preparation, desktop publishing, paint image/editing, clip art/image gallery, home design/landscaping, educational, reference, and entertainment.

Most of the products in this category are relatively inexpensive, often priced less than $100. Figure 3-32 lists popular software packages for many of these applications. The following sections discuss the features and functions of these applications.

POPULAR SOFTWARE PACKAGES FOR HOME/PERSONAL/EDUCATIONAL USE

Software Application	Popular Packages
Integrated Software	• Microsoft Works
Personal Finance	• Intuit Quicken • Microsoft Money
Legal	• E-Z Legal Advisor • Kiplinger's WILL Power • Nolo WillMaker
Tax Preparation	• Intuit TurboTax • Kiplinger TaxCut
Desktop Publishing (Personal)	• Broderbund Print Shop Pro Publisher • Microsoft Publisher
Paint/Image Editing (Personal)	• Adobe PhotoDeluxe • Broderbund Print Shop • Corel PHOTO-PAINT • Jasc Paint Shop Pro • Microsoft PhotoDraw • Microsoft Picture It! Photo
Clip Art/Image Gallery	• Corel GALLERY • Nova Development Art Explosion
Home Design/Landscaping	• Bob Vila's Home Design • Broderbund 3D Home Design Suite • Quality Plans Complete LandDesign
Reference	• Compton's American Heritage Talking Dictionary • Microsoft Encarta • Microsoft Pocket Streets • Microsoft Streets & Trips • Rand McNally StreetFinder • Rand McNally TripMaker

Figure 3-32 Popular software products for home, personal, and educational use.

APPLY IT!
Office and the Web

If you want to create a Web page, but do not have the time to learn HTML, then consider using one of the Office applications. Word, for instance, provides two techniques for creating Web pages. You can save an existing document as a Web page or you can use the Web Page Wizard.

To save an existing document as a Web page:
- Start Word and open the document.
- Click File on the menu bar and then click Save as Web Page.
- When the Save As dialog box displays, type the file name in the File name text box.
- Click the Change Title button, type a title name, and then click the OK button. This name displays in the browser's title bar. Many search engines use the title for cataloging Web pages, so the title should be as descriptive as possible.

By asking you a series of questions, the Web Page Wizard designs a Web page that can contain frames. A frame is a rectangular section of a Web page that can display another separate Web page. A Web page that contains frames can display multiple Web pages simultaneously on the same screen. If you wish to create a Web page that contains frames, use the Word Help system for assistance on using the Web Page Wizard.

Once you have created Web pages, you can publish them. Publishing is the process of making Web pages available to others, for example on the World Wide Web. Using the Office applications, you can publish Web pages by saving them to a Web folder or to an FTP location.

All Office applications provide options for saving files as Web pages. Word, however, is the only application that provides the Web Page Wizard.

For more information on using Office to create Web pages, visit the Discovering Computers 2002 Apply It Web page (**scsite.com/dc2002/apply.htm**) and click Chapter 3 Apply It #3.

Integrated Software

Integrated software is software that combines applications such as word processing, spreadsheet, and database into a single, easy-to-use package. Like a software suite, the applications within the integrated software package use a similar interface and share some common features. Once you learn how to use one application in the integrated software package, you are familiar with the interface in the other applications.

Unlike a software suite, however, you cannot purchase the applications in the integrated software package individually. Each application in an integrated software package is available only through the integrated software package.

The applications within the integrated software package typically do not have all the capabilities of stand-alone productivity software applications such as Microsoft Word and Microsoft Excel. Integrated software thus is less expensive than a more powerful software suite. For many home and personal users, however, the capabilities of an integrated software package more than meet their needs.

Personal Finance Software

Personal finance software is a simplified accounting program that helps home users and small office/home office users balance their checkbook, pay bills, track personal income and expenses, track investments, and evaluate financial plans (Figure 3-33). Using personal finance software can help you determine where, and for what purpose, you are spending money so you can manage your finances. Reports can

Web Link

For more information on personal finance software, visit the Discovering Computers 2002 Chapter 3 WEB LINK page (**scsite.com/dc2002/ch3/ weblink.htm**) and click Personal Finance Software.

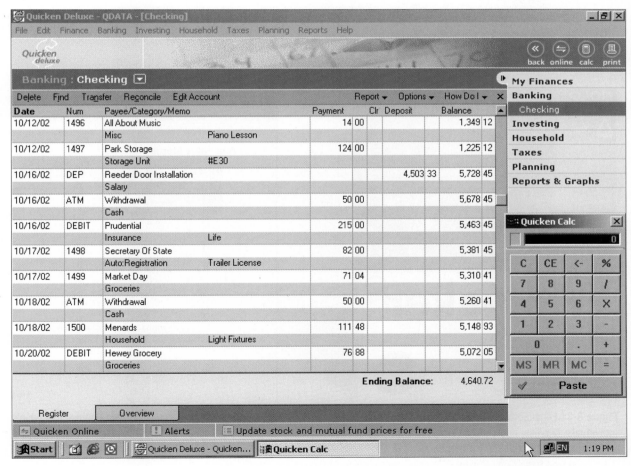

Figure 3-33 Many home users work with personal finance software to assist them with balancing their checkbook and paying bills.

summarize transactions by category (such as dining), by payee (such as the electric company), or by time period (such as the last two months).

Most of these packages offer a variety of online services, which require access to the Web. For example, you can track your investments online, compare insurance rates from leading insurance companies, and even do online banking. With **online banking**, you transfer money electronically from your checking or credit card accounts to payees' accounts. You also can download monthly transactions and statements from the Web right into your computer.

Financial planning features include analyzing home and personal loans, preparing income taxes, and managing retirement savings. Other features found in many personal finance packages include home inventory, budgeting, and tax preparation.

Legal Software

Legal software assists in the preparation of legal documents and provides legal advice to individuals, families, and small businesses (Figure 3-34). Legal software provides standard contracts and documents associated with buying, selling, and renting property; estate planning; marriage and divorce; and preparing a will or living trust. By answering a series of questions or completing a form, the legal software tailors the legal document to your needs.

Once the legal document is created, you can file the paperwork with the appropriate agency, court, or office; or you can take the document to your attorney for his or her review and signature. Before using one of these software packages to create a document, you may want to check with your local bar association for its legality.

Tax Preparation Software

Tax preparation software guides individuals, families, or small businesses through the process of filing federal taxes (Figure 3-35). These software packages offer money saving tax tips, designed to lower your tax bill. After you answer a series of questions and complete basic forms, the software creates and analyzes your tax forms to search for missed potential errors and deduction opportunities.

Once the forms are complete, you can print any necessary paperwork, completed and ready for you to file. Some tax preparation packages even allow you to file your tax forms electronically.

Desktop Publishing (Personal)

Instead of using professional DTP software (as discussed earlier in this chapter), many home and small

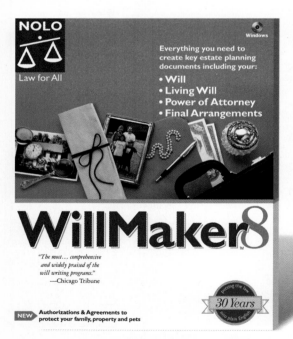

Figure 3-34 Legal software provides legal advice to individuals, families, and small businesses and assists in the preparation of legal documents.

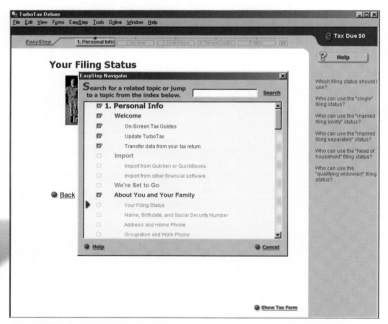

Figure 3-35 Tax preparation software guides individuals, families, or small businesses through the process of filing federal taxes.

business users utilize much simpler, easy-to-understand DTP software designed for smaller-scale desktop publishing projects (Figure 3-36). Using **personal DTP software**, you can create newsletters, brochures, and advertisements; postcards and greeting cards; letterhead and business cards; banners, calendars, and logos; and Web pages.

Personal DTP software packages provide hundreds of thousands of graphical images. You also can import your own digital photographs into the documents. These packages typically guide you through the development of a document by asking a series of questions, offering numerous prede-fined layouts, and providing standard text you can add to documents. In some packages, as you enter text, the personal DTP software checks your spelling. Then, you can print your finished publications on a color printer or place them on the Web.

Many personal DTP packages also include paint/image editing software and photo-editing software.

Paint/Image Editing Software (Personal)

Personal paint/image editing software provides an easy-to-use interface, usually with more simplified capabilities than its professional counterpart, including functions tailored to meet the needs of the home and small business user.

Like the professional versions, personal paint software includes various simplified tools that allow you to draw pictures, shapes, and other images. Personal image editing soft-ware provides the capabilities of paint software and the capability of modify-ing existing graphics. These products also include many templates to assist you in adding an image to documents such as greeting cards, banners, calendars, signs, labels, business cards, and letterhead.

One popular type of image editing software, called **photo-editing software**, allows you to edit digital photographs by removing red-eye (Figure 3-37), adding special effects, or creating electronic photo albums. When the photograph is complete, you can print it on labels, calendars, business cards, and banners; or place it on a Web page. Some of these software packages allow you to send digital photographs to an **online print service**, which will send high-resolution printed images through the postal service. Many have a photo community where you can post photographs on the Web for others to view.

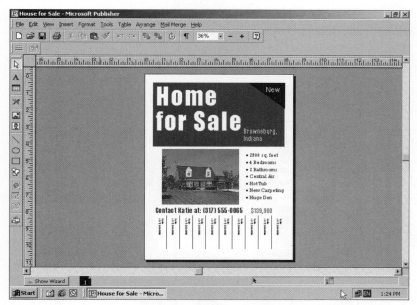

Figure 3-36 With Microsoft Publisher, home and small business users can create professional looking publications such as this announcement.

Figure 3-37 Photo-editing software allows the home user to remove red-eye from digital images.

Clip Art/Image Gallery

Many applications include a **clip art/image gallery**, which is a collection of clip art and photographs (Figure 3-38). Some applications have links to additional clips available on the Web. You also can purchase clip art/image galleries if you need a wider selection of images.

Figure 3-38 Many applications have a clip art/image gallery, such as the one shown in this figure, built in to the package.

In addition to clip art, many clip art/image galleries provide fonts, animations, sounds, video clips, and audio clips. You can use the images, fonts, and other items from the clip art/image gallery in all types of documents, including word processing, desktop publishing, spreadsheet, and presentation graphics.

Home Design/Landscaping Software

Homeowners or potential homeowners can use **home design/landscaping software** to assist with the design or remodeling of a home, deck, or landscape (Figure 3-39). Home design/landscaping software includes hundreds of predrawn plans which you can customize to meet your needs. Once designed, many home design/landscaping packages will print a material list outlining costs and quantities for the entire project.

Educational/Reference/Entertainment Software

Educational software is software that teaches a particular skill. Educational software exists for just about any subject, from learning a foreign language to learning how to cook. Preschool to high school learners also use educational software to assist them with subjects such as reading and math, or to prepare them for class or college entry exams.

Many educational software products use a computer-based training approach. **Computer-based training (CBT)**, also called **computer-aided instruction**, is a type of education in which students learn by using and completing exercises with instructional software. CBT typically consists of self-directed, self-paced instruction on a topic. CBT is popular in business, industry, and schools for teaching new skills or enhancing existing skills of employees, teachers, or students.

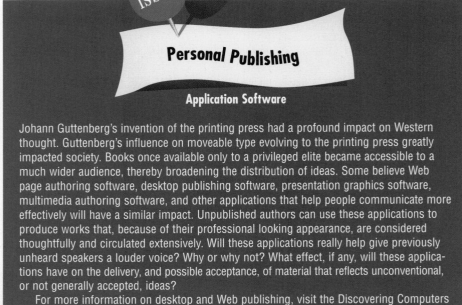

ISSUE

Personal Publishing

Application Software

Johann Guttenberg's invention of the printing press had a profound impact on Western thought. Guttenberg's influence on moveable type evolving to the printing press greatly impacted society. Books once available only to a privileged elite became accessible to a much wider audience, thereby broadening the distribution of ideas. Some believe Web page authoring software, desktop publishing software, presentation graphics software, multimedia authoring software, and other applications that help people communicate more effectively will have a similar impact. Unpublished authors can use these applications to produce works that, because of their professional looking appearance, are considered thoughtfully and circulated extensively. Will these applications really help give previously unheard speakers a louder voice? Why or why not? What effect, if any, will these applications have on the delivery, and possible acceptance, of material that reflects unconventional, or not generally accepted, ideas?

For more information on desktop and Web publishing, visit the Discovering Computers 2002 Issues Web page (**scsite.com/dc2002/issues.htm**) and click Chapter 3 Issue #3.

Reference software provides valuable and thorough information for all individuals (Figure 3-40). Popular reference software includes encyclopedias, dictionaries, health/medical guides, and travel directories.

Entertainment software for personal computers includes interactive games, videos, and other programs designed to support a hobby or provide amusement and enjoyment. For example, you can use entertainment software to play games, make a family tree, compose music, or fly an aircraft.

Web Link

For more information on reference software, visit the Discovering Computers 2002 Chapter 3 WEB LINK page (**scsite.com/dc2002/ch3/ weblink.htm**) and click Reference Software.

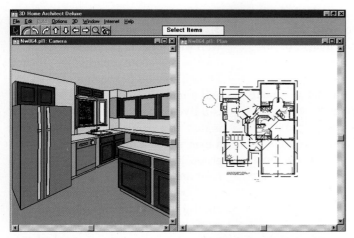

Figure 3-39 Home design/landscaping software can help you design or remodel a home, deck, or landscape.

Figure 3-40 Reference software provides valuable and thorough information for all types of users. This figure shows text you can read about evolution. It includes a variety of pictures, videos, and links to the Web.

ISSUE

How Young Is Too Young?

Educational Software

Software developed for elementary school children, kindergartners, and even preschoolers has won the praise of educators and child psychologists. Yet, controversy has erupted about how young is too young over Knowledge Adventure's® JumpStart Baby™ program, which targets children six- to twenty-four-months old. According to developers, JumpStart Baby™ makes even young children comfortable with computers. The software is tailored to tots and, supporters insist, certainly is more beneficial than an equal amount of time spent watching television. Knowledge Adventure® advocates the software is designed as lapware, meaning it is intended to be used by baby and parent together. It can serve as a springboard to stimulate activities rich in communications and social interaction during the critical developmental years. Critics feel, however, that digital blocks are not a substitute for the real thing. Children need to experience the real world, not a cyber representation. When should children be introduced to computers? Why? How can parents ensure that a child's computer experience is worthwhile?

For more information on children and software, visit the Discovering Computers 2002 Issues Web page (**scsite.com/dc2002/issues.htm**) and click Chapter 3 Issue #4.

SOFTWARE FOR COMMUNICATIONS

One of the main reasons people use computers is to communicate and share information with others. Home and business users have a variety of software options relative to communications. These include e-mail, Web browsers, chat rooms, newsgroups, instant messaging, groupware, and videoconferencing. Chapter 2 presented many of these products. The following sections briefly review these services.

Privacy at Work?

E-Mail

A recent survey indicates that more than 75 percent of Fortune 500 companies routinely monitor employee's e-mail and Web browsing habits. About one company in four has fired an employee based on their discoveries. Some companies even use automated software that searches e-mail messages for derogatory language. One unidentified woman, for example, was fired for using her office e-mail system to complain about her boss. Although she felt her e-mail conversations were private and would not be monitored, she learned, to her chagrin, that she was wrong. Do you think that employers have the right to monitor e-mail? Why or why not? If you knew that a fellow employee criticized the company through the e-mail system, would you tell your boss? What if you heard the same employee planning a theft of company products? Where do you draw the line?

For more information on employee monitoring, visit the Discovering Computers 2002 Issues Web page (**scsite.com/dc2002/issues.htm**) and click Chapter 3 Issue #5.

E-Mail

Today, e-mail quickly is becoming a primary communications method for both personal and business use. **E-mail** (**electronic mail**) is the transmission of messages via a computer network such as a local area network or the Internet. The message can be simple text or can include an attachment such as a word processing document, a graphical image, or an audio or video clip. You use **e-mail software** to create, send, receive, forward, store, print, and delete e-mail messages (see Figure 2-26 on page 2.30). Most e-mail software has a mail notification alert that informs via a message or sound that you have received new mail, even while you are working in another application.

Web Browsers

A software application called a **Web browser**, or **browser**, allows you to access and view Web pages on the Internet (see Figure 2-6 on page 2.9). Today's browsers have graphical user interfaces and are quite easy to learn and use. Browsers have many special features including buttons and navigation to help guide you through Web sites. In addition to displaying Web pages, most browsers allow you to use other Internet services such as e-mail and chat rooms.

Chat Rooms

A **chat room** permits users to chat with each other via the computer (see Figure 2-32 on 2.35). As you type a line of text on your computer, your entered words display on the computer screens of other people in the same chat room. Chats typically are specific to a certain topic, such as computers or cooking. Some chat rooms support **voice chats** and **video chats**, where you hear and see others and they can hear or see you as you chat.

To start a chat session, you connect to a chat server through a chat client. A **chat client** is software on your computer. Most Web browsers include a chat client. If yours does not, you can download one from the Web.

Newsgroups

A **newsgroup**, also called a **discussion**, is an online area on the Web where users conduct written discussions about a particular subject. The difference between a chat room and a newsgroup is that a chat room is a live conversation. The newsgroup is not. To participate in a newsgroup, a user sends a message to the newsgroup. Other users in the newsgroup read and reply to the message.

Some newsgroups require you enter a user name and password to participate in a discussion. These types of newsgroups are used when messages are to be viewed only by authorized members, such as students taking a college course.

To participate in a newsgroup, you use a software program called a **newsreader**. Most browsers include a newsreader.

Instant Messaging

Instant messaging (**IM**) is a real-time communications service that notifies you when one or more people are online and then allows you to exchange messages or files with them or join a private chat room (see Figure 2-33 on page 2.36). Many IM services also can alert you to information such as calendar appointments, stock quotes, weather, or sports scores. People use IM on all types of computers, including desktop computers, notebook computers, handheld computers, and Web-enabled devices.

To use IM, you install software from an instant messaging service, sometimes called an **instant messenger**, onto the computer or device with which you wish to use IM. No standards currently exist for IM. Thus, you and all those individuals on your notification list need to use the same or a compatible instant messenger to guarantee successful communications.

Groupware

Groupware is a software application that helps groups of people work together and share information over a network. To assist with these activities, most groupware provides PIM (personal information manager) functions, such as an address book and appointment calendar. A major feature of groupware is group scheduling, in which a group calendar tracks the schedules of multiple users and helps coordinate appointments and meeting times.

Videoconferencing

A **videoconference** is a meeting between two or more geographically separated people who use a network or the Internet to transmit audio and video data (see Figure 1-44 on page 1.34). A videoconference allows participants to collaborate as if they were in the same room.

To participate in a videoconference, you need videoconferencing software along with a microphone, speakers, and a video camera attached to your computer. As you speak, members of the meeting hear your voice on their speakers. Any image in front of the video camera, such as a person's face, displays in a window on each participant's screen.

Using a similar technology, home users today can make a **video telephone call**, where both parties see each other as they talk.

APPLICATIONS ON THE WEB

As discussed in Chapter 1, you often purchase packaged software from a software vendor, retail store, or Web-based business. In this case, you usually install the software onto your computer before you can run it. Using packaged software has the disadvantages of requiring disk space on your computer and being costly to upgrade as vendors release new versions. Realizing these disadvantages,

some companies today offer products and services on the Web. A **Web application** is a software application that exists on a Web site. Some Web application sites also store your data and information at their site.

To access a Web application, you simply visit the Web site that offers the program. Some Web sites provide access to the program for free. For example, one site creates a map and driving directions when you enter a starting and destination point (Figure 3-41).

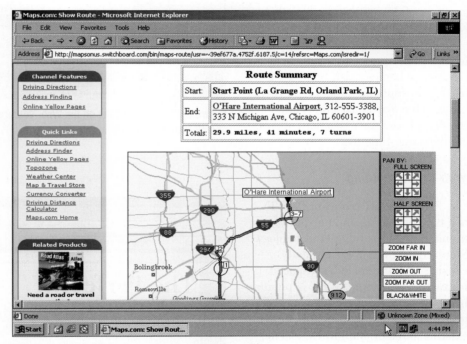

Figure 3-41 This Web site creates a map and provides directions when you enter a starting and destination point.

Other Web sites allow you to use the program for free and pay a fee when a certain action occurs. For example, you can prepare your tax return for free using TurboTax on the Web (Figure 3-42), but if you elect to file it electronically, you pay a small fee (under $10).

Some companies, instead, charge only for service and support — allowing you to use or download the software for free (Figure 3-43). Microsoft's Web applications, called **.NET,** enable users to access Microsoft software on the Web from any type of device or computer that can connect to the Internet.

For those sites that charge for use of the program, a variety of payment schemes exist. Some rent use of the application on a monthly basis, some charge based on the number of user accesses, and others charge a one-time fee.

Web-Based Training

Web-based training (WBT) is a type of CBT (computer-based training) that uses Internet technology. Similarly to CBT, WBT typically consists of self-directed, self-paced instruction on a topic. WBT is popular in business, industry, and schools for teaching new skills or enhancing existing skills of employees, teachers, or students. When using a WBT product, students actively become involved in the learning process instead of passive recipients of information.

Many Web sites offer WBT to the general public. Such training covers a wide range of topics, from how to change a flat tire to creating documents in Word. Many of these Web sites are free. Others ask you to register and pay a fee to take the complete Web-based course.

Figure 3-42 With TurboTax on the Web, you prepare your taxes for free but pay a small fee if you elect to file them electronically.

Figure 3-43 Sun Microsystems only charges for service and support of its StarOffice™ product, which is an integrated word processing, spreadsheet, presentation graphics, database, photo-editing, personal information manager, and communications suite.

WBT often is combined with other materials for distance learning courses. **Distance learning (DL)**, also called **distance education (DE)** or **online learning**, is the delivery of education at one location while the learning takes place at other locations. DL courses provide many time, distance, and place advantages for students who live far from a college campus or work full time. These courses enable students to attend class from anywhere in the world and at times that fit their schedule. Many national and international companies offer DL training. These training courses eliminate the costs of airfare, hotels, and meals for centralized training sessions.

Some Web-based companies specialize in providing instructors with the tools for preparation, distribution, and management of DL courses (Figure 3-44). These tools enable instructors to create rich, educational Web-based training sites and allow the students to interact with a powerful Web learning environment. Through the training site, students can check their progress, take practice tests, search for topics, send e-mail, and participate in discussions and chats. The appeal of these products is they generally are quite easy to learn and use for both the instructors and the students.

Application Service Providers

Storing and maintaining programs can be a costly investment for businesses. Thus, some have elected to outsource one or more facets of their information technology (IT) needs to an application service provider. An **application service provider (ASP)** is a third-party organization that manages and distributes software and services on the Web. For example, Metier is an ASP that provides project management software on the Web (Figure 3-45).

Figure 3-44 WebCT is a tool that enables instructors to create Web-based training courses.

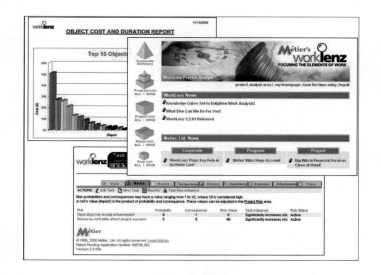

Figure 3-45 WorkLenz is project management software offered by Metier, an application service provider. Using WorkLenz, customers can pinpoint inefficiencies in processes.

Web Link

For more information on distance learning, visit the Discovering Computers 2002 Chapter 3 WEB LINK page (**scsite.com/dc2002/ch3/ weblink.htm**) and click Distance Learning.

Five categories of ASPs have emerged:

- Enterprise ASP: customizes and delivers high-end business applications, such as finance and database
- Local/Regional ASP: offers a variety of software applications to a specific geographic region
- Specialist ASP: delivers applications to meet a specific business need, such as preparing taxes
- Vertical Market ASP: provides applications for a particular industry, such as construction or healthcare
- Volume Business ASP: supplies prepackaged applications, such as accounting, to businesses

Despite the advantages, some companies will wait to outsource to an ASP until they have faster Internet connections.

LEARNING AIDS AND SUPPORT TOOLS WITHIN AN APPLICATION

Learning how to use an application software package effectively involves time and practice. To assist you in the learning process, many software applications provide online Help, links to FAQs, and wizards (Figure 3-46).

Online Help is the electronic equivalent of a user manual. It usually is integrated into an application software package. Online Help provides assistance that can increase your productivity and reduce your frustrations by minimizing the time you spend learning how to use an application software package.

In most packages, a function key or a button on the screen starts the Help feature. When you are using an application and have a question, you can use the Help feature to ask a question or access the Help topics in subject or alphabetical order. Often the Help is **context-sensitive**, meaning that the Help information relates to the current task being attempted. Most online Help also points you to Web sites that provide updates and more comprehensive resources to answer your software questions. These Web sites usually have a **FAQs** (Frequently Asked Questions) page to help you find answers to common questions.

In many cases, online Help has replaced the user manual altogether. Most software developers no longer

Figure 3-46a (online Help)

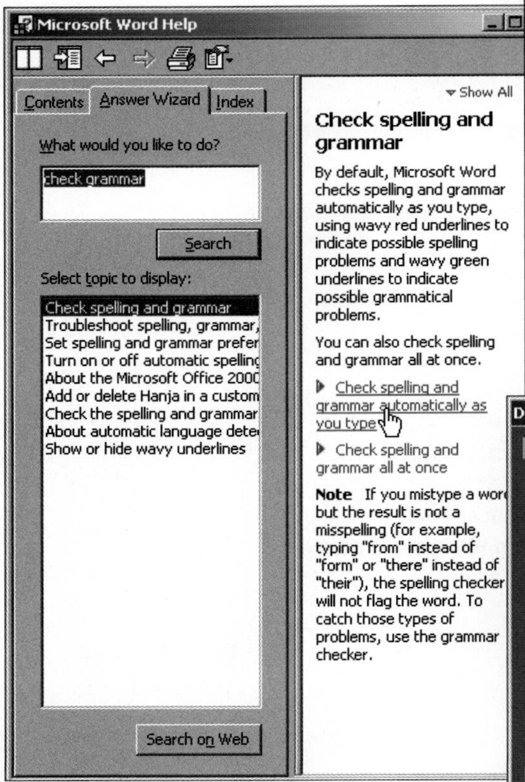

Figure 3-46b (FAQ)

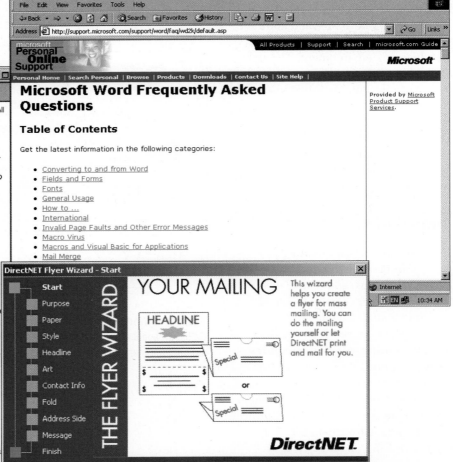

Figure 3-46 Many software applications include online Help, links to FAQs, and wizards.

Figure 3-46c (wizard)

include user's manuals with the software. If you want to learn more about the software package from a printed manual, however, many books are available to help you learn to use the features of personal computer application packages (Figure 3-47). These books typically are available in bookstores and software stores.

A **wizard** is an automated assistant that helps you complete a task by asking you questions and then automatically performing actions based on your answers. Many software applications include wizards. For example, word processing software uses wizards to help you create memorandums, meeting agendas, fax cover sheets, flyers, letters, and resumes. Spreadsheet software includes chart and function wizards. Database software has form and report wizards.

Many colleges and schools provide training on several of the applications discussed in this chapter. If you would like more direction than is provided in online Help, FAQs, wizards, and trade books, contact your local school for a list of class offerings.

CHAPTER SUMMARY

This chapter discussed the role of the system software with respect to application software. It then presented an overview of several productivity software applications, graphic design/multimedia software applications, home/personal/educational software applications, and communications software applications. The chapter identified various Web applications. Finally, learning aids and supports tools within application software products were presented.

Career Corner

Word Processing Technician

Someone with word processing skills can look for career opportunities as a word processing technician or specialist. Other job titles that involve word processing may include word processing operator, clerk typist, general office clerk, data entry clerk, billing clerk, or file clerk. Job responsibilities may include the following:

- Prepares word processing materials that include correspondence, reports, brochures, and other documents.
- Formats and proofreads materials and makes corrections or changes as directed.
- Maintains filing system based on departmental needs as applicable to word processing procedures.

As a word processing technician, you generally work with a team of people. Word processing operators may find employment opportunities in a wide variety of office settings that include business, industry, government agencies, and non-profit agencies. Generally, a high school diploma is the minimum requirement. Entry-level salaries range from $15,000 to $30,000. Microsoft offers the Microsoft Office Users Specialist (MOUS) certification designed to measure and validate users' skills. Those individuals with more experience and advanced skills may find opportunities as word processing supervisors and office supervisors.

To learn more about the field of word processing as a career, visit the Discovering Computers 2002 Careers Web page (**scsite.com/dc2002/careers.htm**) and click Word Processing Technician.

Figure 3-47 Many bookstores sell trade books to help you learn to use the features of personal computer application packages.

E-FINANCE

KA-CHING, KA-CHING

Cashing In on Financial Advice

"Money makes the world go 'round," according to Liza Minnelli and her friends in the 1972 hit musical, *Cabaret*. If that musical were written today, the lyrics would be updated to "Money makes the World Wide Web go 'round," based on the volume of financial Web sites available to Internet users.

When Doug Lebda became thoroughly disgusted with all the red tape he encountered trying to apply for a home mortgage, he took matters into his own hands. He started LendingTree, a Web site that helps consumers conveniently obtain mortgages, loans, and credit cards, as shown in Figure 3-54. This Web site and a growing number of other Internet companies work with hundreds of national lenders to match consumers' needs with the marketplaces' lenders. One of the fastest-growing online banks is Wells Fargo (Figure 3-55), with a Web site that features online banking, tax help, and wanted posters of people who have defrauded the bank.

If you do not have a personal banker or a financial planner, consider a Web adviser to guide your investment decisions. Three highly recognized financial Web

Figure 3-54 Online lending Web sites can help consumers seeking assistance with financial matters, including obtaining loans or comparing mortgage rates.

FINANCE WEB SITES	URL
Advice and Education	
MSN MoneyCentral	moneycentral.msn.com
The Motley Fool	fool.com
Yahoo Finance	finance.yahoo.com
Bankrate.com	bankrate.com
E-Loan	loan.com
LendingTree	lendingtree.com
Wells Fargo	wellsfargo.com
Stock Market	
DLJdirect	dljdirect.com
E*TRADE	etrade.com
Financial Engines	financialengines.com
FreeEdgar	www.freeedgar.com
Merrill Lynch Direct	mldirect.ml.com
MeVC	mevc.com
Morningstar	morningstar.com
Vanguard Group	vanguard.com
Taxes	
IRS - The Digital Daily	www.irs.gov
H&R Block	hrblock.com

For an updated list of finance Web sites, visit scsite.com/dc2002/e-rev.htm.

Figure 3-55 Financial resources Web sites offer general information, stock market analyses, and tax advice, as well as guidance and tips.

sites are MSN MoneyCentral, Yahoo Finance, and The Motley Fool (Figure 3-56) for commentary and education on investing strategies, financial news, and taxes.

You likely have heard stories of people who have made — and lost — their fortunes in the stock market. If you are ready to ride the ups and downs of the NASDAQ and the Dow, an abundance of Web sites can help you pick companies that fit your interests and financial needs. For example, FreeEdgar allows you to read company filings with the SEC. DLJdirect gives you the latest market news from Wall Street's Donaldson, Lufkin & Jenrette.

Figure 3-56 The Fool.com Web site contains strategies and news stories related to personal financing and investing.

Figure 3-57 Income tax forms, employment opportunities, and filing procedures and regulations are posted on the Internal Revenue Service THE DIGITAL DAILY Web page.

When April 15 rolls around, many taxpayers mutter the words, Internal Revenue Service. But the IRS can be a friend, too, when you visit, THE DIGITAL DAILY (Figure 3-57). Claiming to be the fastest, easiest tax publication on the planet, this Web page contains procedures for filing tax appeals, and contains IRS forms, publications, and legal regulations. H&R Block also offers tax information in its Tax Center.

For more information on financial Web sites, visit the Discovering Computers 2002 E-Revolution Web page (scsite.com/dc2002/e-rev.htm) and click Finance.

E·REVOLUTION E-FINANCE *applied:*

1. Visit the three advice and education Web sites listed in Figure 3-55 and read their top business world reports. Write a paragraph on each, summarizing these stories. Which stocks or mutual funds do these Web sites predict as being sound investments today? What are the current market indexes for the DJIA (Dow Jones Industrial Average), S&P 500, and NASDAQ, and how do these figures compare with the previous day's numbers?

2. Using two of the stock market Web sites listed in Figure 3-55, search for information about Microsoft, Adobe Systems, and one other software vendor discussed in this chapter. Write a paragraph on each of these stocks describing the revenues, net incomes, total assets for the previous year, current stock price per share, highest and lowest prices of each stock during the past year, and other relevant investment information.

Student Exercises   Web Links   In Summary   Key Terms   Learn It Online   Checkpoint   In The Lab   Web Work

Special Features   ■ TIMELINE 2002   ■ WWW & E-SKILLS   ■ MULTIMEDIA   ■ BUYER'S GUIDE 2002   ■ WIRELESS TECHNOLOGY   ■ TRENDS 2002   ■ INTERACTIVE LABS   ■ TECH NEWS

Web Instructions: To display this page from the Web, start your browser and enter the URL scsite.com/dc2002/ch3/summary.htm. Click the links for current and additional information. To listen to an audio version of this In Summary, click the Audio button. To play the audio, RealPlayer must be installed on your computer (download by clicking here).

1 What Is Application Software?

Application software, also called a **software application** or an **application**, consists of programs designed to perform specific tasks for users. Application software can be grouped into four major categories: productivity software; graphics design and multimedia software; home, personal, and educational software; and communications software.

2 How Does System Software Interact with Application Software?

System software controls the operations of the computer and its devices. It serves as the interface between the user, the application software, and the computer's hardware. The operating system, one type of system software, contains instructions that allow the user to run application software. The operating system must load from storage into the computer's memory before you can run any application software. A **utility** is a type of system program that performs a specific task.

3 What Is the Role of the User Interface?

Users interact with software through a user interface. Both the Microsoft Windows and the Apple Macintosh operating systems use the concept of a **graphical user interface (GUI)**. This type of interface combines text, graphics, and other visual images to make software easier to use.

4 How Do You Start a Software Application?

The desktop is an onscreen work area with common graphical elements such as **icons**, **buttons**, menus, links, windows, and dialog boxes. A software application can be started by clicking its program name on a **menu** or list of **commands**. Clicking the program name instructs the operating system to transfer the program's instructions from a storage medium into memory. Once started, the application displays in a window on the desktop. A **window** is a rectangular area of the screen used to show the program, data, and/or information.

5 What Are the Widely Used Products and Key Features of Productivity/Business Software Applications and Graphic Design/ Multimedia Software Applications?

Productivity software helps people become more effective and efficient while performing daily activities. **Word processing software** is used for **creating** and **editing** documents that consist primarily of text. In addition, you can **format** a document to improve its appearance and then print and save it to use again. **Spreadsheet software** organizes numeric data in a **worksheet** made up of rows and columns. **Database software** is used to create a **database**, which is an organized collection of data that can be accessed, retrieved, and used. **Presentation graphics software** creates documents called presentations that communicate ideas, messages, and other information to a group. A **personal information manager (PIM)** is software that includes an **appointment calendar**, **address book**, and **notepad** to help organize personal information. **Project management software** is used to plan, schedule, track, and analyze the progress of a project. **Accounting software** helps companies record and report their financial transactions.

Power users often use software that allows them to work with graphics and multimedia. **Computer-aided design (CAD) software** assists in creating engineering, architectural, and scientific designs. **Desktop publishing (DTP) software** is used in designing and producing sophisticated documents. **Paint software** is used to draw graphical images with various tools, while **image editing software** provides the capability of modifying existing images. **Video editing software** and **audio editing software** modify **video** and **audio** segments called clips.

DISCOVERING COMPUTERS 2002

Chapter 1 2 **3** 4 5 6 7 8 9 10 11 12 13 14 15 16 Index HOME 3.41

In Summary

SHELLY CASHMAN SERIES.

Student Exercises Web Links In Summary Key Terms Learn It Online Checkpoint In The Lab Web Work

Special Features ■ TIMELINE 2002 ■ WWW & E-SKILLS ■ MULTIMEDIA ■ BUYER'S GUIDE 2002 ■ WIRELESS TECHNOLOGY ■ TRENDS 2002 ■ INTERACTIVE LABS ■ TECH NEWS

Multimedia authoring software creates electronic interactive presentations that can include text, images, video, audio, and animation. Web page authoring software is designed to help users create Web pages and to organize, manage, and maintain Web sites.

6 What Are the Widely Used Products and Key Features of Home/Personal/Educational Software Applications and Communications Software Applications?

Many applications are designed for use at home, or for personal or educational use. **Integrated software** combines several productivity software applications into a single package. __Personal finance software__ is an accounting program that helps users pay bills, balance a checkbook, track income and expenses, follow investments, and evaluate financial plans. **Legal software** assists in the creation of legal documents and provides legal advice. **Tax preparation software** guides users through the process of filing federal taxes. **Personal DTP software** helps develop conventional documents by asking questions, offering predefined layouts, and providing standard text. **Photo-editing software** is used to edit digital photographs. A **clip art/image gallery** is a collection of clip art and photographs. **Home design/landscaping software** assists with design or remodeling a home, deck, or landscape. **Educational software** teaches a particular skill, **reference software** provides information, and **entertainment software** is designed to support a hobby or provide amusement.

One of the primary reasons people use computers is to communicate and share information. A variety of software options are available. **E-mail software** is used to create, send, receive, forward, store, print, and delete **e-mail** (electronic mail) messages. A **Web browser**, or **browser**, is a software application used to access and view Web pages. **Newsgroups**, or online **discussions**, are areas on the Web where users can participate in discussions about a particular topic. **Instant messaging** provides real-time communications by permitting you to exchange messages or files with other online users. __Groupware__ identifies any type of software that helps groups of people on a network collaborate on projects and share information. A **videoconference** is a meeting between two or more people separated geographically who use a network or the Internet to transmit audio and video data.

7 What Products Are Available as Web Applications?

A **Web application** is a software application that exists on a Web site. To access the program, you visit the Web site that offers the program. Some examples of Web applications include the capability of creating a map and viewing driving directions; viewing your credit card transactions; and preparing your tax return. **Web-based training (WBT)** is a type of __computer-based training__ that uses Internet technology and often is combined with **distance learning (DL)**.

8 What Learning Aids Are Available with Software Applications?

Many software applications and Web sites provide learning aids such as online Help, FAQs, and wizards. __Online Help__ is the electronic equivalent of a user manual. **FAQs** (Frequently Asked Questions) provide answers to common queries. A **wizard** is an automated assistant that helps users complete a task by asking questions and then performing actions based on the answers.

3.42

DISCOVERING
COMPUTERS 2002

Chapter 1 2 3 4 5 6 7 8 9 10 11 12 13 14 15 16 Index HOME

Key Terms

SHELLY
CASHMAN
SERIES.

Student Exercises   Web Links   In Summary   Key Terms   Learn It Online   Checkpoint   In The Lab   Web Work

Special Features   ■ TIMELINE 2002 ■ WWW & E-SKILLS ■ MULTIMEDIA ■ BUYER'S GUIDE 2002 ■ WIRELESS TECHNOLOGY ■ TRENDS 2002 ■ INTERACTIVE LABS ■ TECH NEWS

Web Instructions: To display this page from the Web, start your browser and enter the URL scsite.com/dc2002/ch3/terms.htm. Scroll through the list of terms. Click a term to display its definition and a picture. Click the To WEB button for current and additional information about the term from the Web. To see animations, Shockwave and Flash Player must be installed on your computer (download by clicking here).

accounting software (3.21)
address book (3.20)
antivirus program (3.3)
application (3.2)
application service provider (ASP) (3.35)
application software (3.2)
appointment calendar (3.20)
audio (3.25)
audio editing software (3.25)
authorware (3.25)
bar charts (3.14)
browser (3.32)
button (3.4)
cell (3.12)
charting (3.14)
chat client (3.32)
chat room (3.32)
click (3.4)
clip art (3.8)
clip art/image gallery (3.30)
clip gallery (3.18)
Clipboard (3.10)
color library (3.23)
column charts (3.14)
command (3.5)
computer-aided design (CAD) software (3.22)
computer-aided instruction (3.30)
computer-based training (CBT) (3.30)
context-sensitive (3.36)
context-sensitive menu (3.6)
creating (3.10)
criteria (3.17)
currency (3.16)
data type (3.16)
database (3.15)
database management system (DBMS) (3.16)
database software (3.16)
date (3.16)
desktop (3.4)
desktop publishing (DTP) software (3.23)
dialog box (3.6)
discussion (3.32)
distance education (DE) (3.35)
distance learning (DL) (3.35)
editing (3.10)
educational software (3.30)
e-mail (electronic mail) (3.32)
e-mail software (3.32)
entertainment software (3.31)
FAQs (3.36)
field (3.16)
field size (3.16)
file (3.10)
file name (3.10)
find (3.9)
font (3.10)
font size (3.10)
font style (3.10)
footer (3.9)

format (3.10)
formula (3.12)
function (3.13)
graphical user interface (GUI) (3.4)
groupware (3.33)
header (3.9)
home design/landscaping software (3.30)
hyperlink (3.16)
icon (3.4)
illustration software (3.24)
image editing software (3.24)
import (3.18)
instant messaging (IM) (3.33)
instant messenger (3.33)
integrated software (3.27)
label (3.12)

PRINTING
The process of sending a file to a printer to generate output on a medium such as paper. (3.11)

To WEB

legal software (3.28)
line charts (3.14)
macro (3.13)
margins (3.8)
memo (3.16)
menu (3.5)
multimedia authoring software (3.25)
.NET (3.34)
newsgroup (3.32)
newsreader (3.32)
notepad (3.20)
numeric (3.16)
object (3.16)
online banking (3.28)
online Help (3.36)
online learning (3.35)
online print service (3.29)
operating system (3.3)
page layout (3.23)
paint software (3.24)
personal DTP software (3.29)

personal finance software (3.27)
personal information manager (PIM) (3.20)
photo-editing software (3.29)
pie charts (3.14)
point (3.10)
pointer (3.4)
populating (3.17)
presentation graphics software (3.18)
printing (3.11)
productivity software (3.7)
project management software (3.21)
query (3.17)
record (3.16)
reference software (3.31)
replace (3.9)
saving (3.10)
scrolling (3.9)
search (3.9)
shortcut menu (3.6)
slide show (3.18)
software application (3.2)
software package (3.2)
sort (3.17)
speech recognition (3.11)
spelling checker (3.9)
spreadsheet software (3.12)
structure (3.16)
submenu (3.5)
suite (3.20)
synchronize (3.20)
system software (3.3)
tables (3.16)
tax preparation software (3.28)
text (3.16)
title bar (3.6)
user interface (3.4)
utility (3.3)
utility program (3.3)
validation (3.17)
value (3.12)
video (3.25)
video chats (3.32)
video editing software (3.25)
video telephone call (3.33)
videoconference (3.33)
virus (3.3)
voice chats (3.32)
voice recognition (3.11)
Web application (3.33)
Web browser (3.32)
Web-based training (WBT) (3.34)
what-if analysis (3.14)
window (3.6)
wizard (3.37)
word processing software (3.8)
word processor (3.8)
word wrap (3.9)
worksheet (3.12)

Chapter 1 2 **3** 4 5 6 7 8 9 10 11 12 13 14 15 16 Index **HOME** **3.43**

DISCOVERING
COMPUTERS *2002*

Learn It Online

SHELLY
CASHMAN
SERIES.

Student Exercises   Web Links   In Summary   Key Terms   **Learn It Online**   Checkpoint   In The Lab   Web Work

Special Features   ■ TIMELINE 2002   ■ WWW & E-SKILLS   ■ MULTIMEDIA   ■ BUYER'S GUIDE 2002   ■ WIRELESS TECHNOLOGY   ■ TRENDS 2002   ■ INTERACTIVE LABS   ■ TECH NEWS

Web Instructions: To display this page from the Web, start your browser and enter the URL scsite.com/dc2002/ch3/learn.htm.

1. Web Guide

Click Web Guide to display the Guide to World Wide Web Sites and Searching Techniques Web page. Click Shopping and then click eBay. Search for Software. Use your word processing program to prepare a brief report on the software programs you found. Submit your assignment to your instructor.

2. Scavenger Hunt

Click Scavenger Hunt. Print a copy of the Scavenger Hunt page; use this page to write down your answers as you search the Web. Submit your completed page to your instructor.

3. Who Wants to Be a Computer Genius?

Click Computer Genius to find out if you are a computer genius. Directions on how to play the game will display. When you are ready to play, click the PLAY button. Submit your score to your instructor.

4. Wheel of Terms

Click Wheel of Terms to reinforce important terms you learned in this chapter by playing the Shelly Cashman Series version of this popular game. Directions on how to play the game will display. When you are ready to play, click the PLAY button. Submit your score to your instructor.

5. Career Corner

Click Career Corner to display the Penn State's Career Services Web page. Click a link of your choice. Write a brief report on the information you found. Submit the report to your instructor.

6. Search Sleuth

Click the Search Sleuth to learn search techniques that will help make you a research expert. Submit the completed assignment to your instructor.

7. Crossword Puzzle Challenge

Click Crossword Puzzle Challenge. Complete the puzzle to reinforce skills you learned in this chapter. Directions on how to play the game will display. When you are ready to play, click the PLAY button. Submit the completed puzzle to your instructor.

8. Practice Test

Click Practice Test. Answer each question. When completed, enter your name and click the Grade Test button to submit the quiz for grading. Make a note of any missed questions. If required, print a copy to submit to your instructor.

3.44

DISCOVERING
COMPUTERS *2002*

Chapter 1 2 **3** 4 5 6 7 8 9 10 11 12 13 14 15 16 Index **HOME**

Checkpoint

**SHELLY
CASHMAN
SERIES.**

Student Exercises   Web Links   In Summary   Key Terms   Learn It Online   Checkpoint   In The Lab   Web Work

Special Features ■ TIMELINE 2002 ■ WWW & E-SKILLS ■ MULTIMEDIA ■ BUYER'S GUIDE 2002 ■ WIRELESS TECHNOLOGY ■ TRENDS 2002 ■ INTERACTIVE LABS ■ TECH NEWS

Web Instructions: To display this page from the Web, start your browser and enter the URL scsite.com/dc2002/ch3/check.htm. Click the links for current and additional information. To experience the animation and interactivity, Shockwave and Flash Player must be installed on your computer (download by clicking here.)

LABEL THE FIGURE **Instructions:** Identify the indicated elements in the Windows graphical user interface.

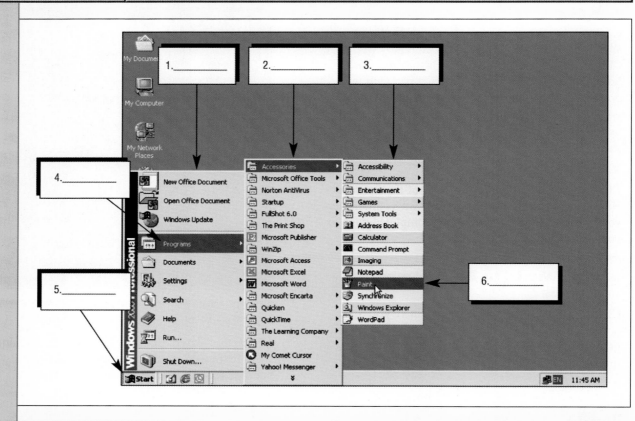

MATCHING **Instructions:** Match each term from the column on the left with the best description from the column on the right.

_____ 1. word wrap
_____ 2. what-if analysis
_____ 3. validation
_____ 4. clip gallery
_____ 5. query

a. Spreadsheet feature that displays data relationships in a graphical, rather than numerical, form.

b. Word processing feature used to locate all occurrences of a particular character, word, or phrase.

c. Word processing feature that allows typing continually without pressing the ENTER key at the end of each line.

d. Database feature that is a specific set of instructions for retrieving data.

e. Database feature that compares data to a set of defined rules or values to determine if it is acceptable.

f. Spreadsheet feature in which certain values are altered to reveal the effects of those changes.

g. Presentation graphics feature consisting of images, pictures, and clips that can be incorporated into slides.

Chapter 1 2 **3** 4 5 6 7 8 9 10 11 12 13 14 15 16 Index HOME **3.45**

DISCOVERING
COMPUTERS *2002*

Checkpoint

SHELLY
CASHMAN
SERIES.

Student Exercises   Web Links   In Summary   Key Terms   Learn It Online   Checkpoint   In The Lab   Web Work

Special Features   ■ TIMELINE 2002   ■ WWW & E-SKILLS   ■ MULTIMEDIA   ■ BUYER'S GUIDE 2002   ■ WIRELESS TECHNOLOGY   ■ TRENDS 2002   ■ INTERACTIVE LABS   ■ TECH NEWS

MULTIPLE CHOICE
Instructions: Select the letter of the correct answer for each of the following questions.

1. A(n) _____ is a utility that prevents, detects, and removes <u>viruses</u> from a computer's memory or storage devices.
   a. macro
   b. operating system
   c. antivirus program
   d. virus program

2. A small <u>symbol</u> on the screen is called a(n) _____ .
   a. pointer
   b. mouse
   c. menu
   d. icon

3. A _____ is a special window a <u>program</u> displays to provide information, present available options, or request a response.
   a. dialog box
   b. shortcut menu
   c. context-sensitive menu
   d. function

4. A _____ is a unique combination of letters of the alphabet, numbers, and other characters that identifies the <u>file</u>.
   a. title bar
   b. file
   c. file name
   d. program name

5. _____ software enables professional designers to design and produce sophisticated documents that contain text, <u>graphics</u>, and brilliant colors.
   a. Spreadsheet
   b. Desktop publishing
   c. Word processing
   d. Paint

SHORT ANSWER
Instructions: Write a brief answer to each of the following questions.

1. How are creating, editing, and formatting a word processing document different? _____ What is the <u>Clipboard</u>? _____ How does the Clipboard work? _____

2. What is a <u>personal information manager</u>? _____ Describe some of the features that are available in a PIM. _____

3. Why do professional designers and graphic artists use <u>DTP software</u> instead of word processing packages? _____ What is a color library? _____ What is page layout? _____

4. What is an Internet <u>e-mail address</u>? _____ What two parts of an e-mail address are separated by the at (@) sign? _____

5. What is online Help? _____ How do <u>FAQs</u> and wizards help software users? _____

WORKING TOGETHER
Instructions: Working with a group of your classmates, complete the following team exercise.

A <u>Web application</u> is a software application that exists on a Web site. With your group, develop a report describing at least three of these Web applications and how an individual could use these various applications effectively. Include in your report a description of each application, a short overview of any online Help or FAQs, and the URL for all applications within your report. Share your findings with your class.

3.46

DISCOVERING
COMPUTERS 2002

Chapter 1 2 3 4 5 6 7 8 9 10 11 12 13 14 15 16 Index HOME

In The Lab

SHELLY
CASHMAN
SERIES.

Student Exercises | Web Links | In Summary | Key Terms | Learn It Online | Checkpoint | In The Lab | Web Work

Special Features ■ TIMELINE 2002 ■ WWW & E-SKILLS ■ MULTIMEDIA ■ BUYER'S GUIDE 2002 ■ WIRELESS TECHNOLOGY ■ TRENDS 2002 ■ INTERACTIVE LABS ■ TECH NEW

Web Instructions: To display this page from the Web, start your browser and enter the URL scsite.com/dc2002/ch3/lab.htm. Click the links for current and additional information.

Working with Application Programs

This exercise uses Windows 98 procedures. Windows is a multitasking operating system, meaning you can work on two or more applications that reside in memory at the same time. To find out how to work with multiple application programs, click the Start button on the taskbar, and then click Help on the Start menu. Click the Contents tab. Click the Exploring Your Computer book. Click the Work with Programs book. Click an appropriate topic to answer each of the following questions:

- How do you start a program?
- How do you switch between programs?
- How do you quit a program that is not responding?
- How do you quit a program?

Close the Windows Help window.

Creating a Word Processing Document

WordPad is a simple word processing program included with the Windows operating system. To create a document with WordPad, click the Start button on the taskbar, point to Programs on the Start menu, point to Accessories on the Programs submenu, and then click WordPad on the Accessories submenu. If necessary, when the WordPad window opens, click its Maximize button. Click View on the menu bar. If a check mark does not display to the left of the Toolbar command, click the toolbar command. Type a complete answer to one of the E-Revolution applied questions posed in this chapter. Your answer should be at least two paragraphs long. Press the TAB key to indent the first line of each paragraph and the ENTER key to begin a new paragraph. To correct errors, press the BACKSPACE key to erase to the left of the insertion point and press the DELETE key to erase to the right. To insert text, position the I-beam mouse pointer at the location where the text should be inserted, and then begin typing. At the end of your document, press the ENTER key twice and then type your name. When your document is complete, save it on a floppy disk inserted into drive A. Click the Save button on the toolbar, type a:\h3-2 in the File name text box in the Save As dialog box, and then click the Save button. Click the Print button on the toolbar to print your document. Quit WordPad.

Using WordPad Help

This exercise uses Windows 98 procedures. Start WordPad as described in In The Lab 2 above. Click Help on the WordPad menu bar and then click Help Topics. When the WordPad Help window opens, click the Index tab. Type saving documents in the text box and then press the ENTER key. Click To save changes to a document in the Topics Found dialog box and then click the Display button.

- How can you save changes to a document?
- How can you save an existing document with a new name?

Close the WordPad Help window and quit WordPad.

Productivity Software Products

What productivity software packages are on your computer? Click the Start button on the taskbar and point to Programs on the Start menu. Scan the Programs submenu (if necessary, point to the arrow at the top or bottom of the submenu to move the submenu up or down) for the names of popular productivity packages. Write the package name and the type of software application (see the chart on page 3.7 for help). When you are finished, click an empty area of the desktop.

Chapter 1 2 3 4 5 6 7 8 9 10 11 12 13 14 15 16 Index HOME 3.47

DISCOVERING
COMPUTERS 2002

SHELLY
CASHMAN
SERIES.

Web Work

Student Exercises   Web Links   In Summary   Key Terms   Learn It Online   Checkpoint   In The Lab   Web Work

Special Features   ■ TIMELINE 2002 ■ WWW & E-SKILLS ■ MULTIMEDIA ■ BUYER'S GUIDE 2002 ■ WIRELESS TECHNOLOGY ■ TRENDS 2002 ■ INTERACTIVE LABS ■ TECH NEWS

Web Instructions: To display this page from the Web, start your browser and enter the URL scsite.com/dc2002/ch3/web.htm. To view At The Movies in exercise 1, RealPlayer must be installed on your computer (download by clicking here). To use the Shelly Cashman Series Word Processing Lab and the Working with Spreadsheets Lab from the Web, Shockwave and Flash Player must be installed on your computer (download by clicking here).

What Is Microsoft?

To view the What Is Microsoft? movie, click the button to the left or click the Play button to the right. Watch the movie, and then complete the exercise by answering the questions below. Founded in 1975, Microsoft is a $25 billion company. It is divided into three main business groups: operating systems, software products, and consumer products, which include games, Web browsers, and other home, personal, and educational products. With this exposure, Microsoft dominates in many markets. Nine out of ten personal computers run some version of the Microsoft Windows operating system. In addition, Microsoft has 90 percent of the office/spreadsheet/graphics software market. Its MSN Internet Explorer comprises more than 60 percent of the Web-browser market. And, because Microsoft bundles and interlocks its systems and programs, organizations with a network of computers are compelled to buy Microsoft products continually. What do you think should be done, if anything, and why?

Shelly Cashman Series Word Processing Lab

Follow the instructions in Web Work 2 on page 1.47 to start and use the Shelly Cashman Series Word Processing Lab. If you are running from the Web, enter the URL www.scsite.com/sclabs/menu.htm or display this Web Work page (see instructions at the top of this page) and then click the button to the left.

Shelly Cashman Series Working with Spreadsheets Lab

Follow the instructions in Web Work 2 on page 1.47 to start and use the Shelly Cashman Series Working with Spreadsheets Lab. If you are running from the Web, enter the URL www.scsite.com/sclabs/menu.htm or display the Web Work page (see instructions at the top of this page) and then click the button to the left.

Setting Up an E-Mail Account

The fastest growing software application may be electronic mail (e-mail). One free e-mail service reports 30 million current subscribers with an additional 80,000 joining every day. To set up a free e-mail account, click the button to the left. Follow the procedures to establish an e-mail account. When you are finished, send yourself an e-mail.

In the News

It is a computer user's nightmare — a button is clicked accidentally or a key is pressed unintentionally and an important message, document, or presentation is deleted. Happily, some software can restore a sound night's sleep by continuously copying open files to the hard drive. Not only are files kept safe, but you always can return to earlier versions of a project. Click the button to the left and read a news article about a new software program. Who is introducing the program? What is the program called? What does it do? Who will benefit from using this software? Why? Where can the software be obtained? Would you be interested in this software? Why or why not?

CHAPTER 4

The Components of the System Unit

The doorbell rings. As you open the door, your niece and nephew politely greet you and then head straight for the computer. Weekend visits have become part of their regular routine. You would like to think it is because of your great personality! The real draw is your computer and all the cool game software.

Lately, though, you have heard complaining. Videos and actions on the screen are choppy. The computer is slow, and it freezes in the middle of some programs.

What can you do? You cannot afford a new computer. A visit to the electronics store where you purchased the computer seems like the solution. After explaining the situation to a technician, she suggests you upgrade the memory inside the computer for a cost of a hundred dollars. It sounds great, but you have one very big problem. You do not have the slightest idea how to install memory inside a computer. The technician assures you the memory upgrade kit includes thorough instructions with detailed pictures. The store also has a 24-hour toll-free help line.

Leaving the store with the upgrade memory kit in hand, you will tackle this project on the weekend — when you can recruit help from your niece and nephew!

THE SYSTEM UNIT

Whether you are a home or a business user, you most likely will make the decision to purchase a new computer or upgrade an existing computer within your lifetime. Thus, understanding the purpose of each component in a computer is important. As discussed in Chapter 1, a computer includes devices used for input, processing, output, storage, and communications. Many of these components reside in the system unit.

The **system unit** is a box-like case that houses the electronic components of the computer used to process data. Sometimes called a **chassis**, the system unit is made of metal or plastic and protects the internal electronic components from damage. All computers have a system unit (Figure 4-1).

On a personal computer, the electronic components and most storage devices reside inside the

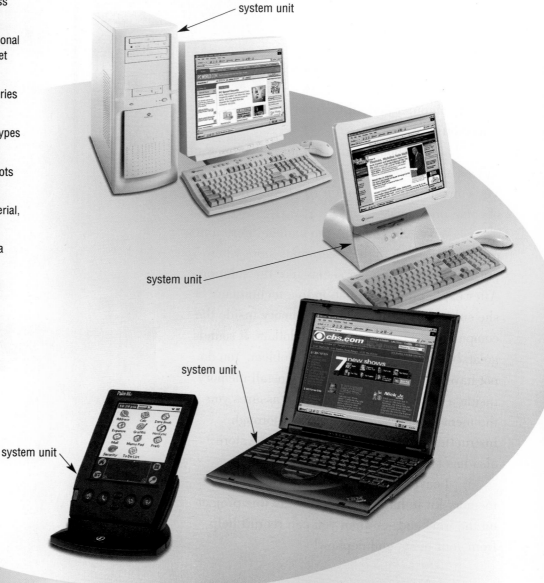

Figure 4-1 All sizes of computers have a system unit.

system unit. Other devices, such as a keyboard, mouse, microphone, monitor, printer, speakers, scanner, and PC camera normally occupy space outside the system unit. On a desktop personal computer, the system unit usually is a device separate from the monitor and keyboard. Some system units sit on top of a desk. Other models, called **tower models**, can stand vertically on the floor.

To conserve on space, an **all-in-one computer** houses the system unit in the same physical case as the monitor. On notebook computers, the keyboard and pointing device often occupy the area on the top of the system unit. The display attaches to the system unit by a hinge. The system unit on a handheld computer usually consumes the entire device. On these devices, the display is part of the system unit too.

At some point, you might have to open the system unit on a desktop personal computer to replace or install a new component. For this reason, you should be somewhat familiar with the inside of the system unit.

Figure 4-2 identifies some of the components inside a system unit on a desktop personal computer. Components inside the system unit include the processor, memory module, cards, ports, and connectors. The

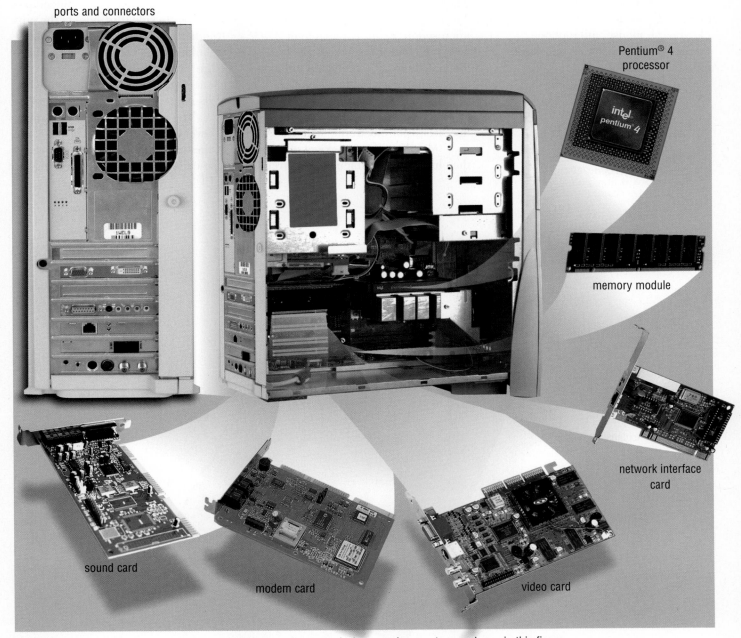

Figure 4-2 Some of the components inside the system unit on a typical personal computer are shown in this figure.

processor interprets and carries out the basic instructions that operate a computer. A memory module is a package that houses memory. Memory temporarily holds data and instructions. A card, also called an expansion card, is a circuit board that adds devices or capabilities to the computer. Four types of cards found in most desktop personal computers today are a sound card, a modem card, a video card, and a network interface card.

Devices outside the system unit attach to a port on the system unit by a cable. These devices may include a keyboard, mouse, microphone, monitor, printer, scanner, speakers, and PC camera.

Web Link

For more information on motherboards, visit the Discovering Computers 2002 Chapter 4 WEB LINK page (**scsite.com/dc2002/ch4/weblink.htm**) and click Motherboards.

The Motherboard

The **motherboard**, sometimes called **system board**, is the main circuit board in the system unit. Figure 4-3 shows a photograph of a desktop personal computer motherboard and identifies some of its components, including different types of chips.

A **chip** is a small piece of semi-conducting material, usually no bigger than one-half-inch square, on which integrated circuits are etched. An **integrated circuit** (**IC**) is a microscopic pathway capable of carrying electrical current. Each integrated circuit can contain millions of elements such as transistors. A **transistor** acts as an electronic switch, or gate, that opens or closes the circuit for electronic signals.

Manufacturers package chips so the chips can be attached to a circuit board such as a motherboard, memory module, or card. A variety of chip packages exist (Figure 4-4). One type, called a **dual inline package** (**DIP**), consists of two parallel rows of downward-pointing thin metal feet (pins). The pins attach the chip package to the circuit board. A **pin grid array** (**PGA**) **package** holds a larger number of pins because the pins are mounted on the surface of the package. A **flip chip-PGA** (**FC-PGA**) **package** is a higher-performance PGA packaging that places the chip on the opposite side (flip side) of the pins. Another high performance packaging technique does not use pins. A **single edge contact** (**SEC**) **cartridge** connects to the motherboard on one of its edges.

The motherboard contains many different types of chips. Of these, one of the most important is the processor, also called the central processing unit (CPU).

Figure 4-3 The motherboard in a desktop personal computer contains chips and many other electronic components.

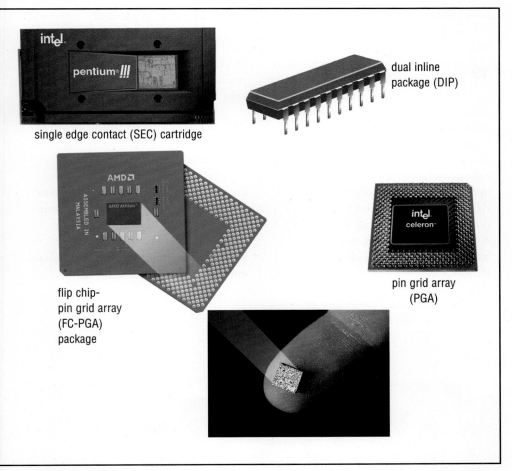

Figure 4-4 Various chip packages.

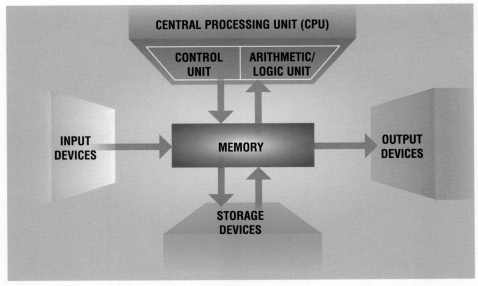

Figure 4-5 Most of the devices connected to the computer communicate with the CPU in order to carry out a task. The arrows in this figure represent the flow of data, instructions, and information.

CENTRAL PROCESSING UNIT

The **central processing unit** (**CPU**), often called a **processor**, interprets and carries out the basic instructions that operate a computer. The CPU significantly impacts overall computing power and manages most of a computer's operations. Most of the devices connected to the computer communicate with the CPU in order to carry out a task (Figure 4-5).

The CPU contains the control unit and the arithmetic/logic unit. These two components work together to perform processing operations.

The Control Unit

The **control unit**, one component of the CPU, directs and coordinates most of the operations in the computer. The control unit has a role much like a traffic cop: it interprets each instruction issued by a program and then initiates the appropriate action to carry out the instruction.

For every instruction, the control unit repeats a set of four basic operations: (1) fetching, (2) decoding, (3) executing, and, if necessary, (4) storing. **Fetching** is the process of obtaining a program instruction or data item from memory. **Decoding** is the process of translating the instruction into commands the computer can execute. **Executing** is the process of carrying out the commands. **Storing** is the process of writing the result to memory.

Together, these four operations (fetching, decoding, executing, and storing) comprise a **machine cycle** or **instruction cycle** (Figure 4-6). **Instruction time (i-time)** is the time it takes the control unit to fetch and decode. **Execution time (e-time)** is the time it takes the control unit to execute and store. You can compute the total time required for a machine cycle by adding together the i-time and e-time.

Some computer professionals measure a CPU's speed according to how many **millions of instructions per second (MIPS)** it can process. Current desktop personal computers, for example, can process more than 300 MIPS. No real standard for measuring MIPS exists, however, because different instructions require varying amounts of processing time.

CPUs use either a CISC or RISC design. **CISC (complex instruction set computing)** supports a large number of instructions. **RISC (reduced instruction set computing)** reduces the instructions to only those used more frequently. A RISC CPU executes simple instructions more quickly than a CISC CPU. A CISC CPU executes complex instructions more quickly than a RISC CPU.

The Arithmetic/Logic Unit

The **arithmetic/logic unit (ALU)**, another component of the CPU, performs arithmetic, comparison, and logical operations.

Arithmetic operations include addition, subtraction, multiplication, and division.

Comparison operations involve comparing one data item to another to determine if the first item is greater than, equal to, or less than the other item. Depending on the result of the comparison, different actions may occur. To determine if an employee should receive overtime

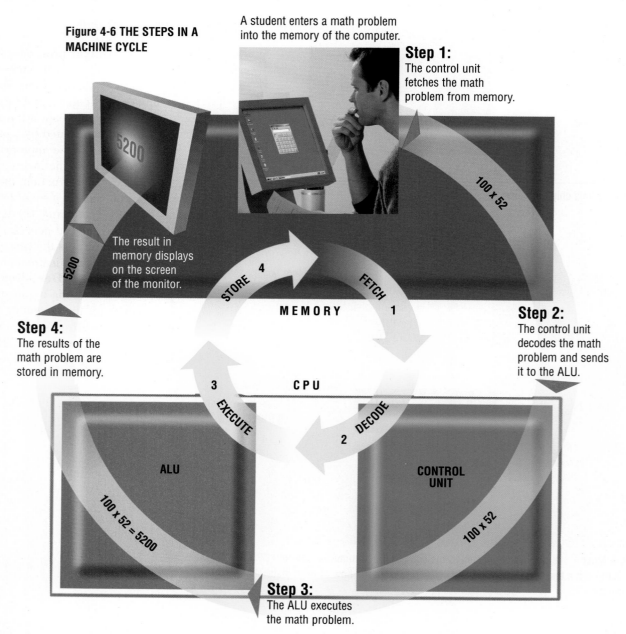

Figure 4-6 THE STEPS IN A MACHINE CYCLE

A student enters a math problem into the memory of the computer.

Step 1: The control unit fetches the math problem from memory.

Step 2: The control unit decodes the math problem and sends it to the ALU.

Step 3: The ALU executes the math problem.

Step 4: The results of the math problem are stored in memory.

The result in memory displays on the screen of the monitor.

STORE 4

FETCH 1

MEMORY

3

CPU

EXECUTE

2 DECODE

ALU

100 x 52 = 5200

CONTROL UNIT

100 x 52

100 x 52

5200

pay, the ALU compares the number of hours an employee worked during the week to the regular time hours allowed (40 hours, for instance). If the hours worked is greater than 40, the ALU calculates an overtime wage. If hours worked is not greater than 40, the ALU does not calculate an overtime wage.

Logical operations use conditions along with logical operators such as AND, OR, and NOT. For example, if only non-salaried employees can receive overtime pay, the ALU must verify that the employee is non-salaried AND worked more than 40 hours before computing an overtime wage.

Pipelining

In some computers, the CPU processes only one instruction at a time. In these computers, the CPU waits until an instruction completes all four stages of the machine cycle (fetch, decode, execute, and store) before beginning work on the next instruction.

With **pipelining**, the CPU begins executing a second instruction before it completes the first instruction. Pipelining results in faster processing because the CPU does not have to wait for one instruction to complete the machine cycle before fetching the next. Think of a pipeline as an assembly line. By the time the first instruction is in the last stage of the machine cycle, three other instructions could have been fetched and started through the machine cycle (Figure 4-7).

Although formerly used only in high-performance computers, today's personal computers commonly use pipelining. Most current personal computer CPU chips can pipeline up to four instructions.

Registers

The CPU contains high-speed storage locations, called **registers**, that temporarily hold data and instructions. A CPU has many different types of registers, each with a specific function. These functions include storing the location from where an instruction was fetched, storing an instruction while the control unit decodes it, storing data while the ALU processes it, and storing the results of a calculation.

Our Brain versus the Computer

Functions of the Control Unit

The control unit's function is to direct and coordinate most of the operations in the computer. For each instruction, the control unit repeats a set of four operations: fetching, decoding, executing, and storing. These four operations may seem new to you, but in a sense you carry out these same operations each time you complete certain ordinary tasks. You input data through one of your five senses; you decode this data, changing it into information; you execute the task in some way; and you store this information for later retrieval. Do people solve problems the same way in which a computer solves a problem? Do you agree that the human brain is similar to a computer? Why or why not? Describe a simple task in which you perform operations like those in the machine cycle. What is different and why? If the human brain can perform all of these functions, do we really need computers? Explain your answer.

For more information on the control unit vs. the human brain, visit the Discovering Computers 2002 Issues Web page (**scsite.com/dc2002/issues.htm**) and click Chapter 4 Issue #1.

MACHINE CYCLE (without pipelining):

| FETCH | DECODE | EXECUTE | STORE | FETCH | DECODE | EXECUTE | STORE |

INSTRUCTION 1   INSTRUCTION 2

MACHINE CYCLE (with pipelining):

| FETCH | DECODE | EXECUTE | STORE |

INSTRUCTION 1
INSTRUCTION 2
INSTRUCTION 3
INSTRUCTION 4

Figure 4-7 Most modern personal computers support pipelining. With pipelining, the CPU begins executing a second instruction before the first instruction is completed. The result is faster processing.

APPLY IT!

Clock Speed – How Much Is Enough?

If you have considered purchasing a computer recently, you are aware of the many available models and that each of these models provides several options from which to choose. The market for personal computer hardware is incredible, making your options on what type of machine you want to buy just as impressive. One primary option to consider is processing power. What clock speed should you purchase? Do you need the latest and greatest dream machine? Is 1 GHz necessary for your processing needs or can you accomplish as much with less power? How fast do you want to go? The answers to these questions are directly related to how you intend to use the computer and what software applications you need. You can select a machine just for the basics or select one used by professional graphic artists or game players.

- Level I – Below 600 MHz
  This computer should provide more than adequate processing power for at least the next couple of years for the typical home user — someone who primarily uses a standard Office suite, edits home photographs, and plays a game now and then.
- Level II – 600 MHz to 1 GHz
  If your interest is in graphics and design, you play some of the multi-media games that include simulated 3-D and virtual reality, or you use voice recognition, your needs would be met best by a Level II computer.
- Level III – 1 GHz and above
  This computer is for the power user. If your goal is to create 3-D applications, run sophisticated graphics software or CAD programs, then you definitely want to purchase the fastest computer you can afford.

For more information on computer processing power, visit the Discovering Computers 2002 Apply It Web page (**scsite.com/dc2002/apply.htm**) and click Chapter 4 Apply It #1.

Web Link

For more information on clock speed, visit the Discovering Computers 2002 Chapter 4 WEB LINK page (**scsite.com/dc2002/ch4/weblink.htm**) and click Clock Speed.

The System Clock

The CPU relies on a small chip called the **system clock** to synchronize, or control the timing of, all computer operations. Just as your heart beats at a regular rate to keep your body functioning, the system clock generates regular electronic pulses, or ticks, that set the operating pace of components in the system unit.

Each tick is a **clock cycle**. In the past, CPUs used one or more clock cycles to execute each instruction. Many of today's CPUs are **superscalar** and can execute more than one instruction per clock cycle.

Clock speed, also called **clock rate**, is the speed at which a processor executes instructions. The faster the clock, the more instructions the CPU can execute per second. Manufacturers state clock speed in megahertz and gigahertz. A **hertz** is one cycle per second. Mega is a prefix that stands for million. Giga is a prefix that stands for billion. Thus, **megahertz** (**MHz**) equates to one million ticks of the system clock, and **gigahertz** (**GHz**) equates to one billion ticks of the system clock. A computer that operates at 933 MHz (*megahertz*) has 933 million (*mega*) clock cycles in one second (*hertz*).

The table in Figure 4-8 identifies these and other prefixes commonly used in the computer industry.

The power of a CPU frequently is determined by how fast it processes data. The system clock is one of the major factors that influence a computer's speed. A CPU with higher clock speed can process more instructions per second than a CPU with a lower clock speed. For example, a 1 GHz CPU is faster than a CPU operating at 800 MHz. Keep in mind that the speed of the system clock affects only the CPU. It has no effect on peripherals such as a printer or disk drive.

The speed of the system clock varies among CPUs. A technological breakthrough by IBM enables CPUs today to operate at speeds well beyond 400 MHz. For nearly 30 years, aluminum was used to create the electronic circuitry on a single chip of silicon crystal. Now, a process exists that uses copper instead of aluminum. CPU chips that use copper run faster because copper is a better conductor of electricity. An added benefit is these chips cost less. They also require less electricity, making them ideal for use in portable computers and other battery-operated devices.

COMMON PREFIXES AND THEIR MEANINGS

Prefixes for Small Amounts	Meaning	Decimal Notation
MILLI	One thousandth of	.001
MICRO	One millionth of	.000001
NANO	One billionth of	.000000001
PICO	One trillionth of	.000000000001

Prefixes for Large Amounts	Meaning	Decimal Notation
KILO	One thousand	1,000
MEGA	One million	1,000,000
GIGA	One billion	1,000,000,000
TERA	One trillion	1,000,000,000,000

Figure 4-8 The table above outlines prefixes commonly used in the computer industry.

Comparison of Personal Computer Processors

On larger computers, such as mainframes and supercomputers, the various functions performed by the CPU, also called a processor, span many separate chips and sometimes multiple circuit boards. On a personal computer, because all functions of the processor usually are on a single chip, some call the chip a **microprocessor**. Most advertisements, however, refer to the chip as a processor. Figure 4-9 shows several popular personal computer processors.

Manufacturers often identify their personal computer processors by a model name or model number. Figure 4-10 summarizes the historical development of the personal computer processor and documents the increases in clock speed and number of transistors in chips since 1982. The greater the number of transistors, the more complex and powerful the chip.

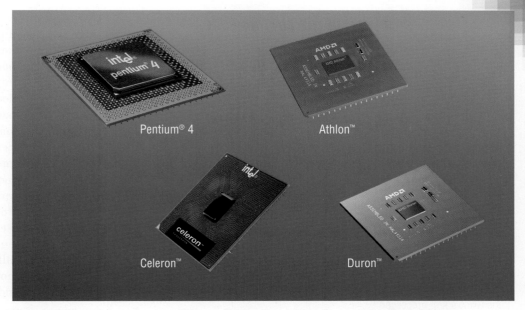

Figure 4-9 Most high-performance PCs use Pentium® and Athlon™ processors. Basic PCs have a Celeron™ or Duron™ processor.

COMPARISON OF WIDELY USED PERSONAL COMPUTER PROCESSORS

NAME	DATE INTRODUCED	MANUFACTURER	CLOCK SPEED	NUMBER OF TRANSISTORS
Pentium® 4	2000	Intel	1.4 GHz and up	42 million
Itanium™	2000	Intel	800 MHz and up	25.4-60 million
Pentium® III Xeon™	1999	Intel	500 MHz - 1 GHz	9.5-28 million
Pentium® III	1999	Intel	400 MHz - 1.2 GHz	9.5-28 million
Athlon™	1999	AMD	500 MHz - 1.2 GHz	22-37 million
Duron™	1999	AMD	600 - 800 MHz	18 million
AMD-K6® III	1999	AMD	400 - 450 MHz	21.3 million
Celeron™	1998	Intel	266 - 800 MHz	7.5-19 million
Pentium® II Xeon	1998	Intel	400 - 450 MHz	7.5-27 million
AMD-K6® II	1998	AMD	366 - 550 MHz	9.3 million
AMD-K6®	1998	AMD	300 MHz	8.8 million
Pentium® II	1997	Intel	234 - 450 MHz	7.5 million
Pentium® with MMX™ technology	1997	Intel	166 - 233 MHz	4.5 million
Pentium® Pro	1995	Intel	150 - 200 MHz	5.5 million
Pentium®	1993	Intel	75 - 200 MHz	3.3 million
80486DX	1989	Intel	25 - 100 MHz	1.2 million
80386DX	1985	Intel	16 - 33 MHz	275,000
80286	1982	Intel	6 - 12 MHz	134,000
PowerPC	1994	Motorola	50 - 500 MHz	Up to 50 million
68040	1989	Motorola	25 - 40 MHz	1.2 million
68030	1987	Motorola	16 - 50 MHz	270,000
68020	1984	Motorola	16 - 33 MHz	190,000
Alpha	1993	Digital; Compaq	150 - 700 MHz	Up to 100 million

Figure 4-10 A comparison of some of the more widely used personal computer processors.

COMPANY ON THE CUTTING EDGE

Chips Dominate Computer Market

Answer: This company's chips power 85 percent of all desktop computers. Question: What is Intel?

Jeopardy television series contestants faced this question in 1994, and today Intel still is the world's largest chip maker. The company also is a major producer of boards, systems, and software for the personal computer, network, and communications industries.

When Gordon Moore and Robert Noyce started Intel in 1968, their goal was to build semiconductor memory to replace magnetic core memory. Intel refined the process of placing thousands of tiny electronic devices on a silicon chip; in 1970, Intel successfully introduced the 1103. One year later, this product became the world's best-selling semiconductor device. In 1971 Intel developed the 4004, the world's first processor.

This innovative spirit and attention to detail remain part of Intel's corporate culture. The company has grown to more than 70,000 employees in more than 40 countries. Intel supports the values of responding to customer needs, working with discipline and quality, taking risks, working in an open and satisfying environment, and striving for optimum results.

For more information on Intel, visit the Discovering Computers 2002 Companies Web page (**scsite.com/dc2002/companies.htm**) and click Intel.

COMPANY ON THE CUTTING EDGE

Intel-Compatible Processor Leader

In the 18th century, philosophers spoke of The Age of Enlightenment. In 1969, The Fifth Dimension sang of The Age of Aquarius. But could today be The Age of Asparagus? In the early 1980s, Advanced Micro Devices (AMD) adopted the phrase to characterize its commitment to develop increasing numbers of proprietary products for the computer industry. Executives identified this goal with asparagus farming because the crop grows slowly, but it is very lucrative once it takes hold.

The company's seeds sprouted and grew into the world's second-largest manufacturer of processors for Microsoft Windows-compatible personal computers. Along with the AMD-K6® and Athlon™ processors with 3DNow!™ technology, AMD also develops flash memory, programmable logic, communications, and networking devices. One-half of the company's nearly $3 billion in revenues is generated from sales outside the United States.

Co-founders Jerry Sanders and John Carey laid the foundation for AMD in Carey's living room in 1968. From the beginning, AMD guaranteed its microchips for every customer would meet or exceed stringent standards. More than three decades later, the company continues this commitment to "parametric superiority."

For more information on AMD, visit the Discovering Computers 2002 Companies Web page (**scsite.com/dc2002/companies.htm**) and click AMD.

Intel is a leading manufacturer of personal computer processors. With their earlier processors, Intel used a model number to identify the various chips. After learning that processor model numbers could not be trade-marked and protected from use by competitors, Intel began identifying their processors with names — thus emerged their series of processors known as the Pentium®. Most high-performance PCs use a **Pentium**® processor. Less expensive, basic PCs use a brand of Intel processor called the **Celeron**™. Two more brands, called the **Xeon**™ and **Itanium**™ processors, are ideal for workstations and low-end servers.

Other companies such as AMD also make **Intel-compatible processors**. These processors have the same internal design or architecture as Intel processors and perform the same functions, but often are less expensive. Intel and Intel-compatible processors are used in PCs.

Apple Macintosh and Power Macintosh systems use a **Motorola processor**, which has a design different from the Intel-style processor. For Apple's PowerPC, Motorola introduced a new processor architecture that increased the speed of the computer.

The **Alpha processor**, which originally was developed by Digital Equipment Corporation, is used primarily in workstations and high-end servers. Current models of the Alpha chip run at clock speeds up to 700 MHz.

A new type of personal computer processor, called an **integrated CPU**, combines functions of a processor, memory, and a video card on a single chip. Lower-costing personal computers and Internet appliances such as a set-top box sometimes use an integrated CPU.

Determining which processor is right for you will depend on how you plan to use the computer. If you purchase a PC (IBM-compatible), you will choose an Intel processor or an Intel-compatible processor. Apple Macintosh and Power Macintosh users will choose a PowerPC processor.

Your intended use also will determine the clock speed of the processor you choose. Processor speed is an important consideration. A home user surfing the Web, for example, will not need as fast a processor as an artist working with

graphics or applications requiring multimedia capabilities such as full-motion video. Figure 4-11 describes guidelines for selecting an Intel processor. Remember, the higher the clock speed, the faster the processor — but also the more expensive the computer.

Today's processors use **MMX**™ (**multimedia extensions**) technology, which is a set of instructions built into the processor that allows it to manipulate and process multimedia data more efficiently. In addition to MMX, Intel's latest processors include **SSE instructions** (**streaming single-instruction, multiple-data instructions**), and AMD's latest processors have **3DNow!**™ technology. These two technologies further improve the processor's performance of multimedia, the Web, and 3-D graphics.

Processor Installation and Upgrades

Instead of buying an entirely new computer, you might be able to upgrade your processor to increase the computer's performance. Processor upgrades are one of three forms: chip for chip, piggyback, or daughterboard. With a **chip for chip upgrade**, you replace the existing processor chip with a new one. With a **piggyback upgrade**, you stack the new processor chip on top of the old one. With a **daughterboard upgrade**, the new processor chip is on a daughterboard. A **daughterboard** is a small circuit board that plugs into the motherboard, often to add additional capabilities to the motherboard.

INTEL PROCESSOR	DESIRED CLOCK SPEED	USE
Itanium™ or Xeon™	1 GHz and up	Power users with workstations; low-end servers on a network
Pentium® family	1 GHz and up	Power users or users that design professional drawings, produce and edit videos, record and edit music, participate in videoconference calls, create professional Web sites, play graphic-intensive multiplayer Internet games
	800 MHz - 1 GHz	Users that design professional documents containing graphics such as newsletters or number intensive spreadsheets; produce multimedia presentations; use the Web as an intensive research tool; edit photographs; send documents and graphics via the Web; watch videos; play graphic-intensive games on CD or DVD; create personal Web sites
	600 - 800 MHz	Home users that manage personal finances; create basic documents with word processing and spreadsheet software; communicate with others on the Web via e-mail, chat rooms, and discussions; shop on the Web; create basic Web pages
Celeron™	600 MHz and up	Home users that manage personal finances; create basic documents with word processing and spreadsheet software; edit photographs; make greeting cards and calendars; use educational or entertainment CD-ROMs; communicate with others on the Web via e-mail, chat rooms, and discussions

Figure 4-11 Determining which processor to obtain when you purchase a computer depends on your computer usage.

The Upgrade Dilemma

If you purchased your computer more than two years ago, then you probably have started to wonder if it is time to buy a new one. You might want one with a few additional options, such as a DVD drive, and a lot more power, especially because today's applications demand speed. The question is should you purchase a new computer or upgrade your current computer. The following list should help with your decision.

- If the processor is a 486 or older, donate it and purchase a new computer.
- If you have a computer with a slow processor, then consider the following upgrade options:
  - If the motherboard will accept a faster processor, replace it.
  - If the motherboard will not accept a faster processor, then consider an upgrade kit. The advantage of buying an upgrade kit is that memory and the processor are pre-installed on the motherboard.
  - Purchase a motherboard and processor of your choice. This option is for the more technical people who know the strengths and weaknesses of the various motherboards and which one will go well with the processor they are purchasing. Also, keep in mind that replacing the motherboard, even using an upgrade kit, is time-consuming.
- Additional items to consider are other devices that may need to be upgraded on your system. Some possibilities include more memory, a new monitor, more video RAM, USB ports, more hard disk storage, new or faster CD-ROM drive, and other storage devices such as a Zip® drive.

For more information on upgrading versus purchasing a new computer, visit the Discovering Computers 2002 Apply It Web page (**scsite.com/dc2002/apply.htm**) and click Chapter 4 Apply It #2.

A processor chip is inserted into an opening, or **socket**, on the motherboard. Many PGA (pin grid array) chips use a zero-insertion force socket. A **zero-insertion force (ZIF) socket** has a small lever or screw that facilitates the installation and removal of processor chips (Figure 4-12). Users easily can upgrade the processor on computers with a ZIF socket because this type of socket requires no force to remove and install a chip. Some motherboards have a second ZIF socket that holds an upgrade chip. In this case, the existing processor chip remains on the motherboard, and you install the upgrade chip into the second ZIF socket.

Heat Sinks and Heat Pipes

Newer processor chips generate a lot of heat, which could cause the chip to burn up. Often, the computer's main fan generates enough airflow to cool the processor. Sometimes, however, the processor requires a heat sink — especially when upgrading to a more powerful processor. A **heat sink** is a small ceramic or metal component with fins on its surface that absorbs and ventilates heat produced by electrical components. Some heat sinks are packaged as part of the processor chip. Others are installed on top or the side of the chip. Because a heat sink consumes a lot of room, a smaller device called a **heat pipe** cools processors in notebook computers.

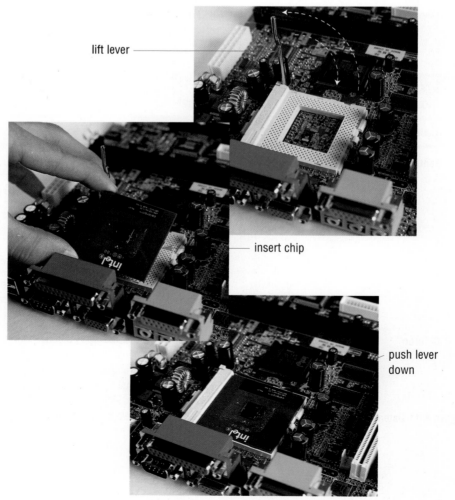

lift lever

insert chip

push lever down

Figure 4-12 A zero-insertion force socket makes it easy to remove and re-install processor chips.

Coprocessors

Another way to increase the performance of a computer is through the use of a coprocessor. A **coprocessor** is a special processor chip or circuit board that assists the processor in performing specific tasks. Users running engineering, scientific, or graphics applications, for instance, will notice a dramatic increase in speed in applications that take advantage of a **floating-point coprocessor**. Floating-point coprocessors sometimes are called math or numeric coprocessors. Most of today's computers include a floating-point coprocessor.

Parallel Processing

Some computers use more than one processor to speed processing times. Known as **parallel processing**, this method uses multiple processors simultaneously to execute a program (Figure 4-13). Parallel processing divides up a problem so that multiple processors work on their assigned portion of the problem at the same time. As you might expect, parallel processing requires special software that recognizes how to divide up the problem and then bring the results back together again. Supercomputers use parallel processing for applications such as weather forecasting.

DATA REPRESENTATION

To understand fully the way a computer processes data, it is important to know how a computer represents data. People communicate through speech by combining words into sentences. Human speech is **analog** because it uses continuous signals that vary in strength and quality. Most computers are **digital**. They recognize only two discrete states: on and off. This is because computers are electronic devices powered by electricity, which also has only two states: on or off.

Web Link

For more information on processors, visit the Discovering Computers 2002 Chapter 4 WEB LINK page (**scsite.com/dc2002/ch4/weblink.htm**) and click Processors.

TECHNOLOGY TRAILBLAZER

ANDY **GROVE**

Psychologists classify paranoia as a serious mental disorder; Intel Chairman Andy Grove classifies it as an essential component of business success. In Grove's book, *Only the Paranoid Survive*, he states that successful corporate managers constantly need to be on the lookout for competitors' threats. He personally worries about flawed products, unproductive factories, and low employee morale.

He advises college students to make career choices based on a variety of factors, including their strengths and weaknesses, their responsibilities at a particular company, to whom they would report, and their ability to adapt to new environments. He explains that after graduating from the University of California at Berkeley in 1963, he chose to work at Fairchild Semiconductor because he desired the California location and he wanted to work with Gordon Moore.

Five years later, he helped found Intel Corporation and was named president in 1979. From 1987 to 1998 he served as chief executive officer. He was named *Time* magazine's Man of the Year in 1997 for his innovative work on microchips, entrepreneurial spirit, and sharp, brilliant mind.

For more information on Andy Grove, visit the Discovering Computers 2002 People Web page (**scsite.com/dc2002/people.htm**) and click Andy Grove.

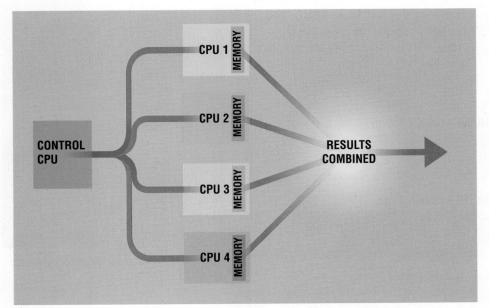

Figure 4-13 Parallel processing divides up a problem so that multiple processors work on their assigned portion of a problem at the same time.

The two digits, zero and one, easily can represent these two states (Figure 4-14). The digit zero (0) represents the electronic state of off (absence of an electronic charge). The digit one (1) represents the electronic state of on (presence of an electronic charge).

When people count, they use the digits in the decimal system (0 through 9). The computer uses a binary system because it only understands two states. The **binary system** is a number system that has just two unique digits, 0 and 1, called bits. A **bit** (short for **bi**nary dig**it**) is the smallest unit of data the computer can represent. By itself, a bit is not very informative.

When eight bits are grouped together as a unit, they form a **byte**. A byte is informative because it provides enough different combinations of 0s and 1s to represent 256 individual

characters. These characters include numbers, uppercase and lowercase letters of the alphabet, punctuation marks, and others such as the letters of the Greek alphabet.

The combinations of 0s and 1s that represent characters are defined by patterns called a coding scheme. In one coding scheme, the number 3 is represented as 00110011, the number 5 as 00110101, and the capital letter T as 01010100 (Figure 4-15). Two popular coding schemes are ASCII and EBCDIC (Figure 4-16). The **American Standard Code for Information Interchange**, or **ASCII** (pronounced ASK-ee), is the most widely used coding system to represent data. Most personal computers and mid-range servers use the ASCII coding scheme. The **Extended Binary Coded Decimal Interchange Code**, or **EBCDIC** (pronounced EB-see-dic) is used primarily on mainframe computers.

The ASCII and EBCDIC coding schemes are sufficient for English and Western European languages but are not large enough for Asian and other languages that use different alphabets. **Unicode** is a coding scheme capable of representing all the world's current languages. The appendix of this book discusses the ASCII, EBCDIC, and Unicode schemes in more depth, along with the parity bit and number systems.

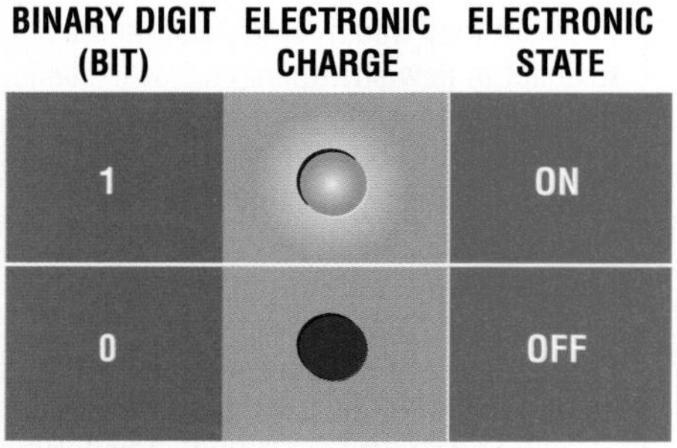

BINARY DIGIT (BIT)	ELECTRONIC CHARGE	ELECTRONIC STATE
1	○	ON
0	●	OFF

Figure 4-14 A computer circuit represents the 0 or the 1 electronically by the presence or absence of an electronic charge.

8-BIT BYTE FOR THE NUMBER 3
0 0 1 1 0 0 1 1

8-BIT BYTE FOR THE NUMBER 5
0 0 1 1 0 1 0 1

8-BIT BYTE FOR THE CAPITAL LETTER T
0 1 0 1 0 1 0 0

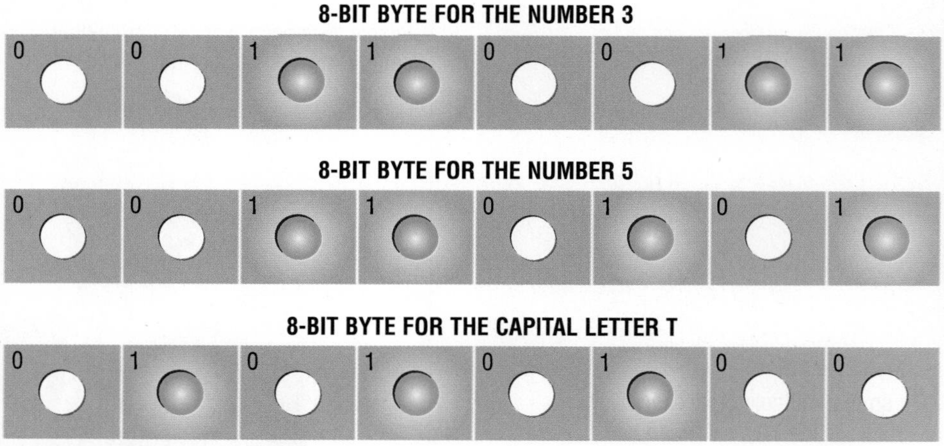

Figure 4-15 Eight bits grouped together as a unit are called a byte. A byte represents a single character in the computer.

ASCII	SYMBOL	EBCDIC
00110000	0	11110000
00110001	1	11110001
00110010	2	11110010
00110011	3	11110011
00110100	4	11110100
00110101	5	11110101
00110110	6	11110110
00110111	7	11110111
00111000	8	11111000
00111001	9	11111001
01000001	A	11000001
01000010	B	11000010
01000011	C	11000011
01000100	D	11000100
01000101	E	11000101
01000110	F	11000110
01000111	G	11000111
01001000	H	11001000
01001001	I	11001001
01001010	J	11010001
01001011	K	11010010
01001100	L	11010011
01001101	M	11010100
01001110	N	11010101
01001111	O	11010110
01010000	P	11010111
01010001	Q	11011000
01010010	R	11011001
01010011	S	11100010
01010100	T	11100011
01010101	U	11100100
01010110	V	11100101
01010111	W	11100110
01011000	X	11100111
01011001	Y	11101000
01011010	Z	11101001
00100001	!	01011010
00100010	"	01111111
00100011	#	01111011
00100100	$	01011011
00100101	%	01101100
00100110	&	01010000
00101000	(	01001101
00101001	)	01011101
00101010	*	01011100
00101011	+	01001110

Figure 4-16 Two popular coding schemes are ASCII and EBCDIC.

Coding schemes such as ASCII make it possible for humans to interact with a digital computer that recognizes only bits. When you press a key on a keyboard, the electronic signal is converted into a binary form the computer recognizes and is stored in memory. Every character is converted to its corresponding byte. The computer then processes the data as bytes, which actually is a series of on/off electrical states. When processing is finished, software converts the bytes back into numbers, letters of the alphabet, or special characters so they can display on a screen or be printed (Figure 4-17). All of these conversions take place so quickly that you do not realize they are occurring.

Standards, such as those defined by ASCII and EBCDIC, make it possible for components within computers to communicate with each other successfully. These and other standards allow various manufacturers to produce a component and be ensured that it will operate correctly in a computer – as long as it meets the defined standard. Standards also enable consumers to purchase components that are compatible with their computer configuration.

MEMORY

During processing, the processor places instructions to be executed and data needed by those instructions into memory. This **memory** is a temporary storage place for data, instructions, and information. Sometimes called primary storage, this and other types of memory consist of one or more chips on the motherboard or some other circuit board in the computer.

Figure 4-17 HOW A LETTER IS CONVERTED TO BINARY FORM AND BACK

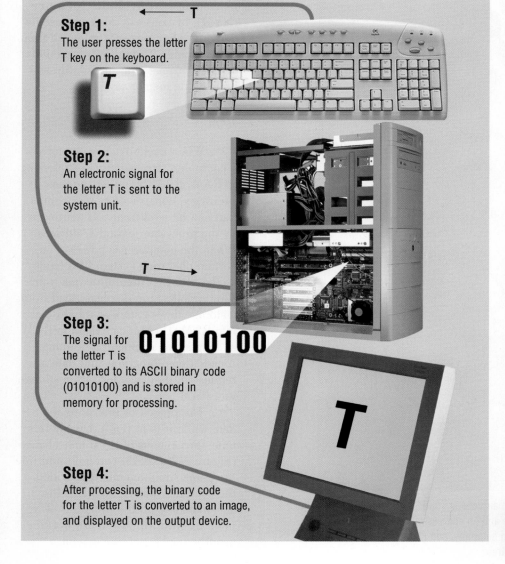

Step 1:
The user presses the letter T key on the keyboard.

Step 2:
An electronic signal for the letter T is sent to the system unit.

Step 3:
The signal for the letter T is 01010100 converted to its ASCII binary code (01010100) and is stored in memory for processing.

Step 4:
After processing, the binary code for the letter T is converted to an image, and displayed on the output device.

TECHNOLOGY TRAILBLAZER

GORDON **MOORE**

A $15 million watch would be extravagant for most people, but not for Gordon Moore, Intel's chairman emeritus. Although he no longer wears his timepiece, it serves as a reminder of Intel's venture into manufacturing and selling digital watches with liquid crystal displays for approximately $150 — until competitors started selling theirs for less than one-tenth the cost. Intel stopped making the watches in 1978.

As a co-founder of Intel in 1968, he witnessed a geometric growth in technology so consistent he could set his watch by it. When writing an article for *Electronics* magazine in 1965 to predict the growth of component technology for the next 10 years, he graphed data about memory chip performance. He predicted the number of transistors and resistors placed on computer chips would double every year, with a proportional increase in computing power and decrease in cost. This principle, Moore's Law, held true until 1975, when he changed the prediction to doubling every two years.

For more information on Gordon Moore, visit the Discovering Computers 2002 People Web page (**scsite.com/dc2002/people.htm**) and click Gordon Moore.

Memory stores three basic items: (1) the operating system and other system software that control the usage of the computer equipment; (2) application programs that carry out a specific task such as word processing; and (3) the data being processed by the application programs. This role of memory to store both data and programs is known as the **stored program concept**.

A byte (character) is the basic storage unit in memory. When application program instructions and data transfer into memory from storage devices, the instructions and data exist as bytes. Each byte resides temporarily in a location in memory, called an **address**. An address is simply a unique number that identifies the location of the byte in memory. The illustration in Figure 4-18 shows how seats in an airplane are similar to addresses in memory: (1) a seat holds one person at a time and an address in memory holds a single byte, (2) both a seat and an address can be empty, and (3) a seat has a unique identifying number and so does a memory address. To access data or instructions in memory, the computer references the addresses that contain bytes of data.

Manufacturers state memory and storage sizes in terms of the number of bytes the device has available for storage (Figure 4-19). A **kilobyte** of memory, abbreviated **KB** or **K**, is equal to exactly 1,024 bytes. To make memory and storage definitions easier to identify, computer users often round a kilobyte down to 1,000 bytes. For example, if a memory chip can store 100 KB, it can hold approximately 100,000 bytes (characters). A **megabyte** (**MB**) is equal to approximately one million bytes. A **gigabyte** (**GB**) equals approximately one billion bytes.

The system unit contains two types of memory: volatile and nonvolatile. When the computer's power is turned off, **volatile memory** loses its contents. **Nonvolatile memory** (**NVM**), by contrast, does not lose its contents when power is removed from the computer. The following sections discuss various types of volatile and nonvolatile memory.

RAM

When users discuss memory in a computer, they usually are referring to RAM. **RAM (random access memory)** consists of memory chips that can be read from and written to by the processor and other devices. When the computer is powered on, certain operating system files (such as the files that determine how your Windows desktop displays) load from a storage device such as a hard disk into RAM. These files remain in RAM as long as the computer is running. As additional programs and data are requested, they also load from storage into RAM.

The processor interprets the data while it is in RAM. During this time, the contents of RAM may change (Figure 4-20). RAM can hold multiple programs simultaneously, provided the computer has enough RAM to accommodate all the programs. The program with which you are working usually displays on the screen.

seat C22   seat B22   seat A22

Figure 4-18 This figure shows how seats in an airplane are similar to addresses in memory: (1) a seat holds one person at a time and an address in memory holds a single byte, (2) both a seat and an address can be empty, and (3) a seat has a unique identifying number and so does a memory address.

MEMORY AND STORAGE SIZES

Term	Abbreviation	Approximate Memory Size	Exact Memory Amount	Approximate Number of Pages of Text
Kilobyte	KB or K	1 thousand bytes	1,024 bytes	1/2
Megabyte	MB	1 million bytes	1,048,576 bytes	500
Gigabyte	GB	1 billion bytes	1,073,741,824 bytes	500,000
Terabyte	TB	1 trillion bytes	1,099,511,627,776 bytes	500,000,000

Figure 4-19 This table outlines terms used to define memory and storage sizes.

Figure 4-20 HOW APPLICATION PROGRAMS TRANSFER IN AND OUT OF RAM

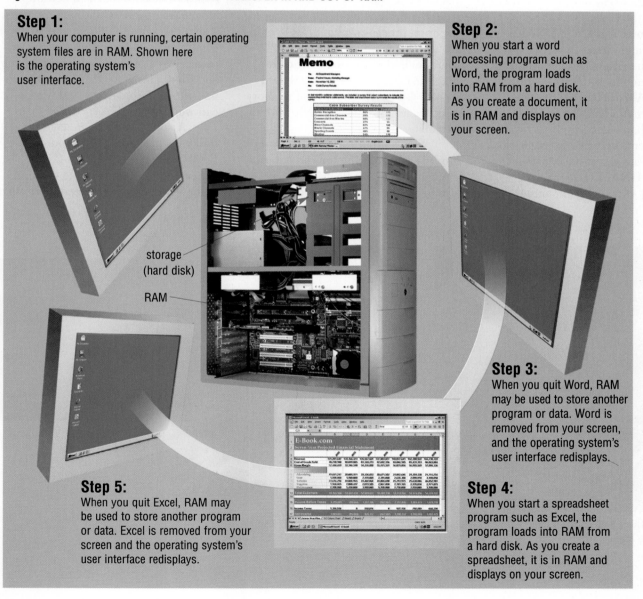

Step 1:
When your computer is running, certain operating system files are in RAM. Shown here is the operating system's user interface.

Step 2:
When you start a word processing program such as Word, the program loads into RAM from a hard disk. As you create a document, it is in RAM and displays on your screen.

storage (hard disk)

RAM

Step 3:
When you quit Word, RAM may be used to store another program or data. Word is removed from your screen, and the operating system's user interface redisplays.

Step 5:
When you quit Excel, RAM may be used to store another program or data. Excel is removed from your screen and the operating system's user interface redisplays.

Step 4:
When you start a spreadsheet program such as Excel, the program loads into RAM from a hard disk. As you create a spreadsheet, it is in RAM and displays on your screen.

Most RAM is volatile. It loses its contents when the power is removed from the computer. For this reason, you must save any items you may need in the future. **Saving** is the process of copying items from RAM to a storage device such as a hard disk.

Two basic types of RAM chips exist: dynamic RAM chips and static RAM chips. Sometimes called **main memory**, dynamic RAM chips are the most common type of RAM. **Dynamic RAM**, or **DRAM** (pronounced DEE-ram), chips must be re-energized constantly or they lose their contents. Many variations of DRAM chips exist, most of which are faster than the basic DRAM. **Synchronous DRAM (SDRAM)** chips are much faster than DRAM chips because they are synchronized to the system clock. **Double data rate SDRAM (DDR SDRAM)** chips, also called **SDRAM II** chips, are faster than SDRAM chips because they transfer data twice for each clock cycle, instead of just once. **Direct Rambus® DRAM (Direct RDRAM®)** chips are yet another type

of DRAM chips that are much faster than SDRAM chips because they use pipelining techniques. Most computers today use some form of SDRAM chips or RDRAM chips.

Static RAM chips, also called **SRAM** (pronounced ESS-ram) chips, are faster and more reliable than any variation of DRAM chips. These chips do not have to be re-energized as often as DRAM chips; thus, the term static is used. SRAM chips, however, are much more expensive than DRAM chips. Special applications such as cache use SRAM chips. A later section in this chapter discusses cache.

RAM chips often are smaller in size than processor chips. RAM chips usually reside on a small circuit board, called a **memory module**, which inserts into the motherboard (Figure 4-21). Three types of memory modules are SIMMs, DIMMs, and RIMMs.

With a **single inline memory module (SIMM)**, the pins on opposite sides of the circuit board connect together to form a single set of contacts.

With a **dual inline memory module (DIMM)**, the pins on opposite sides of the circuit board do not connect and thus form two sets of contacts. SIMMs and DIMMs typically use SDRAM chips. A **Rambus® inline memory module (RIMM)** houses RDRAM chips.

RAM REQUIREMENTS The amount of RAM a computer requires often depends on the types of applications you plan to use on the computer. A computer only can manipulate data that is in memory. RAM is similar to the workspace on the top of your desk. Just as a desktop needs a certain amount of space to hold papers, pens, a stapler, your telephone, and so on, a computer needs a certain amount of memory to store application programs and files. The more RAM a computer has, the more programs and files it can work on at once.

A software package usually indicates the minimum amount of RAM it requires (Figure 4-22). If you want the application to perform optimally, you usually need more than

dual inline memory module

memory chip

Figure 4-21 This photo shows a dual inline memory module (DIMM).

Figure 4-22 The minimum system requirements for a software product usually are printed on the box.

system requirements
Windows®
• 133 MHz Intel Pentium® processor
• Windows 95, 98®, NT 4®, 2000
• 32 MB of RAM
• 40 MB of available disk space
• 256-color monitor capable of 800X600 resolution
• CD-ROM drive
Macintosh®
• Power Macintosh®
• MacOS® 8.5 or later
• 32 MB of free application RAM
• 40 MB of available disk space
• 256-color monitor capable of 800X600 resolution
• CD-ROM drive

the minimum specifications on the software package.

Generally, home users running Windows and using standard application software such as word processing should have at least 32 MB of RAM. Most business users that work with accounting, financial, or spreadsheet programs, voice recognition, and programs requiring multimedia capabilities should have a minimum of 64 MB of RAM. Users composing multimedia presentations or using graphics-intensive applications will want at least 256 MB of RAM.

Figure 4-23a provides guidelines for the amount of RAM for various types of users. Figure 4-23b shows advertisements that match to each user requirement. Advertisements normally list the type of processor, the clock speed of the processor in MHz or GHz, and the amount of RAM in the computer. The amount of RAM in computers purchased today ranges from 64 MB to 512 MB.

The amount of RAM on the computer determines the amount of programs and data a computer can handle at one time, which affects overall performance. The more RAM, the faster the computer will respond.

Cache

Most of today's computers improve processing times with cache (pronounced cash). Two types of **cache** are memory cache and disk cache. This chapter discusses memory cache. Chapter 7 discusses disk cache.

Memory cache, also called a **cache store** or **RAM cache**, helps speed the processes of the computer because it stores frequently used instructions and data. The processor is likely to request these items repeatedly, so the items are stored for quick access. When the processor needs an instruction or data, it first searches cache. If it cannot locate the item in cache, then it searches RAM.

Most modern computers have two or three types, or layers, of memory cache: Level 1, Level 2, and Level 3. **Level 1 (L1) cache**, also called **primary cache** or **internal cache**, is built directly into the processor chip. L1 cache usually has a very small capacity, ranging from 8 KB to 64 KB. The most common size is 16 KB.

When discussing cache, most users are referring to L2 cache. **Level 2 (L2) cache**, or **external cache**, is slightly slower than L1 cache but has a much larger capacity, ranging from 64 KB to 4 MB. On older computers, L2 cache was not part of the processor chip. Instead, it

Web Link
For more information on cache, visit the Discovering Computers 2002 Chapter 4 WEB LINK page (**scsite.com/dc2002/ch4/weblink.htm**) and click Cache.

Figure 4-23a (RAM guidelines)

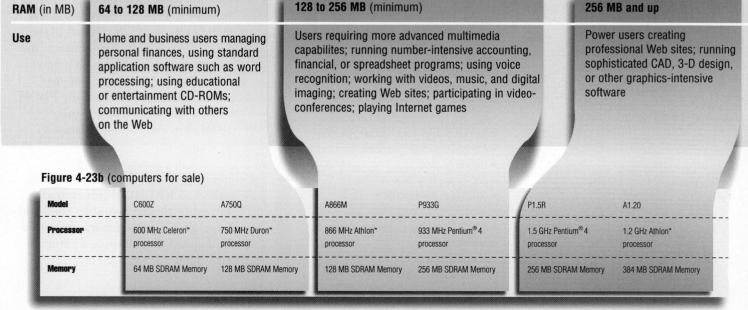

Figure 4-23b (computers for sale)

Figure 4-23 Determining how much RAM you need depends on the applications you intend to run on your computer. Advertisements for computers normally list the type of processor, the speed of the computer measured in MHz or GHz, as well as the amount of RAM installed.

consisted of high-speed SRAM chips on the motherboard or a separate card of chips inserted into a slot in the computer. Current processors include **advanced transfer cache**, a type of L2 cache built directly on the processor chip. Processors that use advanced transfer cache perform at much faster rates than those that do not use it. The common size of advanced transfer cache is 256 KB.

If a processor has L2 advanced transfer cache, it also can use L3 cache. **L3 cache** is a cache separate from the processor chips on the motherboard. L3 cache only exists on computers that use L2 advanced transfer cache.

Cache speeds up processing time because it stores frequently used instructions and data. When the processor needs an instruction or data, it searches memory in this order: L1 cache, then L2 cache, then L3 cache (if it exists), then RAM — with a greater delay in processing for each level of memory it must search. If the instruction or data is not found in memory, then it must search a slower speed storage device such as a hard disk or CD-ROM.

A computer with L2 cache usually performs at speeds 10- to 40-percent faster than those without cache. To realize the largest increase in performance, a desktop computer should have at least 256 KB of L2 advanced transfer cache (Figure 4-24). Servers and workstations have at least 2 MB of L2 advanced transfer cache.

ROM

Read-only memory (ROM pronounced rahm) refers to memory chips storing data that only can be read. The data on ROM chips cannot be modified — hence, the name read only. ROM is nonvolatile. Its contents are not lost when power is removed from the computer.

ROM chips contain data, instructions, or information that is recorded permanently. For example, ROM contains the **basic input/output system (BIOS** pronounced BYE-ohss), which is a sequence of instructions the computer follows to load the operating system and other files when you first turn on the computer. Many other devices also contain ROM chips. For example, ROM chips in many printers contain data for fonts.

Manufacturers of ROM chips often record the data, instructions, or information on the chips when they manufacture the chip. These ROM chips, called **firmware,** contain permanently written data, instructions, or information. The BIOS is firmware that contains the computer's startup instructions.

A variation of the ROM chip, called a **programmable read-only memory (PROM)** chip, is a blank ROM chip on which you can place items permanently. Programmers use **microcode** instructions to program a PROM chip. Once a programmer writes the microcode onto the PROM chip, it functions like a regular ROM chip and cannot be erased or changed.

A programmer can erase microcode on a type of PROM chip, called an **EEPROM (electrically erasable programmable read-only memory)**. Flash memory, discussed in the next section, uses a variation of EEPROM.

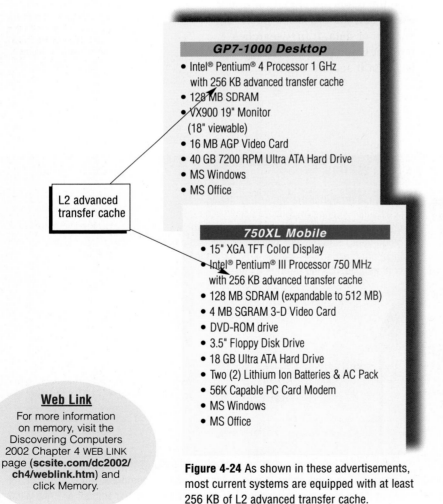

L2 advanced transfer cache

GP7-1000 Desktop
- Intel® Pentium® 4 Processor 1 GHz with 256 KB advanced transfer cache
- 128 MB SDRAM
- VX900 19" Monitor (18" viewable)
- 16 MB AGP Video Card
- 40 GB 7200 RPM Ultra ATA Hard Drive
- MS Windows
- MS Office

750XL Mobile
- 15" XGA TFT Color Display
- Intel® Pentium® III Processor 750 MHz with 256 KB advanced transfer cache
- 128 MB SDRAM (expandable to 512 MB)
- 4 MB SGRAM 3-D Video Card
- DVD-ROM drive
- 3.5" Floppy Disk Drive
- 18 GB Ultra ATA Hard Drive
- Two (2) Lithium Ion Batteries & AC Pack
- 56K Capable PC Card Modem
- MS Windows
- MS Office

Figure 4-24 As shown in these advertisements, most current systems are equipped with at least 256 KB of L2 advanced transfer cache.

Web Link
For more information on memory, visit the Discovering Computers 2002 Chapter 4 WEB LINK page (scsite.com/dc2002/ch4/weblink.htm) and click Memory.

Flash Memory

Flash memory, also known as **flash ROM** or **flash RAM**, is a type of nonvolatile memory that can be erased electronically and reprogrammed. Many current computers use flash BIOS. With **flash BIOS**, the computer easily can update the contents of the BIOS chip, if necessary.

Flash memory chips store data and programs on many handheld computers and devices, such as digital cellular telephones, printers, set-top boxes, digital cameras, automotive devices, digital voice recorders, and pagers (Figure 4-25). **Flash memory cards** store flash memory on a removable device instead of a chip. Removable flash memory allows users to transfer data and information conveniently from these small devices to their desktop computers. A later section in this chapter discusses these cards in more depth. Flash memory is available in sizes up to 128 MB.

CMOS

Another type of memory chip in the system unit is complementary metal-oxide semiconductor memory. **Complementary metal-oxide semiconductor memory**, abbreviated **CMOS** (pronounced SEE-moss), stores configuration information about the computer. This information includes the type of disk drives, keyboard, and monitor; the current date and time; and other startup information needed when you turn on the computer.

CMOS chips use battery power to retain information even when the power to the computer is off. Battery-backed CMOS memory thus keeps the calendar, date, and time current even when the computer is off. Unlike standard ROM, the computer can change information in CMOS, such as when you change from standard time to daylight savings time or when you add new hardware devices to the computer.

APPLY IT!

Your Computer's Battery

Is your computer clock losing time? If so, that is a warning that your CMOS battery is about to go. Moreover, when it does, you will have a difficult time accessing your computer until you change the battery. The CMOS battery powers both the computer's internal clock and a CMOS memory chip that holds all the computer's crucial setup information, such as hard disk parameters, types of floppy drives, and memory size. The battery is easy to replace. Just follow these steps:

1. Obtain a replacement battery from a local vendor or online computer parts dealer.
2. Record your computer's setup information. You can do this by booting your computer and entering its setup mode. Write down all of the settings from the various menus. Alternatively, you can use a software program, such as Norton Utilities, that stores a backup copy of your computer's CMOS settings on a floppy disk.
3. Turn off the computer.
4. Open the case and locate the battery on the motherboard. See your user manual for specifications about the battery and its location.
5. Remove the old battery and replace it with the new one. You may have to move some cables around.
6. Document the date you replaced the battery.
7. Replace the case and turn on the computer. An error message will display.
8. Enter your computer's setup mode.
9. Reenter the settings you recorded from the various setup menus. If you used a program such as Norton Utilities, restore the settings from the floppy disk.

Caution: Do not forget to observe proper anti-static precautions when working inside the case of your computer.

For more information on CMOS and replacing the battery, visit the Discovering Computers 2002 Apply It Web page (**scsite.com/dc2002/apply.htm**) and click Chapter 4 Apply It #3.

Figure 4-25 Flash memory chips are used in personal and handheld computers, digital cellular telephones, printers, set-top boxes, digital cameras, automotive devices, digital voice recorders, and pagers.

Memory Access Times

Access time is the amount of time it takes the processor to read data, instructions, and information from memory. A computer's access time directly affects how fast the computer processes data. Manufacturers use a variety of terminology to state access times (Figure 4-26). Some use fractions of a second, which for memory, occurs in nanoseconds. A **nanosecond** (abbreviated **ns**) is one billionth of a second. A nanosecond is extremely fast (Figure 4-27). In fact, electricity travels about one foot in a nanosecond.

Other manufacturers state access times in MHz, e.g., an 83 MHz SDRAM. If a manufacturer states access time in megahertz, you can convert it to nanoseconds by dividing the megahertz number into 1 billion ns. For example, 133 MHz equals approximately 7.5 ns.

The access time (speed) of memory contributes to the overall performance of the computer. SDRAM chips can have access times up to 133 MHz (7.5 ns). The faster RDRAM chips can have access times up to 800 MHz (1.25 ns). ROM's access times range from 25 to 250 ns. Accessing data in memory can be more than 200,000 times faster than accessing data on a hard disk.

While access times of memory greatly affect overall computer performance, manufacturers and retailers usually list a computer's memory in terms of its size, not its access time. Thus, an advertisement might describe a computer as having 32 MB of SDRAM expandable to 512 MB.

You can expand memory capacity in a number of ways, such as installing additional memory in an expansion slot or inserting a memory card into a card slot.

Chip Recall

Processor Chip Flaws

A glitch within a single computer chip can cause untold problems. In 1994, a design flaw in Intel's Pentium® chip caused a rounding error once in every nine billion division operations. For most users, this would result in a mistake only once in every 27,000 years, so Intel initially ignored the problem. After an unexpected public outcry, Intel supplied replacements to anyone who asked, which cost the company nearly $500 million. Did people overreact? Did the demand for perfection divert funds that could have been spent better elsewhere? (Intel's costs were equivalent to half a year's research and development budget.) How much perfection do consumers have a right to expect? How serious should a problem be before a chip is recalled?

For more information on processor chips and flaw issues, visit the Discovering Computers 2002 Issues Web page (**scsite.com/dc2002/issues. htm**) and click Chapter 4 Issue #2.

ACCESS TIME TERMINOLOGY

TERM	ABBREVIATION	SPEED
Millisecond	ms	One-thousandth of a second
Microsecond	µs	One-millionth of a second
Nanosecond	ns	One-billionth of a second
Picosecond	ps	One-trillionth of a second

Figure 4-26 Access times are measured in fractions of a second. This table outlines terms used to define access times.

10 million operations =
1 blink

Figure 4-27 It takes about one-tenth of a second to blink your eye, which is the equivalent of 100 million nanoseconds. A computer can perform some operations in as little as 10 nanoseconds. In the time it takes to blink your eye, a computer can perform some operations 10 million times.

EXPANSION SLOTS AND EXPANSION CARDS

An **expansion slot** is an opening, or socket, where you can insert a circuit board into the motherboard. These circuit boards add new devices or capabilities to the computer such as more memory, higher-quality sound devices, a modem, or graphics capabilities (Figure 4-28). A variety of terms identify a circuit board that fits in an expansion slot: **card, expansion card, expansion board, board, adapter card, adapter, interface card, add-in,** and **add-on**.

Sometimes a device or feature is built into a card. With other cards, a cable connects the expansion card to a device, such as a scanner, outside the system unit. Figure 4-29 shows someone inserting an expansion card into an expansion slot on a personal computer motherboard.

Four types of expansion cards found in most of today's computers are a video card, a sound card, a network interface card, and a modem card. A **video card**, also called a **video adapter** or **graphics card**, converts computer output into a video signal that is sent through a cable to the monitor, which displays an image on the screen. A **sound card** enhances the sound-generating capabilities of a personal computer by allowing sound to be input through a microphone and output through speakers. A **network interface card** (**NIC** pronounced nick), also called a **network card**, is a communications device that allows the computer to communicate via a network. A **modem card**, also called an **internal modem**, is a communications device that enables computers to communicate via telephone lines or other means.

TYPES OF EXPANSION CARDS

EXPANSION CARD	PURPOSE
Accelerator	To increase the speed of the processor
Controller	To connect disk drives; being phased out because newer motherboards support these connections
Game	To connect a joystick
I/O	To connect input and output devices such as a printer or mouse; being phased out because newer motherboards support these connections
Interface	To connect other peripherals such as a mouse, CD-ROM, or scanner
Memory	To add more memory to the computer
Modem	To connect to other computers through telephone lines
Network Interface	To connect to other computers and peripherals
PC-to-TV converter	To connect to a television
Sound	To connect speakers or microphone
TV Tuner	To view television channels on your monitor
Video	To connect a monitor
Video Capture	To connect a camcorder

Figure 4-28 This table lists some of the types of expansion cards and their functions.

Figure 4-29 This figure shows an expansion card being inserted into an expansion slot on the motherboard of a personal computer.

In the past installing a card was not easy and required you set switches and other elements on the motherboard. Many of today's computers support Plug and Play. With **Plug and Play**, the computer automatically can configure cards and other devices as you install them. Having Plug and Play support means you can plug in a device, turn on the computer, and then use, or *play*, the device without having to configure the computer manually.

PC Cards and Flash Memory Cards

Notebook and other mobile computers have a special type of expansion slot for installing PC Cards. A **PC Card** is a thin credit

Web Link

For more information on PC Cards, visit the Discovering Computers 2002 Chapter 4 WEB LINK page (**scsite.com/dc2002/ch4/weblink.htm**) and click PC Cards.

card-sized device that adds memory, disk drives, sound, fax/modem, communications, and other capabilities to a mobile computer such as a notebook computer (Figure 4-30). Because of their small size and versatility, many consumer electronics products such as digital cameras, cable TV, and automobiles use PC Cards.

All PC Cards conform to standards developed by the **P**ersonal **C**omputer **M**emory **C**ard **I**nternational **A**ssociation (these cards originally were called **PCMCIA cards**). This helps

to ensure that you can interchange PC Cards among handheld computers. PC Cards are all the same length and width, and fit in a standard PC Card slot. A notebook computer usually has a PC card slot on one of its edges.

The three types of PC Cards are Type I, Type II, and Type III. The only difference in size among the three types is their thickness. The thinnest **Type I cards** add memory capabilities to the computer. **Type II cards** contain communications devices such as modems. The thickest **Type III cards** house devices such as hard disks.

Figure 4-30 This picture shows a PC Card sticking out of a PC Card slot on a notebook computer.

ISSUE

Is Cheaper Just as Good?

Personal Computer Prices

Today, you can buy a personal computer for less than $1,000 that has as much functionality as one nearly twice its cost two years ago. These low prices allow consumers today to shop for computer bargains. Many consumers want inexpensive computers that are adequate for basic tasks, such as word processing and Internet access. They feel that spending higher prices on computers with faster processors and more hard disk space is an unnecessary, frivolous expense. As one industry analyst asks, "Why buy a Porsche when you are going to drive only 55 miles per hour?" How might a greater availability of lower costing personal computers change the way schools and businesses use them? Does a higher price mean better quality, with respect to computers? Is it necessary to have the latest and greatest technology in a personal computer?

For more information on prices of personal computers, visit the Discovering Computers 2002 Issues Web page (**scsite.com/dc2002/issues.htm**) and click Chapter 4 Issue #3.

Flash memory cards are available in a variety of sizes (Figure 4-31). Many handheld computers and devices, such as digital computers, digital music players, and cellular telephones, use these memory cards. Some printers and computers have built-in card readers or slots. You also can purchase an external card reader that attaches to any computer. The type of card you have will determine the type of card reader you need.

Unlike other cards that require you to open the system unit and install the card onto the motherboard, you can change a PC Card or flash memory card without having to open the system unit or restart the computer. For example, if you need to connect to the Internet, you can just insert the modem card in the PC Card slot of your notebook computer while the computer is running. The operating system automatically recognizes the new card and allows you to connect to the Internet.

This feature of PC Cards and flash memory cards, called **hot plugging** or **hot swapping**, allows you to add and remove devices while a computer is running.

PORTS

External devices such as a keyboard, monitor, printer, mouse, and microphone, often attach by a cable to the system unit. A **port** is the interface, or point of attachment, to the system unit. The back of the system unit contains many ports (Figure 4-32).

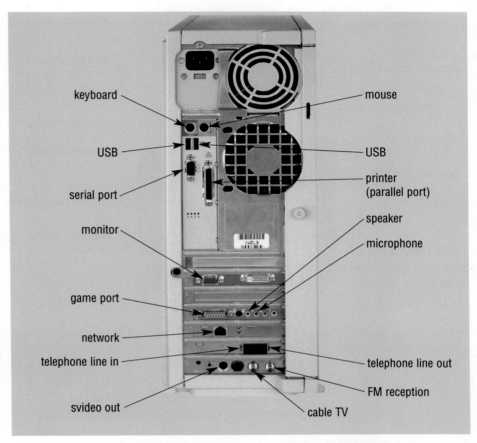

Figure 4-32 A port is an interface that allows you to connect a peripheral device such as a printer, mouse, or keyboard to the computer. The back of the system unit has many ports.

Figure 4-31 Flash memory cards are available in a wide range of sizes.

Web Link

For more information on ports and connectors, visit the Discovering Computers 2002 Chapter 4 WEB LINK page (**scsite.com/dc2002/ch4/weblink.htm**) and click Ports and Connectors.

Ports have different types of connectors. A **connector** joins a cable to a device (Figure 4-33).

One end of a cable attaches to the connector on the system unit and the other end of the cable attaches to a connector on the peripheral device. Most connectors are available in one of two genders: male or female. **Male connectors** have one or more exposed pins, like the end of an electrical cord you plug into the wall. **Female connectors** have matching holes to accept the pins on a male connector, like an electrical wall outlet.

Figure 4-34 shows the different types of connectors on a system unit. Some system units include these connectors when you buy the computer. You add other connectors by inserting cards into the computer. The card has a port that allows you to attach a device to the card.

When you purchase a cable to connect your computer to a peripheral, the manufacturers often identify the cables by their connector types. For example, a printer port might use any

power cord
keyboard connector
USB connector
network connector

mouse connector
printer connector
monitor connector
speaker connector
microphone connector
telephone line in connector

Figure 4-33 A connector attaches an external device to the system unit.

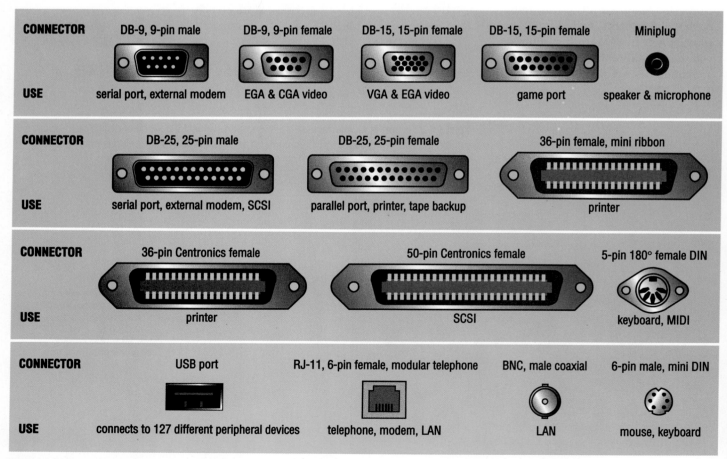

CONNECTOR	DB-9, 9-pin male	DB-9, 9-pin female	DB-15, 15-pin female	DB-15, 15-pin female	Miniplug
USE	serial port, external modem	EGA & CGA video	VGA & EGA video	game port	speaker & microphone

CONNECTOR	DB-25, 25-pin male	DB-25, 25-pin female	36-pin female, mini ribbon
USE	serial port, external modem, SCSI	parallel port, printer, tape backup	printer

CONNECTOR	36-pin Centronics female	50-pin Centronics female	5-pin 180° female DIN
USE	printer	SCSI	keyboard, MIDI

CONNECTOR	USB port	RJ-11, 6-pin female, modular telephone	BNC, male coaxial	6-pin male, mini DIN
USE	connects to 127 different peripheral devices	telephone, modem, LAN	LAN	mouse, keyboard

Figure 4-34 Examples of different types of connectors on a system unit.

one of these connectors: 25-pin female, 36-pin female, 36-pin Centronics female, or USB. Thus, you should understand the differences among connector types.

Sometimes you cannot attach a new peripheral device to the computer because the connector on the system unit is the same gender as the connector on the cable. You can use a gender changer to solve this problem. A **gender changer** is a device that enables you to join two connectors that are either both female or both male.

Most computers have three types of ports: serial, parallel, and USB. The next section discusses each of these ports.

Serial Ports

A **serial port** is one type of interface that connects a device to the system unit by transmitting data one bit at a time (Figure 4-35). Serial ports usually connect devices that do not require fast data transmission rates, such as a mouse, keyboard, or modem. The COM port on the system unit is one type of serial port.

Some modems that connect the system unit to a telephone line use a serial port because the telephone line expects the data in a specific frequency. Serial ports conform to either the RS-232 or RS-422 standard, which specifies the number of pins

used on the port's connector. Two common connectors for serial ports are a male 25-pin connector and a male 9-pin connector.

Parallel Ports

Unlike a serial port, a **parallel port** is an interface that connects devices by transferring more than one bit at a time (Figure 4-36). Parallel ports originally were developed as an alternative to the slower speed serial ports.

Many printers connect to the system unit using a parallel port with a 25-pin female connector. This parallel port can transfer eight bits of data (one byte) simultaneously through eight separate lines in a single cable. A parallel port sometimes is

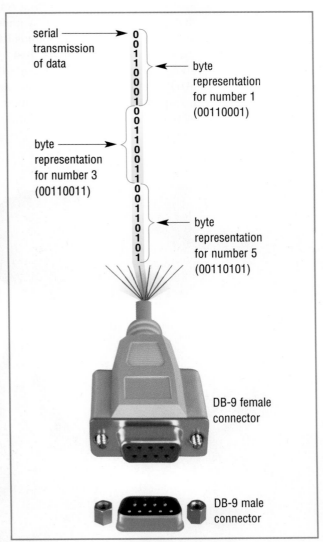

Figure 4-35 A serial port transmits data one bit at a time. One wire sends data; another receives data; and the remaining wires are used for other communications operations.

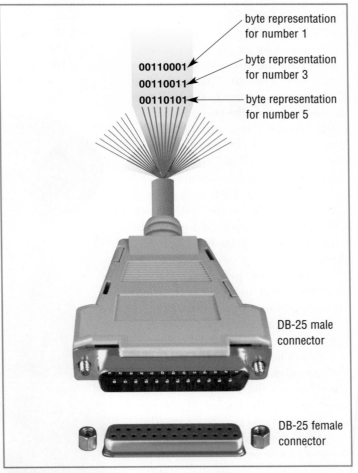

Figure 4-36 A parallel port is capable of transmitting more than one bit at a time. The port shown in this figure has eight wires that transmit data; the remaining wires are used for other communications operations.

called a Centronics interface, after the company that first defined the standard for communications between the system unit and a printer.

Two newer types of parallel ports, the EPP (Enhanced Parallel Port) and the ECP (Extended Capabilities Port), use the same connectors as the Centronics port, but are more than 10 times faster. Both EPP and ECP are part of the IEEE (Institute of Electrical and Electronics Engineers) 1284 standard. The **IEEE 1284** standard specifies how older and newer peripheral devices that use a parallel port should transfer data to and from a computer.

Universal Serial Bus Port

A **universal serial bus (USB) port** can connect up to 127 different peripheral devices with a single connector type. Many system units have one or two USB ports (see Figure 4-32 on page 4.25). To attach multiple devices using a single port, you can daisy chain the devices together outside the system unit. That is, the first USB device connects to the USB port on the computer, the second USB device connects to the first USB device, the third USB device connects to the second USB device, and so on. An alternative to daisy chaining is to use a USB hub. A **USB hub** plugs into the USB port on the system unit and contains multiple USB ports into which you plug cables from USB devices.

Some newer peripheral devices may attach only to a USB port. Others attach to either a serial or parallel port, as well as a USB port. When connecting a device to a USB port, you do not need to install a card in the computer. Simply plug one end of the cable into the USB port and the other end into the device. Having a standard port and connector greatly simplifies the process of attaching devices to a personal computer.

The USB also supports hot plugging and Plug and Play, which means you can attach peripherals while the computer is running. With serial and parallel port connections, by contrast, you often must restart the computer after you attach the device.

Special-Purpose Ports

Four special-purpose ports used on many of today's computers are 1394, MIDI, SCSI, and IrDA. The following section discusses each of these ports.

1394 PORT Similarly to the USB port, the IEEE **1394 port**, also called **FireWire**, can connect multiple types of devices that require faster data transmission speeds such as digital video cameras, digital VCRs, color printers, scanners, digital cameras, and DVD drives to a single connector. You can connect up to 63 devices together using a 1394 port. The 1394 port also supports Plug and Play. The Macintosh G4 computer has a 1394 port.

Many computer professionals believe that ports such as USB and 1394 someday will replace serial and parallel ports completely (Figure 4-37).

MIDI PORT A special type of serial port, called a **musical instrument digital interface**, or **MIDI** (pronounced MID-dee) port, connects the system unit to a musical instrument, such as an electronic keyboard. The electronic music industry has adopted MIDI as a standard to define how devices, such as sound cards and synthesizers, represent sounds electronically. A **synthesizer**, which can be a peripheral or a chip, creates sound from digital instructions.

A system unit with a MIDI port has the capability of recording sounds that have been created by a synthesizer and then processing the sounds (the data) to create new sounds. Just about every sound card supports the MIDI standard, so you can play and manipulate sounds on a computer that were created originally on another computer.

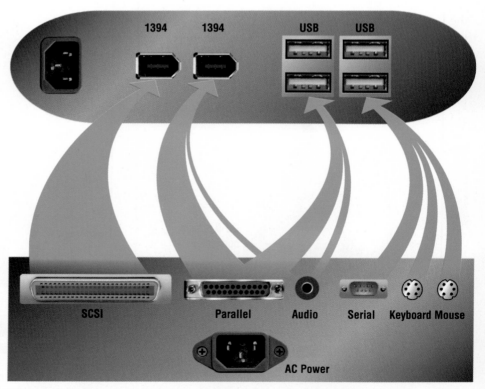

Figure 4-37 Many computer professionals believe that ports such as USB and 1394 someday will replace serial and parallel ports completely.

SCSI PORT A small computer system interface (**SCSI** pronounced skuzzy) port is a special high-speed parallel port that allows you to attach SCSI peripheral devices such as disk drives and printers. Depending on the type of SCSI interface, you can daisy chain either up to 7 or 15 devices together. That is, the first SCSI device connects to the computer, the second SCSI device connects to the first SCSI device, and so on. Some new computers include a SCSI port. Others have a slot that supports a SCSI card.

IrDA PORT Peripheral devices may not use any cables. Instead, some transmit data via infrared light waves. For these wireless devices to transmit signals to a computer, both the computer and the device must have an **IrDA port** (Figure 4-38). These ports conform to standards developed by the **IrDA (Infrared Data Association)**.

Operating similar to a television remote control, you must align the IrDA port on the peripheral device with the IrDA port on the computer so that nothing obstructs the path of the infrared light wave. Devices that use IrDA ports include the keyboard, mouse, printer, digital cameras, digital telephones, and pagers. Several of these devices use a high-speed IrDA port, sometimes called a **FIR (fast infrared)** port.

BUSES

As previously explained, a computer processes and stores data as a series of electronic bits. These bits transfer internally within the circuitry of the computer along electrical channels. Each channel, called a **bus**, allows the various devices inside and attached to the system unit to communicate with each other. Just as vehicles travel on a highway to move from one destination to another, bits travel on a bus (Figure 4-39 on the next page).

Buses transfer bits from input devices to memory, from memory to the processor, from the processor to memory, and from memory to output or storage devices. Buses consist of two parts: a data bus and an address bus. The data bus transfers actual data and the address bus transfers information about where the data should go in memory.

The size of a bus, called the **bus width**, determines the number of bits that the computer can transmit at one time. For example, a 32-bit bus can transmit 32 bits (four bytes) at a time. On a 64-bit bus, bits transmit from one location to another 64 bits (eight bytes) at a time. The larger the number of bits handled by the bus, the faster the computer transfers data.

Web Link

For more information on buses, visit the Discovering Computers 2002 Chapter 4 WEB LINK page (**scsite.com/dc2002/ch4/weblink.htm**) and click Buses.

High-Speed Ports

USB and 1394

In 1996, a few computer manufacturers started to include universal serial bus (USB) support in newer machines. With the release of the iMac in 1998 the USB became widespread. Many consider the USB to be the most important advance to date in connectivity standards for the personal computer. The primary selling point of USB is Plug and Play. Another selling point is that you can daisy chain up to 127 different peripheral devices. It is important to note that 127 is a theoretical limit. In reality, the number of devices is limited by their need for bandwidth and power needs. Another Plug and Play port that supports high speed data transfer rates is the IEEE 1394, also known as FireWire. A 1394 port can handle up to 63 daisy-chained devices. The primary difference between USB and 1394 is that 1394 is more expensive and supports faster data transfer rates. For those with the newest computers and the latest version of Windows 98, USB and 1394 devices should prove much easier to install and use than devices dependent on expansion cards. Will USB and 1394 eventually replace serial and parallel ports? Will consumers be willing to pay more for a 1394 port for faster transfer rates? Why or why not?

For more information on the USB and 1394 devices, visit the Discovering Computers 2002 Issues Web page (**scsite.com/dc2002/issues.htm**) and click Chapter 4 Issue #4.

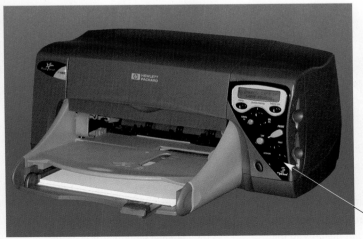

IrDA port on printer

Figure 4-38 Some devices communicate wirelessly through an IrDA port.

Using the highway analogy again, assume that one lane on a highway can carry one bit. A 32-bit bus is like a 32-lane highway. A 64-bit bus is like a 64-lane highway.

If a number in memory occupies 8 bytes, or 64 bits, the computer must transmit it in two separate steps when using a 32-bit bus: once for the first 32 bits and once for the second 32 bits. Using a 64-bit bus, the computer can transmit the number in a single step, transferring all 64 bits at once. The wider the bus, the fewer number of transfer steps required and the faster the transfer of data. Figure 4-40 lists some personal computer processors and their bus widths.

In conjunction with the bus width, many computer professionals discuss a computer's word size. **Word size** is the number of bits the processor can interpret and execute at a given time. That is, a 64-bit processor can manipulate 64 bits at a time. Computers with a larger word size can process more data in the same amount of time than computers with a smaller word size. In most computers, the word size is the same as the bus width.

Every bus also has a clock speed. Just like the processor, manufacturers state the clock speed for a bus in megahertz. Recall that

one megahertz (MHz) is equal to one million ticks per second. Most of today's processors have a bus speed of either 100 MHz or 133 MHz. The higher the bus clock speed, the faster the transmission of data, which results in applications running faster.

A computer has two basic types of buses: a system bus and an expansion bus. A **system bus** is part of the motherboard and connects the processor to main memory. An **expansion bus** allows the processor to communicate with peripheral devices. When computer professionals use the term bus by itself, they usually are referring to the system bus.

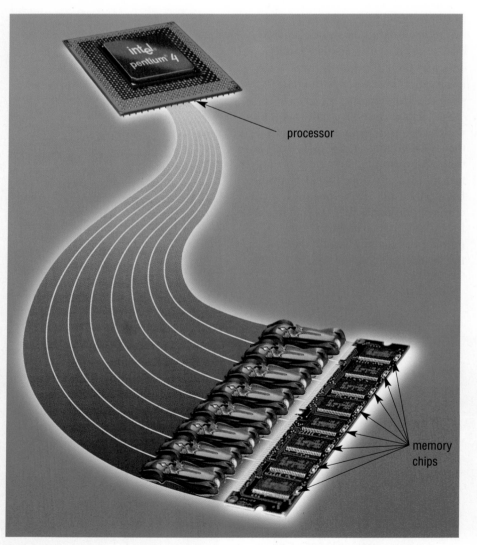

processor

memory chips

COMPARISON OF BUS WIDTHS

NAME	BUS WIDTH*
Pentium® 4	64
Itanium™	64
Pentium® III Xeon™	64
Pentium® III	64
Celeron™	64
Pentium® II Xeon™	64
Pentium® II	64
Pentium® with MMX™ technology	64
Pentium® Pro	64
Pentium®	64
80486DX	32
80386DX	32
80286	16
PowerPC	64
68040	32
68030	32
68020	32

Figure 4-39 Just as vehicles travel on a highway to move from one destination to another, bits travel on a bus. Buses transfer bits from input devices to memory, from memory to the processor, from the processor to memory, and from memory to output or storage devices.

Figure 4-40 A comparison of bus widths on some personal computer processors.

Expansion Bus

Some devices outside the system unit connect to a port on a card, which is inserted into an expansion slot. This expansion slot connects to the expansion bus, which allows the processor to communicate with the peripheral device attached to the card. Data transmitted to memory or the processor travels from the expansion bus via the expansion bus and the system bus (Figure 4-41).

The types of expansion buses on a motherboard determine the types of cards you can add to your computer. Thus, you should understand the following types of expansion buses: ISA bus, PCI bus, AGP bus, USB, 1394 bus, and PC Card bus.

- The most common and slowest expansion bus is the **ISA (Industry Standard Architecture) bus**. A mouse, modem card, sound card, and low-speed network interface card are examples of devices that connect to the ISA bus directly or through an ISA bus expansion slot.
- A **local bus** is a high-speed expansion bus that connects higher speed devices such as hard disks. The first standard local bus was the **VESA local bus**, which was used primarily for video cards. The current local bus standard is the **PCI (Peripheral Component Interconnect) bus** because it is more versatile than the VESA local bus. Types of cards you can insert into a PCI bus expansion slot include video cards, sound cards, SCSI cards, and high-speed network interface cards. The PCI bus transfers data about four times faster than the ISA bus. Most current personal computers have a PCI bus as well as an ISA bus.
- The **Accelerated Graphics Port (AGP)** is a bus designed by Intel to improve the speed with which 3-D graphics and video transmit. With an AGP video card in an AGP bus slot, the AGP bus provides a faster, dedicated interface between the video card and memory. Newer processors support AGP technology.

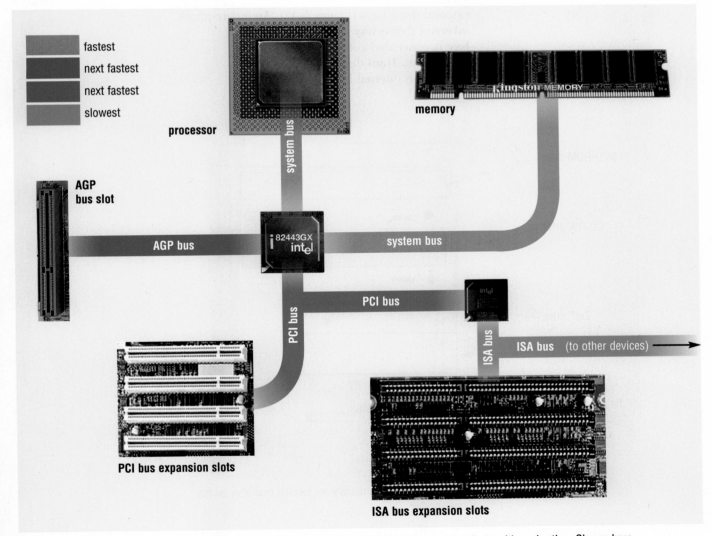

Figure 4-41 Buses allow the various devices inside and attached to the system unit to communicate with each other. Shown here, the buses in order of speed, from fastest to slowest, are the system bus, the AGP bus, the PCI bus, and the ISA bus.

- The **universal serial bus (USB)** and **1394 bus** are buses that eliminate the need to install cards into expansion slots. In a computer with a USB, for example, USB devices connect to each other outside the system unit and then a single cable attaches to the USB port. The USB port then connects to the USB, which connects to the PCI bus on the motherboard. The 1394 bus works in a similar fashion. With these buses, expansion slots are available for devices not compatible with USB or 1394.
- The expansion bus for a PC Card is the **PC Card bus**. With a PC Card inserted into a PC Card slot, data travels on the PC Card bus to the PCI bus.

BAYS

After you purchase a computer, you may want to install an additional device such as a disk drive to add storage capabilities to the system unit. A **bay** is an open area inside the system unit in which you can install additional equipment. A bay is different from a slot, which is used for the installation of cards. These spaces, commonly called **drive bays**, most often hold disk drives.

Two types of drive bays exist: internal and external. An **external drive bay** or **exposed drive bay** allows access to the drive from outside the system unit. Floppy disk drives, CD-ROM drives, DVD-ROM drives, Zip® drives, and tape drives are examples of devices installed in external drive bays (Figure 4-42). An **internal drive bay** or **hidden drive bay** is concealed entirely within the system unit. Hard disk drives are installed in internal bays.

POWER SUPPLY

Many personal computers plug into standard wall outlets, which supply an alternating current (AC) of 115 to 120 volts. This type of power is unsuitable for use with a computer, which requires a direct current (DC) ranging from 5 to 12 volts. The **power supply** is the component in the system unit that converts the wall outlet AC power into DC power.

Some external peripheral devices such as an external modem or tape drive have an **AC adapter**, which is an external power supply. One end of the AC adapter plugs into the wall outlet and the other end attaches to the peripheral device. The AC adapter converts the AC power into DC power that the device requires.

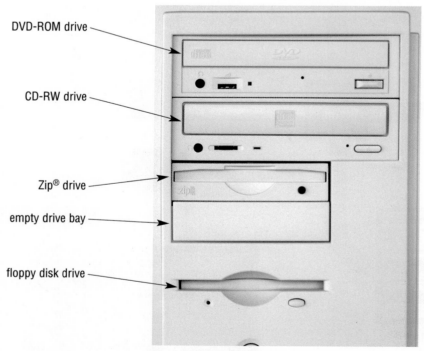

DVD-ROM drive

CD-RW drive

Zip® drive

empty drive bay

floppy disk drive

Figure 4-42 Drive bays usually are located beside or on top of one another.

MOBILE COMPUTERS

As businesses expand to serve customers across the country and around the world, more and more people need to use a computer while traveling to and from a main office to conduct business. As noted in Chapter 1, users with such mobile computing needs — known as mobile users — often have a mobile computer such as a notebook and/or handheld computer (Figure 4-43).

Weighing on average between 4 and 10 pounds, notebook computers can run either using batteries or using a standard power supply. Smaller handheld computers, run strictly on battery.

Like their desktop counterparts, notebook computers and handheld computers have a system unit that contains electronic components that processes data (Figure 4-44). The difference is many other devices also are part of the system unit. In addition to the motherboard, processor, memory, sound card, PC Card slot, and drive bay, the system unit also houses devices such as the keyboard, pointing device, speakers, and display.

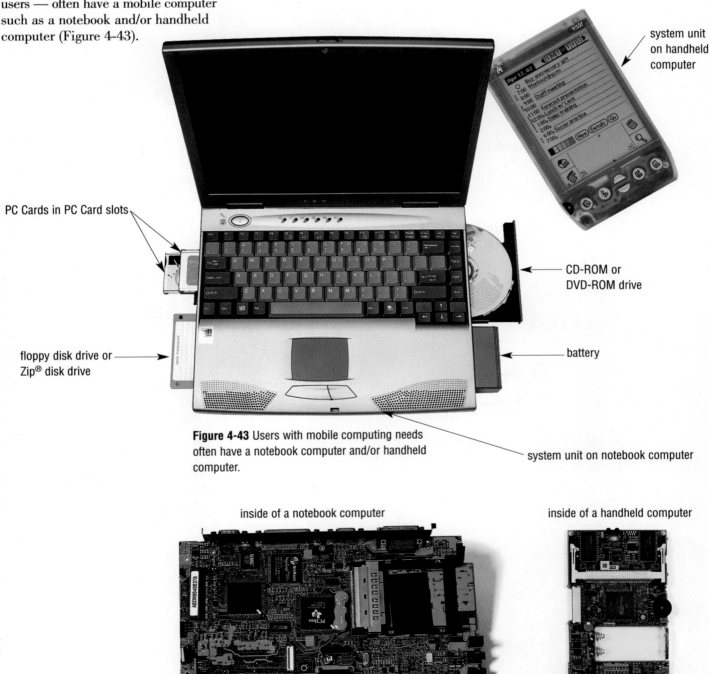

system unit on handheld computer

PC Cards in PC Card slots

CD-ROM or DVD-ROM drive

floppy disk drive or Zip® disk drive

battery

Figure 4-43 Users with mobile computing needs often have a notebook computer and/or handheld computer.

system unit on notebook computer

inside of a notebook computer

inside of a handheld computer

Figure 4-44 Notebook and handheld computers contain electronic components that process data.

A notebook computer usually is more expensive than a desktop computer with the same capabilities. Handheld computers are more affordable, usually costing a few hundred dollars.

The typical notebook computer often has a keyboard/mouse, IrDA, serial, parallel, video, and USB ports (Figure 4-45).

Handheld computers often have an IrDA port so you can communicate wirelessly with other computers or devices such as a printer. Many include a serial port. Handheld computers also can rest in a cradle, so you can transfer data to your desktop computer (Figure 4-46).

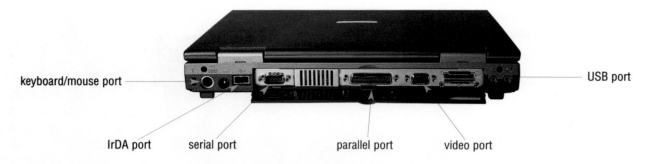

keyboard/mouse port — IrDA port — serial port — parallel port — video port — USB port

Figure 4-45 A notebook computer often has a keyboard/mouse, IrDA, serial, parallel, video, and USB ports.

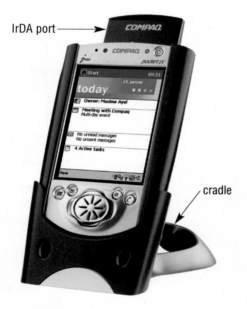

IrDA port — cradle

Figure 4-46 You transfer data from a smaller handheld computer, through a cradle or an IrDA port.

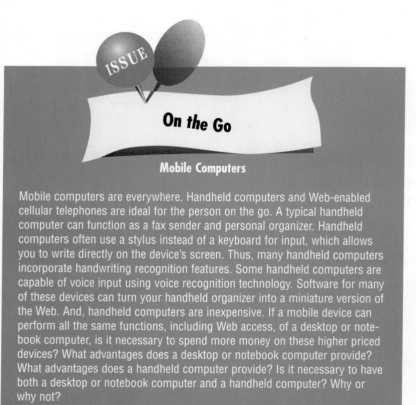

On the Go

Mobile Computers

Mobile computers are everywhere. Handheld computers and Web-enabled cellular telephones are ideal for the person on the go. A typical handheld computer can function as a fax sender and personal organizer. Handheld computers often use a stylus instead of a keyboard for input, which allows you to write directly on the device's screen. Thus, many handheld computers incorporate handwriting recognition features. Some handheld computers are capable of voice input using voice recognition technology. Software for many of these devices can turn your handheld organizer into a miniature version of the Web. And, handheld computers are inexpensive. If a mobile device can perform all the same functions, including Web access, of a desktop or notebook computer, is it necessary to spend more money on these higher priced devices? What advantages does a desktop or notebook computer provide? What advantages does a handheld computer provide? Is it necessary to have both a desktop or notebook computer and a handheld computer? Why or why not?

For more information on mobile computers, visit the Discovering Computers 2002 Issues Web page (**scsite.com/dc2002/issues.htm**) and click Chapter 4 Issue #5.

PUTTING IT ALL TOGETHER

When purchasing a computer, it is important to understand how the components in the system unit work. Many factors inside the system unit influence the speed and power of a computer. The type of computer configuration you require depends on your intended use. The table in Figure 4-47 lists the suggested processor, clock speed, and RAM requirements based on the needs of various types of computer users.

CHAPTER SUMMARY

Chapter 4 presented the components in the system unit, described how memory stores data, instructions, and information, and discussed the sequence of operations that occur when a computer executes an instruction. The chapter included a comparison of various personal computer processors on the market today.

Career Corner

Software Engineer

Software engineering is a dynamic and exciting field. You have your choice of a number of professions from robotics to operating systems and application software development to personal communications systems to intelligent agents to computer animation to computational biology. In many universities, software engineering is a sub-component of computer science. The field of software engineering is concerned with the processes, methods, and tools for the development of high-quality software systems. Students study the application of software specification, design, implementation, testing, and documentation of software.

A minimum of a bachelor's degree is required to work as a software engineer, but many people continue on for their masters and even a Ph.D. A strong mathematics background is required, and the road to the top of this field is a rigorous one. Expect to work hard and put in many years before you obtain your degree. When you finally achieve your goal, do not relax too quickly; computer science is ever changing. To stay in this field, you can expect to upgrade continually your skills and knowledge. The benefits are worth the effort. Software engineers can expect salaries of $75,000 and up.

To learn more about the field of software engineering as a career, visit the Discovering Computers 2002 Careers Web page (**scsite.com/dc2002/careers.htm**) and click Software Engineering.

SUGGESTED CONFIGURATIONS BY USER

USER	PROCESSOR AND CLOCK SPEED	MINIMUM RAM
 Home	Pentium® 4 or Athlon™ 600 MHz or higher; or Celeron™ or Duron™ – 600 MHz or higher	64 MB
 Small Office/Home Office	Pentium® 4 or Athlon™ – 800 MHz or higher	128 MB
 Mobile	Pentium® III or AMD-K6®-2-P 500 MHz or higher	64 MB
 Large Business	Pentium® 4 or Athlon™ – 700 MHz or higher	128 MB
 Power	Pentium® 4 or Itanium™ or Athlon™ – 1 GHz or higher	256 MB

Figure 4-47 This table recommends suggested processor, clock speed, and RAM configurations.

E-RESOURCES

LOOK IT UP

Web Resources Ease System Concerns

Have you heard of a Diffie-Hellman or a mouse potato? If you do not know a JDK from an OSS, then an online computer technology dictionary may be the tool you need. From dictionaries and encyclopedias to online technical support, the Web is filled with a plethora of resources, including those listed in Figure 4-48, to answer your computer questions and resolve specialized problems.

Chapter 4 describes the components of the system unit including the different processors, various types of memory, and other devices associated with it, as well as the components of notebook and handheld computers. With the continual developments in technology and communications, new products reach the marketplace daily.

A way to keep up with the latest developments is to look to online dictionaries that add to their collections of computer and product terms on a regular basis and include thousands of descriptions and designations. An example is the whatis?com Web site listed in the table in Figure 4-48 and shown in Figure 4-49. The whatis?com Web site contains more than 2,500 cyberterms, with daily updates to the words and definitions. This Web site and many other reference Web pages feature a word of the day that identifies a new product or industry standard as well as highlight recently added or revised terms.

Shopping for a new computer can be a daunting experience, but many online guides can help you select the components that best fit your needs and budget. Most of these Web sites, including NetGuide (Figure 4-50),

RESOURCES WEB SITES	URL
Dictionaries and Encyclopedias	
CDT's Guide to Online Privacy	www.cdt.org/privacy/guide/terms
ComputerUser High-Tech Dictionary	computeruser.com/resources/dictionary
Webopedia: Online Computer Dictionary for Internet Terms and Technical Support	webopedia.com
whatis?com	whatis.com
ZD Webopædia	www.zdwebopedia.com
Computer Shopping Guides	
BizRate.com®	bizrate.com/marketplace
Computer Shopper	zdnet.com/computershopper
NetGuide	netguide.com
The CPU Scorecard	cpuscorecard.com
The Online Computer Buying Guide™	grohol.com/computers
Upgrading Guides	
CNET Shopper	shopper.cnet.com
eHow™	ehow.com
PC World.com	pcworld.com/heres_how
Upgrade Source	upgradesource.com
Focus on MacSupport	macsupport.miningco.com/compute/macsupport
Online Technical Support	
Dux Computer Digest	duxcw.com
MSN Computing Central	computingcentral.msn.com
PC911	pcnineoneone.com
PC-Help Online	pchelponline.com
Learnlots.com	www.learnlots.com
Technical and Consumer Information	
CNET	cnet.com
newsday.com	newsday.com/plugin/c101main.htm
The Standard.com	thestandard.com
Wired News	wirednews.com
ZDNet	zdnet.com

For an updated list of resources Web sites, visit scsite.com/dc2002/e-rev.htm.

Figure 4-48 A variety of Web resources can provide information on buying, repairing, and upgrading computers.

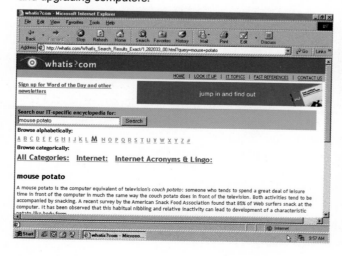

Figure 4-49 Thousands of technology terms are defined at the whatis?com Website.

feature the latest desktop and notebook computer prices, hardware reviews, bargains, and links to popular manufacturers' sale Web pages. If you want to upgrade your present computer, several online guides, such as CNET Shopper and Upgrade Source, give current prices for these components and list the more popular products.

If you are not confident in your ability to work a problem alone, turn to online technical support. Such Web sites, including Learnlots.com (Figure 4-51), often provide streaming how-to video lessons, tutorials, and real-time chats with experienced technicians.

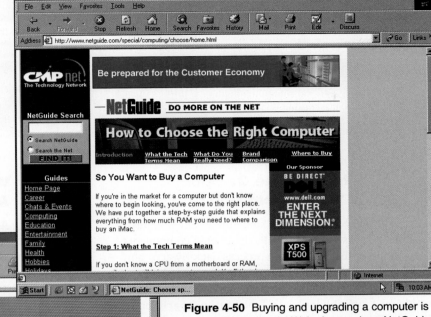

Figure 4-50 Buying and upgrading a computer is simplified with helpful Web sites such as NetGuide.

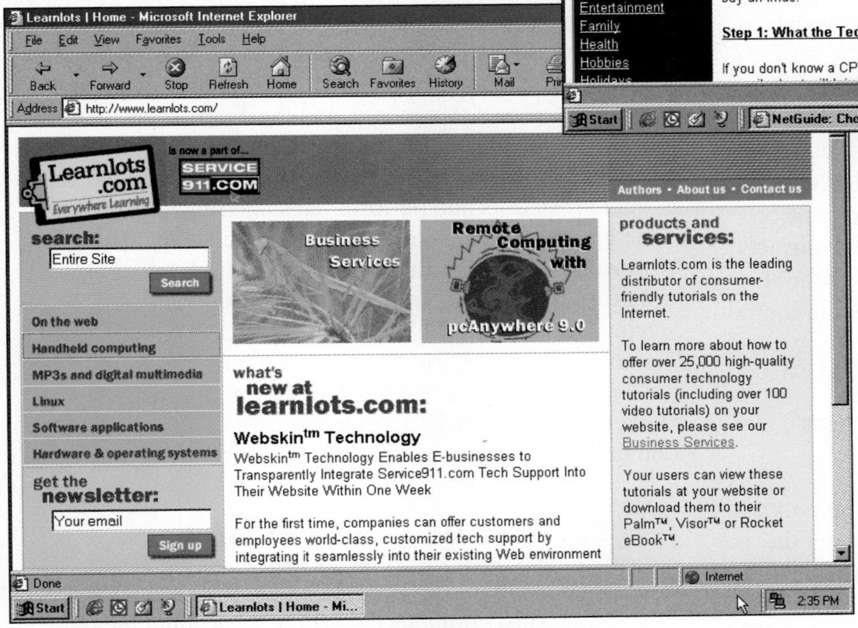

The Web offers a variety of technical and consumer information. Hardware and software reviews, price comparisons, shareware, technical questions and answers, and breaking technology news are found on comprehensive portals such as CNET and ZDNET.

For more information on Web resources sites, visit the Discovering Computers 2002 E-Revolution Web page (scsite.com/dc2002/e-rev.htm) and click Resources.

Figure 4-51 Practical tutorials at the Learnlots.com Web site provide useful technological information.

E-RESOURCES *applied:*

1. Visit the dictionary and encyclopedia Web sites listed in Figure 4-48. Search these resources for five terms. Create a table with two columns: one for the cyberterm and one for the Web definition. Then, create a second table listing five recently added or updated words and their definitions on these sites. Next, visit two of the listed computer shopping guide Web sites to choose the components you would buy if you were building a customized desktop computer and notebook computer. Create a table for both systems listing the computer manufacturer, processor model name or number and manufacturer, clock speed, RAM, cache, number of expansion slots, and number of bays.

2. Visit three upgrading guide Web sites listed in Figure 4-48. Write a paragraph describing available advice for buying a motherboard. Describe the strengths and weaknesses of these Web sites, focusing on such criteria as clarity of instructions, thoroughness, and ease of navigation. Would you use these Web sites as a resource to troubleshoot computer problems? Then, view two technical and consumer information Web sites listed in the table and write a paragraph on each describing the top two news stories of the day.

4.38

DISCOVERING
COMPUTERS 2002

Chapter 1 2 3 4 5 6 7 8 9 10 11 12 13 14 15 16 Index **HOME**

In Summary

SHELLY
CASHMAN
SERIES.

Student Exercises   Web Links   In Summary   Key Terms   Learn It Online   Checkpoint   In The Lab   Web Work

Special Features   ■ TIMELINE 2002 ■ WWW & E-SKILLS ■ MULTIMEDIA ■ BUYER'S GUIDE 2002 ■ WIRELESS TECHNOLOGY ■ TRENDS 2002 ■ INTERACTIVE LABS ■ TECH NEWS

Web Instructions: To display this page from the Web, start your browser and enter the URL scsite.com/dc2002/ch4/summary.htm. Click the links for current and additional information. To listen to an audio version of this In Summary, click the Audio button. To play the audio, RealPlayer must be installed on your computer (download by clicking here).

1 What Are the Components in the System Unit?

The **system unit**, sometimes called a **chassis**, is a box-like case that houses the electronic components of a computer that are used to process data. System unit components include the processor, memory module, expansion cards, ports, and connectors. Many components reside on a circuit board called the **motherboard**, or **system board**. The motherboard contains different types of **chips**, or small pieces of semi-conducting material on which one or more **integrated circuits** (**IC**) are etched. A **transistor** acts as an electronic gate that opens or closes the circuit for electronic signals. One of the more important chips is the central processing unit (CPU).

2 How Does the CPU Process Data?

The **central processing unit** (**CPU**), sometimes referred to as the **processor**, interprets and carries out the basic instructions that operate a computer. The **control unit**, which is one component of the CPU, directs and coordinates most of the operations in the computer. For every instruction, the control unit repeats a set of four basic operations called the **machine cycle**: (1) **fetching** the instruction or data item from memory; (2) **decoding** the instruction into commands the computer understands; (3) **executing**, or carrying out, the commands; and, if necessary, (4) **storing**, or writing, the result to memory. The **arithmetic/logic unit** (**ALU**), another component of the CPU, performs the arithmetic, comparison, and logical operations.

3 What Are Some Processors Available Today?

A personal computer's CPU usually is contained on a single chip called a **processor**. Intel, a leading manufacturer of processors, produces **Pentium®** processors for high-end personal computers, the **Celeron™** processor for less expensive personal computers, and the **Xeon™** and **Itanium™** processors for workstations and servers. **Intel-compatible processors** have the same internal design as Intel processors and perform the same functions, but are made by other companies and often are less expensive. The **Motorola processor** is an alternative to the Intel-style processor and is found in Apple Macintosh and Power Macintosh systems. The **Alpha processor**, originally from Digital Equipment Corporation, is used primarily in workstations and high-end servers. A new type of processor, called an **integrated CPU**, combines functions of a CPU, memory, and a video card on a single chip.

4 How Do Series of Bits Represent Data?

Most computers are **digital**, meaning they understand only two discrete states: on and off. These states are represented using two digits, 0 (off) and 1 (on). Each on or off value is called a **bit** (short for **bi**nary dig**it**), which is the smallest unit of data a computer can handle. Eight bits grouped together as a unit are called a **byte**. A byte can represent 256 individual characters including numbers, letters of the alphabet, punctuation marks, and other characters. Combinations of 0s and 1s used to represent data are defined by patterns called coding schemes. Popular coding schemes are **ASCII**, **EBCDIC**, and **Unicode**.

Chapter 1 2 3 4 5 6 7 8 9 10 11 12 13 14 15 16 Index **HOME** **4.39**

DISCOVERING
COMPUTERS *2002*

In Summary

SHELLY
CASHMAN
SERIES.

Student Exercises   Web Links   In Summary   Key Terms   Learn It Online   Checkpoint   In The Lab   Web Work

Special Features   ■ TIMELINE 2002 ■ WWW & E-SKILLS ■ MULTIMEDIA ■ BUYER'S GUIDE 2002 ■ WIRELESS TECHNOLOGY ■ TRENDS 2002 ■ INTERACTIVE LABS ■ TECH NEWS

What Are Different Types of Memory?

In the processor, a computer's **memory** stores data, instructions, and information. Memory and storage size are measured by the number of bytes — a **kilobyte (K or KB)** is approximately one thousand bytes, a **megabyte (MB)** is approximately one million bytes, and a **gigabyte (GB)** is approximately one billion bytes. **RAM (random access memory)** consists of memory chips that can be read from and written to by the processor and other devices. Two types of RAM chips exist: **dynamic RAM (DRAM)**, which must be reenergized constantly; and **static RAM (SRAM)**, which must be reenergized less often but is more expensive. Most computers improve processing times by using **memory cache** to store frequently used instructions and data. **ROM (read-only memory)** is a memory chip that only can be read; it cannot be modified. **Flash memory**, also called **flash ROM** or **flash RAM**, is nonvolatile memory that can be erased electronically and reprogrammed. **CMOS** memory is used to store configuration information about the computer.

What Are Expansion Slots and Expansion Cards?

An **expansion slot** is an opening, or socket, where a circuit board can be inserted into the motherboard. These circuit boards, sometimes referred to as **expansion boards** or **expansion cards** and several other terms, are used to add new devices or capabilities to the computer, such as a modem or more memory. **Plug and Play** refers to a computer's capability of automatically configuring expansion cards and other devices as they are installed.

How Are Serial Ports, Parallel Ports, and USB Ports Different?

A cable often attaches external devices to the system unit. The interface, or point of attachment, to the system unit is called a **port**. Ports have different types of **connectors** used to join a cable to a device. A **serial port** is an interface that transmits only one bit of data at a time. Serial ports usually connect devices that do not require fast data transmission rates, such as a mouse, keyboard, or modem. A **parallel port** is an interface used to connect devices that are capable of transferring more than one bit at a time. Many printers connect to the system unit using a parallel port. A **universal serial bus (USB) port** can connect up to 127 different peripheral devices with a single connector type. To attach multiple devices to a single port, you daisy chain the devices.

How Do Buses Contribute to a Computer's Processing Speed?

Bits are transferred internally within the circuitry of the computer along electrical channels. Each channel, called a bus, allows various devices inside and attached to the system unit to communicate with each other. The **bus width**, or size of the bus, determines the number of bits that can be transferred at one time. The larger the bus width, the faster the computer transfers data. **Word size** is the number of bits the CPU can process at one time.

What Are the Components in a Notebook Computer?

Notebook computers have a system unit that contains electronic components — the same as those found in a desktop computer. Additionally, the system unit houses the keyboard, pointing device, speakers, and display. A notebook computer often has serial, parallel, keyboard, mouse, USB, video, and IrDA ports.

What Are the Components in a Handheld Computer?

Handheld computers have a system unit that contains electronic components — the same as those found in a desktop computer. Most handheld computers contain an IrDA port to communicate with other handheld computers, desktop and notebook computers, or devices such as a printer.

4.40

DISCOVERING
COMPUTERS 2002

Chapter 1 2 3 4 5 6 7 8 9 10 11 12 13 14 15 16 Index HOME

SHELLY
CASHMAN
SERIES.

Key Terms

Student Exercises | Web Links | In Summary | Key Terms | Learn It Online | Checkpoint | In The Lab | Web Work

Special Features | ■ TIMELINE 2002 ■ WWW & E-SKILLS ■ MULTIMEDIA ■ BUYER'S GUIDE 2002 ■ WIRELESS TECHNOLOGY ■ TRENDS 2002 ■ INTERACTIVE LABS ■ TECH NEWS

Web Instructions: To display this page from the Web, start your browser and enter the URL scsite.com/dc2002/ch4/terms.htm. Scroll through the list of terms. Click a term to display its definition and a picture. Click the To WEB button for current and additional information about the term from the Web. To see animations, Shockwave and Flash Player must be installed on your computer (download by clicking here).

1394 bus (4.32)
1394 port (4.28)
3DNow!™ (4.11)
AC adapter (4.32)
Accelerated Graphics Port (AGP) (4.31)
access time (4.22)
adapter (4.23)
adapter card (4.23)
add-in (4.23)
add-on (4.23)
advanced transfer cache (4.20)
all-in-one computer (4.3)
Alpha processor (4.10)
American Standard Code for Information Interchange (4.14)
analog (4.13)
arithmetic operations (4.6)
arithmetic/logic unit (ALU) (4.6)
ASCII (4.14)
basic input/output system (BIOS) (4.20)
bay (4.32)
binary system (4.14)
bit (4.14)
board (4.23)
bus (4.29)
bus width (4.29)
byte (4.14)
cache (4.19)
cache store (4.19)
card (4.23)
Celeron™ (4.10)
central processing unit (CPU) (4.5)
chassis (4.2)
chip (4.4)
chip for chip upgrade (4.11)
CISC (complex instruction set computing) (4.6)
clock cycle (4.8)
clock rate (4.8)
clock speed (4.8)
CMOS (4.21)
comparison operations (4.6)
complementary metal-oxide semiconductor memory (4.21)
connector (4.26)
control unit (4.5)
coprocessor (4.13)
daughterboard (4.11)
daughterboard upgrade (4.11)
decoding (4.5)
digital (4.13)
Direct Rambus® DRAM (Direct RDRAM®) (4.18)
double data rate SDRAM (DDR SDRAM) (4.18)
DRAM (4.18)
drive bays (4.32)
dual inline memory module (DIMM) (4.18)
dual inline package (DIP) (4.4)
dynamic RAM (4.18)
EBCDIC (4.14)
EEPROM (electrically erasable programmable read-only memory) (4.20)
executing (4.5)
execution time (e-time) (4.6)
expansion board (4.23)
expansion bus (4.30)
expansion card (4.23)
expansion slot (4.23)
exposed drive bay (4.32)
Extended Binary Coded Decimal Interchange Code (4.14)
external cache (4.19)
external drive bay (4.32)
female connectors (4.26)
fetching (4.5)
FIR (fast infrared) (4.29)
FireWire (4.28)
firmware (4.20)

flash BIOS (4.21)
flash memory (4.21)
flash memory cards (4.21)
flash RAM (4.21)
flash ROM (4.21)
flip chip-PGA (FC-PGA) package (4.4)
floating-point coprocessor (4.13)
gender changer (4.27)
gigabyte (GB) (4.16)
gigahertz (GHz) (4.8)
graphics card (4.23)
heat pipe (4.12)
heat sink (4.12)
hertz (4.8)
hidden drive bay (4.32)
hot plugging (4.25)

SYSTEMBOARD
Circuit board that contains most of the electronic components in the system unit. Also called motherboard. (4.4)

To WEB

hot swapping (4.25)
IEEE 1284 (4.28)
instruction cycle (4.6)
instruction time (i-time) (4.6)
integrated circuit (IC) (4.4)
integrated CPU (4.11)
Intel-compatible processors (4.10)
interface card (4.23)
internal cache (4.19)
internal drive bay (4.32)
internal modem (4.23)
IrDA (Infrared Data Association) (4.29)
IrDA port (4.29)
ISA (Industry Standard Architecture) bus (4.31)
Itanium™ (4.10)
K (4.16)
KB (4.16)
kilobyte (4.16)
L3 cache (4.20)
Level 1 (L1) cache (4.19)
Level 2 (L2) cache (4.19)
local bus (4.31)
logical operations (4.7)
machine cycle (4.6)
main memory (4.18)
male connectors (4.26)
megabyte (MB) (4.16)
megahertz (MHz) (4.8)
memory (4.15)
memory cache (4.19)

memory module (4.18)
microcode (4.20)
microprocessor (4.9)
MIDI (4.28)
MIPS (4.6)
MMX™ (multimedia extensions) (4.11)
modem card (4.23)
motherboard (4.4)
Motorola processor (4.10)
musical instrument digital interface (4.28)
nanosecond (ns) (4.22)
network card (4.23)
network interface card (NIC) (4.23)
nonvolatile memory (NVM) (4.16)
parallel port (4.27)
parallel processing (4.13)
PC Card (4.24)
PC Card bus (4.32)
PCI (Peripheral Component Interconnect) bus (4.31)
PCMCIA cards (4.27)
Pentium® (4.10)
piggyback upgrade (4.11)
pin grid array (PGA) package (4.4)
pipelining (4.7)
Plug and Play (4.24)
port (4.25)
power supply (4.32)
primary cache (4.19)
processor (4.5)
programmable read-only memory (PROM) (4.20)
RAM (random access memory) (4.16)
RAM cache (4.19)
Rambus® inline memory module (RIMM) (4.18)
read-only memory (ROM) (4.20)
registers (4.7)
RISC (reduced instruction set computing) (4.6)
saving (4.18)
SDRAM II (4.18)
serial port (4.27)
single edge contact (SEC) cartridge (4.4)
single inline memory module (SIMM) (4.18)
small computer system interface (SCSI) (4.29)
socket (4.12)
sound card (4.23)
SRAM (4.18)
SSE instructions (streaming single-instruction, multiple-data instructions) (4.11)
static RAM (4.18)
stored program concept (4.16)
storing (4.5)
superscalar (4.8)
synchronous DRAM (SDRAM) (4.18)
synthesizer (4.28)
system board (4.4)
system bus (4.30)
system clock (4.8)
system unit (4.2)
tower models (4.3)
transistor (4.4)
Type I cards (4.24)
Type II cards (4.24)
Type III cards (4.24)
Unicode (4.14)
universal serial bus (USB) (4.32)
universal serial bus (USB) port (4.28)
USB hub (4.28)
VESA local bus (4.31)
video adapter (4.23)
video card (4.23)
volatile memory (4.16)
word size (4.30)
Xeon™ (4.10)
zero-insertion force (ZIF) socket (4.12)

Student Exercises   Web Links   In Summary   Key Terms   Learn It Online   Checkpoint   In The Lab   Web Work

Special Features   ■ TIMELINE 2002   ■ WWW & E-SKILLS   ■ MULTIMEDIA   ■ BUYER'S GUIDE 2002   ■ WIRELESS TECHNOLOGY   ■ TRENDS 2002   ■ INTERACTIVE LABS   ■ TECH NEWS

Web Instructions: To display this page from the Web, start your browser and enter the URL scsite.com/dc2002/ch1/learn.htm.

1. Web Guide

Click Web Guide to display the Guide to World Wide Web Sites and Searching Techniques Web page. Click Computers and Computing and then click Virtual Museum of Computing. Scroll down the page and locate General Historical Information. Click a link of your choice. Use your word processing program to prepare a brief report on your tour and submit your assignment to your instructor.

2. Scavenger Hunt

Click Scavenger Hunt. Print a copy of the Scavenger Hunt page; use this page to write down your answers as you search the Web. Submit your completed page to your instructor.

3. Who Wants to Be a Computer Genius?

Click Computer Genius to find out if you are a computer genius. Directions on how to play the game will display. When you are ready to play, click the PLAY button. Submit your score to your instructor.

4. Wheel of Terms

Click Wheel of Terms to reinforce important terms you learned in this chapter by playing the Shelly Cashman Series version of this popular game. Directions on how to play the game will display. When you are ready to play, click the PLAY button. Submit your score to your instructor.

5. Career Corner

Click Career Corner to display the Making College Count page. Click a link of your choice and review the page. Write a brief report describing what you learned. Submit the report to your instructor.

6. Search Sleuth

Click Search Sleuth to learn search techniques that will help make you a research expert. Submit the completed assignment to your instructor.

7. Crossword Puzzle Challenge

Click Crossword Puzzle Challenge. Complete the puzzle to reinforce skills you learned in this chapter. Directions on how to play the game will display. When you are ready to play, click the PLAY button. Submit the completed puzzle to your instructor.

8. Practice Test

Click Practice Test. Answer each question. When completed enter your name and click the Grade Test button to submit the quiz for grading. Make a note of any missed questions. If required, print a copy to submit to your instructor.

Checkpoint

SHELLY
CASHMAN
SERIES.

Student Exercises   Web Links   In Summary   Key Terms   Learn It Online   Checkpoint   In The Lab   Web Work

Special Features   ■ TIMELINE 2002 ■ WWW & E-SKILLS ■ MULTIMEDIA ■ BUYER'S GUIDE 2002 ■ WIRELESS TECHNOLOGY ■ TRENDS 2002 ■ INTERACTIVE LABS ■ TECH NEWS

Web Instructions: To display this page from the Web, start your browser and enter the URL scsite.com/dc2002/ch4/check.htm. Click the links for current and additional information. To experience the animation and interactivity, Shockwave and Flash Player must be installed on your computer (download by clicking here.)

LABEL THE FIGURE   Instructions: Identify these components of the motherboard.

1. _____

2. _____

3. _____

4. _____

5. _____

6. _____

MATCHING   Instructions: Match each term from the column on the left with the best description from the column on the right.

_____1. PC card
_____2. sound card
_____3. expansion slot
_____4. video card
_____5. network interface card

a. Converts computer output into a video signal.
b. A communications device that allows the computer to communicate via a network.
c. Enhances the sound-generating capabilities of a personal computer.
d. A device that can connect up to 127 different peripheral devices with a single connector type.
e. A device that enables you to join two connectors that are either both female or both male.
f. A thin, credit card-sized device.
g. An opening, or socket, where you can insert a circuit board into the motherboard.

DISCOVERING
COMPUTERS 2002

Chapter 1 2 3 4 5 6 7 8 9 10 11 12 13 14 15 16 Index HOME

4.43

Checkpoint

SHELLY
CASHMAN
SERIES.

Student Exercises   Web Links   In Summary   Key Terms   Learn It Online   Checkpoint   In The Lab   Web Work

Special Features ■ TIMELINE 2002 ■ WWW & E-SKILLS ■ MULTIMEDIA ■ BUYER'S GUIDE 2002 ■ WIRELESS TECHNOLOGY ■ TRENDS 2002 ■ INTERACTIVE LABS ■ TECH NEWS

MULTIPLE CHOICE | Instructions: Select the letter of the correct answer for each of the following questions.

1. A(n) _____ is a small piece of semi-conducting material on which one or more integrated circuits are etched.
   a. chip
   b. system board
   c. control unit
   d. arithmetic/logic unit

2. The process of translating instructions into commands is called _____ .
   a. fetching
   b. decoding
   c. executing
   d. storing

3. Most RAM is _____ .
   a. volatile
   b. nonvolatile
   c. read-only
   d. both a and c

4. A _____ cache helps speed the processes of the computer by storing frequently used instructions and data.
   a. disk
   b. memory
   c. ROM
   d. PROM

5. A _____ port can support up to 127 different devices.
   a. serial
   b. parallel
   c. SCSI
   d. USB

SHORT ANSWER | Instructions: Write a brief answer to each of the following questions.

1. What is the purpose of the CPU? _____ What is the control unit's job? _____ What are the four basic operations? _____

2. How is instruction time, or i-time, different from execution time, or e-time? _____ In what unit is a computer's speed measured? _____

3. How are arithmetic operations, comparison operations, and logical operations different? _____ In what part of the CPU do these operations occur? _____

4. What are some of the different processors used in today's personal computers? _____ What is a new type of processor? _____

5. How are the components different among a desktop computer, a notebook computer, and a handheld computer? _____

WORKING TOGETHER | Instructions: Working with a group of your classmates, complete the following team exercise.

Prepare a report on the different types of ports and the way you connect peripheral devices to a computer. As part of your report, include the following subheadings and an overview of each subheading topic: (1) What is a port? (2) What is a connector? (3) What is a serial port and how does it work? (4) What is a parallel port and how does it work? (5) What is a USB port and how does it work? Expand your report so that it includes information beyond that in your textbook. Create a PowerPoint presentation from your report.

4.44

DISCOVERING
COMPUTERS 2002

Chapter 1 2 3 4 5 6 7 8 9 10 11 12 13 14 15 16 Index HOME

In The Lab

SHELLY
CASHMAN
SERIES.

Student Exercises   Web Links   In Summary   Key Terms   Learn It Online   Checkpoint   In The Lab   Web Work

Special Features   ■ TIMELINE 2002   ■ WWW & E-SKILLS   ■ MULTIMEDIA   ■ BUYER'S GUIDE 2002   ■ WIRELESS TECHNOLOGY   ■ TRENDS 2002   ■ INTERACTIVE LABS   ■ TECH NEWS

Web Instructions: To display this page from the Web, start your browser and enter the URL scsite.com/dc2002/ch4/lab.htm. Click the links for current and additional information.

Installing New Hardware

This exercise uses Windows 98 procedures. Plug and Play technology, a key feature of the Windows operating system, allows users to install new devices without having to reconfigure the system manually. To find out how to install a new device with Plug and Play technology, click the Start button on the taskbar, and then click Help on the Start menu. When the Windows Help window displays, if necessary, click the Contents tab. Click the Managing Hardware and Software book and then click the Installing New Hardware and Software book. Click Install a Plug and Play device.

- What are the three steps in installing a Plug and Play device?
- When would Windows not detect a Plug and Play device?
- How is a device that is not Plug and Play installed?

Close Windows Help.

Setting the System Clock

Double-click the time on the taskbar. In the Date/Time Properties dialog box, click the Question Mark button on its title bar, and then click the picture of the calendar. Read the information in the pop-up window and then click the pop-up window to close it.

Repeat this process for other areas of the dialog box and then answer these questions:

- What is the purpose of the calendar?
- How do you change the time zone?
- What is the difference between the Close and Apply buttons?

Close the Date/Time Properties dialog box.

Using Calculator to Perform Number System Conversion

Instead of the decimal (base 10) number system that people use, computers use the binary (base 2) or hexadecimal (base 16) number systems. It is not necessary to understand these number systems to use a computer, but it is interesting to see how decimal numbers look when in binary or hexadecimal form. Click the Start button on the taskbar, point to Programs on the Start menu, point to Accessories on the Programs submenu, and then click Calculator on the Accessories submenu. Click View on the menu bar and then click Scientific to display the scientific calculator. Perform the following tasks:

- Click Dec to select decimal. Enter 35 by clicking the numeric buttons or using the numeric keypad. Click Bin to select binary. What number displays? Click Hex to select hexadecimal. What number displays? Click the C (Clear) button.

- Convert the following decimal numbers to binary and hexadecimal: 7,256, and 3,421.
- What decimal number is equal to 10010 in the binary system? What decimal number is equal to 2DA9 in the hexadecimal system?

Close the Calculator window.

Power Management

This exercise uses Windows 98 or Windows 2000 procedures. Environmental and financial considerations make it important to manage the amount of power a computer uses. Click the Start button on the taskbar, point to Settings on the Start menu, and then click Control Panel on the Settings submenu. Double-click the Power Management icon in the Control Panel window. In the Power Management Properties dialog box, if necessary, click the Power Schemes tab.

- What is a power scheme?
- What power scheme currently is being used on your computer?
- After how many minutes of inactivity is the monitor turned off?
- After how many minutes of inactivity are the hard disks turned off?

Close the Power Management Properties dialog box and the Control Panel window. How can the Power Management Properties dialog box be used to make a computer more energy efficient?

DISCOVERING
COMPUTERS 2002

Chapter 1 2 3 4 5 6 7 8 9 10 11 12 13 14 15 16 Index HOME 4.45

Web Work

SHELLY
CASHMAN
SERIES.

Student Exercises   Web Links   In Summary   Key Terms   Learn It Online   Checkpoint   In The Lab   Web Work

Special Features   ■ TIMELINE 2002   ■ WWW & E-SKILLS   ■ MULTIMEDIA   ■ BUYER'S GUIDE 2002   ■ WIRELESS TECHNOLOGY   ■ TRENDS 2002   ■ INTERACTIVE LABS   ■ TECH NEWS

Web Instructions: To display this page from the Web, start your browser and enter the URL scsite.com/dc2002/ch4/web.htm. To view At The Movies in exercise 1, RealPlayer must be installed on your computer (download by clicking here). To use the Shelly Cashman Series Understanding the Motherboard Lab from the Web, Shockwave and Flash Player must be installed on your computer (download by clicking here).

Andrew Grove

To view the Andrew Grove movie, click the button to the left or click the Play button to the right. Watch the movie, and then complete the exercise by answering the question below. Intel is the leading manufacturer of processors, including the Pentium®, Celeron™, and Xeon™ processors. Intel grew to its present size with more than 60,000 employees because of the outstanding leadership of Andrew Grove. Based on the personal information you learned about Mr. Grove in the movie, describe how his early life struggles, his strong work ethic, and his vision of capitalizing on business trends have been the foundation for Intel's worldwide processor empire. How might Andrew Grove's forward-growth visions for Intel continue to drive the company toward even greater success in the future?

Shelly Cashman Series Understanding the Motherboard Lab

Follow the appropriate instructions in Web Work 2 on page 1.47 to start and use the Shelly Cashman Series Understanding the Motherboard Lab. If you are running from the Web, enter the URL scsite.com/sclabs/ menu.htm, or display the Web Work page (see instructions at the top of this page) and then click the button to the left.

How a Processor Works

After reading about what a processor does and the way it interacts with other system unit components, it still can be difficult to understand how a processor performs even a simple task such as adding two plus three. Click the button to the left, and complete this exercise to learn what a processor does to find the answer.

Newsgroups

Would you like more information about a special interest? Perhaps you would like to share opinions and advice with people who have the same interests. If so, you might be interested in newsgroups, also called discussion groups or forums. A newsgroup offers the opportunity to read articles on a specific subject, respond to the articles, and even post your own articles. Click the button to the left to find out more about newsgroups. What is lurking? What is Usenet? Click the Searching Newsgroups link at the bottom of the page. Read and print the Searching Newsgroups Web page. How can you locate a newsgroup on a particular topic?

In the News

The ENIAC (Electronic Numerical Integrator and Computer) often is considered the first modern computer. Invented in 1946, the ENIAC weighed 30 tons and filled a 30-by-50-foot room, yet its capabilities are dwarfed by current notebook computers. The ENIAC performed fewer than 1,000 calculations per minute; today, personal computers can process more than 300 million instructions per second. The rapid development of computing power and capabilities is astonishing, and that development is accelerating. Click the button to the left and read a news article about the introduction of a new or improved computer component. What is the component? Who is introducing it? Will the component change the way people use computers? If so, how?

CHAPTER 5

Input

As the semester ends, schoolwork is becoming more intense. Your term paper on the American Revolution is due next week. The research is complete, but you still need to type and format your document. Written summaries of biology labs also are due. Your partner just e-mailed you the spreadsheet analysis for your marketing case study. You have to write a report that summarizes these findings.

Before sitting down at the computer, you decide to get some fresh air and take your dog, Bandit, for a walk. First thing out the door, Bandit wraps his leash around your legs as he takes off after a cat. Trying to free yourself, you fall down and break your right arm and two fingers. After a lengthy delay in the emergency room, you now have a cast from your shoulder to your fingertips.

You are beside yourself wondering how you are going to finish all your papers. You barely can type and cannot use the mouse at all. Your friend suggests voice recognition software. Just talk to the computer and it writes what you say. This sounds perfect! You spend some of your savings on the software thinking — this is going to be cool!

WHAT IS INPUT?

Input is any data or instructions you enter into the memory of a computer. Users can input data and instructions using a variety of techniques (Figure 5-1). A keyboard allows you to type characters. Using a mouse, you can click a button or roll a wheel to input instructions to the computer. A microphone allows you to speak into the computer. You can write on some computer screens with a special writing device. With others, you touch the screen to make selections. You can send images into the computer using a digital camera, video camera, or a scanner.

Once input is in memory, the processor can access it and process it into output. As mentioned, two types of input are data and instructions (Figure 5-2).

OBJECTIVES

After completing this chapter, you will be able to:

- Describe the two types of input
- List the characteristics of a keyboard
- Identify various types of keyboards
- Identify various types of pointing devices
- Explain how a mouse works
- Describe different mouse types
- Explain how voice recognition works
- Understand how to input data into a handheld computer
- Identify the uses of a digital camera
- Describe the various techniques used for video input
- Describe the uses of PC video cameras and Web cams
- Explain how scanners and other reading devices work
- Identify alternative input devices for physically challenged users

Figure 5-1 Data can be input into a computer in a variety of ways.

Data is a collection of raw unprocessed facts, figures, and symbols. In addition to words and numbers, data also includes sounds, images, and video. Technically speaking, a datum is a single item of data. The term data, however, commonly is used and accepted as both the singular and plural form of the word.

A computer processes data into information. **Information** is data that is organized, meaningful, and useful to a particular user or group of users. The timecards for a given week are an example of data. A company might process this data into a report (information) that summarizes the total hours worked and the payroll expense for the week.

Instructions can be in the form of programs, commands, and user responses. Following is a description of each type of instruction.

A **program** is a series of instructions that tells a computer how to perform the tasks necessary to process data into information. Programs are kept on storage media such as a floppy disk, hard disk, CD-ROM, or DVD-ROM. Programs are input into the memory of the computer, as they are needed. Programs respond to commands that a user issues.

A **command** is an instruction given to a computer program. Users can issue commands by typing or pressing keys on the keyboard, clicking a mouse button, speaking into a microphone, or touching an area of a screen.

Most programs today are menu driven and have a graphical user interface. A **menu-driven** program provides menus as a means of entering commands. Menus contain a list of options from which you select.

A **graphical user interface (GUI)** has icons, buttons, and other graphical objects that allow you to select and issue commands. A GUI is the most user-friendly way to interact with a computer.

A **user response** is an instruction you issue by replying to a question that a computer program displays. Your response to the question instructs the program to perform certain actions. Assume the program asks the question, Are the timecard entries correct? If you answer Yes, the program saves the timecard entries on a storage device. If you answer No, the program gives you the opportunity to modify the entries.

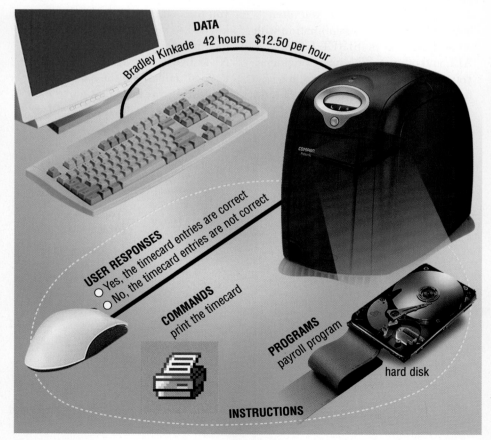

Figure 5-2 Two types of input are data and instructions. Instructions can be in the form of user responses, commands, and programs.

DATA
Bradley Kinkade   42 hours $12.50 per hour

USER RESPONSES
○ Yes, the timecard entries are correct
○ No, the timecard entries are not correct

COMMANDS
print the timecard

PROGRAMS
payroll program

hard disk

INSTRUCTIONS

Watching Your Emotions

Emotional Input and Your Privacy

In addition to data, programs, commands, and user responses, researchers are experimenting with a fifth type of input – human emotions. A development called affective computing uses input devices such as video cameras and skin sensors with software similar to voice recognition programs, allowing a computer to read a user's emotions. For example, a furrowed brow and sweaty palms might indicate frustration. Emotional input could be invaluable in conjunction with computer-aided instruction, letting a computer know whether to speed up or slow down tutorials. Some people, however, see affective computing as an invasion of privacy. Do you agree? In what areas might affective computing be useful? Why? Would you be comfortable with a computer knowing how you feel? Why or why not?

For more information on affective computing, visit the Discovering Computers 2002 Issues Web page (scsite.com/dc2002/issues.htm) and click Chapter 5 Issue #1.

ISSUE

WHAT ARE INPUT DEVICES?

An **input device** is any hardware component that allows you to enter data, programs, commands, and user responses into a computer. Depending on your particular application and requirement, the input device you use may vary. Popular input devices include the keyboard, mouse, stylus, microphone, digital camera, and scanner. The following pages discuss these and other input devices.

Storage devices, such as disk drives, serve as both input and output devices. Chapter 7 discusses storage devices.

THE KEYBOARD

Many people use a keyboard as one of their input devices. A **keyboard** is an input device that contains keys you press to enter data into the computer (Figure 5-3).

Desktop computer keyboards typically have from 101 to 105 keys. Keyboards for smaller computers such as notebook computers contain fewer keys. A computer keyboard includes keys that allow you to type letters of the alphabet, numbers, spaces, punctuation marks, and other symbols such as the dollar sign ($) and asterisk (*). A keyboard also contains other keys that allow you to enter data and instructions into the computer.

All computer keyboards have a typing area that includes the letters of the alphabet, numbers, punctuation

marks, and other basic keys. Many desktop computer keyboards also have a numeric keypad on the right side of the keyboard. A **numeric keypad** is a calculator-style arrangement of keys that includes numbers, a decimal point, and some basic mathematical operators (see Figure 5-3). Many users prefer to use the numbers on the numeric keypad instead of the numbers at the top of the typing area.

Across the top of most keyboards are function keys, which are labeled with the letter F followed by a number (see Figure 5-3). **Function keys** are special keys programmed to issue commands to a computer. The command associated with a function key depends on the program you are using. For example, in many programs, pressing the function key F1 displays a Help window. When instructed to press a function key such as F1, do not press the letter F followed by the number 1. Instead, press the key labeled F1.

To issue commands, you often use function keys in combination with other special keys (SHIFT, CTRL, ALT, and others). With many programs, you can use a button, a menu, a function key, or a combination of keys

to obtain the same result (Figure 5-4).

Keyboards also contain keys that allow you to position the insertion point. The **insertion point** is a symbol that indicates where on the screen the next character you type will display (Figure 5-5). Depending on the program, the symbol may be a vertical bar, a rectangle, or an underline. You can move the insertion point left, right, up, or down by pressing the arrow keys on the keyboard.

Keyboards typically contain at least four **arrow keys**: one pointing up, one pointing down, one pointing left, and one pointing right. Most keyboards also contain keys such as HOME, END, PAGE UP, and PAGE DOWN, that you can press to move the insertion point to the beginning or end of a line, page, or document.

Nearly all keyboards have toggle keys. A **toggle key** is a key that switches between two different states. The NUM LOCK key, for example, is a toggle key (see Figure 5-3). When you press it once, it locks the numeric keypad so you can use this keypad to type numbers. When you press the NUM LOCK key again, the numeric keypad unlocks so the same keys serve as arrow keys that move the

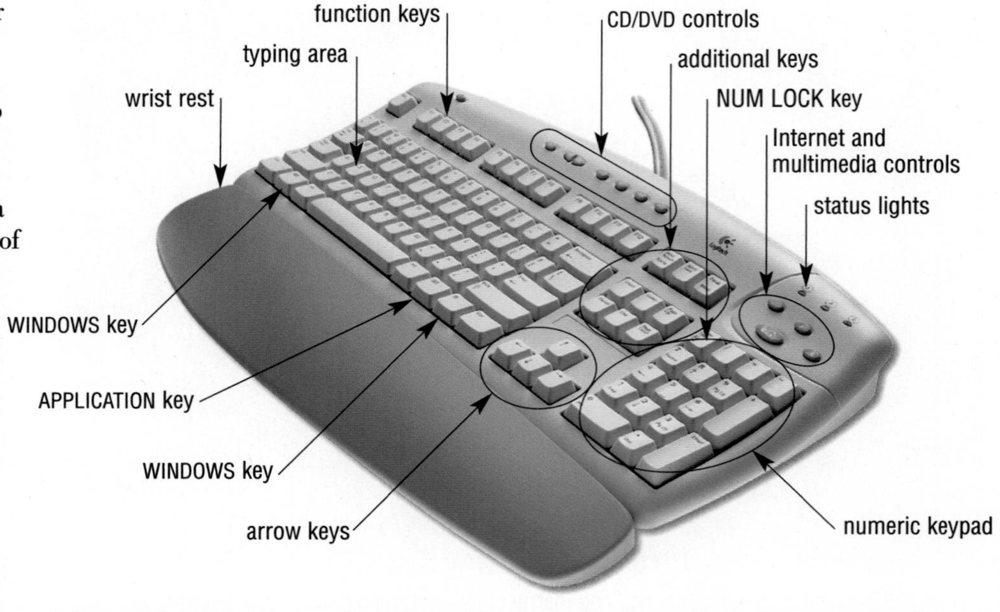

Web Link

For more information on keyboards, visit the Discovering Computers 2002 Chapter 5 WEB LINK page (**scsite.com/dc2002/ch5/ weblink.htm**) and click Keyboards.

Figure 5-3 A desktop computer keyboard. You type using keys in the typing area and on the numeric keypad.

insertion point. Many keyboards have status lights that light up when you activate a toggle key.

Most keyboards have a WINDOWS key and an APPLICATION key. The WINDOWS key displays the Start menu. The APPLICATION key displays an item's shortcut menu.

Newer keyboards also include buttons that allow you to access your CD/DVD drive, adjust speaker volume, open your e-mail program, start your Web browser, and search the Internet. Some keyboards even have USB ports so you can plug USB devices directly into the keyboard instead of the back of the system unit.

Keyboard Types

A standard computer keyboard sometimes is called a **QWERTY keyboard** because of the layout of its typing area. That is, the first six leftmost letters on the top alphabetic line of the keyboard spell QWERTY (pronounced KWER-tee).

Most of today's desktop computer keyboards are enhanced keyboards. An **enhanced keyboard** has 12 function keys along the top, 2 CTRL keys, 2 ALT keys, and a set of arrow and additional keys between the typing area and the numeric keypad (see Figure 5-3).

Most keyboards attach to a serial port, or a keyboard port, or a USB port on the system unit via a cable. Some keyboards, however, do not use wires at all. A **cordless keyboard** is a battery-powered device that transmits data using wireless technology, such as radio waves or infrared light waves. These cordless devices communicate with a receiver that attaches to a port on the system unit. The port type varies depending on the type of wireless technology.

On notebook and many handheld computers, the keyboard is built into the top of the system unit (Figure 5-6). To fit in these smaller computers, the keyboards usually are smaller and have fewer keys. Most desktop computer keyboards have at least 101 keys. A typical notebook computer keyboard, by contrast, usually has about 85 keys. To provide all of the functionality of a desktop computer keyboard, manufacturers design many of the keys to serve two or three different purposes.

Command	Button	Menu	Function Key(s)
Copy		Edit|Copy	SHIFT+F2
Open		File|Open	CTRL+F12
Print		File|Print	CTRL+SHIFT+F12

Figure 5-4 Many programs allow you to use a button, a menu, or a function key to obtain the same result, as shown by these examples from Microsoft Word.

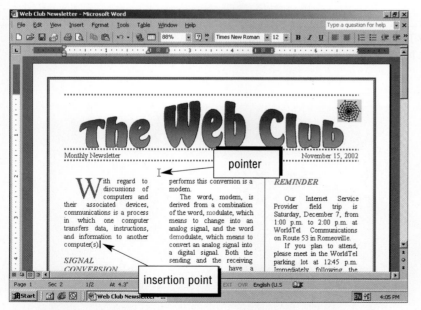

Figure 5-5 In most Windows programs, such as Word, the insertion point is a blinking vertical bar. You can use the keyboard or the mouse to move the insertion point. The pointer, another symbol that displays on the screen, is controlled using a pointing device such as a mouse.

Figure 5-6 On notebook and many handheld computers, the keyboard is built into the top of the system unit.

Users of handheld computers that do not have keyboards sometimes prefer to work with a portable keyboard to enter data. A **portable keyboard** is a full-sized keyboard you conveniently can attach and remove from a handheld computer. Figure 5-7 shows a pocket-sized portable keyboard that unfolds into a full-sized keyboard.

Regardless of size, many keyboards have a rectangular shape with the keys aligned in rows. Users who spend a large amount of time typing on these keyboards sometimes experience repetitive strain injuries

(RSI) of their wrists. For this reason, some manufacturers offer ergonomic keyboards. An **ergonomic keyboard** has a design that reduces the chance of these wrist injuries (Figure 5-8). Even keyboards that are not ergonomically designed attempt to offer a user more comfort. For example, many keyboards today include a wrist rest or palm rest to reduce strain on your wrist while typing (see Figure 5-3 on page 5.4).

The goal of **ergonomics** is to incorporate comfort, efficiency, and safety into the design of items in the workplace. Employees can be injured or develop disorders of the muscles, nerves, tendons, ligaments, and joints from working in an area that is not ergonomically designed. Thus, OSHA (Occupational Safety & Health Administration) has proposed standards whereby employers must establish programs that prevent these types of injuries or disorders.

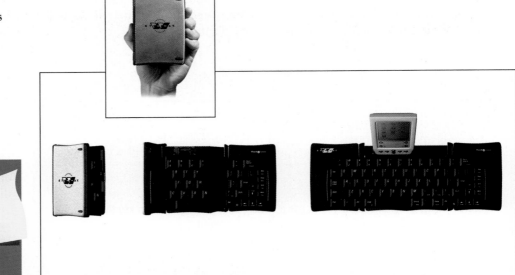

Figure 5-7 This convenient, portable keyboard unfolds into a full-sized keyboard that you can attach to a handheld computer.

Figure 5-8 The Microsoft Natural Keyboard Pro is an ergonomic keyboard designed to minimize strain on your hands and wrists.

POINTING DEVICES

A **pointing device** is an input device that allows you to control a pointer on the screen. In a graphical user interface, a **pointer** is a small symbol on the screen (see Figure 5-5 on page 5.5). A pointer often takes the shape of an I-beam (I), a block arrow ( ), or a pointing hand ( ). Using a pointing device, you can position the pointer to move or select items on the screen. For example, you can use a pointing device to move the insertion point; select text, graphics, and other objects; and click buttons, icons, links, and menu commands.

The following sections discuss common pointing devices.

MOUSE

A **mouse** is a pointing device that fits comfortably under the palm of your hand. The mouse is the most widely used pointing device on desktop computers.

With a mouse, you control the movement of the pointer, often called a **mouse pointer**, on the screen and make selections from the screen. The top of a mouse has one to four buttons; some also have a small wheel. The bottom of a mouse is flat and contains a mechanism that detects movement of the mouse.

Mouse Types

A **mechanical mouse** has a rubber or metal ball on its underside (Figure 5-9). When the ball rolls in a certain direction, electronic circuits in the mouse translate the movement of the mouse into signals the computer understands. You should place a mechanical mouse on a mouse pad. A **mouse pad** is a rectangular rubber or foam pad that provides better traction than the top of a desk. The mouse pad also protects the ball in the mouse from a build up of dust and dirt, which could cause it to malfunction.

An optical mouse, by contrast, has no moving mechanical parts inside. Instead, an **optical mouse** uses devices that emit and sense light to detect the mouse's movement (Figure 5-10). Some use optical sensors; others use laser. You can place an optical mouse that uses optical sensors on nearly all types of surfaces, eliminating the need for a mouse pad. An optical mouse that uses laser usually requires a special mouse pad. An optical mouse is more precise than a mechanical mouse and does not require cleaning like a mechanical mouse, but it also is slightly more expensive.

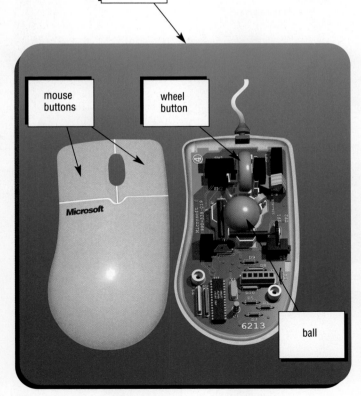

Figure 5-9 A mechanical mouse contains a small ball.

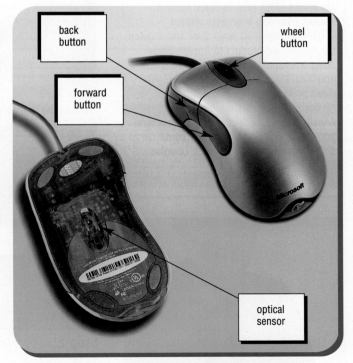

Figure 5-10 This optical mouse uses an optical sensor. It also includes buttons you push with your thumb that enable you to navigate forward and backward through Web pages.

Web Link

For more information on a mouse, visit the Discovering Computers 2002 Chapter 5 WEB LINK page (**scsite.com/dc2002/ch5/ weblink.htm**) and click Mouse.

TECHNOLOGY TRAILBLAZER

DOUGLAS **ENGELBART**

Without Douglas Engelbart, it is unlikely the phrase *point and click* would be part of our vocabulary. As a scientist at the Stanford Research Institute in the 1960s, Engelbart was part of a team that designed the first mouse with funding from NASA and the U.S. Department of Defense. The mouse prototype had a cord in the front, but Engelbart switched it to the rear to move it out of the way. He would tilt or rock that mouse to draw straight lines, and then he would push it and lift it off the desk to let the two perpendicular wheels on the bottom spin, which moved the cursor across the screen.

Even though he filed a patent for his design in 1965, Engelbart's thinking was too ahead of his time to reach fruition. Xerox's Palo Alto engineers refined Engelbart's ideas 10 years later and showed the redesigned product to Apple's Steve Jobs, who applied the concept to his graphical Macintosh and had the mouse mass produced in the mid-1980s.

For more information on Douglas Engelbart, visit the Discovering Computers 2002 People Web page (**scsite.com/ dc2002/people.htm**) and click Douglas Engelbart.

A mouse can connect to your computer in several ways. Most have a cable that attaches to a serial port, a mouse port, or USB port on the computer. A **cordless mouse** or **wireless mouse** is a battery-powered device that transmits data using wireless technology, such as radio waves or infrared light waves. The wireless technology used for a cordless mouse is very similar to that of a cordless keyboard discussed earlier. Some users prefer a cordless mouse because it frees up desk space and eliminates the clutter of a cord.

Using a Mouse

As you move the mouse, the pointer on the screen also moves. For example, when you move the mouse to the left, the pointer moves left on the screen (Figure 5-11). When you move the mouse to the right, the pointer moves right on the screen, and so on. If you have never worked with a mouse, you might find it a little awkward at first. With a little practice, however, you will discover that a mouse is quite easy to use.

Generally, you use the mouse to move the pointer on the screen to an object such as a button, a menu, an icon, a link, or text. Then, you press a mouse button to perform a certain

Figure 5-11 HOW TO MOVE THE POINTER WITH A MOUSE

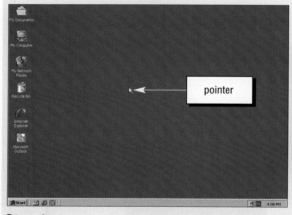 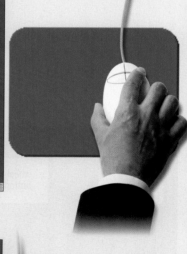

Step 1:
Position the mouse in the middle of the mouse pad.

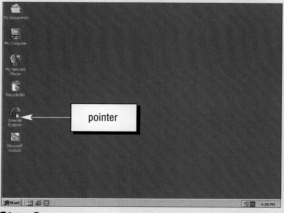 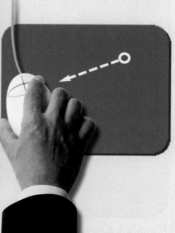

Step 2:
Move the mouse diagonally toward the left until it rests on the Internet Explorer icon.

action on that object. Windows users work with a mouse that has at least two buttons. For example, if you point to the Internet Explorer button on the taskbar and then press, or *click*, the primary mouse button, the browser displays a Web page on the screen. For a right-handed user, the left button usually is the primary mouse button and the right mouse button is the secondary mouse button. Left-handed people, however, can reverse the function of these buttons.

In addition to clicking, you can perform other operations using the mouse. These operations include point, right-click, double-click, drag, and right-drag. The table in Figure 5-12 explains how to perform these and other mouse operations. Some programs also use keys in combination with the mouse to perform certain actions.

As mentioned earlier, sometimes a mouse has a wheel that you can use with certain programs (see Figure 5-9 on page 5.7 and Figure 5-10 on page 5.7). You rotate or press the wheel to move text and objects on the screen. The function of the mouse buttons and the wheel varies depending on the program.

COMPANY ON THE CUTTING EDGE

Logitech

Mice Are Welcome Here

Thinking about a room full of mice can send chills down your spine. But Logitech employees are not bothered by all the mice in their offices; in fact, they smile when they think of these creatures.

Logitech is the world's largest manufacturer of the mouse, having created more than 200-million corded and cordless devices since 1981. The company also designs, produces, and markets a variety of other input devices, including keyboards, optical trackballs, joysticks, gamepads, and Internet video cameras. Cordless products account for more than one-third of the devices sold.

More than one-half of Logitech's engineers are software engineers, and they have used their innovative design and technological expertise to help the company win more than 50 worldwide awards. Among their 25 industry firsts are the cordless and opto-mechanical mouse devices, the color handheld scanner, and the digital still camera.

For more information on Logitech, visit the Discovering Computers 2002 Companies Web page (**scsite.com/dc2002/companies.htm**) and click Logitech.

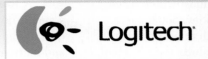

Operation	Mouse Action	Example
Point	Move the mouse across a flat surface until the pointer on the desktop rests on the item of choice.	Position the pointer on the screen.
Click	Press and release the primary mouse button, which usually is the left mouse button.	Select or deselect items on the screen or start a program or program feature.
Right-click	Press and release the secondary mouse button, which usually is the right mouse button.	Display a shortcut menu.
Double-click	Quickly press and release the left mouse button twice without moving the mouse.	Start a program or program feature.
Drag	Point to an item, hold down the left mouse button, move the item to the desired location on the screen, and then release the left mouse button.	Move an object from one location to another or draw pictures.
Right-drag	Point to an item, hold down the right mouse button, move the item to the desired location on the screen, and then release the right mouse button.	Display a shortcut menu after moving an object from one location to another.
Rotate wheel	Roll the wheel forward or backward.	Scroll up or down a few lines.
Press wheel button	Press the wheel button while moving the mouse on the desktop.	Scroll continuously.

Figure 5-12 The more common mouse operations.

OTHER POINTING DEVICES

The mouse is the most widely used pointing device today. Some users, however, work with other pointing devices. These include the trackball, touchpad, pointing stick, joystick, wheel, light pen, touch screen, and stylus. The following sections discuss each of these pointing devices.

Trackball

Whereas a mechanical mouse has a ball on the bottom, a **trackball** is a stationary pointing device with a ball on its top (Figure 5-13). The ball in most trackballs is about the size of a Ping-Pong ball.

To move the pointer using a trackball, you rotate the ball with your thumb, fingers, or the palm of your hand. In addition to the ball, a trackball usually has one or more buttons that work just like mouse buttons.

A trackball requires frequent cleaning because it picks up oils from your fingers and dust from the environment. If you have limited desk space, however, a trackball is a good alternative to a mouse because you do not have to move the entire device.

Touchpad

A **touchpad** or **trackpad** is a small, flat, rectangular pointing device that is sensitive to pressure and motion (Figure 5-14). To move the pointer using a touchpad, you slide your fingertip across the surface of the pad. Some touchpads have one or more buttons around the edge of the pad that work like mouse buttons. On many touchpads, you also can tap the pad's surface to imitate mouse operations such as clicking.

You can attach a stand-alone touchpad to any personal computer. You find them more often on notebook computers.

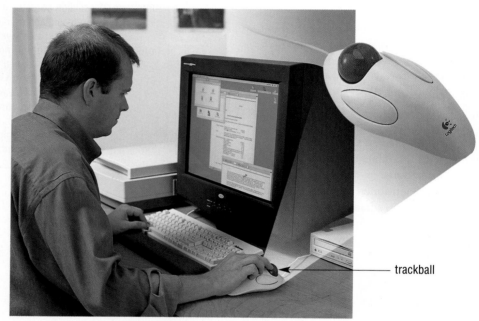

trackball

Figure 5-13 A trackball is like an upside-down mouse. You rotate the ball with your thumb, fingers, or palm of your hand to move the pointer.

touchpad

Figure 5-14 Many notebook computers have a touchpad that you can use to control the movement of the pointer.

Pointing Stick

A **pointing stick** is a pressure-sensitive pointing device shaped like a pencil eraser that is positioned between keys on the keyboard (Figure 5-15). To move the pointer using a pointing stick, you push the pointing stick with your finger. The pointer on the screen moves in the direction you push the pointing stick.

A pointing stick does not require any additional desk space. In addition, it does not require cleaning like a mechanical mouse or trackball. IBM first developed the pointing stick for its notebook computers. Whether you select a notebook computer that has a touchpad or pointing stick is a matter of personal preference.

Joysticks and Wheels

Users running game software or flight and driving simulation software often use a joystick or wheel as a pointing device (Figure 5-16). A **joystick** is a vertical lever mounted on a base. You move the lever in different directions to control the actions of a vehicle or player. The lever usually includes buttons called triggers you can press to activate certain events. Some joysticks also have additional buttons you can set to perform other actions.

A **wheel** is a steering-wheel type input device. You turn the wheel to drive a car, truck, or other vehicle. Most wheels also include foot pedals for acceleration and braking actions. A joystick and wheel typically attach via a cable to the game port on a sound card or game card or to a USB port.

Figure 5-15 Some notebook computers use a pointing stick to control the movement of the pointer.

pointing stick

Web Link

For more information on pointing sticks, visit the Discovering Computers 2002 Chapter 5 WEB LINK page (**scsite.com/dc2002/ch5/ weblink.htm**) and click Pointing Sticks.

joystick

wheel

pedal

Figure 5-16 Joysticks and wheels help the user control the actions of players and vehicles in game and simulation software.

Light Pen

A **light pen** is a handheld input device that contains a light source or can detect light. Some light pens require a specially designed monitor, while others work with a standard monitor. To select objects on the screen, you press the light pen against the surface of the screen or point the light pen at the screen and then press a button on the pen.

Health care professionals, such as doctors and dentists, use light pens because they can slide a protective sleeve over the pen — keeping their fingers free of contaminants (Figure 5-17). Light pens also are ideal for areas where employees hands might contain food, dirt, grease, or other chemicals that could damage the computer. Applications with limited desktop space such as industrial or manufacturing environments find light pens convenient, as well.

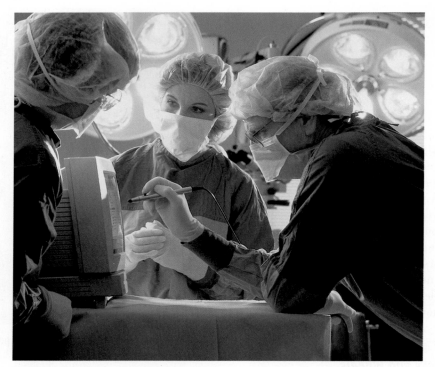

Figure 5-17 To make selections with a light pen, you touch the pen against the surface of the screen or point the pen at the screen and then press a button on the pen.

Touch Screen

A **touch screen** is a touch-sensitive display. You interact with the device by touching areas of the screen with your finger (Figure 5-18). Because they require a lot of arm movements, you do not enter large amounts of data into touch screens. Instead, you touch words, pictures, numbers, or locations identified on the screen.

Kiosks located in stores, hotels, airports, and museums often have touch screens. So you easily can access your bank account from your car, many ATM machines have touch screens. Many computers in restaurants, cafeterias, gift shops, and resorts have touch screens. Some notebook computers even have touch screens.

Instead of using your finger, some touch screens use a stylus. The next section discusses this device.

Figure 5-18 You interact with a touch screen by touching areas of the screen with your finger.

Stylus

A **stylus** looks like a ballpoint pen, but uses pressure, instead of ink, to write text and draw lines. This device, originally called a **pen** or electronic pen, was used in professional graphical applications such as computer-aided design and drafting. The following paragraphs describe how these and many other applications today use a pen, also known as a stylus.

Architects, mapmakers, artists, and designers create drawings and sketches by using an electronic pen on a graphics tablet. A **graphics tablet**, also called a **digitizer** or **digitizing tablet**, is a flat, rectangular, electronic plastic board. Each location on the graphics tablet corresponds to a specific location on the screen. When you draw on the tablet with the pen, the tablet detects and converts the movements into digital signals that are sent into the computer. These pens are quite sophisticated, featuring erasers and programmable buttons. In addition to a pen, some graphics tablets also use a cursor. A **cursor** is a device that looks similar to a mouse, except it has a window with cross hairs, so the user can see through to the tablet (Figure 5-19).

Pens used for handwriting recognition have grown in popularity. Using special software along with a pen and graphics tablet, you can send handwritten notes via e-mail or sign your name electronically (Figure 5-20). Upon receipt, the receiver sees your handwritten note or signature in its original form. Businesses save time using **electronic signatures**, also called **e-signatures**, which are just as legal as an ink signature.

Web Link

For more information on a stylus, visit the Discovering Computers 2002 Chapter 5 WEB LINK page (**scsite.com/dc2002/ch5/weblink.htm**) and click Stylus.

Web Link

For more information on e-signatures, visit the Discovering Computers 2002 Chapter 5 WEB LINK page (**scsite.com/dc2002/ch5/weblink.htm**) and click E-signatures.

Figure 5-20 With digital signatures just as legal as ink signatures, the demand for graphics tablets and pens is growing.

Figure 5-19 Architects, mapmakers, artists, and designers create drawings and sketches with an electronic pen on a graphics tablet. Other tablets use a cursor as the input device.

Some notebook and many handheld computers have touch screens that allow you to input data using a stylus (Figure 5-21). Instead of using a keyboard, you write or make selections on the computer screen with the stylus. These computers use **handwriting recognition software** that translates handwritten letters and symbols into characters that the computer understands. A later section in this chapter discusses handheld computer input and handwriting recognition software in more depth.

COMPANY ON THE CUTTING EDGE

Ubiquitous Palm Is a Phenomenon

Oprah has one. So do Murphy Brown and the media spinners in the hit movie, *Wag the Dog*. Indeed, more than two million people worldwide have a Palm handheld computer in their pocket or purse or briefcase to help them manage and organize their professional and personal lives.

The Palm handheld computer, manufactured by Palm, Inc., commands more than three-fourths of the handheld computer market. More than 43,000 developers are working on new software applications and hardware add-ons for this versatile and stylish product. Currently, software for Palm handhelds enables users to perform a multitude of tasks, including read e-books, record golf scores, and play games.

Palm was founded in 1992 and acquired by U.S. Robotics in 1995. One year later, the company introduced the Pilot 1000 and 5000 products, which blazed a trail for the handheld market. In 1997, 3Com acquired U.S. Robotics and made Palm a subsidiary of the corporation. Two years later, 3Com made Palm an independent, publicly traded company.

For more information on Palm, visit the Discovering Computers 2002 Companies Web page (**scsite.com/dc2002/companies.htm**) and click Palm.

VOICE INPUT

Voice input is the process of entering data by speaking into a microphone that is attached to the sound card on the computer. As an alternative to using a keyboard to input data, many users are talking to their computers.

Voice recognition, also called **speech recognition**, is the computer's capability of distinguishing spoken words (Figure 5-22). Voice recognition programs do not understand speech. They only recognize a vocabulary of pre-programmed words. The vocabulary of voice recognition programs can range from two words to millions of words. The automated telephone system at your bank may ask you to answer questions by speaking the words Yes or No into the telephone. A voice recognition program on your computer, by contrast, may recognize up to two million words!

In the past, voice recognition systems were found only in specialized applications in which a user's hands were occupied or disabled. Today, voice recognition applications are affordable and easy to use, providing all types of users with a convenient form of input. Some productivity software, such as word processing and spreadsheet, include voice recognition as part of the product. For example, you can dictate memos and letters into your word processing program instead of typing them. You can issue commands to your software applications, search the Web, participate in chat rooms, and send and receive e-mail and instant messages — all by speaking into a microphone.

The first voice recognition programs were speaker dependent. Today, most are speaker independent. With **speaker-dependent software**, the computer makes a profile of your voice, which means you have to train the computer to recognize your voice.

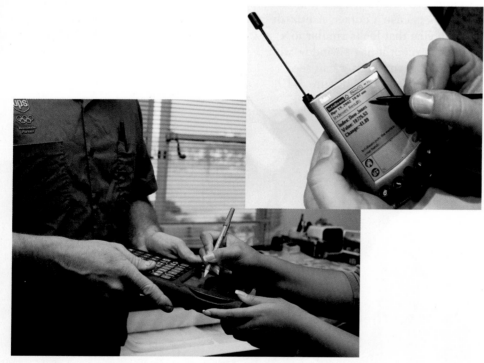

Figure 5-21 Many handheld computers support handwriting input through a stylus.

To train the computer, you must speak each of the words in the vocabulary into the computer repeatedly. After hearing the spoken word repeatedly, the program develops and stores a digital pattern for the word. When you later speak a word, the program compares the spoken word to those stored. **Speaker-independent software** has a built-in set of word patterns. That is, you do not have to train a computer to recognize your voice. Many products today include a built-in set of words that grows as the software learns your words.

Some voice recognition software requires **discrete speech**, which means you have to speak slowly and separate each word with a short pause. Most of today's products, however, allow you to speak in a flowing conversational tone, called **continuous speech**.

ISSUE

Talk to Your Computer

The Accuracy of Voice Recognition Software

Voice recognition is a process accomplished through software that allows users to interact with their computer by voice. Even though improvements have been made within voice recognition software, it still is not perfect. Experts agree voice recognition capability represents the future of software. Experts do not agree, however, that the future is now. The best voice recognition programs are 90 to 95 percent accurate. Yet, advocates admit this assessment is based on expected speech and vocabulary. When confronted with unusual dialogue, accuracy drops. Even a 90 percent accuracy rate means 1 out of 10 words will be wrong. Before we can use voice recognition software effectively, how accurate must it be? When would voice recognition be an advantage? Might it ever be a disadvantage? Why? Would you use voice recognition software?

For more information on voice recognition, visit the Discovering Computers 2002 Issues Web page (**scsite.com/dc2002/issues.htm**) and and click Chapter 5 Issue #3.

Figure 5-22 HOW VOICE RECOGNITION WORKS

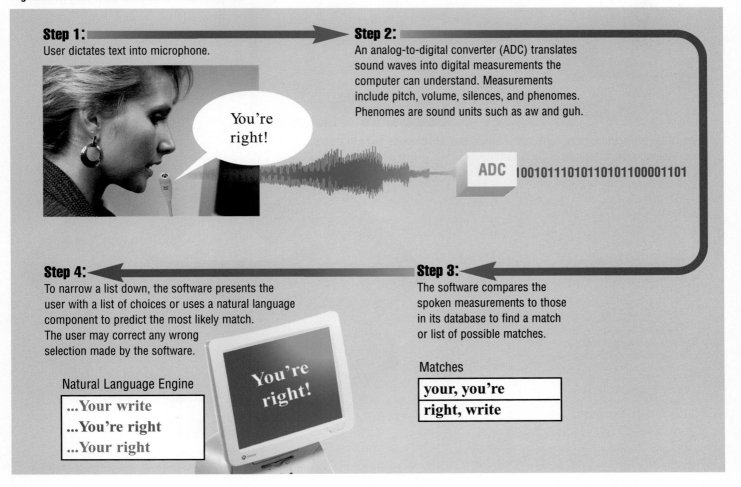

Step 1:
User dictates text into microphone.

You're right!

Step 2:
An analog-to-digital converter (ADC) translates sound waves into digital measurements the computer can understand. Measurements include pitch, volume, silences, and phenomes. Phenomes are sound units such as aw and guh.

ADC 100101110101101011000001101

Step 3:
The software compares the spoken measurements to those in its database to find a match or list of possible matches.

Matches

| your, you're |
| right, write |

Step 4:
To narrow a list down, the software presents the user with a list of choices or uses a natural language component to predict the most likely match. The user may correct any wrong selection made by the software.

Natural Language Engine

| ...Your write |
| ...You're right |
| ...Your right |

You're right!

Audio Input

Voice input is part of a larger category of input called audio input. **Audio input** is the process of entering any sound into the computer such as speech, music, and sound effects. To input high-quality sound, your personal computer must have a sound card. You can input sound via a device such as a microphone, tape player, CD player, or radio, each of which plugs into a port on the sound card.

With a microphone plugged into the microphone port on the sound card, you can record any sound, including speech. Windows stores audio files as **waveforms**, which are

called **WAV** files and have a .wav extension. Once you save the sound in a file, you can play it using the Sound Recorder. You can attach the audio file to an e-mail message or include it in a document such as a word processing report or presentation graphics slide show.

WAV files often are large – requiring more than 1 MB of storage space for a single minute of audio. For this reason, WAV files often are compressed so they take up less storage space.

You can input music and other sound effects using external MIDI devices such as an electronic piano keyboard (Figure 5-23). Discussed in

the previous chapter, in addition to being a port, MIDI (musical instrument digital interface) is the electronic music industry's standard that defines how digital musical devices represent sounds electronically. These devices connect to the sound card on your computer. Software programs that conform to the MIDI standard allow you to compose and edit music and other sounds. For example, you can change the speed, add notes, or rearrange the score to produce an entirely new sound.

INPUT DEVICES FOR HANDHELD COMPUTERS

Handheld computers today are very popular for both home and business users (Figure 5-24). Available in a variety of sleek colors, they include many features such as a calendar, appointment book, calculator, memo pad, and wireless Web and e-mail access.

Figure 5-23 An electronic piano keyboard is an external MIDI device that can record music. You can store the music in the computer.

Web Link

For more information on handheld computer input, visit the Discovering Computers 2002 Chapter 5 WEB LINK page (**scsite.com/dc2002/ch5/ weblink.htm**) and click Handheld Computer Input.

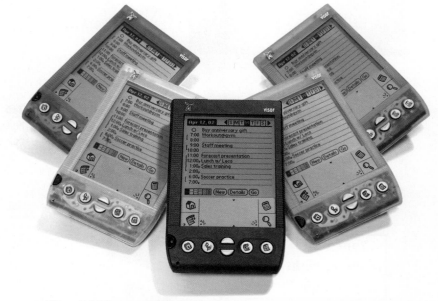

Figure 5-24 Handheld computers today are available in a wide range of colors.

To satisfy the input needs of many different types of users, handheld computers provide many different ways to input data (Figure 5-25). The primary input method on most is the stylus. A handheld computer typically includes a basic stylus. You can purchase more elaborate models that have a ballpoint pen at one end and a stylus at the other. With the stylus, you can enter data in two ways: use an on-screen keyboard or use handwriting recognition software. Each handheld computer uses its own handwriting recognition software. For example, the Palm products use Graffiti®.

Instead of using a stylus, you can attach a full-sized keyboard to your handheld computer. You also can type onto your desktop computer and transfer the data into your handheld computer and vice-versa. As an alternative to typing, many handheld computers support voice input so you can enter data and instructions by speaking into the device. If you want to take photographs and view them on your handheld computer, you can attach a digital camera directly to many handheld computer models.

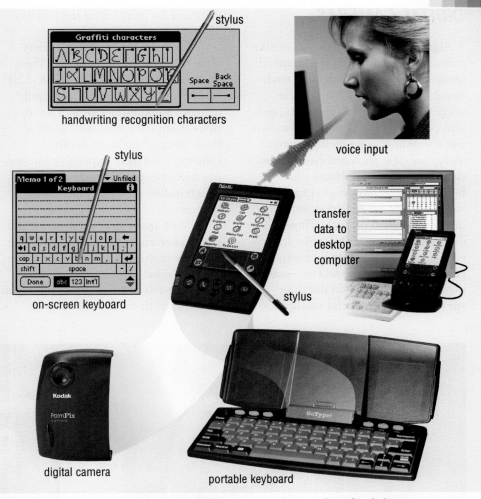

Figure 5-25 Data can be input into a handheld computer using a variety of techniques.

TECHNOLOGY TRAILBLAZER

DONNA **DUBINSKY**

As if being the president and CEO of 3Com's Palm Computing Division were not enough of a challenge, Donna Dubinsky founded Handspring with Jeff Hawkins in 1998 with the goal of becoming the leading handheld computing device maker for the consumer market.

Before coming to Palm Computing, Dubinsky had served as director of distribution at Apple Computer and as an international vice president at Claris. At Palm, she and Hawkins introduced the PalmPilot personal organizer in 1996; sales of more than two million units make it the most-rapidly adopted new computing product ever manufactured. In an effort to learn how consumers actually use the Palm, she watched consumers open the PalmPilot boxes and read the manuals. She even took some technical support calls herself to see what questions they were asking.

Craving her independence and autonomy at Handspring, Dubinsky is using the Palm operating system on its Visor handheld computer. She stresses that size, connectivity to a personal computer, usability, and an economical price are the factors that make handheld computers successful.

For more information on Donna Dubinsky, visit the Discovering Computers 2002 People Web page (scsite.com/dc2002/people.htm) and click Donna Dubinsky.

DIGITAL CAMERAS

A **digital camera** allows you to take pictures and store the photographed images digitally, instead of on traditional film (Figure 5-26). Mobile users such as real estate agents, general contractors, and photojournalists use a digital camera so they immediately can view photographed images right on the camera. Home and business users have digital cameras to save the expense of film developing, duplication, and postage. These users can share images with family, friends, co-workers, and clients by posting the photographs on a Web site or e-mailing them. You also can add dazzling special effects and print multiple copies of an image from the comfort of your home or office.

Digital cameras use a variety of techniques to store images. These include floppy disk, SuperDisk, Clik! disk, PC Card, compact flash card, memory stick, mini-CD, and micro-drive. Chapter 7 discusses each of these storage media in depth. Generally, the more expensive cameras use higher-capacity storage devices, which means they can hold more pictures.

With many digital cameras, you can review and edit the images while they are in the camera. You also can connect some cameras directly to a printer or television. If you prefer, you can work with the images on your desktop personal computer. To do this, you **download**, or transfer a copy of, the pictures from the digital camera to the computer. With some cameras, you connect a cable between the digital camera and a serial port or USB port on the computer and then use special software included with the camera. As a faster alternative, some users purchase a reading device that attaches to a parallel port or USB port on the computer. With the media in a reading device, you can transfer the images from the media to the computer. For cameras that use a floppy disk, you simply insert the disk into the computer's disk drive and then copy the pictures to the computer.

Figure 5-26 Digital cameras are used for a variety of reasons. The images are viewable immediately on the camera. They also can be edited, printed, or posted on a Web page or photo community.

Once the pictures are on your computer, you can edit them with photo-editing software, print them, fax them, send them via e-mail, include them in another document, or post them to a Web site or photo community for everyone to see. You can add pictures to greeting cards, a computerized photo album, a family newsletter, certificates, and awards. Figure 5-27 illustrates how a digital camera transforms the captured image into a screen display on your computer.

The three basic types of digital cameras are studio cameras, field cameras, and point-and-shoot cameras. The most expensive and highest quality of the three, a **studio camera** is a stationary camera used for professional studio work. Often used by photojournalists, a **field camera** is a portable camera that has many lenses and other attachments. Similarly to the studio camera, a field camera can be quite expensive. A **point-and-shoot camera** is more affordable and lightweight and provides acceptable quality photographic images for the home or small business user.

A point-and-shoot camera often features flash, zoom, automatic focus, and special effects. With some, you can record short narrations for your pictures. Several of these cameras have a built-in TV out port that allows

Figure 5-27 HOW A DIGITAL CAMERA WORKS

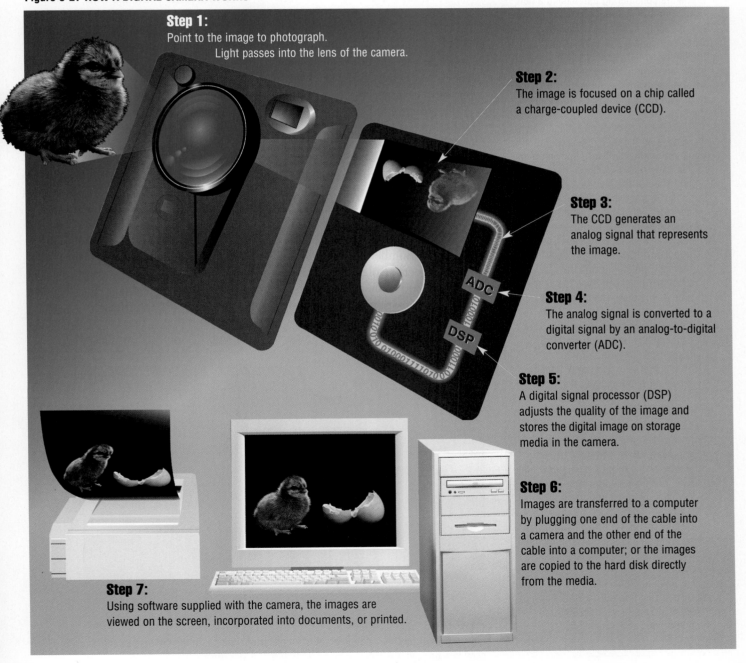

Step 1:
Point to the image to photograph.
Light passes into the lens of the camera.

Step 2:
The image is focused on a chip called a charge-coupled device (CCD).

Step 3:
The CCD generates an analog signal that represents the image.

Step 4:
The analog signal is converted to a digital signal by an analog-to-digital converter (ADC).

Step 5:
A digital signal processor (DSP) adjusts the quality of the image and stores the digital image on storage media in the camera.

Step 6:
Images are transferred to a computer by plugging one end of the cable into a camera and the other end of the cable into a computer; or the images are copied to the hard disk directly from the media.

Step 7:
Using software supplied with the camera, the images are viewed on the screen, incorporated into documents, or printed.

you to display their pictures directly on your television screen. This camera is ideal for the home user and mobile users such as real estate agents, insurance agents, and general contractors.

APPLY IT!

Going Digital with Pictures

If you are considering purchasing a new camera in the near future, then consider going digital. Taking pictures with a digital camera is fast and easy. Similar to a traditional camera, you will find a wide price range for digital cameras. For a better idea of what you should purchase to fit your budget and lifestyle, consider the following:

1. If you want to print or publish your images on the Web, then resolution is important. Similar to your monitor, the higher the resolution, the better and sharper the picture.

2. Image storage is another feature to consider. Most digital cameras include some type of miniature removable storage media. The most popular of these media is flash memory, but some cameras use small hard disks or even the venerable floppy disk. The number of images you can store on one of these devices depends on the capacity, the resolution, and the amount of compression.

3. The type of lens you select affects how your pictures look. If you are going to be backpacking in the Rockies and want to take a close-up picture of a newly bloomed wildflower, then a macro lens is what you need. Or, if you want to take a picture of the moose on the next hill over, consider a zoom lens.

4. Perhaps the most important factor to consider is how much money you plan to spend. Determine your price and do some comparison shopping, using the above listed features as guidelines.

For links to digital camera sites, visit the Discovering Computers 2002 Apply It Web page (**scsite.com/dc2002/apply.htm**) and click Chapter 5 Apply It #1.

One factor that affects the quality of a digital camera is its resolution. **Resolution** describes the sharpness and clearness of an image. The higher the resolution, the better the image quality, but the more expensive the camera. Some digital camera resolutions today exceed three million pixels. A **pixel** (short for *pic*ture *el*ement) is a single point in an electronic image (Figure 5-28). The greater the number of pixels the camera uses to capture an image, the better the quality of the image.

As a rule, a 1-megapixel (million pixel) camera is fine for screen displays such as photo communities, Web pages, and e-mail attachments. These low-end cameras cost a few hundred dollars. If you plan to print photographs larger than 5 x 7 inches, you should have at least a 2-megapixel (million pixel) camera. For images as good as film-based cameras, use a 3-megapixel camera. These high-end point-and-shoot cameras cost less than $1,000.

Some manufacturers use dots per inch to represent a digital camera's resolution. **Dots per inch (dpi)** is the number of pixels in an inch of screen display. For example, a 1,600 x 1,200 (pronounced 1600 by 1200) dpi camera has 1,600 pixels per vertical inch and 1,200 pixels per horizontal inch. If just one number is stated, such as 1,200 dpi, then both the vertical and horizontal numbers are the same. Digital cameras for the consumer range from 640 x 480 dpi to 1,792 x 1,200 dpi. On some cameras, you can adjust the dpi to the resolution you need. With a lower dpi, you can capture more images. For example, a camera set at 800 x 600 dpi might capture and store 61 images. The number of images reduces to 24 on the same camera set at 1,600 x 1,200 dpi.

The actual photographed resolution is known as the **optical resolution**. Some manufacturers state **enhanced resolution**, or **interpolated resolution**, instead of or in addition to optical resolution. Optical resolution is different from enhanced resolution. The enhanced resolution usually is higher because it uses a special formula to add pixels between those generated by the optical resolution.

Another measure of a digital camera's quality is the number of bits it stores in a dot. Each dot consists of one or more bits of data. The more bits used to represent a dot, the more colors and shades of gray that can be represented. One bit per dot is enough for simple one-color images. For multiple colors and shades of gray, each dot requires more than one bit of data. Your point-and-shoot camera should be at least 24 bit.

Figure 5-28 A pixel is a single point in an electronic image. In digital images, the pixel is a tiny square. When images are printed, pixels are circles of color.

VIDEO INPUT

Video input or **video capture** is the process of entering a full-motion recording into a computer and storing it on a storage medium. Many video devices use analog video signals. Computers, by contrast, use digital signals. To input video from these analog devices, the analog signal must be converted to a digital signal. To do this, you plug a video camera, VCR, or other analog video device into a video-in plug that is attached to the computer. One card that has a video-in plug is a video capture card. A **video capture card** is an expansion card that converts the analog video signal into a digital signal that a computer can understand. (Most new computers are not equipped with a video capture card because not all users need this type of card.)

A new generation of video cameras produces digital signals. A **digital video (DV) camera** is a video camera that records video as digital signals, instead of analog signals. In addition to video, you also can capture still frames with these cameras. A DV camera connects directly to a parallel port or USB port on the computer. Many DV cameras have a video-in plug. Thus, with a DV camera, you do not need a video capture card (Figure 5-29).

Once you connect the video device to the computer, you can begin recording. After you save the video on a storage medium, you can play it or edit it using video-editing software.

Just as with audio files, video files can require huge amounts of storage space. A three-minute segment, or clip, of high-quality video can require an entire gigabyte of storage

(equal to approximately 50 million pages of text). To decrease the size of the files, video often is compressed.

Video compression works by recognizing that only a small portion of a video image changes from frame to frame. A video compression program might store the first frame and then store only the changes from one frame to the next. The program assumes the next frames will be almost identical to the first. Before you view the video, the program decompresses the video segment. Instead of using software to decompress video, some computers have a video decoder. A **video decoder** is a card that decompresses video data. A video decoder is more effective and efficient than software.

If you do not want to save an entire video clip on your computer, you can use a **video digitizer** to capture an individual frame from an analog video and then save the still

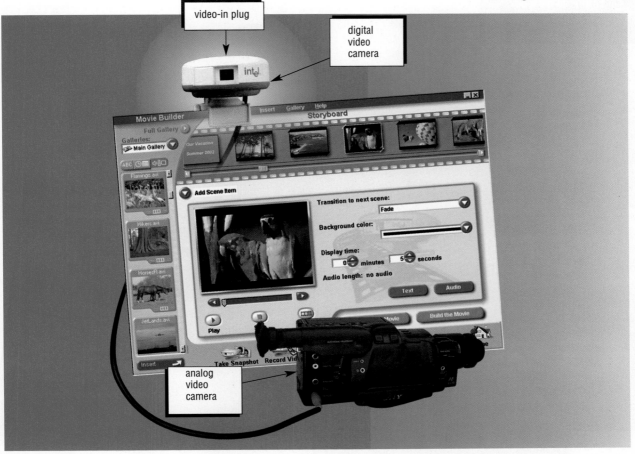

Figure 5-29 You can capture home videos on VHS tapes by attaching an analog video camera to the video-in plug on a digital video camera.

picture in a file. To do this, plug the analog recording device such as a video camera, VCR, or television into the video digitizer. The video digitizer then usually connects to a parallel port or USB port. While watching the video using special software, you can stop it and capture any single frame. The resulting files are similar to those that a digital camera generates.

PC Video Cameras

A **PC video camera**, or **PC camera**, is a DV camera that allows the home user to record, edit, and capture video and still images and to make video telephone calls on the Internet (Figure 5-30). During a **video telephone call**, both parties see each other as they talk. To provide security in your home, the PC camera can be set to take digital photographs at preset time intervals or whenever it detects motion.

Attached to your computer's USB port, a PC camera usually sits on top of your monitor. For more flexibility, some PC cameras are portable. That is, you can detach them from the computer and use them anywhere.

Some PC cameras have a video-in plug, allowing you to attach a video camera or VCR directly to it. This enables you to create movies from existing videos. The cost of these cameras usually is less than a hundred dollars.

Many magazines and textbooks are beginning to use digital watermarks and PC cameras to connect printed media to the Web. A **digital watermark** is a small digital image that when held in front of a PC camera, displays an associated Web page on the computer screen.

PC video camera

Figure 5-30 A PC video camera can be used to capture, edit, and record video and to make video telephone calls on the Internet.

Web Cams

A **Web cam**, also called a **cam**, is a video camera whose output displays on a Web page. A Web cam attracts Web site visitors by showing images that change regularly (Figure 5-31). You could use a Web cam to show a work in progress, weather and traffic information, employees at work, photographs of a vacation, or any other images you wish to display.

Some Web sites have live Web cams that display still pictures and update the displayed image at a specified time or time intervals, such as 30 seconds. Another type of Web cam, called **streaming cam**, shows moving images by sending a continual stream of pictures.

Web cam

Figure 5-31 This Web cam shows the inside of a unique diner. The image is updated every 30 seconds.

ISSUE

Around the World in 80 Clicks

The Value of Web Cams

Consider going around the world in 80 clicks. It is possible. Take an online tour of the world at your leisure. Thousands of Web sites show live images through Web cams. These sites feature real-time (often 24-hour) views from every country in the world, and from places such as beaches, buildings, classrooms, dorm rooms, baby bassinets, fish tanks, taxicab dashboards, even inside a refrigerator. Or, how about a camera mounted on a bike, transmitting images through a cellular telephone? Some people may question the entertainment value and the appeal of the Web cam, especially because many of the sites are rather boring. With the drop in price and the increased ease of installation and use, more people are using Web cams to share the view from their part of the world. What motivates someone to do this? Why would someone want to see a stranger's home movies? In what type of Web cam Web site would you be interested? Why?

For more information on Web cams, visit the Discovering Computers 2002 Issues Web page (**scsite.com/dc2002/issues.htm**) and click Chapter 5 Issue #5.

Videoconferencing

A **videoconference** is a meeting between two or more geographically separated people who use a network or the Internet to transmit audio and video data (Figure 5-32). To participate in a videoconference, you need videoconferencing software along with a microphone, speakers, and a video camera attached to your computer. As you speak, members of the meeting hear your voice on their speakers. Any image in front of the video camera, such as a person's face, displays in a window on each participant's screen.

A **whiteboard** is another window on the screen that can display notes and drawings simultaneously on all participants' screens. This window provides multiple users with an area on which they can write or draw.

Figure 5-32 As you speak, members of a videoconference hear your voice on their speakers. With the video camera facing you, an image of your face displays in a window on each participant's screen.

APPLY IT!

Setting Up a Web Cam

Web cams are the Internet craze of today. Live Web cam images provide Web site visitors an inside view of your world. Setting up a Web cam is much easier than you might think.

1. The first step is to select a camera. If you use an analog camcorder, you need a card such as a video capture card that converts the analog video signal into a digital signal. Another alternative is a digital video camera that connects directly to your computer's USB port or parallel port. If the camera connects to the parallel port, you also will need a device such as a switchbox that enables you to use the camera and printer at the same time.

   Be sure your camera can capture high-quality pictures for areas with poor lighting. A camera with an inadequate sensitivity to light often generates murky Web cam images. Many cameras are on the market, so be sure to read reviews prior to purchasing.

2. To display Web cam images on a Web page, you send the images from your camera to a Web server. With many Web cam software programs, you FTP images (frames) at specified times or time intervals. Some programs also allow you to set up streaming video from the camera. Popular Web cam software products include Webcam32 and Ispy WebCam (see URL below). Price range for this software is from $25 to $75.

3. Next, you create a Web page that will display your Web cam images. On the Web page, you need to add HTML code that instructs the Web server to display your images. Most Web cam software products provide sample code.

4. For the Web cam images to display on the Web, you need access to a Web server. Many ISPs or OSPs provide this service at no cost. With your Web page on the Web server, the world can see your Web cam images.

   Several all-in-one kits also are available that supply the camera, the software, and sometimes access to a Web server. These kits are convenient and easy to use but may not provide the extras that are available when you purchase individual components.

   For more information on Web cams and the Web addresses mentioned above, visit the Discovering Computers 2002 Apply It Web page (**scsite.com/dc2002/apply.htm**) and click Chapter 5 Apply It #2.

The costs of videoconferencing hardware and software continue to decrease. Thus, videoconferencing is becoming a cost-effective way to conduct business meetings, corporate training, and educational classes.

SCANNERS AND READING DEVICES

Some input devices save you time by eliminating the manual entry of data. With these devices, you do not type or speak into the computer. Instead, these devices capture data from a **source document**, which is the original form of the data. Examples of source documents are timecards, order forms, invoices, paychecks, advertisements, brochures, photographs, inventory tags, or any other document that contains data to be processed.

Devices that capture data directly from source documents include optical scanners, optical character recognition devices, optical mark recognition devices, bar code scanners, and magnetic-ink character recognition readers. The following pages discuss each of these devices.

Optical Scanner

An **optical scanner**, usually called a **scanner**, is a light-sensing input device that reads printed text and graphics and then translates the results into a form the computer can use.

One of the more popular types of scanners is a flatbed scanner. A **flatbed scanner** works similarly to a copy machine except it creates a file of the document in memory instead of a paper copy (Figure 5-33). Once an object is scanned, you can display it on the screen, store it on a storage medium, print it, fax it, attach it to an e-mail message, include it in another document, or post it to a Web site or photo community for everyone to see.

For example, you can scan a picture and then include the picture when creating a brochure.

Web Link

For more information on scanners, visit the Discovering Computers 2002 Chapter 5 WEB LINK page (**scsite.com/dc2002/ch5/ weblink.htm**) and click Scanners.

Figure 5-33 HOW A FLATBED SCANNER WORKS

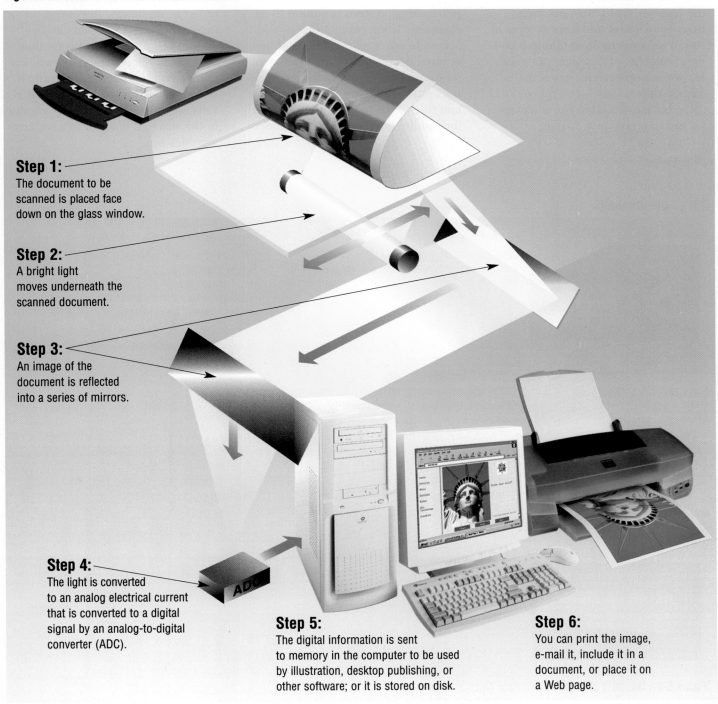

Step 1:
The document to be scanned is placed face down on the glass window.

Step 2:
A bright light moves underneath the scanned document.

Step 3:
An image of the document is reflected into a series of mirrors.

Step 4:
The light is converted to an analog electrical current that is converted to a digital signal by an analog-to-digital converter (ADC).

Step 5:
The digital information is sent to memory in the computer to be used by illustration, desktop publishing, or other software; or it is stored on disk.

Step 6:
You can print the image, e-mail it, include it in a document, or place it on a Web page.

Three other types of scanners are pen, sheet-fed, and drum. The table in Figure 5-34 summarizes the four types of scanners.

As with a digital camera, the quality of a scanner is measured by the number of bits it stores in a dot and the number of dots per inch, or resolution. The higher each number, the better quality, but the more expensive the scanner. Most of today's affordable color desktop scanners for the home or small business range from 30 to 48 bit and have an optical resolution ranging from 600 to 3,000 dpi. Commercial scanners designed for power users range from 4,000 to 12,500 dpi.

Businesses often use scanners for image processing. **Image** **processing**, or **imaging**, consists of capturing, storing, analyzing, displaying, printing, and manipulating images. Image processing allows you to convert paper documents such as reports, memos, and procedure manuals into an electronic form. Once saved electronically, you can distribute these documents electronically.

Many business users store and index these documents with an image processing system. An **image processing system** is similar to an electronic filing cabinet that provides access to exact reproductions of the original documents. The government, for example, uses an image processing system to store property deeds and titles to provide quick access to the public, lawyers, and loan officers.

Many scanners also include OCR (optical character recognition) software. **OCR software** can read and convert many types of text documents. Suppose you need to modify a business report, but do not have the original word processing file. You could scan the document with a flatbed scanner, but you still would not be able to edit the report. The scanner, which does not differentiate between text and graphics, saves the report as an image. To convert the image into a text file that can be edited, you use OCR software that works with the scanner. You will be able to edit the resulting text file in a word processing program. The OCR software typically places any graphics in the scanned image into a separate graphics file.

TYPES OF SCANNERS

Scanner	Method of Scanning/ Use	Scannable Items
Flatbed	• Similar to a copy machine • Scanning mechanism passes under the item to be scanned, which is placed on a glass surface	• Single sheet documents • Bound material • Photographs • Some models include trays for slides, transparencies, and negatives
Pen or handheld	• Move pen over text to be scanned, then transfer data to computer • Ideal for mobile users, students, researchers • Some connect to a handheld computer • Some read Web bar codes	• Any printed text • Web bar codes
Sheet-fed	• Item to be scanned is pulled into a stationary scanning mechanism • Smaller and less expensive than a flatbed scanner	• Single sheet documents • Photographs • Slides (with an adapter)
Drum	• Item to be scanned rotates around a stationary scanning mechanism • Very large and expensive • Used in publishing industry	• Single sheet documents • Photographs • Slides • Negatives

Figure 5-34 This table describes the various types of scanners.

Current OCR software has a very high success rate and usually can identify more than 99 percent of scanned material. OCR software also marks text it cannot read, allowing you to make corrections easily.

Optical Readers

An **optical reader** is a device that uses a light source to read characters, marks, and codes and then converts them into digital data that a computer can process. The following sections discuss three types of optical readers: optical character recognition, optical mark recognition, and bar code scanner.

OPTICAL CHARACTER RECOGNITION **Optical character recognition** (**OCR**) is a technology that involves reading typewritten, computer-printed, or handwritten characters from ordinary documents and translating the images into a form that the computer can understand. Most **OCR devices** include a small optical scanner for reading characters and sophisticated software for analyzing what is read.

OCR devices range from large machines that can read thousands of documents per minute to handheld wands that read one document at a time. OCR devices read characters printed using an OCR font. A widely used OCR font is called OCR-A (Figure 5-35). During the scan of a document, an OCR device determines the shapes of characters by detecting patterns of light and dark. OCR software then compares these shapes with predefined shapes stored in memory and converts the shapes into characters the computer can understand.

Many companies use OCR characters on turnaround documents. A **turnaround document** is a document that you return (turn around) to the company that creates and sends it. For example, when you receive a bill, you tear off a portion of the bill and send it back to the company with your payment (Figure 5-36). The portion of the bill you return usually has your account number, payment amount, and other information printed in optical characters.

ABCDEFGHIJKLMNOPQRSTUVWXYZ
1234567890-=█;',./

Figure 5-35 A portion of the characters in the OCR-A font. Notice how characters such as the number 0 and the letter O are shaped differently so the reading device easily can distinguish between them.

Bostongas
Essexgas Colonialgas
Eastern Enterprises
WHEN PAYING AT OFFICE PLEASE BRING THIS ENTIRE BILL
WHEN PAYING BY MAIL PLEASE ENCLOSE THIS COUPON
AND MAIL PAYMENTS TO: POST OFFICE BOX 4300
WOBURN MA 01888-4300
PLEASE INDICATE AMOUNT PAID
AUTO ************* 3-DIGIT 018
SCOTT GOOD
4934 WEST ST
IPSWICH MA 01938-2253
PAYMENTS RECEIVED BY
AUG 30, 2002
WILL BE REFLECTED ON YOUR NEXT BILL
BOSTON GAS COMPANY
03
MAKE CHECKS PAYABLE TO ABOVE
ACCOUNT NUMBER
02019 23730 910
PAYMENT DUE UPON RECEIPT
AMOUNT DUE
$23.94
12015297300100100000023947
PLEASE DETACH HERE

SERVICE ADDRESS	ACCOUNT NUMBER	BILLING DATE
SCOTT GOOD 4934 WEST ST IPSWICH MA 01938-2253	02019 23730 910	AUG 7, 2002
	METER NUMBER	NEXT READ DATE
	09735042	SEP 5, 2002

FOR BILL INFORMATION OR SERVICE CALL: 1-617-469-2300

GAS USED
Bill for 1 month, Jul 6-Aug 4

Present actual meter read, Aug 4, 2002	0786
Previous actual meter read, Jul 6, 2002	- 0786
Units of gas	0
Therm conversion factor	x1.0550
Therms used this period	0

CHARGES FOR GAS USED
Commercial/Industrial, G-41
Delivery Charges:

GAS USE HISTORY

	Therms		Therms
Aug 02 Actual	0	Jan 02 Actual	27
Jul 02 Actual	0	Dec 01 Actual	3
Jun 02 Actual	1	Nov 01 Actual	7
May 02 Actual	4	Oct 01 Actual	0
Apr 02 Actual	9	Sep 01 Actual	0
Mar 02 Actual	43	Aug 01 Actual	0
Feb 02 Actual	180	Jul 01 Actual	0

BALANCE & PAYMENTS
Balance as of Jul 7, 2002 $23.94

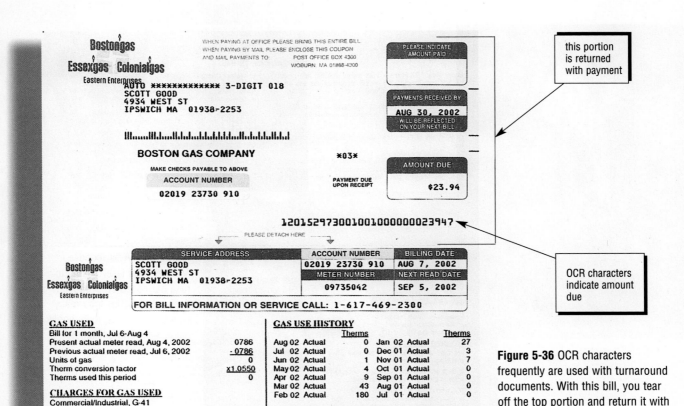

Figure 5-36 OCR characters frequently are used with turnaround documents. With this bill, you tear off the top portion and return it with your payment.

OPTICAL MARK RECOGNITION

Optical mark recognition (OMR) devices read hand-drawn marks such as small circles or rectangles. A person places these marks on a form, such as a test, survey, or question-naire answer sheet (Figure 5-37). With a test, the OMR device first reads the answer key sheet to record correct answers based on patterns of light. The OMR device then reads the remaining documents and matches their patterns of light against the answer key sheet.

BAR CODE SCANNER A **bar code scanner** uses laser beams to read bar codes (Figure 5-38). A **bar code** is an identification code that consists of a set of vertical lines and spaces of different widths. The bar code represents data that identifies the manufacturer and the item. Manufacturers either print a bar code on a product's package or on

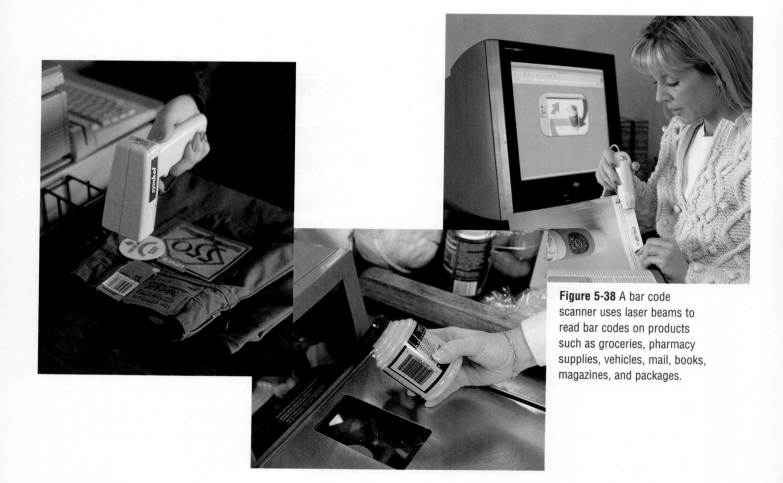

Figure 5-37 On many surveys and questionnaires, you draw small circles to indicate your answers. These forms are read by optical mark recognition (OMR) devices.

Figure 5-38 A bar code scanner uses laser beams to read bar codes on products such as groceries, pharmacy supplies, vehicles, mail, books, magazines, and packages.

a label that is affixed to a product. A bar code scanner reads a bar code by using light patterns that pass through the bar code lines.

A variety of products such as groceries, pharmacy supplies, vehicles, mail, magazines, and books have bar codes. Each industry uses its own type of bar code. The U.S. Postal Service uses a POSTNET bar code. Retail and grocery stores use the Universal Product Code, or UPC (Figure 5-39). The table in Figure 5-40 summarizes some of the more widely used bar codes.

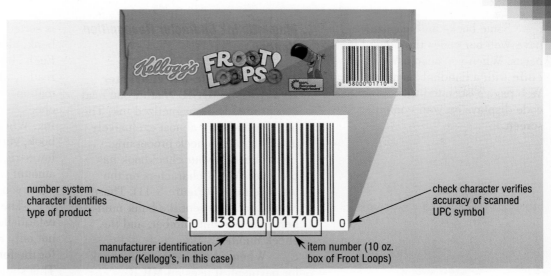

number system character identifies type of product

check character verifies accuracy of scanned UPC symbol

manufacturer identification number (Kellogg's, in this case)

item number (10 oz. box of Froot Loops)

Figure 5-39 This UPC identifies a box of Kellogg's Froot Loops™.

TYPES OF BAR CODES

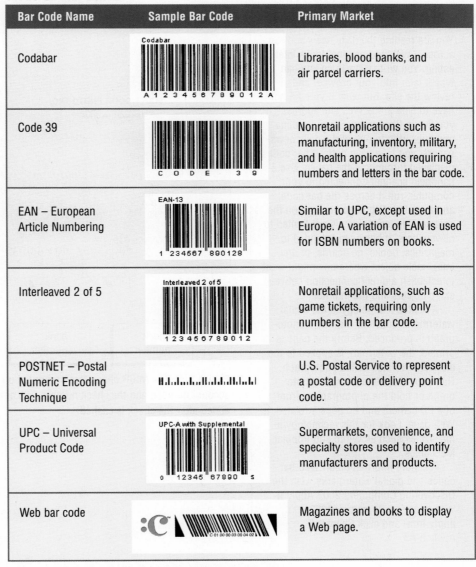

Bar Code Name	Sample Bar Code	Primary Market
Codabar	Codabar A 1 2 3 4 5 6 7 8 9 0 1 2 A	Libraries, blood banks, and air parcel carriers.
Code 39	C O D E 3 9	Nonretail applications such as manufacturing, inventory, military, and health applications requiring numbers and letters in the bar code.
EAN – European Article Numbering	EAN-13 1 234567 890128	Similar to UPC, except used in Europe. A variation of EAN is used for ISBN numbers on books.
Interleaved 2 of 5	Interleaved 2 of 5 1 2 3 4 5 6 7 8 9 0 1 2	Nonretail applications, such as game tickets, requiring only numbers in the bar code.
POSTNET – Postal Numeric Encoding Technique		U.S. Postal Service to represent a postal code or delivery point code.
UPC – Universal Product Code	UPC-A with Supplemental 0 12345 67890 s	Supermarkets, convenience, and specialty stores used to identify manufacturers and products.
Web bar code		Magazines and books to display a Web page.

Figure 5-40 Some of the more widely used types of bar codes.

Some books and magazines have Web bar codes throughout their pages. When you scan a **Web bar code** with a handheld scanner, the Web page associated with the bar code displays on your computer screen.

Magnetic Ink Character Recognition Reader

A **magnetic-ink character recognition (MICR) reader** can read text printed with magnetized ink. The banking industry almost exclusively uses MICR for check processing. Each check in your checkbook has precoded MICR characters on the lower-left edge (Figure 5-41). These characters represent the bank number, your account number, and the check number.

When a bank receives a check for payment, it uses an MICR inscriber to print the amount of the check in MICR characters in the lower-right corner. The check then

is sorted or routed to the customer's bank, along with thousands of others. Each check is inserted into an MICR reader, which sends the check information — including the amount of the check — to a computer for processing. When you balance your checkbook, verify the amount printed in the lower-right corner is the same as the amount written on the check; otherwise, your statement will not balance.

The banking industry has established an international standard not only for bank numbers, but also for the font of the MICR characters. This standardization makes it possible for you to write checks in another country.

APPLY IT!

Web Bar Codes Can Save You Time

You are reading the daily news and run across a Web address that looks interesting. You write it down so you can type it later into your browser and review the site. But what if you did not have to type in the Web site address? If you live in Charleston, South Carolina and subscribe to one of the daily newspapers, you may have noticed bar codes displayed throughout the pages. Use a handheld scanner connected to your computer, run it across the bar code, and a related Web page pops up on the screen. This technology is not limited to newspapers. It has been extended to magazines, books, postcards, or any imaginable object where one might want to establish a direct connection between static objects and the Internet.

A related technology is the digital watermark. Consider the way a photograph is produced. Before the page is printed, the watermark is applied to the electronic version of the photograph. Run your scanner across the photograph or hold the photograph in front of a PC camera and up pops a related Web page. Look for this technology in magazines such as Wired and Popular Mechanics.

For more information on Web bar codes and digital watermarks, visit the Discovering Computers 2002 Apply It Web page (**scsite.com/dc2002/ apply.htm**) and click Chapter 5 Apply It #3.

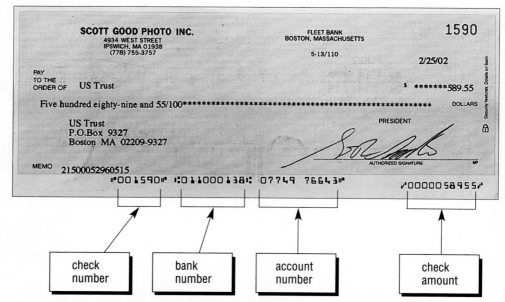

Figure 5-41 The MICR characters preprinted on the check represent the bank number, your account number, and the check number. The amount of the check in the lower-right corner is added after the check is cashed.

Wireless Input

Instead of reading or scanning data from a source document, you can use a wireless input technology to obtain data directly at the location where the transaction or event takes place. Factories, warehouses, the outdoors, or other locations where heat, humidity, and cleanliness are difficult to control use wireless input. The employee uses a handheld computer or device to collect data wirelessly.

As shown in Figure 5-42, an employee can enter product inventory data into a handheld device and then later transfer the data to a desktop computer through a docking station.

Many users have Web-enabled computers and devices such as cellular telephones and pagers, which allow wireless connections to the Web. More and more users today send data wirelessly to central office computers using these devices.

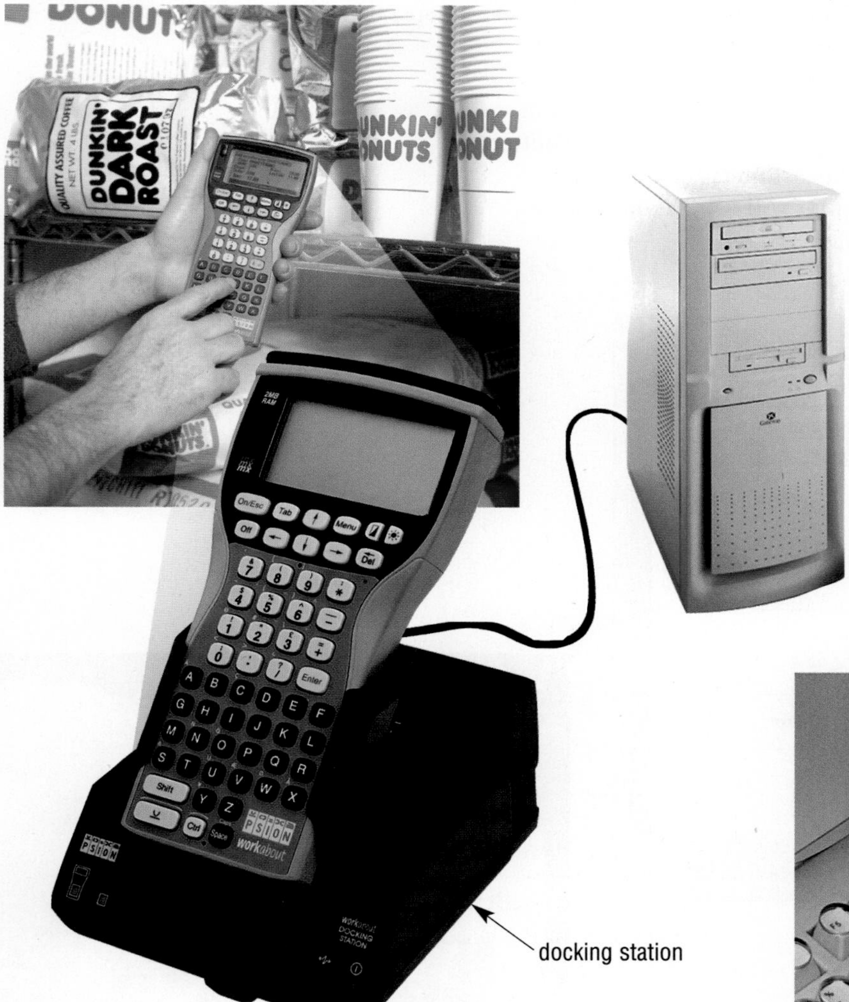

INPUT DEVICES FOR PHYSICALLY CHALLENGED USERS

The growing presence of computers in everyone's lives has generated an awareness of the need to address computing requirements for those with physical limitations. The **Americans with Disabilities Act (ADA)** requires any company with 15 or more employees make reasonable attempts to accommodate the needs of physically challenged workers. Whether at work or at home, you may find it necessary to obtain input devices that address physical limitations. Besides voice recognition, which is ideal for blind or visually impaired users, several other input devices are available.

Users with limited hand mobility that wish to use a keyboard have several options. A **keyguard** is a metal or plastic plate placed over the keyboard that allows users to rest their hands on the keyboard without accidentally pressing any keys. A keyguard also guides a finger or pointing device so a user presses only one key at a time (Figure 5-43).

docking station

Figure 5-42 This employee enters product data into a handheld device and then later transfers the data to a desktop computer through a docking station.

Figure 5-43 A keyguard allows users to rest their hands on the keyboard without accidentally pressing any keys. It also guides a finger or pointing device onto a key so a user presses only a single key at a time.

Keyboards with larger keys also are available. Still another option is the **on-screen keyboard**, in which a graphic of a standard keyboard displays on the user's screen. Figure 5-44 shows an on-screen keyboard in Microsoft Word. In Figure 5-45, a woman uses a pointing device in her lap to press the keys on the on-screen keyboard.

Various pointing devices are available for users with motor disabilities. Small trackballs that you control with a thumb or one finger can be attached to a table, mounted to a wheelchair, or held in a user's hand. People with limited hand movement can use a **head-mounted pointer** to control the pointer or insertion point. To simulate the functions of a mouse button, a user can work with switches that control the pointer. The switch

might be a pad you press with your hand, a foot pedal, a receptor that detects facial motions, or a pneumatic instrument controlled by puffs of air.

Two exciting developments in this area are gesture recognition and computerized implant devices. Both in the prototype stage, they attempt to provide users with a natural computer interface. With **gesture recognition**, the computer will be able to detect human motions. Computers with this capability have the potential to recognize sign language, read lips, track facial movements, or follow eye gazes. For paralyzed or speech impaired individuals, a doctor will implant a computerized device into the brain. This device will contain a transmitter. As the user thinks thoughts, the transmitter will send signals to the computer.

PUTTING IT ALL TOGETHER

When you purchase a computer, you should have an understanding of the input devices included with the computer, as well as those you may need that are not included. Many factors influence the type of input devices you may use: the type of input desired, the hardware and software in use, and the desired cost. The type of input devices you require depends on your intended use. Figure 5-46 outlines several suggested input devices for specific computer users.

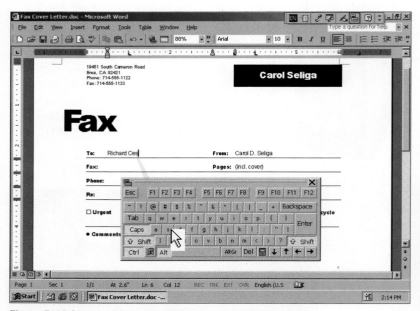

Figure 5-44 As you click letters on the on-screen keyboard, they display in the document at the location of the insertion point.

Figure 5-45 By operating a handheld switch, this user selects keyboard keys that display on the screen of this portable computer, which is mounted to her wheelchair.

SUGGESTED INPUT DEVICES BY USER

USER	INPUT DEVICE
Home	• Enhanced keyboard or ergonomic keyboard • Mouse • Joystick or wheel • 30-bit 600 x 1,200 dpi color scanner • 1- or 2-megapixel digital camera • Microphone • Voice recognition software • PC video camera
Small Office/Home Office	• Enhanced keyboard or ergonomic keyboard • Mouse • Stylus and portable keyboard for handheld computer • 36-bit 600 x 1,200 dpi color scanner • 1- or 2-megapixel digital camera • Microphone • Voice recognition software • PC video camera
Mobile	• Wireless mouse for notebook computer • Trackball, touchpad, or pointing stick on notebook computer • Stylus and portable keyboard for handheld computer • 2- or 3-megapixel digital camera • Voice recognition software
Large Business	• Enhanced keyboard or ergonomic keyboard • Mouse • Touch screen • Light pen for point-of-sale terminals • 42-bit 1,200 x 1,200 dpi color scanner • OCR or OMR or bar code reader or MICR reader • Microphone • Voice recognition software • Video camera for videoconferences
Power	• Enhanced keyboard or ergonomic keyboard • Mouse • Stylus and cursor for graphics tablet • 48-bit 1,200 x 1,200 dpi color scanner • 3-megapixel digital camera • Microphone • PC video camera

Figure 5-46 This table recommends suggested input devices.

Career Corner

Webcasting

Webcasting is a form of communications that features streaming rich media, including audio, video, and Web-based multimedia. It quickly is becoming a mainstream Internet application. Similar to a television broadcast, a Webcast airs exclusively on the Internet. The advantage is Webcasting can be done at anytime, anywhere in the world.

With broadband communications becoming more widely used, digital video and digital audio quickly are becoming in-demand technologies. As a result, Webcasting is a growing niche industry. Because creating and delivering a Webcast requires diverse skills, employment opportunities are available for people with knowledge in a range of fields, including production and camera use, content development and technical writing, audio/visual expertise, engineering, networking, or other technical areas. Dual skill sets are an asset. Salaries within this industry vary widely, anywhere from $25,000 to $100,000 or more, depending on the job and the skills.

Currently no certifications are available in this field, but you can look for these in the near future. The International Webmasters Association (IWA) will most likely sponsor the certifications (see URL below).

To learn more about Webcasting as a career and the Web site mentioned above, visit the Discovering Computers 2002 Careers Web page (**scsite.com/dc2002/ careers.htm**) and click Webcasting.

E-COMMUNITIES

PICTURE THIS!

Share Your Community Pride

The family welcomes a new baby, a cousin graduates from college, good friends tie the knot, and grandma and grandpa celebrate their 50th wedding anniversary. Share these kinds of announcements, memories, and activities, and photographs of each event, by joining a Web community or creating your own. Virtual communities allow family, friends, and others with similar interests to connect and disseminate information with the Internet world.

Web communities connect computer users around the globe and make exchanging ideas and viewpoints easy and convenient. Thousands of virtual communities permit groups to play games, offer support, entertain each other, and work on collective projects.

Several Web sites bridge the gap between conventional and digital photography. These photo-sharing services allow shutterbugs to create virtual photo albums and share these images online.

Most Web sites, such as Zing shown in Figure 5-47, provide free, unlimited storage space with the hope that users will view the advertisements and order paper reprints and personalized gifts. Other photo Web sites are listed in Figure 5-48.

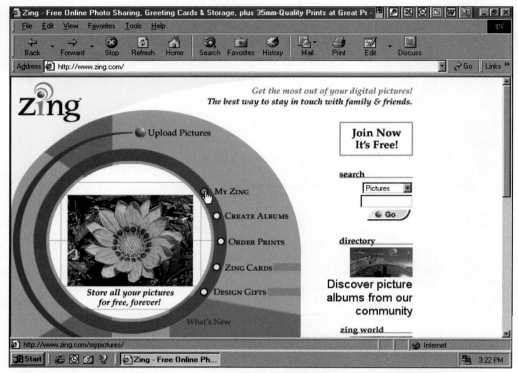

Figure 5-47 Zing and other photo Web sites provide a setting where family and friends can view digital pictures online.

PHOTO AND COMMUNITY WEB SITES	URL
Photos	
GatherRound.com℠	gatherround.com
Kodak PhotoNet Online	www.photonet.com
MSN PictureIt Photo Center	communities.msn.com/photoalbums
PhotoWorks	photoworks.com
Shutterfly	shutterfly.com
Zing	zing.com
Web Communities	
Canterbury Net	www.canterbury.net.nz
CyberErie	cybererie.com
MSN Web Communities	communities.msn.com/webcommunities
Redstone Colorado Online	redstonecolorado.com
Run the Planet	runtheplanet.com
Yahoo! GeoCities Neighborhoods	geocities.yahoo.com/cgi-bin/hood/geo

For an updated list of photo and community Web sites, visit scsite.com/dc2002/e-rev.htm.

Figure 5-48 These photo and community Web sites allow you to share your pictures and meet people with similar interests.

Another type of virtual community allows people with related interests to share information. The categories of these Web communities are wide-ranging and include health support groups and vintage Corvettes to cruise ships and the Chicago Cubs. The Yahoo! GeoCities CollegePark community displayed in Figure 5-49 allows users to converse on such topics as distance learning, sports, and music. Runners can jump to Run the Planet, billed as the largest world-wide running community on the Internet.

Residents in entire towns have developed Web communities that promote businesses, permit parents to communicate with teachers, and inform citizens about the town council's meetings. One of the first communities was developed in Montana in the late 1980s to connect teachers, many of whom taught in one-room schools. Today, residents throughout the world have virtual communities. Citizens in Canterbury, New Zealand, for example, share information on genealogy, psychology, and community activities on their Canterbury Net; Redstone, Colorado, residents share community news and activities by logging on to Redstone Colorado Online (Figure 5-50); and CyberErie citizens in Erie, Pennsylvania, take coffee breaks in their cyber café, share their pets in the virtual zoo, and relax in the CyberLibrary.

For more information on Web communities, visit the Discovering Computers 2002 E-Revolution Web page (scsite.com/dc2002/e-rev.htm) and click Communities.

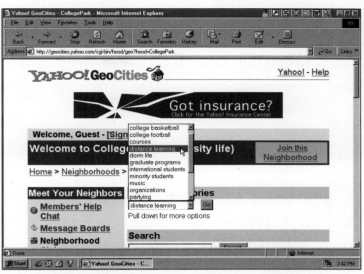

Figure 5-49 Cyber residents of Yahoo!'s GeoCities CollegePark discuss hundreds of collegiate topics, including distance learning, assignments, sports, and activities.

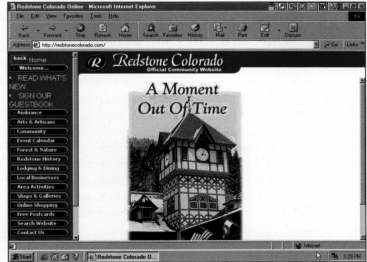

Figure 5-50 Redstone, Colorado, residents share information on local events, shopping, and the environment through their community Web site.

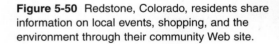

E-COMMUNITIES *applied:*

1. View three of the photos Web sites listed in Figure 5-48. Make a table that lists the Web site names, categories of photo albums, amount of storage space, cost, resolution constraints, and length of time photos are permitted to stay online. Explain why you would or would not like to view photos online.

2. Visit two of the community Web sites listed in Figure 5-48. Write a paragraph on each Web site describing its content, ease of use, and features. Then, describe what content you would include in a Web community of your hometown. Would you, for example, include a Web cam? A list of businesses and services? Hours when public offices are open? What advertisers, if any, would you contact to obtain revenue?

5.36

DISCOVERING
COMPUTERS 2002

Chapter 1 2 3 4 5 6 7 8 9 10 11 12 13 14 15 16 Index HOME

In Summary

SHELLY
CASHMAN
SERIES.

Student Exercises   Web Links   In Summary   Key Terms   Learn It Online   Checkpoint   In The Lab   Web Work

Special Features   ■ TIMELINE 2002   ■ WWW & E-SKILLS   ■ MULTIMEDIA   ■ BUYER'S GUIDE 2002   ■ WIRELESS TECHNOLOGY   ■ TRENDS 2002   ■ INTERACTIVE LABS   ■ TECH NEWS

Web Instructions: To display this page from the Web, start your browser and enter the URL scsite.com/dc2002/ch5/summary.htm. Click the links for current and additional information. To listen to an audio version of this In Summary, click the Audio button. To play the audio RealPlayer must be installed on your computer (download by clicking here).

1 What Are the Two Types of Input?

Input is any data or instructions entered into the memory of a computer. The two types of input are data and programs. **Data** is a collection of unorganized facts that can include words, numbers, pictures, sounds, and video. A computer processes data into information. A **program** is a series of instructions that tell a computer how to process data into information.

2 What Are the Characteristics of a Keyboard?

The **keyboard**, a primary input device on a computer, is an input device that contains keys you press to enter data into the computer. All keyboards have a typing area used to type letters of the alphabet, numbers, punctuation marks, and other basic characters. A keyboard also may include a **numeric keypad** designed to make it easier to enter numbers, **function keys** programmed to issue commands and accomplish certain tasks, **arrow keys** used to move the **insertion point**, and **toggle keys** that can be switched between two different states.

3 Describe the Various Types of Keyboards

A standard computer keyboard sometimes is called a **QWERTY keyboard** because of the layout of its typing area. An **enhanced keyboard** has function keys, CTRL keys, ALT keys, and a set of arrow and additional keys. A **cordless keyboard** transmits data using wireless technology such as infrared light or radio waves. A **portable keyboard** is a full-sized keyboard you can attach and remove from a handheld computer. An **ergonomic keyboard** is designed to reduce the risk of wrist injuries.

4 What Are the Various Types of Pointing Devices?

A pointing device controls the movement of a pointer on the screen. A **mouse** is a pointing device that is moved across a flat surface, controls the movement of the pointer on the screen, and is used to make selections from the screen. A **trackball** is a stationary pointing device with a ball mechanism on its top. A **touchpad** or **trackpad** is a flat, rectangular pointing device that is sensitive to pressure and motion. A **pointing stick** is a pressure-sensitive pointing device shaped like a pencil eraser. Other pointing devices include a **joystick** (a vertical lever mounted on a base), a **wheel** (a steering-wheel type of device), a **light pen** (a handheld device that contains a light source or can detect light), a **touch screen** (a monitor with a touch-sensitive panel on the screen), a **stylus** or **pen** (a pen to write text and draw lines), a **graphics tablet** or **digitizer** or **digitizing tablet** (an electronic plastic board used to input graphical data) and a **cursor** (a mouse-like device that has a window with cross hairs).

5 How Does a Mouse Work?

The bottom of a mouse is flat and contains a multidirectional mechanism, either a small ball or an optical sensor, which detects movement of the mouse. As the mouse is moved across a flat surface, electronic circuits in the mouse translate the movement into signals that are sent to the computer. You use the mouse to move the pointer on the screen. To operate the mouse, you point, click, right-click, double-click, drag, and right-drag.

6 What Are the Different Mouse Types?

A **mechanical mouse** has a rubber or metal ball on its underside. An optical mouse uses devices that emit light to detect the mouse's movement. A **cordless mouse**, or **wireless mouse**, relies on battery power and uses infrared light or radio waves to communicate with a receiver.

Chapter 1 2 3 4 **5** 6 7 8 9 10 11 12 13 14 15 16 Index HOME 5.37

DISCOVERING
COMPUTERS *2002*

In Summary

SHELLY
CASHMAN
SERIES.

Student Exercises | Web Links | In Summary | Key Terms | Learn It Online | Checkpoint | In The Lab | Web Work

Special Features ■ TIMELINE 2002 ■ WWW & E-SKILLS ■ MULTIMEDIA ■ BUYER'S GUIDE 2002 ■ WIRELESS TECHNOLOGY ■ TRENDS 2002 ■ INTERACTIVE LABS ■ TECH NEWS

 ## How Does Voice Recognition Work?

Voice input is the process of entering data by speaking into a computer-attached microphone and is part of a larger category of input called audio input. **Audio input** is the process of entering any sound into the computer such as speech, music, and sound effects. To input voice requires **voice recognition** or **speech recognition** software. The program may be **speaker-dependent** (the computer makes a profile of your voice) or **speaker-independent** (contains a built-in set of word patterns). Some programs require **discrete speech**, which means you have to speak slowly, whereas others support **continuous speech**, allowing you to talk in a normal conversational tone.

 ## How Is Data Input into a Handheld Computer?

Handheld computers are popular for both home and business users. Using the stylus, the primary input method, you can enter data through an onscreen keyboard or use handwriting recognition software. Other input methods include attaching a full-sized keyboard, using voice input, or attaching a digital camera to the handheld computer.

 ## What Are the Uses of a Digital Camera?

You use a digital camera to take pictures and digitally store the photographed images. The three basic types are **studio camera**, **field camera**, and **point-and-shoot camera**. You can **download**, or transfer, the photographed images to a computer by a connecting cable; or they can be stored and copied on a computer. Once on a computer, pictures can be edited with photo-editing software, printed, faxed, sent via electronic mail, included in another document, or posted on a Web site.

What Are Various Techniques Used for Video Input?

Video input or **video capture** is the process of entering a full-motion recording into a computer and storing the video on a hard disk or some other medium. To capture video, a video camera is plugged into a **video capture card**, which is an expansion card that converts the analog video signal into a digital signal. A **digital video (DV) camera** is a video camera that records video as digital signals, instead of analog signals. A **video digitizer** can be used to capture an individual frame from a video and save the still picture in a file.

 ## What Are Uses of PC Video Cameras and Web Cams?

A **PC video camera**, or **PC camera**, is a DV camera that allows the home user to record, edit, and capture video and still images and to make video telephone calls on the Internet. You can use the PC camera for security by setting it to take digital photographs at preset times. To attract visitors to your Web site, use your video camera to display a **Web cam** image on your Web page.

 ## How Do Scanners and Other Reading Devices Work?

A **scanner** is a light-sensing input device that reads printed text and graphics and then translates the results into a form the computer can use. An **optical reader** uses a light source to read characters, marks, and codes and converts them into digital data that can be processed by a computer. Three types of optical readers are **optical character recognition (OCR)**, **optical mark recognition (OMR)**, **bar code scanners**, and **magnetic-ink character recognition (MICR) reader**.

 ## What Are Some Alternative Input Devices for Physically Challenged Users?

Speech recognition, or the computer's capability of distinguishing spoken words, is ideal for blind or visually impaired computer users. A **keyguard**, which is placed over the keyboard, allows people with limited hand mobility to rest their hands on the keyboard and guides a finger or pointing device so a user presses only one key at a time. Keyboards with larger keys and screen-displayed keyboards on which keys are pressed using a pointing device also can help. Pointing devices such as small trackballs that can be controlled with a thumb or one finger and **head-mounted pointers** also are available for users with motor disabilities.

5.38

Chapter 1 2 3 4 5 6 7 8 9 10 11 12 13 14 15 16 Index HOME

DISCOVERING
COMPUTERS 2002

Key Terms

SHELLY
CASHMAN
SERIES.

Student Exercises   Web Links   In Summary   Key Terms   Learn It Online   Checkpoint   In The Lab   Web Work

Special Features ■ TIMELINE 2002 ■ WWW & E-SKILLS ■ MULTIMEDIA ■ BUYER'S GUIDE 2002 ■ WIRELESS TECHNOLOGY ■ TRENDS 2002 ■ INTERACTIVE LABS ■ TECH NEWS

Web Instructions: To display this page from the Web, start your browser and enter the URL scsite.com/dc2002/ch5/terms.htm. Scroll through the list of terms. Click a term to display its definition and a picture. Click the To WEB button for current and additional information about the term from the Web. To see animations, Shockwave and Flash Player must be installed on your computer (download by clicking here).

Americans with Disabilities Act
    (ADA) (5.31)
arrow keys (5.4)
audio input (5.16)
bar code (5.28)
bar code scanner (5.28)
cam (5.23)
command (5.3)
continuous speech (5.15)
cordless keyboard (5.5)
cordless mouse (5.8)
cursor (5.13)
data (5.3)
digital camera (5.18)
digital video (DV) camera (5.21)
digital watermark (5.22)
digitizer (5.13)
digitizing tablet (5.13)
discrete speech (5.15)
dots per inch (dpi) (5.20)
download (5.18)
electronic signatures (5.13)
enhanced keyboard (5.5)
enhanced resolution (5.20)
ergonomic keyboard (5.6)
ergonomics (5.6)
e-signatures (5.13)
field camera (5.19)
flatbed scanner (5.25)
function keys (5.4)
gesture recognition (5.32)
graphical user interface (GUI) (5.3)
graphics tablet (5.13)
handwriting recognition software
    (5.14)
head-mounted pointer (5.32)
image processing (5.26)
image processing system (5.26)
imaging (5.26)
information (5.3)
input (5.2)
input device (5.4)
insertion point (5.4)
instructions (5.3)

interpolated resolution (5.20)
joystick (5.11)
keyboard (5.4)
keyguard (5.31)
light pen (5.12)
magnetic-ink character recognition
    (MICR) reader (5.30)
mechanical mouse (5.7)
menu-driven (5.3)
mouse (5.7)
mouse pad (5.7)
mouse pointer (5.7)
numeric keypad (5.4)
OCR devices (5.27)
OCR software (5.26)
on-screen keyboard (5.32)
optical character recognition (OCR)
    (5.27)
optical mark recognition (OMR) (5.28)
optical mouse (5.7)

SCANNER
Light-sensing input device that reads printed text and graphics, then translates the results into a form the computer can use; similar to a copy machine except it creates a file of the document instead of a paper copy.
Also called an optical scanner. (5.25)

To WEB

optical reader (5.27)
optical resolution (5.20)
optical scanner (5.25)
PC camera (5.22)
PC video camera (5.22)

pen (5.13)
pixel (5.20)
point-and-shoot camera (5.19)
pointer (5.7)
pointing device (5.7)
pointing stick (5.11)
portable keyboard (5.6)
program (5.3)
QWERTY keyboard (5.5)
resolution (5.20)
scanner (5.25)
source document (5.24)
speaker-dependent software (5.15)
speaker-independent software (5.15)
speech recognition (5.14)
streaming cam (5.23)
studio camera (5.19)
stylus (5.13)
toggle key (5.4)
touch screen (5.12)
touchpad (5.10)
trackball (5.10)
trackpad (5.10)
turnaround document (5.27)
user response (5.3)
video capture (5.21)
video capture card (5.21)
video compression (5.21)
video decoder (5.21)
video digitizer (5.21)
video input (5.21)
video telephone call (5.22)
videoconference (5.24)
voice input (5.14)
voice recognition (5.14)
WAV (5.16)
waveforms (5.16)
Web bar code (5.30)
Web cam (5.23)
wheel (5.11)
whiteboard (5.24)
wireless mouse (5.8)

DISCOVERING
COMPUTERS *2002*

Learn It Online

SHELLY
CASHMAN
SERIES.

Student Exercises   Web Links   In Summary   Key Terms   Learn It Online   Checkpoint   In The Lab   Web Work

Special Features   ■ TIMELINE 2002 ■ WWW & E-SKILLS ■ MULTIMEDIA ■ BUYER'S GUIDE 2002 ■ WIRELESS TECHNOLOGY ■ TRENDS 2002 ■ INTERACTIVE LABS ■ TECH NEWS

Web Instructions: To display this page from the Web, start your browser and enter the URL scsite.com/dc2002/ch5/learn.htm.

1. Web Guide

Click Web Guide to display the Guide to World Wide Web Sites and Searching Techniques Web page. Click Reference and then click About.com. Search for data dictionary. In the Find It Now text box, type digital camera. Scroll through the results and then click a link of your choice. Use your word processing program to prepare a brief report on your findings and submit your assignment to your instructor.

2. Scavenger Hunt

Click Scavenger Hunt. Print a copy of the Scavenger Hunt page; use this page to write down your answers as you search the Web. Submit your completed page to your instructor.

3. Who Wants to Be a Computer Genius?

Click Computer Genius to find out if you are a computer genius. Directions on how to play the game will display. When you are ready to play, click the PLAY button. Submit your score to your instructor.

4. Wheel of Terms

Click Wheel of Terms to reinforce important terms you learned in this chapter by playing the Shelly Cashman Series version of this popular game. Directions on how to play the game will display. When you are ready to play, click the PLAY button. Submit your score to your instructor.

5. Career Corner

Click Career Corner to display the Career Magazine page. Review this page. Click the links that you find interesting. Write a brief report on the topics you found to be the most interesting. Submit the report to your instructor.

6. Search Sleuth

Click Search Sleuth to learn search techniques that will help make you a research expert. Submit the completed assignment to your instructor.

7. Crossword Puzzle Challenge

Click Crossword Puzzle Challenge. Complete the puzzle to reinforce skills you learned in this chapter. Directions on how to play the game will display. When you are ready to play, click the PLAY button. Submit the completed puzzle to your instructor.

8. Practice Test

Click Practice Test. Answer each question. When completed, click the Grade Test button to submit the quiz for grading. Make a note of any missed questions. If required, print a copy to submit to your instructor.

5.40

DISCOVERING
COMPUTERS 2002

Chapter 1 2 3 4 **5** 6 7 8 9 10 11 12 13 14 15 16 Index **HOME**

Checkpoint

SHELLY
CASHMAN
SERIES.

Student Exercises   Web Links   In Summary   Key Terms   Learn It Online   **Checkpoint**   In The Lab   Web Work

Special Features ■ TIMELINE 2002 ■ WWW & E-SKILLS ■ MULTIMEDIA ■ BUYER'S GUIDE 2002 ■ WIRELESS TECHNOLOGY ■ TRENDS 2002 ■ INTERACTIVE LABS ■ TECH NEWS

Web Instructions: To display this page from the Web, start your browser and enter the URL scsite.com/dc2002/ch5/check.htm. Click the links for current and additional information. To experience the animation and interactivity, Shockwave and Flash Player must be installed on your computer (download by clicking here.)

LABEL THE FIGURE | **Instructions:** Identify these areas and keys on a typical desktop computer keyboard.

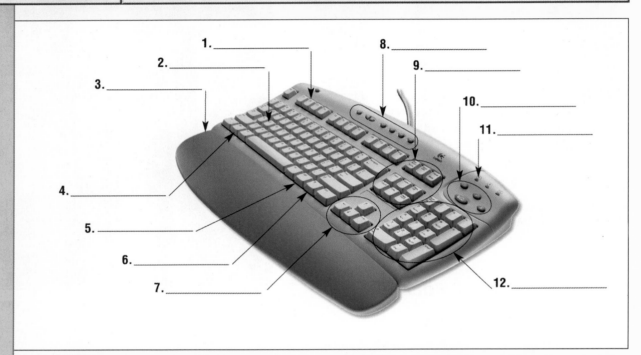

1. _____
2. _____
3. _____
4. _____
5. _____
6. _____
7. _____
8. _____
9. _____
10. _____
11. _____
12. _____

MATCHING | **Instructions:** Match each term from the column on the left with the best description from the column on the right.

_____1. Trackball
_____2. Pointing stick
_____3. Joystick
_____4. Mouse
_____5. Touchpad

a. The most widely used pointing device on desktop computers.
b. A stationary pointing device with a ball on its top.
c. A vertical lever mounted on a base.
d. A steering-wheel type input device.
e. A handheld input device that contains a light source.
f. A small, flat, rectangular pointing device that is sensitive to pressure and motion.
g. A pressure-sensitive pointing device shaped like a pencil eraser that is positioned between keys on the keyboard.

DISCOVERING
COMPUTERS 2002

Chapter 1 2 3 4 5 6 7 8 9 10 11 12 13 14 15 16 Index HOME 5.41

Checkpoint

SHELLY
CASHMAN
SERIES.

Student Exercises Web Links In Summary Key Terms Learn It Online Checkpoint In The Lab Web Work

Special Features ■ TIMELINE 2002 ■ WWW & E-SKILLS ■ MULTIMEDIA ■ BUYER'S GUIDE 2002 ■ WIRELESS TECHNOLOGY ■ TRENDS 2002 ■ INTERACTIVE LABS ■ TECH NEWS

MULTIPLE CHOICE | Instructions: Select the letter of the correct answer for each of the following questions.

1. A(n) _____ is a device that looks similar to a mouse, except it has a window with cross hairs, so the user can see through to the tablet.
   a. optical scanner
   b. cursor
   c. stylus
   d. trackball

2. _____ is speaking slowly and pausing between each word when using voice recognition software.
   a. Discrete speech
   b. Continuous speech
   c. Speaker-independent
   d. Speaker-dependent

3. An architect may use an electronic pen and a _____ to create drawings.
   a. graphics tablet
   c. touchpad
   b. touch screen
   d. trackball

4. The most expensive type of digital camera is a _____ .
   a. field
   b. point-and-shoot
   c. studio
   d. Web cam

5. A light-sensing input device that reads printed text and graphics and then translates the results into a form the computer can use is called a _____ .
   a. camera
   b. microphone
   c. PDA
   d. scanner

SHORT ANSWER | Instructions: Write a brief answer to each of the following questions.

1. Why is resolution important when using a scanner? _____ How is resolution typically measured and stated? _____

2. How is optical character recognition different from optical mark recognition? _____ What is MICR? _____

3. What is a bar code? _____ How are bar codes read? _____ On what products are they used? _____ What is the difference between a bar code and a Web bar code? _____

4. How is speaker-dependent software different from speaker-independent software? _____ How is discrete speech recognition different from continuous speech recognition? _____

5. What is videoconferencing? _____ How does a whiteboard enhance videoconferencing? _____ What hardware is required for a videoconference? _____

WORKING TOGETHER | Instructions: Working with a group of your classmates, complete the following team exercise.

The Occupational and Safety Health Association (OSHA) defines ergonomics as the science of fitting the job to the worker. Investigate the difference between carpal tunnel syndrome and repetitive strain injury. Prepare a report and a PowerPoint presentation to share with the class. Include suggestions on proper workstation ergonomics.

5.42

DISCOVERING
COMPUTERS 2002

Chapter 1 2 3 4 5 6 7 8 9 10 11 12 13 14 15 16 Index HOME

In The Lab

SHELLY
CASHMAN
SERIES.

Student Exercises Web Links In Summary Key Terms Learn It Online Checkpoint In The Lab Web Work

Special Features ■ TIMELINE 2002 ■ WWW & E-SKILLS ■ MULTIMEDIA ■ BUYER'S GUIDE 2002 ■ WIRELESS TECHNOLOGY ■ TRENDS 2002 ■ INTERACTIVE LABS ■ TECH NEWS

Web Instructions: To display this page from the Web, start your browser and enter the URL scsite.com/dc2002/ch5/lab.htm. Click the links or current and additional information.

About Your Computer

This exercise uses Window 95 or Windows 98 procedures. Your computer probably has more than one input device. To learn about the input devices on your computer, right-click the My Computer icon on the desktop. Click Properties on the shortcut menu. When the System Properties dialog box displays, click the Device Manager tab. Click View devices by type. Below Computer, a list of hardware device categories displays. What input devices appear in the list? Click the plus sign next to each category. What specific input devices in each category are connected to your computer? Click the Cancel button in the System Properties dialog box.

Customizing the Keyboard

The Windows operating system provides several ways to customize the keyboard for people with physical limitations. Some of these options are Sticky-Keys, FilterKeys, and ToggleKeys. To discover more about each option, click the Start button on the taskbar, point to Settings on the Start menu, and then click Control Panel on the Settings submenu. Double-click the Accessibility Options icon in the Control Panel window. Click the Keyboard tab in the Accessibility Properties dialog box. Click the Question Mark button in the title bar,

click StickyKeys, read the information on the pop-up window, and then click the pop-up window to close it. Repeat this process for FilterKeys and ToggleKeys. What is the purpose of each option? How might each option benefit someone with a physical disability? Click the Cancel button in the Accessibility Properties dialog box and then click the Close button in the Control Panel window.

Using the Mouse and Keyboard to Interact with an Online Program

See your instructor for the location of the Loan Payment Calculator program. Click the Start button on the taskbar, and then click Run on the Start menu to display the Run dialog box. In the Run text box, type the path and file name of the program. For example, type a:loancalc.exe and then press the ENTER key to display the Loan Payment Calculator window. Type 12500 in the LOAN AMOUNT text box. Click the YEARS right scroll arrow or drag the scroll box until YEARS equals 15. Click the APR right scroll arrow or drag the scroll box until APR equals 8.5. Click the Calculate button. Write down the monthly payment and sum of payments. Click the Clear button. What are the monthly payment and sum of payments for each of these loan amounts, years, and APRs: (1) 28000, 5, 7.25; (2) 98750, 30, 9; (3) 6000, 3,

8.75; (4) 62500, 15, 9.25. Close the Loan Payment Calculator.

MouseKeys

A graphical user interface allows you to perform many tasks with just the point and click of a mouse. Yet, what if you do not have, or cannot use, a mouse? The Windows operating system is prepared to accommodate this possibility with an option called MouseKeys. When the MouseKeys option is turned on, you can use numeric keypad keys to move the mouse pointer, click, right-click, double-click, and drag. To find out how, click the Start button on the taskbar and then click Help on the Start menu. Click the Index tab in the Help window. Type MouseKeys in the text box and then click the Display button. To answer each of the following questions, click an appropriate topic in the Topics Found dialog box, click the Display button, and read the Help information. To display a different topic, click the topic and then click the Display button.

- How do you turn on MouseKeys?
- How do you use MouseKeys to move the mouse pointer?
- How do you perform each of these operations using MouseKeys: click, right-click, double-click, drag?

Click the Close button to close the Help window.

Web Work

Student Exercises   Web Links   In Summary   Key Terms   Learn It Online   Checkpoint   In The Lab   **Web Work**

Special Features ■ TIMELINE 2002 ■ WWW & E-SKILLS ■ MULTIMEDIA ■ BUYER'S GUIDE 2002 ■ WIRELESS TECHNOLOGY ■ TRENDS 2002 ■ INTERACTIVE LABS ■ TECH NEWS

Web Instructions: To display this page from the Web, start your browser and enter the URL scsite.com/dc2002/ch5/web.htm. To view At The Movies in exercise 1, RealPlayer must be installed on your computer (download by clicking here). To use the Shelly Cashman Series Scanning Documents Lab from the Web, Shockwave and Flash Player must be installed on your computer (download by clicking here).

Web Cam Virtual World

To view the Web Cam Virtual World movie, click the button to the left or click the Play button to the right. Watch the movie, and then complete the exercise by answering the questions below. The Internet is where the curious meet the pretentious. With the availability of mobile cameras, Web cams, and PC video cameras, images reach millions of people. From around the globe, you can watch gorillas from Namibia, the miracle of birth at a hospital, or a toddler's birthday party next door. Some of this Web cam virtual world is informative, some serves a useful purpose, some of it is just entertainment, and some of it is intrusive. A more open society sounds like a good thing, but what about the privacy issues? Are there limits to what should be on the Web, or only limits to who should have access? Is access to this virtual world too easy or distracting? Will it help or hinder efforts to solve the problems of the real world?

Shelly Cashman Series Scanning Documents Lab

Follow the appropriate instructions in Web Work 2 on page 1.47 to start and use the Shelly Cashman Series Scanning Documents Lab. If you are running from the Web, enter the URL, www.scsite.com/sclabs/menu.htm; or display the Web Work page (see instructions at the top of this page) and then click the button to the left.

Sending E-Mail

E-mail allows you to send messages anywhere in the world. Use the e-mail account you set up in Web Work 4 in Chapter 3 to send a message. Click the button to the left to display your e-mail service. Log in to your e-mail service and then follow the instructions for composing a message. The subject of the message should be input devices. Type the e-mail address of one of your classmates. In the message itself, type something your classmate should know about input devices, and then send the message. Next, follow the instructions to read and reply to any messages you have received. When you are finished, quit your e-mail service.

In the News

Input devices can enhance user productivity and increase the number of potential users. The U.S. Army recently discovered this by replacing the many buttons used to operate a tank's onboard computer with a joystick and just three buttons. To the Army's delight, tank-driver performance has improved, and even individuals who scored poorly on Army intelligence tests handled the tanks effectively. Click the button to the left and read a news article about a new or improved input device, an input device being used in a new way, or an input device being made more available. What is the device? Who is promoting it? How will it be used? Will the input device change the number, or effectiveness, of potential users? If so, why?

CHAPTER 6

Output

One day a week during a break between classes, you go home to make a nutritious lunch. You enjoy preparing meals now because your refrigerator's screen displays a digital cookbook with recipes suitable for the food currently stored in it.

The telephone rings as you sit down to eat. After taking the call, you turn to the refrigerator's door and press a button on its screen to record a video message: "John, the dealership called. Your car is ready. The number is 555-1029." When John returns home, he will retrieve the message you recorded.

With a few minutes to relax, you press a button on the refrigerator's screen to view your own video messages. John's face appears on the screen. He says, "Samantha called. She needs help with algebra." When the message ends, you press another button to watch the daily news directly on the refrigerator's screen.

Before heading back, you check your e-mail messages with the touch of a button; compose a message to Samantha pressing on-screen keyboard keys; and then reach for a soda.

This not-so-ordinary refrigerator has become communications central at your house. Now, if only your car could drive itself to school, you could study on the way!

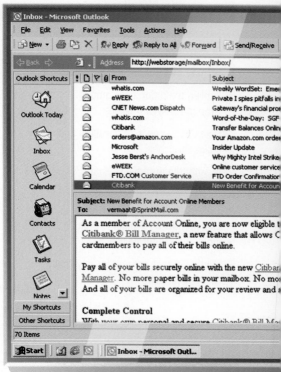

WHAT IS OUTPUT?

Output is data that has been processed into a useful form, called information. That is, computers process input into output. A computer generates several types of output, depending on the hardware and software being used and the requirements of the user.

You view, print, or hear output. Looking at a monitor on your desktop, you see information on the screen. Notebook computers, handheld computers, cellular telephones, and many other similar devices also have screens that allow mobile users to view information such as documents, Web sites, and e-mail messages while away from a desk. Some printers produce black-and-white documents. Others produce brilliant colors, so you can print color documents, photographs, and transparencies. Through the computer's speakers or a headset, you can hear sounds, music, and voice.

While using a computer, you will encounter four basic categories of output: text, graphics, audio, and video (Figure 6-1). Very often, documents and Web sites include more than one of these types of output.

- **Text** consists of characters that create words, sentences, and paragraphs. Examples of text-based documents are memorandums, letters, announcements, press releases, advertisements, newsletters, envelopes, and mailing labels.

  By accessing the Web, you can view and print many other types of text-based documents. These include newspapers, magazines, books, play or television show transcripts, stock quotes, famous speeches, and historical lectures.

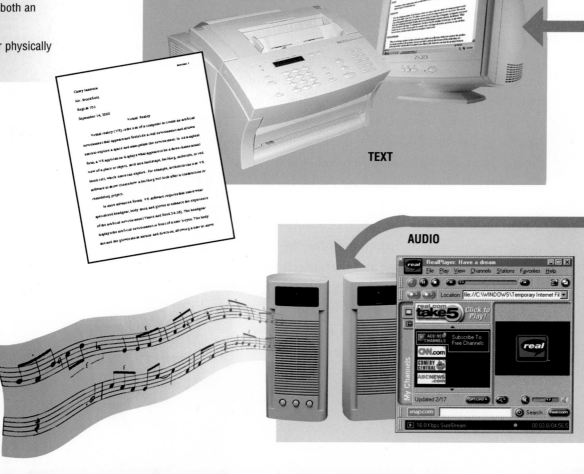

TEXT

AUDIO

- A **graphic**, or **graphical image**, is a digital representation of non-text information such as a drawing, chart, and photograph. Many text-based documents include graphical images to enhance their visual appeal and convey information. Business letters have logos. Reports include charts. Newsletters use drawings, clip art, and photographs. You even can print high-quality photographs right from your digital camera, eliminating the need for film or film developers.

  Many Web sites use animated graphics, giving images the appearance of motion. Some sites have simple animations such as blinking icons and scrolling messages. Others use sophisticated animations such as a simulation that shows how an avalanche starts.

- **Audio** is music, speech, or any other sound. You can put your favorite music CD in the CD-ROM or DVD-ROM drive and listen to the music while working on the computer. Many software programs such as games, encyclopedias, and simulations have musical accompaniments for entertainment and audio clips, such as narrations and speeches, to enhance understanding. For example, you can listen to Martin Luther King recite his "I Have a Dream" speech.

  On the Web, you can tune into radio and television stations and listen to audio clips or live broadcasts of interviews, talk shows, sporting events, news, music, and concerts. You also can have a conversation with a friend, co-worker, or family member over the Web, just as if you were on the telephone.

- **Video** consists of full-motion images that are played back at various speeds. Most video also has accompanying audio. By attaching your video camera to the computer, you can watch home movies on the computer. You also can attach your television's antenna or cable to your computer and watch your favorite television programs right on the computer.

  As with audio, many software programs and Web sites include video clips to enhance your understanding. See doctors perform a life-saving surgery, watch a pre-recorded news report, observe a hurricane in action, or enjoy a live performance of your favorite jazz band — right on your computer!

Figure 6-1 Four common types of output are text, graphics, audio, and video.

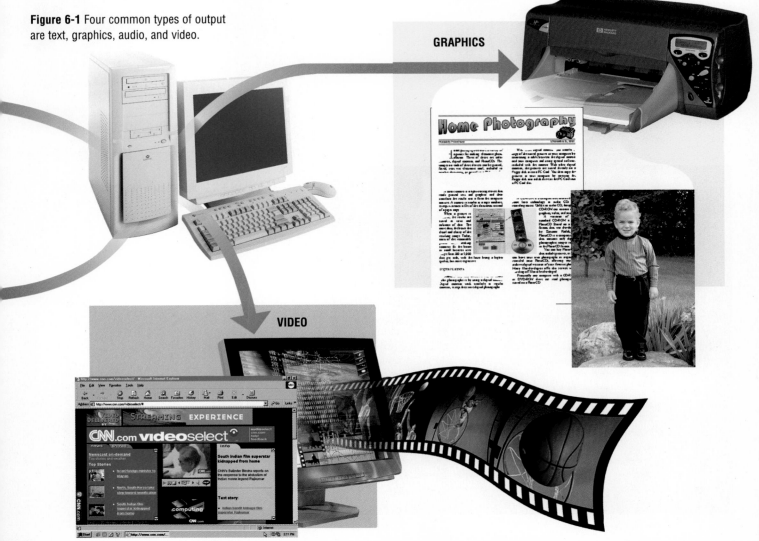

GRAPHICS

VIDEO

WHAT ARE OUTPUT DEVICES?

An **output device** is any hardware component that can convey information to a user. Commonly used output devices include display devices, printers, speakers, headsets, data projectors, facsimile machines, and multifunction devices. The following pages discuss each of these output devices.

DISPLAY DEVICES

A **display device**, or simply **display**, is an output device that visually conveys text, graphics, and video information. Information on a display device, sometimes called **soft copy**, exists electronically and displays for a temporary period of time.

The display device consists of the **screen**, or projection surface, and the components that produce the information on the screen. Many computers use a monitor as their display device. A **monitor** is a separate plastic or metal case that houses the screen. Most mobile computers, however, integrate the display and other components into the same physical case. For example, the display on a notebook computer attaches with a hinge, and the display on a handheld computer is part of the computer case.

Most display devices project text, graphics, and video information in color (Figure 6-2). Some, however, are monochrome. **Monochrome** means the information displays in one color (such as white, amber, green, black, blue, or gray) on a different color background, possibly black or grayish-white. Some handheld computers and devices use monochrome displays to save on battery power. To enhance the quality of their graphics, monochrome displays often use gray scaling. **Gray scaling** involves using many shades of gray from white to black, which provides better contrast on the images.

Figure 6-2 Most desktop monitors display information in color.

Web Link

For more information on monitors, visit the Discovering Computers 2002 Chapter 6 WEB LINK page (**scsite.com/dc2002/ch6/weblink.htm**) and click Monitors.

ISSUE

The Paper Chase

Use a Display Device instead of a Printer

In 1975, George Pake, the head of Xerox Corporation's Research Center in Palo Alto, California, predicted the use of printed paper would decline dramatically as offices turned to electronic files accessed at the touch of a button. Futurist Alvin Toffler wrote in 1970 that making paper copies of anything is a primitive use of machines and violates their very spirit. Instead of these predictions coming true, the opposite happened. Paper use has risen more than 40 percent during the past 30 years. Statistics indicate a major portion of this increase is tied directly to e-mail. Additionally, every office has computer printers, copy machines, and facsimile machines that reproduce documents at an ever-increasing rate. Can and should people and organizations try to reduce paper use? Why or why not? If society cannot create a paperless office, what can be done to promote a less-paper office?

For more information on the paperless office, visit the Discovering Computers 2002 Issues Web page (**scsite.com/dc2002/issues.htm**) and click Chapter 6 Issue #1.

Display devices include CRT monitors, LCD monitors and displays, gas plasma monitors, and televisions. The following sections describe each of these display devices.

CRT Monitors

A **CRT monitor** is a monitor that is similar to a standard television set because it contains a cathode ray tube (Figure 6-3). A **cathode ray tube (CRT)** is a large, sealed, glass tube. The front of the tube is the screen. Tiny dots of phosphor material coat the screen on a CRT. Each dot consists of a red, a green, and a blue phosphor. The three dots combine to make up each pixel. Recall from Chapter 5 that a **pixel** (short for *pic*ture *el*ement) is a single point in an electronic image. Inside the CRT, an electron beam moves back and forth across the back of the screen. This causes the dots on the front of the screen to glow, which produces an image on the screen.

CRT monitors for desktop computers are available in various sizes, with the more common being 15, 17, 19, 21, and 22 inches. You measure a monitor diagonally, from one corner of

the casing to the other. In addition to monitor size, advertisements also list a monitor's viewable size. The **viewable size** is the diagonal measurement of the actual viewing area provided by the monitor. A 21-inch monitor, for example, may have a viewable size of only 19.8 inches.

Determining what size monitor to use depends on your intended use. A large monitor allows you to view more information on the screen at once, but usually is more expensive. If you work on the Web or use multiple applications at one time, you may want to invest in a 19-inch monitor. If you use your computer for intense graphing applications, such as desktop publishing and engineering, you may want an even larger monitor.

In the past, CRT monitor screens were curved slightly. Current models have flat screens. A flat screen reduces glare, reflection, and distortion of images. With a flat screen, you will not have as much eyestrain and fatigue. Thus, a flat screen is an ergonomic screen. Recall from Chapter 5 that the goal of ergonomics is to incorporate comfort, efficiency, and safety into the design of items in the workplace.

LCD Monitors and Displays

LCD monitors and **LCD displays** use liquid crystal, instead of a cathode ray tube, to present information on the screen. A **liquid crystal display (LCD)** has liquid crystals between two sheets of material. When an electric current passes through the crystals, they twist. This causes some light waves to be blocked and allows others to pass through, which creates the images on the screen.

LCD monitors and LCD displays are a type of flat-panel display. A **flat-panel display** has a lightweight, compact screen that consumes less than one-third of the power than does a CRT monitor. This feature makes the LCD monitors and displays ideal for mobile users or users with space limitations.

Like CRT monitors, LCD monitors are available in a variety of sizes, with the more common being 15, 17, 18, and 20 inches. LCD monitors have a much smaller footprint than do traditional CRT monitors; that is, they take up much less desk space (Figure 6-4). You even can mount some LCD monitors on the wall for increased space savings. LCD monitors typically are more expensive than CRT monitors.

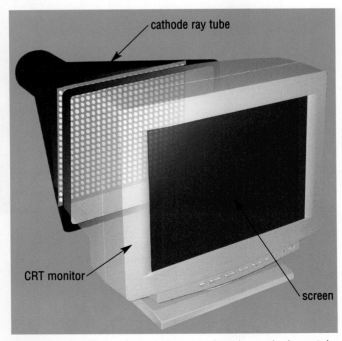

Figure 6-3 The core of many desktop monitors is a cathode ray tube.

Figure 6-4 An LCD monitor is much thinner and lighter than a CRT monitor.

Many current LCD monitors have built-in television tuners. These monitors allow you to watch television programs without having to install a TV tuner card in the system unit. Simply plug your television antenna or cable into the port on the monitor.

Notebook and handheld computers often use LCD displays. The display device is built into these mobile computers (Figure 6-5). The LCD displays for notebook computers are available in a variety of sizes, with the more common being 14.1, 15.0, and 15.4 inches.

Many Web-enabled devices such as cellular telephones and pagers also use LCD displays (Figure 6-6).

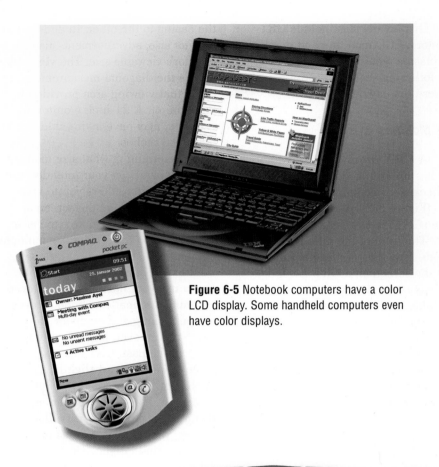

Figure 6-5 Notebook computers have a color LCD display. Some handheld computers even have color displays.

Web Link

For more information on Web-enabled devices, visit the Discovering Computers 2002 Chapter 6 WEB LINK page (**scsite.com/dc2002/ch6/ weblink.htm**) and click Web-enabled Devices.

COMPANY ON THE CUTTING EDGE

 MOTOROLA

Wireless Products for Web Access

The next time you listen to your favorite radio station in your car, give thanks to Paul and Joseph Galvin for making it possible. These two brothers developed the first practical and affordable car radio and created the Galvin Manufacturing Corporation in Chicago in 1928.

Paul Galvin named the company's products Motorola, combining the ideas of motion and radio. This trademark became so familiar that the company officially changed its name in 1947. Although the corporation branched out into other products, such as two-way radios for the military and for police departments, televisions, and microprocessor chips, its development of early communications devices made them the formidable leader they are today in wireless communications.

Today, Motorola's wireless telephones and word pagers allow you to receive Internet content, send e-mail, and connect to personal and company databases. Mya, the cyber-generated personal assistant, even will read you your e-mail, appointments, and weather and traffic reports.

For more information on Motorola, visit the Discovering Computers 2002 Companies Web page (**scsite.com/dc2002/companies.htm**) and click Motorola.

Figure 6-6 Most handheld Web-enabled devices such as cellular telephones and pagers use LCD displays. These devices provide access to the Internet and/or e-mail.

A Web-enabled device is a device that provides access to the Web and/or e-mail. Many Web-enabled handheld computers and devices use monochrome displays to save battery power. Some handheld computers, however, do have a color display.

Another popular handheld Web-enabled device that uses an LCD screen is an electronic book. An **electronic book (e-book)** is a small, book-sized computer that allows users to read, save, highlight, bookmark, and add notes to online text (Figure 6-7). You download new book content to your e-book from the Web.

To improve the quality of reading material on LCD screens, such as an e-book, Microsoft has developed a new technology called ClearType. The goal of **ClearType** is to make onscreen reading as natural as reading from printed material.

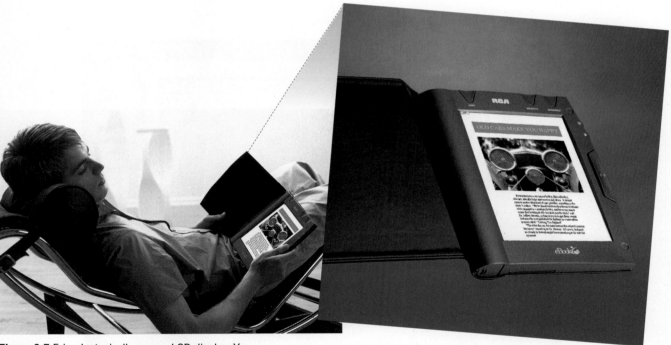

Figure 6-7 E-books typically use an LCD display. You can read books, magazines, newspapers, Web pages, or any other printed material on an e-book, which is about the size of a paperback book.

LCD monitors and displays produce color using either passive matrix or active matrix technology. An **active-matrix display**, also known as a **thin-film transistor (TFT) display**, uses a separate transistor for each color pixel and thus can display high-quality color that is viewable from all angles. Active-matrix displays require more power than passive-matrix displays because they use many transistors.

A **passive-matrix display**, now often called a **dual-scan display**, uses fewer transistors and requires less power than an active-matrix display. The color on a passive-matrix display often is not as bright as an active-matrix display. You can view images on a passive-matrix display best when working directly in front of the display. The latest passive-matrix displays use **high-performance addressing (HPA)**, which provide image quality near that of TFT displays. Passive-matrix displays are less expensive than active-matrix displays.

Gas Plasma Monitors

For even larger displays, some large business or power users prefer gas plasma monitors, which can measure more than 42 inches wide (Figure 6-8). Many of these monitors also can hang directly on a wall.

A **gas plasma monitor** is a flat-panel display that uses gas plasma technology, which substitutes a layer of gas for the liquid crystal material in an LCD monitor. When voltage is applied, the gas releases ultraviolet (UV) light. This UV light causes the pixels on the screen to glow and form an image. Gas plasma monitors offer larger screen sizes and higher display quality than LCD monitors but are much more expensive.

Quality of Display Devices

The quality of a monitor or display depends largely on its resolution, dot pitch, and refresh rate. As described in Chapter 5, **resolution** describes the sharpness and clearness of an image. Manufacturers state the resolution of a display device as dots, or pixels. The greater the number of pixels the display uses, the better the quality of the image. For example, an 800 x 600 monitor can display up to 800 horizontal pixels and 600 vertical pixels, for a total of 480,000 pixels to create a screen image. Most monitors today can display up to 1280 x 1024 pixels, with 800 x 600 typically the standard. High-end monitors can display up to 2048 x 1536 pixels.

Figure 6-8 Large gas plasma monitors can measure more than 42 inches wide.

Displays with higher resolutions use a greater number of pixels, providing a smoother image. As the resolution increases, however, the images on the screen appear smaller (Figure 6-9). For this reason, you would not use a high resolution on a small display, such as a 15-inch monitor, because the small characters would be difficult to read. The display resolution you choose is a matter of preference. Larger monitors typically use a higher resolution, and smaller monitors use a lower resolution. For example, a 21-inch monitor may use a 1600 x 1200 resolution, and a 17-inch monitor may use a resolution of 800 x 600. A higher resolution also is desirable for graphics applications. A lower resolution usually is satisfactory for business applications such as word processing.

Dot pitch is another factor which you can use to measure image clarity. **Dot pitch**, sometimes called **pixel pitch**, is the distance between each pixel on a display. The smaller the distance between the pixels, the sharper the image. Text created with a smaller dot pitch is easier to read. To minimize eye fatigue, you should use a monitor with a dot pitch of .29 millimeters or lower.

Refresh rate is yet another factor in a monitor's quality. **Refresh rate**, also called **vertical frequency** or **vertical scan rate**, is the speed that a monitor redraws images on the screen. Ideally, a monitor's refresh rate should be fast enough to maintain a constant, flicker-free image. A slower refresh rate causes the image to fade and then flicker as it is redrawn. This flicker can lead to eye fatigue and cause headaches for users. Refresh rate is measured according to **hertz**, which is the number of times per second the screen is redrawn. Although most people can tolerate a refresh rate of 60 hertz, a high-quality monitor will provide a refresh rate of at least 75 hertz. This means the image on the screen redraws itself 75 times in a second.

Figure 6-9a (screen resolution at 800 x 600)

Figure 6-9b (screen resolution at 1024 x 768)

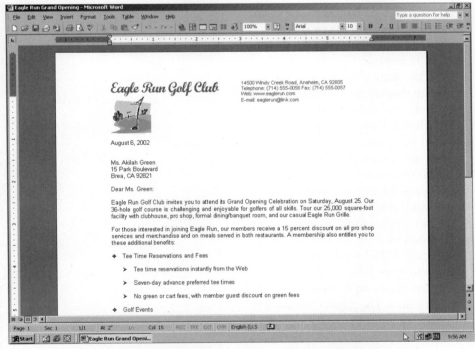

Figure 6-9 The higher a screen's resolution, the smaller the images display on the screen. This figure illustrates that all elements on the screen become smaller when the resolution is increased from 800 x 600 to 1024 x 768. Notice also that more text displays on the screen with the higher resolution.

Video Cards and Monitors

To display color on a monitor, the computer sends a signal through the video card in the system unit. A **video card**, also called a **graphics card** or **video adapter**, converts digital output from the computer into an analog video signal and sends the signal through a cable to the monitor. How the display device produces the picture varies depending on the type of display.

CRT monitors use the analog signal to produce a picture (Figure 6-10). LCD monitors use a digital signal to produce a picture. The LCD monitor contains circuitry that converts the analog signal from the video card back to a digital signal. This is one reason why LCD monitors are more expensive than CRT monitors. Ideally, an LCD monitor should plug into a digital interface on the computer. The **Digital Display Working Group (DDWG)**, which is led by several industry companies, is developing a standard interface for all displays. This new digital interface, called the **Digital Video Interface (DVI)**, provides connections for both CRT and LCD monitors.

The number of colors a video card can display is determined by its bit depth. The video card's **bit depth**, also called the **color depth**, is the number of bits it uses to store information about each pixel. For example, an 8-bit video card (also called 8-bit color) uses 8 bits to store information about each pixel. Thus, this video card can display 256 different colors (computed as 2^8 or $2 \times 2 \times 2 \times 2 \times 2 \times 2 \times 2 \times 2$). A 24-bit video card uses 24 bits to store information about each pixel and can display 2^{24} or 16.7 million colors. The greater the number of bits, the better the resulting image.

Over the years, several video standards have been developed to define the resolution, number of colors, and other display properties. Today, the **Video Electronics Standards Association (VESA)**, which consists of video card and monitor manufacturers, develops video standards. Most current video cards support the **super video graphics array (SVGA)** standard, which also supports resolutions and colors in the VGA standard. The table in Figure 6-11 outlines the suggested resolution and number of displayed colors in the MDA, VGA, XGA, SVGA, and beyond SVGA standards.

For a monitor to display images using the resolution and number of colors defined by a video standard, the monitor must support the same video standard *and* the video card must be capable of communicating appropriate signals to the monitor.

Both the video card and the monitor must support the video standard to generate the desired resolution and number of colors.

Your video card also must have enough memory to generate the resolution and number of colors you want to display. The memory in video cards stores information about each pixel. Video cards use a variety of video memory: VRAM, WRAM, SGRAM, or SDRAM. Manufacturers state video memory in megabytes. The table in Figure 6-12 outlines the amount of video memory required for various screen resolutions and color depth configurations. For example, if you

Figure 6-10 HOW VIDEO TRAVELS FROM THE PROCESSOR TO A CRT MONITOR

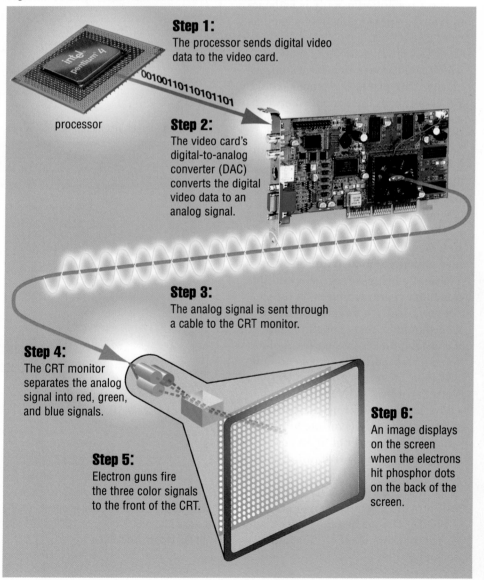

processor

Step 1:
The processor sends digital video data to the video card.

Step 2:
The video card's digital-to-analog converter (DAC) converts the digital video data to an analog signal.

Step 3:
The analog signal is sent through a cable to the CRT monitor.

Step 4:
The CRT monitor separates the analog signal into red, green, and blue signals.

Step 5:
Electron guns fire the three color signals to the front of the CRT.

Step 6:
An image displays on the screen when the electrons hit phosphor dots on the back of the screen.

wanted an 800 x 600 resolution with 24-bit color (16.7 million colors), then your video card should have at least 2 MB of video memory.

Monitor Ergonomics

The goal of ergonomics is to incorporate comfort, efficiency, and safety into the design of items in the workplace. Many monitors have features that help address ergonomic issues. Most monitors have a tilt-and-swivel base, so you can adjust the angle of the screen to minimize neck strain and reduce glare from overhead lighting.

Monitors also have controls that allow you to adjust the brightness, contrast, positioning, height, and width of images. These controls usually are on the front of the monitor for easy access. Newer monitors have digital controls that allow you to fine-tune the display in small increments. An advantage of digital controls is you quickly can return to the default settings by pressing the reset button.

CRT monitors produce a small amount of electromagnetic radiation. **Electromagnetic radiation (EMR)** is a magnetic field that travels at the speed of light. No solid evidence exists to prove that EMR poses a health risk. To be safe, however, all high-quality CRT monitors comply

with MPR II standards. **MPR II** is a set of standards that defines acceptable levels of EMR for a monitor. To protect yourself even further, sit at arm's length from the CRT monitor because EMR only travels a short distance. In addition, EMR is greatest on the sides and back of the CRT monitor. LCD monitors do not pose this risk.

VIDEO STANDARDS

Standard	Suggested Resolution	Possible Simultaneous Colors
Monochrome Display Adapter (MDA)	720 x 350	1 for text
Video Graphics Array (VGA)	640 x 480	16
	320 x 200	256
Extended Graphics Array (XGA)	1024 x 768	256
	640 x 480	65,536
Super Video Graphics Array (SVGA)	800 x 600	16.7 million
	1024 x 768	16.7 million
	1280 x 1024	16.7 million
	1600 x 1200	16.7 million
Beyond SVGA	1920 x 1440	16.7 million
	2048 x 1536	16.7 million

Figure 6-11 The various video standards.

VARIOUS VIDEO CARD CONFIGURATIONS

Video Memory	Color Depth	Number of Colors	Resolution
1 MB	8-bit	256	1024 x 768
	16-bit	65,536	800 x 600
2 MB	8-bit	256	1024 x 768
	16-bit	65,536	1280 x 1024
	24-bit	16.7 million	800 x 600
4 MB	24-bit	16.7 million	1024 x 768
6 MB	24-bit	16.7 million	1280 x 1024
8 MB	32-bit	16.7 million	1600 x 1200
16 MB	32-bit	16.7 million	1920 x 1440
32 MB	32-bit	16.7 million	2048 x 1536

Figure 6-12 The amount of video memory required for various screen resolutions.

APPLY IT!
Monitor Ergonomics – All Strain, No Gain

Your desktop computer can cause you more problems than you know. Many computer users are unaware of computer vision syndrome (CVS). The Mayo Clinic (see URL below) advises that if you have some or all of these symptoms, you may have CVS: sore, tired, burning, itching or dry eyes; blurred or double vision; distance vision blurred after prolonged staring at monitor; headache or sore neck; difficulty shifting focus between monitor and source documents; difficulty focusing on the screen image; color fringes or afterimages when you look away from the monitor; and increased sensitivity to light. Although eyestrain associated with CVS is not thought to have serious or long-term consequences, it is disruptive and unpleasant.

Following are some hints that may help ease the strain:
- Take an eye break – every 10 minutes or so, look away from the monitor
- Close your eyes and rest them for at least a minute
- Blink your eyes – the Mayo Clinic suggests blinking every five seconds
- Place your monitor about an arm's length away from your eyes with the top of the screen at eye level or below
- Use a glare screen
- Use large fonts
- If you wear glasses, ask your doctor for computer glasses
- Adjust the lighting

For links to computer health issues and the Web site mentioned above, visit the Discovering Computers 2002 Apply It Web page (scsite.com/dc2002/apply.htm) and click Chapter 6 Apply It #1.

To help reduce the amount of electricity used by monitors and other computer components, the United States Department of Energy (DOE) and the United States Environmental Protection Agency (EPA) developed the **ENERGY STAR program**. This program encourages manufacturers to create energy-efficient devices that require little power when they are not in use. Monitors and devices that meet ENERGY STAR guidelines display an ENERGY STAR® label (Figure 6-13).

Televisions

Many home and business users have a television set as a monitor for their computer. Connecting a computer to a standard television set requires an **NTSC converter**, which converts the digital signal from the computer into an analog signal that the television set can display. NTSC stands for **National Television Standards Committee** and consists of industry members that have technical expertise about television-related issues.

High-definition television (**HDTV**) is a type of television set that works with digital broadcasting signals and supports a wider screen and higher resolution display than a standard television set. With HDTV, the broadcast signals are digitized when they are sent. Digital television signals provide two major advantages over analog signals. First, digital signals produce a higher-quality picture. Second, many programs

can be broadcast on a single digital channel, whereas only one program can be broadcast on an analog channel. Currently, only a few U.S. television stations broadcast digital signals. By 2006, all stations must be broadcasting digital signals, as mandated by the FCC.

As the cost of HDTV becomes more reasonable, home users will begin to use it as their computer's display device. HDTV also is ideal for presenting material to a large group.

HDTV technology also makes interactive TV more feasible. **Interactive TV** is a two-way communications technology in which users interact with television programming. Instead of adding special equipment to your standard television, HDTV works directly with interactive TV. Uses of interactive TV include selecting a movie from a central library of movies, voting or responding to network questionnaires, banking and shopping, and playing games.

PRINTERS

A **printer** is an output device that produces text and graphics on a physical medium such as paper or transparency film. Printed information, called **hard copy**, exists physically and is a more permanent form of output than that presented on a display device (soft copy).

A hard copy, also called a **printout**, can be portrait or landscape orientation (Figure 6-14). A page in **portrait orientation** is taller than it is wide, with information printed across the shorter width of the paper. A page in **landscape orientation** is wider than it is tall, with information printed across the widest part of the paper. Letters, reports, and books typically use portrait orientation. Spreadsheets, slide shows, and graphics often use landscape orientation.

Figure 6-13 Products with an Energy Star label are energy efficient as defined by the Environmental Protection Agency (EPA).

Figure 6-14a (portrait orientation)

Play Auditions...
... for Grease!

HARBOR THEATRE COMPANY

The Harbor Theat
singing, and dan
for roles in *Greas*
Alumni Hall.

Only Harbor Coll
role in the play. B

To s

Figure 6-14 Portrait orientation is taller than it is wide. Landscape orientation is wider than it is tall.

Figure 6-14b (landscape orientation)

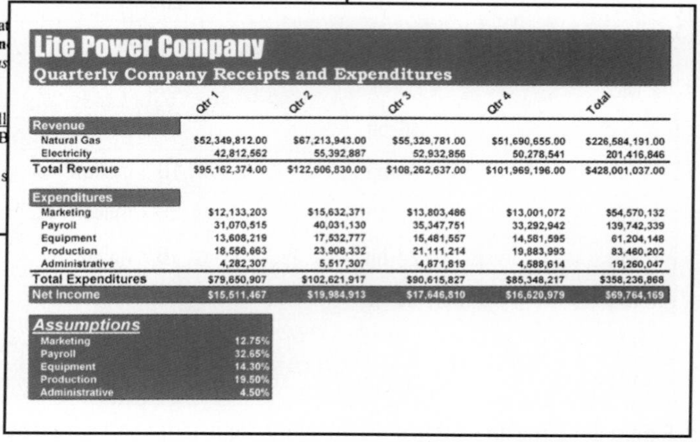

Lite Power Company
Quarterly Company Receipts and Expenditures

	Qtr 1	Qtr 2	Qtr 3	Qtr 4	Total
Revenue					
Natural Gas	$52,349,812.00	$67,213,943.00	$55,329,781.00	$51,690,655.00	$226,584,191.00
Electricity	42,812,562	55,392,887	52,932,856	50,278,541	201,416,846
Total Revenue	$95,162,374.00	$122,606,830.00	$108,262,637.00	$101,969,196.00	$428,001,037.00
Expenditures					
Marketing	$12,133,203	$15,632,371	$13,803,486	$13,001,072	$54,570,132
Payroll	31,070,515	40,031,130	35,347,751	33,292,942	139,742,339
Equipment	13,608,219	17,532,777	15,481,557	14,581,595	61,204,148
Production	18,556,663	23,908,332	21,111,214	19,883,993	83,460,202
Administrative	4,282,307	5,517,307	4,871,819	4,588,614	19,260,047
Total Expenditures	$79,650,907	$102,621,917	$90,615,827	$85,348,217	$358,236,868
Net Income	$15,511,467	$19,984,913	$17,646,810	$16,620,979	$69,764,169

Assumptions	
Marketing	12.75%
Payroll	32.65%
Equipment	14.30%
Production	19.50%
Administrative	4.50%

Home computer users might print a hundred pages or fewer a week. Small business computer users might print several hundred pages a day. Users of mainframe computers, such as large utility companies that send printed statements to hundreds of thousands of customers each month, require printers that are capable of printing thousands of pages per hour.

To meet this range of printing needs, many different printers exist with varying speeds, capabilities, and printing methods. Figure 6-15 presents a list of questions to help you decide on the printer best suited to your needs.

Many printers today handle Internet printing. With **Internet printing**, an Internet service on the Web sends a print instruction to your printer, which may be at a location different from your computer or device that accessed the Web site (Figure 6-16). A printer with Internet printing capability can receive print instructions from an Internet printing service so it can print documents from desktop and wireless computers and devices, such as cellular telephones. For example, you can print items such as postage, package shipping labels, newspaper articles, and event tickets from a Web-enabled cellular telephone. The goal of Internet printing is to make every computer and Web-enabled device capable of printing.

Generally, printers are either impact or nonimpact. The following pages discuss printers in both of these categories.

1. How fast must my printer print?
2. Do I need a color printer?
3. What is the cost per page for printing?
4. Do I need multiple copies of documents?
5. Will I print graphics?
6. Do I want to print photographs?
7. What types of paper does the printer use?
8. What sizes of paper does the printer accept?
9. How much paper can the printer tray hold?
10. Will the printer work with my computer and software?
11. How much do supplies such as ink and paper cost?
12. Can the printer print on envelopes and transparencies?
13. What is my budget?
14. How much do I print now, and what will I be printing in a year or two?

Figure 6-15 Questions to ask when purchasing a printer.

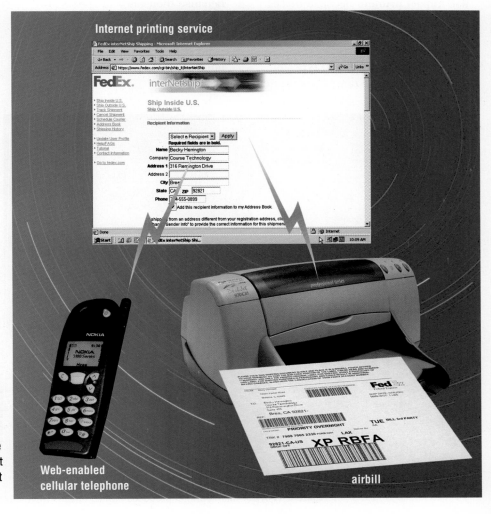

Figure 6-16 Internet printing allows printers to print documents from desktop and wireless computers and devices. The device sends the print instruction to an Internet service, which sends the print instruction to the printer.

Impact Printers

An **impact printer** forms characters and graphics on a piece of paper by striking a mechanism against an ink ribbon that physically contacts the paper. Impact printers generally are noisy because of this striking activity.

Impact printers typically do not provide letter quality print. **Letter quality (LQ)** output is a quality of print acceptable for business letters. Many impact printers produce **near letter quality (NLQ)** print, which is slightly less clear than letter quality. Some companies use NLQ impact printers for routine jobs such as printing mailing labels, envelopes, and invoices.

Impact printers are ideal for printing multipart forms because they easily can print through many layers of paper. Factories and retail counters use impact printers because these printers can withstand dusty environments, vibrations, and extreme temperatures.

Two commonly used types of impact printers are dot-matrix printers and line printers. The following paragraphs discuss each of these printers.

DOT-MATRIX PRINTERS A **dot-matrix printer** is an impact printer that produces printed images when tiny wire pins on a print head mechanism strike an inked ribbon (Figure 6-17). When the ribbon presses against the paper, it creates dots that form characters and graphics.

Most dot-matrix printers use **continuous-form paper**, in which each sheet of paper is connected together. The pages have holes along the sides to help feed the paper through the printer. Perforations along the inside of the holes and at each fold allow you to separate the sheets into standard-sized sheets of paper, such as 8½-by-11-inches. With continuous-form paper, you do not have to change the paper often because thousands of sheets are connected together. You also can adjust many dot-matrix printers to print pages in either portrait or landscape orientation.

The print head mechanism on a dot-matrix printer can contain 9 to 24 pins, depending on the manufacturer and the printer model. A higher number of pins means the printer prints more dots per character, which results in higher print quality.

The speed of a dot-matrix printer is measured by the number of characters per second (cps) it can print. The speed of dot-matrix printers ranges from 50 to 700 characters per second (cps), depending on the desired print quality.

LINE PRINTERS A **line printer** is a high-speed impact printer that prints an entire line at a time (Figure 6-18). The speed of a line printer is measured by the number of lines per minute (lpm) it can print. These printers are capable of printing up to 3,000 lines per minute (lpm).

Figure 6-18 A line printer is a high-speed printer often connected to a mainframe, mid-range server, or network.

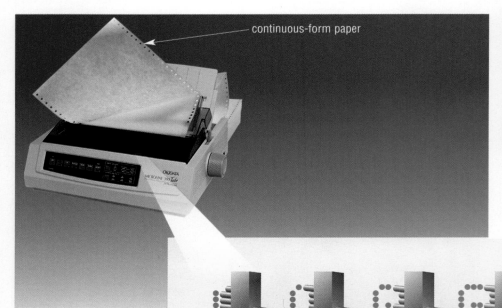

continuous-form paper

Figure 6-17 A dot-matrix printer produces printed images when tiny pins strike an inked ribbon.

Mainframes, mid-range servers, or networked applications, such as manufacturing, distribution, or shipping, often use line printers. These printers typically use 11-by-17-inch continuous-form paper. For example, mainframe computers often use greenbar paper to print reports.

Two popular types of line printers used for high-volume output are band and shuttle-matrix. A **band printer** prints fully-formed characters when hammers strike a horizontal, rotating band that contains shapes of numbers, letters of the alphabet, and other characters. A shuttle-matrix printer works more like a dot-matrix printer. The difference is the **shuttle-matrix printer** moves a series of print hammers back and forth horizontally at incredibly high speeds, as compared to standard line printers. Unlike a band printer, a shuttle-matrix printer can print characters in various fonts and font sizes.

Nonimpact Printers

A **nonimpact printer** forms characters and graphics on a piece of paper without actually striking the paper. Some spray ink, while others use heat and pressure to create images. Because these printers do not strike the paper, they are much quieter than the previously discussed impact printers.

Three commonly used types of nonimpact printers are ink-jet printers, laser printers, and thermal printers. The following sections discuss each of these printers.

Ink-Jet Printers

An **ink-jet printer** is a type of nonimpact printer that forms characters and graphics by spraying tiny drops of liquid ink onto a piece of paper. Ink-jet printers usually use individual sheets of paper stored in a removable or stationary tray.

Ink-jet printers can produce letter-quality text and graphics in both black-and-white and color print on a variety of paper types (Figure 6-19). Available paper types include plain paper, ink-jet, photo paper, glossy paper, and banner paper. Some ink-jet printers can print photographic-quality images on any of these types of paper. Others require the heavier weight ink-jet paper for better-looking color documents.

These printers also print on other materials such as envelopes, labels, index cards, greeting card paper, transparencies, and iron-on t-shirt transfers. Many ink-jet printers include software for creating greeting cards, banners, business cards, letterheads, and transparencies.

Ink-jet printers have become the most popular type of color printer for use in the home because of their lower cost and letter-quality print. You can purchase an ink-jet printer of reasonable quality for a few hundred dollars.

As with many other input and output devices, one factor that determines the quality of an ink-jet printer is its resolution, or sharpness and clarity. Printer resolution is measured by the number of dots per inch (dpi) a printer can output. As shown in Figure 6-20, the higher the dpi, the better the print quality. With an ink-jet printer, a dot is a drop of ink. A higher dpi means the drops of ink are smaller, which provides a higher quality image. Most ink-jet printers have a dpi that ranges from 300 to 2,400 dpi. Printers with a higher dpi usually are more expensive.

The speed of an ink-jet printer is measured by the number of pages per minute (ppm) it can print. Most ink-jet printers print from 1 to 12 pages per minute (ppm). Graphics and colors print at the slower rate.

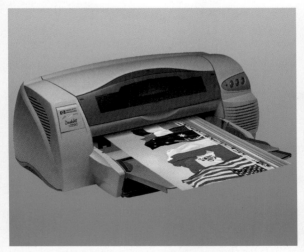

Figure 6-19 Ink-jet printers are the most popular type of color printer used in the home.

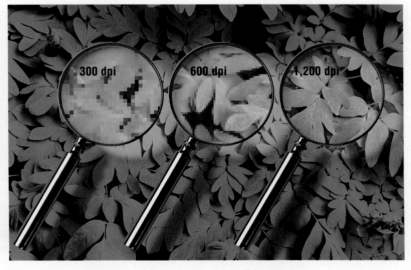

Figure 6-20 The higher the dpi, the better the quality of the image.

The print head mechanism in an ink-jet printer contains ink-filled print cartridges. Each cartridge has fifty to several hundred small ink holes, or nozzles. The steps in Figure 6-21 illustrate how a drop of ink appears on a page. Each nozzle in the print cartridge is similar to an individual pin on a dot-matrix printer. Just as any combination of dot-matrix pins can be activated, heat or pressure propels ink through any combination of the nozzles to form a character or image on the paper.

Web Link

For more information on ink-jet printers, visit the Discovering Computers 2002 Chapter 6 WEB LINK page (**scsite.com/dc2002/ch6/weblink.htm**) and click Ink-Jet Printers.

When the print cartridge runs out of ink, you simply replace the cartridge. Most ink-jet printers have at least two print cartridges: one containing black ink and the other(s) containing colors. These cartridges usually cost from $20 to $40 per cartridge. The number of pages you can print from a single cartridge varies by manufacturer. Some print as few as 20 pages, while others print as many as 300 pages.

On average, it costs from $.03 to $.05 per page for black ink and $.10 to $.15 per page for color ink. When coupled with premium photo paper, the cost for a high-quality photograph can increase to about $1.00 per page.

Laser Printers

A **laser printer** is a high-speed, high-quality nonimpact printer (Figure 6-22). Laser printers for personal computers usually use individual sheets of paper stored in a removable tray that slides into the printer case. Some laser printers have trays that can accommodate different sizes of paper, while others require separate trays for letter- and legal-sized paper. Most laser printers have a manual feed slot where you can insert individual sheets and envelopes. You also can print transparencies on a laser printer.

Figure 6-21 HOW AN INK-JET PRINTER WORKS

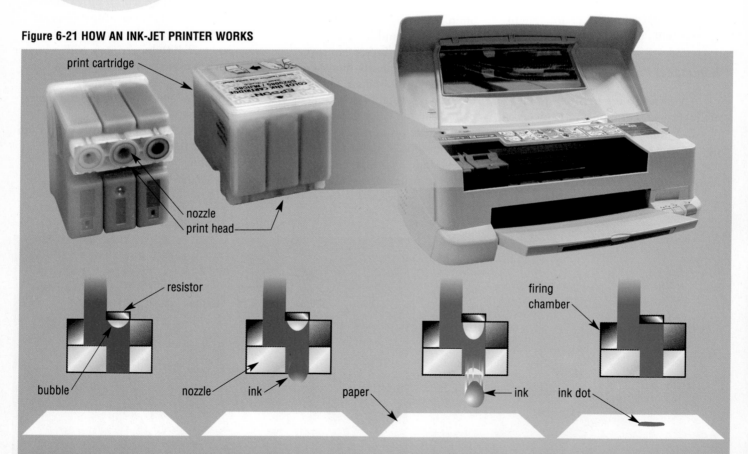

print cartridge

nozzle
print head

resistor

firing chamber

bubble

nozzle   ink   paper   ink   ink dot

Step 1:
A small resistor heats the ink, causing the ink to boil and form a vapor bubble.

Step 2:
The vapor bubble forces the ink through the nozzle.

Step 3:
Ink drops onto the paper.

Step 4:
As the vapor bubble collapses, fresh ink is drawn into the firing chamber.

Figure 6-22 Laser printers are used with personal computers, as well as larger computers.

Laser printers can print text and graphics in very high quality resolutions, ranging from 600 to 1,200 dpi. While laser printers typically cost more than ink-jet printers, they also are much faster. A high-end laser printer can print text at speeds of up to 40 pages per minute.

Depending on the quality and speed of the printer, the cost of a black-and-white laser printer ranges from a few hundred to several thousand dollars. The higher the resolution and speed, the more expensive the printer. Mainframe computers use high-end fast laser printers. Although color laser printers are available, they are relatively expensive, with prices often exceeding a thousand dollars.

Operating in a manner similar to a copy machine, a laser printer creates images using a laser beam and powdered ink, called **toner**. The laser beam produces an image on a special drum inside the printer. The light of the laser alters the electrical charge on the drum wherever it hits. When this occurs, the toner sticks to the drum and then transfers to the paper through a combination of pressure and heat (Figure 6-23).

Web Link

For more information on laser printers, visit the Discovering Computers 2002 Chapter 6 WEB LINK page (**scsite.com/dc2002/ch6/ weblink.htm**) and click Laser Printers.

Figure 6-23 HOW A LASER PRINTER WORKS

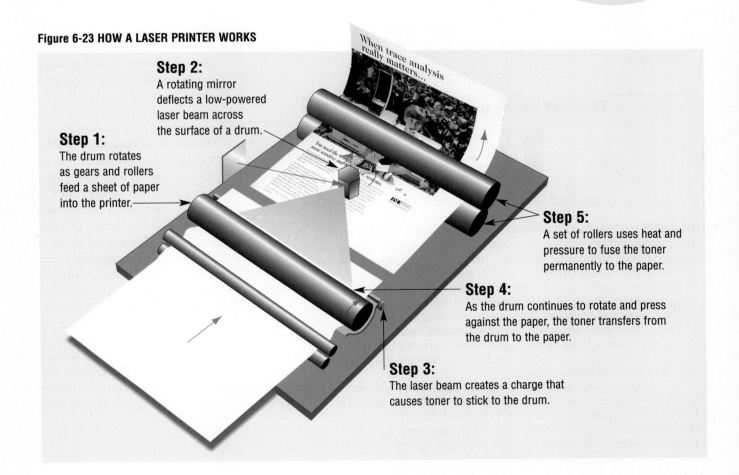

Step 1:
The drum rotates as gears and rollers feed a sheet of paper into the printer.

Step 2:
A rotating mirror deflects a low-powered laser beam across the surface of a drum.

Step 3:
The laser beam creates a charge that causes toner to stick to the drum.

Step 4:
As the drum continues to rotate and press against the paper, the toner transfers from the drum to the paper.

Step 5:
A set of rollers uses heat and pressure to fuse the toner permanently to the paper.

APPLY IT!
Printed Matters

Printers are available in various shapes and sizes and a range of prices. The type of printer you purchase depends on the type of printing you want to do. If the printer is for your business, it either can enhance the professional image you want the world to see — or detract from it. If the printer is for personal use, high-quality output may not be a major factor.

For most people, the choice is between two categories: laser printers and ink-jet printers. A laser printer generally prints at a relatively fast speed and produces high-quality black and white or color output. Resolution continues to improve from the original 300 dots per inch (dpi) to as much as 1,200 dpi. The price per page of a text-oriented document is $.02 to $.03. The printer trays for most laser printers can hold as many as 250 sheets of paper, and the printer can handle thousands of pages of output per month. Color laser printers are available and prices have decreased, but they still are expensive.

Although slower, ink-jet printers are less expensive than laser printers. The big advantage is the availability of color printing and entry-level units with low price tags. The price for a page of black-and-white text is around $.04 per page.

Some factors to consider when purchasing a printer are as follows:
- Primary use
- Space and noise
- Speed or pages per minute (PPM)
- Color capabilities
- Price of consumables
- Print quality and resolution
- Interface – parallel or USB
- Paper handling features

For more information on printers, visit the Discovering Computers 2002 Apply It Web page (**scsite.com/dc2002/apply.htm**) and click Chapter 6 Apply It #2.

COMPANY ON THE CUTTING EDGE

Coin Toss Determines Output Name

Bill Hewlett and Dave Packard, Stanford University graduates, had invented an audio oscillator while working in their garage, and now they needed a name for their partnership. They decided to use their last names, but whose name should be first? The two friends tossed a coin; Bill Hewlett won.

Walt Disney Studios placed an order in 1939 for eight audio oscillators. Hewlett-Packard (HP) shipped the oscillators to Disney, and the movie studios used the invention to test sound equipment for producing the film *Fantasia.*

Hewlett and Packard created the first set of corporate objectives in 1957, which became known as the HP Way. This philosophy embraces the free exchange of information, trust and respect, integrity, teamwork, and what HP calls Management by Walking Around.

The company's initial products were test and measurement equipment. In the 1960s, their product line expanded to include calculators. HP ushered in the first business minicomputer in 1972. In the 1980s, HP turned toward the microcomputer and printer markets. Today, the manufacturer is noted for a range of high-quality products, including personal computers, notebook computers, scanners, and ink-jet and laser printers.

For more information on Hewlett-Packard, visit the Discovering Computers 2002 Companies Web page (**scsite.com/dc2002/companies.htm**) and click HP.

When the toner runs out, you can replace the toner cartridge. Toner cartridge prices range from $50 to $100 for about 5,000 printed pages. On average, the cost per printed page on a black-and-white laser printer is $.02 to $.03.

When printing a document, laser printers process and store the entire page before they actually print it. For this reason, laser printers sometimes are called page printers. Storing a page before printing requires the laser printer has a certain amount of memory in the device.

Depending on the amount of graphics you intend to print, a laser printer can have up to 200 MB of memory. To print a full-page 600-dpi picture, for instance, you might need 16 MB of memory on the printer. If your printer does not have enough memory to print the picture, it either will print as much of the picture as its memory will allow, or it will display an error message and not print any of the picture. You usually can increase the amount of memory in a laser printer by inserting memory cards into the printer's expansion slots.

Laser printers use software that enables them to interpret a **page description language (PDL)**. A PDL tells the printer how to layout the contents of a printed page. When you purchase a laser printer, it comes with at least one of two common page description languages: PCL or PostScript. Developed by Hewlett-Packard, a leading printer manufacturer, **PCL (Printer Control Language)** is a standard printer language that supports the fonts and layout used in standard office documents. Professionals in the desktop publishing and graphic art fields commonly use **PostScript** because it is designed for complex documents with intense graphics and colors.

Thermal Printers

A **thermal printer** generates images by pushing electrically heated pins against heat-sensitive paper. Basic thermal printers are inexpensive, but the print quality is low and the images tend to fade over time. Thermal printers, however, are ideal for use in small devices such as adding machines.

Two special types of thermal printers have a much higher print quality. A **thermal wax-transfer printer**, also called a **thermal transfer printer**, generates rich, nonsmearing images by using heat to melt colored wax onto heat-sensitive paper. Thermal wax-transfer printers are more expensive than ink-jet printers, but less expensive than many color laser printers. A **dye-sublimation printer**, also called a **thermal dye transfer printer**, uses heat to transfer colored dye to specially coated paper.

Costing several thousand dollars, dye-sublimation printers can create images that are of photographic quality (Figure 6-24). Applications requiring very high image quality, such as medical or security applications, use these printers.

Some manufacturers offer a near dye-sublimation quality printer for the home user that costs several hundred dollars. Most home users, however, purchase a photo printer instead of these inexpensive dye-sublimation quality printers. The next page discusses photo printers.

Figure 6-24 This printer uses dye sublimation technology, which creates photographic quality output.

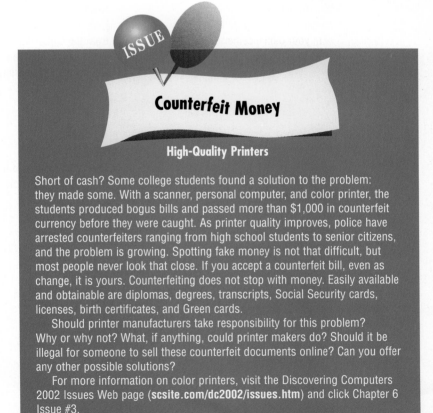

ISSUE

Counterfeit Money

High-Quality Printers

Short of cash? Some college students found a solution to the problem: they made some. With a scanner, personal computer, and color printer, the students produced bogus bills and passed more than $1,000 in counterfeit currency before they were caught. As printer quality improves, police have arrested counterfeiters ranging from high school students to senior citizens, and the problem is growing. Spotting fake money is not that difficult, but most people never look that close. If you accept a counterfeit bill, even as change, it is yours. Counterfeiting does not stop with money. Easily available and obtainable are diplomas, degrees, transcripts, Social Security cards, licenses, birth certificates, and Green cards.

Should printer manufacturers take responsibility for this problem? Why or why not? What, if anything, could printer makers do? Should it be illegal for someone to sell these counterfeit documents online? Can you offer any other possible solutions?

For more information on color printers, visit the Discovering Computers 2002 Issues Web page (**scsite.com/dc2002/issues.htm**) and click Chapter 6 Issue #3.

Web Link

For more information on photo printers, visit the Discovering Computers 2002 Chapter 6 WEB LINK page (**scsite.com/dc2002/ch6/weblink.htm**) and click Photo Printers.

Photo Printers

A **photo printer** is a color printer that can produce photo lab quality pictures as well as printing everyday documents. In addition, many photo printers can read media directly from a digital camera (Figure 6-25). That is, you do not need to attach the printer to your computer. Simply remove the storage device, such as a media card, from the digital camera and insert it into the printer.

Then, push buttons on the printer to select the desired photo, specify the number of copies, and indicate the size of the printed image. Size options for printed photographs can range from 3 x 3 inches to 13 x 19 inches. Some even print panoramic photographs.

Many photo printers use ink-jet technology. Thus, you can connect a photo printer to your computer and use it for all your printing needs. For a few hundred dollars, this printer is ideal for the home or small business user.

Figure 6-25 HOW SOME PHOTO PRINTERS WORK WITH A DIGITAL CAMERA

Step 1: Insert media card into digital camera. Take the photograph with your digital camera.

Step 2: Remove the media card from the digital camera and insert it into the card slot on the photo printer.

Step 3: Select desired image to print, number of copies, and size of print by pushing buttons on the photo printer.

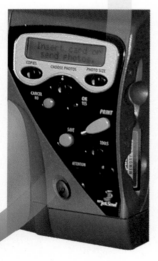

Step 4: Remove the photo from the photo printer.

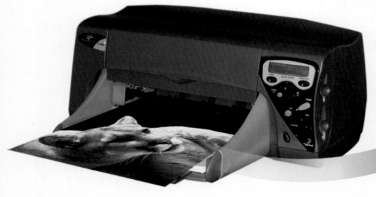

Label and Postage Printers

A **label printer** is a small printer that prints on an adhesive-type material that can be placed on a variety of items such as envelopes, packages, floppy disks, CDs, DVDs, audiocassettes, photographs, file folders, and toys. Most label printers also print bar codes.

Some newer model label printers have built-in digital scales and can print e-stamps (Figure 6-26). An **e-stamp**, also called **Internet postage**, is digital postage you buy and print right from your personal computer. That is, you purchase an amount of postage from an authorized postal service Web site and download it directly to the label printer. As you need stamps, you print them on the label printer.

Figure 6-26 Many label printers have built-in digital scales and can print e-stamps.

ISSUE

Print Your Own Photographs

Digital Cameras and Photo Printers

As with any technology, the price of digital cameras and photo printers continues to decrease. Lower prices are an enticement for more and more people to turn away from traditional cameras and film developing to digital photography. Digital cameras radically have simplified the process of getting your pictures into your personal computer. Even so, all cameras live or die on image quality. Some experts suggest that the 35mm still is king and the traditional camera rules, especially when making photographs for glossy reports or other high-quality publications. How much quality is lost by using a digital camera? Maybe none. Other experts argue that a digital camera produces better quality than a film camera in many important respects and praise the digital camera as the answer to all photographic needs.

So whom can you believe? Does this mean one should throw away the 35mm camera? Is this the end of the traditional camera? What is your opinion of the digital camera? How much longer before the demise of purchasing rolls of films and print development? Alternatively, will traditional cameras continue for many more years?

For more information on digital cameras and photo printers, visit the Discovering Computers 2002 Issues Web page (**scsite.com/dc2002/issues.htm**) and click Chapter 6 Issue #4.

Portable Printers

A **portable printer** is a small, lightweight printer that allows a mobile user to print from a notebook or handheld computer while traveling (Figure 6-27). Barely wider than the paper on which they print, portable printers easily can fit in a briefcase alongside a notebook computer.

Some portable printers use ink-jet technology. Others are thermal or thermal wax-transfer. Many of these printers connect to a parallel port or USB port. Others have a built-in wireless infrared port through which they communicate with the computer.

Plotters and Large-Format Printers

Plotters are sophisticated printers used to produce high-quality drawings such as blueprints, maps, and circuit diagrams. These printers are used in specialized fields such as engineering and drafting, and usually are very costly. Current plotters use a row of charged wires (called styli) to draw an electrostatic pattern on specially coated paper and then fuse toner to the pattern. The printed image consists of a series of very small dots, which provide high-quality output.

Operating like an ink-jet printer, but on a much larger scale, a **large-format printer** creates photo-realistic quality color prints. Used by graphic artists, these high costing, high performance printers are used for signs, posters, and other displays (Figure 6-28).

Plotters and large-format printers typically can handle paper with widths up to 60 inches because blueprints, maps, signs, posters and other such drawings and displays can be quite large. Some plotters and large-format printers use individual sheets of paper, while others take large rolls.

Figure 6-27 A portable printer is a small, compact printer that allows the mobile user to print from a notebook or handheld computer while traveling.

Figure 6-28 Graphic artists use large-format printers to print signs, posters, and other displays.

SPEAKERS AND HEADSETS

An **audio output device** is a component of a computer that produces music, speech, or other sounds, such as beeps. Two commonly used audio output devices are speakers and headsets.

Most personal computers have a small internal speaker that usually outputs only low-quality sound. For this reason, many personal computer users add sophisticated stereo **speakers** to their computers to generate a higher-quality sound (Figure 6-29). Some monitors even have larger speakers built into the sides of the monitor.

To boost the low bass sounds, some users add a **woofer** (also called a subwoofer). You connect the stereo speakers and woofer to ports on the sound card. Most speakers have tone and volume controls so you can adjust settings.

When using speakers, anyone within listening distance can hear the output. If you are in a computer laboratory or some other crowded environment, speakers might not be practical. Instead, you can plug a headset into a port on the sound card. With the **headset**, only you can hear the sound from the computer (Figure 6-30).

speakers

woofer

Figure 6-29 Many personal computer users have high-quality stereo speakers and a woofer for their computers.

Figure 6-30 In a crowded environment where speakers are not practical, you can use a headset for audio output.

Before purchasing a new computer or upgrading an existing one, you should consider the ways in which you will use it. Unless sound plays a minor role in your life, you will want to consider a stand-alone sound card. Most inexpensive computers integrate a sound chip with the motherboard. Look at the back of the computer. If the microphone and speaker ports are grouped together with the keyboard/mouse connector and the serial port, you have an integrated onboard sound chip.

Until recently, Creative Lab's Sound Blaster (see URL below) card has dominated the computer sound market. If a sound card were not Sound Blaster compatible, it would not sell. This is because most games require a Sound Blaster compatible sound card. Even though new technology opened the door for other options, Sound Blaster is still the de facto standard. Today's cards make games and multimedia applications sound great and provide users with the capability to compose, edit, and print their own music; learn to play the piano; record and edit digital audio; and play audio CDs.

The biggest change in sound card architecture was the introduction of 3D-positional audio. Primarily used with games, the 3D-positional audio algorithm fools your brain into thinking sounds are emanating from somewhere other than the speakers sitting in front of you.

Purchasing a sound card is an individual decision. To get a better idea of what you should purchase to fit your budget and lifestyle, consider the following:
1. How much money do you plan to spend?
2. Will you use the sound card for playing games or music, recording digital audio?
3. Select two or three cards and then read online reviews (see URL below).

For more information on computer sound systems and the Web sites mentioned above, visit the Discovering Computers 2002 Apply It Web page (**scsite.com/dc2002/apply.htm**) and click Chapter 6 Apply It #3.

Electronically produced voice output is growing in popularity. **Voice output** occurs when you hear a person's voice or when the computer talks to you through the speakers on the computer. As discussed in Chapter 2, you can listen to interviews, talk shows, sporting events, news, recorded music, and live concerts from many radio and television stations on the Web. Some Web sites dedicate themselves to providing voice output, where you can hear songs, quotes, and historical speeches and lectures (Figure 6-31).

Very often, voice output works with voice input. **Internet telephony**, for example, allows you to have a conversation over the Web, just as if you were on the telephone.

Sophisticated programs enable the computer to converse with you. Talk into the microphone and say, "I'd like today's weather report." The computer replies, "For which city?" You reply, "Chicago." The computer says, "Sunny and 80 degrees."

OTHER OUTPUT DEVICES

Although monitors, printers, and speakers are the more widely used output devices, many other output devices are available for particular uses and applications. These include data projectors, facsimiles, and multifunction devices. The following pages discuss each of these devices.

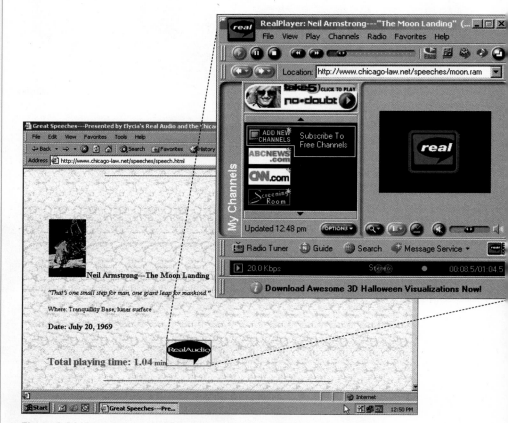

Figure 6-31 You can listen to historical speeches and lectures from the Web. Playing here is an audio broadcast made by Neil Armstrong as he walked on the moon for the first time.

Data Projectors

A **data projector** is a device that takes the image from a computer screen and projects it onto a larger screen so an audience of people can see the image clearly. For example, many classrooms use data projectors so all students easily can see an instructor's presentation on the screen (Figure 6-32).

Some data projectors are large devices that attach to a ceiling or wall in an auditorium. Others are small portable devices. Two types of smaller, lower-cost units are LCD projectors and DLP projectors.

An **LCD projector**, which uses liquid crystal display technology, attaches directly to a computer and uses its own light source to display the information shown on the computer screen. Because LCD projectors tend to produce lower-quality images, some users prefer to use a DLP projector for sharper, brighter images.

A **digital light processing (DLP) projector** uses tiny mirrors to reflect light, which produces crisp, bright, colorful images that remain in focus and can be seen clearly even in a well-lit room.

Facsimile (Fax) Machine

A **facsimile (fax) machine** is a device that transmits and receives documents over telephone lines. The documents can contain text, drawings, or photographs, or can be handwritten. The term fax also refers to a document that you send or receive via a fax machine.

A stand-alone fax machine scans an original document, converts the image into digitized data, and transmits the digitized image (Figure 6-33). A fax machine at the receiving end reads the incoming data, converts the digitized data into an image, and prints or stores a copy of the original image.

Figure 6-33 A stand-alone fax machine.

Figure 6-32 DLP projectors produce sharp, bright images.

Many computers include fax capability by using a fax modem. A **fax modem** is a modem that also allows you to send (and sometimes receive) electronic documents as faxes (Figure 6-34). A fax modem transmits computer-prepared documents, such as a word processing letter, or documents that have been digitized with a scanner or digital camera. A fax modem transmits these faxes to a fax machine or to another fax modem.

When a computer (instead of a fax machine) receives a fax, you can view the fax on the screen, saving the time and expense of printing it. If you wish, you also can print the fax using special fax software. The quality of the viewed or printed fax is less than that of a word processing document because the fax actually is a large image. Optical character recognition (OCR) software enables you to convert the image to text and then edit it.

A fax modem can be an external device that plugs into a port on the back of the system unit or an internal card you insert into an expansion slot on the motherboard.

Multifunction Devices

A **multifunction device** (**MFD**) is a single piece of equipment that looks like a copy machine, but provides the functionality of a printer, scanner, copy machine, and perhaps a fax machine (Figure 6-35). The features of these devices, which are sometimes called multifunction peripherals (MFPs) or all-in-one devices, vary widely. For example, some use color ink-jet printer technology, while others include a black-and-white laser printer.

Figure 6-35 This multifunction device is a color printer, scanner, copy machine, and fax machine all in one.

Web Link

For more information on fax modems, visit the Discovering Computers 2002 Chapter 6 WEB LINK page (**scsite.com/dc2002/ch6/weblink.htm**) and click Fax Modems.

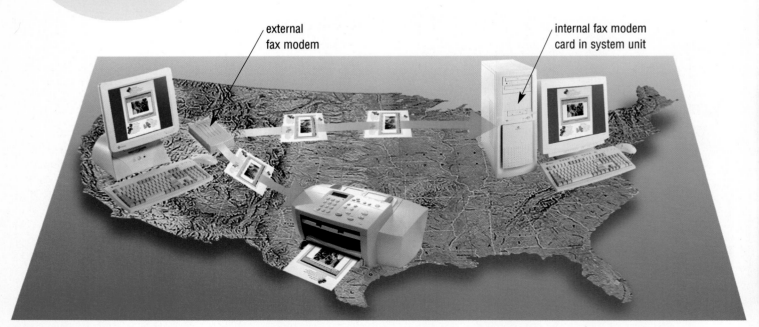

external fax modem

internal fax modem card in system unit

Figure 6-34 A fax modem allows you to send (and sometimes receive) electronic documents as faxes to a fax machine or another computer.

Small offices and home offices (SOHOs) use MFDs because they require less space than having a separate printer, scanner, copy machine, and fax machine. Another advantage of an MFD is that it is significantly less expensive than if you purchase each device separately. If the device breaks down, however, you lose all four functions, which is the primary disadvantage. Given all the advantages, more users are bringing MFDs into their offices and homes.

TERMINALS

A **terminal** is a device that performs both input and output because it consists of a monitor (output), a keyboard (input), and a video card. Terminals fall into three basic categories: dumb terminals, intelligent terminals, and special-purpose terminals.

A **dumb terminal** has no processing power; thus, cannot function as an independent device (Figure 6-36). A dumb terminal can enter and transmit data to, or receive and display information from, a computer to which it is connected. Dumb terminals connect to a **host computer** that performs the processing and then sends the output back to the dumb terminal. The host computer usually is a mid-range server, mainframe, or supercomputer.

Web Link

For more information on multifunction devices, visit the Discovering Computers 2002 Chapter 6 WEB LINK page (**scsite.com/dc2002/ch6/ weblink.htm**) and click Multifunction Devices.

ISSUE

Jack of all Trades

Multifunction Devices

Designing and setting up a home office is a challenge. In addition to a computer, other required hardware most likely includes a printer, fax machine, copy machine, and scanner. When selecting these components, you have several options to consider. One option is to purchase each of these as a separate device. A second option is to purchase a combination printer and scanner or combination printer and fax machine. A third option is to purchase a multifunction device that contains all four of these hardware devices. Generally, a multifunction device represents a convenient and efficient way to expand the type of document input and output facilities. On the other hand, performance offered by multifunction devices rarely matches individual devices that are designed specifically for the job. Which option would be best? How would budget and workspace affect your choice? Why? What advantages or disadvantages are there in relation to connecting these devices to a personal computer?

For more information on multifunction devices, visit the Discovering Computers 2002 Issues Web page (**scsite.com/dc2002/issues.htm**) and and click Chapter 6 Issue #5.

Figure 6-36 Dumb terminals have no processing power and usually are connected to larger computer systems.

In addition to a monitor and keyboard, an **intelligent terminal** also has memory and a processor that has the capability of performing some functions independent of the host computer. Intelligent terminals sometimes are called **programmable terminals** because they can be programmed by the software developer to perform basic tasks. In recent years, personal computers have replaced most intelligent terminals.

Other special-purpose terminals perform specific tasks and contain features uniquely designed for use in a particular industry. Two of these special-purpose terminals are point-of-sale terminals and automated teller machines (Figure 6-37).

A **point-of-sale** (**POS**) terminal records purchases at the point where the consumer purchases a product or service. The POS terminal used in a grocery store, for example, is a combination of an electronic cash register and bar code reader. As described in Chapter 5, grocery store UPC bar codes contain data that identify the manufacturer and item of a product. When the check out clerk scans the bar code on the food product (input), the computer uses the manufacturer and item numbers to look up the price of the item and the complete product name in the database. Then, the price of the item from the database displays on the monitor (output), the name of

the item and its price print on a receipt (output), and the item being sold is recorded so the inventory can be updated. Thus, the output from POS terminals serves as input to other computers to maintain sales records, update inventory, verify credit, and perform other activities associated with the sales transactions that are critical to running the business.

Many POS terminals handle credit card or debit card payments. Simply swipe your card through the reader (input) and the system processes your credit or debit card. Once approved, the terminal usually prints a receipt for a customer (output).

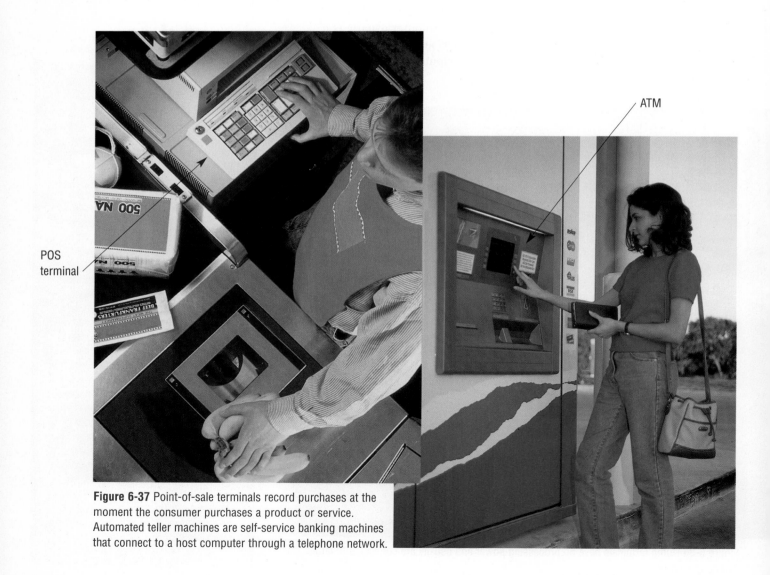

Figure 6-37 Point-of-sale terminals record purchases at the moment the consumer purchases a product or service. Automated teller machines are self-service banking machines that connect to a host computer through a telephone network.

An **automated teller machine** (**ATM**) is a self-service banking machine that connects to a host computer through a telephone network. You insert a plastic bankcard with a magnetic strip into the ATM and enter your password, called a personal identification number (PIN), to access your bank account. Some ATMs have touch screens, while others have special keyboards for input. Using an ATM, you can withdraw cash, deposit money, transfer funds, or inquire about an account balance. When your transaction is complete, the ATM prints a receipt for your records.

OUTPUT DEVICES FOR PHYSICALLY CHALLENGED USERS

As discussed in Chapter 5, the growing presence of computers in people's lives has generated an awareness of the need to address computing requirements for those with physical limitations. For users with mobility, hearing, or vision disabilities, many different types of output devices are available. Hearing-impaired users, for example, can instruct programs to display words instead of sounds. With the Windows operating system, these users also can set options to make programs easier to use. For example, the Magnifier command enlarges text and other items in a window on the screen (Figure 6-38).

Web Link

For more information on POS terminals visit the Discovering Computers 2002 Chapter 6 WEB LINK page (**scsite.com/dc2002/ch6/ weblink.htm**) and click POS Terminals.

Web Link

For more information on automated teller machines, visit the Discovering Computers 2002 Chapter 6 WEB LINK page (**scsite.com/dc2002/ch6/ weblink.htm**) and click Automated Teller Machines.

Figure 6-38a (Magnifier command)

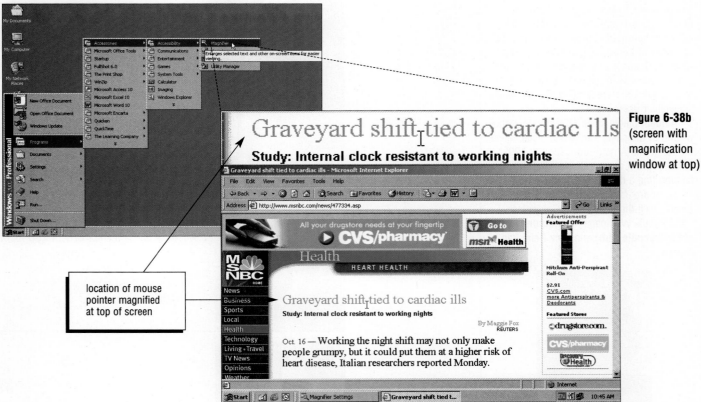

Figure 6-38b (screen with magnification window at top)

location of mouse pointer magnified at top of screen

Figure 6-38 The Magnifier command in Windows enlarges text and other on-screen items for individuals with vision disabilities.

PUTTING IT ALL TOGETHER

Many factors influence the type of output devices you should use: the type of output desired, the hardware and software in use, and the desired cost. Figure 6-40 outlines several suggested monitors, printers, and other output devices for various types of computer users.

CHAPTER SUMMARY

Data is a collection of raw, unprocessed facts, figures, and symbols. Computers process and organize data into information, which has meaning and is useful. This chapter described the various methods of output and several commonly used output devices. Output devices presented included display devices, printers, speakers, data projectors, fax machines, multifunction devices, and terminals.

Career Corner

Graphics Designer/Illustrator

A designer or illustrator is an artist, but generally does not create original works. Instead, their job is to portray visually the ideas of their clients. Illustrators work in fields such as fashion, technical, medical, animation, or even that of a cartoonist. Designers create visual impressions of products and advertisements. Some of these are as follows:

- Graphic designers – design book covers, stationery, CD covers, and CD embossments
- Costume and theater designers – design costumes and settings for theater and television
- Interior designers – design the layout, decor, and furnishings of homes and buildings
- Jewelry designers – design jewelry, including some one of a kind
- Fashion designers – design clothing, shoes, and other fashion accessories

Education-wise, you can find certificate, two-year, four-year, and master level programs within the design area. Many individuals choose to freelance, while others work with ad agencies, publishing companies, design studios, or specialized departments within large companies. Salaries may range anywhere from $25,000 to $75,000 plus, based on experience and educational background.

Adobe (see URL below) offers a Certified Expert Program. To become an Adobe® Certified Expert, you must pass an Adobe Product Proficiency Exam for the product for which you want to be certified.

To learn more about graphics design and illustration as a career and the Web site mentioned above, visit the Discovering Computers 2002 Careers Web page (**scsite.com/dc2002/careers.htm**) and click Graphics Designer/Illustrator.

PRINTER	OTHER
• Ink-jet color printer; *or* • Photo printer • Label printer	• Speakers • Headset
• Multifunction device; *or* • Ink-jet color printer; *or* • Laser printer, black and white • Label printer	• Fax machine • Speakers
• Portable printer • Ink-jet color printer; *or* • Laser printer, black and white, for in-office use; *or* • Photo printer	• Fax modem • Headset • DLP data projector
• Laser printer, black and white • Line printer (for large reports from a mainframe) • Label printer	• Fax machine *or* fax modem • Speakers • DLP data projector • Dumb terminal
• Laser printer, black and white • Plotter • Photo printer; *or* • Dye sublimation printer	• Fax machine *or* fax modem • Speakers • Headset

*e*REVOLUTION

E·GOVERNMENT

STAMP OF APPROVAL

Making a Federal Case for Useful Information

When it is time to buy stamps to mail your correspondence, you no longer need to wait in long lines at your local post office. Instead, log on to the Internet and download a stamp right to your personal computer.

The U.S. Postal Service has authorized several corporations to sell stamps online. Users can download software from a company's Web site, charge the postage fee to a credit card, and then print the postage on a label printer or directly onto envelopes and labels. Some of these Web sites, such as Stamps.com, shown in Figure 6-41, charge a small percentage of each order as a convenience fee.

Although citizens may not be enthusiastic about paying income taxes, April 15 can be more tolerable knowing that some of their hard-earned dollars are spent subsidizing useful government Web sites.

You can recognize these Web sites on the Internet by their .gov top-level domain abbreviation. For example, the Library of Congress Web site is lcweb.loc.gov. As the oldest federal cultural institution in the United States and the largest library in the world, the mission of the Library of Congress is to serve the research needs of the U.S. Congress. Patrons can visit one of 22 reading rooms on Capitol Hill and access more than 115 million items written in 450 languages. The Library of Congress Web site, shown in Figure 6-42, has forms and information from the Copyright Office, an

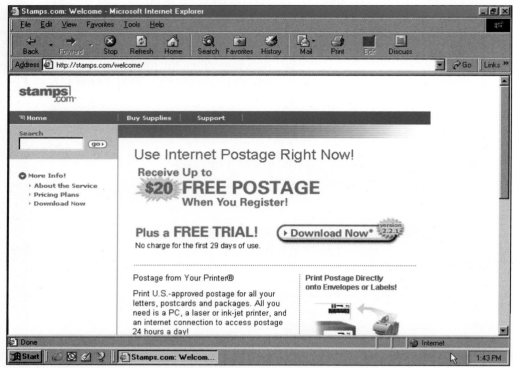

Figure 6-41 Purchasing stamps on the Internet eliminates making a trip to the post office and waiting in long lines.

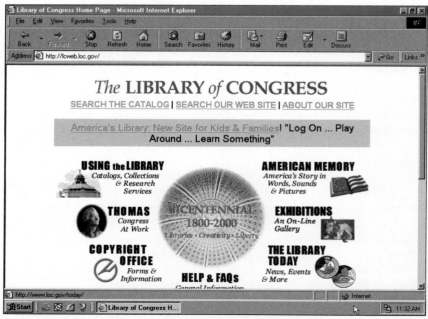

Figure 6-42 The Library of Congress Web site contains more than 115 million items written in 450 languages.

online gallery, and links to a variety of topics, including the National Agricultural Library and the National Library of Medicine. These and other government resources Web sites are listed in Figure 6-43.

Government and military Web sites offer a wide range of information. The Time Service Department Web site will provide you with the correct time. If you are looking for a federal document, the FedWorld Information Network lists thousands of documents distributed by the government on its Web site. For access to the names of your congressional representatives, the president's cabinet members, and the Supreme Court justices; or to read portions of a federal statute or the U.S. Constitution, visit the extensive Hieros Gamos Web site, which is a governmental and legal portal with links to the legislative, judicial, and executive branches of government.

For more information on government resources Web sites, visit the Discovering Computers 2002 E-Revolution Web page (scsite.com/dc2002/e-rev.htm) and click Government.

GOVERNMENT RESOURCES WEB SITES	URL
Postage	
Pitney Bowes	pitneybowes.com
Simply Postage	simplypostage.com
Stamps.com	stamps.com
Government	
FedWorld Information Network	fedworld.gov
Hieros Gamos	hg.org
Library of Congress	lcweb.loc.gov
National Archives and Records Administration	www.nara.gov
National Agricultural Library	www.nal.usda.gov
National Library of Medicine	www.nlm.nih.gov
The White House	www.whitehouse.gov
Thomas Legislative Information	thomas.loc.gov
Time Service Department	tycho.usno.navy.mil
U.S. Department of Education	ed.gov
U.S. Government Printing Office	www.access.gpo.gov
U.S. Patent and Trademark Office	www.uspto.gov
U.S. Treasury	treas.gov
USA Jobs	www.usajobs.opm.gov

For an updated list of government resources Web sites, visit scsite.com/dc2002/e-rev.htm.

Figure 6-43 These Web sites offer information on buying U.S.-approved postage online and researching federal agencies.

E-GOVERNMENT applied:

1. View the three postage Web sites listed in Figure 6-43. Compare and contrast the available services on each one. Consider postage cost, necessary equipment, shipping services, security techniques, and tracking capability. Explain why you would or would not like to use this service.

2. Visit the Hieros Gamos Web site listed in Figure 6-43. What are the names, addresses, and telephone numbers of your two state senators and your local congressional representative? On what committees do they serve? Who is the chief justice of the Supreme Court, and what has been this justice's opinion on two recently decided cases? Who are the members of the president's cabinet? Then, visit two other Web sites listed in Figure 6-43. Write a paragraph on each Web site describing its content and features.

6.34

DISCOVERING
COMPUTERS *2002*

Chapter 1 2 3 4 5 6 7 8 9 10 11 12 13 14 15 16 Index **HOME**

In Summary

SHELLY
CASHMAN
SERIES.

Student Exercises   Web Links   In Summary   Key Terms   Learn It Online   Checkpoint   In The Lab   Web Work

Special Features   ■ TIMELINE 2002 ■ WWW & E-SKILLS ■ MULTIMEDIA ■ BUYER'S GUIDE 2002 ■ WIRELESS TECHNOLOGY ■ TRENDS 2002 ■ INTERACTIVE LABS ■ TECH NEWS

Web Instructions: To display this page from the Web, start your browser and enter the URL scsite.com/dc2002/ch6/summary.htm. Click the links for current and additional information. To listen to an audio version of this In Summary, click the Audio button. To play the audio, RealPlayer must be installed on your computer (download by clicking here).

1 What Are the Four Types of Output?

Output is data that has been processed into a useful form, called information. Four types of output are text, graphics, audio, and video. **Text** consists of characters used to create words, sentences, and paragraphs. A **graphic** or **graphical image** is a digital representation of nontext information such as a drawing, chart, or photograph. **Audio** is music, speech, or any other sound. **Video** consists of full-motion images that are played back at various speeds.

2 What Are the Different Types of Output Devices?

An **output device** is any hardware component capable of conveying information to a user. A **display device** is an output device that visually conveys text, graphics, and video information. A **printer** is an output device that produces text and graphics on a physical medium such as paper or transparency film. An **audio output device** produces music, speech, or other sounds. Other output devices include data projectors, facsimile (fax) machines, and multifunction devices.

3 What Factors Affect the Quality of a Monitor?

A **monitor** is a display device that consists of a screen housed in a plastic or metal case. The quality of the display depends on a monitor's resolution, dot pitch, and refresh rate. **Resolution**, or sharpness, is related to the number of pixels a monitor can display. **Dot pitch**, a measure of image clarity, is the distance between each pixel. **Refresh rate** is the speed with which a monitor redraws images on the screen. Refresh rate should be fast enough to maintain a constant, flicker-free image. A **video card** converts digital output into an analog video signal that is sent through a cable to the monitor. How the picture is produced is determined by the display device. Several standards define resolution, the number of colors, and other monitor

properties. Today, most monitors and video cards support the **super video graphics array** (**SVGA**) standard.

4 What Are Monitor Ergonomic Issues?

Features that address monitor ergonomic issues include controls to adjust the brightness, contrast, positioning, height, and width of images. Many monitors have a tilt-and-swivel base so the angle of the screen can be altered to minimize neck strain and glare. CRT monitors produce a small amount of **electromagnetic radiation** (**EMR**), which is a magnetic field that travels at the speed of light. High-quality CRT monitors should comply with **MPR II** standards, which define acceptable levels of EMR for a monitor.

5 How Are Various Types of Printers Different?

Printers produce printed information, called **hard copy**. Generally printers are grouped into two categories: impact and nonimpact. An **impact printer** forms characters and graphics by striking a mechanism against an ink ribbon that physically contacts the paper. A **dot-matrix printer** is an impact printer that prints images when tiny wire pins on a print head mechanism strike an inked ribbon. A **line printer** is a high-speed impact printer that prints an entire line at one time. A **nonimpact printer** creates characters and graphics without actually striking the paper. An **ink-jet printer** is a high-speed, high-quality nonimpact printer that sprays drops of ink onto a piece of paper. A **laser printer** is a nonimpact printer that operates in a manner similar to a copy machine. A **thermal printer** generates images by pushing electrically heated pins against heat-sensitive paper. A printer capable of **Internet printing** receives print instructions from an Internet service, allowing it to print documents from desktop and wireless devices. Other types of printers include **photo printers**, **label printers**, **portable printers**, and **plotters**.

DISCOVERING COMPUTERS 2002

Chapter 1 2 3 4 5 6 7 8 9 10 11 12 13 14 15 16 Index HOME

6.35

SHELLY CASHMAN SERIES.

Student Exercises Web Links In Summary Key Terms Learn It Online Checkpoint In The Lab Web Work

Special Features ■ TIMELINE 2002 ■ WWW & E-SKILLS ■ MULTIMEDIA ■ BUYER'S GUIDE 2002 ■ WIRELESS TECHNOLOGY ■ TRENDS 2002 ■ INTERACTIVE LABS ■ TECH NEWS

In Summary

6 What Are Various Types of Audio Output Devices?

Two commonly used audio output devices are **speakers** and **headsets**. Most personal computers have an internal speaker that outputs low-quality sound. Many users add high-quality stereo speakers or purchase personal computers with larger speakers built into the sides of the monitor. A woofer can be added to boost low bass sounds. A headset plugged into a port on the sound card allows only the user to hear sound from the computer.

7 Why Are Data Projectors, Fax Machines, and Multifunction Devices Used?

A data projector takes the image on a computer screen and projects it onto a large screen so an audience of people can see the image. A **facsimile (fax) machine** transmits and receives documents over telephone lines. A **fax modem** is a communications device that sends (and sometimes receives) electronic documents as faxes. A **multifunction device (MFD)** is a single piece of equipment that looks like a copy machine, but provides the functionality of a printer, scanner, copy machine, and sometimes a fax machine.

8 How Is a Terminal Both an Input and Output Device?

A **terminal** is a device that consists of a keyboard (input), a monitor (output), and a video card. A terminal is used to input and transmit data to, or receive and output information from, a host computer that performs the processing. Three basic categories of terminals are **dumb terminals**, **intelligent terminals**, and **point-of-sale (POS)** terminals.

9 What Are Output Options for Physically Challenged Users?

For users with mobility, hearing, or vision disabilities, many different types of output devices are available. Hearing-impaired users can instruct programs to display words instead of produce sounds. Visually impaired users can change the size or color of text to make words easier to read. Blind users can utilize voice output, where the computer reads information that displays on the screen. A Braille printer outputs information in Braille onto paper.

Key Terms

SHELLY CASHMAN SERIES.

Student Exercises   Web Links   In Summary   Key Terms   Learn It Online   Checkpoint   In The Lab   Web Work

Special Features ■ TIMELINE 2002 ■ WWW & E-SKILLS ■ MULTIMEDIA ■ BUYER'S GUIDE 2002 ■ WIRELESS TECHNOLOGY ■ TRENDS 2002 ■ INTERACTIVE LABS ■ TECH NEWS

Web Instructions: To display this page from the Web, start your browser and enter the URL scsite.com/dc2002/ch6/terms.htm. Scroll through the list of terms. Click a term to display its definition and a picture. Click the To WEB button for current and additional information about the term from the Web. To see animations, Shockwave and Flash Player must be installed on your computer (download by clicking here).

active-matrix display (6.8)
audio (6.3)
audio output device (6.23)
automatic teller machine (ATM) (6.29)
band printer (6.15)
bit depth (6.10)
Braille printer (6.30)
cathode ray tube (CRT) (6.5)
ClearType (6.7)
color depth (6.10)
continuous-form paper (6.14)
CRT monitor (6.5)
data projector (6.25)
Digital Display Working Group (DDWG) (6.10)
digital light processing (DLP) projector (6.25)
Digital Video Interface (DVI) (6.10)
display (6.4)
display device (6.4)
dot pitch (6.9)
dot-matrix printer (6.14)
dual-scan display (6.8)
dumb terminal (6.27)
dye-sublimation printer (6.19)
electromagnetic radiation (EMR) (6.11)
electronic book (e-book) (6.7)
ENERGY STAR program (6.12)
e-stamp (6.21)
facsimile (fax) machine (6.25)
fax modem (6.26)
flat-panel display (6.5)
gas plasma monitor (6.8)
graphic (6.3)
graphical image (6.3)
graphics card (6.10)
gray scaling (6.4)
hard copy (6.12)
headset (6.23)
hertz (6.9)
high-definition television (HDTV) (6.12)
high-performance addressing (HPA) (6.8)
host computer (6.27)
impact printer (6.14)
ink-jet printer (6.15)
intelligent terminal (6.28)
interactive TV (6.12)
Internet postage (6.21)
Internet printing (6.13)

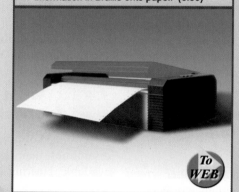

BRAILLE PRINTER
Printer for blind users that outputs information in Braille onto paper. (6.30)

To WEB

Internet telephony (6.24)
label printer (6.21)
landscape orientation (6.12)
large-format printer (6.22)
laser printer (6.16)
LCD displays (6.5)
LCD monitors (6.5)
LCD projector (6.25)
letter quality (LQ) (6.14)
line printer (6.14)
liquid crystal display (LCD) (6.5)
monitor (6.4)
monochrome (6.4)
MPR II (6.11)
multifunction device (MFD) (6.26)
National Television Standards Committee (6.12)
near letter quality (NLQ) (6.14)
nonimpact printer (6.15)
NTSC converter (6.12)
output (6.2)
output device (6.4)
page description language (PDL) (6.18)
passive-matrix display (6.8)
PCL (Printer Control Language) (6.18)
photo printer (6.20)
pixel (6.5)
pixel pitch (6.9)
plotters (6.22)
point-of-sale (POS) terminal (6.28)
portable printer (6.22)
portrait orientation (6.12)

PostScript (6.18)
printer (6.12)
printout (6.12)
programmable terminals (6.28)
refresh rate (6.9)
resolution (6.8)
screen (6.4)
shuttle-matrix printer (6.15)
soft copy (6.4)
speakers (6.23)
super video graphics array (SVGA) (6.10)
terminal (6.27)
text (6.2)
thermal dye transfer printer (6.19)
thermal printer (6.19)
thermal transfer printer (6.19)
thermal wax-transfer printer (6.19)
thin-film transistor (TFT) display (6.8)
toner (6.17)
vertical frequency (6.9)
vertical scan rate (6.9)
video (6.3)
video adapter (6.10)
video card (6.10)
Video Electronics Standards Association (VESA) (6.10)

LARGE FORMAT PRINTER
Nonimpact printer that creates photo-realistic quality color prints; operates like an ink-jet printer, but on a much larger scale. (6.22)

To WEB

viewable size (6.5)
voice output (6.24)
woofer (6.23)

DISCOVERING COMPUTERS 2002

Learn It Online

SHELLY CASHMAN SERIES.

Student Exercises   Web Links   In Summary   Key Terms   Learn It Online   Checkpoint   In The Lab   Web Work

Special Features   ■ TIMELINE 2002   ■ WWW & E-SKILLS   ■ MULTIMEDIA   ■ BUYER'S GUIDE 2002   ■ WIRELESS TECHNOLOGY   ■ TRENDS 2002   ■ INTERACTIVE LABS   ■ TECH NEWS

Web Instructions: To display this page from the Web, start your browser and enter the URL scsite.com/dc2002/ch6/learn.htm.

1. Web Guide

Click Web Guide to display the Guide to World Wide Web Sites and Searching Techniques Web page. Click Computers and Computing. Click PC Guide and then search for monitors. Click monitors and then review the information. Use your word processing program to prepare a brief report on your findings and submit your assignment to your instructor.

2. Scavenger Hunt

Click Scavenger Hunt. Print a copy of the Scavenger Hunt page; use this page to write down your answers as you search the Web. Submit your completed page to your instructor.

3. Who Wants to Be a Computer Genius?

Click Computer Genius to find out if you are a computer genius. Directions on how to play the game will display. When you are ready to play, click the PLAY button. Submit your score to your instructor.

4. Wheel of Terms

Click Wheel of Terms to reinforce important terms you learned in this chapter by playing the Shelly Cashman Series version of this popular game. Directions on how to play the game will display. When you are ready to play, click the PLAY button. Submit your score to your instructor.

5. Career Corner

Click Career Corner to display the MSN Career page. Review this page. Click the links that you find interesting. Write a brief report on the topics you found to be the most helpful. Submit the report to your instructor.

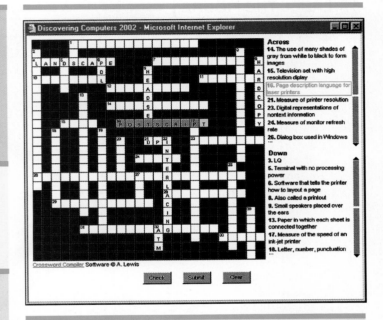

6. Search Sleuth

Click Search Sleuth to learn search techniques that will help make you a research expert. Submit the completed assignment to your instructor.

7. Crossword Puzzle Challenge

Click Crossword Puzzle Challenge. Complete the puzzle to reinforce skills you learned in this chapter. Directions on how to play the game will display. When you are ready to play, click the PLAY button. Submit the completed puzzle to your instructor.

8. Practice Test

Click Practice Test. Answer each question. When completed, enter your name and click the Grade Test button to submit the quiz for grading. Make a note of any missed questions. If required, print a copy to submit to your instructor.

6.38

DISCOVERING
COMPUTERS *2002*

Chapter 1 2 3 4 5 **6** 7 8 9 10 11 12 13 14 15 16 Index **HOME**

Checkpoint

SHELLY
CASHMAN
SERIES.

Student Exercises Web Links   In Summary   Key Terms   Learn It Online   **Checkpoint**   In The Lab   Web Work

Special Features ■ TIMELINE 2002 ■ WWW & E-SKILLS ■ MULTIMEDIA ■ BUYER'S GUIDE 2002 ■ WIRELESS TECHNOLOGY ■ TRENDS 2002 ■ INTERACTIVE LABS ■ TECH NEWS

Web Instructions: To display this page from the Web, start your browser and enter the URL scsite.com/dc2002/ch6/check.htm. Click the links for current and additional information. To experience the animation and interactivity, Shockwave and Flash Player must be installed on your computer (download by clicking here.)

LABEL THE FIGURE | **Instructions:** Identify each step in how a laser printer works.

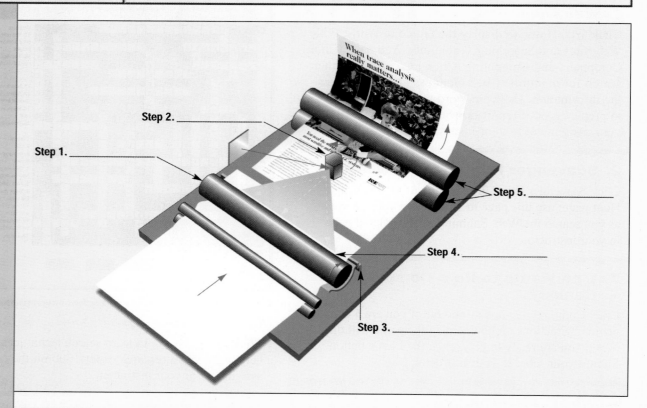

MATCHING | **Instructions:** Match each term from the column on the left with the best description from the column on the right.

_____ 1. thermal
_____ 2. dot-matrix
_____ 3. laser
_____ 4. portable
_____ 5. ink-jet

a. Generates images by pushing electrically heated pins against heat-sensitive paper.
b. Uses heat to transfer colored dye to specially coated paper.
c. An impact printer.
d. Sprays droplets of ink to form characters and graphics.
e. Prints an entire line at one time.
f. Processes and stores the entire page before printing it.
g. Lightweight printer for a mobile user.

Chapter 1 2 3 4 5 6 7 8 9 10 11 12 13 14 15 16 Index **HOME**

6.39

DISCOVERING
COMPUTERS *2002*

Checkpoint

SHELLY
CASHMAN
SERIES.

Student Exercises   Web Links   In Summary   Key Terms   Learn It Online   Checkpoint   In The Lab   Web Work

Special Features   ■ TIMELINE 2002 ■ WWW & E-SKILLS ■ MULTIMEDIA ■ BUYER'S GUIDE 2002 ■ WIRELESS TECHNOLOGY ■ TRENDS 2002 ■ INTERACTIVE LABS ■ TECH NEWS

MULTIPLE CHOICE   Instructions: Select the letter of the correct answers for each of the following questions.

1. Output is data that has been processed into a useful form, called _____ .
   a. ClearType
   b. MPR II
   c. information
   d. gray scaling

2. A display device _____ .
   a. displays in two colors on a black background
   b. is an output device that visually conveys text, graphics, and video information
   c. meets ENERGY STAR guidelines
   d. none of the above

3. A display screen that uses a separate transistor for each color pixel is a(n) _____ .
   a. dual-scan display
   b. passive-matrix display
   c. terminal
   d. active-matrix display

4. A printer produces _____ .
   a. soft copy
   b. hard copy
   c. both hard copy and soft copy
   d. color depth

5. Using _____ , you can have a conversation over the Web.
   a. DLP
   b. EMR
   c. the ENERGY STAR program
   d. Internet telephony

SHORT ANSWER   Instructions: Write a brief answer to each of the following questions.

1. How is an active-matrix display different from a passive-matrix display? _____ What is a gas plasma monitor? _____

2. How do LCD monitors and LCD displays present information on the screen? _____ What is a flat-panel display? _____ What is an electronic book (e-book) and how does it use ClearType? _____

3. What is high-definition television (HDTV)? _____ What advantages does HDTV provide over analog signals? _____

4. What is monitor ergonomics? _____ Why is monitor ergonomics important? _____ What is the ENERGY STAR program? _____

5. How is a dumb terminal different from an intelligent terminal? _____ For what purpose is a point-of-sale terminal used? _____ What is a programmable terminal? _____

WORKING TOGETHER   Instructions: Working with a group of your classmates, complete the following team exercise.

A group of business employees would like to set up a small accounting office, with 10 to 12 employees. They have hired you and your group as consultants to help with the setup. Your primary responsibility is to determine the type of output devices you think they will need within the office. Items to consider are type and number of printers, type and number of display devices, audio and video devices, and whether fax machines, fax modems, and/or multifunction devices are needed. Use the Internet to research information for this project. Prepare a report to share with the class. Include a table listing the pros and cons of the various devices and a short explanation why you selected each device.

In The Lab

SHELLY
CASHMAN
SERIES.

Student Exercises   Web Links   In Summary   Key Terms   Learn It Online   Checkpoint   **In The Lab**   Web Work

Special Features   ■ TIMELINE 2002   ■ WWW & E-SKILLS   ■ MULTIMEDIA   ■ BUYER'S GUIDE 2002   ■ WIRELESS TECHNOLOGY   ■ TRENDS 2002   ■ INTERACTIVE LABS   ■ TECH NEWS

Web Instructions: To display this page from the Web, start your browser and enter the URL scsite.com/dc2002/ch1/lab.htm. Click the links or current and additional information.

About Your Computer

This exercise uses Windows 98 procedures. Your computer probably has more than one output device. To learn about the output devices on your computer, right-click the My Computer icon on the desktop. Click Properties on the shortcut menu. When the System Properties dialog box displays, click the Device Manager tab. If necessary, click View devices by type. Below Computer, a list of hardware device categories displays. What output devices display in the list? Click the plus sign next to each category. What specific output devices in each category are connected to your computer? Close the System Properties dialog box.

Accessibility Options

This exercise uses Windows 98 procedures. The Windows operating system offers several output options for people with hearing or visual impairments. Three of these options are SoundSentry, Show-Sounds, and High Contrast. To find out more about each option, click the Start button, point to Settings on the Start menu, and then click Control Panel on the Settings submenu. Double-click the Accessibility Options icon in the Control Panel window. Click the Sound tab in the Accessibility Properties dialog box. Click the Question Mark button on

the title bar, click SoundSentry, read the information in the pop-up window, and then click the pop-up window to close it. Repeat this process for ShowSounds. Click the Display tab. Click the Question Mark button on the title bar and then click High Contrast. Read the information in the pop-up window, and then click the pop-up window to close it. What is the purpose of each option? Click the Cancel button. Click the Close button to close the Control Panel window.

Self-Portrait

Windows includes a drawing program called Paint. The quality of graphics produced with this program depends on a variety of factors, including the quality of your printer, your understanding of the software, and (to some extent) your artistic talent. In this exercise, you use Paint to create a self-portrait. To access Paint, click the Start button, point to Programs on the Start menu, point to Accessories on the Programs submenu, and then click Paint on the Accessories submenu. When the Paint window opens, the Paint toolbox displays on the left side of the window. Point to a toolbox button to see a tool's name; click a button to use that tool. Use the tools and colors available in Paint to draw a picture of yourself. If you make a mistake, you can click Undo on the Edit menu to undo your most recent action, you can erase part of your picture using

the Eraser/Color Eraser tool, or you can clear the entire picture by clicking Clear Image on the Image menu. When your self-portrait is finished, print it by clicking Print on the File menu. Close Paint.

Magnifier

This exercise uses Windows 2000 procedures. Magnifier is a Windows utility for the visually impaired. To find out about the Magnifier capabilities, click the Start button on the taskbar and then click Help on the Start menu. Click the Index tab in the Windows 2000 window and then type `magnifier` in the Type in the keyword to find text box. Click the overview subentry below the Magnifier entry in the list of topics and then click the Display button. Click Magnifier overview in the Topics Found dialog box and then click the Display button. Read the Help information in the right pane of the Windows 2000 window and answer the following questions:

- How does Magnifier make the screen more readable for the visually impaired?
- What viewing options does Magnifier have?
- What tracking options does Magnifier have?

Click the Close button to close the Windows 2000 window.

DISCOVERING
COMPUTERS *2002*

Chapter 1 2 3 4 5 **6** 7 8 9 10 11 12 13 14 15 16 Index **HOME**

6.41

Web Work

SHELLY
CASHMAN
SERIES.

Student Exercises   Web Links   In Summary   Key Terms   Learn It Online   Checkpoint   In The Lab   Web Work

Special Features   ■ TIMELINE 2002   ■ WWW & E-SKILLS   ■ MULTIMEDIA   ■ BUYER'S GUIDE 2002   ■ WIRELESS TECHNOLOGY   ■ TRENDS 2002   ■ INTERACTIVE LABS   ■ TECH NEWS

Web Instructions: To display this page from the Web, start your browser and enter the URL scsite.com/dc2002/ch6/web.htm. To view At The Movies in exercise 1, RealPlayer must be installed on your computer (download by clicking here). To use the Shelly Cashman Series Setting Up to Print Lab and the Configuring Your Display Lab from the Web, Shockwave and Flash Player must be installed on your computer (download by clicking here).

E-Books

To view the E-Books movie, click the button to the left or click the Play button to the right. Watch the movie, and then complete the exercise by answering the questions below. Electronic books are here. Holding a half-dozen novels, a semester's worth of textbooks, or a library of sales and service manuals, they promise a new world of portability, access, and convenience. Book files can be downloaded easily from the Internet. Prices range from $300 to $500 for the e-book itself, with thousands of titles currently available for $5 to$25 each. The technology and the market for e-books continue to improve in parallel. Better screens and voice recognition already are in the works. What other features might you suggest? What, if anything, do you think inhibits consumer acceptance of this technology?

Shelly Cashman Series Setting Up to Print Lab

Follow the appropriate instructions in Web Work 2 on page 1.47 to start and use the Shelly Cashman Series Setting Up to Print Lab. If you are running from the Web, enter the URL, www.scsite.com/sclabs/menu.htm; or display the Web Work page (see instructions at the top of this page) and then click the button to the left.

Shelly Cashman Series Configuring Your Display Lab

Follow the appropriate instructions in Web Work 2 on page 1.47 to start and use the Shelly Cashman Series Configuring Your Display Lab. If you are running from the Web, enter the URL, www.scsite.com/sclabs/menu.htm; or display the Web Work page (see instructions at the top of this page) and then click the button to the left.

Choosing a Monitor

The monitor is a key component of any new personal computer that you purchase. Everything you see is influenced by the monitor you select. Determining which monitor is best for your individual needs requires some research. Monitors are available in a range of sizes and a variety of resolutions. Click the button to the left for a tutorial on how to select the monitor that is best for your particular requirements.

In the News

Monitors continue to grow clearer and thinner. A newly introduced 50-inch gas plasma display presents near-photographic images and is less than four inches thick. At a cost of $25,000, the monitors probably will be seen first at stadiums, in airports, and as touch screens in stores. Yet, as prices fall, consumers surely will purchase the monitors for HDTV and crystal-clear Internet access. Click the button to the left and then read a news article about a new or improved output device. What is the device? Who manufactures it? How is the output device better than, or different from, earlier devices? Who do you think is most likely to use the device? Why?

6.42

scsite.com/dc2002/ch6/multimedia.htm

MULTIMEDIA
a VIRTUAL experience

Web Instructions: To gain World Wide Web access to additional and up-to-date information regarding this special feature, launch your browser and enter the URL shown at the top of this page.

INTERACTIVE MULTIMEDIA
Changing the Way People Work, Learn, and Play

Watch the Air Force Thunderbirds perform their daring aerobatic feats. Travel to Egypt and view King Tut's tomb. Watch the space shuttle blast into orbit. With multimedia, you can have all these adventures without setting foot outside your house (Figure 1). **Multimedia** refers to using computers to integrate text, graphics, animation, audio, and video into one application.

Unlike television, which combines and presents these media in a predefined order, most multimedia applications are interactive. Users participate directly with the application. **Interactive multimedia** presents information in various ways with a variety of media elements. Users choose the material to view, define the order in which it is presented, and obtain feedback on their actions. The computer accepts input through a keyboard, voice, or pointing device — such as a mouse — and performs an action in response.

Interactivity makes multimedia well suited for applications such as video games, flight simulators, virtual reality, electronic magazines, and educational and training tutorials. The multimedia application shown in Figure 2, for example, allows you to select from numerous geographical locations to learn about diving expeditions into the U.S. National Marine Sanctuaries and other regions.

Figure 1
Today, interactive multimedia plays an increasingly important role in business, industry, education, and entertainment.

MULTIMEDIA APPLICATIONS

A **multimedia application** uses technology for business, education, and entertainment. Businesses use multimedia, for example, in interactive advertisements and for job- and skill-training applications. Teachers use multimedia applications to deliver classroom presentations that enhance student learning.

Students, in turn, use multimedia applications to learn by reading, seeing, hearing, and interacting with the subject content. A wide variety of computer games and other types of entertainment also use multimedia applications.

Another important application of multimedia is to create **simulations**, which are computer-based models of real-life situations. Multimedia simulations often replace costly and sometimes hazardous demonstrations and training in areas such as chemistry, biology, medicine, and aviation.

The following sections provide a more detailed look at the various types of multimedia applications, such as business presentations, computer- and Web-based training, distant learning, classroom and special education, electronic books and references, how-to guides, and newspapers and magazines. These sections also address the use of multimedia for entertainment and edutainment, virtual reality, and kiosks, as well as its importance on the World Wide Web.

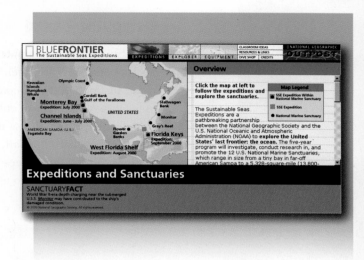

Figure 2
This National Geographic Web site consists of text, graphics, and links to diving expeditions.

Business Presentations

Many businesses and industries use multimedia to create marketing presentations that advertise and sell products. Advertisers, for instance, save time and money by using this software to produce television commercials with unique media effects. Sales representatives also use multimedia in marketing presentations created using presentation graphics software. To deliver these presentations to a large audience, users can connect their computer to a video projector that displays the presentation on a full screen (Figure 3).

Figure 3
Video projectors connected to a computer can display images brightly and clearly. Some projectors are as small and lightweight as a notebook computer.

WORK • LEARN • PLAY

6.44

Computer-Based Training

Students use **computer-based training** (**CBT**) to learn and complete exercises with instructional software, such as the Learn By Series shown in Figure 4. Also called **computer-aided instruction** (**CAI**), computer-based training is popular in business, industry, and schools to teach new skills or to enhance the existing skills of employees, teachers, or students. Athletes, for example, use multimedia computer-based training programs to learn the intricacies of baseball, football, soccer, tennis, and golf, while airlines use multimedia CBT simulations to train employees for emergency situations. Schools use CBT to train teachers in various disciplines and to teach students math, language, and software skills. Interactive CBT software called **courseware** usually is available on CD-ROM or DVD-ROM or shared over a network.

Computer-based training allows for flexible, on-the-spot training. Businesses, for example, can set up corporate training labs, so employees can update their skills without leaving the workplace. Installing CBT software on an employee's computer or on the company network provides even more flexibility by allowing employees to update their job skills at their desks, at home, or while traveling.

Computer-based training provides a unique learning experience because learners receive instant feedback in the form of positive responses for correct answers or actions, additional information on incorrect answers, and immediate scoring and results. Testing and self-diagnostic features allow instructors to verify that a learner has mastered curriculum objectives and identify those who need additional instruction or practice. CBT is especially effective for teaching software skills if the CBT is integrated with the software application because it allows students to practice using the software as they learn.

Some of the many other advantages of CBT over traditional training include self-paced study, reduced training time and costs, and unique multimedia content. Many CBT trainers find they can increase their time helping trainees because computers handle test delivery and grading.

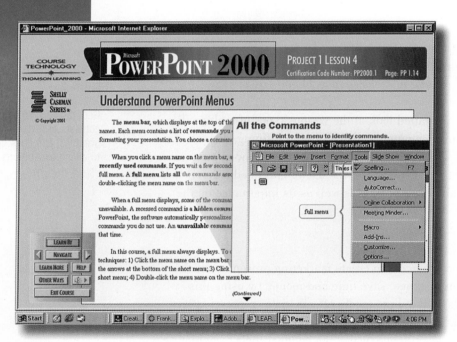

Figure 4
Computer-based training, such as the Learn By Series, is designed so students can choose learning activities that complement their learning styles.

Web-Based Training (WBT) and Distance Learning

Web-based training (**WBT**) is an approach to computer-based training (CBT) that employs the technologies of the Internet and the World Wide Web. As with CBT, Web-based training typically consists of self-directed, self-paced instruction on a topic. Because it is delivered via the Web, however, WBT has the advantage of being able to offer up-to-date content on any type of computer platform.

During the past few years, the number of organizations using Web-based training has exploded. Today, many major corporations in the United States provide employees with some type of Web-based training to teach new skills or to upgrade their current skills.

Web-based training, computer-based training, and other materials often are used as materials for distance learning courses. **Distance learning**, also called **distance education**, is the delivery of education from one location while the learning takes place at other locations. Some national and international corporations also save millions of dollars by using distance learning to train employees, thus eliminating the costs of airfare, hotels, and meals for centralized training sessions.

Many colleges and universities offer numerous distance learning courses, usually in the form of Web-based or Web-enhanced courses (Figure 5). Web-based courses offer many advantages for students who live far from a college campus or work full time, allowing them to complete coursework from home or at any time that fits their schedules. A number of colleges and universities now offer master's and doctorate degree programs in which every required course is taught over the Web.

Web-based training also is available for individuals at home or at work. Today, anyone with access to the Web can take advantage of hundreds of multimedia tutorials offered online. Such tutorials cover a wide range of topics, from how to change a flat tire to creating presentations in Microsoft PowerPoint. Many of these Web sites are free (Figure 6); others ask users to register and pay a fee to take the complete Web-based course.

Classroom and Special Education

Multimedia applications are used to teach students of all ages. From interactive CD-ROMs and DVD-ROMs to presentations, multimedia can be an effective tool for delivering educational material to potential learners, making learning more exciting and interesting. Often, isolated rural schools are leaders in connecting classrooms to the Internet and using multimedia applications to enhance learning.

Figure 5
Many colleges and universities offer some of their classes in a distance learning format.

Figure 6
This Learn2 2torial explains how to install the best sound for your computer system in 10 minutes. The Web site offers practical and straightforward steps for a variety of activities on such diverse topics as obtaining a line of credit and repairing a surfboard ding.

This software makes the learning process more interesting, allows students to perform experiments in a risk-free environment, and provides instant feedback and testing. Virtual dissection of a frog is possible, for example, as shown in Figure 7. CBT also appeals to various learning styles and provides a new type of learning experience. A student using a CBT study guide, for example, could listen to a speaker reciting French vocabulary to help with the pronunciation of difficult words. You can buy many CBT programs such as these on CD-ROM or DVD-ROM from a local retailer or merchant on the Web.

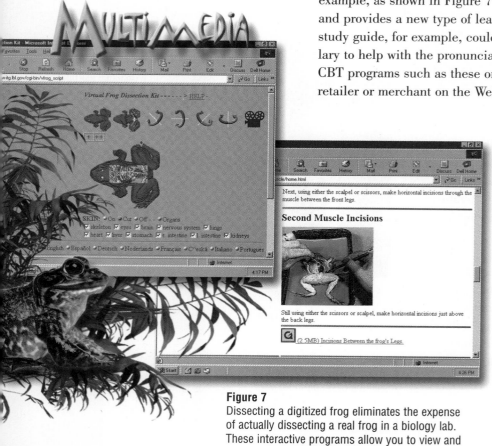

Figure 7
Dissecting a digitized frog eliminates the expense of actually dissecting a real frog in a biology lab. These interactive programs allow you to view and remove organs and to make a movie of your progress. The Web pages are available in various languages.

Research has shown that, when properly evaluated and integrated into teaching at the point of instruction, multimedia applications are a highly effective teaching tool. When using a multimedia application, students become actively involved in the learning process instead of passive recipients of information. Interactive multimedia applications engage students by asking them to define their own paths through an application, which often lead them to explore many related topics.

Multimedia applications also are well suited for both physically impaired and learning disabled students. Students who are visually impaired, for example, benefit from the audio capabilities of multimedia applications, as well as the use of graphics and larger font sizes (Figure 8). Visual materials, such as graphics, animation, and video, also make learning easier for students who are hearing impaired. Many educational software companies offer multimedia products with closed captioning or sign language to enhance the learning experience for hearing-impaired students. The ability of individuals to work, practice, and review at their own pace is a major benefit for the learning disabled.

FIGURE 8
Physically impaired and learning disabled students benefit from multimedia software rich in graphics, animation, and video. These students are using software developed by ClickIt!, which allows them to choose objects on the screen without using a mouse.

Electronic Books

One type of **electronic book** is a digital text that gives the user access to information through links, which often are bold or underlined words. These electronic books have many of the elements of a regular book, including pages of text and graphics. Users generally click icons to turn pages of this type of electronic book. A table of contents, glossary, and index also are available at the click of a button. To display a definition or a graphic, play a sound or a video sequence, or connect to a Web site, users simply can click a link.

A newer type of electronic book, called an **e-book**, uses a small book-sized computer that can hold up to 4,000 pages, or about 10 book's worth of text and small graphics. By clicking a button, users move forward or backward, add notes, and highlight text stored in the e-book. Figure 6-7 on page 6.7 shows a photograph of an e-book. Readers also can view e-books on a small personal computer, such as a Palm™ handheld computer, with the text supplied from various sources. One of these sources is **Project Gutenberg**, which makes thousands of literary and reference books and materials available free to the general public (Figure 9).

Publishers are developing innovative methods of getting authors' words to the public. Some publishers, for example, create purely digital books sold online or in single copies when customers place orders through online booksellers' and organizations' Web sites. These e-books are not sold in bookstores. For example, readers desiring chapters of Stephen King's novel, *The Plant*, ordered them for $1 each through Amazon.com. Other publishers are creating **electronic paper**, which feels like real paper but is coated with electronic ink so that the characters can change. When you finish reading one of these books, you can plug it into a telephone line or a wireless receiver and then download another book.

Electronic Reference Texts

An **electronic reference text**, sometimes called an **e-text**, is a digital version of a reference book, which uses text, graphics, sound, animation, and video to explain a topic or to provide additional information. The multimedia encyclopedia, Microsoft Encarta, for example, includes the complete text of a multivolume encyclopedia. In addition to text-based information, Microsoft Encarta includes thousands of photographs, animations, audio and video clips, and detailed illustrations (Figure 10). This array of multimedia information is accessible via menus and links.

FIGURE 9
Geoffrey Chaucer's
Canterbury Tales is among the thousands of public domain reference and literary works available from Project Gutenberg. One new book is added to the Web site almost daily.

FIGURE 10
Microsoft Encarta is a popular multimedia encyclopedia that includes graphics, audio, video, and Web links.

Many other reference texts are used in a variety of fields and professions (Figure 11). Health and medicine are two areas in which multimedia reference texts play an important role. Instead of using volumes of books, health professionals and students rely on reference CD-ROMs and DVD-ROMs for information, illustrations, animations, and photographs on hundreds of health and first-aid topics.

ELECTRONIC REFERENCE TEXTS

Name	Publisher	URL	Description
American Heritage Talking Dictionary	Compton's NewMedia, Inc.	www.comptons.com	Uses a human-sounding voice to pronounce more than 90,000 words; contains more than 200,000 definitions, an integrated thesaurus, and 3,000 images, photographs, maps, and flags.
Compton's® Encyclopedia	Compton's NewMedia, Inc.	www.comptons.com	Features more than 40,000 articles, interactive science activities, monthly updates via the Internet, 360-degree views and virtual tours, more than 8,000 photos, and 100 videos, animations, and slide shows.
Encarta Encyclopedia Deluxe	Microsoft	microsoft.com	Contains more than 42,000 articles, 170 videos and animations, a natural language search function, a dynamic timeline, virtual tours, 360-degree views, and text-to-speech capabilities.
Library of the Future	AbleSoft	kidsoft.com	Contains descriptions of more than 5,000 literary works, authors' biographies, and film clips.
American Sign Language for Kids	Multimedia 2000	m-2k.com	Uses text, QuickTime video, animations, and illustrations to teach 2,600 signs, and includes learning games and lessons on fingerspelling.

For an updated list of electronic reference text Web sites, enter the URL at the top of this page.

FIGURE 11 These e-texts use multimedia to clarify topics and supply additional information on thousands of subjects.

How-To Guides

Numerous interactive multimedia applications are available to help individuals in their daily lives. These multimedia applications fall into the broad category of how-to guides. **How-to guides** are multimedia applications that include step-by-step instructions and interactive demonstrations to teach practical new skills (Figure 12). Much like the computer-based training applications used by businesses, how-to guides allow users to acquire and test new skills in a risk-free environment. The skills learned with a how-to guide, however, usually are oriented toward personal enrichment, rather than workplace skills.

How-to guides can help with activities such as buying a home or a car, designing a garden, planning a vacation, improving a home, and repairing a car or computer. The CD-ROM how-to-guides listed in Figure 13 show the wide variety of instructional guides. Multimedia how-to guides also are available on DVD-ROM and the Web.

FIGURE 12
Web users can learn American Sign Language via the HandSpeak online dictionary. This Web site features video clips of individuals signing words, including words with several definitions.

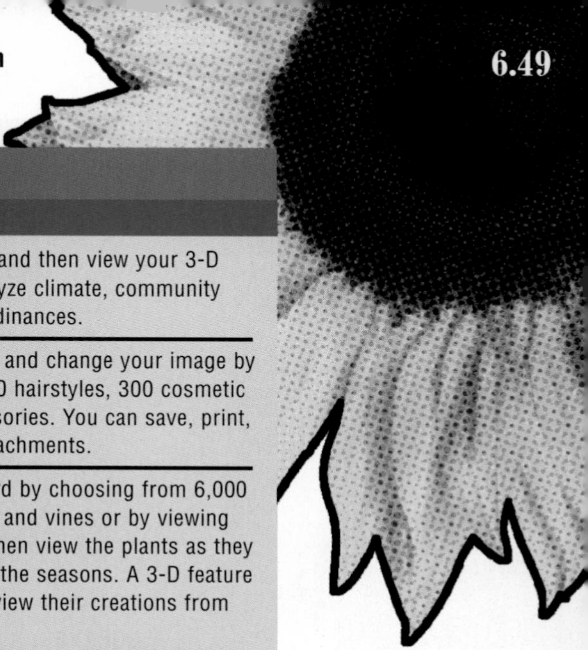

CD-ROM HOW-TO GUIDES

Name	Publisher	URL	Description
3D Home Architect®	Mattel Interactive™	www.mattelinteractive.com	Customize floor plans and then view your 3-D design. The plans analyze climate, community growth, and zoning ordinances.
Cosmopolitan™ Virtual Makeover™	Mattel Interactive™	www.mattelinteractive.com	Input your photograph and change your image by experimenting with 500 hairstyles, 300 cosmetic colors, and 200 accessories. You can save, print, and send as e-mail attachments.
Complete LandDesigner 3D	SierraHome Network	sierra.com/sierrahome	Design a garden or yard by choosing from 6,000 trees, shrubs, flowers, and vines or by viewing sample gardens, and then view the plants as they grow and change with the seasons. A 3-D feature lets virtual gardeners view their creations from any angle.
MasterCook Deluxe	SierraHome Network	sierra.com/sierrahome	Prepare one of 5,000 dishes based on nutritional value and ingredients on hand. Watch instructional videos, and adjust the portions to the number of servings needed.
Teach Yourself PC Maintenance	Learn2.com, Inc.	learn2.com	Learn such computer concepts as motherboard ports, the OS and processor, hardware, installing SIMMs, modem standards, baud vs. bit rates, maintenance tools, keyboard cleaning, and the ScanDisk utility from four interactive multimedia CD-ROM tutorials.

For an updated list of CD-ROM how-to guide Web sites, enter the URL at the top of this page.

FIGURE 13
These how-to guides teach useful skills by using videos, interactive demonstrations, and animations.

Newspapers and Magazines

A **multimedia newspaper** and a **multimedia magazine** are digital versions of a newspaper or magazine distributed on CD-ROM, DVD-ROM, or via the World Wide Web. Today, many print-based magazines and newspapers have companion Web sites that provide multimedia versions of some or all of their printed content (Figure 14). An **electronic magazine**, or **e-zine**, is a digital publication available via the Web (Figure 15 on the next page).

Multimedia newspapers and magazines usually include the sections and articles found in their print-based versions, including departments, editorials, and more. Unlike printed publications, however, multimedia magazines and newspapers use many types of media to convey information. Audio and video clips, for example, can showcase recent album or movie releases, and animations can depict weather patterns or election results.

MULTIMEDIA MAGAZINES AND NEWSPAPERS

Name	URL
Independent Newspapers (South Africa)	iol.co.za
Kyodo News (Tokyo)	home.kyodo.co.jp
National Geographic	nationalgeographic.com
Newsweek	newsweek.msnbc.com
The Daily Telegraph (London)	www.telegraph.co.uk
The Globe and Mail (Canada)	globeandmail.ca
The New York Times	nytimes.com
The Wall Street Journal	wsj.com
Time	time.com
USA TODAY	usatoday.com
Washington Post	washingtonpost.com

For an updated list of multimedia magazine and newspaper Web sites, enter the URL at the top of this page.

FIGURE 14
Multimedia magazines and newspapers from various countries use video and audio clips, animations, and other interactive multimedia tools to bring the world to personal computers.

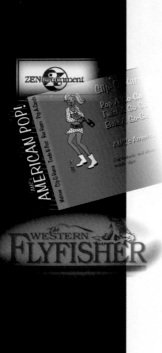

E-ZINES		
Name	URL	Description
AMC's American Pop!	ampop.com	Programming devoted to vintage music, movies, toys, fashions, and pop culture. Shockwave and Flash are used extensively.
OS/2 eZine	www.os2ezine.com	Articles and forums focusing on IBM's OS/2 multitasking operating system.
The Western Flyfisher	westernflyfisher.com	Numerous audio and video clips for flyfishing enthusiasts.
WebReference.com	webreference.com	Reference material on a wide variety of Web topics, including effective authoring, browsing, coding HTML, and designing Web sites.
ZENtertainment	zentertainment.com	Latest entertainment news, including sections for music, TV, movies, toys, comics, and food.

For an updated list of e-zines Web sites, enter the URL at the top of this page.

FIGURE 15
E-zines are produced for the Web and often contain multimedia applications.

Entertainment and Edutainment

Multimedia combines the media elements of television and interactivity, thus making it ideal for entertainment. Multimedia computer games, for example, use a combination of graphics, audio, and video to create a realistic and entertaining game situation. Often the game simulates a real or fictitious world, in which users play the role of a character and have direct control of what happens in the game. The music industry also sells interactive multimedia applications on CD-ROM and DVD-ROM. Some interactive music CD-ROMs, for example, allow budding musicians to play musical instruments along with their favorite musician, read about the musician's life and interests, and even create their own versions of popular songs. Like interactive games, these applications give users a character role and put them in control of the application (Figure 16).

ENTERTAINMENT APPLICATIONS			
Name	Publisher	URL	Description
Backyard Baseball	Humongous Entertainment	humongous.com	Select players from 30 Major League Baseball teams or create your own team colors, ballpark, and strategy. Play online with other Windows users.
Dogz®	Mattel Interactive™	www.mattelinteractive.com	Use voice recognition to train your Dogz to sit, fetch, or roll over; create custom scenes with the Play Scene Editor.
Motocross Madness	Microsoft	microsoft.com	Perform stunts on your motorbike while you race up to eight opponents online via the MSN Gaming Zone.
RollerCoaster Tycoon™	Hasbro Interactive	hasbro-interactive.com	Use 14 styles to construct roller coasters with accurate motion dynamics and physics principles. Analyze their excitement and nausea ratings.
The Sims	Electronic Arts	thesims.com	Develop characters in a neighborhood, build their homes, and display your creations on the World Wide Web with these open-ended games.

For an updated list of entertainment application Web sites, enter the URL at the top of this page.

FIGURE 16
Entertainment applications, rich in multimedia content, provide fun and relaxation for children and adults.

Other multimedia applications are used for **edutainment**, which is an experience meant to be both educational and entertaining. Many edutainment CD-ROMs and DVD-ROMs provide content for individuals of all ages, while others are created specifically to teach children in a fun and appealing way. Some of these edutainment applications are listed in Figure 17.

EDUTAINMENT APPLICATIONS

Name	Publisher	URL	Description
Carmen Sandiego	Mattel Interactive	www.mattelinteractive.com	Discover geography by searching for criminals in various locales using foreign languages and Internet links to maps and satellite pictures. The police chief gives updates using real-time video.
James Cameron's Titanic Explorer	20th Century Fox	foxinteractive.com/games/titanicexplorer	Witness James Cameron's diving expedition of the Titanic and use interactive 3-D models to examine the ship and the wreck. View a computer simulation of how the ship sank, and then browse through more than 1,200 pages of survivors' testimony.
Kaplan GMAT, LSAT, and GRE™	Encore Software	encoresoftware.com	View personalized interactive lessons and links to graduate schools.
Reader Rabbit	Mattel Interactive	www.mattelinteractive.com	Teaches young children problem solving, decision making, and logic skills; learning technology monitors performance, offers help, and prints reports.
The New Way Things Work	DK Multimedia	www.dk.com	Discover how more than 150 machines work by viewing animations, illustrations, and videos.

For an updated list of edutainment application Web sites, enter the URL at the top of this page.

FIGURE 17
Edutainment applications offer adults and children both education and entertainment.

Virtual Reality

Virtual reality (VR) is the use of a computer to create an artificial environment that appears and feels like a real environment and allows users to explore a space and manipulate the surroundings (Figure 18). In its simplest form, a virtual reality application displays a three-dimensional view of a place or object, such as a landscape, building, molecule, or red blood cell, which users can explore. Architects use this type of software to show clients how a building will look after a construction or remodeling project.

In more advanced forms, VR software users wear specialized headgear, body suits, and gloves to enhance the experience of the artificial environment (Figure 19). The headgear displays the artificial environment in front of both eyes. The body suit and the gloves sense motion and direction, allowing users to move, pick up, and hold virtually displayed items. Experts predict that eventually the body suits will provide tactile feedback, so users can experience the touch and feel of the virtual world.

Your first encounter with VR likely will be a virtual reality game such as a flight simulator. In these games, special

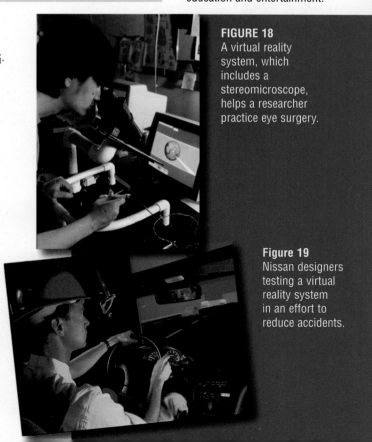

FIGURE 18
A virtual reality system, which includes a stereomicroscope, helps a researcher practice eye surgery.

Figure 19
Nissan designers testing a virtual reality system in an effort to reduce accidents.

FIGURE 20
The U.S. Capitol Virtual Tours Web site give visitors 360-degree views of the Senate and House of Representative chambers, also included are details about objects found in those rooms and historical information.

FIGURE 21
Lexus is one of the auto manufacturers that allows Internet users to build a specific car, including selecting colors and accessories, and then price their designed vehicle. Nearly one-half of U.S. households that buy vehicles turn to the Internet to research their purchases.

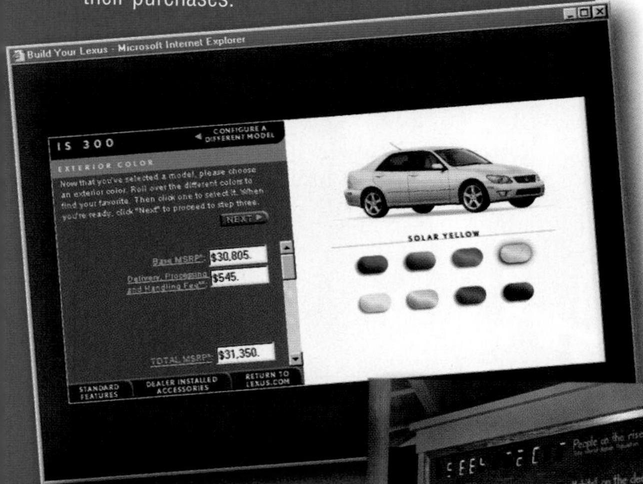

visors allow you to see the computer-generated environment. As you walk around the game's electronic landscape, sensors in the surrounding game machine record your movements and change your view of the landscape accordingly. You also might use a Web-based VR application developed using **virtual reality modeling language (VRML)**. Web sites, such as the U.S. Capitol Web site shown in Figure 20, use virtual reality to allow you to take tours of a city, view real estate for sale, or interact with local attractions.

Some companies use VR for more practical, commercial applications, as well. Automobile companies, for example, have created virtual showrooms in which customers can view the exterior and interior of vehicles (Figure 21). In addition, airplane manufacturers are using virtual prototypes to test new models and shorten product design time. Telecommunications firms use personal computer-based VR applications for employee training. As computing power and the use of the Web increase, practical applications of VR will continue to emerge in education, business, and entertainment.

Kiosks

A **kiosk** is a computerized information or reference center that allows users to select various options to browse through or find specific information. A typical kiosk is a self-service structure equipped with computer hardware and software. Kiosks often use touch screen monitors or keyboards for input devices and contain all of the data and information needed for the application stored directly on the computer.

Kiosks often provide information in public places where visitors or customers have common questions. Locations such as shopping centers, airports, museums, and libraries, for example, use kiosks to provide information on available services, product and exhibit locations, maps, and other information (Figure 22). Kiosks also are used for marketing. A kiosk might contain an interactive multimedia application that allows you to try options and explore scenarios related to a product or service. For example, you might be able to try different color combinations or take short quizzes to determine which product best meets your needs. The interactive multimedia involves customers with the product, thus increasing the likelihood of purchase.

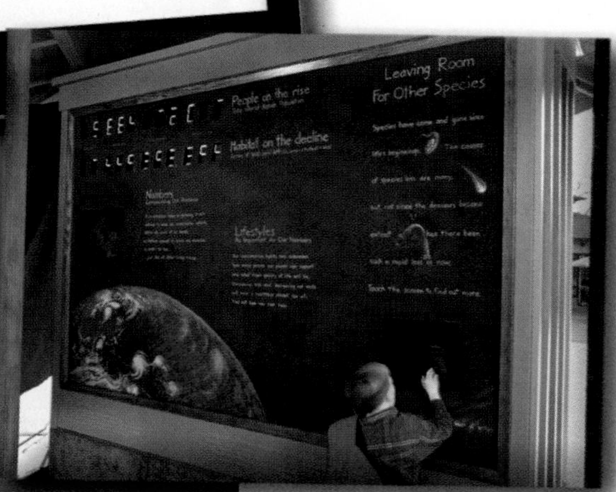

FIGURE 22
Seattle's Woodland Park Zoo features an interactive kiosk for its *Touch the Earth . . . Gently* exhibit. The 11-by-9-foot exhibit contains a laser disc player, touch screen monitor, and counters that calculate the net gain in world population and the net loss of wild animals' habitats.

The World Wide Web

Multimedia applications also play an important role on the **World Wide Web**, which is the part of the Internet that supports multimedia. In fact, much of the information on the Web today relies on multimedia. Using multimedia brings a Web page to life, increases the types of information available on the Web, expands the Web's potential uses, and makes the Internet a more entertaining place to explore. As described in Chapter 2, the Web uses many types of media to deliver information and enhance a user's Web experience (Figure 23). Graphics and animations reinforce text-based content and provide updated information. Online radio stations, movie rental Web sites, and games use audio and video clips to provide movie and music clips or to deliver the latest news.

Many of the multimedia applications previously described, including computer- and Web-based training, newspapers, e-zines, games, and virtual reality, are deliverable via the Web. New multimedia authoring software packages include tools for creating and delivering multimedia applications via the World Wide Web. Some of these authoring software packages allow users to create applications in the Windows environment and then convert them to HTML and Java for Web use.

DEVELOPING MULTIMEDIA APPLICATIONS

You can create a multimedia application using a variety of software applications. With PowerPoint, for example, you can create a presentation that combines text, graphics, animation, and audio and video clips (Figure 24). Developing these applications follows a standard process with several phases. While some

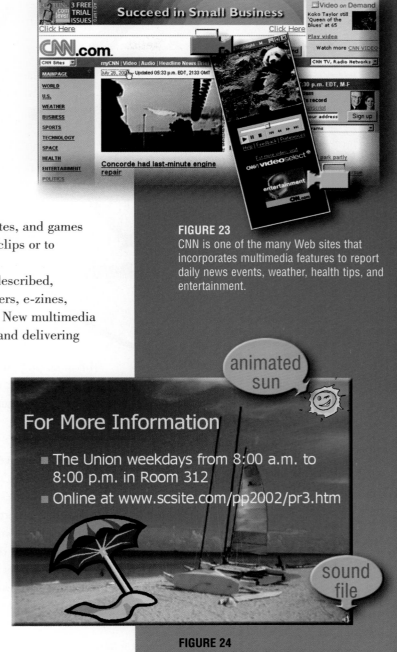

FIGURE 23
CNN is one of the many Web sites that incorporates multimedia features to report daily news events, weather, health tips, and entertainment.

FIGURE 24
This PowerPoint slide features an animated sun and a sound file with the crash of waves.

6.54

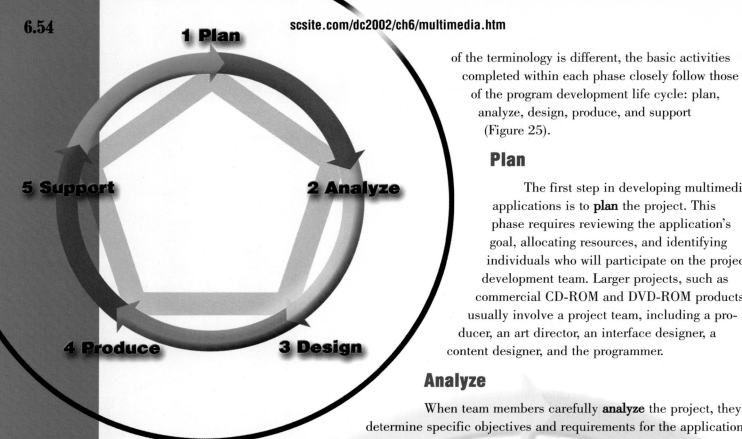

FIGURE 25
Developing
effective
multimedia
presentations
involves a five-
step process.

of the terminology is different, the basic activities completed within each phase closely follow those of the program development life cycle: plan, analyze, design, produce, and support (Figure 25).

Plan

The first step in developing multimedia applications is to **plan** the project. This phase requires reviewing the application's goal, allocating resources, and identifying individuals who will participate on the project development team. Larger projects, such as commercial CD-ROM and DVD-ROM products, usually involve a project team, including a producer, an art director, an interface designer, a content designer, and the programmer.

Analyze

When team members carefully **analyze** the project, they determine specific objectives and requirements for the application. For small projects, the developer may play a variety of roles, which may include content developer, interface designer, and programmer. For larger projects with specific learning objectives, analysis is extremely important.

Design

Once basic requirements have been determined, the **design** phase begins. A vital tool for the project team is a flowchart, or map, which includes all of the various media elements in the application and serves as a blueprint to which the project team or individual developer can refer. Another important tool is the **project script**, which provides detailed information to supplement the flowchart and records how the various media elements will be used in the production. Screen design is another crucial part of designing an effective multimedia application. The colors and layout used for individual screens greatly influence the overall effect of the finished product.

Produce

Project team members **produce** the multimedia application by creating the various media elements used in the application and combining them using multimedia authoring software. Artists develop original graphics and animations using drawing and illustration software, add photographs by using a digital camera, a PhotoCD, or a scanner, and record digital video and audio clips using recording devices and a video capture or sound card. Authoring begins when they have obtained all of the media elements. Finally, the developer tests the program to verify it performs according to design specifications.

Support

During the **support** phase, the developer reviews the project to ensure all objectives have been met. In addition, errors are identified and corrected. At this point, plans may be made to modify or enhance the application with additional features. If so, the cycle begins again at the planning phase.

Multimedia Authoring Software

Developing an interactive multimedia application involves using **multimedia authoring software** to combine text, graphics, animation, audio, and video into an application. Authoring programs also allow you to design interactive areas on the screen that respond to user input. Once various media elements are added to the program, the multimedia authoring software assigns relationships and actions to elements. The programs also help create a structure that lets the user navigate through the material presented.

One of the more important activities of the production phase of multimedia development is selecting the multimedia authoring software package. Factors to consider when selecting a multimedia authoring software package are quality of application developed, ease of use, clear documentation, responsiveness of vendor's service and technical support, compatibility with other applications, ease of programming, functionality, and system requirements for both user and developer.

Most popular authoring packages share similar features and are capable of creating similar applications. The major differences exist in the ease of use for development. Four popular multimedia authoring packages — Authorware, Director, Flash, and ToolBook — are described in Figure 26. Developers can use these products to create spectacular Web sites.

FIGURE 26
These popular multimedia authoring software packages allow users to create interactive elements that respond to user input.

MULTIMEDIA AUTHORING SOFTWARE			
Product	Publisher	URL	Use
Authorware	Macromedia	macromedia.com	Uses flowchart metaphor to build a multimedia application.
Director	Macromedia	macromedia.com	Uses a theater or movie production metaphor to build a multimedia application. Three integrated windows — Cast, Score, and Stage — are used to create and sequence text and other media elements.
Flash	Macromedia	macromedia.com	Creates dazzling Web sites that display across a user's entire screen — regardless of monitor size — and include input, interactivity, sounds, music, graphics, and animations.
ToolBook	click2learn.com	click2learn.com	Uses a graphical user interface and an object-oriented approach to design applications using basic objects such as buttons, fields, graphics, backgrounds, and pages.

For an updated list of multimedia authoring software Web sites, enter the URL at the top of this page.

FEATURE SUMMARY

Interactive multimedia distributed on CD-ROM, DVD-ROM, and via the World Wide Web influences people's everyday experiences in the workplace, at school, and in recreational activities. In today's office, employees and clients prepare and view multimedia business presentations. Using drill-and-practice or exploration activities, learners of all ages are able to define their own learning paths, investigate topics in depth, and get immediate feedback. Students gain knowledge of the world in and out of the classroom using computer-based training, Web-based training, distance learning, electronic books and reference texts, how-to guides, virtual reality, and multimedia magazines and newspapers. Entertainment and edutainment interactive multimedia programs enrich the way people relax and have fun. Interacting with well-designed multimedia applications is a positive experience and engages and challenges users, thus encouraging them to think independently and creatively.

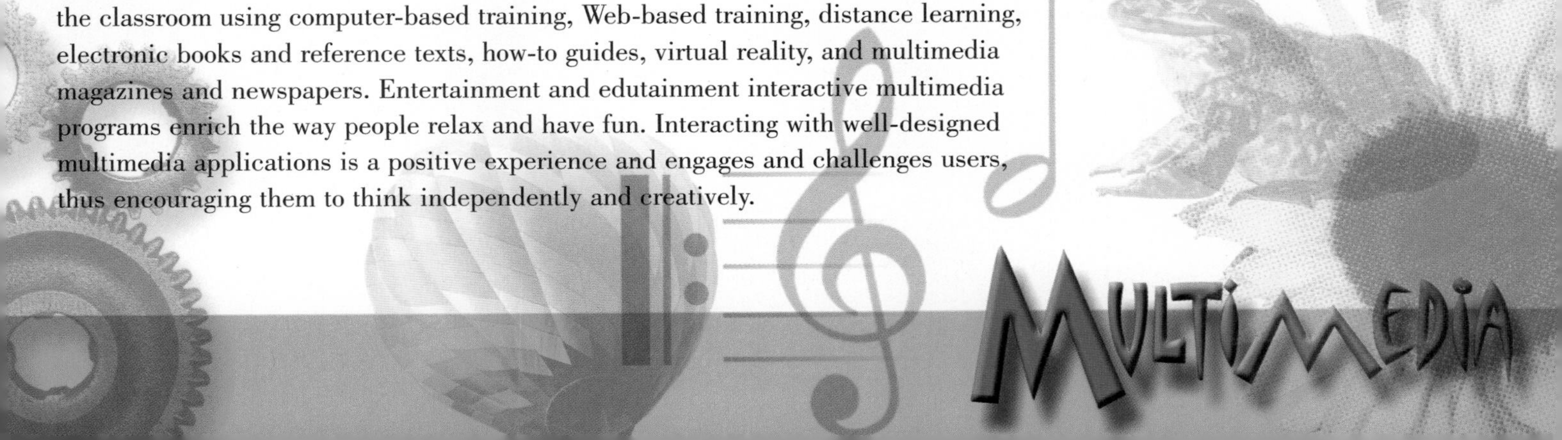

CHAPTER 7

Storage

Wedding bells are ringing. It is just two weeks until your big day! With all your wedding arrangements confirmed, the reception planned, and the honeymoon booked, you are happily humming the tune... "Going to the chapel and we're gonna get married."

Of the 247 invited family members and friends, 192 guests have responded, yes. Most of the regrets are guests who live too far away and cannot afford airfare and hotel expenses.

Even though you knew this would happen, it is disappointing that anyone must miss this special occasion. That is why you ordered digital photographs as part of your wedding package. At the end of your big day, the photographer will present you with a memory card containing at least 30 digital photographs of the wedding. You plan to post these photographs to your Internet hard drive before you leave for your Caribbean cruise.

For this very reason, your wedding invitations requested a reply with your guests' e-mail addresses. With the response cards in hand, you sit down at the computer and e-mail the Web address of your Internet hard drive to all those on your guest list. As you finish the first e-mail message, you hum, "Today's the day we'll say I do."

7.2

CHAPTER 7 STORAGE

MEMORY VERSUS STORAGE

Storage refers to the media on which data, instructions, and information are kept, as well as the devices that record and retrieve these items (Figure 7-1). It is important you understand the difference between storage and memory, which was discussed in Chapter 4. The next section reviews the definition of memory and then discusses basic storage concepts.

OBJECTIVES

After completing this chapter, you will be able to:

- Differentiate between storage and memory
- Identify various types of storage media and storage devices
- Explain how a floppy disk stores data
- Identify the advantages of using high-capacity disks
- Describe how a hard disk organizes data
- Identify the advantages of using an Internet hard drive
- Explain how a compact disc stores data
- Understand how to care for a compact disc
- Differentiate between CD-ROMs, CD-RWs, and DVD-ROMs
- Identify the uses of tape
- Understand how an enterprise storage system works
- Explain how to use PC Cards and other miniature storage media
- Identify uses of microfilm and microfiche

Figure 7-1 Data, instructions, and information are stored on a variety of storage media.

floppy disk

miniature mobile storage media

PC Card

tape library

Memory

During processing, the processor places instructions to be executed and data needed by those instructions into memory. Memory is a temporary holding place for data and instructions. Sometimes called primary storage, memory consists of one or more chips on the motherboard or some other circuit board in the computer.

The two basic types of memory are volatile and nonvolatile. When the computer's power is turned off, **volatile memory** loses its contents. Almost all RAM is volatile.

Nonvolatile memory, by contrast, does not lose its contents when power is removed from the computer. For example, when a manufacturer permanently records data and instructions onto a non-volatile ROM chip, the contents of the chip remain intact when you turn off the computer.

hard disk

RAID

o • Pictures • Text • Graphics • Audio • Video
res • Text • Graphics • Audio • Video • Pictures
Video • Pictures • Text
res • Text • Graphics
ext • Graphics • Audio
raphics • Audio • Video
res • Text • Graphics • Audio • Video • Pictures
• Graphics • Audio • Video • Pictures • Text
cs • Audio • Video • Pictures • Text • Graphics
lio • Video • Pictures • Text • Graphics • Audio

Storage

CD-ROM, DVD-ROM, or CD-RW

tape backup

CD-ROM jukeboxes

Storage

Storage, also called **secondary storage**, **auxiliary storage**, **permanent storage**, or **mass storage**, holds items such as data, instructions, and information for future use.

Think of storage as a filing cabinet that holds file folders, and memory as the top of your desk. When you want to work with a file, you remove it from the filing cabinet (storage) and place it on your desk (memory). When you are finished with the file, you remove it from your desk (memory) and return it to the filing cabinet (storage).

Storage is nonvolatile. Items in storage remain intact even when power is removed from the computer (Figure 7-2). A **storage medium** (media is the plural) is the physical material on which a computer keeps data, instructions, and information. Examples of storage media are floppy disks, hard disks, compact discs, and tape. A **storage device** is the computer hardware that records and retrieves items to and from a storage medium.

Storage devices serve as a source of input when they read and a source of output when they write. **Reading** is the process of transferring data, instructions, and information from a storage medium into memory. **Writing** is the process of transferring these items from memory to a storage medium.

The speed of a disk storage device is defined by its access time. **Access time** is the amount of time it takes the device to locate an item on a disk. The access time of storage devices is slow, compared with memory. Memory devices access items in billionths of a second (nanoseconds). Storage devices, by contrast, access items in thousandths of a second (milliseconds).

Capacity is the number of bytes (characters) a storage medium can hold. Figure 7-3 lists the terms

AN ILLUSTRATION OF VOLATILITY

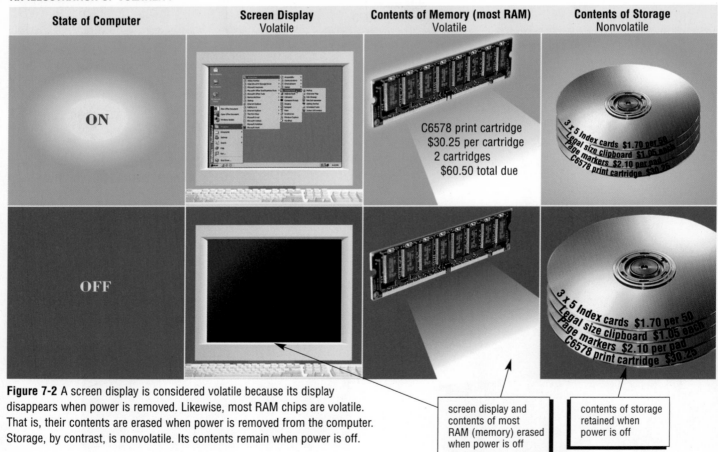

Figure 7-2 A screen display is considered volatile because its display disappears when power is removed. Likewise, most RAM chips are volatile. That is, their contents are erased when power is removed from the computer. Storage, by contrast, is nonvolatile. Its contents remain when power is off.

STORAGE TERMS

Storage Term	Abbreviation	Number of Bytes
Kilobyte	KB	1 thousand
Megabyte	MB	1 million
Gigabyte	GB	1 billion
Terabyte	TB	1 trillion
Petabyte	PB	1 quadrillion

Figure 7-3 The capacity of a storage device is measured by the amount of bytes it can hold.

manufacturers use to define the capacity of storage media. A typical floppy disk can store up to 1.44 MB of data (approximately 1.4 million bytes) and a typical hard disk stores 30 GB of data (approximately 30 billion bytes).

Storage requirements among users vary greatly. Small office home office (SOHO) users might need to store a relatively small amount of data. A field sales representative might have a list of names, addresses, and telephone numbers of 50 customers, which he or she uses on a daily basis. Such a list might require no more than a few thousand bytes of

storage. Large business users, such as banks, libraries, or insurance companies, often process data for millions of customers and thus might need to store trillions of bytes worth of historical or financial records in their archives.

Numerous types of storage media and storage devices exist to meet a variety of users' needs. Figure 7-4 shows how different types of storage media and memory compare in terms of relative cost and speed. This chapter discusses the storage media in the pyramid, as well as other media.

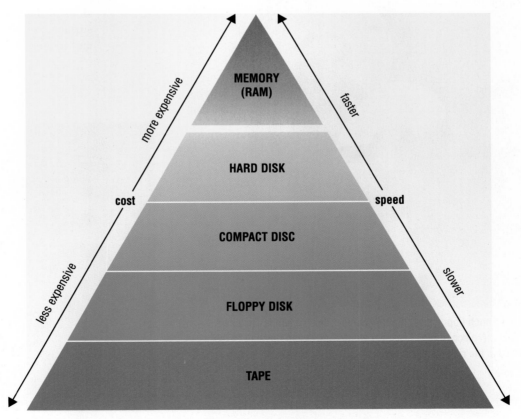

Figure 7-4 This pyramid shows how different types of storage media and memory compare in terms of relative cost and speed. Memory is faster than storage, but is expensive and not practical for all storage requirements. Storage is less expensive but is slower than memory.

FLOPPY DISKS

A **floppy disk**, or **diskette**, is a portable, inexpensive storage medium that consists of a thin, circular, flexible plastic disk with a magnetic coating enclosed in a square-shaped plastic shell (Figure 7-5). In the early 1970s, IBM introduced the floppy disk as a new type of storage. These 8-inch wide disks were known as floppies because they had flexible plastic covers. The next generation of floppies looked much the same, but they were only 5.25-inches wide.

Today, the standard floppy disk is 3.5-inches wide and has a rigid plastic outer cover. Although the exterior of the 3.5-inch disk is not floppy, users still refer to them as floppy disks.

A floppy disk is a portable storage medium. When discussing a storage medium, the term portable means you can remove the medium from one computer and carry it to another computer. For example, most personal computers have a floppy disk drive, in which you insert and remove a floppy disk (Figure 7-6).

Floppy Disk Drives

A **floppy disk drive (FDD)** is a device that can read from and write on a floppy disk. Desktop personal computers and many notebook computers have a floppy disk drive installed inside the system unit. Some notebook computers have a removable floppy disk drive, where you can remove the entire drive and replace it with another type of drive or device.

Computers with one floppy disk drive refer to it as *drive A*. Computers that have two floppy disk drives designate the second one as *drive B*.

On a 3.5-inch floppy disk, a piece of metal called the **shutter** covers an opening in the rigid plastic shell (see Figure 7-5). When you insert a floppy disk into a floppy disk drive, the drive slides the shutter to the side to expose a portion of both sides of the floppy disk's recording surface. Never open the disk's shutter and touch its recording surface.

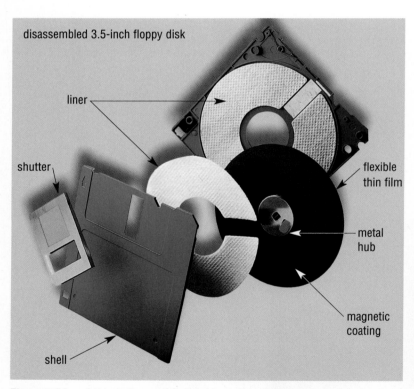

Figure 7-5 In a 3.5-inch floppy disk, the thin circular flexible film is enclosed between two liners. A piece of metal called a shutter covers an opening to the recording surface in the rigid plastic shell.

Figure 7-6 On a personal computer, you insert and remove a floppy disk from a floppy disk drive.

On the front of most floppy disk drives is a light emitting diode (LED) that lights up when the drive is accessing the floppy disk. You should not remove a floppy disk when the LED is lit.

The read/write head in the floppy disk drive is the mechanism that actually reads items from or writes items on the floppy disk. Figure 7-7 illustrates the steps for reading from and writing on a floppy disk. The average time it takes a current floppy disk drive to locate an item on a disk is 84 milliseconds, or approximately 1/12 of a second.

Sometimes, a floppy disk drive will malfunction when it is attempting to access a floppy disk and will display an error message on the screen. If the same error occurs with multiple floppy disks, the read/write heads in the floppy disk drive may have a buildup of dust or dirt. In this case, you can try cleaning the read/write heads using a floppy disk cleaning kit.

To read from or write on a floppy disk, a floppy disk drive must support that floppy disk's density. **Density** is the number of bits in an area on a storage medium. A disk with a higher density has more bits in an area and thus has a larger storage capacity. Most disks today are high density (HD). To access an HD floppy disk, you must have an HD floppy disk drive. An HD floppy disk has a capacity of 1.44 MB. That is, an HD floppy disk can hold up to approximately 1.44 million bytes.

Floppy disk drives are **downward compatible**, which means they recognize and can use earlier media. Floppy disk drives are not **upward compatible**, and thus cannot recognize newer media. For example, a lower-density floppy disk drive cannot read from or write on a high-density floppy disk.

TECHNOLOGY TRAILBLAZER

AL **SHUGART**

Al Shugart has more than 45 years experience in the technology industry.

In 1951, Shugart joined IBM as a customer engineer. In 1955, he became part of a product development program that would have a profound impact on the computer industry. As the company's product manager for random-access memory projects worldwide, Shugart supervised a team in 1967 responsible for developing a removable, portable data storage device. This effort led to the construction of an 8-inch, read-only disk and later to the first read-write disk drive. Shugart left IBM in 1969 and spent the next four years as vice president of product development for Memorex. He founded Shugart Associates in 1973 with the mission to popularize the 8-inch disk drive and mass produce it for the commercial market. The following year, Shugart left the company bearing his name and worked as a private consultant to the technology industry until 1979, when he founded Seagate Technology.

For more information on Al Shugart, visit the Discovering Computers 2002 People Web page (**scsite.com/dc2002/people.htm**) and click Al Shugart.

Figure 7-7 HOW A FLOPPY DISK DRIVE WORKS

Step 1:
When you insert the floppy disk into the drive, the shutter moves to the side to expose the recording surface on the disk.

Step 2:
When you initiate a disk access, the circuit board on the drive sends signals to control movement of the read/write heads and the disk.

Step 6:
The read/write heads read data from and write data on the floppy disk.

Step 5:
A motor positions the read/write heads over the correct location on the recording surface of the disk.

Step 4:
A motor causes the floppy disk to spin.

Step 3:
If disk access is a write instruction, the circuit board verifies whether the disk can be written to or not.

Web Link
For more information on floppy disks, visit the Discovering Computers 2002 Chapter 7 WEB LINK page (**scsite.com/dc2002/ch7/weblink.htm**) and click Floppy Disks.

How a Floppy Disk Stores Data

A floppy disk is a type of magnetic media. **Magnetic media** uses magnetic patterns to store items such as data, instructions, and information on a disk's surface. Most magnetic disks are read/write storage media. This enables you to access (read) data from and place (write) data on a magnetic disk any number of times, just as you can with an audiocassette tape.

A floppy disk stores data in tracks and sectors (Figure 7-8). A **track** is a narrow recording band that forms a full circle on the surface of the disk. The disk's storage locations consist of pie-shaped sections, which break the tracks into small arcs called **sectors**. A sector can store up to 512 bytes of data. A typical floppy disk stores data on both sides of the disk, has 80 tracks on each side of the recording surface, and 18 sectors per track.

You can compute a disk's storage capacity by multiplying together the number of sides on the disk, the number of tracks on the disk, the number of sectors per track, and the number of bytes in a sector. For example, the formula for a high-density 3.5-inch floppy disk is as follows: 2 (sides) x 80 (tracks) x 18 (sectors per track) x 512 (bytes per sector) = 1,474,560 bytes (Figure 7-9). Some disks store system files in some tracks, which means the available capacity on a disk may be less than the total possible capacity.

Given the actual number of available bytes on a floppy disk (1,474,560), you may question why manufacturers call them 1.44 MB disks. The 1.44 MB is not a rounding of the 1,474,560. Instead, it is a result of doubling 720 MB, which is the capacity of a low-density 3.5-inch floppy disk.

For reading and writing purposes, sectors are grouped into clusters. A **cluster** is the smallest unit of disk space that stores data. Each cluster, also called an **allocation unit**, consists of two to eight sectors (the number varies depending on the operating system). Even if a file consists of only a few bytes, it uses an entire cluster. Each cluster holds data from only one file. One file, however, can span many clusters.

Sometimes, a sector has a flaw and cannot store data. When you format a disk, the operating system marks these bad sectors as unusable. **Formatting** is the process of preparing a disk for reading and writing. Chapter 8 discusses the formatting process in more depth.

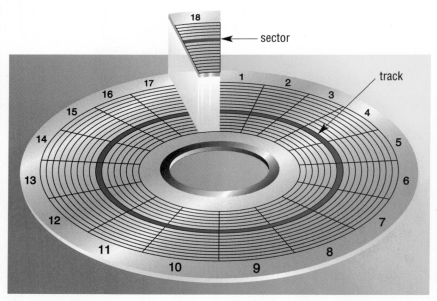

Figure 7-8 A track is a narrow recording band that forms a full circle on the surface of a disk. The disk's storage locations then are divided into pie-shaped sections, which break the tracks into small arcs called sectors.

CHARACTERISTICS OF A 3.5-INCH HIGH-DENSITY FLOPPY DISK

Capacity	1.44 MB
Sides	2
Tracks	80
Sectors per track	18
Bytes per sector	512
Sector per disk	2880

Figure 7-9 Most of today's personal computers use high-density disks.

Care of Floppy Disks

Floppy disks provide an inexpensive and reliable form of storage. Disk manufacturers state that a floppy disk can last at least seven years, with reasonable care. In many cases, the disks do not have that long of a life span.

To maximize a disk's life, you should take proper care of it. When handling a floppy disk, avoid exposing it to heat, cold, magnetic fields, and contaminants such as dust, smoke, or salt air. Exposure to any of these elements could damage or destroy the data, instructions, and information stored on the floppy disk. To protect disks further, keep the disks in a storage tray when not using them.

To protect floppy disks from accidentally being erased, the disk's plastic outer cover has a write-protect notch in its corner. A **write-protect notch** is a small opening that has a tab you slide to cover or expose the notch (Figure 7-10). The write-protect notch works much like the recording tab on a VHS tape: if you remove the recording tab, a VCR cannot record onto the VHS tape.

On a floppy disk, if the write-protect notch is open, the drive cannot write on the floppy disk. If the write-protect notch is covered, or closed, the drive can write on the floppy disk. The write-protect notch only affects the floppy disk drive's capability of *writing* on the disk. A floppy disk drive can read from a floppy disk whether the write-protect notch is open or closed. Some floppy disks have a second opening on the opposite side of the disk that does not have the small tab. This opening identifies the disk as an HD (high-density) floppy disk.

HIGH-CAPACITY DISKS

A **high-capacity disk drive** is a disk drive that uses disks with capacities of 100 MB and greater. High-capacity disks allow you easily to transport a large number of files from one computer to another. These disks also can store large graphics, audio, or video files. Another popular use of these disks is to back up important data and information. A **backup** is a duplicate of a file, program, or disk that you can use if the original is lost, damaged, or destroyed.

Three types of high-capacity disk drives are the SuperDisk™ drive, the HiFD™ drive, and the Zip® drive. The first two are downward compatible with floppy disks. That is, SuperDisk™ and HiFD™ drives can read from and write on standard 3.5-inch floppy disks, as well as their own high-capacity disks.

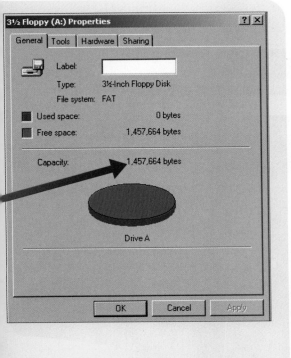

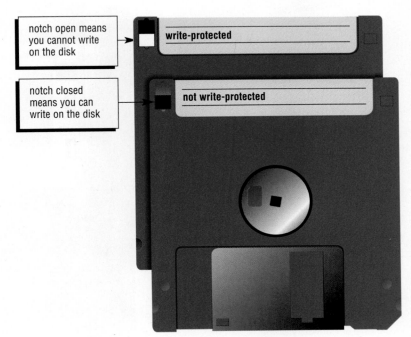

Figure 7-10 To protect data from being erased accidentally, floppy disks have a write-protect notch. By sliding a small tab, you either can cover or expose the notch.

Many notebook computers offer a SuperDisk™ drive or a HiFD™ drive as an option. Developed by Imation, a **SuperDisk™ drive** reads from and writes on a 120 MB or a 250 MB SuperDisk™. Some digital cameras have built-in SuperDisk drives to allow storage of hundreds of photographs on a single disk. The **HiFD™ (High-Capacity Floppy Disk) drive**, developed by Sony Electronics Inc., reads from and writes on a 200 MB HiFD™ disk.

A **Zip® drive** is a high-capacity disk drive developed by Iomega Corporation that uses a Zip® disk. A **Zip® disk** is slightly larger than and about twice as thick as a 3.5-inch floppy disk, and can store 100 MB or 250 MB of data. Many desktop computers have a built-in Zip® drive as a standard feature (Figure 7-11). Others offer it as an option. You also can connect an external Zip® drive to a notebook or desktop computer to provide even more portability.

HARD DISKS

When personal computers were introduced, software programs and their related files fit easily on a single floppy disk. With these programs, you simply inserted the disk to use the program. Throughout time, software became more complex and included graphical user interfaces and multimedia. Users no longer could run programs from a floppy disk. Instead, they installed the program, which consumed many floppy disks, onto the hard disk. Hard disks provide far greater storage capacities and much faster access times than floppy disks.

A **hard disk**, also called a **hard disk drive**, consists of several inflexible, circular platters that store items electronically. Made of aluminum, glass, or ceramic, a **platter** is coated with a material that allows items to be recorded magnetically on its surface. The platters, along with the read/write heads, and

the mechanism for moving the heads across the surface of the hard disk, are enclosed in an airtight, sealed case to protect them from contamination.

Most desktop personal computers contain at least one hard disk. The hard disk inside the system unit, sometimes called a **fixed disk**, is not portable (Figure 7-12). A section later in this chapter discusses another type of hard disk: a removable hard disk.

Current personal computer hard disks can store from 10 to 75 GB of data, instructions, and information. Like floppy disks, these hard disks store data magnetically. Hard disks also are read/write storage media. That is, you can both read from and write on a hard disk any number of times. A recently developed hard disk, called an **optically-assisted hard drive**, combines laser and optic technologies with the magnetic media. These optically-assisted hard drives have potential storage capacities of up to 280 GB.

Figure 7-11 Many new computers have a built-in Zip® drive.

Web Link

For more information on Zip® drives, visit the Discovering Computers 2002 Chapter 7 WEB LINK page (**scsite.com/dc2002/ch7/ weblink.htm**) and click Zip® Drives.

hard disk installed in system unit

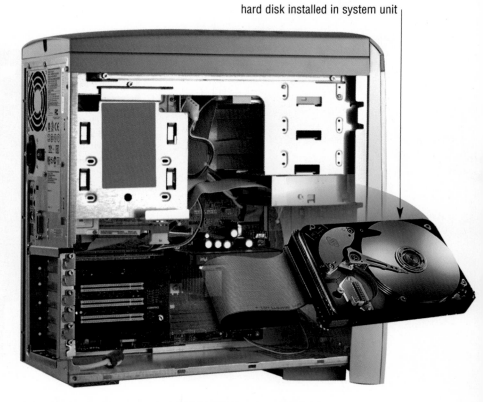

Figure 7-12 The hard disk in a desktop personal computer normally resides permanently inside the system unit. That is, it is not portable.

How a Hard Disk Works

Most hard disks have multiple platters stacked on top of one another. Each platter has two read/write heads, one for each side. The hard disk has arms that move the read/write heads to the proper location on the platter (Figure 7-13).

The location of the read/write heads often is referred to by its cylinder. A **cylinder** is the location of a single track through all platters (Figure 7-14). For example, if a hard disk has 4 platters (8 sides), each with 1,000 tracks, then it will have 1,000 cylinders with each cylinder consisting of 8 tracks (2 for each platter). A single movement of the read/write head arms can read all the platters of data.

While your computer is running, the platters in the hard disk rotate at a high rate of speed, usually 5,400 to 7,200 revolutions per minute. The platters typically continue spinning until power is removed from the computer. (On some computers, the hard disk turns off after a specified time period to save power.) The spinning motion creates a cushion of air between the platter and its read/write head. This cushion ensures that the read/write head floats above the platter instead of making direct contact with the platter surface. The distance between the read/write head and the platter is approximately two millionths of an inch.

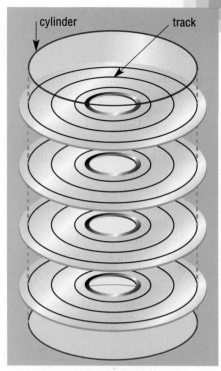

Figure 7-14 A cylinder is the location of a single track through all platters on a hard disk.

Figure 7-13 HOW A HARD DISK WORKS

Step 1:
The circuit board controls the movement of the head actuator and a small motor.

Step 2:
A small motor spins the platters while the computer is running.

Step 3:
When software requests a disk access, the read/write heads determine the current or new location of the data.

Step 4:
The head actuator positions the read/write head arms over the correct location on the platters to read or write data.

As shown in Figure 7-15, this close clearance leaves no room for any type of contamination. Dirt, hair, dust, smoke, and other contaminants could cause the hard disk to have a head crash. A **head crash** occurs when a read/write head touches the surface of a platter, usually resulting in a loss of data or sometimes loss of the entire drive. Today's hard disks are built to withstand shocks and are sealed tightly to keep out contaminants, which means head crashes are less likely to occur.

Access time for today's hard disks ranges from approximately 5 to 11 milliseconds. A hard disk's access time is significantly faster than a floppy disk for two reasons: (1) a hard disk spins much faster than a floppy disk and (2) a hard disk spins constantly, while a floppy disk starts spinning only when it receives a read or write command.

Some computers improve hard disk access time by using disk caching. **Disk cache** (pronounced cash) is a portion of memory that the processor uses to store frequently accessed items (Figure 7-16). Disk cache works similarly to memory cache. When a program needs data, instructions, or information, the processor checks the disk cache. If the item is in disk cache, the processor uses that item and completes the process. If the processor does not find the requested item in the disk cache, then the processor must wait for the hard disk drive to locate and transfer the item from the disk to the processor.

A **cache controller** manages cache and thus determines which items cache should store. On newer processors, the cache controller is part of the processor.

Some disk caching systems also attempt to predict what data, instructions, or information might be needed and place them into cache before the processor requests them. Almost all new disk drives work with some amount of disk cache because it significantly improves disk access times.

You can divide a formatted hard disk into separate areas called **partitions** by issuing a special operating system command. Each partition functions as if it were a separate hard disk drive. Users often partition a hard disk so they can install multiple operating systems on the same hard disk.

If a hard disk has only one partition, the operating system designates it as *drive C*. If the hard disk has two partitions, the first partition is *drive C* and the second is *drive D*. Unless specifically requested by the consumer, most manufacturers define a single partition (drive C) on the hard disk.

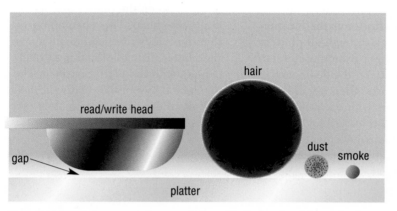

Figure 7-15 The clearance between a disk read/write head and the platter is about two millionths of an inch. Contaminants, such as a smoke particle, dust particle, or human hair, could render the drive unusable.

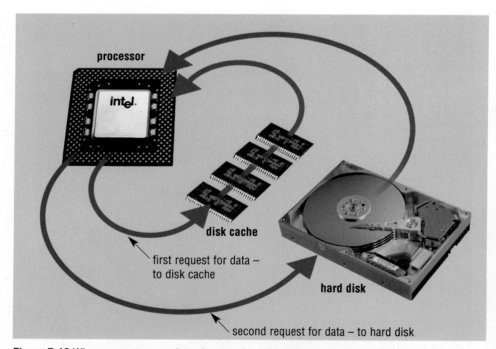

Figure 7-16 When a program needs an item such as data, instructions, or information, the processor checks the disk cache. If the item is located, the processor uses it. If the processor does not find the item in the disk cache, then the processor must wait for the disk drive to locate and transfer the item from the disk.

Hard Disk Controllers

A **disk controller** is a special-purpose chip and associated electronic circuits that control the transfer of data, instructions, and information from a disk to the rest of the computer. Some users refer to the disk controller as an interface.

On a personal computer, a **hard disk controller (HDC)** is the interface for a hard disk. The HDC may be part of a disk drive or may be a separate card inside in the system unit. Many external hard drives use a USB port as their interface.

Vendors usually state the HDC interface in their computer advertisements. Thus, you should understand the types of available interfaces. In addition to USB, two types of HDCs for personal computers are EIDE and SCSI.

EIDE One of the most widely used controllers for hard disks is the **Enhanced Integrated Drive Electronics (EIDE)** controller. EIDE controllers can support up to four hard disks at 137 GB per disk. They can transfer data, instructions, and information to and from the disk at rates of up to 66 MB per second.

An earlier type of EIDE controller was **ATA**, which is short for AT Attachment. Some manufacturers market their EIDE controllers as Fast ATA. EIDE controllers are backward compatible with earlier IDE and ATA controllers. Various versions include ATA, ATA-4, Ultra ATA, Ultra DMA, and ATA/66.

SCSI Small computer system interface, or **SCSI**, (pronounced scuzzy) controllers can support multiple disk drives, as well as other peripherals such as scanners high-capacity disk drives, CD-ROM drives, CD-RW drives, DVD-ROM drives, tape drives, printers, scanners, network interface cards, and much more. When using SCSI devices, you can daisy chain devices together by connecting the first SCSI device to the computer, the second SCSI device to the first SCSI device, and so on. Some computers have a built in SCSI controller, while others use an expansion card to add a SCSI controller.

SCSI controllers are faster than EIDE controllers, providing up to 160 MB per second transfer rates. SCSI controllers typically cost a few hundred dollars more than do EIDE controllers. Many versions of SCSI controllers exist, including SCSI-3, Wide SCSI, Fast SCSI, Fast Wide SCSI, Ultra SCSI, Ultra2 SCSI, and Ultra 160 SCSI. These SCSI controllers typically are backward compatible with earlier SCSI devices.

Removable Hard Disks

Some hard disks are removable, which enables you to insert and remove the hard disk from a hard disk drive, much like a floppy disk. A **removable hard disk**, also called a **disk cartridge**, is a disk drive in which a plastic or metal case surrounds the hard disk so you can remove it from the drive (Figure 7-17). A popular, reasonably priced, removable hard disk is the **Jaz® disk** by Iomega. A Jaz® disk can store up to 2 GB of data, instructions, and information.

Figure 7-17 The Jaz® disk by Iomega is a removable hard disk with a storage capacity of up to 2 GB.

COMPANY ON THE CUTTING EDGE

Kingston TECHNOLOGY COMPUTING WITHOUT LIMITS

Memory in the Making

Ever sit down to take a test, have your mind go blank, and wonder if you were losing your memory?

The computer industry also thought it was losing its memory in 1987. At that time, memory for personal computers was scarce. John Tu and David Sun knew they could help solve the problem. They founded Kingston Technology and designed a standard single inline memory module (SIMM) using a readily available alternative chip.

As the memory shortage eased a few years later, Kingston branched into manufacturing processor upgrades, storage subsystems, and networking solutions. Today, Kingston is the world's leading independent manufacturer of memory products for computers, servers, digital cameras, and other electronic devices. With annual sales of more than $1.5 million in 1999, Kingston markets more than 2,000 products.

Fortune magazine has honored Kingston as one of the 100 Best Companies to Work for in the United States. Part of this honor is due to Kingston's company philosophy of treating all employees as family members and of displaying such traits as courtesy, honesty, and compassion.

For more information on Kingston Technology, visit the Discovering Computers 2002 Companies Web page (**scsite.com/dc2002/companies.htm**) and click Kingston.

Portable media, such as floppy disks and other removable disks, have several advantages over fixed disks. First, you can use a removable disk to transport a large number of files or to make backup copies of important files. You also can use removable disks when data security is an issue. For example, at the end of a work session, you can remove the hard disk and lock it up, leaving no data in the computer.

RAID

For applications that depend on reliable data access, it is crucial the data is available when a user attempts to access it. Some manufacturers develop a type of hard disk system that connects several smaller disks into a single unit that acts like a single large hard disk. A group of two or more integrated hard disks is called a **RAID (redundant array of independent disks)**. Although quite expensive, a RAID system is more reliable than a traditional disk system (Figure 7-18). Thus, networks and Internet servers often use RAID.

RAID duplicates data, instructions, and information to improve data reliability. RAID systems implement this duplication in different ways, depending on the storage design, or level, used. (These levels are not hierarchical. That is, higher levels are not necessarily better than lower levels.) The simplest RAID storage design is **level 1**, called **mirroring**, which has one backup disk for each disk (Figure 7-19a). A level 1 configuration enhances system

reliability because, if a drive should fail, a duplicate of the requested item is available elsewhere within the array of disks.

Levels beyond level 1 use a technique called **striping**, which splits data, instructions, and information across multiple disks in the array (Figure 7-19b). Striping improves disk access times, but does not offer data duplication. For this reason, some RAID levels combine both mirroring and striping.

Figure 7-18 A group of two or more integrated hard disks, called a RAID (redundant array of independent disks), often is used with network servers. Shown here is a desktop RAID. Figure 7-1 on page 7.3 shows a rack-mount RAID.

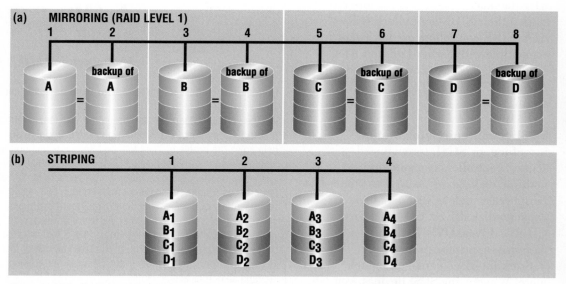

Figure 7-19 In RAID level 1, called mirroring, a backup disk exists for each disk. Higher RAID levels use striping; that is, portions of each disk are placed on multiple disks.

Maintaining Data Stored on a Hard Disk

Most manufacturers guarantee their hard disks to last somewhere between three and five years. Many last much longer with proper care. To prevent the loss of items stored on a hard disk, you should perform preventative maintenance such as defragmenting or scanning the disk for errors. As shown in the table in Figure 7-20, operating systems such as Windows provide many maintenance and monitoring utilities. Chapter 8 discusses these and other utilities in more depth.

Web Link

For more information on disk utilities, visit the Discovering Computers 2002 Chapter 7 WEB LINK page (**scsite.com/dc2002/ch7/ weblink.htm**) and click Disk Utilities.

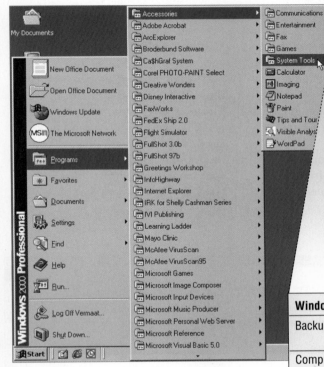

Figure 7-20 Windows provides many maintenance and monitoring utilities on the System Tools submenu. The table in this figure briefly describes some of these utilities.

Windows Utility	Function
Backup	Creates a copy of files on a hard disk in case the original is damaged or destroyed.
Compression Agent	Recompresses files according to settings in DriveSpace (see below).
Disk Cleanup	Frees up space on a hard disk by listing files that can be deleted safely.
Disk Defragmenter	Reorganizes files and unused space on a hard disk so programs run faster.
Drive Converter (FAT 32)	Improves the FAT method of storing data, which frees up hard disk space and makes programs load faster.
DriveSpace	Compresses a hard disk or floppy disk to create free space on the disk.
Maintenance Wizard	Runs utilities that optimize your computer's performance.
Net Watcher	Monitors users and disk/file usage when computers are networked.
Resource Meter	Monitors system, user, and graphics resources being used by programs.
ScanDisk	Detects errors on a disk and then repairs the damaged areas.
Scheduled Tasks	Automatically runs a utility at a specified time.
System Monitor	Monitors disk access, the processor, memory, and network usage.

Internet Hard Drives

Instead of storing data locally on your fixed or removable hard disk, you can opt to store it on an Internet hard drive. An **Internet hard drive**, sometimes called **online storage**, is a service on the Web that provides

APPLY IT!

Use an Internet Hard Drive to Extend Your Disk Drive Space

If you are looking for extra disk drive space, a file backup service, or a way to share files with others, you may want to consider one of the free Internet hard drive services. One of the most popular of these is i-drive (see URL below). Using i-drive, you can do the following:
- Save music files, create a play list, and play the songs from i-drive
- Create an online photo album to share with your family and friends
- Save games and other software programs
- Save entire Web pages

To use i-drive, first set up your free account by filling out a short online form. Record your ID and password, log on, and you are ready to go. Click a button to access, setup, and use the following features:

1. Add an i-drive icon to your desktop so that you can drag-and-drop files to your i-drive the same way you drag-and-drop within Windows.
2. Create a Play List folder or a New Photo Album and make these available for public, private, or shared access.
3. Download and install Filo, free downloadable software that lets you clip Web pages, images, files, and links straight to your i-drive or bookmark directly to your i-drive.
4. Use i-drive and access your files from any computer with Web access.

For links to Internet hard drive services and the Web site mentioned above, visit the Discovering Computers 2002 Apply It Web page (**scsite.com/dc2002/apply.htm**) and click Chapter 7 Apply It #1.

storage to computer users (Figure 7-21). Many offer storage free of charge to the consumer. Revenues come from advertisers on the site.

Users store data and information on an Internet hard drive for a variety of reasons:

- You no longer need to transport files while away from your desktop computer. Simply copy files to an Internet hard drive and access them from any computer or device that has Web access.
- As you surf the Web, you may spend a lot of time downloading or saving files on your computer's hard disk. Instead, you can save the large audio, video, and graphics files on an Internet hard drive instantaneously.
- As an alternative to e-mailing attachments to family, friends, co-workers, and customers, you

can save the attachment on an Internet hard drive. Recipients of your e-mail message can visit your Internet hard drive to play an audio file, watch the video clip, or view a picture.
- View time-critical data and images immediately while away from the main office or location. For example, doctors can view x-ray images from another hospital, home, office, or while on vacation.
- You easily can store offsite backups of data. Chapter 8 presents this and other backup strategies.

In addition to storage space, these Web sites offer other services. These services often include e-mail, calendar, address book, and task list applications. As with other files on the Internet hard drive, you can share your calendars, address books, and tasks lists with others that have Web access.

Figure 7-21 Shown here is an example of a free Internet hard drive service.

COMPACT DISCS

In the past, when you purchased software, you received one or more floppy disks that contained the files needed to install or run the software program. As software programs became more and more complex, the number of floppy disks required to store the programs increased, sometimes exceeding 30 disks. These more complex programs required a storage medium with greater capacity. This is why most manufacturers today distribute software programs on compact discs.

A **compact disc** (**CD**), also called an **optical disc**, is a flat,

round, portable, metal storage medium that usually is 4.75 inches in diameter and less than one-twentieth of an inch thick. Just about every personal computer today includes some type of compact disc drive installed in a drive bay. These drives read compact discs, including audio CDs.

On these drives, you push a button to slide out a tray, insert your compact disc with the label side up, and then push the same button to close the tray (Figure 7-22). Other convenient features on most of these drives include a volume control button and a headphone jack so you can use stereo headphones to listen to audio without disturbing others nearby.

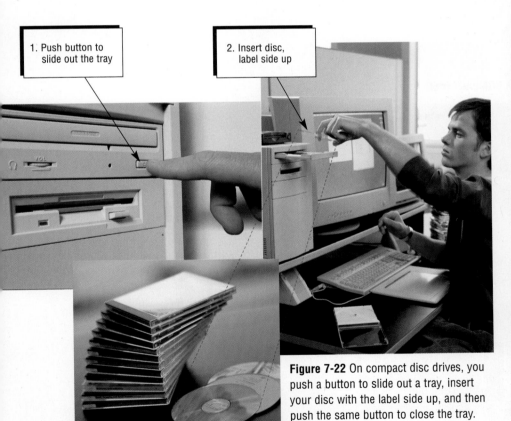

1. Push button to slide out the tray

2. Insert disc, label side up

Figure 7-22 On compact disc drives, you push a button to slide out a tray, insert your disc with the label side up, and then push the same button to close the tray.

Recall that a floppy disk drive is designated as drive A. The drive designation of a compact disc drive usually follows alphabetically after that of the hard disk. For example, if the hard disk is drive C, then the compact disc is drive D.

Compact discs store items such as data, instructions, and information by using microscopic pits (indentations) and land (flat areas) that are in the middle layer of the disc (Figure 7-23). (Most manufacturers place a silk-screened label on the top layer of the disc so you can identify it.) A high-powered laser light creates the pits. A lower-powered laser light reads items from the compact disc by reflecting light through the bottom of the disc, which usually is either solid gold or silver in color. The reflected light is converted into a series of bits

the computer can process. Land causes light to reflect, which is read as binary digit 1. Pits absorb the light; this absence of light is read as binary digit 0.

A compact disc typically stores items in a single track that spirals from the center of the disc to the edge of the disc. As with a hard disk, this single track is divided into evenly sized sectors in which items are stored (Figure 7-24).

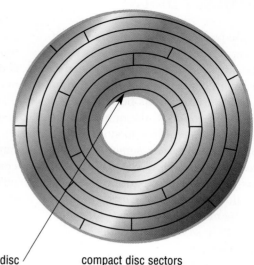

single track
spirals to edge of disc

compact disc sectors

Figure 7-24 The data on a compact disc often is stored in a single track that spirals from the center of the disc to the edge of a disc.

Figure 7-23 HOW A LASER READS DATA ON A COMPACT DISC

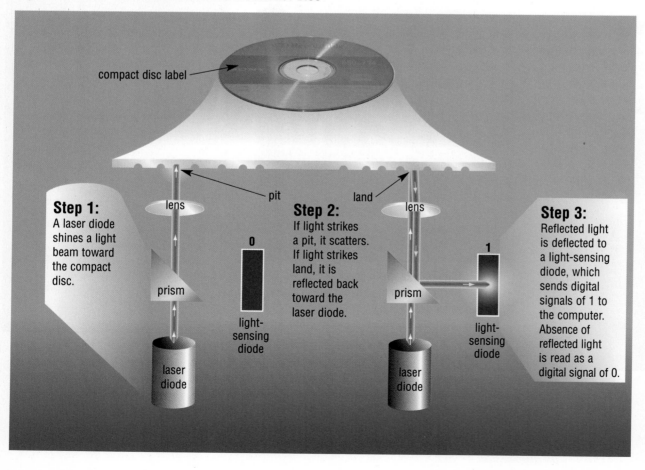

compact disc label

pit   land

lens   lens

Step 1:
A laser diode shines a light beam toward the compact disc.

prism

0

light-sensing diode

laser diode

Step 2:
If light strikes a pit, it scatters. If light strikes land, it is reflected back toward the laser diode.

prism

1

light-sensing diode

laser diode

Step 3:
Reflected light is deflected to a light-sensing diode, which sends digital signals of 1 to the computer. Absence of reflected light is read as a digital signal of 0.

Manufacturers guarantee that a properly cared for compact disc will last five years, but could last up to 50 years. To protect data on any type of compact disc, you should place it in its protective case, called a **jewel box**, when you are finished using it (Figure 7-25). When handling compact discs, you should avoid stacking them and exposing them to heat, cold, and contaminants. Figure 7-26 outlines some guidelines for the proper care of compact discs.

Figure 7-25 To protect data on a CD, you should place it in a jewel box when you are finished using it.

jewel box

You can clean the bottom surface of a compact disc with a soft cloth and warm water or a specialized compact disc cleaning kit. You also can repair scratches on the bottom surface with a specialized compact disc repair kit.

Compact discs are available in a variety of formats, including CD-ROM, CD-R, CD-RW, and DVD-ROM. The following pages discuss these basic formats.

Do not expose the disc to excessive heat or sunlight.

Do not eat, smoke, or drink near a disc.

Do not stack discs.

Do not touch the underside of the disc.

Do store the disc in a jewel box when not in use.

Do hold a disc by its edges.

Figure 7-26 Some guidelines for the proper care of compact discs.

CD-ROMs

A **CD-ROM** (pronounced SEE-DEE-rom), or **compact disc read-only memory,** is a silver-colored compact disc that uses the same laser technology as audio CDs for recording music. In addition to audio, a CD-ROM can contain text, graphics, and video. The manufacturer writes, or **records**, the contents of standard CD-ROMs. You only can read the contents of these discs. That is, you cannot erase or modify their contents — hence, the name read-only.

For a computer to read items on a CD-ROM, you must place it into a **CD-ROM drive** or **CD-ROM player**. Because audio CDs and CD-ROMs use the same laser technology, you also can use your CD-ROM drive to listen to an audio CD while working on your computer.

A typical CD-ROM holds about 650 MB of data, instructions, and information. This is about 450 times more than you can store on a high-density 3.5-inch floppy disk. Manufacturers use CD-ROMs to store and distribute today's multimedia and other complex software because these

discs have such high storage capacities (Figure 7-27). Some programs even require that the disc be in the drive each time you use the program.

CD-ROM Drive Speed

The speed of a CD-ROM drive is extremely important when viewing animation or video such as those found in multimedia encyclopedias and games. A slower CD-ROM drive results in choppy images or sound. The data transfer rate is the time it takes a drive to transmit data, instructions, and information from the

Web Link

For more information on CD-ROMs, visit the Discovering Computers 2002 Chapter 7 WEB LINK page (**scsite.com/dc2002/ch7/ weblink.htm**) and click CD-ROMs.

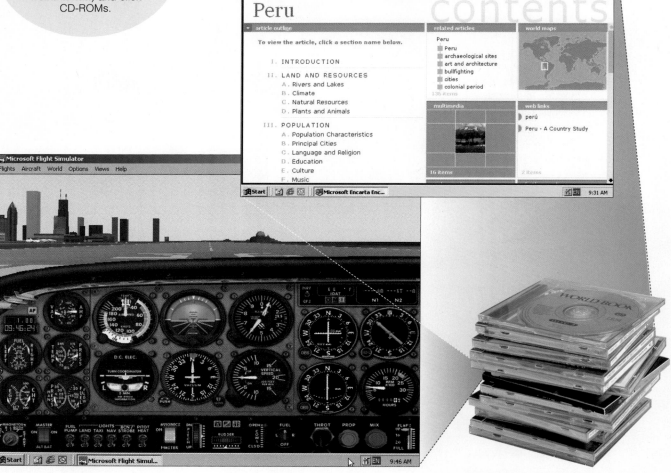

Figure 7-27 CD-ROMs are used to store and distribute multimedia and other complex software.

drive to another device. The original CD-ROM drives were single-speed drives with a data transfer rate of 150 KB per second. Manufacturers measure all CD-ROM drives relative to the first CD-ROM drive. An X denotes the original transfer rate of 150 KB per second. For example, a 40X CD-ROM drive has a data transfer rate of 6,000 (40 x 150) KB per second or 6 MB per second.

Current CD-ROM drives have data transfer rates, or speeds, ranging from 40X to 75X. The higher the number, the faster the CD-ROM drive, which results in smoother playback of images and sounds. Faster CD-ROM drives, however, are more expensive than slower drives.

PhotoCDs and Picture CDs

Based on a file format developed by Eastman Kodak, a **PhotoCD** is a compact disc that contains digital photographic images saved in the PhotoCD format. Commercial and professional users work with PhotoCDs. Most professional desktop publishing software packages can read the PhotoCD format.

A PhotoCD is a **multisession** disc, which means you can write additional data, instructions, and information to the disc at a later time. Thus, as users capture more photographs, they can add them to the PhotoCD. (Most standard CD-ROMs are **single-session** because manufacturers write all items to the disc at one time.)

For the home user, Kodak has a Picture CD. A **Picture CD** is a single-session disc that stores digital versions of photographs for consumers. Many film developers offer this service when you drop off film to be developed. That is, in addition to printed photographs and negatives, you also receive a disc containing your pictures (Figure 7-28). The additional cost for a Picture CD is about $10 per roll of film.

Figure 7-28 Many film developers offer a Picture CD service when you drop off film to be developed.

ISSUE

And Your Choice Is?

CD-ROM or Printed Brochure

Instead of printed brochures, companies increasingly now mail or give marketing CD-ROMs to their potential customers. CD-ROMs are more expensive than conventional advertisements, but the companies feel the storage medium's interactivity is worth the cost in most instances. Some automobile manufacturers, for example, offer a CD-ROM that introduces new vehicles to prospective buyers. The CD-ROM shows photographs, statistics, option packages, and pricing information. Using a mouse, automobile shoppers can *walk around and kick the tires*, view the car from different angles, obtain close-ups of special features, and even go on a figurative test drive. Should companies advertise on CD-ROMs and mail the CD-ROMs to the public? Do people install and read the information on these CD-ROMs? Is a printed brochure more effective? What products are best suited to promotion on CD-ROM? Why? What products are least suited? Why? Will marketing CD-ROMs ever replace printed advertising materials? Why or why not?

For more information on CD-ROMs, visit the Discovering Computers 2002 Issues Web page (**scsite.com/dc2002/issues.htm**) and click Chapter 7 Issue #2.

Using photo-editing software and the photographs on the Picture CD, you can remove red eye, crop the photograph, trim away edges, enhance colors, adjust the lighting, and edit just about any aspect of a photograph. You also can print copies of the photographs on glossy paper with your ink-jet printer. If you want to share the photographs, you can e-mail them, copy them to an Internet hard drive, or post them on a photo community.

CD-R AND CD-RW

Most computers today include either a CD-R or CD-RW drive as a standard feature. Others offer one of these drives as an option. Unlike standard CD-ROM drives, you can record, or write, your own data onto a disc with a CD-R or CD-RW drive.

A **CD-R (compact disc-recordable)** is a multisession compact disc onto which you can record your own items such as text, graphics, and audio. With a CD-R, you can write on part of the disc at one time and another part at a later time. Once you have recorded the CD-R, you can read from it as many times as you wish. You can write on each part only one time, and you cannot erase the disc's contents. Most CD-ROM drives can read a CD-R.

You write on the CD-R using a **CD recorder** or a **CD-R drive** and special software. A CD-R drive can read and write both audio CDs and standard CD-ROMs. These drives

read at speeds of up to 24X and write at speeds of up to 8X. Manufacturers often list the write speed first, for example, as 8/24. CD-R drives are slightly more expensive than standard CD-ROM drives.

Instead of CD-R drives, many users opt for CD-RW drives. A **CD-RW (compact disc-rewritable)** is an erasable disc you can write on multiple times. Originally called an **erasable CD (CD-E)**, a CD-RW overcomes the major disadvantage of CD-R disks, which is you can write on them only once. With CD-RW, the disc acts like a floppy or hard disk, allowing you to write and rewrite data, instructions, and information onto it multiple times. To write on a CD-RW disc, you must have CD-RW software and a **CD-RW drive**. These drives have a write speed up to 12X, rewrite speed up to 4X, and a read speed up to 32X. Manufacturers typically state the speeds in this order, for example, as 12/4/32.

CD-RW discs can be read only by multiread CD-ROM drives. A **multiread CD-ROM drive** is a drive that can read audio CDs, data CDs, CD-Rs, and CD-RWs. Most recent CD-ROM drives are multiread.

APPLY IT!

Digital Photographs

Internet evangelists have long predicted the move to digital and online photograph storage. These predictions now are coming true. One does not even need a scanner or digital camera to participate in the fun.

Picture CD is a new film digitation service from Kodak (see URL below). This technology bridges the film-digital gap by providing a solution that gives people the benefit of both film and digital pictures. Use a Picture CD to view pictures on your computer. You can print or modify, improve, and enhance your photographs, and send e-mail postcards. To purchase a Picture CD, just check the box for KODAK Picture CD on your processing envelope when you take in your film or one-time-use cameras for processing.

Many sites on the Web allow you to create a photo album similar to an album you may have at home. Most of these sites offer free unlimited storage. If you choose, you can share your albums with friends, family, or the entire Internet community. Some sites provide the option of sending electronic greeting cards or postcards.

For more information on Picture CDs, online photograph storage, and the Web site mentioned above, visit the Discovering Computers 2002 Apply It Web page (**scsite.com/dc2002/apply.htm**) and click Chapter 7 Apply It #2.

Using a CD-RW disc, you easily can backup large files from your hard disk. You also can share data and information with other users that have a CD-ROM drive.

A very popular use of CD-RW and CD-R discs is to create audio CDs.

That is, you can make your own music disc. Users have two basic options to create an audio CD: copy the song(s) from an existing audio CD or download the song(s) from the Web. The steps in Figure 7-29 illustrate these techniques.

Figure 7-29 HOW TO CREATE AN AUDIO CD

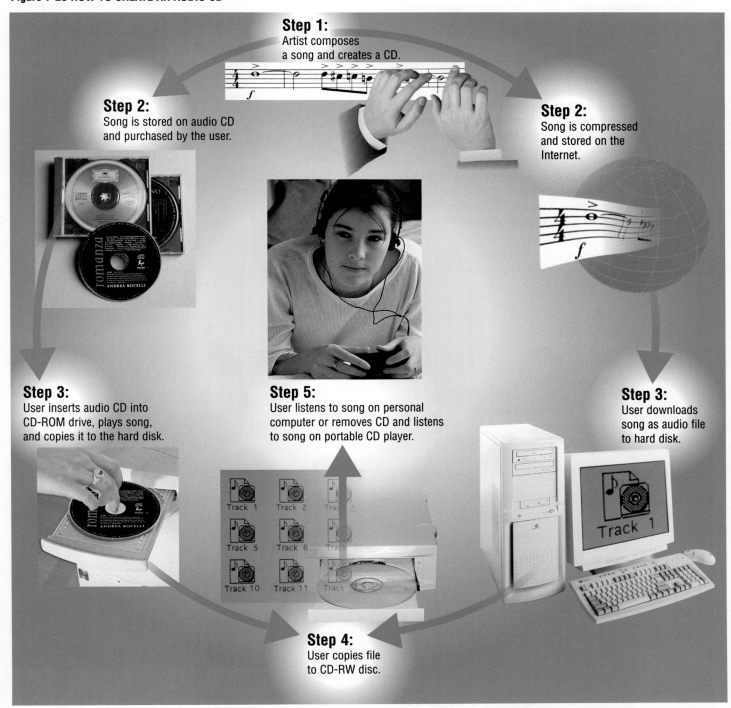

Step 1: Artist composes a song and creates a CD.

Step 2: Song is stored on audio CD and purchased by the user.

Step 2: Song is compressed and stored on the Internet.

Step 3: User inserts audio CD into CD-ROM drive, plays song, and copies it to the hard disk.

Step 5: User listens to song on personal computer or removes CD and listens to song on portable CD player.

Step 3: User downloads song as audio file to hard disk.

Step 4: User copies file to CD-RW disc.

APPLY IT!

The Future of CD-RW Discs

You probably have seen ads and read about CD-R and CD-RW discs. You may have considered purchasing one of these drives, but wondered how you could use this technology. Consider that 10 years ago the common method of sharing files was via a 5.25-inch floppy disk. Depending on the disk's density, you could store either 360 or 1.2 million characters. With today's increasing need for removable storage, CD-R and CD-RW may become as popular as the floppy disk in its heyday. These drives have more than 400 times the capacity of a floppy disk. They combine the compatibility, flexibility, and storage capacity of a CD with the drag-and-drop ease of a floppy.

CD-R and CD-RW add a new dimension to CD use in computers. You use CD technology to store your data and record your own CDs. With CD-RW, you can erase and rewrite data repeatedly on the same disc. The number of times the disc can be rewritten depends upon the quality of the disc.

Adding one of these drives to any new or existing computer is easy to do. You may find that this technology is perfect for backing up a large set of files, creating music CDs, or creating multimedia presentations. CD-RW drives are able to write both CD-R and CD-RW disc formats. CD-RW discs, however, have two disadvantages: a) they cannot be read by all CD drives; and b) CD-RW discs cannot be written to by CD-R drives.

For more information on CD-R and CD-RW discs, visit the Discovering Computers 2002 Apply It Web page (scsite.com/dc2002/apply.htm) and click Chapter 7 Apply It #3.

ISSUE

Make Your Own Music

CD-RW Storage

The CD-RW disc opened new possibilities. For multimedia designers and home recording artists, the recordable CD format offers a range of powerful storage applications. Price decreases and ease of use make these devices even more attractive. Along with almost any new technology, negatives exist. At many schools, for example, some students use college servers to create their own music sites and download copyrighted music. Using CD-RW storage, they record the songs and distribute unauthorized copies. Many people think the Internet is a new frontier and copyright rules do not apply. Do you agree with this? Is it ethical to copy a CD and share it with a friend? Is it the responsibility of schools to educate students about such ethical issues? Why or why not?

For more information on CD-RWs, visit the Discovering Computers 2002 Issues Web page (scsite.com/dc2002/issues.htm) and click Chapter 7 Issue #3.

DVD-ROMS

Although CD-ROMs have huge storage capacities, even a CD-ROM is not large enough for many of today's complex programs. Some multimedia software, for example, requires five or more CD-ROMs. To meet these tremendous storage requirements, some manufacturers store and distribute software using a DVD-ROM (Figure 7-30). The goal of DVD technology is to meet the needs of home entertainment, computer usage,

DVD-ROM

DVD-ROM drive

Figure 7-30 A DVD-ROM is an extremely high-capacity compact disc capable of storing 4.7 GB to 17 GB.

and business data and information storage with a single medium. When you rent or buy a DVD movie, it uses a DVD-Video format to store the motion picture digitally.

A **DVD-ROM (digital video disc-ROM)** is an extremely high capacity compact disc capable of storing from 4.7 GB to 17 GB. The storage capacity of a DVD-ROM is more than enough to hold a telephone book containing every resident in the United States. Not only is the storage capacity of a DVD-ROM greater than a CD-ROM, a DVD-ROM's quality also far surpasses that of a CD-ROM.

In order to read a DVD-ROM, you must have a **DVD-ROM drive** or **DVD player**. These drives can read at speeds up to 40X. Newer DVD-ROM drives also can read audio CDs, CD-ROMs, CD-Rs, and CD-RWs.

At a glance, a DVD-ROM looks just like a CD-ROM. Although the size and shape are similar, a DVD-ROM stores data, instructions, and information in a slightly different manner and thus achieves a higher storage capacity.

A DVD-ROM uses one of three storage techniques. The first technique involves making the disc more dense by packing the pits closer together. A second technique involves using two layers of pits. For this technique to work, the lower layer of pits is semitransparent so the laser can read through it to the upper layer. This technique doubles the capacity of the disc. Finally, some DVD-ROMs are double-sided, which means you remove the DVD-ROM and turn it over to read the other side. The storage capacities of various types of DVD-ROMs are shown in the table in Figure 7-31.

DVD Variations

DVDs are available in a variety of formats, one of which stores digital motion pictures. To view a movie on a DVD, insert the DVD movie disc into a DVD player connected to your television set or into a DVD-ROM drive to view the movie on your computer screen. Movies on DVD have near-studio-quality video, which far surpasses VHS tapes. When music is stored on a DVD, it includes surround sound and has a much better quality than that on an audio CD.

You also can obtain recordable and rewritable versions of DVD. With a **DVD-R (DVD-recordable)**, you can write once on it and read (play) it many times. A DVD-R is similar to a CD-R. DVD-R drives have a read speed of up to 32X and a write speed of up to 8X. With a rewritable DVD, called a **DVD-RAM**, you can erase and record on the disc multiple times. A DVD-RAM is similar to a CD-RW, except it has storage capacities up to 5.2 GB. DVD-RAM drives typically can read DVD-ROM, DVD-R, and all CD media. A competing technology to DVD-RAM is **DVD+RW**. As the cost of DVD technologies becomes more reasonable, many industry professionals expect that DVD eventually will replace all CD media.

DVD-ROM STORAGE CAPACITIES

Sides	Layers	Storage Capacity
1	1	4.7 GB
1	2	8.5 GB
2	1	9.4 GB
2	2	17 GB

Figure 7-31 Storage capacities of DVD-ROMS.

TECHNOLOGY TRAILBLAZER

MARK DEAN

Not many first graders can handle algebra problems. But Mark Dean was no ordinary first grader. Along with solving fourth-grade math equations in his first year of school, he also tutored older students. In high school, he was a straight-A student and a star athlete.

He also spent hours inventing new products. As a youth, he and his dad built a tractor from scratch. After graduating at the top of his class from the University of Tennessee, he joined IBM and helped design the improvements in architecture that allow components, such as modems and printers, to communicate with personal computers. This technology is used in more than 40 million personal computers manufactured each year. After earning his Ph.D. degree at Stanford, he headed a team at IBM that invented the first CMOS microprocessor chip to operate at one gigahertz (1,000 MHz). As an IBM idea man, he currently is developing an electronic tablet that functions as an e-book, DVD player, radio, wireless telephone, and Web-enabled device.

Dean is the first African-American to receive an IBM Fellowship, the company's highest technical ranking. He has been inducted into the National Inventor's Hall of Fame, an honor he shares with fewer than 150 other people.

For more information on Mark Dean, visit the Discovering Computers 2002 People Web page (**scsite.com/dc2002/people.htm**) and click Mark Dean.

TAPES

One of the first storage media used with mainframe computers was tape. **Tape** is a magnetically coated ribbon of plastic capable of storing large amounts of data and information at a low cost.

Similar to a tape recorder, a **tape drive** reads from and writes data and information on a tape.

Web Link

For more information on tapes, visit the Discovering Computers 2002 Chapter 7 WEB LINK page (**scsite.com/dc2002/ch7/weblink.htm**) and click Tapes.

Although older computers used reel-to-reel tape drives, today's tape drives use tape cartridges. A **tape cartridge** is a small, rectangular, plastic housing for tape (Figure 7-32). Tape cartridges containing one-quarter-inch wide tape are slightly larger than audiocassette tapes. Business and home users sometimes backup personal computer hard disks onto tape.

Some personal computers have external tape units. Others have the tape drive built into the system unit. On larger computers, tape cartridges are mounted in a separate cabinet called a tape library.

Three common types of tape drives are quarter-inch cartridge (QIC), digital audio tape (DAT), and digital linear tape (DLT). The fastest and most expensive of the three is DLT. The table in Figure 7-33 summarizes each of these types of tapes.

Tape storage requires **sequential access**, which refers to reading or writing data consecutively. Like a music tape, you must forward or rewind the tape to a specific point to access a specific piece of data. For example, to access item W, you must pass sequentially through points A through V.

Floppy disks, hard disks, and compact discs all use direct access. **Direct access**, also called **random access**, means you can locate a particular data item or file immediately, without having to move consecutively through items stored in front of the desired data item or file. Sequential access is much slower than direct access. Tapes no longer are used as a primary method of storage. Instead, business and home users utilize tapes most often for long-term storage and backup.

Figure 7-32 A tape cartridge and a tape drive.

POPULAR TYPES OF TAPES

Name	Abbreviation	Storage Capacity
Quarter-inch cartridge	QIC	40 MB to 20 GB
Digital audio tape	DAT	2 to 40 GB
Digital linear tape	DLT	20 to 80 GB

Figure 7-33 Common types of tapes.

ENTERPRISE STORAGE SYSTEMS

Many companies use networks. Data, information, and instructions stored on the network must be accessible easily to all authorized users. The data, information, and instructions also must be secure, so unauthorized users do not have access. An **enterprise storage system** is a strategy that focuses on the availability, protection, organization, and backup of storage in a company. The goal of an enterprise storage system is to consolidate storage so operations run as efficiently as possible. Large business users often utilize an enterprise storage system strategy.

To implement an enterprise storage system, a company uses a combination of techniques. As shown in Figure 7-34, an enterprise storage system may use servers, a RAID system, a tape library, CD-ROM jukeboxes, Internet backup, NAS devices, and/or a storage area network. The following paragraphs briefly discuss each of these storage techniques.

- A server stores data, information, and instructions needed by users on the network.
- A RAID system ensures that data is not lost if one drive fails.
- A **tape library** is a high-capacity tape system that works with multiple tape cartridges for storing backups of data, information, and instructions.

- A CD-ROM server, also called a **CD-ROM jukebox**, holds hundreds of CD-ROMs that can contain application programs and data.
- Companies using **Internet backup** store data, information, and instructions on the Web.
- A **network-attached storage** (**NAS**) device is an easy way to add additional hard disk space to the network.
- A **storage area network** (**SAN**) is a high-speed network that connects storage devices.

Some companies manage an enterprise storage system in house. Other larger applications elect to offload all (or at least the backup) storage management to an outside

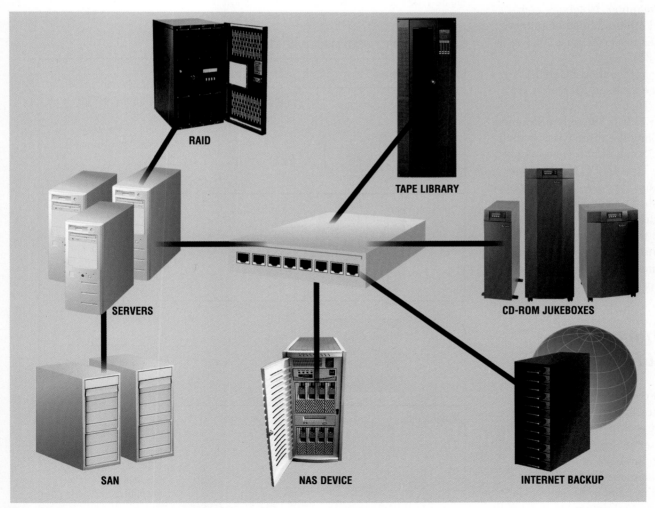

Figure 7-34 An enterprise storage system uses a variety of storage techniques.

organization or online Web service. Some vendors focus on providing enterprise storage systems to clients. A data warehouse might seek this type of outside service. A **data warehouse** is a huge database system that stores and manages historical and current transaction data. For example, a credit card company that stores and manages millions of customer transactions probably uses a data warehouse.

PC CARDS

As discussed in Chapter 4, a **PC Card** is a thin, credit card-sized device that fits into a PC Card slot on a notebook or other personal computer. Different types and sizes of PC Cards add storage, additional memory, communications, and sound capabilities to a computer. Notebook computers and other mobile computers and devices most often use PC Cards (Figure 7-35).

Originally called PCMCIA cards, three kinds of PC Cards are available: Type I, Type II, and Type III (Figure 7-36). The only difference in size among the three types is their thickness. Some digital cameras use a Type II or Type III PC Card to store photographs. Type III cards can house a hard disk. The advantage of a PC Card for storage is portability. You easily can transport large amounts of data, instructions, and information from one machine to another using a Type II or Type III PC Card.

MINIATURE MOBILE STORAGE MEDIA

Handheld computers and digital cameras are wonderful devices that provide the mobile user with immediate access to technology. These handheld devices do not have much internal storage. Some use PC Cards. As shown in the table in Figure 7-37, other types of miniature storage media also are available.

Figure 7-35 PC Cards normally are used with notebook computers and other mobile devices.

PC CARDS

Category	Thickness	Use
Type I	3.3 mm	RAM, SRAM, flash memory
Type II	5.0 mm	Modem, LAN, SCSI, sound, TV tuner, storage
Type III	10.5 mm	Rotating storage such as a hard disk

Figure 7-36 The above table outlines the various uses of PC Cards.

SOME COMMONLY USED MINIATURE STORAGE MEDIA

Device Name	Storage Capacity	Type, Use
Clik! Disk 	40 MB	Cartridge Digital cameras, notebook computers
CompactFlash 	2 to 256 MB	Memory Card Digital cameras, handheld computers, notebook computers, printers, cellular telephones
Microdrive 	1 GB	Memory Card Digital cameras, handheld computers, music players, video cameras
SmartMedia 	2 to 128 MB	Memory Card Digital cameras, handheld computers, photo printers, cellular telephones

Figure 7-37 Miniature storage used with digital cameras and other handheld devices.

To view images and other information captured on a miniature mobile medium, you can transfer its contents to your desktop computer or other device. Some printers read PC cards and other miniature storage media. Handheld devices, such as players and wallets, read or display the contents of miniature storage media such as memory cards (Figure 7-38).

Figure 7-38 This wallet displays the contents of a memory card.

Smart Cards

A **smart card**, which is similar in size to a credit card or ATM card, stores data on a thin microprocessor embedded in the card (Figure 7-39). When you insert the smart card into a specialized card reader, the information on the smart card is read and, if necessary, updated.

Two types of smart cards exist: intelligent and memory. An **intelligent smart card** contains a processor and has input, process, output, and storage capabilities. A **memory card**, by contrast, has only

storage capabilities. A memory card can store a variety of data and information including photographs, music, books, and video clips. As shown earlier, many digital cameras and other handheld devices use memory cards.

One popular use of smart cards is to store a prepaid dollar amount, as in a prepaid telephone calling card. You receive the card with a specific dollar amount stored in the microprocessor. Each time you use the card, it reduces the available amount of money. Using these cards provides convenience to the caller, eliminates the telephone company's need to collect coins from telephones, and reduces vandalism of pay telephones. Other uses of smart cards include storing patient records, vaccination data, and other health-care information; tracking information such as customer purchases or employee attendance; and storing a prepaid amount such as electronic money.

Electronic money (e-money), also called **digital cash**, is a means of paying for goods and services over the Internet. As discussed in Chapter 2, a bank issues unique digital cash

smart card

Figure 7-39 This doctor of pediatrics looks up the confidential patient records on her computer by sliding the smart card through a smart card reader. The smart card reader attaches to the serial port on the computer.

numbers that represent an amount of money. When you purchase digital cash, the amount of money is withdrawn from your bank account. One implementation of e-money places the digital cash on a smart card. To use the card, you swipe it through a card reader on your computer or one that is attached to your computer.

ISSUE

Will Money Become Obsolete?

E-Money Society

The first e-commerce transaction from one personal computer to another computer occurred in May 1994. When you conduct a business activity online, you are participating in e-commerce. One method of paying for the goods or services purchased online is e-money. Digital signatures and encryption techniques make e-money possible. This technology is recognized widely by banks as the most secure measure for protecting financial information. Financial institutions tout the many benefits of e-money for the consumer. Some of these include convenient and easy one-button payment, easy refunds, shop online without a credit card, privacy protection, and wireless access. With all of these benefits of e-money, will paper money disappear? Is e-money just a step on the way to tomorrow's payment system technology or is it already here? Would you feel comfortable using e-money? Will society in general accept this technology?

For more information on e-money, visit the Discovering Computers 2002 Issues Web page (**scsite.com/dc2002/ issues.htm**) and click Chapter 7 Issue #4.

Web Link

For more information on PC Cards, visit the Discovering Computers 2002 Chapter 7 WEB LINK page (**scsite.com/dc2002/ch7/ weblink.htm**) and click PC Cards.

MICROFILM AND MICROFICHE

Microfilm and microfiche store microscopic images of documents on roll or sheet film (Figure 7-40). **Microfilm** uses a 100- to 215-foot roll of film. **Microfiche** uses a small sheet of film, usually about four inches by six inches. A **computer output microfilm (COM) recorder** is the device that records the images on the film. The stored images are so small that you only can read them with a microfilm or microfiche reader.

Applications of microfilm and microfiche are widespread. Libraries use these media to store back issues of newspapers, magazines, and genealogy records. Large organizations use microfilm and microfiche to archive inactive files. Banks use it to store transactions and cancelled checks. The U.S. Army uses it to store personnel records.

Using microfilm and microfiche provides a number of advantages. It greatly reduces the amount of paper firms must handle. It is inexpensive, and it has the longest life of any storage medium (Figure 7-41).

Nothing Lasts Forever

Digital Information Deterioration

This aphorism is true even with respect to computer storage. The industry has just begun to realize the magnitude of digital information deterioration. NASA discovered almost 20 percent of the data collected during the Viking mission was lost on decaying magnetic tape. Veterans' files, census statistics, and toxic-waste records also have been lost on deteriorating storage media. One computer scientist admits that digital information lasts forever or five years — whichever comes first. A major problem with digital data is that, unlike the visible deterioration in a faded document, the extent of decay on a storage medium such as a CD-ROM may be invisible until it is too late. If you were the leader of an information-intensive organization, what medium would you choose to store your records? Why? What steps would you take to ensure the records were intact 10 years from now? Twenty years from now?

For more information on digital storage, visit the Discovering Computers 2002 Issues Web page (**scsite.com/dc2002/issues.htm**) and click Chapter 7 Issue #5.

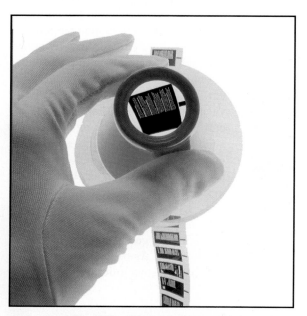

Figure 7-40 Microfilm and microfiche store microscopic images of documents on roll or sheet film.

MEDIA LIFE EXPECTANCIES

Media Type	Guaranteed Life Expectancy	Potential Life Expectancy
Tape	2 to 5 years	20 years
Compact Disc	5 years	50 to 100 years
Microfilm	100 years	200 years

Figure 7-41 Microfilm is the medium with the longest life.

PUTTING IT ALL TOGETHER

Many factors influence the type of storage devices you should use: the amount of data, instructions, and information to be stored; the hardware and software in use; and the desired cost. The table in Figure 7-42 outlines several suggested storage devices for various types of computer users.

CHAPTER SUMMARY

Storage refers to the media on which data, instructions, and information are kept, as well as the devices that record and retrieve these items. This chapter explained various storage media and storage devices. Storage media covered included floppy disks, high-capacity disks, hard disks, CD-ROMs, CD-RWs, DVD-ROMs, tape, and PC Cards and other miniature forms of storage. Enterprise storage systems also were covered.

USER	STORAGE DEVICE
Home 	• 3.5-inch HD floppy disk drive • 250 MB Zip® drive • 30 GB hard disk • Internet hard drive • DVD-ROM drive • CD-RW drive
Small Office/Home Office 	• 3.5-inch HD floppy disk drive • 40 GB hard disk • Internet hard drive • DVD-ROM drive • CD-RW drive • 2 GB Jaz® drive
Mobile 	• 3.5-inch HD floppy disk drive • 1 GB PC Card hard disk • 10 GB hard disk • Internet hard drive • DVD-ROM drive *or* 40X CD-ROM drive
Large Business 	• 3.5-inch HD floppy disk drive • 75 GB hard disk • DVD-ROM drive • CD-RW drive • Microfilm or microfiche • Smart card reader • RAID • Tape drive • Enterprise storage system
Power	• 3.5-inch HD floppy disk drive • DVD-ROM drive • CD-RW drive • 75 GB hard disk • Internet hard drive • 2 GB Jaz® drive

Figure 7-42 This table recommends suggested storage devices.

Career Corner

Computer Technician

Computer technicians are in great demand in every organization and industry. For many, this is the entry point for a career in the computer/information technology field. The responsibilities of a computer technician or a computer service technician can include a variety of duties. Most companies who employ someone with this title expect the technician to have basic across-the-board knowledge of concepts in the computer electronics field. Some of these tasks are hardware repair and installation; software installation, upgrade, and configuration; and troubleshooting client and/or server problems.

Technicians generally work with a variety of users, so people skills are an important asset, especially the ability to work with groups of non-technical users. Because this is an entry-level position, salaries are not quite as high as other more demanding and skilled positions. Individuals with these skills can expect an average annual starting salary of around $25,000 to $35,000.

The Electronics Technicians Association (see URL below) provides a Computer Service Technician (CST) certification program.

To learn more about the field of computer technician as a career and the Web site mentioned above, visit the Discovering Computers 2002 Careers Web page (**scsite.com/dc2002/careers.htm**) and click Computer Technician.

E-SHOPPING

CYBERMALL MANIA

Let Your Mouse Do Your Shopping

From groceries to clothing to computers, you can buy just about everything you need with just a few clicks of your mouse. Electronic retailers (e-tailers), especially those listed in Figure 7-43, are cashing in from cybershoppers' purchases with books, computer software and hardware, and music being the hottest commodities. Online sales in the United States exceed $60 billion yearly. E-shoppers can browse for a variety of goods at these popular Web sites.

Holiday sales account for a large portion of Internet purchases with nearly nine million households doing some of their holiday shopping online. During the holiday season, some Web sites such as KBkids.com (Figure 7-44) have more than 235,000 hits per day. Macy's, Bloomingdale's, and other e-tailers ship more than 300,000 boxes daily out of warehouses that are the size of 20 football fields and are stocked with five million items.

The two categories of Internet shopping Web sites are those with physical counterparts, such as Eddie Bauer (Figure 7-45),

SHOPPING WEB SITES	URL
Apparel	
Eddie Bauer	eddiebauer.com
J. Crew	jcrew.com
Lands' End	landsend.com
Books and Music	
Amazon.com	amazon.com
Barnes & Noble	barnesandnoble.com
Borders	borders.com
Computers and Electronics	
Crutchfield	crutchfield.com
Best Buy	bestbuy.com
Buy.com	buy.com
Miscellaneous	
1-800-Flowers.com	1800flowers.com
drugstore.com	drugstore.com
Toys "R" Us	toysrus.com
Wal-Mart	walmart.com

For an updated list of shopping Web sites, visit scsite.com/dc2002/e-rev.htm.

Figure 7-43 Popular Web shopping sites.

Figure 7-44 Shopping for popular toys online eliminates waiting in long lines in stores.

Figure 7-45 Stores such as Eddie Bauer have both a physical and an Internet presence.

Wal-Mart, and Nordstrom, and those with only a Web presence, such as Egghead.com (Figure 7-46), and amazon.com.

Figure 7-46 Egghead.com is a business with only an Internet presence.

Some e-shoppers, however, are finding online shopping even more frustrating than finding a convenient parking space at the neighborhood mall on Saturday afternoon. Delayed shipments, out-of-stock merchandise, poor customer service, and difficult return policies have left some savvy shoppers with a poor impression of their Internet experience. As e-tailers rush to set up an Internet site, they sometimes overlook important considerations, such as customer service telephone numbers and e-mail addresses, adequate staff to answer queries quickly and courteously, and sufficient in-stock merchandise.

Paying for the merchandise online causes concern for many e-shoppers. Although online merchants promise secure transactions, some users are wary of cyberthieves. One way of calming their fears may be through the use of e-money, which is a payment system that allows consumers to purchase goods and services anonymously. Several computer companies, Web merchants, and credit card companies are collaborating to develop a standard method of transferring money securely and quickly from electronic wallets, which verify a user's identity.

For more information on shopping Web sites, visit the Discovering Computers 2002 E-Revolution Web page (scsite.com/dc2002/e-rev.htm) and click Shopping.

E-SHOPPING applied:

1. Visit two of the three apparel Web sites listed in the table in Figure 7-43 and select a specific pair of jeans and a shirt from each one. Create a table with these headings: e-tailer, style, fabric, features, price, tax, and shipping fee. Enter details about your selections in the table. Then, visit two of the books and music Web sites and search for a CD you would consider purchasing. Create another table with the names of the Web site, artist, and CD, as well as the price, tax, and shipping fee.

2. Visit two of the computers and electronics and two of the miscellaneous Web sites listed in Figure 7-43. Write a paragraph describing the features these Web sites offer compared with the same offerings from stores. In another paragraph, describe any disadvantages of shopping at these Web sites instead of actually seeing the merchandise. Then, describe their policies for returning unwanted merchandise and for handling complaints.

7.34

DISCOVERING
COMPUTERS 2002

Chapter 1 2 3 4 5 6 7 8 9 10 11 12 13 14 15 16 Index HOME

In Summary

SHELLY
CASHMAN
SERIES.

Student Exercises   Web Links   In Summary   Key Terms   Learn It Online   Checkpoint   In The Lab   Web Work

Special Features   ■ TIMELINE 2002   ■ WWW & E-SKILLS   ■ MULTIMEDIA   ■ BUYER'S GUIDE 2002   ■ WIRELESS TECHNOLOGY   ■ TRENDS 2002   ■ INTERACTIVE LABS   ■ TECH NEWS

Web Instructions: To display this page from the Web, start your browser and enter the URL scsite.com/dc2002/ch7/summary.htm. Click the links for current and additional information. To listen to an audio version of this In Summary, click the Audio button. To play the audio, RealPlayer must be installed on your computer (download by clicking here).

1 How Is Storage Different from Memory?

Memory, which is composed of one or more chips on the motherboard, holds data and instructions while they are being interpreted and executed by the processor. Memory can be **volatile** or **nonvolatile**. Storage holds items such as data, instructions, and information for future use.

2 What Are Storage Media and Storage Devices?

A **storage medium** (media is the plural) is the physical material on which items such as data, instructions, and information are kept. A **storage device** is the mechanism used to record and retrieve items to and from a storage medium. When a storage device transfers items from a storage medium into memory — a process called reading — it functions as an input device. When a storage device transfers items from memory to a storage medium — a process called **writing** — it functions as an output device.

3 How Is Data Stored on a Floppy Disk?

A **floppy disk** is a portable, inexpensive storage medium that consists of a thin, circular, flexible disk with a plastic magnetic coating enclosed in a square-shaped plastic shell. Formatting prepares a disk for reading and writing by organizing the disk into storage locations called **tracks** and **sectors**. A **floppy disk drive (FDD)** is a device that reads from and writes on a floppy disk. The drive slides the **shutter** to the side to expose a portion of both sides of the floppy disk's recording surface. A circuit board on the drive sends signals to control the movement of the read/write head, which is the mechanism that reads items from or writes items on the floppy disk. A motor causes the floppy disk to spin and positions the read/write head over the correct location on the recording surface. The read/write head

then writes data on the floppy disk. Floppy disks should not be exposed to heat, cold, magnetic fields, or contaminants such as dust, smoke, or salt air. The disk's shutter should not be opened and the recording surface should not be touched. Floppy disks should be inserted carefully into the disk drive and kept in a storage tray when not in use.

4 What Are the Advantages of Using High-Capacity Disks?

A disk with capacities of 100 MB or greater is called a high-capacity disk. To store large graphics, audio, video, or other large files and for data **backup**, high-capacity disks are the best choice for storage. Three types of high-capacity disk drives are the **SuperDisk™ drive**, the **HiFD™** (High-Capacity Floppy Disk) **drive**, and the **Zip® drive**.

5 How Does a Hard Disk Organize Data?

A **hard disk** consists of several inflexible, circular disks called platters on which items are stored electronically. A hard disk can be divided into separate areas called **partitions** with each partition functioning as if it were a separate hard disk drive. An **optically-assisted hard drive** combines laser and optic technologies with the magnetic media.

6 What Are the Advantages of Using an Internet Hard Drive?

An **Internet hard drive** is a service on the Web that provides storage to computer users. Many offer this service without charge. Users may store information on an **Internet hard drive** so they can access files from any computer or device that has Web access, download and save large files, share files with others, view time-critical data and images, and store offsite backup of data.

Chapter 1 2 3 4 5 6 **7** 8 9 10 11 12 13 14 15 16 Index HOME 7.35

DISCOVERING
COMPUTERS 2002

In Summary

SHELLY
CASHMAN
SERIES.

Student Exercises   Web Links   **In Summary**   Key Terms   Learn It Online   Checkpoint   In The Lab   Web Work

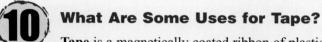
Special Features ■ TIMELINE 2002 ■ WWW & E-SKILLS ■ MULTIMEDIA ■ BUYER'S GUIDE 2002 ■ WIRELESS TECHNOLOGY ■ TRENDS 2002 ■ INTERACTIVE LABS ■ TECH NEWS

7 How Is Data Stored on Compact Discs?

A **compact disc (CD)** is a flat, round, portable metal storage medium that usually is 4.75 inches in diameter and less than one-twentieth of an inch thick. Compact discs store items in microscopic pits (indentations) and land (flat areas) that are located in the middle layer, usually under the printed label on the disc. A high-powered laser light creates the pits in a single track, divided into evenly sized sectors, that spirals from the center of the disc to the edge of the disc. A lower-powered laser reads items from the compact disc by reflecting light through the bottom of the disc surface. The reflected light is converted into a series of bits that the computer can process.

8 How Do You Care for a Compact Disc?

Compact discs should not be stacked or exposed to heat, cold, and contaminants. The underside should not be touched. A compact disc should be held by its edges and placed in its protective case, called a **jewel box**, when it is not being used. The bottom surface of the compact disc can be cleaned with a soft cloth and warm water or a specialized CD cleaning kit.

9 How Are CD-ROMs, CD-RWs, and DVD-ROMs Different?

A **CD-ROM** is a compact disc that uses the same laser technology as audio CDs for recording music. A typical CD-ROM can hold about 650 MB of data, instructions, and information. A **CD-RW** is an erasable disc on which you can write multiple times. These discs can be read only by multiread CD-ROM drives. A **DVD-ROM** is an extremely high capacity compact disc capable of storing from 4.7 GB to 17 GB. Both the storage capacity and quality of a DVD-ROM surpass that of a CD-ROM. A DVD-ROM stores data in a different manner than a CD-ROM, making the disc more dense by packing pits closer together, by using two layers of pits, or by using both sides of the disc. You must have a **DVD-ROM drive** or **DVD player** to read a DVD-ROM disc.

10 What Are Some Uses for Tape?

Tape is a magnetically coated ribbon of plastic capable of storing large amounts of data and information at a low cost. Tape storage requires sequential access, which refers to reading or writing data consecutively. Tape mainly is used for long-term storage and backup.

11 How Does an Enterprise Storage System Work?

An **enterprise storage system** is a strategy that focuses on the availability, protection, organization, and backup of storage in a company. It is implemented using the following techniques: a server for the users, a RAID system, a **storage area network (SAN)**, a **network-attached storage (NAS)** device, a CD-ROM jukebox, **Internet backup**, and a **tape library**.

12 How Do You Use PC Cards and Other Miniature Storage Media?

A **PC Card** is a thin, credit card-sized device that fits into a PC Card slot on a notebook computer or personal computer. PC Cards are used to add storage, memory, communications, and sound capabilities. A smart card, similar in size to an ATM card, stores data on a thin processor embedded in the card. Smart cards are used to store prepaid dollar amounts, such as electronic money; patient records in the health-care industry; and tracking information, such as customer purchases.

13 What Are Some Uses for Microfilm and Microfiche?

Microfilm and microfiche store microscopic images of documents on roll (microfilm) or sheet (microfiche) film. Libraries and large organizations use microfilm and microfiche to archive relatively inactive documents and files.

7.36

DISCOVERING
COMPUTERS 2002

Chapter 1 2 3 4 5 6 7 8 9 10 11 12 13 14 15 16 Index HOME

Key Terms

SHELLY
CASHMAN
SERIES.

Student Exercises Web Links   In Summary   Key Terms   Learn It Online   Checkpoint   In The Lab   Web Work

Special Features ■ TIMELINE 2002 ■ WWW & E-SKILLS ■ MULTIMEDIA ■ BUYER'S GUIDE 2002 ■ WIRELESS TECHNOLOGY ■ TRENDS 2002 ■ INTERACTIVE LABS ■ TECH NEW

Web Instructions: To display this page from the Web, start your browser and enter the URL scsite.com/dc2002/ch7/terms.htm. Scroll through the list of terms. Click a term to display its definition and a picture. Click the To WEB button for current and additional information about the term from the Web. To see animations, Shockwave and Flash Player must be installed on your computer (download by clicking here).

access time (7.4)
allocation unit (7.8)
ATA (7.13)
auxiliary storage (7.4)
backup (7.9)
cache controller (7.12)
capacity (7.4)
CD recorder (7.22)
CD-R (compact disc-recordable) (7.22)
CD-R drive (7.22)
CD-ROM (7.20)
CD-ROM drive (7.20)
CD-ROM jukebox (7.27)
CD-ROM player (7.20)
CD-RW (compact disc-rewritable) (7.23)
CD-RW drive (7.23)
cluster (7.8)
compact disc (CD) (7.17)

PhotoCD
Compact disc that contains only digital photographic images saved in PhotoCD format. PhotoCDs containing pictures can be purchased, or a user can have his or her own pictures or negatives recorded on a PhotoCD in order to have digital versions of photographs. (7.21)

compact disc read-only memory (7.20)
computer output microfilm (COM) recorder (7.30)
cylinder (7.11)
data warehouse (7.28)
density (7.7)
digital cash (7.29)
direct access (7.26)
disk cache (7.12)
disk cartridge (7.13)
disk controller (7.13)

diskette (7.6)
downward compatible (7.7)
DVD player (7.25)
DVD+RW (7.25)
DVD-R (DVD-recordable) (7.25)
DVD-RAM (7.25)
DVD-ROM (digital video disc-ROM) (7.25)
DVD-ROM drive (7.25)
electronic money (e-money) (7.29)
Enhanced Integrated Drive Electronics (EIDE) (7.13)
enterprise storage system (7.27)
erasable CD (CD-E) (7.23)
fixed disk (7.10)
floppy disk (7.6)
floppy disk drive (FDD) (7.6)
formatting (7.8)
hard disk (7.10)
hard disk controller (HDC) (7.13)
hard disk drive (7.10)
head crash (7.12)
HiFD™ (High-Capacity Floppy Disk) drive (7.10)
high-capacity disk drive (7.9)
intelligent smart card (7.29)
Internet backup (7.27)
Internet hard drive (7.16)
Jaz® disk (7.13)
jewel box (7.19)
level 1 (7.14)
magnetic media (7.8)
mass storage (7.4)
memory card (7.29)
microfiche (7.30)
microfilm (7.30)
mirroring (7.14)
multiread CD-ROM drive (7.23)
multisession (7.21)
network-attached storage (NAS) (7.27)
nonvolatile memory (7.3)
online storage (7.16)
optical disc (7.16)
optically-assisted hard drive (7.10)
partitions (7.12)
PC Card (7.28)
permanent storage (7.4)
PhotoCD (7.21)
Picture CD (7.21)
platter (7.10)
RAID (redundant array of independent disks) (7.14)

Floppy Disk
Portable, inexpensive storage medium that consists of a thin, circular, flexible plastic disk with a magnetic coating. (7.5)

random access (7.26)
reading (7.4)
records (7.20)
removable hard disk (7.13)
secondary storage (7.4)
sectors (7.8)
sequential access (7.26)
shutter (7.6)
single-session (7.21)
small computer system interface (SCSI) (7.13)
smart card (7.29)
storage (7.4)
storage area network (SAN) (7.27)
storage device (7.4)
storage medium (7.4)
striping (7.14)
SuperDisk™ drive (7.10)
tape (7.26)
tape cartridge (7.26)
tape drive (7.26)
tape library (7.27)
track (7.8)
upward compatible (7.7)
volatile memory (7.3)
write-protect notch (7.9)
writing (7.4)
Zip® disk (7.10)
Zip® drive (7.10)

DISCOVERING COMPUTERS *2002*

Chapter 1 2 3 4 5 6 **7** 8 9 10 11 12 13 14 15 16 Index **HOME**

7.37

SHELLY
CASHMAN
SERIES.

Learn It Online

Student Exercises Web Links In Summary Key Terms **Learn It Online** Checkpoint In The Lab Web Work

Special Features ■ TIMELINE 2002 ■ WWW & E-SKILLS ■ MULTIMEDIA ■ BUYER'S GUIDE 2002 ■ WIRELESS TECHNOLOGY ■ TRENDS 2002 ■ INTERACTIVE LABS ■ TECH NEWS

Web Instructions: To display this page from the Web, start your browser and enter the URL scsite.com/dc2002/ch7/learn.htm.

1. Web Guide

Click Web Guide to display the Guide to World Wide Web Sites and Searching Techniques Web page. Click Reference and then click Webopedia. Search for optical disc. Click one of the optical disc links. Use your word processing program to prepare a brief report on your findings and submit your assignment to your instructor.

2. Scavenger Hunt

Click Scavenger Hunt. Print a copy of the Scavenger Hunt page; use this page to write down your answers as you search the Web. Submit your completed page to your instructor.

3. Who Wants to Be a Computer Genius?

Click Computer Genius to find out if you are a computer genius. Directions on how to play the game will display. When you are ready to play, click the PLAY button. Submit your score to your instructor.

4. Wheel of Terms

Click Wheel of Terms to reinforce important terms you learned in this chapter by playing the Shelly Cashman Series version of this popular game. Directions on how to play the game will display. When you are ready to play, click the PLAY button. Submit your score to your instructor.

5. Career Corner

Click Career Corner to display the Campus Career page. Click a link of an area of interest and review the information. Write a brief report describing what you discovered. Submit the report to your instructor.

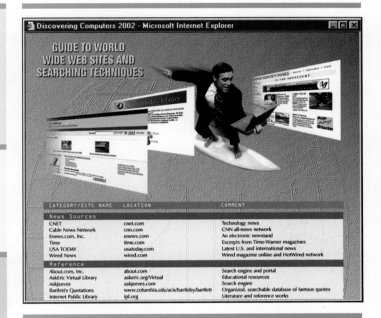

6. Search Sleuth

Click Search Sleuth to learn search techniques that will help make you a research expert. Submit the completed assignment to your instructor.

7. Crossword Puzzle Challenge

Click Crossword Puzzle Challenge. Complete the puzzle to reinforce skills you learned in this chapter. Directions on how to play the game will display. When you are ready to play, click the PLAY button. Submit the completed puzzle to your instructor.

8. Practice Test

Click Practice Test. Answer each question. When completed, enter your name and click the Grade Test button to submit the quiz for grading. Make a note of any missed questions. If required, print a copy to submit to your instructor.

7.38

DISCOVERING
COMPUTERS 2002

Chapter 1 2 3 4 5 6 7 8 9 10 11 12 13 14 15 16 Index **HOME**

Checkpoint

SHELLY
CASHMAN
SERIES.

Student Exercises   Web Links   In Summary   Key Terms   Learn It Online   Checkpoint   In The Lab   Web Work

Special Features   ■ TIMELINE 2002   ■ WWW & E-SKILLS   ■ MULTIMEDIA   ■ BUYER'S GUIDE 2002   ■ WIRELESS TECHNOLOGY   ■ TRENDS 2002   ■ INTERACTIVE LABS   ■ TECH NEWS

Web Instructions: To display this page from the Web, launch your browser and enter the URL scsite.com/dc2002/ch7/check.htm. Click the links for current and additional information. To experience the animation and interactivity, Shockwave and Flash Player must be installed on your computer (download by clicking here.)

LABEL THE FIGURE   **Instructions:** Identify each step of how a hard disk works.

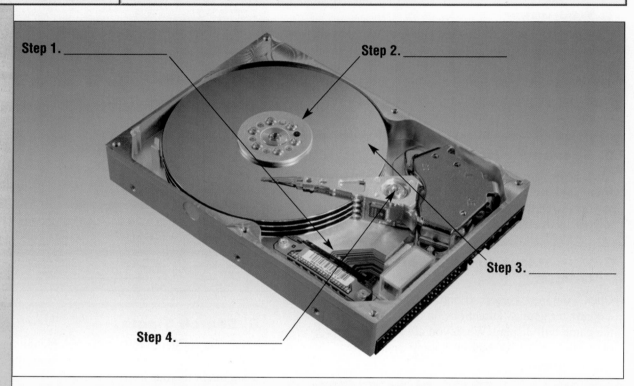

Step 1. _____

Step 2. _____

Step 3. _____

Step 4. _____

MATCHING   **Instructions:** Match each term from the column on the left with the best description from the column on the right.

_____ 1. CD-ROM
_____ 2. hard disk
_____ 3. floppy disk
_____ 4. Zip® disk
_____ 5. CD-RW

a. Typically stores data on both sides of the disk, has 80 tracks on each side of the recording surface, and 18 sectors per track.
b. An erasable optical disc you can write on multiple times.
c. A silver-colored compact disc that uses the same laser technology as audio CDs.
d. Consists of several inflexible, circular platters that store items electronically.
e. A drive that can read audio CDs, data CD-ROMs, CD-Rs, and CD-RWs.
f. Slightly larger than and about twice as thick as a 3.5-inch floppy disk, and can store 100 MB or 250 MB of data.
g. A multisession compact disc onto which you can record your own items such as text, graphics, and audio.

DISCOVERING
COMPUTERS *2002*

Checkpoint

SHELLY
CASHMAN
SERIES.

Student Exercises   Web Links   In Summary   Key Terms   Learn It Online   Checkpoint   In The Lab   Web Work

Special Features   ■ TIMELINE 2002 ■ WWW & E-SKILLS ■ MULTIMEDIA ■ BUYER'S GUIDE 2002 ■ WIRELESS TECHNOLOGY ■ TRENDS 2002 ■ INTERACTIVE LABS ■ TECH NEWS

MULTIPLE CHOICE   Instructions: Select the letter of the correct answer for each of the following questions.

1. Secondary storage is _____ .
   a. volatile
   b. nonvolatile
   c. permanent
   d. both b and c
2. The amount of time it takes the device to locate an item on a disk is called _____ .
   a. reading time
   b. writing time
   c. access time
   d. locating time
3. Most _____ have multiple platters stacked on top of one another.
   a. hard disks
   b. floppy disks
   c. CD-ROMs
   d. Zip® disks

4. An Internet hard drive is a service on the Web that provides _____ to computer users.
   a. a multiread CD-ROM drive
   b. a CD-ROM jukebox
   c. online storage
   d. sectors
5. A _____ is an extremely high-capacity compact disc capable of storing from 4.7 GB to 17 GB.
   a. CD-RW
   b. DVD-ROM
   c. CD-R
   d. PhotoCD

SHORT ANSWER   Instructions: Write a brief answer to each of the following questions.

1. What is access time? _____ Why is hard disk access time faster than floppy disk access time? _____
2. What is disk density? _____ What does it mean to say that floppy disk drives are downward compatible but not upward compatible? _____
3. What is a head crash? _____ How does a disk cache improve hard disk access time? _____
4. How does an Internet hard drive work? _____ Why would someone want to use one of these? _____ What disadvantages could there be? _____
5. How are multisession CD-ROMs different from single-session CD-ROMs? _____ What are the four basic formats of compact discs? _____ How are CD-Rs and CD-RWs different? _____

WORKING TOGETHER   Instructions: Working with a group of your classmates, complete the following team exercise.

Data and information backup is as important for people with personal computers as it is for companies. Develop a report detailing what your group would consider to be the ideal backup system and devices for the following scenarios: (1) a home computer for personal use; (2) a computer used in a home-based business; (3) a small business with six to eight computers; (4) a business or organization with up to 100 computers; and (5) a business or organization with more than 100 computers. Include information that supports why you selected the particular options. Develop a PowerPoint presentation and present your information to the class.

7.40

DISCOVERING
COMPUTERS *2002*

Chapter 1 2 3 4 5 6 **7** 8 9 10 11 12 13 14 15 16 Index **HOME**

In The Lab

SHELLY
CASHMAN
SERIES.

Student Exercises   Web Links   In Summary   Key Terms   Learn It Online   Checkpoint   In The Lab   Web Work

Special Features   ■ TIMELINE 2002 ■ WWW & E-SKILLS ■ MULTIMEDIA ■ BUYER'S GUIDE 2002 ■ WIRELESS TECHNOLOGY ■ TRENDS 2002 ■ INTERACTIVE LABS ■ TECH NEWS

Web Instructions: To display this page from the Web, start your browser and enter the URL scsite.com/dc2002/ch7/lab.htm. Click the links for current and additional information.

Examining My Computer

How many disk drives does your computer have? What letter is used for each? To find out more about the disk drives on your computer, right-click the My Computer icon on the desktop. Click Open on the shortcut menu. What is the drive letter for the floppy disk drive on your computer? What letter(s) are used for the hard disk drives on your computer? If you have a CD-ROM drive, what letter is used for it? Double-click the Hard disk (C:) drive icon in the My Computer window. The Hard disk (C:) window shows the file folders (yellow folder icons) stored on your hard disk. How many folders are on the hard disk? Click the Close button to close the Hard disk (C:) window. Close the My Computer window.

Working with Files

Insert the Discover Data Disk into drive A. See the Preface at the front of this book for instructions for downloading the Data Disk or see your instructor for information on accessing the files required in this book. Double-click the My Computer icon on the desktop. When the My Computer window opens, right-click the 3½ Floppy (A:) icon. Click Open

on the shortcut menu. Click View on the menu bar and then click Large Icons. Right-click the h3-2 icon. If h3-2 is not on the floppy disk, ask your instructor for a copy. Click Copy on the shortcut menu. Click Edit on the menu bar and then click Paste. How has the 3½ Floppy (A:) window changed? Right-click the new icon (Copy of h3-2) and then click Rename on the shortcut menu. Type h7-2 and then press the ENTER key. Right-click the h7-2 icon and then click Print on the shortcut menu. Close the 3½ Floppy (A:) window. Close the My Computer window.

Learning About Your Hard Disk

What are the characteristics of your hard disk? To find out, right-click the My Computer icon on the desktop. Click Open on the shortcut menu. Right-click the Hard disk (C:) icon in the My Computer window. Click Properties on the shortcut menu. If necessary, click the General tab and then answer the following questions:

- What Label is on the disk?
- What Type of disk is it?
- How much of the hard disk is Used space?
- How much of the hard disk is Free space?

- What is the total Capacity of the hard disk?

Close the Hard disk (C:) Properties dialog box and the My Computer window.

Disk Cleanup

This exercise uses Windows 2000 procedures. Just as people maintain they never can have too much money, computer users insist that you never can have too much hard disk space. Fortunately, Windows includes a utility program called Disk Cleanup that can increase available hard disk space. To find out more about Disk Cleanup, click the Start button on the taskbar and then click Help on the Start menu. Click the Index tab in the Windows 2000 window and then type disk cleanup in the Type in the keyword to find text box. Click the overview subentry below the Disk Cleanup entry in the list of topics and then click the Display button. Read the Help information in the right pane of the Windows 2000 window and answer the following questions:

- How does Disk Cleanup help to free up space on the hard disk?
- How do you start Disk Cleanup using the Start button?

Click the Close button to close the Windows 2000 window.

DISCOVERING COMPUTERS 2002

Chapter 1 2 3 4 5 6 **7** 8 9 10 11 12 13 14 15 16 Index HOME **7.41**

Web Work

SHELLY CASHMAN SERIES.

Student Exercises   Web Links   In Summary   Key Terms   Learn It Online   Checkpoint   In The Lab   Web Work

Special Features ■ TIMELINE 2002 ■ WWW & E-SKILLS ■ MULTIMEDIA ■ BUYER'S GUIDE 2002 ■ WIRELESS TECHNOLOGY ■ TRENDS 2002 ■ INTERACTIVE LABS ■ TECH NEWS

Web Instructions: To display this page from the Web, start your browser and enter the URL scsite.com/dc2002/ch7/web.htm. To view At The Movies in exercise 1, RealPlayer must be installed on your computer (download by clicking here). To use the Shelly Cashman Series Maintaining Your Hard Drive Lab from the Web, Shockwave and Flash Player must be installed on your computer (download by clicking here).

Pocket Card

To view the Pocket Card movie, click the button to the left or click the Play button to the right. Watch the movie, and then complete the exercise by answering the questions below. The dangers of too-easy credit are all too obvious, and often personally painful. Addressing these dangers, the pocket card (actually a debit card) was developed to provide access to a fixed-dollar limit, corresponding to a pre-deposited amount. In emergencies (or perhaps with a heartrending story to one's parent) it is possible to increase the amount with a deposit or transfer, either online or using a Touch-Tone telephone. Pocket cards also offer monitoring and accountability, because purchases trigger e-mail notification to the card's owner. The budgeting and monitoring features have attracted two prime markets: parents of out-of-town students, and employers of salespeople. Why these two markets? What other target opportunities can you see?

Shelly Cashman Series Maintaining Your Hard Drive Lab

Follow the appropriate instructions in Web Work 2 on page 1.47 to start and use the Shelly Cashman Series Maintaining Your Hard Drive Lab. If you are running from the Web, enter the URL, www.scsite.com/sclabs/menu.htm; or display the Web Work page (see instructions at the top of this page) and then click the button to the left.

Digital Video Disc (DVD)

A DVD can hold almost 25 times more data than a CD. This translates into richer sound and images than ever seen or heard before. The quality of DVD storage is beginning to have a major impact on the market. Some expect that the sales of DVD optical drives soon will pass the $4 billion mark. Click the button to the left and complete this exercise to learn more about DVDs.

Personal Information Management

Are you tired of forgetting birthdays, missing meetings, overlooking appointments, or neglecting to complete important tasks? If so, then personal information management software may be perfect for you. Click the button to the left to find out about a free, Internet-based calendar. How could this calendar help you organize your life? How might the calendar help you have more fun? After reading the information, you may sign up to create your own Internet-based calendar.

In the News

IBM recently unveiled a small disk drive, about the size of a quarter, that is capable of storing 1 GB of information, as much as 690 floppy disks. The drive will be used in devices such as digital cameras. What other storage devices are on the horizon? Click the button to the left and read a news article about a new or improved storage device. What is the device? Who manufactures it? How is the storage device better than, or different from, earlier devices? How will the device be used? Why?

CHAPTER 8

Operating Systems and Utility Programs

At last, your chemistry lab is finished. Now you have time to relax and respond to e-mail messages, some of which relate to your distance learning course. As you click the Send button, replying to the first of 22 unread messages, the computer freezes. You click the button on the mouse. Nothing happens. You press a key on the keyboard. The computer beeps. You click the mouse again. Still no response. With reluctance, you restart the computer.

While you are waiting, you ponder the work ahead and hope nothing is wrong. After all, you no longer can get by in school without your computer. By now, you expect to see the Windows desktop. Something *is* wrong. It is time to call for help. You dial the toll-free number for technical support, but the automated system places you on hold. Your thoughts turn to that distance learning homework.

Finally, a live person answers your call! You explain the problem to the technician. She tells you the first step in solving this problem is to start the computer again — this time with the boot disk in the floppy disk drive. Now you know you are in trouble... what's a boot disk?

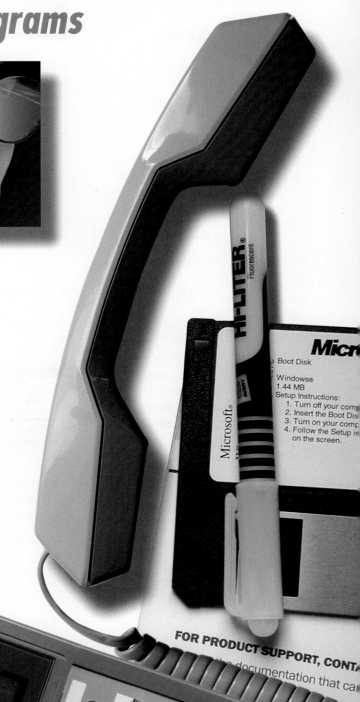

8.2

SYSTEM SOFTWARE

Software is the series of computer-language coded instructions that tells the computer how to perform tasks. Two types of software are application software and system software. Like most computer users, you probably interact with a variety of application software products such as a word processing program, an e-mail program, and a Web browser. You also interact with system software.

System software consists of the programs that control the operations of the computer and its devices. System software serves as the interface between the user, the application software, and the computer's hardware.

Two types of system software include operating systems and utility programs. This chapter discusses the operating system and its functions, as well as several utility programs for personal computers.

OBJECTIVES

After completing this chapter, you will be able to:

- Describe the two types of software
- Understand the startup process for a personal computer
- Describe the term user interface
- Explain features common to most operating systems
- Know the difference between stand-alone operating systems and network operating systems
- Identify various stand-alone operating systems
- Identify various network operating systems
- Recognize devices that use embedded operating systems
- Discuss the purpose of the following utilities: file viewer, file compression, diagnostic, uninstaller, disk scanner, disk defragmenter, backup, and screen saver

Figure 8-1 Most operating systems perform the functions illustrated in this figure.

start up the computer

administer security

control a network

OPERATING SYSTEMS

An **operating system** (**OS**) is a set of programs containing instructions that coordinate all the activities among computer hardware resources. For example, the operating system recognizes input from an input device such as the keyboard, mouse, microphone, or PC camera; coordinates the display of output on the monitor; instructs a printer how and when to print information; and manages data and instructions in memory and information stored on disk. A computer needs an operating system to work.

Many different operating systems exist. Most perform similar functions that include starting the computer, providing a user interface, managing programs, managing memory, scheduling jobs, configuring devices, accessing the Web, monitoring performance, and providing housekeeping services (Figure 8-1). Some operating systems also allow you to control a network and administer security.

In most cases, the operating system resides on the computer's hard disk. On smaller handheld computers, the operating system may reside on a ROM chip.

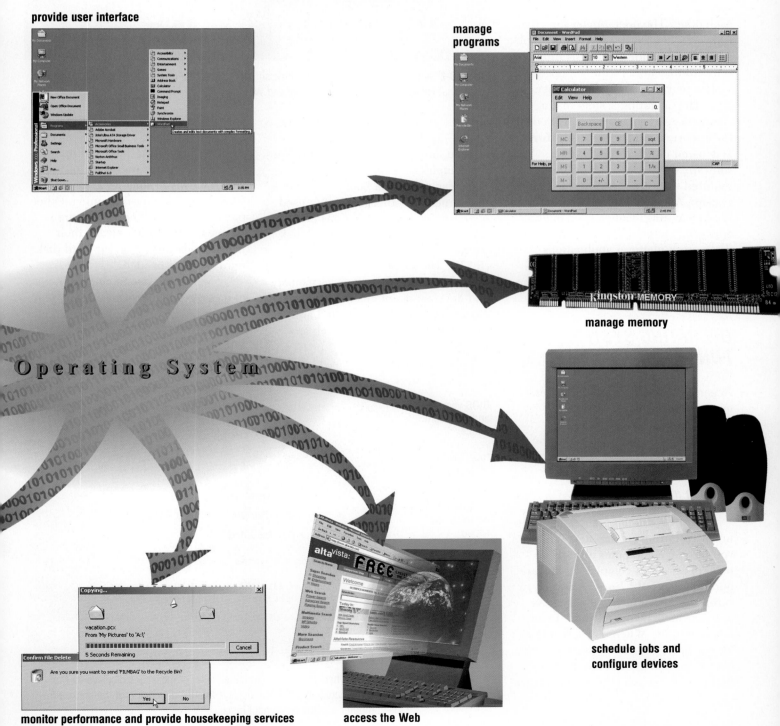

provide user interface

manage programs

manage memory

Operating System

schedule jobs and configure devices

monitor performance and provide housekeeping services

access the Web

Different sizes of computers typically use different operating systems. For example, a mainframe computer does not use the same operating system as a desktop computer. Even the same types of computers, such as desktop computers, may not use the same operating system. One personal computer may use Windows and another may use Mac OS. Furthermore, these various operating systems often are not compatible with each other. The operating system that runs on a PC will not run on an Apple computer. In addition, application software that works with one operating system may not work with another.

The operating system that a computer uses sometimes is called the **software platform** or **platform**. When you purchase application software, the package identifies the required software platform (operating system). A **cross-platform** application is one that runs identically on multiple operating systems (Figure 8-2). Often, these cross-platform applications have multiple versions, each corresponding to a different operating system.

OPERATING SYSTEM FUNCTIONS

Regardless of the size of computer, most operating systems provide similar functions. The following sections discuss functions common to operating systems.

Starting a Computer

Booting is the process of starting or restarting a computer. When you turn on a computer after it has been powered off completely, you are performing a **cold boot**. A **warm boot** or **warm start** is the process of restarting a computer that already is powered on. When using Windows, for example, you can perform a warm boot by pressing a combination of keyboard keys, selecting options from

Figure 8-2 Some applications run on multiple software platforms (operating systems). This box shows that FileMaker runs on Windows 98 and Windows NT.

a menu, or pressing a Reset button on the computer.

Each time you boot a computer, the kernel and other frequently used operating system instructions are *loaded*, or copied from the hard disk (storage) to the computer's memory (RAM). The **kernel** is the core of an operating system that manages memory and devices; maintains the computer's clock; starts applications; and assigns the computer's resources, such as

devices, programs, data, and information. The kernel is **memory resident**, which means it remains in memory while the computer is running. Other parts of the operating system are **nonresident**, which means their instructions remain on the hard disk until they are needed.

When you boot a computer, a set of messages displays on the screen (Figure 8-3). The actual information

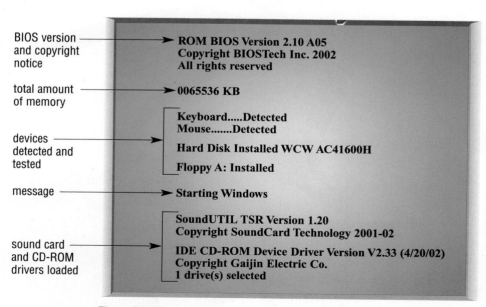

Figure 8-3 When you boot a computer, a set of messages displays on the screen. The actual information displayed varies depending on the make of the computer and the equipment installed.

displayed varies depending on the make of the computer and the equipment installed. The boot process, however, is similar for large and small computers.

The following steps explain what occurs during a cold boot on a personal computer using the Windows operating system (Figure 8-4).

1. When you turn on the computer, the power supply sends an electrical signal to the motherboard and the other devices located in the system unit.

2. The surge of electricity causes the processor chip to reset itself and look for the ROM chip(s) that contains the BIOS. The **BIOS** (pronounced BYE-ohss), which stands for **basic input/output system**, is firmware that contains the computer's startup instructions.

Figure 8-4 HOW A PERSONAL COMPUTER BOOTS UP

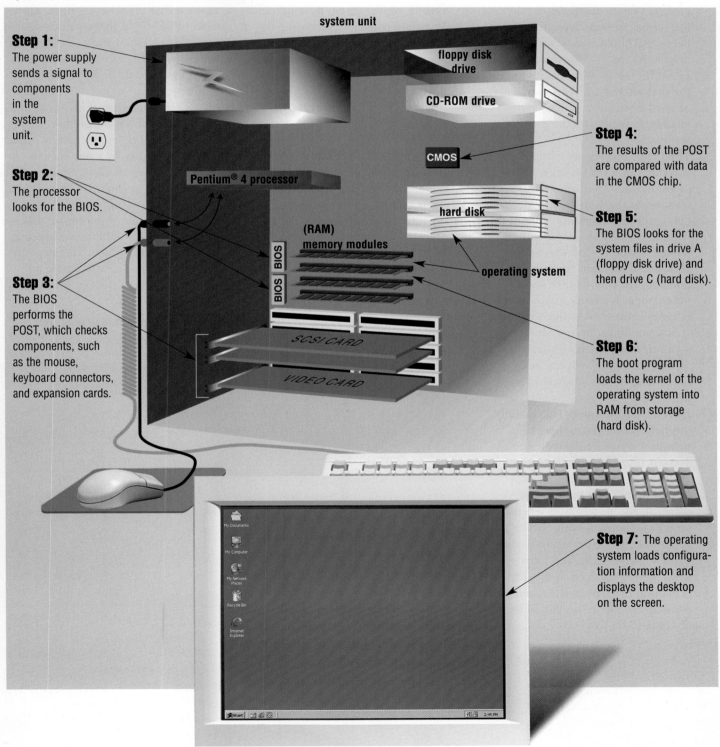

Step 1: The power supply sends a signal to components in the system unit.

Step 2: The processor looks for the BIOS.

Step 3: The BIOS performs the POST, which checks components, such as the mouse, keyboard connectors, and expansion cards.

system unit

floppy disk drive

CD-ROM drive

Pentium® 4 processor

CMOS

hard disk

BIOS BIOS

(RAM) memory modules

operating system

SCSI CARD

VIDEO CARD

Step 4: The results of the POST are compared with data in the CMOS chip.

Step 5: The BIOS looks for the system files in drive A (floppy disk drive) and then drive C (hard disk).

Step 6: The boot program loads the kernel of the operating system into RAM from storage (hard disk).

Step 7: The operating system loads configuration information and displays the desktop on the screen.

As discussed in Chapter 4, firmware consists of ROM chips that contain permanently written instructions.

3. The BIOS executes a series of tests to make sure the computer hardware is connected properly and operating correctly. The tests, collectively called the **power-on self test** (**POST**), check the various system components such as the buses, system clock, expansion cards, RAM chips, keyboard, and drives. As the POST executes, LEDs flicker on devices, including the disk drives and keyboard. Several beeps also sound, and messages display on the monitor's screen.

4. The POST results are compared with data in a CMOS chip on the motherboard. As discussed in Chapter 4, the CMOS chip stores configuration information about the computer, such as the amount of memory; type of disk drives, keyboard, and monitor; the current date and time; and other startup information. It also detects any new devices connected to the computer. If any problems are found, the computer may beep, display error messages, or cease operating — depending on the severity of the problem.

5. If the POST completes successfully, the BIOS searches for specific operating system files called **system files**. Usually, the operating system will look first in drive A (the designation for a floppy disk drive). If the system files are not on a disk in drive A, the BIOS looks in drive C (the designation usually given to the first hard disk). If neither drive A nor drive C contain the system files, some computers look to the CD-ROM or DVD-ROM drive.

6. Once located, the system files load into memory and execute. Next, the kernel of the operating system loads into memory. Then, the operating system in memory takes control of the computer.

7. The operating system loads system configuration information. In Windows, the **registry** consists of several files that contain the system configuration information. Windows constantly accesses the registry during the computer's operation for information such as installed hardware and software devices and individual user preferences for mouse speed, passwords, and other user-specific information.

Necessary operating system files load into memory. When complete, the Windows desktop and icons display on the screen. The operating system executes programs in the StartUp folder. The **StartUp folder** contains a list of programs that open automatically when you boot the computer.

EMERGENCY REPAIR DISK A **boot drive** is the drive from which your personal computer boots (starts). In most cases, drive C (the hard disk) is the boot drive. Sometimes a hard disk becomes damaged and the computer cannot boot from the hard disk. In this case, you can boot from a special disk. An **emergency repair disk**, sometimes called a **boot disk** or a **rescue disk**, is a floppy disk, Zip® disk, or CD-ROM that contains system files that will start the computer. For this reason, it is crucial you have an emergency repair disk available and ready for use.

When you install an operating system, one of the installation steps involves making an emergency repair disk. Often when you purchase a computer, the manufacturer pre-installs the operating system. If you did not install the operating system, you may not have an emergency repair disk. In this case, you should create one and keep it in a safe place. The steps in Figure 8-5 show how to create an emergency repair disk in Windows.

Figure 8-5 HOW TO CREATE AN EMERGENCY REPAIR DISK IN WINDOWS

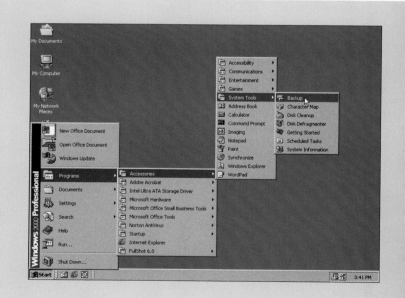

Step 1:
Click the Start button on the taskbar, point to Programs on the Start menu, point to Accessories on the Programs submenu, point to System Tools on the Accessories submenu, and then point to Backup.

The User Interface

You interact with software through its user interface. A **user interface** controls how you enter data and instructions and how information displays on the screen. Two types of user interfaces are command-line and graphical (Figure 8-6). Many operating systems use a combination of these two interfaces to define how you interact with your computer.

Figure 8-6b (graphical user interface)

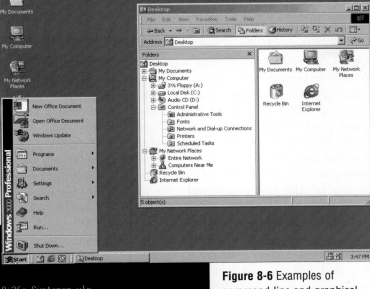

Figure 8-6a (command-line interface)

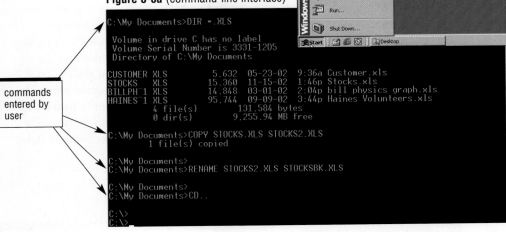

commands entered by user

Figure 8-6 Examples of command-line and graphical user interfaces.

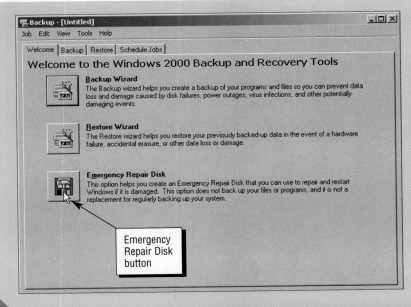

Emergency Repair Disk button

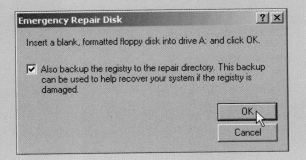

Step 2:
Click Backup on the System Tools submenu to open the Backup window. Point to the Emergency Repair Disk button.

Step 3:
Click the Emergency Repair Disk button to create the emergency repair disk. Follow the on-screen instructions.

With a **command-line interface**, you type keywords or press special keys on the keyboard to enter data and instructions. As described in Chapter 3, a keyword is a special word, phrase, or code that a program understands as an instruction. Some keyboards also include keys that send a command to a program when you press them. When working with a command-line interface, the set of commands you use to interact with the computer is called the **command language**. Command-line interfaces often are difficult to use because they require exact spelling, grammar, and punctuation. Minor errors, such as a missing period, will generate an error message.

A graphical user interface typically is easier to learn and use than a command-line interface because it does not require you memorize a command language. As discussed in Chapter 1, a **graphical user interface (GUI)** allows you to use menus and visual images such as icons, buttons, and other graphical objects to issue commands. A **menu** is a set of commands from which you choose. An **icon** is a small image that represents a program, an instruction, a file, or some other object. You can use a keyboard, mouse, or any other pointing device to interact with menus, icons, buttons, and other onscreen objects.

Today, many GUIs incorporate features similar to that of a Web browser. For example, icons function as Web links, and Web pages can be delivered or *pushed* automatically to your screen (Figure 8-7).

Managing Programs

Some operating systems have single-user functionality and can support only one running program. Others support thousands of users running multiple programs. How an operating system handles programs directly affects your productivity.

A **single user/single tasking** operating system allows only one user to run one program at a time. Suppose, for example, you are creating a poster in a graphics program and then decide to check your e-mail messages. With a single tasking operating system, you must quit the graphics program before you can run the e-mail program. You then must close the e-mail program and restart the graphics program to finish the poster. Early systems were single user. Most operating systems today are multitasking.

ISSUE

OS Innovations

Types of Operating Systems

Today's operating systems include a variety of features. They support a graphical user interface, monitor performance, and administer security. Most operating systems also include a variety of utility programs. These utilities offer functions such as compressing files, diagnosing problems, scanning disks, defragmenting disks, checking for viruses, backing up files and disks, and displaying screen savers. Do you think an operating system should include these features? Are these features useful? What other features should be included in an operating system? If you were to write an overview of the perfect operating system, which innovative features would you include?

For more information on operating systems and operating systems features, visit the Discovering Computers 2002 Issues Web page (**scsite.com/dc2002/issues.htm**) and click Chapter 8 Issue #1.

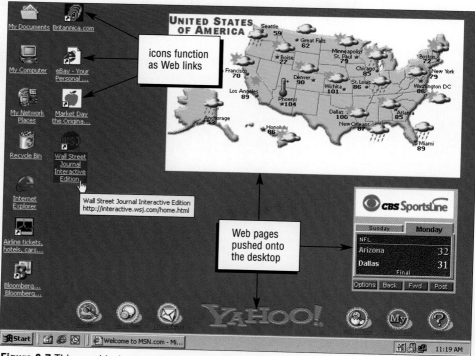

Figure 8-7 This graphical user interface incorporates icons that function like Web links, and Web pages that are *pushed* onto the desktop.

A **multitasking** operating system allows a single user to work on two or more applications that reside in memory at the same time. Using the example just cited, if you are working with a multitasking operating system, you do not have to quit the graphics program to run your e-mail program. Both programs can run concurrently.

Most users today run multiple programs simultaneously. It is common to have an e-mail program and Web browser open at all times, while working in applications such as word processing or graphics.

When you run multiple applications at the same time, one is in the foreground and others are in the background (Figure 8-8). The **foreground** contains the active application; that is, the one you currently are using. The others that are

running, but not in use, are in the **background**. You easily can switch between foreground and background applications. To make an application active (in the foreground), you click its name on the taskbar. This causes the operating system to place all other applications in the background.

A **multiuser** operating system enables two or more users to run a program simultaneously. Networks, mid-range servers, mainframes, and supercomputers allow hundreds to thousands of users to connect at the same time, and thus are multiuser.

A **multiprocessing** operating system can support two or more processors running programs at the same time. Multiprocessing works much like parallel processing, which was discussed in Chapter 3. Multi-processing involves the coordinated

processing of programs by more than one processor. As with parallel processing, multi-processing increases a computer's processing speed.

A computer with separate processors also can serve as a fault-tolerant computer. A **fault-tolerant computer** continues to operate even if one of its components fails. Fault-tolerant computers have duplicate components such as processors, memory, and disk drives. If any one of these components fails, the computer switches to the duplicate component and continues to operate. Airline reservation systems, communications networks, and automated teller machines and other systems that must be operational at all times use fault-tolerant computers.

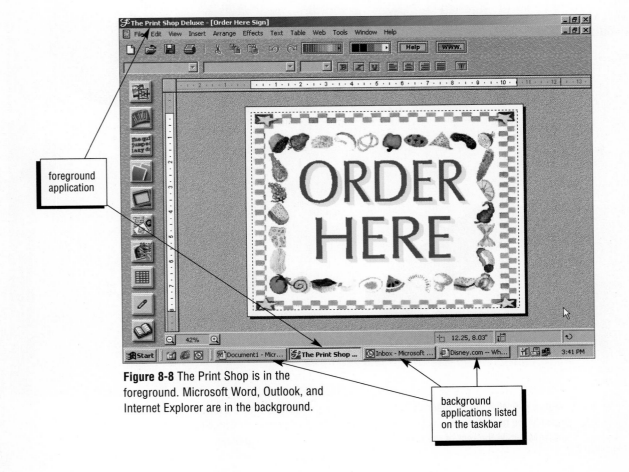

Figure 8-8 The Print Shop is in the foreground. Microsoft Word, Outlook, and Internet Explorer are in the background.

foreground application

background applications listed on the taskbar

Managing Memory

The purpose of **memory management** is to optimize use of random access memory (RAM). As discussed in Chapter 4, RAM consists of one or more chips on the motherboard that temporarily hold items such as data and instructions while the processor interprets and executes them. The operating system allocates, or assigns, these items to an area of memory while they are being processed. Then, it carefully monitors the contents of memory. Finally, the operating system clears these items from memory when the processor no longer requires them.

Some operating systems use virtual memory to optimize RAM. With **virtual memory (VM)**, the operating system allocates a portion of a storage medium, usually the hard disk, to function as additional RAM (Figure 8-9). As you interact with a

program, part of it may be in RAM, while the rest of the program is on the hard disk as virtual memory.

The area of the hard disk used for virtual memory is called a **swap file** because it swaps (exchanges) data, information, and instructions between memory and storage. A **page** is the amount of data and program instructions that can swap at a given time. Thus, the technique of swapping items between memory and storage often is called **paging**.

When an operating system spends much of its time paging, instead of executing application software, it is said to be **thrashing**.

If application software, such as a Web browser, has stopped responding and your hard disk's LED blinks repeatedly, the operating system probably is thrashing. To stop it from thrashing, quit the application that stopped responding. If thrashing occurs frequently, one possibility is you may need to install more RAM in your computer.

Scheduling Jobs

The operating system determines the order in which jobs are processed. A **job** is an operation the processor manages. Jobs include receiving data from an input device, processing

VIRTUAL MEMORY MANAGEMENT

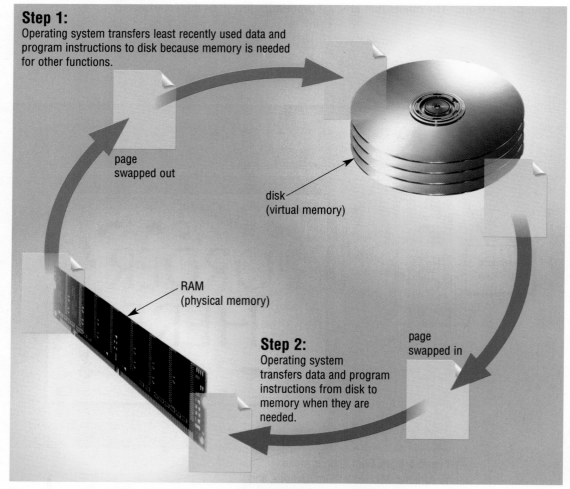

Step 1:
Operating system transfers least recently used data and program instructions to disk because memory is needed for other functions.

page swapped out

disk (virtual memory)

RAM (physical memory)

Step 2:
Operating system transfers data and program instructions from disk to memory when they are needed.

page swapped in

Figure 8-9 With virtual memory (VM), the operating system allocates a portion of a storage medium, usually the hard disk, to function as additional RAM. As you interact with a program, part of it may be in RAM, while the rest of the program is on the hard disk as virtual memory.

instructions, sending information to an output device, and transferring items from storage to memory and from memory to storage.

The operating system does not always process jobs on a first-come, first-served basis. Sometimes, one user may have higher priority than other users. In this case, the operating system has to adjust the schedule of jobs. Other times, a device may already be busy processing one job when it receives another job. This occurs because the processor operates at a much faster rate of speed than peripheral devices. For example, if the processor sends five print jobs to a printer, the printer only can print one document at a time.

While waiting for devices to become idle, the operating system places items in buffers. A **buffer** is an area of memory or storage in which items are placed while waiting to be transferred to or from an input or output device.

The operating system commonly uses buffers with print jobs. This process, called **spooling,** sends print jobs to a buffer instead of sending them immediately to the printer. The buffer holds the information waiting to print while the printer prints from the buffer at its own speed. By spooling print jobs to a buffer, the processor can interpret and execute instructions while the printer is printing documents. Once a print job is in the buffer, you can use the computer for other tasks.

Another advantage of spooling is it allows you to send a second job to the printer without waiting for the first job to finish printing. Multiple print jobs line up in a **queue** within the buffer. A program, called a **print spooler**, intercepts print jobs from the operating system and places them in the queue (Figure 8-10).

Configuring Devices

To communicate with each device in the computer, the operating system relies on device drivers. A **device driver**, also called a **driver**, is a small program that tells the operating system how to communicate with a device. Each device on a computer, such as the mouse, keyboard, monitor, and printer, has its own specialized set of commands and thus requires its own specific driver. When you boot a computer, the operating system loads each device's driver. These devices will not function without their correct drivers. In Windows environments, most device drivers have a .drv extension.

Web Link

For more information on device drivers, visit the Discovering Computers 2002 Chapter 8 WEB LINK page (**scsite.com/dc2002/ch8/ weblink.htm**) and click Device Drivers.

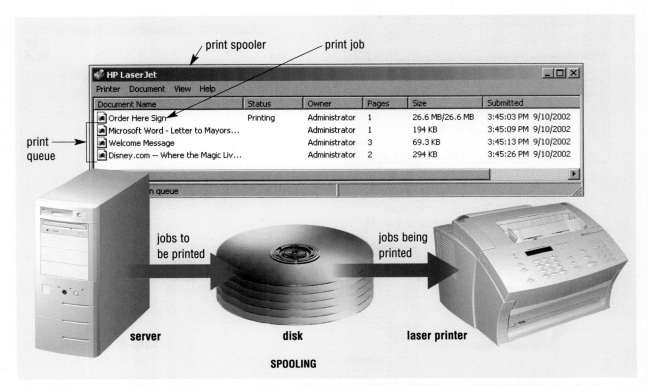

Figure 8-10 Spooling increases both processor and printer efficiency by writing print jobs to a disk before they are printed. In this figure, three jobs are in the queue and one is printing.

If you attach a new device to your computer, such as a printer or scanner, its driver must be installed before you can use the device. Windows provides a wizard to guide you through the installation steps. Figure 8-11 shows how to install a device driver for a Kodak digital camera. You follow the same general steps to install device drivers for any type of hardware. For many devices, your computer's operating system already may include the necessary drivers. If it does not, you can install the drivers from the disk included with the device upon purchase.

If you need a driver for your device and do not have the original disk, you can obtain the driver by contacting the vendor that sold you the device or contacting the manufacturer directly. Many manufacturers post device drivers on their Web site for anyone to download.

Figure 8-11 HOW TO INSTALL DRIVERS FOR NEW HARDWARE IN WINDOWS

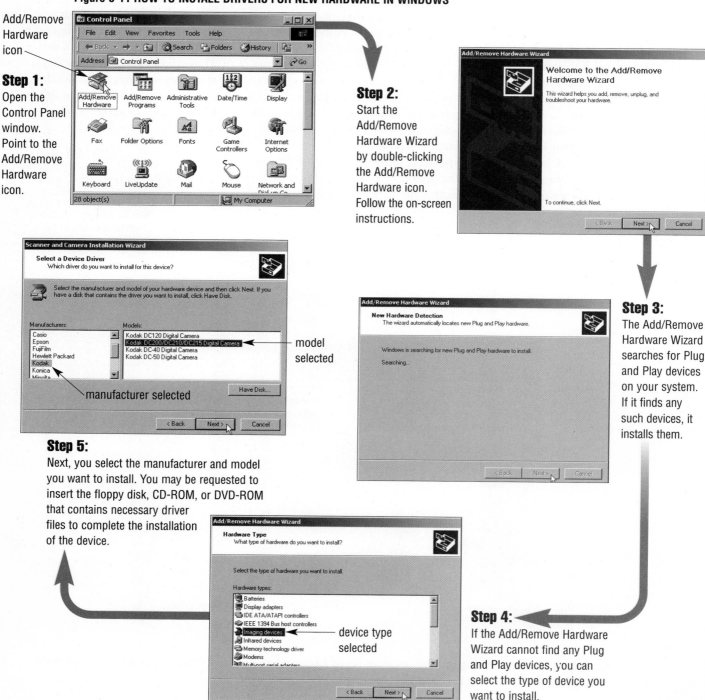

In the past, installing a new hardware device often required setting switches and other elements on the motherboard. Today, installation is easier because most devices and operating systems support Plug and Play. As discussed in Chapter 4, **Plug and Play** means the computer can recognize a new device and assist you in its installation by loading the necessary drivers automatically and checking for conflicts with other devices. With Plug and Play, a user can plug in a device, turn on the computer, and then use, or play, the device without having to configure the system manually.

When installing some components, occasionally you have to know which interrupt request the device should use for communications. An **interrupt request (IRQ)** is a communications line between a device and the processor. Most computers have 16 IRQs, numbered 0 through 15 (Figure 8-12). With Plug and Play, the operating system determines the best IRQ to use for these communications.

If your operating system uses an IRQ that already is assigned to another device, an IRQ conflict will occur and the computer will not work properly. If an IRQ conflict occurs, you will have to obtain the correct IRQ for the device. You usually can find this information in the installation directions that accompany the device.

Accessing the Web

Operating systems typically provide a means to establish Web connections. For example, Windows includes an Internet Connection Wizard that guides you through the process of setting up a connection between your computer and your Internet service provider (Figure 8-13).

Some operating systems include a Web browser and an e-mail program, enabling you to begin using the Web and communicate with others as soon as you set up the connections. This feature saves time because you do not have to install any additional software.

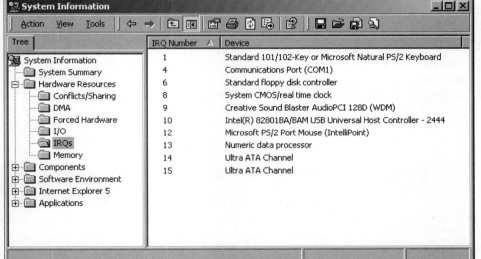

Figure 8-12 An interrupt request (IRQ) is a communication line between a device and the processor. In this example, only 10 of the 16 IRQs are being used (1, 4, 6, 8, 9, 10, 12, 13, 14, and 15).

Web Link
For more information on Plug and Play, visit the Discovering Computers 2002 Chapter 8 WEB LINK page (**scsite.com/dc2002/ch8/weblink.htm**) and click Plug and Play.

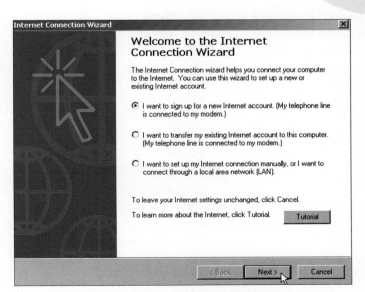

Figure 8-13 The Internet Connection Wizard allows you to set up a connection between your computer and your Internet service provider.

Monitoring Performance

Operating systems typically contain a performance monitor. A **performance monitor** is a program that assesses and reports information about various system resources and devices (Figure 8-14). For example, you can monitor the processor, disks, memory, and network usage. A performance monitor also can check the number of reads and writes to a file.

The information in performance reports can help you identify problems with resources so you can attempt to resolve the problem. If your computer is running extremely slow, the performance monitor may determine that you are using the computer's memory to its maximum. Thus, you might consider installing additional memory.

Providing Housekeeping Services

Operating systems contain a program called a file manager. A **file manager** performs functions related to storage and file management (Figure 8-15). Some of the storage and file management functions that a file manager performs are formatting and copying disks; displaying a list of files on a storage medium; checking the amount of used or free space on a storage medium; organizing, copying, renaming, deleting, moving, and sorting files; and creating shortcuts. A **shortcut** is an icon on the desktop that runs a program when you click it.

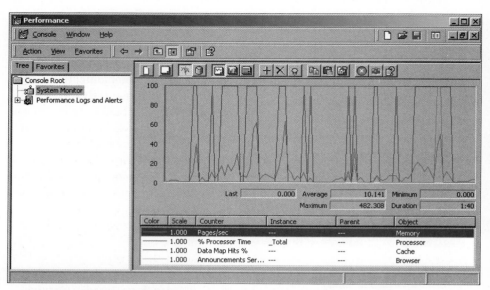

Figure 8-14 A performance monitor is a program that assesses and reports information about various system resources and devices. The System Monitor is a performance monitor in Windows. Shown above it is tracking memory, processor, cache, and browser usage.

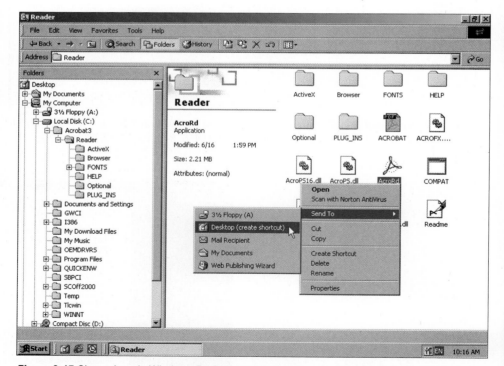

Figure 8-15 Shown here is Windows Explorer, which is a file manager included with Windows. In this figure, the user is creating a shortcut for the Acrobat Reader program. The shortcut will display as an icon on the desktop.

Formatting is the process of preparing a disk for reading and writing. Most floppy and hard disk manufacturers preformat their disks. If you must format a floppy disk, do so by issuing a formatting command to the operating system. Various operating systems format disks differently. Thus, you typically cannot use a disk formatted in one operating system in a computer that has a different operating system. For example, you cannot use a Mac OS floppy disk in a computer that uses the Windows operating system — without special hardware and software.

With the Windows operating system, the formatting process also defines the file allocation table. The **file allocation table** (**FAT**) is a table of information that the operating system uses to locate files on a disk. The FAT is like a library card catalog for your disk, which contains a listing of all files, file types, and locations. If you format a disk that already contains data, instructions, or information,

the formatting process erases the file location information and redefines the file allocation table for these items. Thus, formatting does not erase the actual files on the disk. For this reason, if you accidentally format a disk, you often can unformat it with a utility program.

Controlling a Network

Some operating systems are network operating systems. A **network operating system**, also called a **network OS** or **NOS** (pronounced nauce), is an operating system that supports a network. As discussed in Chapter 1, a **network** is a collection of computers and devices connected together via communications media and devices such as cables, telephone lines, and modems. Some networks are wireless, that is, use no physical lines or wires.

In some networks, the **server** is the computer that controls access to the hardware and software on the

network and provides a centralized storage area for programs, data, and information. The other computers on the network, called **clients**, rely on the server(s) for resources such as files, devices, processing power, and storage (Figure 8-16).

A network OS organizes and coordinates how multiple users access and share resources on the network. Resources include programs, files, and devices such as printers and drives. The network administrator uses the network OS to add and remove users, computers, and other devices to and from the network.

Some operating systems have network features built into them. In other cases, the network OS is a set of programs separate from the operating system on the client computers. When they are not connected to the network, the client computers use their own operating system. When connected to the network, the network OS assumes most of the functions of the operating system.

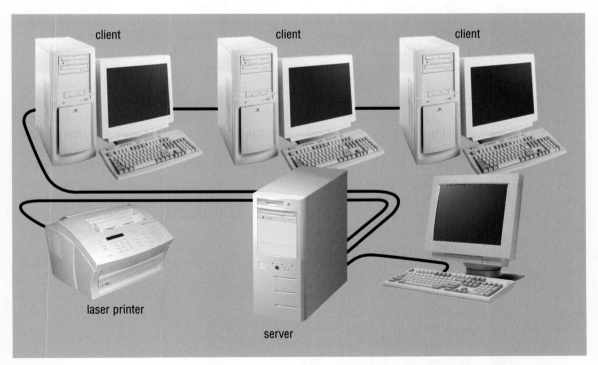

Figure 8-16 On a client/server network, one or more computers are designated as a server, and the other computers on the network are called clients.

Administering Security

When network administrators establish user accounts, each account typically requires a user name and password to access, or **log on**, to the network (Figure 8-17). A **user name**, or **user ID**, is a unique combination of characters, such as letters of the alphabet or numbers, that identifies one specific user. Many users select a combination of their first and last names as their user name. A user named Katy Bollini might choose kbollini as her user name.

Figure 8-17 Most multiuser operating systems allow each user to log on, which is the process of entering a user name and a password into the computer.

A **password** is a combination of characters associated with the user name that allows access to certain computer resources. To prevent unauthorized users from accessing those computer resources, you should keep your password confidential. As you enter your password, most computers hide, or mask, the actual password characters by displaying some other characters, such as asterisks (*).

After entering your user name and password, the operating system compares your entries with a list of authorized user names and passwords. If your entries match the user name and password kept on file, the operating system grants you access. If the entries do not match, the operating system denies you access. The operating system also records successful and unsuccessful logon attempts in a file. This allows the network administrator to review who is using or attempting to use the computer. Network administrators also use these files to monitor computer usage.

The network administrator uses the network OS to establish permissions to resources. These permissions define who can access certain resources and when they can access those resources. Some operating systems allow the network administrator to assign passwords to files and commands, restricting access to only authorized users.

Network administrators using Windows 2000 Server easily manage user access and resources through its Active Directory service. **Active Directory (AD)** is a feature of Windows 2000 Server that allows network administrators to manage all network information including users, devices, settings, and connections from a central environment — even if components of the network are not located in the same physical areas. A later section in this chapter discusses Windows 2000 Server in more depth.

TYPES OF OPERATING SYSTEMS

Many of the first operating systems were device dependent and proprietary. A **device-dependent** software product is one that runs only on a specific type of computer. **Proprietary software** is privately owned and limited to a specific vendor or computer model. When manufacturers introduced a new computer or model, they often produced an improved and different proprietary operating system. Problems arose, however, when a user wanted to switch computer models or manufacturers. The user's application software often would not work on the new computer because the applications were designed to work with a specific operating system.

Some operating systems still are device dependent. The trend today, however, is toward **device-independent** operating systems that run on many manufacturers' computers. The advantage of device independent operating systems is you can retain existing application software and data files even if you change computer models or vendors. This feature generally represents a sizable savings in time and money.

New versions of an operating system usually are downward compatible. A **downward-compatible** operating system is one that recognizes and works with application software written for an earlier version of the operating system. The application software, by contrast, is said to be upward compatible. An **upward-compatible** product is written for an earlier version of the operating system, but also runs with the new version.

Three basic categories of operating systems exist today: stand-alone, network, and embedded. The table in Figure 8-18 lists examples of operating systems in each category. The following pages discuss the operating systems listed in the table.

STAND-ALONE OPERATING SYSTEMS

A **stand-alone operating system** is a complete operating system that works on a desktop or notebook computer. Some stand-alone operating systems, called **client operating systems**, also work in conjunction with a network operating system. That is, client operating systems can operate with or without a network.

Examples of stand-alone operating systems are DOS, Windows 3.x, Windows 95, Windows NT Workstation, Windows 98, Windows 2000 Professional, Windows Millennium Edition, Mac OS, OS/2 Warp, UNIX, and Linux. The following paragraphs briefly discuss most of these operating systems. The section that covers network operating systems discusses UNIX and Linux.

DOS

The term **DOS (Disk Operating System)** refers to several single user operating systems developed in the early 1980s for personal computers. The two more widely used versions of DOS were PC-DOS and MS-DOS. Microsoft Corporation developed both PC-DOS and MS-DOS. The functionality of these two operating systems was essentially the same. The basic difference was the type of computer on which they were installed. Microsoft developed PC-DOS (Personal Computer DOS) for IBM, which in turn installed and sold PC-DOS on its computers. At the same time, Microsoft marketed and sold MS-DOS (Microsoft DOS) to makers of IBM-compatible PCs.

CATEGORIES OF OPERATING SYSTEMS

Category	Examples
Stand-alone	• DOS • Windows 3.x • Windows 95 • Windows NT Workstation • Windows 98 • Windows 2000 Professional • Windows Millennium Edition • Mac OS • OS/2 Warp • UNIX • Linux
Network	• NetWare • Windows NT Server • Windows 2000 Server • OS/2 Warp Server for E-business • UNIX • Linux • Solaris
Embedded	• Windows CE • Pocket PC OS • Palm OS

Figure 8-18 Examples of stand-alone, network, and embedded operating systems.

DOS used a command-line interface when Microsoft first developed it. Later versions included both command-line and menu-driven user interfaces, as well as improved memory and disk management.

At its peak, DOS was a widely used operating system, with an estimated 70 million computers running it. Today, DOS no longer is widely used because it does not offer a graphical user interface (GUI) and it cannot take full advantage of modern 32-bit personal computer processors.

Windows 3.x

To meet the need for an operating system that had a GUI, Microsoft developed **Windows**. **Windows 3.x** refers to three early versions of Microsoft Windows: Windows 3.0, Windows 3.1, and Windows 3.11. These Windows 3.x versions were not operating systems. They were operating environments. An **operating environment** is a GUI that works in combination with an operating system to simplify its use. Windows 3.x was designed to work as an operating environment with DOS.

Windows 95

With **Windows 95**, Microsoft developed a true multitasking operating system — not an operating environment like early versions of Windows. Windows 95 thus did not require DOS to run. It did include, however, some DOS and Windows 3.x features to allow for downward compatibility.

One advantage of Windows 95 was its improved GUI, which made working with files and programs easier than the earlier versions. In addition, most programs ran faster under

Windows 95 because it was written to take advantage of the processing speed in 32-bit processors (versus 16-bit processors). Windows 95 also included support for networking, Plug and Play technology, longer file names, and e-mail.

Windows NT Workstation

Microsoft developed **Windows NT Workstation** as a client operating system that could connect to a Windows NT Server. **Windows NT**, also referred to as **NT**, was an operating system designed for client/server networks. Windows NT Workstation had a Windows 95 interface. Thus, users familiar with Windows 95 easily could migrate to Windows NT Workstation. Businesses most often used Windows NT Workstation.

Windows 98

Microsoft developed an upgrade to the Windows 95 operating system, called Windows 98. The **Windows 98** operating system was more integrated with the Internet than Windows 95. For example, Windows 98 included Microsoft **Internet Explorer**, a popular Web browser. The Windows 98 file manager, called **Windows Explorer**, also had a Web browser look and feel. With Windows 98, you could have an **Active Desktop**™ interface, which allowed you to set up Windows so icons on the desktop and file names in Windows Explorer worked similar to Web links.

Windows 98 also provided faster system startup and shutdown, better file management, and support for multimedia technologies such as DVD and WebTV™. Windows 98 supported the Universal Serial Bus (USB) so you easily could add and remove devices on your computer.

Windows 2000 Professional

Microsoft Windows 2000 Professional is an upgrade to the Windows NT Workstation operating system. **Windows 2000 Professional** is a complete multitasking client operating system that has a GUI (Figure 8-19). Windows 2000 Professional is a reliable operating system for desktop and laptop business computers.

Windows 2000 Professional includes features of previous Windows versions (Figure 8-20). Additionally, Windows 2000 Professional includes these features:

- Windows Installer Service guides you through installation or upgrade of applications
- Windows File Protection safeguards operating system files from being overwritten during installation of applications
- Certifies device drivers to safeguard them from tampering
- Faster performance than Windows 98
- Adapts Start menu to display applications you use most frequently
- Preview multimedia files in Windows Explorer before opening them
- Enhanced technology to increase efficiency and productivity of mobile users

Windows 2000 does require more disk space, memory, and a faster processor than previous versions of Windows because its features are more complex.

Web Link

For more information
on Windows, visit the
Discovering Computers 2002
Chapter 8 WEB LINK page
(**scsite.com/dc2002/ch8/
weblink.htm**) and click
Windows.

Figure 8-19 Microsoft Windows 2000 is easy to use, fast, and integrated with the Internet.

WINDOWS FEATURES

Feature	Description
1. Active Desktop™	Active Desktop™ allows you to set up Windows so icons on the desktop and file names in Windows Explorer work like links (single-click), and create real-time windows that display television-style news or an animated ticker that provides stock updates, news, or other information.
2. Taskbar/toolbars	Several new toolbars can be added to the taskbar by right-clicking the taskbar.
3. Windows Explorer has a Web browser look and feel	Several Web browser tools have been added to Windows Explorer so your hard disk is viewed as an extension of the World Wide Web. For example, Back and Forward buttons allow you easily to revisit folders you have selected previously. A Favorites menu enables you to view quickly your favorite folders.
4. Increased speed	Faster startup and shutdown of Windows. Also, loads 32-bit applications faster.
5. Tune-Up Wizard	Makes your program run faster, checks for hard disk problems, and frees up hard disk space.
6. Multiple display support	Makes it possible for you to use several monitors at the same time to increase the size of your desktop, run different programs on separate monitors, and run programs or play games with multiple views.
7. Universal Serial Bus	Add devices to your computer easily without having to restart.
8. Accessibility Settings Wizard	Accessibility options, such as StickyKeys, ShowSounds, and MouseKeys, are Wizard designed to help users with specific disabilities make full use of the computer.
9. Update Wizard	Reviews device drivers and system software on your computer, compares findings with a master database on the Web, and then recommends and installs updates specific to your computer.
10. Registry Checker	Maintenance program that finds and fixes Registry problems.
11. FAT32	FAT32 is an improved version of the File Allocation Table (file system) that allows hard drives larger than 2 GB to be formatted as a single drive.
12. Hardware support	Supports a variety of new hardware devices, such as DVD, force-feedback joysticks, digital audio speakers, and recording devices. Improved Plug and Play capabilities make installing new hardware easy.

Figure 8-20 Most of the Windows operating systems include these features.

ISSUE

To Change or Not?

Operating Systems

At a recent technical conference, a speaker from a noted software company told an audience of IT professionals that upgrading to a new operating system would be seamless. His listeners responded with uncontrollable laughter. Adopting a new operating system seldom is easy. As a result, no matter what the benefits, people often are reluctant to give up their old operating systems. Although reviewers agree each new Windows version offers several advantages over previous versions, one of the earlier versions of the operating system, Windows 95, is still in use. Why might people be unwilling to embrace new operating system versions? How could developers hasten acceptance of a new operating system? If you generally are satisfied with your current operating system, would you upgrade? Why or why not?

For more information on operating systems and Windows, visit the Discovering Computers 2002 Issues Web page (**scsite.com/dc2002/issues.htm**) and click Chapter 8 Issue #3.

Windows Millennium Edition

Windows Millennium Edition is an upgrade to the Windows 98 operating system. **Windows Millennium Edition**, also called **Windows Me** (pronounced EM-ee), is an operating system that has features specifically for the home user (Figure 8-21). In addition to providing the capabilities in Windows 98, Windows Me offers these additional features:

- Digitize, edit, and store home movies and still photographs using Windows Movie Maker
- Easily transfer photographs from a digital camera with Windows Image Acquisition
- Listen to audio CDs or Web radio stations with Windows Media Player
- Use Windows Restore to recover previous computer settings when a problem occurs
- Deliver the latest system updates automatically to your desktop when you are connected to the Internet
- Easily set up a home network
- Use Internet Connection Sharing so that multiple members of the house can all connect to the Internet at the same time
- Send instant messages
- Use NetMeeting to have a video telephone call

Figure 8-21 Windows Millennium Edition is an operating system designed specifically for the home user that includes many graphic, audio, and video applications.

Mac OS

Apple's **Macintosh operating system** was the first commercially successful GUI. It was released with Macintosh computers in 1984. Since then, it has set the standard for operating system ease of use and has been the model for most of the new GUIs developed for non-Macintosh systems.

Recently, Apple changed the name of the operating system from Macintosh operating system to Mac OS. **Mac OS** is a multitasking operating system available only for computers manufactured by Apple. Figure 8-22 shows a screen of the latest version of Mac OS. This version includes two popular Web browsers: Netscape Navigator and Microsoft Internet Explorer. It also has the capability of opening, editing, and saving files created using the Windows and DOS platforms. Other features of the latest version of Mac OS include large photo-quality icons, built-in networking support, electronic mail, online shopping, enhanced speech recognition, and enhanced multimedia capabilities.

Web Link

For more information on Mac OS, visit the Discovering Computers 2002 Chapter 8 WEB LINK page (**scsite.com/dc2002/ch8/ weblink.htm**) and click Mac OS.

Figure 8-22 Mac OS is the operating system used with Apple Macintosh computers.

COMPANY ON THE CUTTING EDGE

Apple Computer, Inc.

Mac OS X Introduces Technologies

Actor Richard Dreyfuss says his Apple Macintosh makes him a thousand times more productive. Humanitarian and boxing champion Muhammed Ali uses his Mac for philanthropic efforts. Comedian Sinbad would select Apple's QuickTime software if he could have only one application. These AppleMasters praise Apple's hardware and software virtues, as do millions of users in more than 120 countries.

Steven Jobs and Stephen Wozniak formed Apple in 1976 when they decided to market the Apple I, a circuit board they had developed in Jobs' garage. They incorporated one year later and introduced the Apple II, the personal computer that helped generate more than $1 billion in annual sales.

The Apple II product line was discontinued in 1993, and the following year Apple introduced the high-performance Power Macintosh line. Apple then licensed its operating system to other computer manufacturers. This decision was reversed later, however, as other manufacturers reduced Apple's market share and revenues dropped. After a series of personnel changes, Jobs became Apple's CEO. Under his direction, Apple introduced the iBook, the PowerMac G4, and the Mac OS X, which includes iTools, an Internet search feature called Sherlock, and QuickTime TV.

For more information on Apple Computers, visit the Discovering Computers 2002 Companies Web page (**scsite.com/dc2002/companies.htm**) and click Apple.

OS/2 Warp

OS/2 Warp is IBM's GUI multitasking client operating system that supports networking, the Internet, Java, and speech recognition (Figure 8-23). In addition to running programs written specifically for OS/2 (pronounced OH-ESS-too), the operating system also can run DOS and most Windows programs.

OS/2 has been used by businesses because of IBM's long association with business computing and OS/2's strong networking support.

NETWORK OPERATING SYSTEMS

As discussed earlier in this chapter, a network operating system is an operating system that supports a network. A network operating system typically resides on a server. Recall the server is the computer that controls access to the hardware and software on the network and provides a centralized storage area for programs, data, and information. The client computers on the network rely on the server(s) for resources. Many of the client operating systems discussed in the previous section work in conjunction with a network operating system.

Examples of network operating systems include NetWare, Windows NT Server, Windows 2000 Server, OS/2 Warp Server for E-business, UNIX, Linux, and Solaris™. The following pages briefly discuss these operating systems.

NetWare

Novell's **NetWare** is a widely used network operating system designed for client/server networks. NetWare has a server portion that resides on the network server and a client portion that resides on each

Figure 8-23 OS/2 is IBM's multitasking GUI operating system designed to work with 32-bit personal computer processors.

client computer connected to the network. The server portion of NetWare allows you to share hardware devices attached to the server (such as a printer), as well as any files or application software stored on the server. The client portion of NetWare communicates with the server. Client computers also have their own stand-alone operating system such as Windows or Mac OS.

Windows NT Server

As previously mentioned, Microsoft developed Windows NT as an operating system for client/server networks. The server in this environment used **Windows NT Server**. The client computers used Windows NT Workstation or some other stand-alone version of Windows.

Windows 2000 Server

Windows 2000 Server is an upgrade to Windows NT Server. To meet various levels of server requirements, the **Windows 2000 Server family** consists of three products:

Windows 2000 Server, Windows 2000 Advanced Server, and Windows 2000 Datacenter Server. **Windows 2000 Server** is the operating system for the typical business network. **Windows 2000 Advanced Server** is an operating system designed for e-commerce applications. **Windows 2000 Datacenter Server** is best for demanding, large-scale applications such as data warehousing.

Windows 2000 Server offers these features:

- Host and manage Web sites
- Windows Distributed interNet Applications (DNA) Architecture provides a tool for easy application development across platforms
- Deliver and manage multimedia across intranets and the Internet
- Enable users to store documents in Web folders
- Manage information about network users and resources with Active Directory™
- Support clients using Windows 2000 Professional, Windows NT, Windows 98, Windows 95, Windows 3.x, Mac OS, and UNIX

OS/2 Warp Server for E-business

OS/2 Warp Server for E-business is IBM's network operating system designed for all sizes of business. Many e-commerce applications use OS/2 Warp Server for E-business. For its Web browser and e-mail program, OS/2 Warp Server for E-business includes Netscape. Clients use OS/2 Warp or some version of Windows.

UNIX

UNIX (pronounced YOU-nix) is a multitasking operating system developed in the early 1970s by scientists at Bell Laboratories. Bell Labs (a subsidiary of AT&T) was prohibited from actively promoting UNIX in the commercial marketplace because of federal regulations. Bell Labs instead licensed UNIX for a low fee to numerous colleges and universities, where UNIX obtained a wide following. UNIX was implemented on many different types of computers. After deregulation of the telephone companies in the 1980s, UNIX was licensed to many hardware and software companies.

UNIX lacks interoperability across multiple platforms. Several versions of this operating system exist, each slightly different. When you move application software from one UNIX version to another, you must rewrite some of the programs. Another weakness of UNIX is that it has a command-line interface (Figure 8-24).

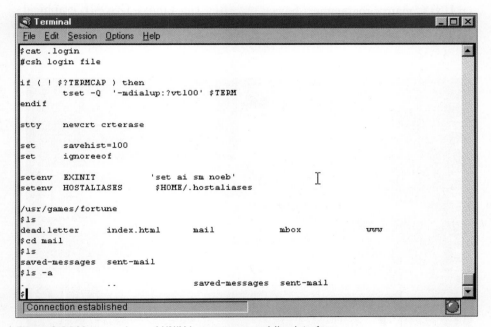

Figure 8-24 Many versions of UNIX have a command-line interface.

Many of the UNIX commands are difficult to remember and use. To help reduce this problem, some versions of UNIX offer a GUI.

Today, a version of UNIX is available for most computers of all sizes. Power users often work with UNIX because of its flexibility and power. In addition to being a stand-alone operating system, UNIX also is a network operating system. That is, UNIX is capable of handling a high volume of transactions in a multiuser environment and working with multiple processors using multiprocessing. Some call UNIX a **multipurpose operating system** because it is both a stand-alone and network operating system.

Linux

Linux is one of the fastest growing operating systems. **Linux** (pronounced LINN-uks) is a popular, free, multitasking UNIX-type operating system. In addition to the basic operating system, Linux also includes many programming languages — all for free.

Linux is not proprietary software like the operating systems discussed thus far. Instead, Linux is **open-source software**, which means its code is available to the public. Based on UNIX, many programmers have donated time to make Linux the best possible version of UNIX. Promoters of open-source software state two main advantages: users that modify the software share their improvements with others, and customers can personalize the software to meet their needs.

Some versions of Linux are command-line. Others are GUI. The two most popular GUIs available for Linux are GNOME and KDE.

You can obtain Linux in a variety of ways. You can download it from the Web free of charge. Many Linux books include a CD-ROM containing Linux. Some vendors sell a CD-ROM version of Linux. If you are purchasing a new computer, some retailers will pre-install Linux on the hard disk. Some companies market software applications that run on their own version of Linux. Figure 8-25 shows Red Hat Linux's GNOME graphical user interface.

PRODUCT ON THE CUTTING EDGE

Users Embrace Free Operating System

Linux belongs to everybody, according to its creator, Linus Torvalds. Although he owns the trademark for the name and is in charge of development, a large, friendly community distributes the operating system. These individuals are driven to offer an alternative to Microsoft Windows and Apple Mac OS, and they have an extensive number of user groups, mailing lists, newsletters, and forums.

Linux' GNU General Public License allows anyone to obtain and modify the source code and then redistribute the revised product. Torvalds encourages this creativity and productivity, believing that the refinements ultimately stimulate more interest in the product and increase its popularity.

He admits he is not opposed to commercial software because the revenue it generates helps support the development of new incentives that help create a polished product, which most free software does not have. For example, commercial software packages — especially word processing — usually have a better user interface than free software does. But many Linux applications and games are available.

For more information on Linux, visit the Discovering Computers 2002 Companies Web page (**scsite.com/dc2002/companies. htm**) and click Linux.

Figure 8-25 Red Hat provides a version of Linux called Red Hat Linux. Shown here is the GNOME graphical user interface.

Solaris

Solaris™, a version of UNIX developed by Sun Microsystems, is a network operating system designed specifically for e-commerce applications. Solaris™ can manage high-traffic accounts and incorporate security necessary for Web transactions. Client computers use a version of Solaris™, called CDE (Common Desktop Environment), that specifically works with the Solaris™ operating system.

EMBEDDED OPERATING SYSTEMS

The operating system on most handheld computers and small devices, called an **embedded operating system**, resides on a ROM chip.

Popular embedded operating systems include Windows CE, Pocket PC OS, and Palm OS. The following pages discuss these operating systems.

Windows CE

Windows CE is a scaled-down Windows operating system designed for use on wireless communications devices and smaller computers such as handheld computers, in-vehicle devices, and Web-enabled devices. On most of these devices, the Windows CE interface incorporates many elements of the Windows GUI. The operating system also supports color, sound, multitasking, e-mail, and Internet capabilities. Many applications, such as Microsoft Word and Microsoft Excel, have scaled-down versions that run with Windows CE.

Web Link

For more information on UNIX, visit the Discovering Computers 2002 Chapter 8 WEB LINK page (**scsite.com/dc2002/ch8/ weblink.htm**) and click UNIX.

ISSUE

UNIX versus Windows

Choosing an Operating System

A question that confronts the IT management, individuals, and companies worldwide when upgrading computers is "What operating system should we select?" Price is certainly a consideration. Determining price, however, includes the original operating system cost, maintenance, and upgrade. Microsoft Windows definitely has the edge as far as the most widely used and popular operating system. UNIX, which includes a family of operating systems such as Linux, AIX, OpenBSD, and others, is a free open-source program. UNIX is a mature system, developed in the early 1970s, long before Microsoft even existed. Why then, would a company select Microsoft instead of UNIX or one of the operating systems from the UNIX family? Which one would you select? Why? Is Microsoft a better operating system than UNIX? What operating system factors would you consider when purchasing a new personal computer? Would you buy a computer with a UNIX-based operating system?

For more information on operating systems and upgrading operating systems, visit the Discovering Computers 2002 Issues Web page (**scsite.com/ dc2002/issues.htm**) and click Chapter 8 Issue #4.

TECHNOLOGY TRAILBLAZER

LINUS **TORVALDS**

Free is good, in the mind of Linus Torvalds and the millions of people who benefit from his free operating system, Linux.

The software's roots began when Torvalds was a student in Finland and began writing an operating system for a study he was performing. He believes that Finland's high level of technology and superior educational system gave him the advantages of being able to concentrate on his brainstorm instead of worrying about economic issues.

Today he considers himself the operating system's lead technical developer and still spends time writing code. Due to Linux' success, however, he now has to delegate tasks and spend more time answering e-mail messages and coordinating work efforts. He knows that everyone agrees that he is in charge and is solely responsible for project management, setting milestones, and making radical decisions.

Torvalds states that he does not worry about the future of Linux and that it will continue to be refined. His sole long-range plan is to improve the software.

For more information on Linus Torvalds, visit the Discovering Computers 2002 People Web page (**scsite.com/dc2002/people.htm**) and click Linus Torvalds.

The **Auto PC** is a device mounted onto a vehicle's dashboard that is powered by Windows CE (Figure 8-26). Using an automobile equipped with Auto PC, the driver can obtain information such as driving directions, traffic conditions, weather, and stock quotes; access and listen to e-mail; listen to the radio or an audio CD; and share information with a handheld or notebook computer. The Auto PC is ideal for the mobile user because it is directed through voice commands.

Pocket PC OS

Pocket PC OS is a scaled-down operating system developed by Microsoft that works on a specific type of handheld computer, called a **Pocket PC** (Figure 8-27). With this operating system and a Pocket PC

device, you have access to all the basic PIM functions such as contact lists, schedules, tasks, calendars, and notes. These devices also provide many other features. For example, you can check e-mail, browse the Web, listen to music, send and receive instant messages, record a voice message, manage your finances, read an e-book, or create a word processing document or spreadsheet. These devices also support handwriting recognition.

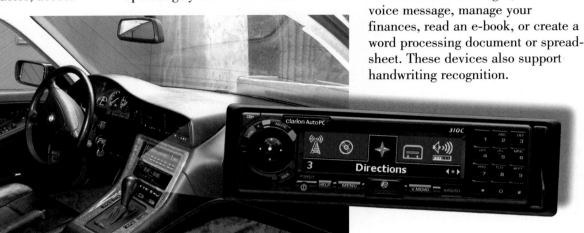

Figure 8-26 Auto PC is powered by Windows CE.

APPLY IT!

Pocket PC OS versus Palm OS

You are ready to purchase a handheld computer. Next is the difficult part — which operating system to choose. The Palm OS® currently runs on many handheld computers, including all Palms, PalmPilots, and Handspring™ Visors. Microsoft's Pocket PC, however, is creating stiff competition. To make a decision, you first must evaluate your own personal needs and then determine which OS is for you. Some features you may want to consider are as follows:

- Your use as a student may be to take notes, keep track of your class schedule, play music, and play games.
- For business needs, you may need to keep a contact list, an appointment schedule, and keep in touch with clients via e-mail.
- For personal use, you may want to keep track of birthdays, maintain a list of addresses, keep a calendar, and access news.

After establishing your goals, your next step is to compare the two operating systems and determine which one has the features that best meet your needs. Some features to consider in your comparison are as follows:
- Ease of use
- Synchronizing with your personal computer
- Application availability (calendar, games, notes, appointments, music, e-mail, contacts, and so on.)
- Price
- Color display
- Battery life
For more information and links to Palm OS and Pocket PC, visit the Discovering Computers 2002 Apply It Web page (**scsite.com/dc2002/apply.htm**) and click Chapter 8 Apply It #2.

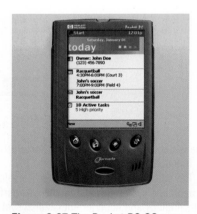

Figure 8-27 The Pocket PC OS runs on any Pocket PC device.

Palm OS

The Palm handheld computers from Palm, Inc., and Visor handheld computers from Handspring™ use an operating system called **Palm OS®**. With this operating system and a compatible handheld computer, you can manage schedules and contacts and easily synchronize this information with a desktop computer. With some handheld computers, you also have wireless access to the Internet and your e-mail. These handheld computers contain handwriting recognition software, called Graffiti®. They also have software that allows you to manage many different types of information such as telephone messages, project notes, reminders, task and address lists, and important dates and appointments.

UTILITY PROGRAMS

A **utility program**, also called a **utility**, is a type of system software that performs a specific task, usually related to managing a computer, its devices, or its programs. Most operating systems include several utility programs. You also can buy stand-alone utilities that offer improvements over those included with the operating system.

Some vendors offer **utility suites** that combine several utility programs into a single package.

Others offer Web-based utility services. To use a **Web-based utility service**, you usually pay an annual fee that allows you to access and use the vendor's utility programs on the Web. McAfee and Norton offer utility suites and Web-based utility services.

Popular utility programs offer these functions: viewing files, compressing files, diagnosing problems, uninstalling software, scanning disks, defragmenting disks, backing up files and disks, and displaying screen savers. The following paragraphs briefly discuss each of these utilities.

File Viewer

A **file viewer** is a utility that allows you to display and copy the contents of a file. An operating system's file manager often includes a file viewer. For example, Windows Explorer has a viewer called **Imaging Preview** that displays the contents of graphics files (Figure 8-28). The title bar of the file viewer window displays the name of the file being viewed.

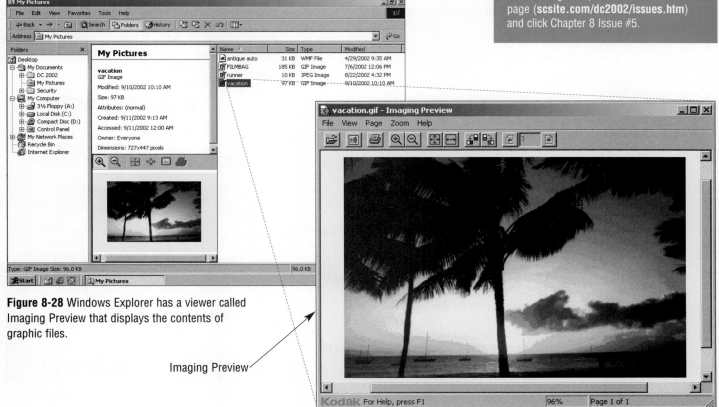

Figure 8-28 Windows Explorer has a viewer called Imaging Preview that displays the contents of graphic files.

Imaging Preview

File Compression

A **file compression utility** shrinks the size of a file. A compressed file takes up less storage space than the original file. Compressing files frees up room on the storage media and improves system performance. Attaching a compressed file to an e-mail message reduces the time needed for file transmission. Uploading and downloading compressed files to and from the Internet reduces the file transmission time.

Compressed files, sometimes called **zipped files**, usually have a .zip extension. When you receive or download a compressed file, you must uncompress it. To **uncompress**, or **unzip**, a file, you restore it to its original form. Two popular stand-alone file compression utilities are PKZIP™ and WinZip® (Figure 8-29).

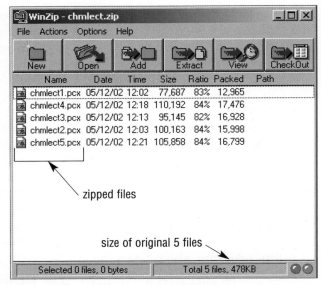

zipped files

size of original 5 files

Figure 8-29 WinZip® is a popular stand-alone file compression utility. This zipped file (chmlect) contains 5 files. Without being zipped, these files consume 478 KB. Zipping the files reduced the amount of storage to 79 KB.

APPLY IT!

File Compression – Zipped Files

You may have received an e-mail file attachment or downloaded a file with a .zip extension. The .zip extension indicates the file has been compressed. People use file compression to reduce the size of a file, to combine several files and/or folders into a single file, and to reduce Internet download/upload time.

One of the most popular Windows file compression programs is WinZip. Because WinZip is shareware, you can download an evaluation copy.

Downloading and installing WinZip:
1. Access the WinZip Web site (see URL below).
2. Follow the instructions at the WinZip Web site to download and install the program.

Compressing a group of files:
1. Start WinZip.
2. Click I Agree when the Licensing Agreement displays.
3. Click the New button to display the New Archive dialog box.
4. Click the box arrow to the right of the Create text box and then select the folder in which you wish to save the zipped file.
5. In the File name text box, type the name of the zipped file. Do not type the extension .zip.
6. Click the OK button to display the Add dialog box.
7. If necessary, change folders and then select the files you wish to add.
8. Click the Add button.
9. You can add additional files from the same or other folders by clicking the Add button again.

To unzip or decompress a zipped file:
1. Start Windows Explorer and double-click the file name. This starts WinZip.
2. Click the Extract button to display the Extract dialog box.
3. Select the folder in which you wish to save the extracted file(s).
4. Click the Extract button.
5. After the files are extracted, close the WinZip program.
Note: After Step 1, if you want to open a single file, double-click the file name instead of clicking the Extract button.

For more information on WinZip, links to other WinZip tutorials, and the Web site mentioned above, visit the Discovering Computers 2002 Apply It Web page (**scsite.com/dc2002/apply.htm**) and click Chapter 8 Apply It #3.

Diagnostic Utility

A **diagnostic utility** compiles technical information about your computer's hardware and certain system software programs and then prepares a report outlining any identified problems. For example, Windows includes the diagnostic utility, **Dr. Watson**, which diagnoses problems as well as suggests courses of action (Figure 8-30).

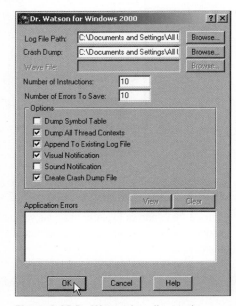

Figure 8-30 Dr. Watson is a diagnostic utility included with Windows.

Uninstaller

An **uninstaller** is a utility that removes an application, as well as any associated entries in the system files (Figure 8-31). When you install an application, the operating system records the information it uses to run the software in the system files. The system file entries will remain, if you attempt to remove the application from your computer by deleting the files and folders associated with the program without running the uninstaller. Most operating systems include an uninstaller. You also can purchase a stand-alone program, such as McAfee's UnInstaller.

Disk Scanner

A **disk scanner** is a utility that (1) detects and corrects both physical and logical problems on a hard disk or floppy disk and (2) searches for and removes unnecessary files. A physical problem is one with the media such as a scratch on the surface of the disk. A logical problem is one with the data, such as a corrupted file allocation table (FAT). Windows includes two disk scanner utilities. One detects problems and the other searches for and removes unnecessary files such as temporary files (Figure 8-32).

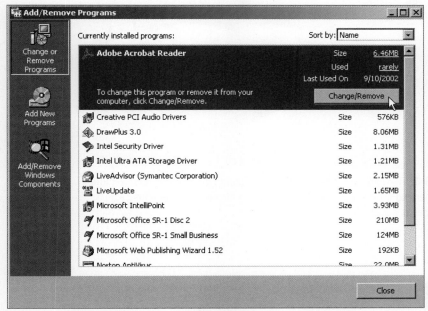

Figure 8-31 An uninstaller removes software applications and associated system file entries from your hard disk.

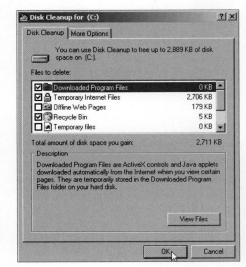

Figure 8-32 Disk Cleanup searches for and removes unnecessary files.

TECHNOLOGY TRAILBLAZER

PHILLIP **KATZ**

It happens every time you are packing for your vacation: you have too much stuff crammed in your suitcase, and you cannot close the zipper. Phillip Katz had a similar problem: too much stuff to cram onto a floppy disk. He decided to do something about this situation and developed PKZIP, using his initials as the first letters in the software's name.

As a high school student in suburban Milwaukee, Katz was brilliant and creative. He was enrolled in advanced math and physics classes and participated on the math team.

Six years after graduation, he quit his job as a software design engineer and started his business, PKWARE, with his mother at their kitchen table.

The innovative PKZIP shareware cornered the data compression market, and PKWARE has steady annual sales of $5 million. This success, however, was not enough to fulfill Katz' life. He lived his life alone and as a transient, never attending computer conferences or lectures and losing contact with his mother. He died unexpectedly in 2000 at the young age of 37.

For more information on Phillip Katz, visit the Discovering Computers 2002 People Web page (**scsite.com/dc2002/people.htm**) and click Phillip Katz.

Disk Defragmenter

A **disk defragmenter** is a utility that reorganizes the files and unused space on a computer's hard disk so the operating system can access data more quickly and programs can run faster. When an operating system stores data on a disk, it places the data in the first available sector on the disk. Although it attempts to place data in sectors that are contiguous (next to each other), this is not always possible. When the contents of a file are scattered across two or more noncontiguous sectors, the file is **fragmented**. Fragmentation slows down disk access and thus the performance of the entire computer. **Defragmenting** the disk, or reorganizing it so the files are stored in contiguous sectors, solves this problem (Figure 8-33). Windows includes a disk defragmenter, called **Disk Defragmenter**.

Backup Utility

A **backup utility** allows you to copy, or backup, selected files or your entire hard disk onto another disk or tape. During the backup process, the backup utility monitors progress and alerts you if it needs additional disks or tapes. Many backup programs will compress files during this process, so the backup files require less storage space than the original files.

For this reason, you usually cannot use backup files in their backed up form. In the event you need to use one of these files, a **restore program** reverses the process and returns backed up files to their original form. Backup utilities include restore programs.

You should back up files and disks regularly in the event your originals are lost, damaged, or destroyed. Windows includes a backup utility (Figure 8-34). Some users opt to back up their files to an Internet hard drive. As described in Chapter 7, an Internet hard drive, sometimes called online storage, is a service on the Web that provides storage to computer users.

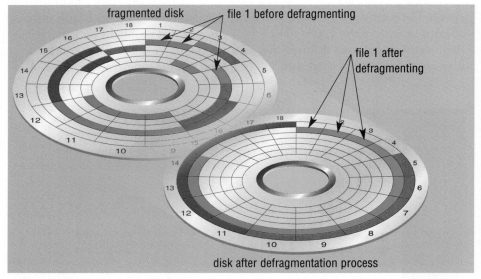

Figure 8-33 A fragmented disk has many files stored in noncontiguous sectors. Defragmenting reorganizes the files, so they are located in contiguous sectors, which speeds access time.

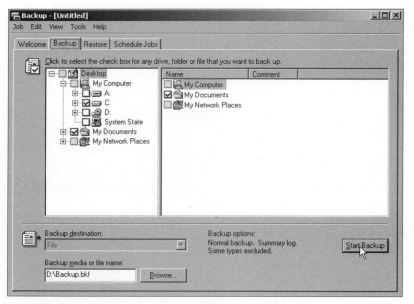

Figure 8-34 A backup utility allows you to copy files or your entire hard disk to another disk or tape.

Screen Saver

A **screen saver** is a utility that causes a monitor's screen to display a moving image or blank screen if no keyboard or mouse activity occurs for a specified time period (Figure 8-35). When you press a key on the keyboard or move the mouse, the screen returns to the previously displayed image.

Screen savers originally were developed to prevent a problem called **ghosting**, in which images could be permanently etched on a monitor's screen. Ghosting is not a problem with today's monitors. Still, screen savers are popular for security, business, or entertainment purposes. To secure a computer, you can configure your screen saver so a user must enter a password to stop the screen saver and redisplay the previous image. Some screen savers use push technology, enabling you to receive updated

and new information each time the screen saver displays. As described in Chapter 2, push technology occurs when Web-based content downloads automatically to your computer at a regular interval or whenever the Web site updates.

An operating system often includes several screen savers. You also can purchase screen savers or download them from the Web.

CHAPTER SUMMARY

This chapter defined an operating system and then discussed the functions common to most operating systems. The chapter also presented a variety of stand-alone operating systems, network operating systems, and embedded operating systems. Finally, the chapter discussed several utility programs used with today's personal computers.

Figure 8-35 When you press a key on the keyboard or move the mouse, the screen saver stops and the previously displayed image shows on the screen.

Career Corner

Network Administrator

Networking professionals are in high demand. A network administrator (NA) must have a thorough knowledge of operating system software and generally has a multi-function position. Some of the tasks an NA may be asked to complete are as follows:
- Ensure servers and workstations function properly
- Implement system backups, upgrades, and security policies
- Identify and resolve connectivity issues
- Install and maintain software on clients and servers
- Perform support of network hardware components such as terminals, servers, hubs, and routers
- Participate in technical group projects to provide networking related support and keep abreast of new developments in networking, systems, and office automation technologies
- Suggest new solutions to increase network productivity

Many network administrators have some type of networking certification, which is the first step in establishing a career as a networking professional. Some of the more popular of these certifications include Microsoft Certified System Engineer (MCSE) (see URL below), Certified Novell Engineer (CNE) (see URL below), and Cisco Certified Network Associate (CCNA) (see URL below).

Salaries within these positions vary greatly and are based on job responsibilities. Those individuals with certifications, however, can expect an approximate starting salary between $35,000 to $75,000.

To learn more about the field of a network administrator as a career and the Web sites mentioned above, visit the Discovering Computers 2002 Careers Web page (**scsite.com/dc2002/careers.htm**) and click Network Administrator.

e REVOLUTION

E·WEATHER E·SPORTS E·NEWS

WHAT'S NEWS?

Weather, Sports, and News Web Sites Score Big Hits

Rain or sun? Hot or cold? Do you toss a coin to determine tomorrow's forecast? Or, do you study weather maps displayed on television and Internet sites? The world seems neatly divided into these two camps, with Web sites such as The Weather Channel (Figure 8-36) receiving more than 10 million hits each day. Weather is the leading online news item, with at least 10,000 Web sites devoted to this field. A few of the more popular Web sites are listed in Figure 8-37. A multitude of news, sports, and weather Web sites resides on the Internet.

Baseball may be the national pastime, but sports aficionados yearn for major league football, basketball, and hockey along with everything from auto racing to cricket. Although television has four major networks and two live, 24-hour all-sports channels, these media outlets do not provide enough action to quench the thirst of fans across the globe. The Internet fills this void with such Web sites as CBS SportsLine.com (Figure 8-38), with more than one million pages of multimedia sports news, entertainment, and merchandise, and Sports.com, which covers rugby, cricket, Formula One racing, tennis, and golf. CBS SportsLine.com creates the official Major League Football and the PGA Tour Web sites and provides content for America Online, Netscape, and Excite.

Olympics fans are hungry for sports action, results, and athlete profiles. The biggest event ever delivered on the Internet was the 2000 Olympic Games in Sydney, Australia. The official Olympics Web site received more than 6.5 billion hits during the 17-day event. That number is 10 times the number of Internet visitors at the 1998 Nagano Winter Olympic Games Web site.

Figure 8-36 Local, national, and international weather conditions, along with details on breaking weather stories, are available on The Weather Channel Web pages.

REPORTING WEB SITES	URL
Weather	
Information Please Weather Page	infoplease.com/weather.html
STORMFax®	stormfax.com
The Weather Channel	weather.com
Weatherplanner	weatherplanner.com
Wx.com	wx.com
Sports	
Athletes Direct	athletesdirect.com
CBS SportsLine	cbs.sportsline.com
ESPN.com	espn.com
Halife E-Sports	halife.com/sports/esports.html
Live Internet Sports Radio Stations	www.csi.ukns.com/radios.html
Todays Sports	todayssports.com
Sports.com	sports.com
News	
APBnews	apbnews.com
MSNBC	msnbc.com
New York Post	newyorkpost.com
Online Newspapers	onlinenewspapers.com
Silicon Valley News	mercurycenter.com/svtech/news
Starting Page Best News Sites	startingpage.com/html/news.html
The Washington Post	washingtonpost.com
The Web Cowboy	thewebcowboy.com

For an updated list of reporting Web sites, visit scsite.com/dc2002/e-rev.htm.

Figure 8-37 Numerous weather, sports, and news Web sites reside on the Internet.

The IBM-run Web site also permitted fans to send e-mail to the 10,500 competitors.

The Internet has emerged as a major source for news, with one-third of Americans going online at least once a week and 15 percent going online daily for reports of major news events. These viewers, who tend to be under the age of 50 and college graduates, are attracted to the Internet's flashy headline format, immediacy, and in-depth reports.

Users are attracted to Web news sites that have a corresponding print or television presence. MSNBC, CNN, ABC News, *USA TODAY*, *The Washington Post*, and *The New York Times* are among the more popular Internet news destinations. The technology content in the Silicon Valley News Web site (Figure 8-39) and crime, justice, and safety news in APBnews.com appeal to users.

For more information on weather, sports, and news sites, visit the Discovering Computers 2002 E-Revolution Web page (scsite.com/dc2002/e-rev.htm) and click Weather, Sports, and News.

Figure 8-38
Sports fans can catch the latest scores and player profiles on sports Web sites.

Figure 8-39 The Silicon Valley News Web site posts feature stories with details on the ever-changing world of technology.

E-WEATHER E-SPORTS E-NEWS *applied:*

1. Visit two of the weather Web sites listed in the table in Figure 8-37. Do they contain the same local and five-day forecasts for your city? What similarities and differences do they have in coverage of a national weather story? Next visit two of the sports Web sites in the table and write a paragraph describing the content these Web sites provide concerning your favorite sport.

2. Visit the Online Newspapers and Starting Page Best News Sites Web sites listed in Figure 8-37 and select two newspapers from each site. Write a paragraph describing the top national news story featured in each of these four Web pages. Then, write another paragraph describing the top international news story displayed at each Web site. In the third paragraph, discuss which of the four Web sites is the most interesting in terms of story selection, photographs, and Web page design.

8.34

Chapter 1 2 3 4 5 6 7 **8** 9 10 11 12 13 14 15 16 Index **HOME**

DISCOVERING
COMPUTERS *2002*

In Summary

SHELLY
CASHMAN
SERIES.

Student Exercises   Web Links   In Summary   Key Terms   Learn It Online   Checkpoint   In The Lab   Web Work

Special Features   ■ TIMELINE 2002   ■ WWW & E-SKILLS   ■ MULTIMEDIA   ■ BUYER'S GUIDE 2002   ■ WIRELESS TECHNOLOGY   ■ TRENDS 2002   ■ INTERACTIVE LABS   ■ TECH NEWS

Web Instructions: To display this page from the Web, start your browser and enter the URL scsite.com/dc2002/ch8/summary.htm. Click the links for current and additional information. To listen to an audio version of this In Summary, click the Audio button. To play the audio, RealPlayer must be installed on your computer (download by clicking here).

1 What Are the Two Types of System Software?

System software consists of the programs that control the operations of the computer and its devices. System software performs a variety of functions, such as running applications and storing files, and serves as the interface between a user, the application software, and the computer's hardware. The two types of system software are operating systems and utility programs. An **operating system (OS)** is a set of programs containing instructions to coordinate all of the activities among computer hardware resources. A utility program is a type of system software that performs a specific task, usually related to managing a computer, its devices, or its programs.

2 What Is the Startup Process for a Personal Computer?

Starting a computer involves loading an operating system into memory — a process called **booting**. When the computer is turned on, the power supply sends an electrical signal to devices located in the system unit. The processor chip resets itself and looks for the ROM chip that contains the **BIOS (basic input/output system)**, which is firmware that holds the startup instructions. The BIOS executes the **power-on self test (POST)** to make sure hardware is connected properly and operating correctly. Results of the POST are compared with data in a CMOS chip on the motherboard. If the POST is completed successfully, the BIOS looks for **system files**. Once located, the system files load into memory and execute. The boot program next loads the **kernel** of the operating system into memory. The operating system loads system configuration information from the **registry** for each device. The remainder of the operating system is loaded into RAM, the desktop and icons display on the screen, and programs in the **StartUp folder** are executed.

3 What Is a User Interface?

The part of the OS software with which you interact is the **user interface**. Two types of user interfaces are command-line and graphical. With a **command-line interface**, you type keywords or press special keys on the keyboard to enter data and instructions. A **graphical user interface (GUI)** allows you to use **menus** and visual images such as **icons** and buttons to issue commands. Many of today's GUIs incorporate Web browser-like features.

4 What Are the More Common Features of Operating Systems?

Various capabilities of operating systems are described as single user, multitasking, multiuser, and multiprocessing. A **single user** operating system allows only one user to run one program at a time. A **multitasking** operating system allows a single user to work on two or more applications that reside in memory at the same time. A **multiuser** operating system enables two or more users to run a program simultaneously. A **multiprocessing** operating system can support two or more processors running programs at the same time.

Operating systems manage memory, schedule jobs, configure devices, establish Web connections, monitor system performance, control networks, administer security, and manage storage media and files. **Memory management** optimizes use of random access memory (RAM). **Spooling** increases efficiency by placing print jobs in a buffer until the printer is ready, freeing the processor for other tasks. A **device driver** is a small program that configures devices by accepting commands and converting them into commands the device understands. **Plug and Play** is the computer's capability of recognizing any new device and assisting in the installation of the device. A **performance monitor** assesses and reports information about various system resources and devices. A type of program called a **file manager** performs functions related to storage and file management.

Chapter 1 2 3 4 5 6 7 8 9 10 11 12 13 14 15 16 Index HOME 8.35

DISCOVERING
COMPUTERS *2002*

In Summary

SHELLY
CASHMAN
SERIES.

Student Exercises | Web Links | In Summary | Key Terms | Learn It Online | Checkpoint | In The Lab | Web Work

Special Features ■ TIMELINE 2002 ■ WWW & E-SKILLS ■ MULTIMEDIA ■ BUYER'S GUIDE 2002 ■ WIRELESS TECHNOLOGY ■ TRENDS 2002 ■ INTERACTIVE LABS ■ TECH NEWS

5 What Is the Difference between Stand-Alone Operating Systems and Network Operating Systems?

A stand-alone operating system is an operating system that works on a desktop or notebook computer. Some stand-alone operating systems, called **client operating systems**, also work in conjunction with a network operating system. A **network operating system (NOS)** supports a **network**. In some networks, the **server** controls access to the network hardware and software. **Clients**, which are other computers on the network, rely on the server for resources. The network OS organizes and coordinates how multiple users access and share resources on the network. Most multiuser operating systems administer security by allowing each user to **log on**, which is the process of entering a **user name** and **password**.

6 What Are Some Stand-Alone Operating Systems?

DOS (Disk Operating System) refers to several single user, command-line and menu-driven operating systems developed in the early 1980s for personal computers. **Windows 3.x** refers to three early **operating environments** that provided a graphical user interface to work in combination with DOS and simplify its use. **Windows 95** is a true multitasking operating system — not an operating environment. The **Windows 98** operating system is easier to use than Windows 95 and is more integrated with the Internet. Windows 2000 Professional is an upgrade to **Windows NT**, which is an operating system designed for client-server networks. **Windows Millennium Edition** is an updated version of Windows 98 that contains features specifically designed for home computer users. The **Macintosh OS**, a descendant of the first commercially successful graphical user interface, is available only on Macintosh computers. **OS/2 Warp** is IBM's network operating system. **UNIX** is a multitasking operating system developed by scientists at Bell Laboratories. **Linux** is a popular, free, multitasking, UNIX-like operating system.

7 What Are Some Network Operating Systems?

A network OS supports a network and generally resides on a server. Examples of network operating systems include Novel **Netware**; Microsoft **Windows NT Server** and **Windows 2000 Server family**; IBM **OS/2 Warp** and **OS/2Warp Server; UNIX**, which is a **multipurpose operating system; Linux**, which is a multitasking, UNIX-type operating system; and **Solaris™**, a version of UNIX developed by Sun Microsystems specifically for e-commerce applications.

8 What Devices Use Embedded Operating Systems?

Most handheld computers and small devices use an embedded operating system. **Windows CE** is a scaled-down Windows operating system designed for use on wireless communications devices and smaller computers. **Pocket PC OS** is a scaled-down Microsoft operating system that works on a specific type of handheld computer, called a **Pocket PC**. **Palm OS®** is a popular operating system used with handheld computers from Palm, Inc. and Handspring™.

9 What Are Some Common Utility Programs?

A **file viewer** displays the contents of a file. A **file compression utility** reduces the size of a file. A **diagnostic utility** compiles technical information about a computer's hardware and certain system software programs and then prepares a report outlining any identified problems. An **uninstaller** removes an application, as well as any associated entries in the system files. A **disk scanner** detects and corrects problems on a disk and searches for and removes unwanted files. A disk defragmenter reorganizes files and unused space on a computer's hard disk so data can be accessed more quickly and programs can run faster. A **backup utility** copies or backs up selected files or the entire hard drive onto another disk or tape. A **screen saver** causes the monitor's screen to display a moving image on a blank screen if no keyboard or mouse activity occurs for a specific time.

8.36

Chapter 1 2 3 4 5 6 7 8 9 10 11 12 13 14 15 16 Index HOME

DISCOVERING
COMPUTERS 2002

Key Terms

SHELLY
CASHMAN
SERIES.

Student Exercises   Web Links   In Summary   Key Terms   Learn It Online   Checkpoint   In The Lab   Web Work

Special Features   ■ TIMELINE 2002   ■ WWW & E-SKILLS   ■ MULTIMEDIA   ■ BUYER'S GUIDE 2002   ■ WIRELESS TECHNOLOGY   ■ TRENDS 2002   ■ INTERACTIVE LABS   ■ TECH NEW

Web Instructions: To display this page from the Web, start your browser and enter the URL scsite.com/dc2002/ch8/terms.htm. Scroll through the list of terms. Click a term to display its definition and a picture. Click the To WEB button for current and additional information about the term from the Web. To see animations, Shockwave and Flash Player must be installed on your computer (download by clicking here).

Active Desktop™ (8.18)
Active Directory (AD) (8.16)
Auto PC (8.26)
background (8.9)
backup utility (8.30)
basic input/output system (8.5)
BIOS (8.5)
boot disk (8.6)
boot drive (8.6)
booting (8.4)
buffer (8.11)
client operating systems (8.17)
clients (8.15)
cold boot (8.4)
command language (8.8)
command-line interface (8.8)
cross-platform (8.4)
defragmenting (8.30)
device-dependent (8.17)
device driver (8.11)
device-independent (8.17)
diagnostic utility (8.28)
disk defragmenter (8.30)
Disk Defragmenter (8.30)
disk scanner (8.29)
DOS (Disk Operating System) (8.17)
downward-compatible (8.17)
Dr. Watson (8.28)
driver (8.11)
embedded operating system (8.25)
emergency repair disk (8.6)
fault-tolerant computer (8.9)
file allocation table (FAT) (8.15)
file compression utility (8.28)
file manager (8.14)
file viewer (8.27)
foreground (8.9)
formatting (8.15)
fragmented (8.30)
ghosting (8.31)
graphical user interface (GUI) (8.8)
icon (8.8)
Imaging Preview (8.27)
Internet Explorer (8.18)
interrupt request (IRQ) (8.13)
job (8.10)
kernel (8.4)
Linux (8.24)
log on (8.16)
Mac OS (8.21)
Macintosh operating system (8.21)

memory management (8.10)
memory resident (8.4)
menu (8.8)
multiprocessing (8.9)
multipurpose operating system (8.24)
multitasking (8.9)
multiuser (8.9)
NetWare (8.22)
network (8.15)
network operating system (8.15)
network OS (8.15)
nonresident (8.4)
NOS (8.15)
NT (8.18)
open-source software (8.24)
operating environment (8.18)
operating system (OS) (8.3)
OS/2 Warp (8.22)
OS/2 Warp Server (8.23)
page (8.10)
paging (8.10)
Palm OS® (8.26)
password (8.16)
performance monitor (8.14)
platform (8.4)
Plug and Play (8.13)
Pocket PC (8.26)
Pocket PC OS (8.26)
power-on self test (POST) (8.6)
print spooler (8.11)
proprietary software (8.17)
queue (8.11)
registry (8.6)
rescue disk (8.6)
restore program (8.30)
screen saver (8.31)
server (8.15)
shortcut (8.14)
single user/single tasking (8.8)
software platform (8.4)
Solaris™ (8.25)
spooling (8.11)
stand-alone operating system (8.17)
StartUp folder (8.6)
swap file (8.10)
system files (8.6)
system software (8.2)
thrashing (8.10)
uncompress (8.28)
uninstaller (8.29)
UNIX (8.23)

unzip (8.28)
upward-compatible (8.17)
user ID (8.16)
user interface (8.7)
user name (8.16)

PALM OS®
An operating system used with handheld computers such as Palm and Visor. (8.26)

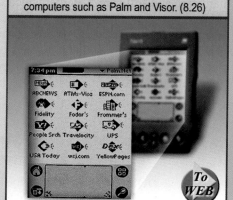

utility (8.27)
utility program (8.27)
utility suites (8.27)
virtual memory (VM) (8.10)
warm boot (8.4)
warm start (8.4)
Web-based utility service (8.27)
Windows (8.18)
Windows 2000 Advanced Server (8.22)
Windows 2000 Datacenter Server (8.22)
Windows 2000 Professional (8.18)
Windows 2000 Server (8.22)
Windows 2000 Server family (8.22)
Windows 3.x (8.18)
Windows 95 (8.18)
Windows 98 (8.18)
Windows CE (8.25)
Windows Explorer (8.18)
Windows Me (8.20)
Windows Millennium Edition (8.20)
Windows NT (8.18)
Windows NT Server (8.22)
Windows NT Workstation (8.18)
zipped files (8.28)

DISCOVERING
COMPUTERS *2002*

Learn It Online

SHELLY
CASHMAN
SERIES.

Student Exercises   Web Links   In Summary   Key Terms   Learn It Online   Checkpoint   In The Lab   Web Work

Special Features   ■ TIMELINE 2002   ■ WWW & E-SKILLS   ■ MULTIMEDIA   ■ BUYER'S GUIDE 2002   ■ WIRELESS TECHNOLOGY   ■ TRENDS 2002   ■ INTERACTIVE LABS   ■ TECH NEWS

Web Instructions: To display this page from the Web, start your browser and enter the URL scsite.com/dc2002/ch8/learn.htm.

1. Web Guide

Click Web Guide to display the Guide to World Wide Web Sites and Searching Techniques Web page. Click Reference and then click Webopedia. Search for operating systems. Click one of the operating system links. Prepare a brief report on your findings and submit your assignment to your instructor.

2. Scavenger Hunt

Click Scavenger Hunt. Print a copy of the Scavenger Hunt page; use this page to write down your answers as you search the Web. Submit your completed page to your instructor.

3. Who Wants to Be a Computer Genius?

Click Computer Genius to find out if you are a computer genius. Directions on how to play the game will display. When you are ready to play, click the PLAY button. Submit your score to your instructor.

4. Wheel of Terms

Click Wheel of Terms to reinforce important terms you learned in this chapter by playing the Shelly Cashman Series version of this popular game. Directions on how to play the game will display. When you are ready to play, click the PLAY button. Submit your score to your instructor.

5. Career Corner

Click Career Corner to display the QuintEssential Careers page. Click one of the tutorial links and complete the tutorial. Prepare a brief report describing what you learned. Submit the report to your instructor.

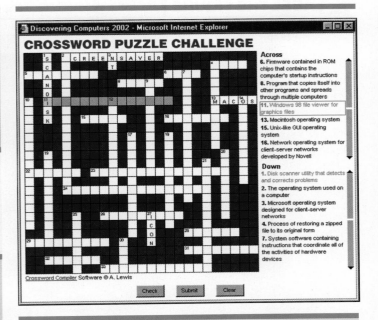

6. Search Sleuth

Click Search Sleuth to learn search techniques that will help make you a research expert. Submit the completed assignment to your instructor.

7. Crossword Puzzle Challenge

Click Crossword Puzzle Challenge. Complete the puzzle to reinforce skills you learned in this chapter. Directions on how to play the game will display. When you are ready to play, click the PLAY button. Submit the completed puzzle to your instructor.

8. Practice Test

Click Practice Test. Answer each question. When completed, enter your name and click the Grade Test button to submit the quiz for grading. Make a note of any missed questions. If required, print a copy to submit to your instructor.

8.38

DISCOVERING
COMPUTERS *2002*

Chapter 1 2 3 4 5 6 7 **8** 9 10 11 12 13 14 15 16 Index **HOME**

Checkpoint

SHELLY
CASHMAN
SERIES.

Student Exercises   Web Links   In Summary   Key Terms   Learn It Online   Checkpoint   In The Lab   Web Work

Special Features   ■ TIMELINE 2002   ■ WWW & E-SKILLS   ■ MULTIMEDIA   ■ BUYER'S GUIDE 2002   ■ WIRELESS TECHNOLOGY   ■ TRENDS 2002   ■ INTERACTIVE LABS   ■ TECH NEWS

Web Instructions: To display this page from the Web, start your browser and enter the URL scsite.com/dc2002/ch8/check.htm. Click the links for current and additional information. To experience the animation and interactivity, Shockwave and Flash Player must be installed on your computer (download by clicking here).

✎ LABEL THE FIGURE | **Instructions:** Identify each step of how a personal computer boots up.

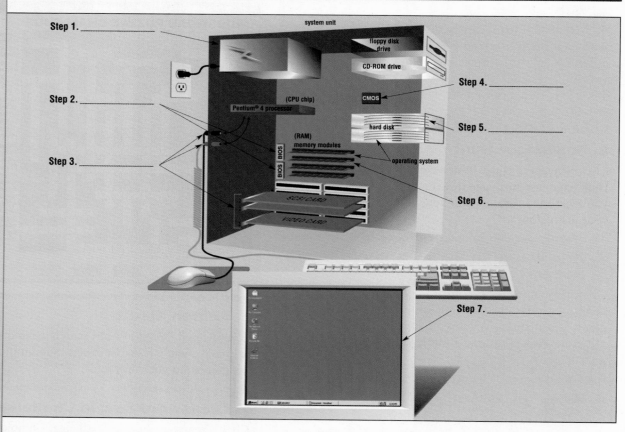

✎ MATCHING | **Instructions:** Match each term from the column on the left with the best description from the column on the right.

_____ 1. OS/2 Warp
_____ 2. Windows 2000 Professional
_____ 3. Windows NT
_____ 4. Linux
_____ 5. Windows Me

a. Operating environment that works in combination with an operating system to simplify its use.
b. An operating system designed for client/server networks.
c. An upgrade to Windows 98 that has features specifically for the home user.
d. A complete multitasking client operating system for desktop and notebook business computers.
e. IBM's multitasking client operating system that supports networking, the Internet, Java, and speech recognition.
f. An open-source operating system.

Chapter 1 2 3 4 5 6 7 **8** 9 10 11 12 13 14 15 16 Index HOME

8.39

DISCOVERING
COMPUTERS *2002*

Checkpoint

SHELLY
CASHMAN
SERIES.

Student Exercises   Web Links   In Summary   Key Terms   Learn It Online   Checkpoint   In The Lab   Web Work

Special Features ■ TIMELINE 2002 ■ WWW & E-SKILLS ■ MULTIMEDIA ■ BUYER'S GUIDE 2002 ■ WIRELESS TECHNOLOGY ■ TRENDS 2002 ■ INTERACTIVE LABS ■ TECH NEWS

MULTIPLE CHOICE | Instructions: Select the letter of the correct answer for each of the following questions.

1. The two types of system software include operating systems and _____ .
   a. file viewers
   b. utility services
   c. utility programs
   d. compression programs
2. Stand-alone operating systems that work in conjunction with a network operating system are called _____ .
   a. client operation systems
   b. DOS
   c. Linux
   d. operating environments
3. One weakness of the _____ operating system is its command-line interface.
   a. Mac OS
   b. OS/2 Warp
   c. UNIX
   d. Windows 2000 Professional

4. An embedded operating system usually resides on a _____ .
   a. hard drive
   b. ROM chip
   c. RAM chip
   d. removable disk
5. A _____ combines several utility programs into a single package.
   a. utility service
   b. zipped file
   c. disk scanner
   d. utility suite

SHORT ANSWER | Instructions: Write a brief answer to each of the following questions.

1. How is a command-line interface different from a graphical user interface? _____ Why is a graphical user interface described as user-friendly? _____ List two operating systems with graphical user interfaces and two with command-line interfaces. _____
2. What are networking operating systems? _____ How are networking operating systems different from stand-alone operating systems? _____
3. How is a single user operating system different from a multiuser operating system? _____ How is a multitasking operating system different from a multiprocessing operating system? _____
4. What is a boot disk? _____ Why is it important to have a boot disk available? _____
5. What is a file compression utility? _____ When and why would you use a file compression utility program? _____ What are some other utility programs you would find useful? _____

WORKING TOGETHER | Instructions: Working with a group of your classmates, complete the following team exercise.

You and your group have been hired as consultants for ABC Importing. ABC has offices throughout the world — each using a multitude of different operating systems. Many times, it is very difficult to transfer data and information among these systems. ABC's CEO would like your consulting group to recommend a solution for this problem. Prepare a written report and a PowerPoint presentation explaining your solution. Share your report and presentation with your class.

8.40

DISCOVERING
COMPUTERS *2002*

Chapter 1 2 3 4 5 6 7 8 9 10 11 12 13 14 15 16 Index HOME

In The Lab

SHELLY
CASHMAN
SERIES.

Student Exercises   Web Links   In Summary   Key Terms   Learn It Online   Checkpoint   In The Lab   Web Work

Special Features   ■ TIMELINE 2002   ■ WWW & E-SKILLS   ■ MULTIMEDIA   ■ BUYER'S GUIDE 2002   ■ WIRELESS TECHNOLOGY   ■ TRENDS 2002   ■ INTERACTIVE LABS   ■ TECH NEWS

Web Instructions: To display this page from the Web, start your browser and enter the URL scsite.com/dc2002/ch8/lab.htm. Click the links for current and additional information.

About Windows

This exercise uses Windows 98 procedures. Double-click the My Computer icon on the desktop. When the My Computer window displays, click Help on the menu bar and then click About Windows 98. Answer the following questions:

- To whom is Windows licensed?
- How much physical memory is available to Windows?
- What percent of the system resources are free?

Click the OK button in the About Windows dialog box. Close the My Computer window.

Using a Screen Saver

Right-click an empty area on the desktop and then click Properties on the shortcut menu. When the Display Properties dialog box displays, click the Screen Saver tab. Click the Screen Saver box arrow and then click Mystify Your Mind or any other selection. Click the Preview button to display the actual screen saver. Move the mouse to make the screen saver disappear. Answer the following questions:

- How many screen savers are available in your Screen Saver list?
- How many minutes does your system wait before activating a screen saver?

Click the Cancel button in the Display Properties dialog box.

Changing Desktop Colors

Right-click an empty area on the desktop and then click Properties on the shortcut menu. When the Display Properties dialog box displays, click the Appearance tab. Perform the following tasks: (1) Click the Question Mark button on the title bar and then click the Scheme box. When the pop-up window displays, right-click it. Click Print Topic on the shortcut menu and then click the OK button in the Print dialog box. Click anywhere to remove the pop-up window. (2) Click the Scheme box arrow and then click Rose to display the Rose color scheme shown in Figure 8.40. Select a color scheme you like. Click the Cancel button in the Display Properties dialog box.

Figure 8-40

Customizing the Desktop for Multiple Users

This exercise uses Windows 98 procedures. If more than one person uses a computer, how can you customize the desktop for each user? Click the Start button on the taskbar and then click Help on the Start menu. Click the Contents tab. Click the Exploring Your Computer book. Click The Windows Desktop book. Click the Customizing for Multiple Users book. Click an appropriate Help topic and read the information to answer each of the following questions:

- How can you display a list of users at startup?
- How can you add personalized settings for a new user?
  - How can you change desktop settings for multiple users?

Click the Close button to close the Windows Help window.

Web Work

udent Exercises   Web Links   In Summary   Key Terms   Learn It Online   Checkpoint   In The Lab   Web Work

cial Features ■ TIMELINE 2002 ■ WWW & E-SKILLS ■ MULTIMEDIA ■ BUYER'S GUIDE 2002 ■ WIRELESS TECHNOLOGY ■ TRENDS 2002 ■ INTERACTIVE LABS ■ TECH NEWS

Web Instructions: To display this page from the Web, start your browser and enter the URL scsite.com/dc2002/ch8/web.htm. To view At The Movies in exercise 1, RealPlayer must be installed on your computer (download by clicking here). To use the Shelly Cashman Series Evaluating Operating Systems Lab and Working at Your Computer Lab from the Web, Shockwave and Flash Player must be installed on your computer (download by clicking here).

Linux Gets Personal

To view the Linux Gets Personal movie, click the button to the left or click the Play button to the right. Watch the movie, and then complete the exercise by answering the question below. It looks like Microsoft Windows has some meaningful competition. The Linux operating system has shown itself to be easy to transition to from Windows, apparently more reliable in networking situations, and, at the price of free, it decidedly is less expensive. Though Linux is free, aligned companies make their money by providing customization services and selling new applications. Major companies, including IBM, Compaq, and HP, have formed an alliance to develop desktop office software that competes with Microsoft. Is Linux a boon to, or will it just complicate things for, computer users?

Shelly Cashman Series Evaluating Operating Systems Lab

Follow the instructions in Web Work 2 on page 1.47 to start and use the Shelly Cashman Series Evaluating Operating Systems Lab. If you are running from the Web, enter the URL, www.scsite.com/ sclabs/menu.htm; or display the Web Work Web page (see instructions at the top of this page) and then click the button to the left.

Shelly Cashman Series Working at Your Computer Lab

Follow the instructions in Web Work 2 on page 1.47 to start and use the Shelly Cashman Series Working at Your Computer Lab. If you are running from the Web, enter the URL, www.scsite.com/sclabs/menu.htm; or display the Web Work Web page (see instructions at the top of this page) and then click the button to the left.

A Picture's Worth a Thousand Words

Although she is not a programmer, Susan Kare's impact on the modern graphical user interface has been substantial. Kare is the person responsible for many of the icons used in modern graphical interfaces. According to Forbes magazine, "When it comes to giving personality to what otherwise might be cold and uncaring office machines, Kare is the queen of look and feel." Click the button to the left to learn more about Susan Kare and her approach to developing icons.

In the News

When Windows 2000 was launched in March 2000, hundreds queued up at computer outlets. It is unclear, however, whether the anticipation was caused by the new operating system or by the promotions many dealers offered — one vendor gave computer buyers the chance also to purchase a computer for $20. Click the button to the left and read a news article about the impact, quality, or promotion of an operating system. What operating system was it? What was done to sell the operating system? Is the operating system recommended? Why or why not?

The decision to buy a personal computer is an important one — and finding and purchasing a personal computer suited to your needs will require an investment of both time and money. As with many buyers, you may have little computer experience and find yourself unsure of how to proceed. The following guidelines are presented to help you purchase, install, and maintain a desktop computer. These guidelines also apply to the purchase of a notebook computer or handheld computer. Purchasing a notebook computer or handheld computer also involves some additional considerations, which are addressed later in this special feature.

Buyer's Guide 2002

How to Purchase, Install, and Maintain a Personal Computer

How to Purchase a Desktop Personal Computer

Determine what application products you will use on your computer. Knowing what application products you plan to use will help you decide on the type of computer to buy, as well as to define the memory, storage, and other requirements. Certain application products, for example, can run only on Macintosh computers, while others run only on a personal computer with the Windows operating system. Further, some application products require more memory and disk space than others, as well as additional input/output and storage devices. For example, if you want to efficiently create copies of CDs with your computer, then you will need to include two CD drives: one that reads from a CD, and one that reads from and writes to a CD.

WEB INSTRUCTIONS: *To gain World Wide Web access to additional and up-to-date information regarding this special feature, launch your browser and enter the URL shown at the top of this page.*

When you purchase a computer, it may come bundled with several software products. At the very least, you probably will want software for word processing and a browser to access the World Wide Web. If you need additional applications, such as a spreadsheet, a database, or presentation graphics, consider purchasing a software suite that offers reduced pricing on several applications, such as Microsoft Works or Microsoft Office.

Before selecting a specific package, be sure the software contains the features necessary for the tasks you want to perform. Many Web sites and magazines, such as those listed in Figure 1, provide reviews of software products. These Web sites frequently have articles that rate computers and software on cost, performance, and support.

Type of Computer	Web Site	URL
PC	Computer Shopper	zdnet.com/computershopper/edit/howtobuy
	PC World Magazine	pcworld.com
	Byte Magazine	byte.com
	Smart Business for New Economy	zdnet.com/smartbusinessmag/
	PC Magazine	zdnet.com/pcmag
	Yahoo! Computers	computers.yahoo.com
	FamilyPC Magazine	familypc.zdnet.com
	Microsoft Network	eshop.msn.com
	Dave's Guide to Buying a PC	css.msu.edu/pc-guide.html
Macintosh	TechWeb News	www.techweb.com/wire/apple
	ZDNet News	zdnet.com/mac
	Macworld Magazine	macworld.zdnet.com
	Apple	apple.com

For an updated list of hardware and software reviews and their Web sites, visit scsite.com/dc2002/ch8/buyers.htm.

Figure 1 Hardware and software reviews.

2 Before buying a computer, do some research. Talk to friends, coworkers, and instructors about prospective computers. What type of computers did they buy? Why? Would they recommend their computer and the company from which they bought it? You also should visit the Web sites or read reviews in the magazines listed in Figure 1. As you conduct your research, consider the following important criteria:

- Speed of the processor

- Size and types of memory (RAM) and storage (hard disk, floppy disk, CD-ROM, CD-RW, DVD-ROM, Zip® drive)

- Input/output devices included with the computer (e.g., mouse, keyboard, monitor, printer, sound card, video card)

- Communications devices included with the computer (modem, network interface card)

- Any software included with the computer

Adobe Illustrator 9.0
The industry-standard vector graphics creation software for print and the Web

Adobe PageMaker 6.5 Plus
New Version
Professional page layout for business

Award-Winning Software Now Includes:
• Professional templates for newsletters, brochures, and more
• Adobe Photoshop 5.0 LE!

Adobe

3 Look for free software. Many computer vendors include free software with their systems. Some sellers even let you choose which software you want. Remember, however, that free software has value only if you would have purchased the software even if it had not come with the computer.

4 If you are buying a new computer, you have several purchasing options: buying from your school bookstore, a local computer dealer, a local large retail store, or ordering by mail via telephone or the World Wide Web. Each purchasing option has certain advantages. Many college bookstores, for example, sign exclusive pricing agreements with computer manufacturers and, thus, can offer student discounts. Local dealers and local large retail stores, however, more easily can provide hands-on support. Mail-order companies that sell computers by telephone or online via the Web (Figure 2) often provide the lowest prices but extend less personal service. Some major mail-order companies, however, have started to provide next-business-day, onsite services. A credit card usually is required to buy from a mail-order company. Figure 3 lists some of the more popular mail-order companies and their Web site addresses.

Figure 2   Some mail-order companies, like Gateway, sell computers online.

Type of Computer	Company	URL	Telephone Number
PC	Computer Shopper	computershopper.com	Not Available
	Compaq	compaq.com	1-800-888-0220
	CompUSA	compusa.com	1-800-266-7872
	dartek.com	dartek.com	1-800-531-4622
	Dell	dell.com	1-800-678-1626
	Gateway	gateway.com	1-800-846-4208
	Micron	micron.com	1-800-964-2766
Macintosh	Apple Computer	store.apple.com	1-800-795-1000
	Club Mac	www.clubmac.com	1-800-258-2622
	MacConnection	macconnection.com	1-888-213-0260
	MacExchange	macx.com	1-888-650-4488

For an updated list of new computer mail-order companies and their Web sites, visit scsite.com/dc2002/ch8/buyers.htm.

Figure 3   New computer mail-order companies.

5 If you are buying a used computer, stick with name brands. Although brand-name equipment can cost more, most brand-name computers have longer, more comprehensive warranties, are better supported, and have more authorized centers for repair services. As with new computers, you can purchase a used computer from local computer dealers, local large retail stores, or mail order via the telephone or the Web. Classified ads and used computer brokers offer additional outlets for purchasing used computers. Figure 4 lists several major used computer brokers and their Web site addresses.

Company	URL	Telephone Number
American Computer Exchange	www.amcoex.com	1-800-786-0717
Custom Edge, Inc.	bocoex.com	1-617-625-7722
U.S. Computer Exchange, Inc.	www.uscomputerexchange.com	1-800-711-9000
eBay	ebay.com	Not Available

For an updated list of used computer mail-order companies and their Web sites, visit scsite.com/dc2002/ch8/buyers.htm.

Figure 4   Used computer mail-order companies.

6 Use a worksheet to compare computers, services, and other considerations. You can use a separate sheet of paper to take notes on each vendor's computer and then summarize the information on a spreadsheet, such as the one shown in Figure 5. Most companies advertise a price for a base computer that includes components housed in the system unit (processor, RAM, sound card, video card), disk drives (floppy disk, hard disk, CD-ROM, CD-RW, and DVD-ROM), a keyboard, mouse, monitor, printer, speakers, and modem. Be aware, however, that some advertisements list prices for computers with only some of these components. Monitors, printers, and modems, for example, often are not included in a base computer's price. Depending on how you plan to use the computers, you may want to invest in additional or more powerful components. When you are comparing the prices of computers, make sure you are comparing identical or similar configurations.

Microsoft Excel - Computer Cost Comparison

Items to Purchase	Desired Computer	Local Dealer #1	Local Dealer #2	Online Dealer #1	Online Dealer #2	Comments
				Price		

Computer Cost Comparison Worksheet

Most dealers list prices for computers with most of these components (instead of listing individual component costs). To compare prices, enter the overall computer price in row 5, and enter a 0 (zero) for components included in computer cost. For any additional components not covered in the computer price, enter the price in the appropriate cells.

Items to Purchase	Desired Computer	Local Dealer #1	Local Dealer #2	Online Dealer #1	Online Dealer #2	Comments
				Price		
Computer Price	< $2,000					
Processor	Pentium III at 800 MHz					
RAM	128 MB					
Cache	256 KB L2					
Hard Disk	20 GB					
Monitor	17 Inch					
Video Card	32 MB					
Floppy Drive	3.5 Inch					
CD/CD-RW/DVD Drive	CD-RW with Software					
Speakers	Stereo					
Sound Card	Soundblaster Compatible					
USB Ports	2					
1394 Port	2					
Fax/Modem*	56 K					
Microphone	Yes					
Backup	250 MB Zip					
Keyboard	Standard					
Pointing Device	IntelliMouse					
Joystick	Yes					
Printer	Color Inkjet					
Printer Cable	Yes					
Video Camera	Yes					
Scanner	Yes					
Surge Protector	Yes					
Operating System	Windows Me					
Application Software	Office Small Business Edition					
Antivirus Software	Yes					
Internet Connection	1-year					
Warranty	3-year Onsite Service					
Total Cost		$ -	$ -	$ -	$ -	

* Cable, DSL, and ISDN users should consider purchasing a Network card or specialized modem, rather than a Fax/Modem.

Figure 5 A spreadsheet is an effective tool for summarizing and comparing the prices and components of different computer vendors. A copy of the Computer Cost Comparison Worksheet is on the Discover Data Disk. To obtain a copy of the Discover Data Disk, see the preface of this book for instructions.

Consider more than just price. The lowest cost computer may not be the best buy. Consider such intangibles as the vendor's time in business, the vendor's regard for quality, and the vendor's reputation for support. If you need to upgrade your computer often, you may want to consider a leasing arrangement, in which you pay monthly lease fees but upgrade or add on to your computer as your equipment needs change. If you are a replacement buyer, ask if the vendor will buy your old computer; an increasing number of companies are taking trade-ins. No matter what type of buyer you are, insist on a 30-day, no questions-asked return policy on your computer.

Be aware of hidden costs. Before purchasing, be sure to consider any additional costs associated with buying a computer, such as an additional telephone line, an uninterruptible power supply (UPS), computer furniture, floppy disks and paper, or computer training classes you may want to take. Depending on where you buy your computer, the seller may be willing to include some or all of these in the computer purchase price.

Avoid restocking fees. Some companies charge a restocking fee of 10 to 20 percent as part of their money-back return policy. In some cases, there is no restocking fee for hardware, but there is for software. Ask about the existence and terms of any restocking policies before you buy.

10 Select an Internet service provider (ISP) or online service provider (OSP). You can access the Internet in one of two ways: via an ISP or an OSP. Both provide Internet access for a monthly fee that ranges from $5 to $20. Some OSPs offer free Internet access. Local ISPs offer Internet access through local telephone numbers to users in a limited geographic region. National ISPs provide access for users nationwide (including mobile users), through local and toll-free telephone numbers and cable. Because of their size, national ISPs offer more services and generally have a larger technical support staff than local ISPs. OSPs furnish Internet access as well as members-only features for users nationwide. Figure 6 lists several national ISPs and OSPs. Before you choose an Internet access provider, compare such features as the number of access hours, monthly fees, available services (e-mail, Web page hosting, chat), and reliability.

Company	Service	URL	Telephone Number
America Online	OSP	aol.com	1-800-827-6364
AT&T Data and IP Services	ISP	att.com/wss	1-800-288-3199
CompuServe	OSP	compuserve.com	1-800-848-8990
Earthlink Network	ISP	www.earthlink.com	1-800-395-8425
Juno	Free OSP	juno.com	1-888-829-5866
MCI	ISP	mciworldcom.com	1-800-888-0800
Microsoft Network	OSP	msn.com	1-800-386-5550
NetZero	Free OSP	netzero.com	Not Available
Prodigy	ISP/OSP	prodigy.com	1-800-776-3449

For information on local ISPs or to learn more on any ISPs and OSPs listed here, visit The List™ at thelist.internet.com. The List™ — the most comprehensive and accurate directory of ISPs and OSPs on the Web — compares dial-up services, access hours, and fees for over 9,000 access providers.

For an updated list of ISPs and OSPs, visit scsite.com/dc2002/ ch8/buyers.htm.

Figure 6   National ISPs and OSPs.

11 Buy a computer compatible with the ones you use elsewhere. If you use a personal computer at work or in some other capacity, make sure the computer you buy is compatible. For example, if you use a PC at work, you may not want to purchase a Macintosh for home use. Having a computer compatible with the ones at work or school will allow you to transfer files and spend time at home on work- or school-related projects.

12 Consider purchasing an onsite service agreement. If you use your computer for business or are unable to be without your computer, consider purchasing an onsite service agreement through a local dealer or third-party company. Most onsite service agreements state that a technician will come to your home, work, or school within 24 hours. If your computer includes onsite service only for the first year, think about extending the service for two or three years when you buy the computer.

13 Use a credit card to purchase your new computer. Many credit cards now offer purchase protection and extended warranty benefits that cover you in case of loss of or damage to purchased goods. Paying by credit card also gives you time to install and use the computer before you have to pay for it. Finally, if you are dissatisfied with the computer and are unable to reach an agreement with the seller, paying by credit card gives you certain rights regarding withholding payment until the dispute is resolved. Check your credit card for specific details.

Avoid buying the smallest computer available. Computer technology changes rapidly, meaning a computer that seems powerful enough today may not serve your computing needs in a few years. In fact, studies show that many users regret they did not buy a more powerful computer. Plan to buy a computer that will last you for two to three years. You can help delay obsolescence by purchasing the fastest processor, most memory, and largest hard drive you can afford. If you must buy a smaller computer, be sure you can upgrade it with additional memory and auxiliary devices as your computer requirements grow. Figure 7 includes minimum recommendations for each category of user discussed in this book: Home User, Small Business User, Mobile User, Large Business User, and Power User. The Home User category is divided into two groups: Application Home User and Game Home User.

BASE COMPONENTS	Application Home User	Game Home User	Small Business User	Mobile User	Large Business User	Power User
HARDWARE						
Processor	Celeron at 600 MHz	Pentium 4 at 1.4 GHZ	Pentium III at 1 GHZ	Pentium III at 700 MHZ	Pentium 4 at 1.4 GHZ	Pentium 4 at 1.4 GHZ
RAM	96 MB	128 MB	128 MB	128 MB	384 MB	512 MB
Cache	256 KB L2	512 KB L2	512 KB L2	512 KB L2	512 KB L2	2 MB L2
Hard Drive	10 GB	20 GB	20 GB	10 GB	80 GB	80 GB
Video Graphics Card	32 MB	64 MB	32 MB	16 MB	64 MB	64 MB
Monitor	17"	19"	17"	15" active matrix	19"	21"
DVD/CD-ROM Drive	48X CD-ROM	12X DVD with Decoder Card	48X CD-ROM	6X DVD	48X CD-ROM	12X DVD with Decoder Card
CD-RW 2nd Bay	Yes	Yes	Yes	Not Applicable	Yes	Yes
Floppy Drive	3.5"	3.5"	3.5"	3.5"	3.5"	3.5"
Printer	Color inkjet	Color inkjet	8 ppm laser	Portable inkjet	24 ppm laser	8 ppm laser
Fax/Modem or Network Card	Yes	Yes	Yes	Yes	Yes	Yes
Sound Card	Soundblaster Compatible	Soundblaster Compatible	Soundblaster Compatible	Built-In	Soundblaster Compatible	Soundblaster Compat
Speakers	Stereo	Full-Dolby surround	Stereo	Stereo	Stereo	Full-Dolby surround
TV-Out Connector	Yes	Yes	Yes	Yes	Yes	Yes
USB Port	Yes	Yes	Yes	Yes	Yes	Yes
1394 Port	No	Yes	No	No	Yes	Yes
Pointing Device	IntelliMouse or Optical Mouse	Optical mouse and Joystick	IntelliMouse or Optical Mouse	Touchpad or Pointing Stick and Optical Mouse	IntelliMouse or Optical Mouse	IntelliMouse or Optical Mouse and Joystick
Keyboard	Yes	Yes	Yes	Built-In	Yes	Yes
Backup Disk/Tape Drive	250 MB Zip	1 GB Jaz	1 GB Jaz and Tape	250 MB Zip	2 GB Jaz and Tape	2 GB Jaz and Tape
SOFTWARE						
Operating System	Windows ME	Windows ME	Windows 2000 Professional	Windows 2000 Professional	Windows 2000 Professional	Windows 2000 Professional
Application Software Suite	Office Standard	Office Standard	OfficeSmall Business Edition	Office Small Business Edition	Office Premium	Office Premium
Internet Access	Cable, Online Service, or ISP	Cable, Online Service, or ISP	Cable	Online Service or ISP	LAN/WAN (T1/T3)	LAN
OTHER						
Surge Protector	Yes	Yes	Yes	Portable	Yes	Yes
Warranty	3-Year Limited, 1-Year Next Business Day On-Site Service	3-Year Limited, 1-Year Next Business Day On-Site Service	3-year on-site service	3-Year Limited, 1-Year Next Business Day On-Site Service	3-year on-site service	3-year on-site service
Other		Headset		Docking Station Carrying case		
Optional Components for all Categories						
digital camera						
multifunction device (MFD)						
scanner						

Figure 7 Base computer components and optional components.

How to Purchase a Notebook Computer

If you need computing capability when you travel, you may find a notebook computer to be an appropriate choice. The guidelines mentioned in the previous section also apply to the purchase of a notebook computer (Figure 8). The following are additional considerations unique to notebook computers.

Figure 8   A notebook computer.

1 Purchase a notebook computer with a sufficiently large active-matrix screen.
Active-matrix screens display high-quality color that is viewable from all angles. Less expensive, passive-matrix screens sometimes are difficult to see in low-light conditions and cannot be viewed from an angle. Notebook computers typically come with a 12.1-inch, 13.3-inch, 14.1-inch, or 15.4-inch display. For most users, a 14.1-inch display is satisfactory. If you intend to use your notebook computer as a desktop replacement, however, you may opt for a 15.4-inch display. If you travel a lot and portability is essential, consider that most of the lightest machines are equipped with a 13.3-inch display. Regardless of size, the resolution of the display should be at least 800 x 600 pixels.

2 Experiment with different pointing devices and keyboards. Notebook computer keyboards are far less standardized than those for desktop computers. Some notebook computers, for example, have wide wrist rests, while others have

none. Notebook computers also use a range of pointing devices, including pointing sticks, touchpads, and trackballs. Before you purchase a notebook computer, try various types of keyboard and pointing devices to determine which is easiest for you to use. Regardless of the pointing device you select, you also may want to purchase a regular mouse unit to use when you are working at a desk or other large surface.

3 Make sure the notebook computer you purchase has a CD-ROM or DVD-ROM drive. Loading software, especially large software suites, is much faster if done from a CD-ROM, CD-RW, or DVD-ROM. Today, most notebook computers come with an internal CD-ROM drive. Some notebook computers even come with a CD-ROM drive and a CD-RW drive or both a DVD-ROM drive and a CD-RW drive. Some users prefer a DVD-ROM drive to a CD-ROM drive. Although DVD-ROM drives are more expensive, they allow you to read CD-ROMs and to play movies using your notebook computer.

If necessary, upgrade memory and disk storage at the time of purchase. As with a desktop computer, upgrading your notebook computer's memory and disk storage usually is less expensive at the time of initial purchase. Some disk storage is custom designed for notebook computer manufacturers, meaning an upgrade might not be available a year or two after you purchase your notebook computer.

If you are going to use your notebook computer on an airplane, purchase a second battery. Two batteries should provide enough power to last through most airplane flights. If you anticipate running your notebook computer on batteries frequently, choose a computer that uses lithium-ion batteries (they last longer than nickel cadmium or nickel hydride batteries).

Purchase a well-padded and well-designed carrying case. An amply padded carrying case will protect your notebook computer from the bumps it will receive while traveling. A well-designed carrying case will have room for accessories such as spare floppy disks, CD-ROMs, a user manual, pens, and paperwork (Figure 9).

Figure 9 Well-designed carrying case.

If you travel overseas, obtain a set of electrical and telephone adapters. Different countries use different outlets for electrical and telephone connections. Several manufacturers sell sets of adapters that will work in most countries (Figure 10).

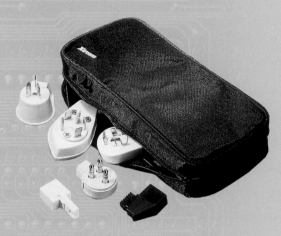

Figure 10 Set of electrical and telephone adapters.

If you plan to connect your notebook computer to a video projector, make sure the notebook computer is compatible with the video projector. Some notebook computers will not allow you to display an image on the notebook computer and projection device at the same time (Figure 11). Either of these factors can affect your presentation negatively.

Figure 11 Video projector.

How to Purchase a Handheld Computer

If you need to stay organized when you are on the go, then a lightweight, palm-size or pocketsize computer, called a handheld computer, may be the right choice. Handheld computers typically are categorized by the operating system they run. Although several are available, the two primary operating systems are Palm OS (Figure 12) and Pocket PC (Figure 13). Listed in this section are a few points you will want to consider when purchasing a handheld computer. You also should visit the Web sites listed in Figure 14.

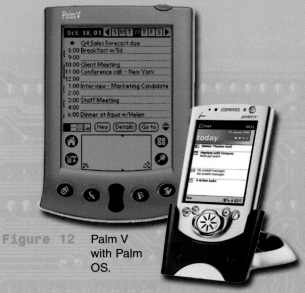

Figure 12   Palm V with Palm OS.

Figure 13   Compaq iPaq Pocket PC.

1 Determine the applications you plan to run on your handheld computer. All handheld computers can handle basic organizer-type applications, such as calendar, address book, and notepad. The availability of other applications is dependent on the operating system you choose. With more than 5,000 applications, the depth of software applications for the Palm OS is unmatched. Handheld computers that run Pocket PC have fewer applications available, but they do run a Windows-like operating system and applications you probably are familiar with, such as Word and Excel.

2 What do you want to pay? The price of handheld computers runs from $100 to $1,000, depending on their capabilities. In general, Palm OS devices are at the lower end of the cost spectrum and Pocket PC devices are at the higher end. The average selling price for handheld computers is in the $300 to $500 range. For the latest handheld computer prices, capabilities, and accessories, visit the Web sites listed in Figure 14.

Web Site	URL
Compaq	compaq.com/products/handhelds
Computer Shopper	computershopper.com
Handspring	handspring.com
Microsoft	pocketpc.com
Mobile Computing	mobilecomputing.com
Palm	palm.com
PDA Buyers Guide	pdabuyersguide.com
smaller.com	smaller.com
Wireless Developer Network	wirelessdevnet.com

For an updated list of handheld computer Web sites, visit *scsite.com/ dc2002/ch8/buyers.htm*.

Figure 14   Reviews and information on handheld computers.

3 Practice with the touch screen and handwriting recognition before deciding on a model. You use a pen-like stylus to handwrite on the screen. The handheld computer then translates the handwriting into a computerized font. You also can use the stylus as a pointing device to select items on the screen and enter data using a transparent on-screen key board. Some handheld computers are easier to use than others. You can buy third-party software to improve a handheld computer's handwriting recognition.

4 Decide if you want a color screen. Pocket PC devices have color screens (as many as 65,536 colors), while most Palm OS devices have monochrome screens (4 to 16 shades of gray). More colors result in greater detail. Resolution also influences the quality of the display.

5 Compare battery life. Any mobile device is good only if it has the power to run. Palm OS devices with black-and-white screens tend to have a much longer battery life than Pocket PC devices with color screens. To help alleviate this problem, both Palm OS and Pocket PC devices have incorporated rechargeable batteries, but this only works if you are near a recharger.

6 Check out the accessories. You need to consider what accessories you want for your handheld computer. Handheld computer accessories include carrying cases, portable keyboards, removable storage, car chargers, GPS systems, dashboard mounts, replacement styli, synchronization cradles and cables, and more.

7 Decide if you want additional functionality. You will find that off-the-shelf Pocket PC devices have broader functionality than Palm OS devices. For example, voice-recording capability, e-book player, MP3 (music) player, and video player are standard on most Pocket PC devices. If you are leaning towards a Palm OS device and still want these additional functions, they can be added later if you find you really need them.

8 Is synchronization of data with other handheld computers, personal computers, or printers important? Most handheld computers come with a cradle that connects to the USB or serial port on your computer so that you can synchronize data. An infrared port, however, allows you to synchronize data with any device, including other handheld computers that have a similar infrared port.

9 If you travel often, then consider e-mail and Web access from your handheld computer. Some handheld computers come with a modem that can send and receive data across telephone lines. Other handheld computers allow you to connect to your cellular telephone and use it as a modem. More expensive handheld computers have wireless capabilities built in. In either case, for a monthly network connection fee you can access your e-mail, company Web sites, and any other information on the World Wide Web from anywhere.

WEB SITE	URL
Getting Started/Installation	
Computers 101	newsday.com/plugin/c101main.htm
HelpTalk Online	helptalk.com
Ergonomics	
Ergonomic Computing	cobweb.creighton.edu/training/ergo.htm
Healthy Choices for Computer Users	www-ehs.ucsd.edu/ergo/ergobk/vdt.htm
Video Display Terminal Health and Safety Guidelines	uhs.berkeley.edu/Facstaff/Ergonomics

For an updated list of reference materials, visit *scsite.com/dc2002/ch8/ buyers.htm*.

Figure 15   Web references on setting up and using your computer.

How to Install a Personal Computer

It is important that you spend time planning for the installation of your computer. Follow these steps to ensure your installation experience will be a pleasant one and that your work area is safe, healthy, and efficient.

1 Read the installation manuals before you start to install your equipment. Many manufacturers include separate installation instructions with their equipment that contain important information. You can save a great deal of time and frustration if you make an effort to read the manuals.

2 Do some research. To locate additional instructions on installing your computer, review the computer magazines or Web sites listed in Figure 15 to search for articles on installing a computer.

3 Set up your computer in a well-designed work area, with adequate workspace around the computer. Ergonomics is an applied science devoted to making the equipment and its surrounding work area safer and more efficient. Ergonomic studies have shown that using the correct type and configuration of chair, keyboard, monitor, and work surface will help you work comfortably and efficiently, and help protect your health. For your computer workspace, experts recommend an area of at least two feet by four feet. Figure 16 illustrates additional guidelines for setting up your work area.

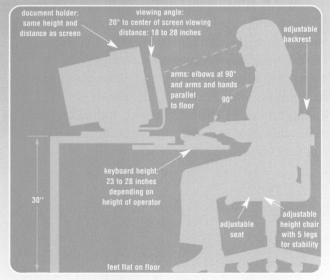

Figure 16   A well-designed work area should be flexible to allow adjustments to the height and build of different individuals. Good lighting and air quality also are important considerations.

Install bookshelves. Bookshelves above and/or to the side of your computer area are useful for keeping manuals and other reference materials handy.

Have a telephone outlet and telephone or cable connection near your workspace so you can connect your modem and/or place calls while using your computer. To plug in your modem to dial up and access the World Wide Web, you will need a telephone outlet or cable connection close to your computer. Having a telephone nearby also helps if you need to place business or technical support calls while you are working on your computer. Often, if you call a vendor about a hardware or software problem, the support person can talk you through a correction while you are on the telephone. To avoid data loss, however, do not place floppy disks on the telephone or near any other electrical or electronic equipment.

While working at your computer, be aware of health issues. Working safely at your computer requires that you consider several health issues. To minimize neck and eye discomfort, for instance, obtain a document holder that keeps documents at the same height and distance as your computer screen. To provide adequate lighting that reduces eye strain, use non-glare light bulbs that illuminate your entire work area. Figure 17 lists additional computer user health guidelines.

Computer User Health Guidelines

1. Work in a well-designed work area. See Figure 16 on the previous page.

2. Alternate work activities to prevent physical and mental fatigue. If possible, change the order of your work to provide some variety.

3. Take frequent breaks. Every fifteen minutes, look away from the screen to give your eyes a break. At least once per hour, get out of your chair and move around. Every two hours, take at least a fifteen-minute break.

4. Incorporate hand, arm, and body stretching exercises into your breaks. At lunch, try to get outside and walk.

5. Make sure your computer monitor is designed to minimize electromagnetic radiation (EMR). If it is an older model, consider adding EMR reducing accessories.

6. Try to eliminate or minimize surrounding noise. Noisy environments contribute to stress and tension.

7. If you frequently use the telephone and the computer at the same time, consider using a telephone headset. Cradling the telephone between your head and shoulder can cause muscle strain.

8. Be aware of symptoms of repetitive strain injuries: soreness, pain, numbness, or weakness in neck, shoulders, arms, wrists, and hands. Do not ignore early signs; seek medical advice.

Figure 17 Following these health guidelines will help computer users maintain their health.

Obtain a computer tool set. Computer tool sets include any screwdrivers and other tools you might need to work on your computer. Computer dealers, office supply stores, and mail-order companies sell these tool sets. To keep all the tools together, get a tool set that comes in a zippered carrying case.

Save all the paperwork that comes with your computer. Keep the documents that come with your computer in an accessible place, along with the paperwork from your other computer-related purchases. To keep different-sized documents together, consider putting them in a manila file folder, large envelope, or sealable plastic bag.

9 **Record the serial numbers of all your equipment and software.** Write the serial numbers of your equipment and software on the outside of the manuals packaged with these items. As noted in the next section, you also should create a single, comprehensive list that contains the serial numbers of all your equipment and software.

10 **Complete and send in your equipment and software registration cards.** When you register your equipment and software, the vendor usually enters you in its user database. Being a registered user not only can save you time when you call with a support question, it also makes you eligible for special pricing on software upgrades.

11 **Keep the shipping containers and packing materials for all your equipment.** Shipping containers and packing materials will come in handy if you have to return your equipment for servicing or must move it to another location.

12 **Identify device connectors.** At the back of your computer, you will find a number of connectors for your printer, monitor, mouse, telephone line, and so forth (Figure 18). If the manufacturer has not identified them for you, use a marking pen to write the purpose of each connector on the back of the computer case.

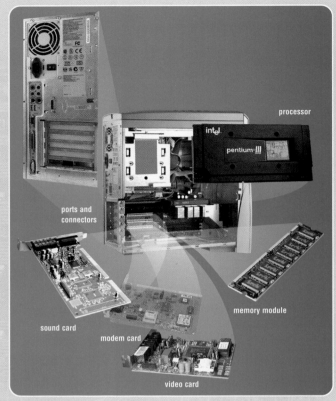

Figure 18 Inside the system unit and the connectors at the back.

13 **Install your computer in an area where you can maintain the temperature and humidity.** You should keep the computer in an area with a constant temperature between 60°F and 80°F. High temperatures and humidity can damage electronic components. Be careful when using space heaters, for example, as the hot, dry air they generate can cause disk problems.

14 **Keep your computer area clean.** Avoid eating and drinking around your computer. Also, avoid smoking. Cigarette smoke can damage the floppy disk drives and floppy disk surfaces.

15 **Check your home or renter's insurance policy.** Some renter's insurance policies have limits on the amount of computer equipment they cover. Other policies do not cover computer equipment at all if it is used for business. In this instance, you may want to obtain a separate insurance policy.

How to Maintain Your Computer

Even with the most sophisticated hardware and software, you will need to do some type of maintenance to keep everything working properly. You can simplify and minimize the maintenance by following the steps listed below.

Start a notebook that includes information on your computer. Keep a notebook that provides a single source of information about your entire computer, both hardware and software. Each time you make a change to your computer, such as adding or removing hardware or software or altering computer parameters, record the change in your notebook. Include the following items in your notebook:

- Vendor support numbers from your user manuals

- Serial numbers of all equipment and software

- User IDs, passwords, and nicknames for your ISP or OSP, network access, Web sites, and so on

- Vendor and date of purchase for all software and equipment

- Trouble log that provides a chronological history of equipment or software problems

- Notes on any discussions with vendor support personnel

Figure 19 provides a suggested outline for the contents of your notebook.

PC OWNER'S NOTEBOOK OUTLINE

1. Vendors
   Vendor
   City/State
   Product
   Telephone #
   URL

2. Internet and online
      services information
   Service provider name
   Logon telephone number
   Alternate logon
      telephone number
   Technical support
      telephone number
   User ID
   Password

3. Web site information
   Web site name
   URL
   User ID
   Password
   Nickname

4. Serial numbers
   Product
   Manufacturer
   Serial #

5. Purchase history
   Date
   Product
   Manufacturer
   Vendor
   Cost

6. Software log
   Date installed/uninstalled

7. Trouble log
   Date
   Time
   Problem
   Resolution

8. Support calls
   Date
   Time
   Company
   Contact
   Problem
   Comments

9. Vendor paperwork

Figure 19 To keep important information about your computer on hand and organized, use an outline such as this sample outline.

Before you work inside your computer, turn off the power and disconnect the equipment from the power source. Working inside your computer with the power on can affect both you and the computer adversely. Thus, you should turn off the power and disconnect the equipment from the power source before you open a computer to work inside. In addition, before you touch anything inside the computer, you should touch an unpainted metal surface such as the power supply. Doing so will help discharge any static electricity that could damage internal components.

3 **Keep the area surrounding your computer dirt and dust free.** Reducing the dirt and dust around your computer will reduce the need to clean the inside of your computer. If dust builds up inside the computer, remove it carefully with compressed air and a small vacuum. Do not touch the components with the vacuum.

4 **Back up important files and data.** Use the operating system or utility program to create an emergency or rescue disk to help you restart your computer if it crashes. You also regularly should copy important data files to disks, tape, or another computer.

5 **Protect your computer from viruses.** A computer virus is a potentially damaging computer program designed to infect other software or files by attaching itself to the software or files with which it comes in contact. Virus programs are dangerous because often they destroy or corrupt data stored on the infected computer. You can protect your computer from viruses by installing an antivirus program.

6 **Keep your computer tuned.** Most operating systems include several computer tools that provide basic maintenance functions. One important tool is the disk defragmenter. Defragmenting your hard disk reorganizes files so they are in contiguous (adjacent) clusters, making disk operations faster. Some programs allow you to schedule maintenance tasks for times when you are not using your computer. If necessary, leave your computer on at night so it can run the required maintenance programs. If your operating system does not provide the tools, you can purchase a stand-alone utility program to perform basic maintenance functions.

7 **Learn to use diagnostic tools.** Diagnostic tools help you identify and resolve problems, thereby helping to reduce your need for technical assistance. Diagnostic tools help you test components, monitor resources such as memory and processing power, undo changes made to files, and more. As with basic maintenance tools, most operating systems include diagnostic tools; you also can purchase or download many stand-alone diagnostic tools.

APPENDIX

Coding Schemes and Number Systems

CODING SCHEMES

As discussed in Chapter 4, a computer uses a coding scheme to represent characters. This section presents the ASCII, EBCDIC, and Unicode coding schemes and discusses parity.

ASCII and EBCDIC

Two widely used codes that represent characters in a computer are the ASCII and EBCDIC codes. **The American Standard Code for Information Interchange,** called ASCII (pronounced ASK-ee), is the most widely used coding system to represent data. Many personal computers and mid-range servers use ASCII. The **Extended Binary Coded Decimal Interchange Code**, or EBCDIC (pronounced EB-see-dic) is used primarily on mainframe computers. Figure A-1 summarizes these codes. Notice how the combination of bits (0s and 1s) is unique for each character.

When the ASCII or EBCDIC code is used, each character that is represented is stored in one byte of memory. Other binary formats exist, however, that the computer sometimes uses to represent numeric data. For example, a computer may store, or pack, two numeric characters in one byte of memory. The computer uses these binary formats to increase storage and processing efficiency.

Unicode

The 256 characters and symbols that are represented by ASCII and EBCDIC codes are sufficient for English and western European languages but are not large enough for Asian and other languages that use different alphabets. Further compounding the problem is that many of these languages use symbols, called **ideograms**, to represent multiple words and ideas. One solution to this situation is Unicode. **Unicode** is a 16-bit code that has the capacity of representing more than 65,000 characters and symbols.

ASCII	SYMBOL	EBCDIC
00110000	0	11110000
00110001	1	11110001
00110010	2	11110010
00110011	3	11110011
00110100	4	11110100
00110101	5	11110101
00110110	6	11110110
00110111	7	11110111
00111000	8	11111000
00111001	9	11111001
01000001	A	11000001
01000010	B	11000010
01000011	C	11000011
01000100	D	11000100
01000101	E	11000101
01000110	F	11000110
01000111	G	11000111
01001000	H	11001000
01001001	I	11001001
01001010	J	11010001
01001011	K	11010010
01001100	L	11010011
01001101	M	11010100
01001110	N	11010101
01001111	O	11010110
01010000	P	11010111
01010001	Q	11011000
01010010	R	11011001
01010011	S	11100010
01010100	T	11100011
01010101	U	11100100
01010110	V	11100101
01010111	W	11100110
01011000	X	11100111
01011001	Y	11101000
01011010	Z	11101001
00100001	!	01011010
00100010	"	01111111
00100011	#	01111011
00100100	$	01011011
00100101	%	01101100
00100110	&	01010000
00101000	(	01001101
00101001	)	01011101
00101010	*	01011100
00101011	+	01001110

Figure A-1

Unicode represents all the world's current languages using more than 34,000 characters and symbols (Figure A-2). In Unicode, 30,000 codes are reserved for future use, such as ancient languages, and 6,000 codes are reserved for private use. Existing ASCII coded data is fully compatible with Unicode because the first 256 codes are the same. Unicode currently is implemented in several operating systems, including Windows NT and OS/2, and major system developers have announced plans eventually to implement Unicode.

	041	042	043	044	045	046	047
0	А	Р	а	р		ꙩ	Ѱ
1	Б	С	б	с	ě	ѡ	ѱ
2	В	Т	в	т	ђ	ꙃ	ѳ
3	Г	У	г	у	ѓ	ꙅ	ѻ
4	Д	Ф	д	ф	є	ꙉ	ѵ
5	Е	Х	е	х	ѕ	ю	ѷ
6	Ж	Ц	ж	ц	і	Ꙃ	ѷ
7	З	Ч	з	ч	ї	ꙗ	ѷ
8	И	Ш	и	ш	ј	ꙙ	Оу
9	Й	Щ	й	щ	љ	ꙙ	оу
A	К	Ъ	к	ъ	њ	Ꙗ	Ꙩ
B	Л	Ы	л	ы	ћ	ꙗ	ꙩ
C	М	Ь	м	ь	ќ	Ꙕ	ꙛ
D	Н	Э	н	э		ꙕ	ꙝ
E	О	Ю	о	ю	ў	ꙕ	ꙡ
F	П	Я	п	я	џ	ꙑ	ꙟ

Figure A-2

Parity

Regardless of whether ASCII, EBCDIC, or other binary methods are used to represent characters in memory, it is important that the characters be stored accurately. For each byte of memory, most computers have at least one extra bit, called a **parity bit**, that is used by the computer for error checking. A parity bit can detect if one of the bits in a byte has been changed inadvertently. While such errors are extremely rare (most computers never have a parity error during their lifetime), they can occur because of voltage fluctuations, static electricity, or a memory failure.

Computers are either odd- or even-parity machines. In computers with odd parity, the total number of on bits in the byte (including the parity bit) must be an odd number. In computers with even parity, the total number of on bits must be an even number (Figure A-3). The computer checks parity each time it uses a memory location. When the computer moves data from one location to another in memory, it compares the parity bits of both the sending and receiving locations to see if they are the same. If the system detects a difference or if the wrong number of bits is on (e.g., an odd number in a system with even parity), an error message displays. Many computers use multiple parity bits that enable them to detect and correct a single-bit error and detect multiple-bit errors.

NUMBER SYSTEMS

This section describes the number systems that are used with computers. Whereas thorough knowledge of this subject is required for technical computer personnel, a general understanding of number systems and how they relate to computers is all most users need.

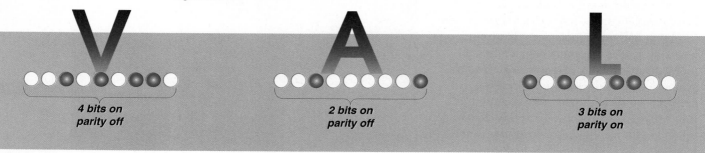

Figure A-3

The binary (base 2) number system is used to represent the electronic status of the bits in memory. It also is used for other purposes such as addressing the memory locations. Another number system that commonly is used with computers is **hexadecimal** (base 16). The computer uses the hexadecimal system to communicate with a programmer when a problem with a program exists, because it would be difficult for the programmer to understand the 0s and 1s of binary code. Figure A-4 shows how the decimal values 0 through 15 are represented in binary and hexadecimal.

The mathematical principles that apply to the binary and hexadecimal number systems are the same as those that apply to the decimal number system. To help you better understand these principles, this section starts with the familiar decimal system, then progresses to the binary and hexadecimal number systems.

The Decimal Number System

The decimal number system is a base 10 number system (deci means ten). The base of a number system indicates how many symbols are used in it. The decimal number system uses 10 symbols: 0 through 9. Each of the symbols in the number system has a value associated with it. For example, 3 represents a quantity of three and 5 represents a quantity of five.

The decimal number system also is a positional number system. This means that in a number such as 143, each position in the number has a value associated with it. When you look at the decimal number 143, the 3 is in the ones, or units, position and represents three ones or (3 x 1); the 4 is in the tens position and represents four tens or

DECIMAL	BINARY	HEXADECIMAL
0	0000	0
1	0001	1
2	0010	2
3	0011	3
4	0100	4
5	0101	5
6	0110	6
7	0111	7
8	1000	8
9	1001	9
10	1010	A
11	1011	B
12	1100	C
13	1101	D
14	1110	E
15	1111	F

Figure A-4

(4 x 10); and the 1 is in the hundreds position and represents one hundred or (1 x 100). The number 143 is the sum of the values in each position of the number (100 + 40 + 3 = 143). The chart in Figure A-5 shows how you can calculate the positional values (hundreds, tens, and units) for a number system. Starting on the right and working to the left, the base of the number system, in this case 10, is raised to consecutive powers (10^0, 10^1, 10^2). These calculations are a mathematical way of determining the place values in a number system.

When you use number systems other than decimal, the same principles apply. The base of the number system indicates the number of symbols that are used, and each position in a number system has a value associated with it. By raising the base of the number system to consecutive powers beginning with zero, you can calculate the positional value.

power of 10	10^2	10^1	10^0	1	4	3	=	
				(1×10^2) +	(4×10^1) +	(3×10^0)	=	
positional value	100	10	1	(1×100) +	(4×10) +	(3×1)	=	
number	1	4	3	100 +	40 +	3	=	143

Figure A-5

The Binary Number System

As previously discussed, binary is a base 2 number system (bi means two), and the symbols it uses are 0 and 1. Just as each position in a decimal number has a place value associated with it, so does each position in a binary number. In binary, the place values, moving from right to left, are successive powers of two (2^0, 2^1, 2^2, 2^3) or (1, 2, 4, 8). To construct a binary number, you place ones in the positions where the corresponding values add up to the quantity you want to represent; you place zeros in the other positions. For example, in a four-digit binary number, the binary place values are (from right to left) 1, 2, 4, and 8. The binary number 1001 has ones in the positions for the values 1 and 8 and zeros in the positions for 2 and 4. Therefore, the quantity represented by binary 1001 is 9 (8 + 0 + 0 + 1) (Figure A-6).

The Hexadecimal Number System

The hexadecimal number system uses 16 symbols to represent values (hex means six, deci means ten). These include the symbols 0 through 9 and A through F (Figure A-4 on page A.3). The mathematical principles previously discussed also apply to hexadecimal (Figure A-7).

The primary reason why the hexadecimal number system is used with computers is because it can represent binary values in a more compact and readable form and because the conversion between the binary and the hexadecimal number systems is very efficient.

An eight-digit binary number (a byte) can be represented by a two-digit hexadecimal number. For example, in the ASCII code, the character M is represented as 01001101. This value can be represented in hexadecimal as 4D. One way to convert this binary number (4D) to a hexadecimal number is to divide the binary number (from right to left) into groups of four digits; calculate the value of each group; and then change any two-digit values (10 through 15) into the symbols A through F that are used in hexadecimal (Figure A-8).

Figure A-6

power of 2	2^3	2^2	2^1	2^0
positional value	8	4	2	1
binary	1	0	0	1

1 0 0 1 =

$$(1 \times 2^3) + (0 \times 2^2) + (0 \times 2^1) + (1 \times 2^0) =$$

$$(1 \times 8) + (0 \times 4) + (0 \times 2) + (1 \times 1) =$$

$$8 + 0 + 0 + 1 = 9$$

power of 16	16^1	16^0
positional value	16	1
hexadecimal	A	5

A 5 =

$$(10 \times 16^1) + (5 \times 16^0) =$$

$$(10 \times 16) + (5 \times 1) =$$

$$160 + 5 = 165$$

Figure A-7

positional value	8421	8421
binary	0100	1101
decimal	4	13
hexadecimal	4	D

Figure A-8

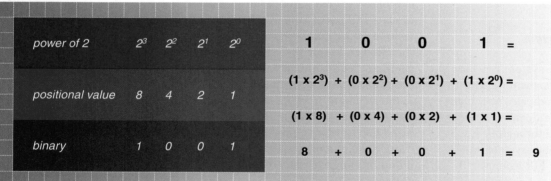

INDEX

1394 bus: Bus that connects multiple types of devices to each other outside the system unit and then a single cable attaches to the 1394 port. **4.32**

1394 port: Port that can connect multiple types of devices that require fast transmission speeds, such as digital video cameras, digital VCRs, color printers, scanners, digital cameras, and DVD drives to a single connector. Also called FireWire. **4.28**, 4.29

3DNow!™: Technology included in AMD processors that further improves the processor's performance of multimedia, the Web, and 3-D graphics. **4.11**

AC adapter: External power supply that converts AC power into DC power, used by some external peripheral devices such as an external modem or tape drive. **4.32**, 4.33

Accelerated Graphics Port (AGP): Bus designed by Intel to improve the speed with which 3-D graphics and video transmit. **4.31**

Access time (disk): The amount of time it takes the device to locate an item on a disk. **7.4**, 7.12

Access time (processor): Amount of time it takes the processor to read data, instructions, and information from memory, directly affecting how fast a computer processes data. **4.22**

Accounting software: Software used by companies to record and report their financial transactions. **3.21**

Active Desktop™: Windows 98 interface used to set up Windows so icons on the desktop and file names in Windows Explorer worked similar to Web links. **8.18**

Active Directory (AD): Feature of Windows 2000 Server that allows network administrators to manage all network information. **8.16**

Active-matrix display: Display technology in LCD monitors and displays that uses a separate transistor for each color pixel and thus can display high-quality color viewable from all angles; also called thin-film transistor (TFT) display. **6.8**, 8.53

Adapter: Circuit board that fits in an expansion slot. **4.23**

Adapter card: Circuit board that fits in an expansion slot. **4.23**

Add-in: Circuit board that fits in an expansion slot. **4.23**

Add-on: Circuit board that fits in an expansion slot. **4.23**

Address: Unique number that identifies the location of a byte in memory. **4.16**

Address book (e-mail): List of names and e-mail addresses, contained in an e-mail program. **2.31**

Address book (groupware), 3.33

Address book (personal information manager): Component of personal information manager software used to enter and maintain names, addresses, and telephone numbers of customers, coworkers, family members, and friends. **3.20**

Address bus, 4.29

Adobe systems, 3.23

Advanced Micro Devices (AMD), 4.10, 4.11

Advanced Research Projects Agency (ARPA): Agency of the U.S. Department of Defense that started a networking project that evolved into the Internet. **2.3**-4

Advanced transfer cache: Type of L2 cache built directly on the processor cache; the most common size is 256 KB. **4.20**

Advocacy Web page: Web page containing content that describes a cause, opinion, or idea. **2.16**-17

Allen, Paul, 3.5, 3.7

All-in-one computer: Computer that houses the system unit in the same physical case as the monitor, used to save space. **1.21**, **4.3**

Allocation unit, *see* **Cluster**

Alpha processor: Processor originally developed by Digital Equipment Corporation that is used primarily in workstations and high-end servers. **4.10**

America Online (AOL), 1.18, 2.6, 2.17

American Standard Code for Information Interchange (ASCII): The most widely used coding system to represent data; used by most PCs and mid-range servers. **4.14**

Americans with Disabilities Act (ADA): Federal law that requires any company with 15 or more employees to make reasonable attempts to accommodate the needs of physically challenged workers. **5.31**

Analog: Continuous signals that vary in strength and quality; example is human speech. **4.13**, 5.21

Animated GIF: Popular type of animation that uses computer animation and graphics software to combine several images into a single GIF file. **2.19**

Animation: Appearance of motion created by displaying a series of still images in rapid sequence. **2.19**, 6.3

Anonymous FTP: Allows anyone to transfer some, if not all, available files using FTP. **2.33**

Antivirus program: Utility program that prevents, detects, and removes viruses from a computer's memory or storage devices. **3.3**

Apple Computer, Inc., 8.21

Application, *see* **Application software**

APPLICATION key, 5.5

Application program, *see* **Application software**

Application service provider (ASP): Third-party company that manages and distributes software and services on the Internet. Instead of installing software on a computer, the user runs the programs from the Internet. Some ASPs provide access to the software at no cost and others charge for use of the program. **1.14**

Application service provider (ASP): Third-party organization that manages and distributes software and services on the Web. **3.35**

categories of, 3.36

Application software: Programs that are used to perform specific tasks, such as: productivity/business tools; to assist with graphics and multimedia projects; to support household activities, for personal business, or for education; and to facilitate communications and include word processing software, spreadsheet software, database software, and presentation graphics software. Also called a software application or an application. **1.13, 3.2**-37

categories of, 3.2

communications, 3.32-33

memory and, 4.16

operating system managing, 8.8-9

starting, 3.4-7

uninstalling, 8.29

Appointment calendar (groupware), 3.33

Appointment calendar (personal information manager): Component that allows scheduling of activities for a particular day and time. **3.20**

Arithmetic operations: Operations of the arithmetic/logic unit, including addition, subtraction, multiplication, and division. **4.6**

Arithmetic/logic unit (ALU): Component of the CPU that performs arithmetic, comparison, and logical operations. 4.5, **4.6**-7

ARPANET: Network built by the Advanced Research Projects Agency that linked scientific and academic researchers. **2.4**

Arrow keys: Keys on a keyboard: one pointing up, one pointing down, one pointing left, and one pointing right. **5.4**

Article: Previously entered message in a newsgroup. **2.33**

ASCII, *see* **American Standard Code for Information Interchange**

ATA: An earlier type of EIDE controller was ATA. **7.13**

Audio: Any music, speech, or other sound stored and produced by a computer. **2.20, 3.25, 6.3**

streaming, 2.21

word processing software, 3.8

Audio CDs, 7.17, 7.23, 24

Audio chats, 6.3

Audio clips, 3.18, 6.3

Audio editing software: Software used to modify audio clips and produce studio quality soundtracks. **3.25**

Audio files, 5.16

Audio input: Process of entering any sound into a computer such as speech, music, and sound effects. **5.16**

Audio output device: Output component that produces music, speech, or other sounds, such as beeps. Two commonly used audio output devices are speakers and headsets. **6.23**

Authorware, *see* **Multimedia authoring software**

Auto PC: Device mounted onto a vehicle's dashboard that is powered by Windows CE; provides driver information such as driving directions, traffic conditions, weather, and stock quotes; access to e-mail; radio or audio CD; and shares information with a handheld or notebook computer. **8.26**

Automated teller machine (ATM): Self-service banking machine that provides access to a bank account by connecting to a host computer through a telephone network. **6.29**

Auxiliary storage, *see* **Storage**

Discovering Computers 2002: Concepts for a Digital World, Web Enhanced

B2B, *see* **Business to business**
Backbone: Communications lines that carry the heaviest amount of traffic on the Internet. **2.7**
Background: When running multiple applications, describes the applications that are running, but not in use. **8.9**
Backup: Duplicate of a file, program, or disk that can be used if the original is lost, damaged, or destroyed. **7.9,** 8.61
  CD-RW, 7.23
  Internet hard drive, 7.16
  removable disk, 7.14
Backup utility: Program used to copy, or backup, selected files or an entire hard disk onto another disk or tape. **8.30**
Band printer: Line printer that prints fully-formed characters when hammers strike a horizontal, rotating band that contains shapes of numbers, letters of the alphabet, and other characters. **6.15**
Banking
  ATM and, 6.29
  e-money and, 7.29
  magnetic-ink character recognition and, 5.30
  online, 3.28
Bar chart, *see* **Column chart**
Bar code: Product identification code that consists of a set of vertical lines and spaces of different widths, representing data that identifies a manufacturer and item. **5.28**
  Web, 5.30
Bar code scanner: Scanner that uses laser beams to read bar codes. **5.28**
Basic input/output system (BIOS): Sequence of instructions a computer follows to load the operating system and other files when the computer is first turned on. **4.20**
Battery power
  CMOS and, 4.21
  handheld computers, 8.56
  notebook computer, 8.54
Bay: Open area inside the system unit in which additional equipment can be installed; commonly called a drive bay. The two types of drive bays are: external, or exposed drive bay and internal, or hidden drive bay. **4.32**
Berners-Lee, Tim, 2.4
Binary system: Number system that has just two unique digits, 0 and 1, called bits. **4.14**
BIOS (basic input/output system): Firmware that contains a computer's startup instructions. **8.5-6**
Bit: Short for binary digit, the smallest unit of data a computer can represent. A bit represents one of two values, on or off. Eight bits are grouped together to form a byte. **4.14**
  bus and, 4.30
Bit depth: The number of bits a video card uses to store information about each pixel; determines the number of colors the video card can display. Also called color depth. **6.10**
Board: Circuit board that fits in an expansion slot. **4.23**
Boot disk, *see* **Emergency repair disk**
Boot drive: Drive from which a personal computer boots (starts), in most cases Drive C. **8.6**

Booting: Process of starting or restarting a computer. **8.4**
Bot, *see* **Spider**
Braille printer: Printer that outputs information in Braille onto paper. **6.30**
Bricklin, Dan, 3.14
Browser, *see* **Web browser**
B-to-B, *see* **Business to business**
B-to-C, *see* **Business to consumer**
Buffer: Area of memory or storage in which items are placed while waiting to be transferred to or from an input or output device. **8.11**
Bus: Electrical channel that allows the various devices inside and attached to the system unit to communicate with each other. Buses transfer bits and consist of two parts: a data bus, which transfers actual data and an address bus, which transfers information about where the data should go in memory. Two types of buses are system buses and expansion buses. **4.29-32**
Bus width: Size of a bus; determines the number of bits that a computer can transmit at one time. **4.29-30**
Business to business (B-to-B or B2B): E-commerce that occurs when businesses provide goods and services to other businesses. **2.25**
Business to consumer (B-to-C or B2C): E-commerce that consists of the sale of goods to the general public. **2.25**
Business/marketing Web page: Web page containing content that promotes or sells products or services. **2.17**
Button: Graphical element that a user activates to cause a specific action to take place. **3.4**
Byte: Eight bits grouped together as a unit, representing a single character in the computer, such as numbers, uppercase and lowercase letters of the alphabet, punctuation marks, and others such as the letters of the Greek alphabet. **4.14,** 4.16

ClearType: Technology developed by Microsoft for LCD screens, such as e-books, to make onscreen reading as natural as reading from printed material. **6.7**
C2C, *see* **Consumer to consumer**
Cable modem: Modem that provides high-speed Internet connections through the cable television network. **2.6**
Cache: Type of memory that improves processing time by storing the contents of frequently accessed RAM locations. When the processor needs an instruction or data, it first searches the cache, then it searches the more slowly accessed RAM. Two types of cache are memory cache and disk cache. **4.19,** 7.12
Cache controller: Controller that manages cache and thus determines which items cache should store. On newer processors, the cache controller is part of the processor. **7.12**
Cache store, *see* **Memory cache**
Calculations, spreadsheet, 3.12, 13
Cam, *see* **Web cam**
Camera
  digital, *see* Digital camera

  digital video, 5.21-24
  PC video, 5.22
  Web cams, 5.23
Capacity: The number of bytes (characters) a storage medium can hold. **7.4**
Card: Circuit board that fits in an expansion slot. 4.3, 4.4, **4.23**
  expansion, *see* **Expansion card**
  storage media, 1.8
Career, 1.27
  choices, 4.13
  computer technician, 7.31
  graphics designer/illustrator, 6.31
  help desk, 1.37
  network administrator, 8.30
  software engineer, 4.35
  Webcasting, 5.33
  Webmaster, 2.37
Cathode ray tube (CRT): Display device that is a large, sealed, glass tube in a CRT monitor. The front of the tube is the screen. Tiny dots of phosphor material coat the screen and each dot consists of a red, a green, and a blue phosphor. The three dots combine to make up each pixel, which is a single point in an electronic image. **6.5**
CD recorder: Device used to write on a CD-R. **7.22**
CD-R (compact disc-recordable): Multisession compact disc that can be recorded onto only once, but can be read from as many times as a user wishes. One part of the disc can be written on at one time and another part at a later time. **7.22**
CD-R drive: Drive that can read and write both audio CDs and standard **CD-ROM (compact disc read-only memory):** Silver-colored compact disc that uses the same laser technology as audio CDs for recording music. In addition to audio, a CD-ROM can contain text, graphics, and video. The manufacturer writes, or records the contents of standard CD-ROMs. You only can read the contents of these discs, not erase or modify their contents. 1.8, **7.20, 7.22**
  notebook computer, 8.54
CD-ROM drive: Drive that reads CD-ROMs. 1.8, **7.20**
CD-ROM jukebox: Device that holds hundreds of CD-ROMs that can contain application programs and data. Also called a CD-ROM server. **7.27**
CD-ROM player: Device that reads CD-ROMs. **7.20**
CD-RW (compact disc-rewritable): Erasable compact disc that can be written on multiple times; originally called an erasable CD (CD-E). 1.8, **7.22-24**
CD-RW drive: Drive that writes on and reads CD-RW discs. **7.22**
Celeron™: Intel processor used by less expensive, basic PCs. **4.10**
Cell: The intersection of a column and row in a spreadsheet. **3.12**
Central processing unit (CPU): Component of the system unit that interprets and carries out the basic instructions that operate a computer. The CPU significantly impacts overall computing power and manages most of a computer's operations. Most of

the devices connected to the computer communicate with the CPU in order to carry out a task. The CPU contains the control unit and the arithmetic/logic unit; these two components work together to perform processing operations. Also called a processor. **1.6**, 4.4, **4.5**-13
installation and upgrades, 4.11-12
memory and, 7.3
personal computer, 4.9-11
purchasing computer and, 8.49
starting computer, 8.5
Charting: Feature of spreadsheet software that allows the display of data in a chart; charts show the relationship of data in graphical form. **3.14**
Chassis, *see* **System unit**
Chat: Real-time typed conversation that takes place on a computer. **2.35**
Chat client: Software that allows connection to a chat server to start a chat session; included in most Web browsers. **2.36, 3.32**
Chat room: Service that permits users on the Web to chat with each other via the computer. As a line of text is typed, the entered words display on the computer screens of other people in the same chat room. Chats typically are specific to a certain topic, such as computers or cooking. Some chat rooms support voice chats and video chats, where people can be seen and heard during the chat. **2.35, 3.32**
Chip: Small piece of semiconducting material, usually no bigger than one-half-inch square, on which integrated circuits are etched. 1.6, **4.4**
CMOS, 4.21
flaws, 4.22
RAM, 4.18-20
ROM, 4.20
Chip for chip upgrade: Processor upgrade that replaces the existing processor chip with a new one. **4.11**
CISC (complex instruction set computing): Design used by the CPU that supports a large number of instructions. **4.6**
Click: Process of pressing and releasing a button on the mouse that activates an object on the screen. **3.4**-5
Client: Computer on a network that relies on servers for resources such as files, devices, processing power, and storage. **2.6, 8.15**
Client operating system: Operating system that works in conjunction with a network operating system. **8.17**
Clip art: Collection of drawings, diagrams, and photographs that can be inserted into documents. **3.8**
Clip art/image gallery: Collection of clip art and photographs that can be used in all types of documents. Many clip art/image galleries also provide fonts, animations, sounds, video clips, and audio clips. **3.30**
Clip gallery: Clip art images, pictures, video clips, and audio clips, typically organized by categories. **3.18**
Clipboard: Temporary storage location for portions of a document during cut, copy, and paste operations. **3.10**

Clock cycle: Describes each tick generated by the system clock. **4.8**
Clock rate, *see* **Clock speed**
Clock speed: The speed at which a processor executes instructions, measured in megahertz and gigahertz. Also called clock rate. **4.8**, 4.11, 4.30
Cluster: Smallest unit of disk space that stores data, consisting of two to eight sectors. Also called an allocation unit. **7.8**
CMOS, *see* **Complementary metal-oxide semiconductor memory**
Coding schemes, 4.14-15
Cold boot: Process of turning on a computer after it has been powered off completely. **8.4**
Color depth, *see* **Bit depth**
Color library: Standard set of colors used by designers and printers to ensure that colors will print exactly as specified. **3.23**
Column chart: Chart that displays bars of various lengths to show the relationship of data. The bars can be horizontal, vertical, or stacked on top of one another. Also called bar chart. **3.14**
Command: Instruction that causes a computer program to perform a specific action. **3.5, 5.3,** 5.4
Command language: Set of commands used to interact with a computer when working with a command-line interface. **8.8**
Command-line interface: Interface that works when user types keywords or presses special keys on the keyboard to enter data and instructions. **8.8**
Communications, 1.5, 1.9-10
purchasing computer and, 8.49
software for, 3.32-33
Communications devices: Devices that enable computer users to communicate and to exchange items such as data, instructions, and information with another computer. **1.8**
Communications lines, Internet and, 2.7
Compact disc (CD): Flat, round, portable, metal storage medium usually 4.75 inches in diameter and less than one-twentieth of an inch thick that store information using microscopic pits (indentations) and land (flat areas) that are in the middle layer of the disc. A high-powered laser light creates the pits and a lower-powered laser light reads items from the compact disc by reflecting light through the bottom of the disc. The reflected light is converted into a series of bits the computer can process. Compact discs are available as CD-ROM, CD-R, CD-RW, and DVD-ROM. A compact disc also is called an optical disc. 1.8, 7.4, **7.17**-25
Compact disc read-only memory, *see* **CD-ROM**
Comparison operations: Operations of the arithmetic/logic unit that involve comparing one data item to another to determine if the first item is greater than, equal to, or less than the other item. **4.6**
Complementary metal-oxide semiconductor memory (CMOS): Type of memory chip that stores configuration information about

a computer, needed when the computer is turned on. CMOS chips use battery power to retain information even when power to the computer is turned off. **4.21**, 8.6
Computer: Electronic machine, operating under the control of instructions stored in its own memory, that can accept data, manipulate the data according to specified rules, produce results, and store the results for future use. **1.4**
categories of, 1.19-25
components of, 1.5-8
examples of usage, 1.28-35
introduction to, 1.1-37
leasing, 1.23
power of, 1.8-10
purchasing, 1.23
starting, 8.4-6
upgrading, 4.12
Computer literate: Phrase that means a user has knowledge and understanding of computers and their uses. **1.4**, 1.9
Computer output microfilm (COM) recorder: Device that records images on microfilm. **7.30**
Computer program: Series of instructions that tells a computer how to perform the tasks necessary to process data into information; also called a program. **1.4, 1.10**-15, **5.3**
application, *see* Application software
custom, 1.14
downloading, 1.14, 15
home users, 1.29
laser printers, 6.18
packaged, 1.13
productivity, 3.7-21
purchasing, 1.13-15
purchasing computer and, 8.49
registration, 8.59
running, 1.11
system, 1.12
Computer programmer: Someone who writes software programs; also called a programmer. **1.14**
Computer technicians, 7.31
Computer vision syndrome, 6.11
Computer-aided design (CAD) software: Sophisticated type of application software used to create engineering, architectural, and scientific designs. **3.22**
Computer-aided instruction, *see* **Computer-based training**
Computer-based training (CBT): Type of education in which students learn by using and completing exercises with instructional software; typically consists of self-directed, self-paced instruction on a topic. Also called computer-aided instruction. **3.30**
Configuration information, 8.6
Connector: Port hardware that joins a cable to a device. Connectors are male or female. 4.3, 4.4, **4.26**
identifying, 8.59
monitors, 6.10
Consumer to consumer (C-to-C or C2C): E-commerce that occurs when one consumer sells directly to another, such as in an online auction. **2.25**

Context-sensitive: Refers to Help information that relates to the current task being attempted. **3.36**

Context-sensitive menu, *see* **Shortcut menu**

Continuous speech: Process of speaking in a flowing conversational tone, which is recognized by most voice recognition software. **5.15**

Continuous-form paper: Paper used by dot-matrix printers in which each sheet of paper is connected together. **6.14**

Control unit, 4.5-6

Control unit: Component of the CPU that directs and coordinates most of the operations in the computer, interpreting each instruction issued by a program and then initiating the appropriate action to carry out the instruction. **4.5**

Coprocessor: Special processor chip or circuit board that assists the processor in performing specific tasks, thereby increasing application speed. **4.13**

Copyrighted material, downloading, 2.23

Cordless keyboard: Battery-powered keyboard that transmits data using wireless technology, such as radio waves or infrared light waves, communicating with a receiver that attaches to a port on the system unit. **5.5**

Cordless mouse: Battery-powered mouse that transmits data using wireless technology, such as radio waves or infrared light waves. Also called wireless mouse. **5.8**

CPU, *see* **Central processing unit**

Crawler, *see* **Spider**

Creating: Process of developing a document by entering text or numbers, inserting graphical images, and performing other tasks using an input device. **3.10**

Criteria: Restrictions data must meet in a query. **3.17**

Cross-platform: Application that runs identically on multiple operating systems. **8.4**

CRT monitor: Monitor that is similar to a standard television set because it contains a cathode ray tube. **6.5,** 6.10

C-to-C, *see* **Consumer to consumer**

Currency: Field data type that contains dollar and cent amounts. **3.16**

Cursor: Input device used with a graphics tablet that looks similar to a mouse, except it has a window with cross hairs, so the user can see through to the tablet. **5.13**

Custom software: Software written by a programmer that is a tailor-made program developed at a user's request to perform specific functions. **1.14**

Cylinder: The location of a single track through all platters on a hard disk. **7.11**

Data: Collection of raw unprocessed facts, figures, and symbols, processed by a computer to create information. In addition to words and numbers, data also includes sounds, images, and video. **1.4, 5.3**

representation, 4.13-14

traveling the Internet, 2.6-7

Data bus, 4.29

Data projector: Output device that takes the image from a computer screen and projects it onto a larger screen so an audience of people can see the image clearly. **6.25**

Data type: Specifies the kind of data a field can contain and how the field is used. Common data types include text, numeric, currency, date, memo, hyperlink, and object. **3.16**

Data warehouse: Huge database system that stores and manages historical and current transaction data. **7.28**

Database: Collection of data organized in a manner that allows access, retrieval, and use of that data. **3.15**

Database management system (DBMS), *see* **Database software**

Database software: Software used to create, access, and manage a database. Also called database management system (DBMS). 1.13, **3.16-17**

Date: Field data type that contains month, day, and year information. **3.16**

Daughterboard: Small circuit board that plugs into the motherboard, often to add capabilities to the motherboard. **4.11**

Daughterboard upgrade: Processor upgrade in which the new processor chip is on a daughterboard. **4.11**

Dean, Mark, 7.25

Decoding: Control unit operation that translates program instructions into commands the computer can execute; part of the machine cycle. **4.5**

Defragmenting: Process of reorganizing a disk to the files are stored in contiguous sectors, which speeds up disk access and thus improves the performance of the entire computer. **8.30**

Density: Number of bits in an area on a storage medium. **7.7**

Desktop: Onscreen work area that can display graphical elements such as icons, buttons, windows, menus, links, and dialog boxes. **3.4**

keyboards, 5.4, 5

shortcuts, 8.23

starting computer and, 8.6

windows, 3.4-6

Desktop computer: Personal computer designed so the system unit, input devices, output devices, and any other devices fit entirely on or under a desk or table. **1.20-22**

processors, 4.10

purchasing, 8.48-53

Desktop publishing

personal, 3.28-29

professional, 3.23

Desktop publishing (DTP) software: Software used by professional designers to design and produce sophisticated documents that contain text, graphics, and brilliant colors. **3.23**

Device dependent: Operating system that runs only on a specific type of computer. **8.17**

Device driver: Small program that tells the operating system how to communicate with a device; also called a driver. **8.11-13**

Device-independent: Operating systems that run on many manufacturers' computers. **8.17**

Diagnostic utility: Utility program that compiles technical information about a computer's hardware and certain system

software programs and then prepares a report outlining any identified problems. **8.28**

Dialog box: Special window a program displays to provide information, present available options, or request a response. **3.6**

Dial-up access: Slow-speed connection to the Internet using a computer, modem, and regular telephone line to dial into an ISP or OSP. **2.6**

Digital: Signals that have only two discrete states: on and off; describes computers because they are electronic devices powered by electricity, which also has only two states: on or off. **4.13, 5.21**

Digital camera: Input device used to take pictures and store the photographed images digitally, instead of on traditional film. 1.5, 1.6, **5.18-20**

handheld computer, 5.17

photo printers and, 6.20

Picture CD and, 7.22

storage, 7.28

SuperDisk™ drive, 7.10

Web publishing and, 1.36, 2.26

Digital cash, *see* **Electronic money**

Digital Display Working Group (DDWG): Organization led by several industry companies that is developing a standard interface for all displays, called the Digital Video Interface (DVI). **6.10**

Digital divide: Phrase used to describe the idea that people of the world can be divided into two distinct groups: (1) those that have access to technology with the ability to use it and (2) those that do not have access to technology or are without the ability to use it. **1.30**

Digital light processing (DLP) projector: Projector that uses tiny mirrors to reflect light, which produces crisp, bright, colorful images that remain in focus and can be seen clearly even in a well-lit room. **6.25**

Digital revolution, 1.2-4, 1.9

Digital video (DV) camera: Video camera that records video as digital signals; also can capture still frames. **5.21-24**

Digital Video Interface (DVI): New digital interface, being developed by the Digital Display Working Group that provides connections for both CRT and LCD monitors. **6.10**

Digital watermark: Small digital image that when held in front of a PC camera, displays an associated Web page on the computer screen. **5.22**

Digitizer, *see* **Graphics tablet**

Digitizing tablet, *see* **Graphics tablet**

Direct access: Ability to locate a particular data item or file immediately, without having to move consecutively through items stored in front of the desired data item or file, used by floppy disks, hard disks, and compact discs. Also called random access. **7.26**

Direct Rambus® DRAM (Direct RDRAM®): Chips that are much faster than SDRAM chips because they use pipelining techniques. **4.18**

Directory: Organized set of topics about Web sites. **2.15**

Discrete speech: Process of speaking slowly and separating each word with a short pause, required by some voice recognition software. **5.15**

Discussion board, *see* **Message board**

Discussion, *see* **Newsgroup**

Disk cache: Portion of memory that a processor uses to store frequently accessed items, which speeds disk access time. When a program needs data, instructions, or information, the processor checks the disk cache. If the item is in disk cache, the processor uses that item and completes the process. If the processor does not find the requested item in the disk cache, then the processor must wait for the hard disk drive to locate and transfer the item from the disk to the processor. **7.12**

Disk cartridge, *see* **Removable hard disk**

Disk controller: Special-purpose chip and associated electronic circuits that control the transfer of data, instructions, and information from a disk to the rest of the computer. Sometimes referred to as an interface. **7.13**

Disk defragmenter: Utility program that reorganizes file and unused space on a hard disk to the operating system can access data more quickly and programs can run faster. **8.30**

Disk Defragmenter: Windows disk defragmenting utility. **8.30**

Disk scanner: Utility program that detects and corrects both physical and logical problems on a hard disk or floppy disk and searches for and removes unnecessary files. **8.29**

Diskette, *see* **Floppy disk**

Display, *see* **Display device**

Display device: Output device that visually conveys text, graphics, and video information; also called a display. Information on a display device, sometimes called soft copy, exists electronically and displays for a temporary period of time. **6.4-12**

Distance education (DE), *see* **Distance learning (DL)**

Distance learning (DL): Delivery of education at one location while the learning takes place at other locations; also called distance education (DE) or online learning. **3.35**

DNS server: Internet server that translates a domain name into its associated IP address, so that when a user types in a domain name, data is routed to the correct computer. **2.8**

Domain name: Text version of an IP address. **2.8**

Domain name system (DNS): System on the Internet that stores the domain names and their corresponding IP addresses. **2.8**

DOS (Disk Operating System): Several single user operating systems developed in the early 1980s for PCs; most widely used versions were PC-DOS and MS-DOS. **8.17**

Dot com: Name sometimes used to describe an organization the have a top-level domain of com. **2.8**

Dot pitch: The distance between each pixel on a display, used as a measure of image clarity; sometimes called pixel pitch. The smaller the distance between the pixels, the sharper the image. Text created with a smaller dot pitch is easier to read. **6.9**

Dot-matrix printer: Impact printer that produces printed images when tiny wire pins on a print head mechanism strike an inked ribbon. When the ribbon presses against the paper, it creates dots that form characters and graphics. **6.14**

Dots per inch (dpi): The number of pixels in an inch of screen display. **5.20**

Double data rate SDRAM (DDR SDRAM): Chips that are faster than SDRAM chips because they transfer data twice for each clock cycle, instead of just once; also called SDRAM II chips. **4.18**

Download (digital camera): Process of transfer a copy of pictures from a digital camera to a computer. **5.18**

Downloading (Web information): Process of receiving information, such as a Web page, onto a computer from a server on the Internet. **2.11**

copyrighted material, 2.23

music, 1.30, 7.23, 24

viruses and, 3.4

Downward compatible (drives): Describes drives that can recognize and use earlier media. **7.7**

Downward-compatible (operating system): Operating system that recognizes and works with application software written for an earlier version of the operating system. **8.17**

Dr Watson: Windows utility program that diagnoses problems as well as suggests courses of action. **8.28**

DRAM, *see* **Dynamic RAM**

Drive bay, *see* **Bay**

Driver, *see* **Device driver**

DSL (digital subscriber line): High-speed connection to the Internet using a regular copper telephone line. **2.6**

Dual inline memory module (DIMM): Type of memory module where the pins on opposite sides of the circuit board do not connect and thus form two sets of contacts; typically use SDRAM chips. **4.18**

Dual inline package (DIP): Chip package consisting of two parallel rows of downward pointing thin metal feet (pins). The pins attach a chip package to the circuit board. **4.4**

Dual-scan display, *see* **Passive-matrix display**

Dubinsky, Donna, 5.17

Dumb terminal: Terminal that has no processing power; it can enter and transmit data to, or receive and display data from, a computer to which it is connected. **6.27**

DVD player: Player reads DVD-ROMs. **7.25**

DVD-R (DVD-recordable): DVD that can be written on once and read (played) many times. **7.25**

DVD-RAM: Rewritable DVD that can be erased and recorded on multiple times. **7.25**

DVD-ROM (digital video disc-ROM): Extremely high capacity compact disc capable of storing from 4.7 GB to 17 GB. 1.8, **7.25**

notebook computer, 8.54

DVD-ROM drive: Drive that reads DVD-ROMs; newer drives also can read audio CDs, CD-ROMs, CD-Rs, and CD-RWs. **7.25**

DVD-RW: Rewritable DVD that can be erased and recorded on multiple times. **7.25**

Dye-sublimation printer: Nonimpact thermal printer that uses heat to transfer colored dye to specially coated paper, creating images that are of photographic quality. Also called a thermal dye transfer printer. **6.19**

Dynamic RAM (DRAM): Most common type of RAM, chips that must be re-energized constantly or they lose their contents; sometimes called main memory. **4.18**

EBCDIC, *see* **Extended Binary Coded Decimal Interchange Code**

E-commerce, *see* **Electronic commerce**

Editing: Process of making changes to a document's existing content, including inserting, deleting, cutting, copying, and pasting items. **3.10**

Educational software: Software that teaches a particular skill. 3.26, **3.30**

EEPROM (electrically erasable programmable read-only memory): Type of PROM chip that a programmer can erase microcode from; used by flash memory. **4.20**

Electromagnetic radiation (EMR): Magnetic field that travels at the speed of light, emitted in small amounts by CRT monitors. **6.11**

Electronic book (e-book): Small, book-sized computer that allows users to read, save, highlight, bookmark, and add notes to online text. New book content is downloaded to an e-book from the Web. **6.7**

Electronic commerce (e-commerce): Financial business transaction that occurs over an electronic network such as the Internet. **1.31, 2.24-25,** 7.29, 8.23

Electronic money (e-money): Means of paying for goods and services over the Internet. When digital cash is purchased, money is withdrawn from a user's bank account, then the bank issues unique digital cash numbers that represent the amount of money withdrawn. One implementation places the digital cash on a smart card, which can be swiped on a reader on a user's computer. Also called digital cash. **7.29**

Electronic signature: Signature made using a graphics tablet and pen; also called an e-signature. **5.13**

Electronic storefront: Method by which a customer (consumer) visits an online business; obtains product descriptions, graphics, and a shopping cart. **2.25**

E-mail (electronic mail): Transmission of messages and files via a computer network such as a local area network or the Internet. **2.30, 3.32**

attachments, 3.4, 7.16

Internet hard drive, 7.16

viruses and, 3.4

voice, 2.31

Web-enabled device, 6.7

E-mail address: Combination of a user name and a domain name that identifies a user, so he or she can receive Internet e-mail. **2.31**

E-mail program, *see* **E-mail software**

E-mail software: Software used to create, send, receive, forward, store, print, and delete e-mail messages. **2.30, 3.32**
operating systems, 8.13
Embedded operating system: Operating system on most handheld computers and small devices. **8.25**
Emergency repair disk: Floppy disk, Zip® disk, or CD-ROM that contains system files that will start the computer. Also called boot disk, or rescue disk. 3.4, **8.6,** 8.61
Emoticons: Symbols used to express emotion when communicating on the Internet. **2.37**
ENERGY STAR program: Program developed by the United States Department of Energy and the United States Environmental Protection Agency that encourages manufacturers to create energy-efficient devices that require little power when they are not in use. Monitors and devices that meet ENERGY STAR guidelines display an ENERGY STAR® label. **6.12**
E-news, 8.32-33
Engelbart, Douglas, 5.8
Enhanced Integrated Drive Electronics (EIDE): One of the most widely used controllers for hard disks, can support up to four hard disks at 137 GB per disk. **7.13**
Enhanced keyboard: Keyboard that has 12 function keys along the top, 2 CTRL keys, 2 ALT keys, and a set of arrow and additional keys between the typing area and the numeric keypad. **5.5**
Enhanced resolution: Measure of photographed resolution, used by some manufacturers instead of or in addition to optical resolution. Enhanced resolution usually is higher because it uses a special formula to add pixels between those generated by the optical resolution. Also called interpolated resolution. **5.20**
Enterprise ASP, 3.36
Enterprise storage system: Strategy that focuses on the availability, protection, organization, and backup of storage in a company. The goal of enterprise storage is to consolidate storage so operations run as efficiently as possible. **7.27**
Entertainment
DVD, 7.24, 25
home users, 1.30
Internet and, 1.17
Entertainment software: Software for personal computers that includes interactive games, videos, and other programs designed to support a hobby or provide amusement and enjoyment. **3.31**
Erasable CD (CD-E), *see* **CD-RW**
Ergonomic keyboard: Keyboard with a design that reduces the chance of wrist injuries. **5.6**
Ergonomics: Design and modifications that can be made to incorporate comfort, efficiency, and safety into items in the workplace. **5.6,** 6.5, 6.11, 8.57
E-signature, *see* **Electronic signature**
E-sports, 8.32-33
E-stamp: Digital postage that can be bought and printed from a personal computer. Also called Internet postage. **6.21**

E-weather, 8.32-33
Executes: Process of computer carrying out program instructions by first placing, or loading, the instructions in the memory of the computer. **1.10**
Executing: Control unit operation that carries out commands; part of the machine cycle. **4.5**
Execution time (e-time): The time it takes the control unit to execute and store. **4.6**
Expansion board: Circuit board that fits in an expansion slot. **4.23**
Expansion bus: Bus that allows the processor to communicate with peripheral devices. **4.30-32**
Expansion card, 4.4
Expansion card: Circuit board that fits in an expansion slot; examples are a video card, sound card, network interface card, or modem card. 4.4, **4.23-25**
Expansion slot: Opening, or socket in the motherboard, into which a circuit board can be inserted, such as additional memory, higher-quality sound devices, a modem, or graphics capabilities. **4.23**
Exposed drive bay, *see* **External drive bay**
Extended Binary Coded Decimal Interchange Code (EBCDIC): Coding system used primarily on mainframe computers. **4.14**
External cache, *see* **Level 2 (L2) cache**
External drive bay: Drive bay that allows access to the drive from outside the system unit; also called exposed drive bay. **4.32**

Facsimile (fax) machine: Device that transmits and receives documents over telephone lines. Stand-alone fax machines scan an original document, convert the image into digitized data, and transmit the digitized image to a receiving fax, while fax modems send and receive electronic documents from a computer as faxes. **6.25-26**
Fanning, Shawn, 1.30
FAQs (Frequently Asked Questions): Page that assists a user in finding answers to common questions. **3.36**
FAQs: Stands for frequently asked questions. **2.37**
Fault-tolerant computer: Computer that continues to operate even if one of its components fails. **8.9**
Fax machine, *see* **Facsimile (fax) machine**
Fax modem: Modem used to send (and sometimes receive) electronic documents as faxes. **6.26**
Female connector: Connector that has matching holes to accept the pins on a male connector, similar to an electrical wall outlet. **4.26**
Fetching: Control unit operation that obtains a program instruction or data item from memory; part of the machine cycle. **4.5**
Field camera: Portable digital camera that has many lenses and other attachments, often used by photojournalists. **5.19**
Field: Column in a table that contains a specific piece of information within a record. **3.16**
Field size: The maximum number of characters that a particular field can contain. **3.16**

File: Named collection of data, instructions, or information. **3.10**
graphics, 2.18
File allocation table (FAT): Table of information that the operating system uses to locate files on a disk. **8.15**
File compression utility: Utility program that shrinks the size of a file. **8.28**
File manager: Operating system program that performs functions related to storage and file management. **8.14**
File name: Unique combination of letters of the alphabet, numbers, and other characters that identifies a file. **3.10**
File viewer: Utility program used to display and copy the contents of a file. **8.27**
Filo, David, 2.17
Find or search: Feature that locates all occurrences of a certain character, word, or phrase. **3.9**
FIR (fast infrared): High-speed IrDA port. **4.29**
FireWire, *see* **1394 port**
Firmware: ROM chips that contain permanently written data, instructions, or information, recorded on the chips when they are manufactured. **4.20**
Fixed disk: Hard disk inside the system unit of a desktop personal computer. **7.10**
Flame wars: Exchanges of flames. **2.37**
Flames: Abusive or insulting messages sent over the Internet. **2.37**
Flash BIOS: Type of BIOS that allows a computer easily to update the contents of the BIOS chip, if necessary. **4.21**
Flash memory cards: Removable device used in handheld computers and devices that stores flash memory, allowing the convenient transfer of data from those devices to a desktop computer. **4.21,** 4.25
Flash memory: Type of nonvolatile memory that can be erased electronically and reprogrammed; also known as flash ROM or flash RAM. 4.10, **4.21**
Flash RAM, *see* **Flash memory**
Flash ROM, *see* **Flash memory**
Flatbed scanner: Scanner that works similar to a copy machine except it creates a file of a document in memory instead of a paper copy. **5.25**
Flat-panel display: Display used by devices such as LCD monitors and LCD displays, using a lightweight, compact screen that consumes less than one-third of the power of a CRT monitor, making it ideal for mobile users or users with space limitations. **6.5**
Flip chip-PGA (FC-PGA) package: Higher-performance PGA chip package that places the chip on the opposite side (flip side) of the pins. **4.4**
Floating-point coprocessor: Coprocessor used to speed up engineering, scientific, or graphics applications; sometimes called a math or numeric coprocessor. **4.13**
Floppy disk: Portable, inexpensive storage medium that consists of a thin, circular, flexible plastic disk with a magnetic coating enclosed in a square-shaped plastic shell. Also called diskette. 1.7, 7.4, **7.6-9**
capacity of, 7.5, 7, 8

formatting, 8.15
viruses and, 3.4
Floppy disk drive (FDD): Device that can read from and write on a floppy disk. 1.7, **7.6**
Font: Name assigned to a specific design of characters. **3.10**
Font size: The size of the characters in a particular font, gauged by a measurement system called points. **3.10**
Font style: Emphasis added to a font, such as **bold**, *italic*, and underline. **3.10**
Footer: Text that appears at the bottom of each page. **3.9**
Foreground: When running multiple applications, describes the active application. **8.9**
Format: Process of changing a document's appearance. **3.10**
Formatting: Process of preparing a disk for reading and writing, usually performed in advance by floppy and hard disk manufacturers. **7.8, 8.15**
Formula: Group of symbols that performs calculations on data in a worksheet and displays the resulting value in a cell. **3.12**
Fragmented: Describes file that has contents scattered across two or more noncontiguous sectors, slowing down disk access and thus the performance of the entire computer. **8.30**
Freeware: Copyrighted software provided at no cost to a user by an individual or company; it cannot be resold by a user. **1.14**
FTP (File Transfer Protocol): Internet standard used to upload and download files with other computers on the Internet. **2.32**
FTP server: Computer used to upload and download files using FTP. **2.33**
FTP site: Collection of files including text, graphics, audio, video, and program files that reside on an FTP server. **2.33**
Function keys: Special keys on a keyboard marked F1, F2, and so on, that are programmed to issue commands to a computer. **5.4**
Function: Predefined formula that performs common calculations such as adding the values in a group of cells or generating a value such as the time or date. **3.13**

Garbage in, garbage out (GIGO): Computing phrase that points out that the accuracy of a computer's output depends on the accuracy of the input. **1.9**
Gas plasma monitor: Flat-panel display that uses gas plasma technology, which has a layer of gas contained between two sheets of material. When voltage is applied, the gas releases ultraviolet (UV) light. This UV light causes the pixels on the screen to glow and form an image. **6.8**
Gates, Bill, 1.9, 1.21, 3.5, 3.7
GB, *see* **Gigabyte**
Gender changer: Device that enables two connectors to be joined that are either both female and both male. **4.26**
Gesture recognition: Process that allows a computer to detect human motions, such as recognizing sign language, reading lips, tracking facial movements, or following eye gazes; still in the prototype stage. **5.32**

Ghosting: Etching of images permanently on a monitor's screen. **8.31**
GIF (Graphics Interchange Format): File format for graphical images that uses compression techniques to reduce a file's size, which results in faster downloading of Web pages. GIF works best for images with only a few distinct colors. **2.19**
Gigabyte (GB): Approximately one billion bytes. **4.16**
Gigahertz (GHz): One billion ticks of the system clock. **4.8**
Graphic: Digital representation of nontext information such as a drawing, chart, or photograph; also called a graphical image. **2.18**-19, 3.22-24, **6.3**
creating, 3.18
desktop publishing, 3.29
printing and, 6.18
word processing software, 3.8
Graphical image, *see* **Graphic**
Graphical user interface: User interface, which controls how a user enters data and instructions and how information displays on the screen; uses visual images such as icons, buttons and other graphical objects. **1.12, 3.4-7, 5.3, 8.8**
Graphics card, *see* **Video card**
Graphics designer/illustrator, 6.31
Graphics Interchange Format, *see* **GIF**
Graphics tablet: Flat, rectangular, electronic plastic board, used with an electronic pen to create drawings and sketches. Also called a digitizer, or digitizing tablet. **5.13**
Gray scaling: Monochrome displays that use many shades of gray from white to black, which provides better contrast for the images. **6.4**
Groupware: Software application that helps groups of people work together and share information over a network, most often using personal information manager functions. A major feature of groupware is group scheduling, in which a group calendar tracks the schedules of multiple users and helps coordinate appointments and meeting times. **3.33**
Grove, Andy, 4.13
Handheld computer: Small computer that fits in a user's hand; also called a palmtop computer. Some have small keyboards and others have no keyboard at all and they usually do not have disk drives. Instead, programs and data are stored on chips inside the system unit or on miniature storage media. **1.23,** 5.14
drawbacks, 1.25
input devices, 5.6, 5.16-17
keyboard, 5.6
operating system, 8.3, 25-27
purchasing, 8.55-57
storage, 7.28
system unit, 4.33
Handwriting recognition software: Software that translates handwritten letters and symbols into characters that the computer understands. **5.14**
Hard copy: Printed information that exists physically and is a more permanent form of output than that presented on a display device (soft copy). Also called printout. **6.12**

Hard disk: Storage medium that consists of several inflexible, circular platters that store items electronically. The platter is made of aluminum, glass, or ceramic and is coated with a material that allows items to be recorded magnetically on its surface. The platters, along with the read/write heads, and the mechanism for moving the heads across the surface of the hard disk, are enclosed in an airtight, sealed case to protect them from contamination. Hard disks can be fixed or removable. Also called a hard disk drive. 1.7, 7.4, **7.10**
Internet, 7.16, 17, 22
capacity of, 7.5
controllers, 7.13
formatting, 8.15
how it works, 7.11-12
RAID, 7.14
removable, 7.13
Hard disk controller (HDC): Special-purpose chip and associated electronic circuits that are the interface for a hard disk on a personal computer; may be part of a disk drive or a separate card inside the system unit. **7.13**
Hard disk drive, *see* **Hard disk**
Hardware: Electric, electronic, and mechanical equipment that makes up a computer. **1.4,** 1.5-8
input, 5.1-33
maintenance, 8.60-61
operating system and, 3.3
output, 6.1-31
purchasing, 8.48-50
registration, 8.59
starting computer and, 8.5-6
storage, 7.1-31
system software and, 1.12
system unit, 4.1-35
Web site, 2.26
Head crash: Event that occurs to a hard disk when a read/write head touches the surface of a platter, usually resulting in a loss of data or sometimes loss of the entire drive. **7.12**
Header: Text that appears at the top of each page. **3.9**
Head-mounted pointer: Device used to control a pointer or insertion point. The switch that controls the pointer might be a pad pressed by hand, a foot pedal, a receptor that detects facial motions, or a pneumatic instrument controlled by puffs of air. Head-mounted pointers are used by people with limited hand movement. **5.32**
Headset: Audio output device plugged into a port on the sound card and worn on a user's head, that allows sound to be heard only by the user. **6.23**
Health issues, 8.58
handheld devices, 1.25
keyboard, 5.6
monitor, 6.5, 6.11
See also Ergonomics
Heat pipe: Device that cools processors in notebook computers. **4.12**
Heat sink: Small ceramic or metal component with fins on its surface that absorbs and ventilates heat produced by electrical components; used to cool processors. **4.12**
Help Desk Specialist, 1.37

Hertz: Measure of a screen's refresh rate, hertz is the number of times per second the screen is redrawn. **6.9**

Hertz: One cycle per second. **4.8**

Hewlett, Bill, 6.18

Hewlett-Packard, 6.18

Hidden drive bay, *see* Internal drive bay

HiFD™ (High-Capacity Floppy Disk) drive: High-capacity disk drive developed by Sony that reads from and writes on a 200 MB HiFD™ disk. 7.9, **7.10**

High-capacity disk drive: Disk drive that uses disks with capacities of 100 MB and greater. **7.9**-10

High-definition television (HDTV): Type of television set that works with digital broadcasting signals and supports a wider screen and higher resolution display than a standard television set. **6.12**

High-performance addressing (HPA): Technology used in the latest passive-matrix displays, which provides image quality near that of TFT displays. **6.8**

Hit: Any Web page name that lists as the result of a search. **2.14**

Home design/ landscaping software: Software used by homeowners or potential homeowners to assist with the design or remodeling of a home, deck, or landscape. **3.30**

Home page: Starting Web page for a browser; provides information about a site's purpose and content. Some Web sites also refer to their starting page as a home page. **2.10**-11

Home user: User that spends time on a computer at home for purposes of research and education, budgeting and personal financial management, home business management, entertainment, personal and business communications, and Web access. 1.2, 1.21, **1.29**

software and, 3.26

storage and, 7.31

Host computer: Computer that dumb terminal connects to; performs the processing and sends the output back to the dumb terminal. **6.27**

Host computer (Internet): Internet server that contains files and services. **2.6**

Host, *see* **Node**

Hot plugging: Feature of PC Cards that allows it to be changed without having to open the system unit or restart the computer; also called hot swapping. **4.25**

Hot swapping, *see* **Hot plugging**

HTML (hypertext markup language): Set of special codes, called tags that format a file for use as a Web page. **2.29**

http (hypertext transfer protocol): Communications standard that enables pages to transfer on the Web. **2.13**

Hyperlink: Web address that links to a document or a Web page. **2.11, 3.16**

Hypertext transfer protocol, *see* **http**

IBM, 1.26

Icon: Small image that displays on the screen to represent a program, document, or some other object. **1.12, 3.4, 8.8**

I-drive, 7.16

IEEE 1284: Institute of Electrical and Electronics Engineers standard that specifies how older and newer peripheral devices that use a parallel port should transfer data to and from a computer. **4.28**

IEEE 1394, 4.28, 29

Illustration software, *see* **Paint software**

Image editing software: Software that has the capabilities of paint software as well as the capability to modify existing images. **3.24**

Image processing: Process of capturing, storing, analyzing, displaying, printing, and manipulating images; also called imaging. Image processing allows the conversion of paper documents such as reports, memos, and procedure manuals into an electronic form. Once saved electronically, the documents can be distributed electronically. **5.26**

Image processing system: System used to store and index documents, similar to an electronic filing cabinet that provides access to exact reproductions of original documents. **5.26**

Imaging, *see* **Image processing**

Imaging Preview: Windows Explorer utility that displays the contents of graphics files. **8.27**

Impact printer: Printer that forms characters and graphics on a piece of paper by striking a mechanism against an ink ribbon that physically contacts the paper; they generally are noisy because of this striking activity and typically do not provide letter quality print. **6.14**-15

Import: Process of bringing clip art or other objects into an application. **3.18**

Information: Data that is organized, meaningful, and useful to a particular user or group of users. **1.4**, 1.27, **5.3**

Informational Web page: Web page that contains factual information. **2.17**

Information appliance, *see* **Internet appliance**

Information processing cycle: The series of input, process, output, and storage activities. **1.5**, 1.9

Information system: System of hardware, software, data, people, and procedures that allows a person to obtain useful and timely information from a computer. **1.27**

Ink-jet printer: Nonimpact printer that forms characters and graphics by spraying tiny drops of liquid ink onto a piece of paper. **6.15**-16

Input: Any data or instructions entered into the memory of a computer; once in memory, input can be accessed by the processor and processed into output. **1.5**, **5.2**-33

digital cameras, 5.18-20

handheld computers, 1.23, 5.16-17

keyboard, 5.4-6

mouse, 5.7-9

physically challenged users, 5.31-32

pointing devices, 5.7-14

purchasing computer and, 8.49

storage devices as, 7.4

video, 5.21-24

voice, 5.14-16, 6.24

Input device: Any hardware component that allows a user to enter data, programs, commands, and user responses into a computer.

Popular input devices include the keyboard, mouse, stylus, microphone, digital camera, scanner, and PC camera. 1.5, 5.4

Insertion point: Symbol that indicates where on the screen the next character that is typed will display. Depending on the program, the symbol may be a vertical bar, a rectangle, or an underline. **5.4**

Install: Process of loading software on a computer's hard disk in order to use a program. **1.11**

Installing personal computer, 8.57-59

Instant messaging (IM): Real-time Internet communications service that notifies users when one or more people are online and then allows them to exchange messages or files or join a private chat room with each other. Many instant messaging services also can alert a user to information such as calendar appointments, stock quotes, weather, or sports scores. **2.36, 3.32**

Instant messenger: Software from an instant messaging service. **2.36, 3.33**

Instruction cycle, *see* **Machine cycle**

Instruction time (I-time): The time it takes the control unit to fetch and decode. **4.6**

Instructions: Programs, commands, and user responses. **5.3**

Integrated circuit (IC): Microscopic pathway capable of carrying electrical current; can contain millions of elements such as transistors. **4.4**

Integrated CPU: New type of processor that combines the functions of a processor, memory, and a video card on a single chip; sometimes used by lower-costing PCs and Internet appliances. **4.11**

Integrated software: Software that combines applications such as word processing, spreadsheet, and database into a single, easy-to-use package. The applications within the integrated software package use a similar interface and share some common features. **3.27**

Intel, 4.10, 4.11, 4.13, 4.15

Intel-compatible processors: Processors made by companies such as AMD that have the same internal design or architecture as Intel processors and perform the same functions, but often are less expensive; used in PCs. **4.10**

Intelligent smart card: Smart card that contains a processor and has input, process, output, and storage capabilities. **7.29**

Intelligent terminal: Terminal that has a monitor, keyboard, memory, and a processor that has the capability of performing some functions independent of the host computer; sometimes called programmable terminals because they can be programmed to perform basic tasks. **6.28**

Interactive TV: Two-way communications technology in which users interact with television programming. **6.12**

Interface card: Circuit board that fits in an expansion slot. **4.23**

Internal cache, *see* **Level 1 (L1) cache**

Internal drive bay: Drive bay concealed entirely within the system unit; also called hidden drive bay. **4.32**

Internal modem, *see* **Modem card**

Internet: The world's largest network, a worldwide collection of networks that links together millions of businesses, government agencies, educational institutions, and individuals. Also called the Net. 1.10, **1.17, 2.2**-37
accessing, 1.17
addresses, 2.8
chat rooms, 2.35-36
connecting to, 2.6
electronic commerce and, 2.24-25
e-mail, see, E-mail
etiquette, 2.37
FTP, 2.32-33
history of, 2.3-4
instant messaging, 2.36, 3.32
mailing lists, 2.34-35
message board, 2.34
newsgroups, 2.33-34
number of users, 1.17
operation of, 2.4-8
paying for goods and services over, 7.29
sharing photos on, 1.36
software on, 1.14, 15
viruses and, 3.4
Web publishing, 2.26-29
See also World Wide Web
Internet appliance: Computer with limited functionality whose main purpose is to connect to the Internet from home; also called an information appliance. **1.24**
processors, 4.11
Internet backup: Use of the Web to store data, information, and instructions. **7.27**
Internet Corporation for Assigned Names and Numbers (ICANN): Group that assigns and controls top-level domains. **2.8**
Internet Explorer: Microsoft Web browser included with Windows 98. 1.9, **8.18**
Internet hard drive: Service on the Web that provides storage to computer users; sometimes called online storage. **7.16**, 7.17, 7.22
Internet postage, *see* **E-stamp**
Internet printing: Type of printing in which an Internet service on the Web sends a print instruction to a printer; the printer may be at a location different from the computer or device that accessed the Web site. **6.13**
Internet service provider (ISP): Business that has a permanent Internet connection and provides temporary connections to individuals and companies for free or for a fee. 1.18, 1.36, **2.5**
selecting, 8.51-52
Internet telephony: Technology that allows users to converse over the Web, just as if they were on the telephone. **6.24**
Internet2 (I2): Internet-related research and development project that uses an extremely high-speed network to develop and test advanced Internet technologies for research, teaching, and learning. **2.4**
Interpolated resolution, *see* **Enhanced resolution**
Interrupt request (IRQ): Communications line between a device and the processor. **8.13**
IP address: Short for Internet protocol address, a number that uniquely identifies each computer or device connected to the Internet, consisting or four groups of numbers, each separated by a period. **2.8**

IrDA (Infrared Data Association): Organization that sets standards for IrDA ports. **4.29**
IrDA port: Port that communicates with the system unit by transmitting data via infrared light waves instead of cables; used by wireless devices. **4.29**
ISA (Industry Standard Architecture) bus: Most common and slowest expansion bus, used to connect devices such as a mouse, modem card, sound card, and low-speed network interface card. **4.31**
IT personnel, *see* Career
Itanium™: Intel processor used in workstations and low-end servers. **4.10**

JavaScript, 1.14
Jaz® disk: Removable hard disk that can store up to 2 GB. **7.13**
Jewel box: Protective case for a compact disc. **7.19**
Job: Operations the processor manages, including receiving data from an input device, processing instructions, sending information to an output device, and transferring items from storage to memory and from memory to storage. **8.10**-11
Jobs, Steven, 8.21
Joint Photographic Experts Group, *see* **JPEG**
Joystick: Pointing device that is a vertical lever mounted on a base, moved in different directions to control the actions of a vehicle or player; used with games or flight and driving simulations. **5.11**
JPEG (Joint Photographic Experts Group): File format for graphical images that uses compression techniques to reduce a file's size, which results in faster downloading of Web pages. **2.19**

K, *see* **Kilobyte**
Katz, Philip, 8.29
KB, *see* **Kilobyte**
Kernel: Core of an operating system that manages memory and devices; maintains the computer's clock; starts applications; and assigns the computer's resources. **8.4**
Keyboard: Input device that contains keys a user presses to enter data into the computer. 1.5, **5.4**-6
connecting, 4.27
handheld computer, 5.17
notebook computer, 8.54
Keyguard: Metal or plastic plate placed over a keyboard that allows users to rest their hands on the keyboard without accidentally pressing any keys; also guides a finger or pointing device so only one key at a time is pressed. Keyguards are used by people with limited hand mobility. **5.31**
Keywords, *see* **Search text**
Kilobyte (KB or K): 1,024 bytes. **4.16**
Kingston Technology, 7.13
Kiosk: Freestanding computer used to provide information to the public that usually has a touch screen for input; advanced kiosks allow customers to place orders, make payments, and access the Web. **1.34**, 5.12
Kodak, 7.21

Label: Text entered in a cell that identifies data and helps organize a worksheet. **3.12**
Label printer: Small nonimpact printer that prints on an adhesive-type material that can be placed on a variety of items such as envelopes, packages, floppy disks, CDs, DVDs, audiocassettes, photographs, file folders, bar codes, and e-stamps. **6.21**
Landscape orientation: Page that is wider than it is tall, with information printed across the widest part of the paper. **6.12**
Laptop computer, *see* **Notebook computer**
Large business user: User in a business that has hundreds or thousands of employees across a region, a country, or the world. 1.28, **1.33**
storage and, 7.5, 7.31
Large-format printer: Printer that creates large-scale, photo-realistic quality color prints. **6.22**
Laser printer: High-speed, high-quality nonimpact printer that creates images using a laser beam and powdered ink, called toner. The laser beam produces an image on a special drum inside the printer. The light of the laser alters the electrical charge on the drum wherever it hits, causing toner to stick to the drum and then transfer to paper through a combination of pressure and heat. **6.16**-18
LCD (liquid crystal display): Display method used in LCD displays and monitors that has liquid crystals contained between two sheets of material. When an electric current passes through the crystals, they twist. This causes some light waves to be blocked and allows others to pass through, which creates the images on the screen. **6.5**-8, 6.10
LCD displays: Flat-panel displays that use liquid crystal to present information on the screen. The liquid crystal is contained between two sheets of material. When an electric current passes through the crystals, they twist. This causes some light waves to be blocked and allows others to pass through, which creates the images on the screen. Because they are lightweight and consume less than one-third of the power of a CRT monitor, LCD displays are ideal for mobile users or users with space limitations and are often used in notebook and handheld computers. **6.5**-8, 6.10
LCD monitors: Flat-panel display device that uses liquid crystal to present information on the screen. The liquid crystal is contained between two sheets of material. When an electric current passes through the crystals, they twist. This causes some light waves to be blocked and allows others to pass through, which creates the images on the screen. LCD monitors are lightweight, consume less than one-third of the power of a CRT monitor, and save space on a desktop. **6.5**-8, 6.10
LCD projector: Projector that uses liquid crystal technology, attaches directly to a computer, and uses its own light source to display information shown on the computer screen. **6.25**
Leasing computer, 1.23

Legal software: Software that assists in the preparation of legal documents and provides legal advice to individuals, families, and small businesses. **3.28**

Letter quality (LQ): Describes print output that is a quality acceptable for business letters. **6.14**

Level 1: Simplest RAID storage design, called mirroring, which has one backup disk for each disk, thereby offering data duplication. **7.14**

Level 1 (L1) cache: Cache built directly into the processor chip; it usually has a very small capacity, ranging from 8 KB to 64 KB but the most common size is 16 KB. Also called primary cache or internal cache. **14.19**

Level 2 (L2) cache: Cache that is slightly slower than L1 cache but has a much larger capacity, ranging from 64 KB to 4 MB; also called external cache. When discussing cache, most users are referring to L2 cache. **4.20**

Level 3 (L3) cache: Cache separate from processor chips on the motherboard and exists only on computers that use L2 advanced transfer cache. **4.20**

Light pen: Handheld input device that contains a light source or can detect light. Some light pens require a specially designed monitor, while others work with a standard monitor. Objects on the screen are selected by pressing the light pen against the surface of the screen or by pointing the light pen at the screen and then pressing a button on the pen. **5.12**

Line chart: Chart that shows a trend during a period of time, as indicated by a rising or falling line. **3.14**

Line printer: High-speed impact printer that prints an entire line at a time. **6.14**

Line printers, 6.14-15

Link, *see* **Hyperlink**

Linux: Popular, free, multitasking UNIX-type operating system. In addition, Linux also includes many programming languages for free. **8.24**

Liquid crystal display, *see* **LCD**

LISTSERVs: Name given to some mailing lists, after a popular mailing list software product. **2.34**

Local area network (LAN), 1.16, 1.33

Local bus: High-speed expansion bus that connects higher speed devices such as hard disks. **4.31**

Local/Regional ASP, 3.36

Log on: Process of accessing a network. **8.16**

Logical operations: Operations of the arithmetic/logic unit that use conditions along with logical operators such as AND, OR, and NOT. **4.7**

Logitech, 5.9

Luquis, Lavonne, 2.35

Mac OS: Multitasking operating system available only for computers manufactured by Apple. **8.21**

Machine cycle: Comprised of fetching, decoding, executing, and storing operations; also called instruction cycle. The total time required for a machine cycle is computed by adding together instruction time and execution time. **4.6**

Macintosh, 1.19

processors, 4.10

Macintosh operating system: Apple operating system that was the first commercially successful GUI. **8.21**

Macro: Sequence of keystrokes and instructions that a user records and saves. When the macro is run, it performs the sequence of saved keystrokes and instructions. **3.13**

Magnetic media: Storage media that uses magnetic patterns to store data, instructions, and information on a disk's surface. Most magnetic disks are read/write storage media. **7.8**

Magnetic-ink character recognition (MICR) reader: Device that can read text printed with magnetized ink, used by the banking industry for check processing. **5.30**

Mail server: Server that contains e-mail mailboxes. **2.31**

Mailbox: Storage location for e-mail that usually resides on the computer that is connected to the Internet, such as the server operated by an ISP or OSP. **2.31**

Mailing list: Group of e-mail names and addresses given a single name. When a message is sent to a mailing list, every person on the list receives a copy of the message in his or her mailbox. **2.34**

Main memory, *see* **Dynamic RAM**

Mainframe: Large, expensive, very powerful computer that can handle hundreds or thousands of connected users simultaneously and can store tremendous amounts of data, instructions, and information. **1.26**

Maintenance, 8.60-61

Maintenance utilities, 7.15

Male connector: Connector that has one or more exposed pins, similar to the end of an electrical cord that would be plugged into a wall. **4.26**

Margins: In a document, the portion of a page outside the main body of text, including the top, the bottom, and both sides of the paper. **3.8**

Marquee: Text that animates by scrolling across a screen. **2.19**

Mass storage, *see* **Storage**

Math coprocessor, *see* **Floating-point coprocessor**

MB, *see* **Megabyte**

M-commerce (mobile commerce): E-commerce that takes place using mobile devices. **2.24**

Mechanical mouse: Mouse that has a rubber or metal ball on its underside. When the ball rolls in a certain direction, electronic circuits in the mouse translate the movement of the mouse into signals the computer. **5.7**

Megabyte (MB): Approximately one million bytes. **4.16**

Megahertz (MHz): One million ticks of the system clock. **4.8**

Memo: Field data type that contains lengthy text entries. **3.16**

Memory: Temporary storage place for data, instructions, and information, consisting of one or more chips on the motherboard or some other circuit board in the computer. Sometimes called primary storage. **1.6, 4.15**

access times, 4.22

nonvolatile, 7.3

notebook computer, 8.54

operating system and, 1.12, 3.3, 8.10

printing and, 6.18

processor and, 7.3

purchasing computer and, 8.49

starting computer and, 8.6

storage versus, 7.2-5

types of, 4.15-22

virtual, 8.10

volatile, 7.3

Memory cache: Type of cache that helps speed the processes of the computer by storing frequently used instructions and data; also called cache store or RAM cache. **4.19**

Memory card: Smart card that has only storage capabilities; used in digital cameras and other handheld devices. **7.29**

Memory management: Process of the operating system optimizing the use of random access memory. **8.10**

Memory module, 4.3, 4

Memory module: Small circuit board that RAM chips reside on, which inserts into the motherboard. Three types of memory modules are SIMMs, DIMMs, and RIMMs. **4.18**

Memory resident: Part of operating system that remains in memory while the computer is running. **8.4**

Menu: Screen display containing a list of commands from which a user can select. **3.5, 8.8**

shortcut, 3.6

Menu-driven: Program that provides menus as a means of entering commands. **5.3**

Message board: Popular Web-based type of discussion group; also called a discussion board. **2.34**

Microbrowser: Special type of browser designed for Web-enabled handheld computers and devices such as cellular telephones; accesses and displays Web pages that contain mostly text. Also called mini-browser. **2.11**

Microcode: Instructions to program a PROM chip. **4.20**

Microfiche: Four by six inch sheet of film used to store microscopic images of documents. **7.30**

Microfilm: 100 to 215-foot roll of film used to store microscopic images of documents. **7.30**

Microphone, 1.5, 1.6, 2.26, 5.14, 5.16

Microprocessor: Name sometimes given to a personal computer processor, because all the functions are on a single chip. **4.9**

Microsoft, 1.9

history of, 3.5, 7

operating systems, 8.17-20

Web application, 3.34

See also Windows

Microsoft Network, The, 1.18
MIDI, *see* **Musical instrument digital interface (MIDI)**
Mid-range server: Computer that is more powerful and larger than a workstation computer and often can support up to 4,000 connected users at the same time; in the past, mid-range servers were known as a minicomputers. **1.25**
Minibrowser, *see* **Microbrowser**
Minicomputer, *see* **Mid-range server**
MIPS: Millions of instructions per second; measure of a CPU's speed. **4.6**
Mirroring, *see* **Level 1**
MMX™ (multimedia extensions): Set of instructions built into a processor that allows it to manipulate and process multimedia data more efficiently. **4.11**
Mobile user: User that travels to and from a main office to conduct business. 1.23, **1.32**
  e-commerce, 2.24
  hardware, 1.28, 4.33
  software, 1.28
  storage, 7.28-29, 7.31
  See also Handheld computer
Modem, 1.8, 1.9
  connecting, 4.27
  fax, 6.26
  Internet access, 2.6
  notebook computer, 1.32
Modem card: Expansion card which is a communications device that enables computers to communicate via telephone lines or other means; also called an internal modem. 4.4, **4.23**
Moderated newsgroup: Newsgroup that has a moderator who reviews the content of newsgroup articles and posts them, if appropriate. **2.34**
Moderator: Person who reviews the content of newsgroup articles and posts them, if appropriate. **2.34**
Monitor: Display device that is a separate plastic or metal case that houses a screen. 1.6, **6.4**
  CRT, 6.5, 10
  gas plasma, 6.8
  LCD, 6.5-8, 10
  television as, 6.12
  video cards and, 6.10-11
Monitoring utilities, 7.15
Monochrome: Display information that displays in one color on a different color background. **6.4**
Moore, Gordon, 4.15
Moore's Law, 4.15
Motherboard: Main circuit board in the system unit; sometimes called the system board. 1.6, **4.4**
Motorola, 6.6
Motorola processor: Processor used by Apple Macintosh and Power **Mouse:** Pointing device that fits comfortably under the palm of a user's hand; the most widely used pointing device on desktop computers. 1.5, **5.7**
  connecting, 4.27
  types, 5.7-8
  using, 5.8-9

Mouse pad: Rectangular rubber or foam pad that provides traction for a mouse and protects the ball in the mouse from a buildup of dust and dirt. **5.7**
Mouse pointer: Pointer that moves when the mouse is moved. **5.7**
Movies, DVD, 7.25
Moving Pictures Experts Group (MPEG): Popular video compression standard. **2.22**
MP3: Technology that compresses an audio file to about one-tenth of its original size, while preserving the original quality of the sound. **2.20**
MP3 players: Portable audio devices that can play MP3 files stored on a CD or miniature storage media. **2.20**
MPEG, *see* **Moving Pictures Experts Group**
MPR II: Set of standards that defines acceptable levels of electromagnetic radiation for a monitor. **6.11**
Multifunction device (MFD): Single piece of equipment that looks like a copy machine, but provides the functionality of a printer, scanner, copy machine, and sometimes a fax machine. Sometimes called multifunction peripherals or all-in-one devices. **6.26**-27
Multimedia: Any application that integrates text with one or more of the following elements: graphics, sound, video, virtual reality, or other media elements. **1.35, 2.18**-22
  processors and, 4.11
Multimedia authoring software: Software used to combine text, graphics, audio, video, and animation into an interactive presentation. Sometimes called authorware. **3.25**
Multiprocessing: Operating system that can support two or more CPUs running programs at the same time. **8.9**
Multipurpose operating system: Operating system that works for both stand-alones and networks. **8.24**
Multiread CD-ROM drive: Drive that can read audio CDs, data CDs, CD-Rs, and CD-RWs. **7.22**
Multisession: Disc on which additional data, instructions, and information can be written to at a later time. **7.21**
Multitasking: Operating system that allows a single user to work on two or more applications that reside in memory at the same time. **8.9**
Multiuser: Operating system that enables two or more users to run a program simultaneously. **8.9**
Music
  downloading, 1.30, 7.23, 24
  input, 5.16
  MP3, 2.20
Musical instrument digital interface (MIDI): Serial port that connects the system unit to a musical instrument, such as an electronic keyboard. **4.28**

Nanosecond (ns): One billionth of a second; used to state access times. **4.22**
Napster, 1.30

National ISP: Type of ISP that provides access to the Internet through local telephone numbers in most major cities and towns nationwide and usually offer more services and generally have a larger technical support staff than regional ISPs. **2.5**
National Television Standards Committee (NTSC): Industry members that have technical expertise about television-related issues. **6.12**
Near letter quality (NLQ): Describe print output that is slightly less clear than letter quality. **6.14**
Net, *see* **Internet**
NET: Microsoft's Web applications that enable users to access Microsoft software on the Web from any type of device or computer that can connect to the Internet. **3.34**
Netiquette: Short for Internet etiquette, the code of acceptable behaviors users should follow while on the Internet. **2.37**
NetWare: Novell's widely used network operating system designed for client/server networks. **8.22**
Network: Collection of computers and devices connected together via communications devices and media such as modems, cables, telephone lines, and satellites. 1.10, **1.16, 2.2, 8.15**
Network administrator, 8.30
Network card, *see* **Network interface card**
Network interface card (NIC): Expansion card that is a communications device, which allows a computer to communicate via a network; also called a network card. 4.4, **4.23**
Network operating system: Operating system that supports a network; also called a network OS or NOS. **8.15,** 8.22-24
Network OS, *see* **Network operating system**
Network-attached storage (NAS): Device that adds additional hard disk space to a network. **7.27**
News server: Computer that stores and distributes newsgroup messages. **2.33**
News Web page: Web page that contains newsworthy material. **2.17**
Newsgroup: Online area on the Web where users conduct written discussions about a particular subject; also called a discussion. **2.33, 3.32**
Newsreader: Software used to participate in a newsgroup; included in most browsers. **2.33, 3.32**
Node: Any computer that directly connects to a network; also called host. **2.4**
Nonimpact printer: Printer that forms characters and graphics on a piece of paper without actually striking the paper. Some spray ink, while others use heat and pressure to create images. **6.15**-22
Nonresident: Part of operating system that remains on the hard disk until it is needed. **8.4**
Nonvolatile memory: Memory that does not lose its contents when power is removed from the computer; includes ROM, flash memory, and CMOS. **4.16, 7.3**
NOS, *see* **Network operating system**

Notebook computer: Portable, personal computer small enough to fit on a lap; also called a laptop computer. **1.22**
displays, 6.6-7
floppy disk drive, 7.6
keyboards, 5.4, 5
mobile users, 1.32, 34
PC Cards, 7.28
system unit, 4.3, 4.33
Notepad: Component of personal information manager software used to record ideas, reminders, and other important information. **3.20**
ns, *see* **Nanosecond**
NSFnet: National Science Foundation's network of five supercomputer centers. **2.4**
NT, *see* **Windows NT**
NTSC (National Television Standards Committee) converter: Device used to connect a computer to a standard television set that converts the digital signal from the computer into an analog signal that the television set can display. **6.12**
Numeric: Field data type that contains numbers only. **3.16**
Numeric coprocessor, *see* **Floating-point coprocessor**
Numeric keypad: Calculator-style arrangement of keys on the keyboard that includes numbers, a decimal point, and some basic mathematical operators. **5.4**

Object: Picture, audio, video, or a document created in other applications such as word processing or spreadsheet. **3.16**
OCR (optical character recognition): Technology that involves reading typewritten, computer-printed, or handwritten characters from ordinary documents and translating the images into a form that a computer can understand. **5.27**
OCR devices: Devices that include a small optical scanner for reading characters and sophisticated software for analyzing what is read. **5.27**
OCR software: Software that can read and convert many types of text documents; included with many scanners. **5.26**
Offline: State of not being connected to the Internet. **2.24**
Online: Describes condition of computer being connected to a network. **1.16**
Online auction: Online sale that allows people to bid on items being sold by other people. The highest bidder at the end of the bidding period purchases the item. **2.25**
Online banking: Use of computer to transfer money electronically from checking or credit card accounts to payees' accounts; also can be used to download monthly transactions and statements from the Web. **3.28**
Online Help: Electronic equivalent of a user manual that assists in learning how to use an application software package; usually integrated into an application software package. **3.36**
Online learning, *see* **Distance learning (DL)**
Online service provider (OSP): Business that not only supplies Internet access, but also has many members-only features that offer a variety of special content and services. 1.18, 1.36, **2.5-6**

Online service providers (OSP), 1.36
Online storage, *see* **Internet hard drive**
Online-print service: Service used to send high resolution printed images through the postal service. Many have a photo community where photographs can be posted on the Web for others to view. **3.29**
On-screen keyboard: Keyboard in which a graphic of a standard keyboard displays on a user's screen; a pointing device can be used to press the keys. On-screen keyboards are used by people with limited hand mobility. **5.32**
Onsite service agreement, 8.52
Open-source software: Software whose code is available to the public. **8.24**
Operating environment: GUI that works in combination with an operating system to simplify its use. **8.18**
Operating system (OS): Set of programs containing instructions that coordinate all the activities among computer hardware resources; also contains instructions that allow a user to run application software. Most operating systems perform similar functions that include starting the computer, providing a user interface, managing programs, managing memory, scheduling jobs, configuring devices, accessing the Web, monitoring performance, and providing housekeeping services; some also control networks and administer security. Also called software platform, or platform. **1.12, 3.3, 8.3**-27
embedded, 8.25-27
functions, 8.4-16
handhelds and, 8.3, 25-27
maintenance functions, 8.61
multiprocessing, 8.9
multitasking, 8.9, 8.23, 8.24
multiuser, 8.9
network, 8.15, 8.22-24
personal computer, 1.20
single user/single tasking, 8.8
stand-alone, 8.17-22
types of, 8.17-27
Optical character recognition, *see* **OCR**
Optical disc, *see* **Compact disc**
Optical mark recognition (OMR): Devices that read hand-drawn marks such as small circles or rectangles. **5.28**
Optical mouse: Mouse that has no moving mechanical parts inside, instead, it uses devices that emit and sense light to detect the mouse's movement. Some use optical sensors; others use laser. **5.7**
Optical reader: Device that uses a light source to read characters, marks, and codes and then converts them into digital data that a computer can process. Thee types of optical readers are: optical character recognition, optical mark recognition, and bar code scanner. **5.27-30**
Optical resolution: Measure of actual photographed resolution. **5.20**
Optical scanner: Light-sensing input device that reads printed text and graphics and then translates the results into a form the computer can use. Also called a scanner. 1.5, 1.36, **5.25-27**

Optically-assisted hard drive: Hard disk that combines laser and optic technologies with the magnetic media and have potential storage capacities of up to 280 GB. **7.10**
OS/2 Warp: IBM's GUI multitasking client operating system that supports networking, the Internet, Java, and speech recognition. **8.22**
OS/2 Warp Server: IBM network operating system for e-business. **8.23**
Output: Data that has been processed into a useful form, called information; computers process input into output. Types of output are: text, graphic, audio, and video. **1.5, 6.2-31**
audio, 6.23-24
date projectors, 6.25
display devices, 6.4-12
fax, 6.25-26
multifunction devices, 6.26-27
physically challenged users, 6.29-30
printers, 6.12-22
purchasing computer and, 8.49
speakers, 6.23
storage devices as, 7.4
terminals, 6.27-29
types of, 6.2-3
voice, 6.24
Output device: Any hardware component that can convey information to a user. Commonly used output devices include display devices, printers, monitors, speakers, headsets, data projectors, facsimile machines, and multifunction devices. **1.6, 6.4-30**

Packaged software: Copyrighted retail software that meets the needs of a wide variety of users. **1.13**
Packard, David, 6.18
Page: Amount of data and program instructions that can swap at a given time. **8.10**
Page description language (PDL): Printer language that tells a printer how to lay out the contents of a printed page. Two common page description languages are PCL and PostScript. **6.18**
Page layout: Process of arranging text and graphics in a document. **3.23**
Paging: Technique of swapping items between memory and storage. **8.10**
Paint software: Software used to draw pictures, shapes, and other graphical images with various onscreen tools such as a pen, brush, eyedropper, and paint bucket; sometimes called illustration software. **3.24**
Paint/image editing software
personal, 3.29
professional, 3.24
Palm handheld computer, 5.14, 5.17
Palm OS®: Operating system for Palm and Visor handheld computers. **8.26**
Palm OS devices, 8.56
Palmtop computer, *see* **Handheld computer**
Parallel port: Interface that connects devices to the system unit by transmitting more than one bit at a time; used for a device that requires fast data transmission rates, such as a printer. **4.27**
Parallel processing: Use of multiple processors simultaneously to execute a program, which speeds processing times. **4.13**

Partitions: Separate areas that a formatted hard disk is divided into by issuing a special operating system command. Each partition functions as if it were a separate hard disk drive. Users often partition a hard disk so they can install multiple operating systems on the same hard disk. **7.12**

Passive-matrix display: Display technology that uses fewer transistors and requires less power than an active-matrix display, resulting in color that often is not as bright as that in an active-matrix display. Images on a passive-matrix display are viewed best when working directly in front of the display. Also called dual-scan display. **6.8**

Password: Combination of characters associated with a user name that allows access to certain computer resources. **8.16**

PC camera, *see* **PC video camera**

PC Card: Thin credit card-sized device that adds memory, disk drives, sound, fax/modem, communications, and other capabilities to a mobile computer; formerly known as PCMCIA cards. **4.24-25, 7.28**

PC Card bus: Bus for a PC card. **4.32**

PC video camera: Digital video camera that allows a home user to record, edit, and capture video and still images and to make video telephone calls on the Internet. Also called PC camera. 1.5, 1.6, 1.36, **5.22**

PCI (Peripheral Component Interconnect) bus: Current local bus standard. **4.31**

PCL (Printer Control Language): Standard printer language, developed by Hewlett-Packard, that supports the fonts and layout used in standard office documents. **6.18**

PCMCIA card, *see* **PC Card**

PDA (Personal Digital Assistant): One of the most popular handheld computers in use today, providing personal organizer functions such as a calendar, appointment book, address book, calculator, and notepad; most also offer basic software applications such as word processing and spreadsheet. **1.23**-24

Pen, *see* **Stylus**

Pentium®: Intel processor used by most high-performance PCs. **4.10**

Performance monitor: Operating system program that assesses and reports information about various system resources and device; also can check the number of reads and writes to a file. **8.14**

Peripheral: Any external device that attaches to the system unit. **1.6**
connecting, 4.27-29

Permanent storage, *see* **Storage**

Personal computer: Computer that can perform all of its input, processing, output, and storage activities by itself. Two major categories of personal computers are desktop computers and notebook computers. **1.19**, 4.3
categories, 1.20-22
processors, 4.10
installing, 8.57-59
maintenance, 8.60-61
processors, 4.9-11
purchasing, 8.48-53

Personal Computer Memory Card International Association (PCMCIA): Organization that develops standards for PC cards. **4.24**

Personal DTP software: Software used to create newsletters, brochures, and advertisements; postcards and greeting cards; letterhead and business cards; banners, calendars, and logos; and Web pages. **3.29**

Personal finance software, 1.29

Personal finance software: Simplified accounting program that helps home users and small office/ home office users balance their checkbook, pay bills, track personal income and expenses, track investments, and evaluate financial plans. **3.27**

Personal information manager (PIM): Software application that includes an appointment calendar, address book, notepad, and other features used to organize personal information. **3.20**

Personal use, software for, 3.26

Personal Web page: Web page maintained by a private individual who normally is not associated with any organization. **2.17**

Photo communities: Name given to some Web sites that allow a user to create an online photo album and store digital photographs free of charge. **1.36**

Photo printer: Nonimpact color printer that can produce photo lab quality pictures as well as printing everyday documents; many use ink-jet technology. In addition, many photo printers can read media directly from a digital camera. **6.20**

PhotoCD: Compact disc that contains digital photographic images saved in the PhotoCD format. **7.21**

Photo-editing software: Software used to edit digital photographs by removing red-eye, adding special effects, or creating electronic photo albums. **3.29**, 7.22

Physically challenged users
input devices, 5.31-32
output devices, 6.29-30

Picture CD: Single-session disc that stores digital versions of photographs for consumers. 1.8, **7.21**

Pie chart: Chart that has the shape of round pies cut into pieces or slices, showing the relationship of parts to a whole. **3.14**

Piggyback upgrade: Processor upgrade that stacks the new processor chip on top of the old one. **4.11**

Pin grid array (PGA) chips, 4.12

Pin grid array (PGA) package: Chip package that holds a larger number of pins because the pins are mounted on the surface of the package. **4.4**

Pipelining: Process of the CPU beginning to execute a second instruction before it completes the first instruction, which results in faster processing because the CPU does not have to wait for one instruction to complete the machine cycle before fetching the next. **4.7**

Pixel: Short for picture element, a single point in an electronic image. The greater the number of pixels, the better the quality of an image. **5.20**, 6.9
scanner, 5.26
video cards, 6.10

Pixel pitch, *see* **Dot pitch**

PKZIP, 8.29

Platform, *see* **Operating system**

Platter: Item inside a hard disk that is made of aluminum, glass, or ceramic and is coated with a material that allows items to be recorded magnetically on its surface. **7.10**

Player: Program contained in operating systems that can play the audio in MP3 files on a computer. **2.20**

Plotters: Sophisticated printers that produce high-quality drawings by using a row of charged wires (called styli) to draw an electrostatic pattern on specially coated paper and then fuses toner to the pattern. **6.22**

Plug and Play: Technology in a computer that automatically configures cards and other devices as they are installed. **4.24**, 4.28, 4.29, **8.13**

Plug-in: Program that extends the capability of a browser. **2.28**

Pocket PC: Handheld computer. **8.26**, 8.56

Pocket PC OS: Scaled-down operating system developed by Microsoft that works on a Pocket PC handheld computer. **8.26**

Point: Measurement of font size, equal to approximately 1/72 of an inch in height. **3.10**

Point of presence (POP): Access point on the Internet that is connected to by dialing a telephone number supplied by an Internet service provider. **2.5**

Point-and-shoot camera: Digital camera that is affordable and lightweight and provides acceptable quality photographic images for the home or small business user. **5.19**

Pointer: Small symbol on the screen in a graphical user interface that moves when the mouse is moved, often taking the shape of an I-beam, a block arrow, or a pointing hand. 3.4, **5.7**

Pointing device: Input device that allows a user to control a pointer to move or select items on the screen. **5.7**
handheld computers, 8.56
notebook computer, 8.54

Pointing stick: Pressure-sensitive pointing device shaped like a pencil eraser that is positioned between keys on the keyboard. The pointer moves when the pointing stick is pushed using a finger. **5.11**

Point-of-sale (POS): Terminal that records purchases at the point where the consumer purchases a product or service, serving as input to other computers that perform activities associated with sales transactions. **6.28**

POP (Post Office Protocol): Communications technology for retrieving e-mail from a mail server. **2.32**

POP3 (Post Office Protocol 3): Newest version of POP. **2.32**

Populating: Process of entering individual records into a table. **3.17**

Port: Interface, or point of attachment, for external devices to a system unit. 4.3, 4.4, **4.25**
keyboards, 5.5
mouse, 5.8
types of, 4.27-29

Portable keyboard: Full-sized keyboard that conveniently can be attached and removed from a handheld computer. **5.6**

Portable media, 7.14

Portable printer: Small, lightweight printer that allows a mobile user to print from a notebook or handheld computer while traveling. **6.22**

Portable storage medium, 7.6

Portal, *see* **Portal Web page**

Portal Web page: Web page that offers a variety of Internet services from a single, convenient location. Also called a portal. **2.17**

Portrait orientation: Page that is taller than it is wide, with information printed across the shorter width of the paper. **6.12**

Post Office Protocol 3, *see* **POP3**

Post: Process of adding an article to a newsgroup. **2.33**

Postage printer, 6.21

PostScript: Printer language designed for complex documents with intense graphics and colors, commonly used by professionals in the desktop publishing and graphic art fields. **6.18**

Power, processor, 4.8, 11

Power supply: Component in the system unit that converts the wall outlet AC power to DC power. **4.32**, 4.33, 8.5, 8.60

Power users: Users that require the capabilities of a workstation or other powerful computer, such as engineers, architects, desktop publishers, and graphic artists. 1.28, **1.35**

storage, 7.31

software, 3.22

Power-on self test (POST): Series of tests executed by BIOS to make sure computer hardware is connected properly and operating correctly; checks the various system components such as buses, system clock, expansion cards, RAM chips, keyboard, and drives. **8.6**

Presentation graphics software: Software used to create documents called presentations, which are used to communicate ideas, messages, and other information to a group. The presentations can be viewed as slides, sometimes called a slide show, that display on a large monitor or on a projection screen. 1.13, 1.32, **3.18**

Primary cache, *see* **Level 1 (L1) cache**

Primary storage, *see* **Memory**

Print spooler: Program that intercepts print jobs from the operating system and places them in a queue. **8.11**

Printer, 1.6

Printer: Output device that produces text and graphics on a physical medium such as paper or transparency film. **6.12-22**

connecting, 4.27

impact, 6.14-15

label, 6.21

large-format, 6.22

laser, 6.16-18

nonimpact, 6.15-22

photo, 6.20

portable, 6.22

postage, 6.21

thermal, 6.19

Printing: Process of sending a file to a printer to generate output on a medium such as paper. **3.11**

Internet, 6.13

Printout, *see* **Hard copy**

Processor, *see* **Central processing unit (CPU)**

Productivity software: Software that assists people in becoming more effective and efficient while performing their daily activities; includes applications such as word processing, spreadsheet, database, presentation graphics, personal information manager, software suite, accounting, and project management. **3.7-21**

Program, *see* **Computer program**

Programmable logic, 4.10

Programmable read-only memory (PROM): ROM chip on which items, called microcode, can be placed permanently; once a programmer writes the microcode onto the chip, it functions like a regular ROM chip and cannot be erased or changed. **4.20**

Programmable terminal, *see* **Intelligent terminal**

Programmer, *see* **Computer programmer**

Project management software: Software used to plan, schedule, track, and analyze the events, resources, and costs of a project. **3.21**

Proprietary software: Operating system that is privately owned and limited to a specific vendor or computer model. **8.17**

Public-domain software Free software that has been donated for public use and has no copyright restrictions. **1.14**

Publishing: Process of making a Web page available on the Internet. **1.36**

Pull technology: Obtaining information from a Web site by requesting it, which relies on a client such as a computer to request a Web page from a server. **2.22**

Purchasing

computer, 1.23

desktop personal computer, 8.48-53

digital cameras, 5.20

handheld computer, 8.55-57

notebook computer, 8.53-55

printers, 6.18

software, 1.13-15

sound card, 6.24

Push technology: Obtaining information from a Web site by having a server automatically download content to a computer at regular intervals or whenever updates are made to the site; also called Webcasting. **2.23**, 5.33

Query: Request for specific data from a database. **3.17**

Queue: Location in buffer where multiple print jobs line up. **8.11**

QWERTY keyboard: Name given to a standard computer keyboard because the first six leftmost letters on the top alphabetic line of the keyboard spell QWERTY. **5.5**

RAID (redundant array of independent disks): Group of two or more integrated hard disks, often used by networks and Internet servers to duplicate data, instructions, and information to improve data reliability. **7.14**

RAM (random access memory): Memory chips that can be read from and written to by the processor and other devices; a type of volatile memory. Two basic types of RAM are dynamic RAM and static RAM. **4.16**, 7.3

operating and, 8.4

requirements, 4.18-19

types of, 4.18

RAM cache, *see* **Memory cache**

Rambus® inline memory module (RIMM): Type of memory module that houses RDRAM chips. **4.18**

Random access, *see* **Direct access**

Reading: Process of transferring data, instructions, and information from a storage medium into memory. **7.4**

Read-only memory, *see* **ROM**

Read/write head

floppy disk drive, 7.7

hard disk, 7.11-12

Real-time: Describes process of people conversing online at the same time. **2.35**

Recalculation, 3.13-14

Record: Row in a table that contains information about a given person, product, or event. **3.16**

Records: Process of writing data, instructions, and information on a CD-ROM. **7.20**

Reference software: Software that provides valuable and thorough information for all individuals; includes encyclopedias, dictionaries, health/medical guides, and travel directories. 1.30, **3.31**

Refresh rate: The speed that a monitor redraws images on the screen, which should be fast enough to maintain a constant, flicker-free image; measured in hertz. Also called vertical frequency or vertical scan rate. **6.9**

Regional ISP: ISP that provides access to the Internet through one or more telephone numbers local to a specific geographic area. **2.5**

Registers: High-speed storage locations contained in the CPU that temporarily hold data and instructions. **4.7**

Registry: In Windows, several files that contain the system configuration information. Windows constantly accesses the registry during the computer's operation for information such as installed hardware and software devices and individual user preferences for mouse speed, passwords, and other user-specific information. **8.6**

Removable hard disk: Disk drive in which a plastic or metal case surrounds the hard disk so it can be removed from the drive; also called a disk cartridge. **7.13**

Replace: Feature that substitutes existing characters or words with new ones. **3.9**

Rescue disk, *see* **Emergency repair disk**

Resolution: Description of the sharpness and clearness of an image. The higher the resolution, the better the image quality. **5.20**, **6.8**

ink-jet printers, 6.15

laser printer, 6.17

monitors, 6.8-9

scanner, 5.26

Resources: Hardware devices, software programs, data, and information that can be shared by users on a network. **1.16**

Restore program: Utility program that reverses the backup process, restoring backed up files to their original form. **8.30**

RISC (reduced instruction set computing): Design used by CPU that reduces the instructions to only those used more frequently. **4.6**

ROM (read-only memory): Memory chips storing data, instructions, or information that only can be read, not modified; the data is recorded permanently on the chips. ROM is nonvolatile memory, meaning its contents are not lost when power is removed from the computer. **4.20**, 7.3
embedded operating systems, 8.25
starting computer and, 8.5-6

Saving: Process of copying a items from RAM to a storage medium such as a floppy disk or hard disk. **3.10, 4.18**

Scanner, *see* **Optical scanner**
Schools, computers in, 1.3

Screen: Display device that consists of a projection surface. **6.4**

Screen saver: Utility program that causes a monitor's screen to display a moving image or blank screen if no keyboard or mouse activity occurs for a specified time period. **8.31**

Scrolling: Process of moving different portions of a document on the screen into view. **3.9**

SCSI, *see* **Small computer system interface**
SCSI, *see* **Small computer system interface**
SDRAM II, *see* **Double data rate SDRAM**
Search, *see* **Find or search**

Search engine: Software program used to find Web sites, Web pages, and Internet files. **2.14**

Search text: Word or phrase entered in a search engine's text box; used to find a Web page or pages. Also called keywords. **2.14**

Secondary storage, *see* **Storage**
Sector: Small arc on a disk that can store up to 512 bytes of data. **7.8**
Security, 7.14
operating system and, 8.16

Sequential access: Process of reading or writing data consecutively, used in tape storage. **7.26**

Serial port: Interface that connects devices to the system unit by transmitting data one bit at a time; used for a device that does not require fast data transmission rates, such as a mouse, keyboard, or modem. **4.27**

Server: Computer that controls access to the hardware and software on a network and provides a centralized storage area for programs, data, and information. **1.21, 2.6, 8.15**
processors, 4.10
Web, *see* Web server

Shareware Copyrighted software distributed free for a trial period; if wanted beyond that period of time, the user sends a payment to the person or company that developed the program. **1.14**

Shopping cart: Method that allows a customer at an electronic storefront to collect purchases. **2.25**

Shortcut: Icon on a desktop that runs a program when it is clicked. **8.14**

Shortcut menu: Menu that displays a list of commonly used commands for completing a task related to the current activity or selected item; also called a context-sensitive menu. **3.6**
Shugart, Al, 7.7

Shutter: Piece of metal on a 3.5 inch floppy disk that covers an opening in the rigid plastic shell; when a floppy disk is inserted into a floppy disk drive, the drive slides the shutter to the side to expose a portion of the disk. **7.6**

Shuttle-matrix printer: Line printer that moves a series of print hammers back and forth horizontally at incredibly high speeds, as compared to standard line printers. **6.15**

Single edge contact (SEC) cartridge: Chip package that connects to the motherboard on one of its edges. **4.4**

Single inline memory module (SIMM): Type of memory module where the pins on opposite sides of the circuit board connect together to form a single set of contacts; typically use SDRAM chips. **4.18**, 7.13

Single user/single tasking: Operating system that allows only one user to run one program at a time. **8.8**

Single-session: Disc on which additional data, instructions, and information can be written to only once. **7. 21**

Slide show: Presentations that are viewed as slides. **3.18**

Small computer system interface (SCSI): High-speed parallel port used to attach SCSI peripheral devices such as disk drives and printers to the system unit. **4.29, 7.13**

Small office/home office (SOHO): Any company with fewer than 50 employees, as well as self-employed people that work out of their homes. 1.28, **1.31**
MFDs, 6.27
storage and, 7.5, 7.31

Smart card: Medium that stores data on a thin microprocessor inserted into a card that is similar in size to a credit card. Two types of smart cards are an intelligent smart card and a memory card. **7.29**

Smart pager, *see* **Web-enabled pager**
Smart phone, *see* **Web-enabled cellular telephone**

Socket: Opening on a motherboard where the processor chip is inserted. **4.12**

Soft copy: Information on a display device. **6.4**

Software, *see* **Computer program**
Software application, *see* **Application software**
Software engineer, 4.35

Software package: Specific software product, such as Microsoft Word, which can be purchased, but also packages that are available as shareware, freeware, and public-domain software. These packages, however, usually have fewer capabilities than retail software packages. **3.2**

Software platform, *see* **Operating system**

Solaris™: Version of UNIX developed by Sun Microsystems that is a network operating system designed specifically for e-commerce applications. **8.25**
Son, Masayoshi, 2.25

Sort: Process of organizing a set of records in a particular order, such as alphabetical or by date. **3.17**
Sound Blaster, 6.24

Sound card: Expansion card that enhances the sound-generating capabilities of a computer by allowing sound to be input through a microphone and output through speakers. 2.26, 4.4, **4.23**, 5.14, 6.24

Source document: Original form of a document to be processed. **5.24**

Spam: Unsolicited e-mail or newsgroup posting sent to many recipients at once. **2.37**

Speaker-dependent software: Voice recognition software that works by having the computer make a profile of a user's voice. The user speaks words into the computer repeatedly, causing the software to develop and store a digital pattern for the words. **5.14-15**

Speaker-independent software: Voice recognition software that has a built-in set of word patterns, meaning the computer does not have to be trained to recognize a user's voice. **5.15**

Speakers: Audio output device that produces sounds. 1.6, **6.23**
Specialist ASP, 3.36

Speech recognition, *see* **Voice recognition**
Speed
access times, 4.22
bus, 4.30
cache, 4.20
processor, 4.8, 11
RAM and, 4.19
storage device, 7.4

Spelling checker: Feature that reviews the spelling of individual words, sections of a document, or the entire document. **3.9**

Spider: Used by search engines, a program that reads pages on Web sites in order to create a catalog, or index, of hits. Also called crawler, or bot. **2.14**

Spoiler: Internet message that reveals a solution to a game or ending to a movie or program. **2.37**

Spooling: Process of operating system sending print jobs to a buffer instead of sending them immediately to the printer; allows the processor to interpret and execute instructions while the printer is printing documents. **8.11**

Spreadsheet software: Software that organizes data in rows and columns and performs calculations on this data. The rows and columns collectively are called a worksheet. 1.13, **3.13-15**

SRAM, *see* **Static RAM**

SSE instructions (streaming single-instruction, multiple-data instructions): Technology included in Intel processors that further improves the processor's performance of multimedia, the Web, and 3-D graphics. **4.11**

Stand-alone computer: Desktop computer that can perform the information processing cycle operations (input, process, output, and storage) without being connected to a network; most also have networking capabilities. **1.21**

Stand-alone operating system: Operating system that is complete and works on a desktop or notebook computer; some, called client operating systems also work in conjunction with a network operating system. **8.17**

Starting computer, 8.4-6

StartUp folder: Folder that contains a list of programs that open automatically when a computer boots. **8.6**

Static RAM (SRAM): Chips that are faster and more reliable than any variation of DRAM chips; they do not have to be re-energized as often as DRAM chips, however, SRAM is much more expensive than DRAM. **4.18**

Storage: Device that holds items such as data, instructions, and information for future use. Storage is nonvolatile, meaning items in storage remain intact even when power is removed from the computer. Also called secondary storage, auxiliary storage, permanent storage, or mass storage. **1.5**, 7.1-3, **7.4-31**

  audio files, 5.16
  compact discs, 7.17-25
  DVD-ROM, 7.24
  enterprise storage system, 7.27
  floppy disks, 7.4, 6-9
  hard disks, 7.10-16
  high-capacity disks, 7.9-10
  memory vs., 7.2
  microfiche, 7.30
  microfilm, 7.30
  miniature mobile, 7.28-29
  online, 7.16, 7.17, 7.22
  PC Card, 7.28
  tape, 7.26
  video files, 5.21

Storage area network (SAN): High-speed network that connects storage devices. **7.27**

Storage device: Device that records and retrieves items to and from a storage medium; often functions as a source of input because it transfers items from storage into memory. 1.7, 1.9, **7.4**

Storage medium (media is the plural): The physical material on which a computer keeps data, instructions, and information; examples are floppy disks, hard disks, compact discs, and tape. **7.4**

Stored program concept: The role of memory to store both data and programs. **4.16**

Storing: Control unit operation that writes the result to memory; part of the machine cycle. **4.5**

Streaming: Process of transferring data in a continuous and even flow, allowing users to access and use a file while it is transmitting. **2.20**

Streaming audio: Data transfer that allows sound (data) to be listened to as it downloads to a computer. Also called streaming sound. **2.21**

Streaming cam: Web cam that shows moving images by sending a continual stream of pictures. **5.23**

Streaming sound, *see* **Streaming audio**

Streaming video: Data transfer that allows recorded or live video images to be watched as they download to a computer. **2.22**

Striping: RAID storage design that splits data, instructions, and information across multiple disks in an array, improving disk access times, but not offering data duplication. **7.14**

Structure: General description of the records and fields in a table, including the number of fields, field names, field sizes, and data types. **3.16**

Studio camera: Stationary digital camera used for professional studio work. **5.19**

Stylus: Input device that looks like a ballpoint pen, but uses pressure, instead of ink, to write text and draw lines; originally called a pen or electronic pen. **5.13**, 5.17, 8.56

Submenu: Menu that displays when a user points to a command on a previous menu. **3.5**

Submission service: Web-based business that offers a package for a fee to register with hundreds of search engines. **2.29**

Subscribe (mailing list): Process of adding an e-mail name and address to a mailing list. **2.34**

Subscribe (newsgroup): Process of saving a newsgroup in a newsreader for easy future access. **2.34**

Suite: Collection of individual applications sold as a single package; typically includes word processing, spreadsheet, database, and presentation graphics applications. 1.13, 3.27, **3.20**, 8.49
  utility, 8.27

Super video graphics array (SVGA): Video standard that supports resolutions and colors in the VGA standard. **6.10**

Supercomputer: Fastest, most powerful, and expensive computer that is capable of processing more than 12 trillion instructions a second; used by applications requiring complex, sophisticated mathematical calculations. **1.26**

SuperDisk™ drive: High-capacity disk drive developed by Imation that reads from and writes on a 120 MB or 250 MB SuperDisk™; used in notebook computers and some digital cameras. 7.9, **7.10**

Superscalar: Computers that can execute more than one instruction per clock cycle. **4.8**

Surfing the Web: Process of jumping from one Web page to another. **2.12**

Swap file: Area of a hard disk used for virtual memory, so called because it swaps (exchanges) data, information, and instructions between memory and storage. **8.10**

Synchronize: Process of transferring information between a handheld computer and a desktop computer so the same information is available on both computers. **3.20**

Synchronous DRAM (SDRAM): Chips that are much faster than DRAM chips because they are synchronized to the system clock. **4.18**

Synthesizer: A peripheral or chip that creates sound from digital instructions. **4.28**

System board, *see* **Motherboard**

System bus: Bus that is part of the motherboard and connects the processor to main memory. **4.30**

System clock: Small chip used by the CPU to synchronize, or control the timing of all computer operations. The system clock generates regular electronic pulses, or ticks that set the operating pace of components in the system unit. **4.8**

System files: Specific operating system files that BIOS searches for during startup. **8.6**

System software: Programs that control the operations of a computer and its devices, serving as the interface between a user, the application software, and the computer's hardware. Two types of system software are the operating system and utility programs. **1.12, 3.3**3, **8.2-31**
  memory and, 4.16
  operating systems, see Operating systems
  role of, 3.3-4
  utility programs, see Utility programs

System unit: Box-like case that houses the electronic components of the computer used to process data, protecting the internal electronic components of the computer from damage. Sometimes called a chassis, the system unit is made of metal or plastic and protects the internal electronic components from damage. **1.6, 4.2**, 8.5
  buses, 4.29-32
  components, 4.1-35
  CPU, 4.5-13
  expansion slots and expansion cards, 4.23-25
  floppy disk drive, 7.6
  memory, 4.15-22
  mobile computers, 4.33
  ports, 4.25-29

Systems analyst: Person who designs a software program by working with both a user and a programmer to determine the desired output of the program. **1.14**

Tables: Data organized in rows and columns. **3.16**

Tags: Special codes used in HTML that specify how text and other elements display in a browser and where the links lead. **2.29**

Tape: Storage media that is a magnetically coated ribbon of plastic capable of storing large amounts of data and information at a low cost; one of the first storage media used with mainframe computers. **7.26**

Tape cartridge: Small, rectangular, plastic housing for tape. **7.26**

Tape drive: Drive that reads from and writes data and information on a tape. **7.26**

Tape library: High-capacity tape system that works with multiple tape cartridges for storing backups of data, information, and instructions. **7.27**

Tax preparation software: Software that guides individuals, families, or small businesses through the process of filing federal taxes. The software offers money saving tax tips, designed to lower tax bills. **3.28**

Telecommuting: Work arrangement in which employees work away from a company's standard workplace and often communicate with the office using some communications technology. **1.34**

Telephone call, video, 1.6, 3.33, 5.22

Telephone line, Internet access and, 2.6

Telephone outlet, 8.58

Television

  DVD player and, 7.25

  monitor and, 6.3, 6.12

Terminal: Device that performs both input and output because it consists of a monitor (output), a keyboard (input), and a video card. Three categories of terminals are: dumb terminals, intelligent terminals, and special-purpose terminals. **6.27-29**

  intelligent, 6.28

Terminal (dumb terminal): Device with a monitor and keyboard; sometimes called a dumb terminal because it has no processing power, cannot act as a stand-alone computer, and must be connected to a server to operate. **1.25**, 6.27

Text: Output consisting of characters that create words, sentences, and paragraphs. **6.2**

Text (spreadsheet): Field data type that contains letters, numbers, or special characters. **3.16**

Thermal dye transfer printer, *see* **Dye-sublimation printer**

Thermal printer: Nonimpact printer that generates images by pushing electrically heated pins against heat-sensitive paper. **6.19**

Thermal transfer printer, *see* **Thermal wax-transfer printer**

Thermal wax-transfer printer: Nonimpact thermal printer that generates rich, nonsmearing images by using heat to melt colored wax onto heat-sensitive paper. Also called a thermal transfer printer. **6.19**

Thin-film transistor (TFT) display, *see* **Active-matrix display**

Thrashing: Process that occurs when an operating system spends much of its time paging, instead of executing application software. **8.10**

Thread: Original article and all subsequent related replies in a newsgroup. Also called threaded discussion. **2.33**

Threaded discussion, *see* **Thread**

Thumbnail: Small version of a larger graphical image that can be clicked to display the full-sized image. **2.19**

Title bar: Horizontal space that contains a window's name. **3.6**

Toggle key: Key on a keyboard that switches between two different states. **5.4**

Toner: Powdered ink used in laser printers. **6.17**

Top-level domain (TLD): Contained in a domain name, an abbreviation that identifies the type of organization associated with the domain. **2.8**

Torvalds, Linus, 8.25

Touch screen: Touch-sensitive display that users interact with by touching areas of the screen. **5.12**

Touchpad: Small, rectangular pointing device that is sensitive to pressure and motion; the pointer is moved when a user slides their finger across the surface of the pad. Also called a trackpad. **5.10**

Tower model: Desktop computer that has a tall and narrow system unit that can sit on the floor vertically, if space is limited on a desktop. **1.20**, 4.3

Track: Narrow recording band that forms a full circle on the surface of a disk. **7.8**

Trackball: Stationary pointing device with a ball on its top, like an upside-down mouse. **5.10**

Trackpad, *see* **Touchpad**

Traffic: Communications activity on the Internet. **2.4**

Transistor: Device that acts as an electronic switch, or gate that opens or closes the circuit for electronic signals. **4.4**

Turnaround document: Document that is returned (turned around) to the company that created and sent it. **5.27**

Type I cards: PC Cards that add memory capabilities to a computer. **4.24**

Type II cards: PC Cards that contain communications devices such as modems. **4.24**

Type III cards: PC Cards that house devices such as hard disks. **4.24**

Uncompress: Process of restoring a compressed file to its original form. Also called unzip. **8.28**

Unicode: Coding scheme capable of representing all the world's current languages. **4.14**

Uniform Resource Locator (URL): Unique address for a Web page; also called Web address. **2.12-13**

Uninstaller: Utility program that removes an application as well as any associated entries in the system files. **8.29**

Universal serial bus (USB): Bus that eliminates the need to install cards into expansion slots. Devices connect to each other outside the system unit and then a single cable attaches to the USB port. The USB port then connects to the USB, which connects to the PCI bus on the motherboard. 4.38, 4.29, **4.32**

  hard drives and, 7.13

Universal serial bus (USB) port: Port that can connect up to 127 different peripheral devices to the system unit with a single connector type. **4.28**

UNIX: Multitasking operating system developed in the early 1970s at Bell Laboratories. **8.23**

  Windows vs., 8.25

Unsubscribe: Process of removing an e-mail name and address from a mailing list. **2.34**

Unzip, *see* **Uncompress**

Upload: Process of copying information from a computer to a Web server. **2.29**

Upward compatible (drive): Describes drives that can recognize and use newer media. **7.7**

Upward compatible (software): Product that is written for an earlier version of the operating system, but also runs with the new version. **8.17**

USB hub: Device that plugs into a USB port on the system unit and contains multiple USB ports that cables from USB devices can be plugged into. **4.28**

USB, *see* **Universal serial bus port**

Usenet: Entire collection of Internet newsgroups. **2.33**

User(s): Someone that communicates with a computer or uses the information it generates. **1.4**

  types of, 1.28-35

User ID, *see* **User name**

User interface: Controls how data and instructions are entered and how information displays on a screen. Two types of user interfaces are command-line and graphical. 1.12, **3.4**, **8.7**

User name: Unique combination of characters, such as letters of the alphabet or numbers, that identifies one specific user. Also called a user ID. **2.31**, **8.16**

User response: Instruction a user issues by replying to a question that a computer program displays. **5.3**

User-ID, *see* **User name**

Utility, *see* **Utility program**

Utility program: System software that performs a specific task, usually related to managing a computer, its devices, or its programs; included in operating systems. Also called utility. **1.12, 3.3,** 7.15, **8.27-31**

Utility suites: Several utility programs that are combined into a single package. **8.27**

Validation: Process of comparing data to a set of rules or values to determine if the data is correct. **3.17**

Value: Number contained in worksheet cells. **3.12**

Vendor, purchasing computer and, 8.51

Vertical frequency, *see* **Refresh rate**

Vertical Market ASP, 3.36

Vertical scan rate, *see* **Refresh rate**

VESA local bus: First standard local bus, which was used primarily for video cards. **4.31**

Video: Output that consists of full-motion images that are played back at various speeds, often with accompanying audio. **2.22, 3.25, 6.3**

  streaming, 2.22

  Web cam, 1.31

  word processing software, 3.8

Video adapter, *see* **Video card**

Video camera, 6.3

  Web, 2.22

Video capture, *see* **Video input**

Video capture card: Expansion card that converts an analog video signal into a digital signal that a computer can understand. **5.21**

Video card: Expansion card that converts digital output from a computer into an analog video signal and sends the signal through a cable to the monitor, which displays an image on the screen. Also called a graphics card or video adapter. 4.4, **4.23, 6.10**

Video chats: Chats where participants can see and hear each other as they chat. **2.35, 3.32**

Video clips, 3.18, 6.3

Video compression: Process used to decrease the size of video files that works by recognizing that only a small portion of a video image changes from frame to frame. A video compression program might store the first frame and then store only the changes from one frame to the next. The program assumes the next frames will be almost identical to the first. Before the video is viewed, the program decompresses the video segment. **5.21**

Video decoder: Card that decompresses video data; more effective and efficient than decompression software. **5.21**

Video digitizer: Device that captures an individual frame from an analog video and then saves the still picture in a file; used when an entire video clip is not needed. **5.21-22**

Video editing software: Software used to modify a segment of a video, called a clip. **3.25**

Video Electronics Standards Association (VESA): Association of video card and monitor manufacturers that develops video standards. **6.10**

Video input, 5.21-24

Video input: The process of entering a full-motion recording into a computer and storing it on a storage medium. Also called video capture. **5.21-24**

Video projector, notebook computers and, 8.55

Video telephone call: Telephone call placed using special software along with a microphone, speakers, and a video camera attached to a computer that allows both parties see each other as they talk; can be made on the Internet. **3.33, 5.22**

Videoconference: Meeting between two or more geographically separated people who use a network or the Internet to transmit audio and video data. **3.33, 5.24**

Viewable size: Diagonal measurement of the actual viewing area provided by a monitor. **6.5**

Virtual memory (VM): Operating system allocates a portion of a storage medium, usually the hard disk, to function as additional RAM. **8.10**

Virtual reality (VR): The use of computers to simulate a real or imagined environment that appears as a three-dimensional (3-D) space. **2.22**

Virus: Program that copies itself into other programs and spreads through multiple computers. **3.3-4, 8.61**

VisiCalc, 3.14

Voice chats: Chats where participants can hear each other as they chat. **2.35, 3.32**

Voice e-mail, 2.31

Voice input: The process of entering data by speaking into a microphone that is attached to the sound card on the computer. **5.14**

Voice output: Audio output of a person's voice or a computer talking through speakers. **6.24**

Voice recognition: Computer's capability of distinguishing spoken words; also called speech recognition. **3.11, 5.14**

Volatile memory: Memory that loses its contents when the computer's power is turned off; includes RAM and cache. **4.16, 7.3**

Volume Business ASP, 3.36

VR, *see* **Virtual reality**

VR world: Entire 3-D Web site that contains infinite space and depth. **2.22**

Warm boot: Process of restarting a computer that already is powered on; also called a warm start. **8.4**

Warm start, *see* **Warm boot**

WAV: Waveform audio files that have a .wav extension. **5.16**

Waveforms: Windows storage format for audio files, called WAV files

Web, *see* **World Wide Web (WWW)**

Web address, *see* **Uniform Resource Locator (URL)**

Web application: Software application that exists on a Web site and is accessed by visiting the Web site. Some companies provide access to the application for free, while others allow the program to be used for free and charge a fee only when a certain action occurs. Other companies charge only for service and support, allowing the software to be used or downloaded for free. **3.34**

Web bar code: Bar code in some books and magazines; when scanned with a handheld scanner, the Web page associated with the bar code displays on the computer screen. **5.30**

Web browser: Software used to access and view Web pages on the Internet; also called a browser. **2.9-11, 3.32**

multimedia and, 2.28

operating systems, 8.13

Web cam: Video camera with output that can be displayed on a Web page; also called a cam. **1.31, 2.22, 5.23**

setting up, 5.24

Web community: Web site that joins a specific group of people with similar interests or relationships. **2.17**

Web hosting service: Storage for Web pages provided by companies for a reasonable monthly fee. **2.29**

Web page: Electronic document on the Web that can contain text, graphics, sound, and video, as well as built-in connections to other documents. 1.18, **2.9**

creating, 2.28, 3.26

navigating, 2.11-12

types of, 2.16-17

Web page authoring: Process of creating a Web site. **2.28**

Web page authoring software: Software used to create Web pages. **2.28**, 3.25

Web publishing: Development and maintenance of Web pages. 1.36, **2.26-29**

Web server: Computer that delivers (serves) Web pages requested by a user. **2.13**

Web site: Collection of related Web pages. 1.18, **2.9**

creating, 2.28-29

deploying, 2.29

designing, 2.26-28

maintaining, 2.29

news, 8.32-33

planning, 2.26

Web-based training (WBT): Type of computer-based training that uses Internet technology and typically consists of self-directed, self-paced instruction on a topic. **3.34**

Web-based utility service: Service that charges an annual fee to access and use a vendor's utility programs on the Web. **8.27**

Webcasting, *see* **Push technology**

Web-enabled cellular telephone: Device that allows a user to send and receive messages on the Internet and browse Web sites specifically configured for display on the telephone; sometimes called a smart phone. **1.24**

Web-enabled devices, 1.32

displays, 6.6-7

Internet access, 2.6

Web-enabled pager: Two-way radio that allows a user to send and receive messages on the Internet; also called a smart pager. **1.24**

Webmaster: Individual responsible for maintaining a Web site and developing Web pages. **2.29**, 2.37

What-if analysis: Process in which certain values are changed in a spreadsheet in order to reveal the effects of those changes. **3.14**

Wheel: Pointing device that is a type of steering wheel, which is turned to drive a car, truck, or other vehicle. **5.11**

Whiteboard: Window on a videoconference screen that can display notes and drawings simultaneously on all participants' screens, providing multiple users with an area on which they can write or draw. **5.24**

Wide area network (WAN), 1.16, 1.33

Window: Rectangular area of the screen that displays a program, data, and/or information. **3.6**

Windows: Microsoft operating system with a graphical user interface. 1.9, 1.20, **8.18**

desktop, 3.4-5

features of, 8.19

graphical user interface, 1.12

starting computer and, 8.6

UNIX vs., 8.25

Windows 2000 Advanced Server: Microsoft operating system designed for e-commerce applications. **8.22**

Windows 2000 Datacenter Server: Microsoft operating system used for demanding, large-scale applications usch as data warehousing. **8.22**

Windows 2000 Professional: Upgrade to Windows NT Workstation operating system that is a complete multitasking client operating system that has GUI. **8.18**

Windows 2000 Server: Microsoft operating system that is an upgrade to Windows NT Server, used for a typical business network. **8.22**

Windows 2000 Server family: Microsoft operating system products that meet various levels of server requirements; include Windows 2000 Server, Windows 2000 Advanced Server, and Windows 2000 Datacenter Server. **8.22**

Windows 3.x: Three early versions of Microsoft Windows: Windows 3.0, Windows 3.1, and Windows 3.11 that were operating environments, not operating systems. **8.18**

Windows 95: Microsoft multitasking operating system, written to be a true operating system and take advantage of the processing speed in 32-bit processors. **8.18**

Windows 98: Microsoft operating system that was an upgrade to Windows 95 and was more integrated with the Internet, provided faster system startup and shutdown, better file management, and support for multimedia technologies and the Universal Serial Bus (USB). **8.18**

Windows CE: Scaled-down Windows operating system designed for use on wireless communications devices and smaller computers. **8.25**

Windows Explorer: Windows 98 file manager. **8.18**

WINDOWS key, 5.5

Windows Me, *see* **Windows Millennium Edition**

Windows Millennium Edition: Upgrade to Windows 98 operating system that has features specifically for the home user; also called Windows Me. **8.20**

Windows NT: Microsoft operating system designed for client/server networks; also called NT. **8.18**

Windows NT Server: Microsoft operating system for the server in client/server networks. **8.22**

Windows NT Workstation: Microsoft client operating system that could connect to a Windows NT Server. **8.18**

WinZip, 8.28

Wireless mouse, *see* **Cordless mouse**

Wireless portal: Portal specifically designed for Web-enabled handheld computers and devices. **2.17**

Wireless service provider (WSP): Company that provides wireless Internet access to users with wireless modems or Web-enabled handheld computers or devices. **2.6**

Wizard: Automated assistant used to complete a task by asking a user questions and then automatically performing actions based on the answers; included in many software applications. **3.37**

Woofer: Audio output device that produces low bass sounds. **6.23**

Word processing software, 3.8-9

Word processing software: One of the most widely used types of application software; allows users to create and manipulate documents that contain text and graphics. Sometimes called a word processor. **3.8**

Word processing technician, 3.37

Word processor, *see* **Word processing software**

Word size: The number of bits a processor can interpret and execute at a given time. **4.30**

Word wrap: Automatic positioning of text by a program at the beginning of the next line, if text is typed that extends beyond the right page margin. **3.9**

Workplace, computers in, 1.3

Worksheet: The collection of rows and columns in a spreadsheet. **3.12**

Workstation: More expensive and powerful desktop computer designed for work that requires intense calculations and graphics capabilities. **1.21**

processors, 4.10

World Wide Web (WWW): Also called the Web, a worldwide collection of electronic documents. **2.9**-24

audio, 6.3

graphics, 6.3

home users, 1.29

multimedia on, 2.18-22

operating system and, 8.13

processors and, 4.11

searching for information on, 2.14-15

selling on, 1.37

See also Internet

World Wide Web Consortium (W3C): Group that oversees research and sets standards and guidelines for many areas of the Internet. **2.4**

Wozniak, Stephen, 8.21

Write-protect notch: Small opening on a floppy disk with a tab that slides to cover or expose the notch, used to protect the floppy disk from being accidentally erased. **7.9**

Writing: Process of transferring data, instructions, and information from memory to a storage medium. **7.4**

Xeon™: Intel processor used in workstations and low-end servers. **4.10**

Yahoo, 2.17

Yang, Jerry, 2.17

Zero-insertion force (ZIF) socket: Socket on a motherboard with a small lever or screw that facilitates the installation and removal of processor chips; used by many PGA (pin grid array) chips. **4.12**

Zip® disk: 100 MB or 250 MB disk that is read from and written on using a Zip® drive. 1.7, **7.10**

viruses and, 3.4

Zip® drive: High-capacity disk drive developed by Iomega that reads from and writes on a 100 MB or 250 MB Zip® disk. 7.9, **7.10**

Zipped files: Compressed files that have a .zip extension. **8.28**

PHOTO CREDITS

Chapter 1: *Chapter opener Figures* Courtesy of Microsoft Corporation; IBM and the IBM Logo are Trademarks of International Business Machines Corporation. Courtesy of International Business Machines Corporation; AP/ Wide World Photos; Gateway and the Gateway stylized logo are trademarks of Gateway, Inc. Courtesy of Gateway, Inc.; *Figure 1-1a* Michael Newman/PhotoEdit; *Figure 1-1b* David Young-Wolff/PhotoEdit; *Figure 1-1c (c)* Bob Daemmrich/The Image Works; *Figure 1-1d* Hunter Freeman/Stone; *Figure 1-1e (c)* Thomas Schweizer/The Stock Market; *Figure 1-2* Courtesy of ADP; *Figure 1-3a* Courtesy of International Business Machines Corporation; *Figure 1-3b* Courtesy of Intel Corporation; *Figure 1-3c* Courtesy of Labtec, Inc.; *Figure 1-3d* Courtesy of Gateway, Inc.; *Figure 1-3e* Courtesy of Eastman Kodak Company; *Figure 1-3f* Courtesy of Thomson Multimedia; *Figure 1-3g* Courtesy of Microsoft Corporation; *Figure 1-3h* Courtesy of Labtec, Inc.; *Figure 1-4a* Courtesy of Intel Corporation; *Figure 1-4b* Courtesy of Advanced Micro Devices, Inc.; *Figure 1-4c* Courtesy of Intel Corporation; *Figure 1-4d* Courtesy of Intel Corporation; *Figure 1-4e* Phil A. Harrington/Peter Arnold, Inc.; *Figure 1-4f* PhotoDisc; *Figure 1-5* Scott Goodwin Photography; *Figure 1-6* Courtesy of Seagate Technology; *Figure 1-7* Courtesy of Iomega Corporation; *Figure 1-8* Scott Goodwin Photography; *Figure 1-9* Courtesy of Eastman Kodak Company; *Figure 1-11* Scott Goodwin Photography; *Figure 1-14* Scott Goodwin Photography; *Figure 1-21* Courtesy of International Business Machines Corporation; *Figure 1-22* Courtesy of Apple Computer, Inc.; *Figure 1-23a* Courtesy of Toshiba America Information Systems, Inc.; *Figure 1-23b* Courtesy of Toshiba America Information Systems, Inc.; *Figure 1-24a* Courtesy of Gateway, Inc.; *Figure 1-24b* Courtesy of Apple Computer, Inc.; *Figure 1-26* Courtesy of Dell Computer; *Figure 1-27* Courtesy of Hewlett Packard Company; *Figure 1-28* Fisher/Thatcher/Stone; *Figure 1-29a* Courtesy of Compaq Computer Corporation; *Figure 1-29b* Courtesy of Nokia; *Figure 1-29c* Scott Goodwin Photography; *Figure 1-30* Courtesy of Intel Corporation; *Figure 1-31* Courtesy of Thomson Multimedia; *Figure 1-32* Courtesy of Hewlett Packard Company; *Figure 1-33* Courtesy of International Business Machines Corporation; *Figure 1-34* Courtesy of International Business Machines Corporation; *Figure 1-36a* PhotoDisc; *Figure 1-36b* PhotoDisc; *Figure 1-36c* Corbis; *Figure 1-36d* PhotoDisc; *Figure 1-36e* Bob Daemmrich/Stock Boston; *Figure 1-38* PhotoEdit; *Figure 1-40a* Corbis; *Figure 1-40b* Bob Daemmrich/Stock Boston; *Figure 1-40c* Courtesy of Nokia; *Figure 1-40d* David Young Wolff/PhotoEdit; *Figure 1-40e* Paul Barton/The Stock Market; *Figure 1-43* Courtesy of Kiosk Information Systems, Inc.; *Figure 1-44* Zigy Kaluzny/Stone; *Figure 1-45a* Bob Daemmrich/Stock Boston; *Figure 1-45b* Linda Phillips/Photo Researchers, Inc.; *Figure 1-45c* Frank Pedrick/The Image Works; *Figure 1-45d* James King-Holmes/Science Photo Library/Photo Researchers, Inc.; *Figure 1-46* Walter Hodges/Stone; **Timeline** 1937 Courtesy of Iowa State University; 1943 The Computer Museum History Center; 1945 Courtesy of the Institute for Advanced Studies; 1946 Courtesy of the University of Pennsylvania Archives; 1947 Courtesy of International Business Machines Corporation; 1951 Courtesy of Unisys Corporation; 1952 Hagley Museum and Library; 1953 Courtesy of M.I.T. Archives; 1957 Courtesy of International Business Machines Corporation; 1957 Courtesy of the Deparment of the Navy; 1958 Courtesy of M.I.T. Archives; 1959 Courtesy of International Business Machines Corporation; 1960 Hagley Museum and Library; 1964 Courtesy of International Business Machines Corporation; 1965 Courtesy of Dartmouth College News Service; 1965 Courtesy of Digital Equipment Corporation; 1970 Courtesy of International Business Machines Corporation; 1971 Courtesy of Intel Corporation; 1975 Courtesy of InfoWorld; 1975 The Computer Museum History Center; 1976 Courtesy of Apple Computer, Inc.; 1979 The Computer Museum History Center; 1980 Courtesy of International Business Machines Corporation; 1980 Courtesy of Microsoft Corporation; 1981 Courtesy of International Business Machines Corporation; 1983 Courtesy of Lotus Development Corporation; 1983 (c) 1982 Time Inc.; 1984 Courtesy of International Business Machines Corporation; 1984 Courtesy of Apple Computer, Inc.; 1984 Courtesy of Hewlett Packard Company; 1987 Courtesy of International Business Machines Corporation; 1989 Courtesy of Intel Corporation; 1989 Courtesy (c) 1997-1998 W3C (MIT,INRIA, Keio). All rights reserved; 1992 Courtesy of Microsoft Corporation; 1993 Courtesy of Intel Corporation; 1993 Jim Clark/ The Liaison Agency; 1993 Courtesy of Netscape Communications Corporation; 1994 Courtesy of Netscape Communications Corporation; 1995 Courtesy of Sun Microsystems, Inc.; 1995 Courtesy of Microsoft Corporation; 1996 Courtesy of Palm Computing, Inc.; 1996 Courtesy of Microsoft Corporation; 1996 Reuters/Rick T. Wilking/Archive Photos; 1996 Courtesy of WebTV Networks Inc.; 1997 I. Uimonen/CORBIS Sygma; 1997 Motion Picture & Television Archives; 1997 Courtesy of Denon Electronics; 1997 Courtesy of International Business Machines Corporation; 1998 Courtesy of Microsoft Corporation; 1998 Courtesy of Apple Computer, Inc.; 1999 Courtesy of Microsoft Corporation; 2000 Courtesy of Microsoft Corporation; 2000 Courtesy of Intel Corporation; 2001 Courtesy of RCA; **Chapter 2:** *Chapter opener Figures* Courtesy of Yahoo!, Inc.; Courtesy of America Online, Inc.; AP/Wide World Photos; Courtesy of Max Ramirez (c) 2000; AP/ Wide World Photos; *Figure 2-3b* Courtesy of Juniper Networks, Inc.; *Figure 2-8a* Scott Goodwin Photography; *Figure 2-8b* Courtesy of Motorola, Inc.; *Figure 2-18a* Courtesy of RCA; *Figure 2-18b* AP/Wide World Photos; *Figure 2-23* PhotoDisc; *Figure 2-26* PhotoDisc; *Figure 2-28* Courtesy of Juniper Networks, Inc.; *Figure 2-29* Jeff Zaruba/The Stock Market; **Chapter 3:** *Chapter opener Figures* (c) 1999 Kathleen King; Courtesy of Dan Bricklin; Courtesy of Microsoft Corporation; Courtesy of Adobe Systems, Inc.; *Figure 3-2* Courtesy of International Business Machines Corporation; *Figure 3-2* Figure Courtesy of Compaq Computer Corporation; *Figure 3-24* Courtesy of Microsoft Corporation; *Figure 3-27* Courtesy of Autodesk's Manufacturing Division; *Figure 3-29* Courtesy of Adobe Systems, Inc.; *Figure 3-30 (c)* Luke Wolbach; *Figure 3-31* Courtesy of click2learn; *Figure 3-33* Courtesy of Intuit; *Figure 3-34* Courtesy of Nolo Software; *Figure 3-35* Courtesy of Broderbund; *Figure 3-39* Courtesy of Metier Ltd.; *Figure 3-47* Scott Goodwin Photography; *Figure 3-48* Jose L. Pelaez/The Stock Market; **Chapter 4:** *Chapter opener Figures* Courtesy of Intel Corporation; Courtesy of Advanced Micro Devices, Inc.; Courtesy of Intel Corporation; Courtesy of Intel Corporation; *Figure 4-1a* Courtesy of Gateway, Inc.; *Figure 4-1b* Courtesy of Gateway, Inc.; *Figure 4-1c* Courtesy of International Business Machines Corporation; *Figure 4-1d* Courtesy of Palm, Inc.; *Figure 4-2a* Courtesy of Intel Corporation; *Figure 4-2b* Courtesy of Kingston Technology, Inc.; *Figure 4-2c* Courtesy of SMC Corporation; *Figure 4-2d* Courtesy of ATI Technologies, Inc.; *Figure 4-2g* Courtesy of the author; *Figure 4-3* Scott Goodwin Photography; *Figure 4-4a* Courtesy of Intel Corporation; *Figure 4-4b* PhotoDisc; *Figure 4-4c* Courtesy of Intel Corporation; *Figure 4-4d* Phil A. Harrington/ Peter Arnold, Inc.; *Figure 4-4e* Courtesy of Advanced Micro Devices, Inc.; *Figure 4-9a* Courtesy of Advanced Micro Devices, Inc.; *Figure 4-9b* Courtesy of Intel Corporation; *Figure 4-9b* Courtesy of Advanced Micro Devices, Inc.; *Figure 4-9d* Courtesy of Intel Corporation; *Figure 4-12* Scott Goodwin Photography; *Figure 4-18* George Schiavone/The Stock Market; *Figure 4-21* Scott Goodwin Photography; *Figure 4-25* Courtesy of Intel Corporation; *Figure 4-29* Scott Goodwin Photography; *Figure 4-30* Scott Goodwin Photography; *Figure 4-31* Courtesy of Sandisk, Inc.; *Figure 4-33* Courtesy of the author; *Figure 4-37* Courtesy of the author; *Figure 4-38* Courtesy of Hewlett Packard Company; *Figure 4-39* Courtesy of Intel Corporation; *Figure 4-42* Courtesy of the author; *Figure 4-43a* Scott Goodwin Photography; *Figure 4-43b* Courtesy of Handspring, Inc.; *Figure 4-44* Scott Goodwin Photography; *Figure 4-45* Scott Goodwin Photography; *Figure 4-46* Courtesy of Compaq Computer Corporation; *Figure 4-47a* PhotoDisc; *Figure 4-47b* PhotoDisc; *Figure 4-47c* Corbis; *Figure 4-47d* PhotoDisc; *Figure 4-47e* Bob Daemmrich/Stock Boston; *Figure 4-48* AP/Wide World Photos; **Chapter 5:** *Chapter opener Figures* Courtesy of Logitech, Inc.; Courtesy of Handspring, Inc.; Courtesy of Doug Englebart; (c) Carol J. Kaelson and Robert Pearcy of Animals/Animals; *Figure 5-1a* PhotoDisc; *Figure 5-1b* Dick Blume/The Image Works; *Figure 5-1c* Dan Bosler/Stone; *Figure 5-1d* Michael Newman/PhotoEdit; *Figure 5-1e* David Young Wolff/PhotoEdit; *Figure 5-1f* PhotoDisc; *Figure 5-2* Courtesy of Compaq Computer Corporation; *Figure 5-3* Courtesy of Logitech, Inc.; *Figure 5-6a* Courtesy of Toshiba America Information Systems, Inc.; *Figure 5-6b* Courtesy of Hewlett Packard Company; *Figure 5-7* Courtesy of Think Outside, Inc.; *Figure 5-8* Courtesy of Microsoft Corporation; *Figure 5-10* Scott Goodwin Photography; *Figure 5-13* Scott Goodwin Photography; *Figure 5-14* Scott Goodwin Photography; *Figure 5-15* Scott Goodwin Photography; *Figure 5-16* Courtesy of Microsoft Corporation; *Figure 5-17* Courtesy of Fastpoint Technologies; *Figure 5-18* AP/ Wide World Photos; *Figure 5-19a* Michael Newman/PhotoEdit; *Figure 5-19b* PhotoDisc; *Figure 5-20* Courtesy of Wacom Technology Corporation; *Figure 5-21a* AP/ Wide World Photos; *Figure 5-21b* Raquel Ramirez/PhotoEdit; *Figure 5-23* David Hanover/Stone; *Figure 5-24* Courtesy of Handspring, Inc.; *Figure 5-25a* Courtesy of Palm, Inc; *Figure 5-25b* Courtesy of Palm. Inc.; *Figure 5-25c* Courtesy of Think Outside, Inc.; *Figure 5-25d* Courtesy of Eastman Kodak Company; *Figure 5-26a* Courtesy of Casio, Inc.; *Figure 5-26b* Courtesy of Eastman Kodak Company; *Figure 5-29* Courtesy of Intel Corporation; *Figure 5-30* Courtesy of Intel Corporation; *Figure 5-32* Steven Peters/Stone; *Figure 5-34a* Courtesy of Microtek Lab, Inc.; *Figure 5-34c* Courtesy of Visioneer, Inc.; *Figure 5-34d* Courtesy of Howtek, Inc.; *Figure 5-36* Scott Goodwin Photography; *Figure 5-37* Courtesy of Scantron; *Figure 5-38a* Scott Goodwin Photography; *Figure 5-38b* Chuck Savage/The Stock Market; *Figure 5-38c* Tony Freeman/PhotoEdit; *Figure 5-41* Scott Goodwin Photography; *Figure 5-42* Courtesy of Psion; *Figure 5-43* Courtesy of Orcca Technologies, Inc.; *Figure 5-45* Courtesy of Prentke Romich Company; *Figure 5-46a* PhotoDisc; *Figure 5-46b* PhotoDisc; *Figure 5-46c* Corbis; *Figure 5-46d* PhotoDisc; *Figure 5-46e* Bob Daemmrich/Stock Boston; *Figure 5-47* David Young-Wolff/PhotoEdit; **Chapter 6:** *Chapter opener Figures* Courtesy of Hewlett Packard Company; Courtesy of Hewlett Packard Company; Motorola and the Motorola logo are registered trademarks of Motorola, Inc. Courtesy of Motorola, Inc.; Courtesy of Heidi Van Arnem; Scott Goodwin Photography; *Figure 6-1b* Courtesy of Eastman Kodak Company; *Figure 6-1c* Courtesy of ViewSonics Corporation; *Figure 6-1d* Courtesy of Hewlett Packard Company; *Figure 6-1e* Courtesy of ViewSonics Corporation; *Figure 6-2* Courtesy of ViewSonics Corporation; *Figure 6-3* Courtesy of InFocus Corporation; *Figure 6-4* Courtesy of ViewSonics Corporation; *Figure 6-5a* Courtesy of International Business Machines Corporation; *Figure 6-5b* Courtesy of Compaq Computer Corporation; *Figure 6-6* Courtesy of Motorola, Inc.; *Figure 6-7* Courtesy of RCA; *Figure 6-8* Courtesy of Fujitsu General America, Fujitsu Plasmavision SlimScreen (r) ; *Figure 6-10* Courtesy of ATI Technologies,Inc.; *Figure 6-16a* Courtesy of Nokia; *Figure 6-16a* Courtesy of Nokia; *Figure 6-16b* Courtesy of Hewlett Packard Company; *Figure 6-17* Courtesy of Okidata Americas, Inc.; *Figure 6-18* Courtesy of Genicom Corporation; *Figure 6-19* Courtesy of Hewlett Packard Company; *Figure 6-21* Courtesy of the author; *Figure 6-22* Courtesy of Hewlett Packard Company; *Figure 6-24* Courtesy of Mitsubishi Digital Electronics America, Inc.; *Figure 6-26* Courtesy of Neopost Online; *Figure 6-27* Courtesy of Citizen America Corporation, www.citizen-america.com; *Figure 6-28* Corbis; *Figure 6-29* Courtesy of Dell Computer ; *Figure 6-30* AP/ Wide World Photos; *Figure 6-32* Courtesy of InFocus Corporation; *Figure 6-32* Courtesy of InFocus Corporation; *Figure 6-33* Stephen Welstead/The Stock Market; *Figure 6-35* Courtesy of Hewlett Packard Company; *Figure 6-36* Charlie Westerman/Stone; *Figure 6-37a* Steve Krongard/The Image Bank; *Figure 6-37b (c)* Bob Daemmrich Photo, Inc.; *Figure 6-39* Courtesy of Freedom Scientific, Inc.; *Figure 6-40a* PhotoDisc; *Figure 6-40b* PhotoDisc; *Figure 6-40c* Corbis; *Figure 6-40d* PhotoDisc; *Figure 6-40e* Bob Daemmrich/Stock Boston; **Multimedia** *Figure 8* AP/Wide World Photos; *Figure 18* Hank Morgan/Photo Researchers, Inc.; *Figure 6-19* Sam Ogen/Science Photo Library/Photo Researchers, Inc.; *Figure 22* Courtesy of Vance Design and Associates; **Chapter 7:** *Chapter opener Figures* Courtesy of EMC Corporation; Courtesy of Kingston Technology Company, Inc.; Courtesy of International Business Machines Research; Courtesy of Alan Shugart; *Figure 7-1a* eyewire.com; *Figure 7-1b* Courtesy of Maxtor Corporation; *Figure 7-1c* Courtesy of Advanced Computer and Netware Company; *Figure 7-1d* COGU2259; *Figure 7-1e* Courtesy of Excel/Meridian Data, Inc. (www.excelcdrom.com); *Figure 7-1f* Courtesy of Imation Corporation; *Figure 7-1g* Courtesy of Exabyte Corporation; *Figure 7-1g* Courtesy of Exabyte Corporation; *Figure 7-1h* Courtesy of Kingston Technology Company, Inc.; *Figure 7-1i* Courtesy of Sandisk, Inc.; *Figure 7-6* Corbis; *Figure 7-11* Courtesy of the author; *Figure 7-12* Courtesy of Seagate Technologies; *Figure 7-13* Courtesy of Maxtor Corporation; *Figure 7-17a* Courtesy of Iomega Corporation; *Figure 7-17b* Courtesy of Iomega Corporation; *Figure 7-18* Courtesy of Advanced Computer and Netware Company; *Figure 7-22* PhotoDisc; *Figure 7-25* PhotoDisc; *Figure 7-29* Sylvie Villegler/Explorer/Photo Researchers; *Figure 7-32a* Courtesy of Imation Corporation; *Figure 7-32b* Courtesy of Seagate Technologies; *Figure 7-34a* Courtesy of Advanced Computer and Netware Company; *Figure 7-34b* Courtesy of Exabyte Corporation; *Figure 7-34c* Courtesy of Excel/Meridian Data, Inc. (www.excelcdrom.com); *Figure 7-34e* Courtesy of Excel/Meridian Data, Inc. (www.excelcdrom.com); *Figure 7-35a* Courtesy of Nokia; *Figure 7-35b* Courtesy of Nokia; *Figure 7-37a* Scott Goodwin Photography; *Figure 7-37b* Courtesy of Sandisk, Inc.; *Figure 7-37c* Courtesy of International Business Machines Corporation; *Figure 7-37d* Courtesy of Sandisk, Inc.; *Figure 7-38* Courtesy of Brenner/Lennon Photo Productions; *Figure 7-39* Courtesy of International Business Machines Corporation; *Figure 7-40* Courtesy of Eastman Kodak Company; *Figure 7-42a* PhotoDisc; *Figure 7-42c* Corbis; *Figure 7-42d* PhotoDisc; *Figure 7-42e* Bob Daemmrich/Stock Boston; *Figure 7-43* The Image Bank; **Chapter 8:** *Chapter opener Figures* Courtesy of (c) 1999, 2000 Linux.com; AP/Wide World Photos; Courtesy of Hildegard Katz; *Figure 8-1a* Scott Goodwin Photography; *Figure 8-1b* Courtesy of Kingston Technology Company, Inc.; *Figure 8-2* Scott Goodwin Photography; *Figure 8-21* Courtesy of Microsoft Corporation; *Figure 8-22* Courtesy of Apple Computer, Inc.; *Figure 8-23* Courtesy of International Business Machines Corporation; *Figure 8-25* Courtesy of (c) 1999 Red Hat, Inc.; *Figure 8-26* Courtesy of Clarion Corporation; *Figure 8-27* Courtesy of Compaq Computer Corporation; *Figure 8-27* Courtesy of Hewlett Packard Company; **Buyer's Guide** *Page 8.43* Courtesy of Adobe Systems, Inc.; *Page 8-45* Scott Goodwin Photography; *Page 8.56* Courtesy of Seagate Technologies, Inc.; *Figure 8* Courtesy of Compaq Computer Corporation; *Figure 9* Courtesy of Toshiba America Information Systems, Inc.; *Figure 10* Courtesy of Toshiba America Information Systems, Inc.; *Figure 11* Courtesy of InFocus Corporation; *Figure 13* Courtesy of Palm, Inc.; *Figure 14* Courtesy of Compaq Computer Corporation.